ANNUAL REPORT

COMMISSIONER OF INDIAN AFFAIRS

TO THE

SECRETARY OF THE INTERIOR

FOR

THE YEAR 1873.

WASHINGTON:
GOVERNMENT PRINTING OFFICE.
1874.

CONTENTS.

LIST OF PAPERS ACCOMPANYING THE ANNUAL REPORT.

REPORT

OF THE

COMMISSIONER OF INDIAN AFFAIRS.

DEPARTMENT OF THE INTERIOR,
OFFICE OF INDIAN AFFAIRS,
November 1, 1873.

I have the honor, in accordance with law, to forward herewith the annual report of Indian affairs of the country.

In respect to the general question of civilization of Indians, the record of the year is a good one. In many of the agencies gratifying progress has been made, as shown in increased interest in the education of children, a disposition to labor, the desire for allotment of lands, and in the increase of stock and ordinary farm products, and other personal property. At other agencies serious efforts in the same direction have developed more decidedly the difficulties which lie in the way of progress. Among these hinderances six are specially noticeable.

FICTION IN INDIAN RELATIONS.

First. A radical hinderance is in the anomalous relation of many of the Indian tribes to the Government, which requires them to be treated as sovereign powers and wards at one and the same time. The comparative weakness of the whites made it expedient, in our early history, to deal with the wild Indian tribes as with powers capable of self-protection and fulfilling treaty obligations, and so a kind of fiction and absurdity has come into all our Indian relations. We have in theory over sixty-five independent nations within our borders, with whom we have entered into treaty relations as being sovereign peoples; and at the same time the white agent is sent to control and supervise these foreign powers, and care for them as wards of the Government. This double condition of sovereignty and wardship involves increasing difficulties and absurdities, as the traditional chieftain, losing his hold upon his tribe, ceases to be distingushed for anything except for the lion's share of goods and moneys which the Government endeavors to send, through him, to his nominal subjects, and as the necessities of the Indians, pressed on every side by civilization, require more help and greater discrimination in the manner of distributing the tribal funds. So far, and as rapidly as possible, all recognition of Indians in any other relation than strictly as subjects of the Government should cease. To provide for this, radical legislation will be required.

EVILS OF PAYMENTS BY CASH ANNUITIES.

The second hinderance, growing directly out of the first, is found in the form in which the benefactions of the Government reach the Indian. In treaties heretofore made with many of the tribes, large sums are stipulated to be paid in cash annuities. Facts show that ordinarily the Indians who have received the most money in this form are in the most unfavorable condition for civilization. The bounty of the Government has pauperized them, and in some cases has tended to brutalize more than to civilize. There are instances where for many years tribes have been receiving from $300 to $500 cash annually to each family of four or five persons, and in all such cases the Indians have made no use of the soil which they possess, and are annually reduced to extreme want within a short time after receiving annuities. These Indians would probably have been far better off to have had only their lands, out of which they might have dug a living, if compelled by hunger, than to have received this bounty in a form that tends to perpetuate idleness and poverty. I recommend that hereafter the appropriations to fulfill these promises for annuities of cash in hand be made for the same amounts, to be expended, in each case, under the direction of the Secretary of the Interior, for purposes of civilization of the tribe, reserving to the discretion of the Secretary the power to pay cash annuities whenever, in his judgment, it is found expedient.

If the objection should be made that this is a violation of a treaty stipulation, the answer is, that the Government is bound to consider the best interests of its wards. And if, in previous years, wrong methods have been adopted, or if the present condition and exigencies require a different method of dealing with the Indians in order to secure their improvement and greatest good, then both justice and humanity require that the change be made.

A satisfactory experiment of this method has been made under a treaty with the Sisseton and Wahpeton Sioux, in accordance with which the moneys paid to these tribes, in payment for their lands sold to the Government, have been expended in goods and provisions, which have been issued to Indians only in return for labor on their part, the labor being, in most cases, for themselves; and thus a threefold benefit has been procured. They have actually received the value of the money; they have received the products of their own labor, and, best of all, they have learned to labor. If a similar use can be made of sums of money now paid to vagrant Indians, and practically squandered by them within a few days, a large incentive to industry will be gained.

WANT OF INDIVIDUAL PROPERTY-RIGHTS.

The third hinderance is found in the want of individual property-rights among Indians. A fundamental difference between barbarians and a civilized people is the difference between a herd and an individual. All barbarous customs tend to destroy individuality. Where everything is held in common, thrift and enterprise have no stimulus of reward, and thus individual progress is rendered very improbable, if not impossible. The starting-point of individualism for an Indian is the personal possession of his portion of the reservation. Give him a house within a tract of land, whose corner-stakes are plainly recognized by himself and his neighbors, and let whatever can be produced out of this landed estate be considered property in his own name, and the first principle of industry and thrift is recognized. In order to this first step, the survey and allotment in severalty of the lands belonging to the Indians must be provided for by congressional legislation.

LAW AMONG INDIANS.

The fourth hinderance is the absence of law for Indians. The first condition of civilization is protection of life and property through the administration of law. As the Indians are taken out of their wild life, they leave behind them the force attaching to the distinctive tribal condition. The chiefs inevitably lose their power over Indians in proportion as the latter come in contact with the Government or with white settlers, until their government becomes, in most cases, a mere form, without power of coercion and restraint. Their authority is founded only on "the consent of the governed," and only as they pander to the whims or vices of the young men of the tribe can they gain such consent. As a police restraint upon lawlessness they are of no avail, being themselves subject to the control of the worst element in the tribe. An Indian murdering another Indian is accountable only to the law of retaliation. The State authorities do not concern themselves in punishing the murders among Indians, even when such murder is committed under the shadow of their criminal courts.

I submit, for the consideration of the honorable Secretary, whether it is not necessary that crimes among Indians shall be defined by United States law, and made punishable before United States courts, or whether it may not be practicable to invest magisterial powers in agents and superintendents, by which they may summon a jury among the Indians or other persons residing at the agencies by authority of law, before whom any serious offense against law and order may be tried. Such a court would be the beginning of administration of justice, out of the workings of which would gradually grow a code of laws, which would cover these cases arising in the Indian country, and come to be enforced by a police among themselves.

At the same time, ample provision should be made for the prosecution of citizens who attempt to encroach upon the rights of Indians, or to debauch them by the sale of intoxicating liquors. The employment of detectives, through the Department of Justice, has worked satisfactorily, so far as the limited appropriation of last year has allowed. The difficulty of securing conviction of parties who are known to be engaged in selling whisky to Indians, makes the prosecution, when attempted by the agent alone, expensive and more frequently unsuccessful. In order to induce information and secure efficiency in these prosecutions, I recommend that such legislation be procured as will insure to the informant all fines arising from conviction under the law.

REFUSAL OF INDIANS TO REMAIN ON RESERVATIONS.

The fifth hinderance, the persistent refusal of a portion of some of the tribes to remain upon their reservation according to treaty, has been mainly experienced with five tribes, viz, the Sioux, Arapahoes, Cheyennes, Kiowas, and Comanches. A portion of the Arapahoes and Cheyennes are identified with the Sioux in their depredations. The remainder are living on a reservation in the Indian Territory.

SIOUX.

The actual depredations committed by the Sioux have been comparatively few, but a portion of the tribe have assumed a hostile attitude toward the Government by attacking the surveying expedition on the Northern Pacific Railroad. According to the best information of this office, the greater number of Indians engaged in these hostilities were a band of Northern Sioux, who have hitherto declined to treat with the Government, and with them a large re-enforcement from different agencies along the Missouri River, as also from Spotted Tail's and Red

Cloud's camps. There is no doubt that the majority of the Indians whom General Stanley encountered in Dakota have been at different times in the year on reservations, and have drawn rations from the Government, some occasionally and some regularly. It is to be regretted that these hostiles could not have been met and defeated by military force. Their actual punishment, in the loss of four or five warriors, was so slight that they seem to regard it at least a drawn fight, if not a victory on their side. The Sioux at Red Cloud and Spotted Tail agencies have also assumed impudent manners and made hostile threats, which have prevented the proper administration of agency affairs. It has been impossible for the agents to issue rations upon actual count of lodges, the Indians refusing to have a count made, and demanding the issue of rations upon the returns brought in by themselves. The agents, not having a force at hand to restrain the demands of the Indians, have been obliged to yield, and, as a consequence, there has often been over-issue, and the Indians have grown bold by successful resistance to authority. Such a course of treatment is unwise and unsafe.

Hitherto the military have refrained from going on this reservation because of the express terms of the treaty with the Sioux, in which it is agreed that no military force shall be brought over the line. I respectfully recommend that provision be made at once for placing at each of the Sioux reservations a military force sufficient to enable the agents to enforce respect for their authority, and to conduct agency affairs in an orderly manner. Also, that all Sioux Indians be required to remain on the Sioux reservation, and that any found off, or refusing to come in and treat with the Government, be forced in and brought to obedience by the military. I am confident that steady progress towards civilization is being made at the different agencies among the Sioux, and, if the turbulent element of this nation can be subdued, the question whether they can be induced to live quietly and to adopt habits of civilization, so as to become self-supporting, will be one only of time and patience.

If it should become necessary to reduce the hostile portion of these Sioux to submission by military force, the Government will find faithful and efficient allies in the several Indian tribes around, the Crows, Black Feet, Gros Ventres, and Arickarees. From these Indians a sufficient number of scouts can be enlisted to break the power of the Sioux Nation.

ARAPAHOES AND CHEYENNES.

The attempt is being made to induce the Northern Arapahoes and Cheyennes to join their respective tribes in the Indian Territory. Those now in the Territory are affiliated to such a degree as to be in one agency, and to occupy together the same reservation. They number 3,500. The union of the northern tribes with them would swell the number to 4,500. There is also a portion of the Cheyennes living upon the staked plains which have never yet come in. They subsist entirely on buffalo, and plunder in Colorado, Mexico, and Texas. Not a little of the raiding in Texas which has been charged upon the Kiowas and Comanches during the past year has been done by these Cheyennes. A company of surveyors, four in number, were murdered by them upon their reservation in June last. The demand made upon the tribe to surrender the murderers has not been complied with, and it is not impossible that, if the Government proceeds to enforce compliance, war will result.

KIOWAS AND COMANCHES.

The Kiowas and Comanches are affiliated in like manner as the Arapahoes and Cheyennes, occupying a common reservation with the same agency. The conduct of the Kiowas during the past year has been comparatively exemplary, under promise of receiving their chiefs Satanta and Big Tree. These prisoners were in the executive control of the governor of Texas, and, on account of the peculiar atrocity of the crimes of which they were convicted, there was strong opposition on the part of the citizens of Texas to their release. But the pledge of the Government having been given to the Kiowas, and the Kiowas having reason to expect its fulfillment because of their own good conduct for the year past, an appeal was made to the courtesy of the governor of Texas to relieve the Government from its embarrassment by the release of the prisoners; and a pledge was made that the Government would use every means to protect the border of Texas, and would require the Comanches to surrender a certain number of raiders from their tribe who have been depredating in Texas during the past summer. Governor Davis accepted the pledge of the Government, in lieu of the further retention of the chiefs as a means of procuring safety for the citizens of Texas, and Satanta and Big Tree were sent to their tribe. The following day the Comanches were brought into council and required to surrender five (5) of their raiders. The chiefs did not deny that some of their young men had been raiding in Texas, nor that they had been committing theft and murder, but they declared it to be impossible for them to arrest and surrender the marauders, and desired to have one more trial in the way of peace. This I declined to give, except on the conditions already made with the governor of Texas, that the raiders should be surrendered. Some of the Comanches then volunteered to accompany the cavalry into Texas to arrest some of their own tribe whom they knew to be engaged at that time in plunder. A cavalry force was at once sent out, with these Indians enlisted as scouts. But they were unable to find the raiders, and returned without any prisoners to surrender in compliance with the requirement made upon them. The conduct of the Comanches is especially flagrant because of their solemn pledge, made one year ago and renewed in July, not to raid any more, on which their captive women and children were surrendered to them.

But it is a serious problem how to punish the guilty ones without striking the innocent. It is also certain that, on the opening of hostilities, a large portion of the tribe would leave the agency and take to the plains, when the difficulty of reaching and controlling them by military force becomes greatly increased. It is believed, however, that there is no alternative. The reservation cannot be made a refuge for thieves and murderers. No policy can assume the name of peace and kindness that expressly provides for immunity of crime. If the military force cannot be made strong enough to follow these Indians whenever they leave the reservation, and strike them while in the act of depredating, then the whole tribe, on refusal to surrender guilty parties, must be held responsible. And while there will be a loss of results already reached in gathering around the agencies these Indians from the plains, and many innocent ones will perhaps suffer with the guilty, yet I am persuaded that vigorous treatment will be kindness in the end. An attempt to restrain and punish the turbulent element in these three different tribes, to be successful, will require a larger military force than merely to strike their camps, destroying them in part, and scattering the remainder on the plains; but the Government can better afford to use a larger force than to undertake a warfare after the savage method of indiscriminate slaughter of women and children.

INTERTRIBAL WARFARE.

Intertribal warfare presents a sixth hinderance in the way of civilization. In view of the hostilities among the different tribes of Indians, and the frequent attacks by some of the tribes, requiring a constant state of defense on the part of others, an order has been issued that no Indians be allowed to leave their reservation without permit from the agent, and the Secretary of War has been requested to direct the commanders of military posts to prevent Indians from passing from one agency to another without such permit; and if they find Indians marauding, or engaged in any hostile expedition against any other tribe, to strike them without parley. A satisfactory execution of this arrangement will probably require either an increased enlistment of scouts from friendly Indians, or an increased military force in the different portions of the Indian country.

On account of their massacre of the Pawnees during the last buffalo hunt in Nebraska, the Sioux have been forbidden to leave their reservation for such hunting. This prohibition is likely to cause complaint and dissatisfaction among the Indians, but the increasing annoyance and peril from wandering Indians in Nebraska seem to justify the office in making the violation of their treaty by the Sioux the occasion of prohibiting their hunting in Nebraska hereafter; and I recommend that this matter be laid before Congress, in order that this prohibition may be enforced, by declaring that that portion of the treaty of 1868, allowing them to hunt within a certain range of country where buffalo are found, be rendered null and void by the act of the Sioux in attacking the Pawnees, and also by their refusal to surrender the members of their tribe who are guilty, while marauding off their reservation, of the wanton murder of the Hall family.

ISSUE OF ARMS AND AMMUNITION.

In several instances tribes entirely friendly to Government and well disposed to civilization have been kept in terror by their marauding neighbors, and prevented from attempting civilized life during the year. In such instances, if the friendly Indians could have been armed they would have defended themselves without assistance from the United States, and I recommend that steps be taken to procure legislation authorizing the Secretary of War to issue arms and ammunition for the self-protection of friendly tribes, on the request of this office, such arms to be accounted for by the agent to whom they are delivered.

MANUAL LABOR SCHOOLS.

Upon no other subject or branch of the Indian service is there such entire agreement of opinion from all agents and persons, connected directly and indirectly with Indian civilization, as upon the necessity of labor schools for Indian children. It is manifest that barbarism can be cured only by education. Instruction in the day-school merely, except among Indians who are already far along in civilization, is attempted at great disadvantage on every hand. Indian children cannot come from the wigwam suitably clad for the school-room. If clothes are provided for them the supply must be frequently repeated. The habits also of wigwam life are entirely irregular. The Indian has no regular habits or hours. He eats and sleeps when and where he will or can, and no school attendance, which depends upon regular home habits of the parents or children, can be relied upon. It is also well nigh impossible to teach Indian children the English language when they spend twenty hours out of the twenty-four in the wigwam, using only their native tongue. The boarding school, on the contrary, takes the youth under constant care, has him always at hand, and surrounds him by an English-speaking community, and above all, gives him instruction in the first lessons of civilization, which can be found only in a well-ordered home.

Any plan for civilization which does not provide for training the young, even though at a largely increased expenditure, is short-sighted and expensive. A large expenditure for a few years in the proper direction will be more economical than a smaller expenditure perpetuated; and it is believed that at least one-half of the Indian children, now growing up in barbarism, could be put during the coming year in such processes of education in home schools, if the means were at hand for supporting such schools. Four or five years of this appliance of civilization cures one-half of the barbarism of the Indian tribe permanently. For these children thus trained, though many of them might lapse into nomadic ways, would never go back so far as to be dangerous or troublesome to the citizens of the Government, and within that length of time it is reasonable to be expected that the other tribes, whose children could not at first be obtained for such schools, will be brought within the reach of the Government, and thus be ready to receive their turn at this training process. I most earnestly recommend that this appropriation for education be made on a scale commensurate with the urgent necessities of the case.

CO-OPERATION WITH RELIGIOUS SOCIETIES.

The arrangement by which, in accordance with the direction of the President, all agents are appointed on the nomination of some religious body is working with increasing satisfaction. In proportion as these religious societies gain assurance that this plan of co-operation with the Government is likely to be permanent, they are generally entering heartily into operations that contemplate earnest educational and religious work in the respective agencies allotted them. They are also learning from experience what are the essential qualifications of an Indian agent, and also the serious nature of the responsibility to the Government which they assume in these nominations. The result is a greater care in the selection of men, and increased watchfulness over their official actions. Out of the sixty-five agents thus nominated there have been several failures during the year, from want of adaptation to the service, or from want of integrity. But in nearly every case the religious society represented by these men has been the first to make the discovery of unfitness, and to ask for a change of agents.

INADEQUATE SALARIES.

There is a serious complaint on the part of these religious bodies that they are not able, at the salary of $1,500, to find competent men willing to accept the service, and that when such men have been secured it has often been found impossible to retain them. The service has lost several of the most competent and reliable agents during the year from this cause. No man capable of managing the business of an agency ranging from $15,000 to $200,000 ought to be asked to give full service to the Government for $1,500 a year. I recommend that the salary of agents be increased to $2,000 per annum for the more eastern agencies, and $2,500 for those remote and inaccessible.

CONDITIONS OF PROGRESS.

In estimating the actual progress attained, under the operation of what has been termed the peace policy, it is necessary to keep in mind the constant change in the position of the Indians toward the white settlers. Tribes which a few years ago were so far removed from all white settlements as to render any annoyance or conflict between the two races improbable and almost impossible, have now, by the tide of emigration, been brought in close proximity to, and almost daily contact with, settlers. Naturally the difficulties in the Indian problem are largely increased by such contact. The clashing interests of both parties produce irritation and make complaints more numerous.

But the peace policy is not to be charged with these increasing troubles, nor to be connected with them except by the inquiry as to what would probably have been the difficulties, in the same circumstances, under any other policy.

The question of the civilization of Indians reduced to its last analysis is twofold. First, whether the Government is willing to make sufficient appropriation to teach barbarous men how to live in a civilized way; and, second, whether the expenditure of such an appropriation can be fairly made through the administration of persons fitted to become their teachers. Without suitable provision for the necessary expenditures the best efforts of the best men will be comparatively futile; and with the most abundant provision that the resources of the nation can make, nothing will be accomplished worthy of the effort unless there can be found persons ready and fitted to go to these Indians, in the spirit of kindness and Christian love, with a faith in God and a faith in man strong enough to sustain them amid the degradation and perversities of barbarism, and cheer them on in the full conviction that no being made in God's image is incapable of improvement. No effort for lifting the poor and degraded can succeed which is not guided by the enthusiasm which comes from this faith. The agent and his employés will not give full work without it, and the Indian will not throw off his suspicion and wake out of his indolence until he feels this touch of human sympathy.

For this reason the Government is specially to be congratulated on the response which the Christian people of the country have made to the proposition of the President that they should take a certain supervision of Government labor for the Indians, by nominating agents and furnishing employés suitable to represent the Government in its beneficent efforts with these tribes, as well as in sending missionaries and teachers for religious labor among them.

THE INDIAN TERRITORY.

The affairs of this Territory will doubtless receive the serious consideration of Congress during the coming session. The practical absence of law as between the inhabitants of the Territory and the citizens of the United States; the general state of unthrift from lack of competition and every incitement to labor incident to ordinary life in this country; the unwillingness of the Indians to take their lands in severalty; the persistent refusal of the Choctaws to give negroes their rights as citizens of the Territory, together with the strong pressure from parties interested in railroad enterprises and investments in lands, will be quite likely to induce legislation of some kind for this country.

If the inhabitants of the Territory would adopt the Okmulgee constitution with the amendments suggested by the President, upon this a satisfactory government could be created for this country. Then if the Indians would have their lands surveyed and allotted to them in severalty, the first steps toward citizenship would be fairly taken. Every consideration of justice seems to require that the treaty obligation which the Government has assumed toward these nations shall be observed. No circumstances can be supposed to exist that will justify the nullification of these obligations, but if it is found, on careful examination, that the highest interests of both the United States and the Indian nations of this Territory require a change in their relations which is not provided for by the different treaties, then the question is fairly raised whether the Government may not assume the responsibility of making the changes in such form as shall secure every right which these Indians can reasonably ask for themselves, and as will also commend itself to the moral sense of the country. The attempt to administer justice for all the Territory through the United States courts at Fort Smith has been largely a failure, and sometimes worse. If the adoption of a territorial constitution by the Indians does not provide a remedy, then a United States court should be established, at some convenient point in the Territory, to take cognizance of all cases of complaint arising between the citizens of the United States and inhabitants of the Territory, and between members of the different tribes and nations in the Territory.

MISSON INDIANS IN SOUTHERN CALIFORNIA.

Special attention is invited to the report of John G. Ames, who was appointed a special commissioner to inquire into the condition and necessities of the Mission Indians in Southern California. These Indians, under the Mexican government, enjoyed civil and property rights, and were abundantly able to take care of themselves from the products of the soil. But under our Government these rights were not considered as transferred, and they now find themselves liable to have the lands which they have cultivated for generations taken from them by white settlers. It would seem that there is no alternative, in any just settlement with these Indians, but to secure for them, in the way proposed in the report of Agent Ames, the land to which they are entitled, or its equivalent, upon which they will be able to subsist themselves without help from the Government.

WEAVING.

The effort during the year to instruct the Indian women among the Chippewas in Wisconsin and Minnesota in the art of weaving has already succeeded so far as to make it certain that, by the introduction of looms among all Indians where the herding of sheep is practicable, a new industry may be brought within the reach of the Indians, which will be of large service in the slow process of civilization.

ARICKAREES, MANDANS, AND GROS VENTRES.

An attempt has been made to induce the Arickarees, Mandans, and Gros Ventres, who occupy the reservation at Fort Berthold, to remove to the Indian Territory, but they have declined to send a delegation to prospect for the tribe, and seem averse to removal from their present grounds, where they are exposed to raids from the Sioux, and their crops are alternately cut off by the grasshopper and the drought. Their crops generally this year are reported as a failure, and it is not unlikely that, without help through a deficiency appropriation, they will suffer severely during the winter. The Indians on these agencies deserve more from the Government than any other tribes in Dakota, on account of their fidelity to the Government and the faithful service rendered by them as scouts in compelling other Indians to keep the peace.

MINNESOTA CHIPPEWAS.

The wandering bands of Chippewas in Minnesota require the attention of the Government. There are two permanent reservations in the State, at Leech Lake and White Earth, and the different bands remaining among the settlements of Pembina and Otter-Tail should be gathered upon the White Earth reservation. For these bands the Government has acquired, by purchase from the Mississippi Chippewas, the right to settle upon this reservation; but in order to establish them there a special appropriation will be required. The appropriation of $10,000, made by last Congress for the removal of the Pembinas, being too limited for the purpose, has not been used.

The Mille Lac band of Chippewas in Minnesota remains in its anomalous position. They have sold their reservation, retaining a right to occupy it during good behavior. With this title to the soil it is not deemed expedient to attempt permanent improvements at Mille Lac, unless a title to the reservation can be returned to them on condition that they surrender to Government all moneys acquired in consideration of their cession of the Mille Lac reservation. If this cannot be done, their Indians should be notified that they belong at White Earth, and be required to remove. In their present location, on its present tenure, nothing can be done looking toward their civilization.

UTES.

In consideration of the condition of the scattered bands of different tribes of Utes in Nevada, Colorado, and Utah, it was deemed advisable to send a commission to inquire as to their numbers and the possibility of gathering them upon one or more reservations, where they would be more immediately under the care of the Government, and removed from the white settlers. Agent G. W. Ingalls and Major J. W. Powell were appointed on this commission. They seem to have adopted the exhaustive method, and the interesting report of their labors for the summer is herewith submitted, and attention invited to their recommendations, which are heartily indorsed by this office.

THE CAUSES WHICH LED TO THE MODOC WAR.

October 14, 1864, a treaty was concluded with the Klamath and Modoc tribes and Yahooskin band of Snake Indians in Oregon, by the first article of which said Indians ceded to the United States all their right, title, and claim to all the country claimed by them, and accepted a reservation described in said article by natural boundaries, upon which they agreed and bound themselves to locate immediately after the ratification of the treaty.

The ratification of this treaty was advised and consented to by the Senate, July 2, 1866, and the same was proclaimed by the President February 17, 1870. At the date of proclamation the Modocs were found on their reservation, where they remained until April, 1870, and then left for their camp on Lost River.

There is evidence that Captain Jack and his band were prepared at this time to remain upon the reservation and settle down in the way of civilization, if there had been ordinary encouragement and assistance, and if the Klamaths, who largely outnumbered Captain Jack's band, and who were their hereditary enemies, had allowed them so to do. This band began to split rails for their farms, and in other ways to adopt civilized habits; but the Klamaths demanded tribute from them for the land they were occupying, which the Modocs were obliged to render. Captain Jack then removed to another part of the reservation, and began again to try to live by cultivating the ground. But he was followed by the same spirit of hostility by the Klamaths, from which he does not seem to have been protected by the agent. The issue of rations seems also to have been suspended for want of funds, and for these reasons Captain Jack and his band returned to their old home on Lost River, where they became a serious annoyance to the whites, who had in the meanwhile settled on their ceded lands.

This annoyance led to serious apprehensions on the part of the military authorities, and under date of the 19th of March, 1872, the honorable Secretary of War transmitted to this Department copies of correspondence between the military in regard to the matter. A copy of this correspondence was sent to Superintendent Odeneal by the Indian Office, April 12, 1872, with directions to have the Modocs removed, if practicable, to their reservation; and if removed, to see that they were properly protected from the Klamaths.

The superintendent was then instructed, in case they could not be removed, to report the practicability of locating them at some other point. The superintendent reported on the 17th June that their reservation was the best place for them to be located, but that he did not believe it practicable to remove them without using the military for that purpose, and that if they should resist, he doubted whether there was force enough in the country to compel them to go. In reply, the superintendent was directed, July 6, 1872, to remove them to the Klamath reservation. The attempt to execute this order resulted in a conflict between the Modocs and the troops and the white settlers. For the purpose of examining into the same, and, if possible, to procure a peaceable solution of the difficulties, a commission was appointed by the Secretary of the Interior in January last. This commission, as finally composed, consisted of A. B. Meacham, late superintendent Indian affairs for Oregon, L. S. Dyar, agent for the Klamath agency, and Rev. E. Thomas, and by direction of the Secretary of the Interior, under date of March 22, 1873, they were put under the direction of General Canby. While engaged in a conference with Captain Jack, chief of the Modocs, and other representative men of the tribe, on the 11th of April, General Canby and Dr. Thomas were brutally murdered by these Indians, and Mr. Meacham severely wounded.

Thus ended the negotiations with the Modocs, who, after seven months' fighting, were subdued by the military, and Captain Jack and three of his principal men were tried by court-martial and executed. The remnant of this Modoc band has been transferred to the Indian Territory, and located for the present on the Quapaw Indian reservation, where they have gladly availed themselves of the privilege of putting their children in school, and have entered upon industrial life with such readiness and good will as to warrant the conclusion that if these Indians could have had this opportunity of gaining their support out of soil upon which an ordinary white man could get a living, and had received just treatment, there would have been no cause of trouble with them. The report of the commission, prepared by the surviving member, A. B. Meacham, is herewith submitted.

COMMISSIONS UNDER INDIAN LEGISLATION BY CONGRESS.

Kansas or Kaw Indians.

The Kansas Indian lands in Kansas, embracing 137,658$\frac{13}{100}$ acres of unsold "trust lands," and a part of the 80,409$\frac{60}{100}$ acres of what is known as the "diminished reserve," were, in 1871, offered for sale under the provisions of the treaty concluded with said Indians October 5, 1859. The bids received in pursuance of said offering were considered and rejected by the Department, and the whole subject again referred to Congress, in order that the Indians might be better protected. An act passed Congress, and was approved May 8, 1872. Provision was made by this act for the appraisement of all of these lands, both "trust" and "diminished reserve," and actual settlers on the trust-lands are given the privilege of purchasing tracts of 160 acres within one year from the date of appraisal. The unoccupied trust-lands are to be sold at public sale, after due advertisement, to the highest bidder, for cash, in tracts not exceeding 160 acres, under such rules and regulations as the Secretary of the Interior may prescribe. The diminished reserve is provided to be sold in tracts not exceeding 160 acres, on sealed bids, after due advertisement. A commission was appointed in pursuance of said act, and made and reported an appraisement of all the lands, which appraisement was approved by the Secretary of the Interior, under date of March 3, 1873. The land in the diminished reserve was offered for sale, but not enough of this land having been bid for to pay the expenses of the sale, the appraisement was set aside by the Secretary of the Interior as being too high, and a new appraisement ordered, and for this purpose a commission was appointed. This commission proceeded to Kansas, and, after consultation with the superintendent of Indian affairs, and an examination of the lands, the chairman reported that he did not regard the former appraisement in excess of the real value of the lands; the former appraisement was, therefore, restored by the Department, and the commission appointed to re-appraise dissolved. Further legislation to enable the sale of this land to actual settlers has been recommended, for the details of which reference is made to that portion of this report relative to "legislation recommended."

SISSETON AND WAHPETON.

The commission appointed last year, under the act of June 7, 1872, to inquire into the title of the Sisseton and Wahpeton bands of Sioux Indians to land in Dakota, was intrusted with the duty of procuring the ratification by said Indians of the agreement made last year by the commission with these Indians, as amended by the act of February 14, 1873. This duty has been performed, the Indians agreeing to the amendments.

WINNEBAGOES IN MINNESOTA.

The treaty concluded with the Winnebago tribe of Indians, April 15, 1859, provided for allotments to said Indians. Owing, however, to the

Sioux outbreak in the year 1862, an act of Congress, approved February 21, 1862, made provision for the peaceable removal of the Winnebagoes beyond the limits of State the of Minnesota, and the sale of their allotments. Some of said Indians, however, refused to remove, and continued to reside upon what they supposed to be their allotments under the treaty of 1859. For the purpose of securing to such the benefit of allotments as contemplated by said treaty, and their pro-rata share of the tribal funds, Congress, by the 9th and 10th sections of the Indian appropriation act, approved July 15, 1870, and the explanatory clause contained in the Indian appropriation act, approved May 29, 1872, provided for an investigation and settlement of their claims. A special commissioner was accordingly appointed, in 1872, for the purpose; but his report being unsatisfactory, Mr. Walter T. Burr was appointed the present year to finally close up the whole subject. Special Commissioner Burr's report has been approved by the Secretary of the Interior, and these claims, which have been the subject of consideration by the Department for some time past, have been finally disposed of.

PAWNEES.

The commission appointed last year under the act of Congress of June 10, 1872, to appraise a portion of this reserve lying south of Loup Fork, did not meet until this year, when the survey of said land was completed. They have just submitted their appraisement, which will be duly examined, and, if found to be correct, will be transmitted to the honorable Secretary of the Interior for his approval.

UTES IN COLORADO TERRITORY.

The commission appointed last year under the act of Congress of April 23, 1872, to negotiate with the Ute Indians for the extinguishment of their right to the south part of their reservation in Colorado, failing in their efforts to this end, the Hon. Felix R. Brunot, president of the board of Indian commissioners, was appointed to visit them in August last and to renew the negotiations. He succeeded in making an agreement with them, by which they relinquish their right to a large tract of valuable mining country, estimated to contain about three million four hundred and fifty thousand (3,450,000) acres. Reference is made to the report of the commission, printed herewith.

RESERVATION OF ME-SHIN-GO-ME-SIA, IN INDIANA.

Provision was made in the treaties with the Miami Indians of November 6, 1838, and November 28, 1840, for a reservation for Chief Me-shin-go-me-sia and his band in Northern Indiana. By act of Congress of June 10, 1872, the Secretary of the Interior was directed to ascertain what persons constituted the band of said chief, their survivors and descendants, and to partition said reserve to them. A commission was appointed for this purpose, who made investigation, and partitioned said land to 63 persons, which partition was reported in due form, and approved by the Secretary of the Interior, and patents are being issued to the parties.

MODOCS.

Owing to difficulties between the military and the Modoc Indians in Oregon, arising out of the refusal of these Indians to remove to their reservation, a committee, of which A. B. Meacham, late superintendent of Indian affairs for Oregon, was chairman, was appointed to investigate into the origin of such difficulties, and to endeavor to adjust the same. This commission was assisted by Gen. E. R. S. Canby, U. S.

Army, commanding the Department of the Columbia, and Rev. D. Thomas, both of whom were most brutally murdered while carrying on negotiations with the Modocs, who were thereupon turned over to the military for punishment, and further negotiations discontinued.

COEUR D'ALÈNES.

The commission appointed to visit certain Bannock Indians, near Fort Hall, Idaho, were directed, under instructions from this office of the 1st of July last, to visit the Cœur d'Alène Indians, to hear complaints, with a view to their cure or removal, and to induce them to abandon a roving life and to consent to confine themselves to a reservation. They succeeded in having a council with these Indians, and as a result of their negotiations, the Indians agreed to go upon a reservation which was, at the time, described to them, and which has since been set apart temporarily by the President until legislation can be had thereon by Congress. For further particulars attention is invited to article entitled "Legislation recommended."

NORTHERN PACIFIC RAILROAD.

A commission was appointed on the 11th of March last to visit the roving Indians likely to oppose the construction of the Northern Pacific Railroad, through the valley of the Yellowstone, and instructed to open negotiations with them having in view the removal of all such opposition, and as far as possible obtaining the consent of said Indians to withdraw all further obstacles to its construction. The commission reported on the 9th of May that they had met nearly all the bands of Indians residing in the locality of the proposed route of said railroad, and after submitting to them the object of their visit, felt assured that there would be no combined action on the part of the Indians against its further construction.

FOND DU LAC.

A commission has been appointed under the act of Congress approved May 29, 1872, to appraise the Fond du Lac Indian reserve in Minnesota. The commission met, but owing to the advanced season, consequent upon the delay in the completion of the survey of the reserve, they concluded not to undertake the appraisement this winter.

KICKAPOOS.

The effort made two years ago, under the acts of July 15, 1870, and March 3, 1871, to remove the Kickapoos and other roving bands of Indians from the border of Texas and the republic of Mexico, having failed, a commission was appointed to make another attempt to accomplish the object desired, namely, to remove said Indians to some point within the limits of the Indian Territory, where they could be kept from depredating on and annoying the inhabitants of Texas, and started in the pursuits of civilized life. After repeated councils with the Indians, and overcoming numerous obstacles caused by the action of some of the citizens of Mexico, the commission, with the valuable assistance rendered by Senor Montero, succeeded in getting some three or four hundred to consent to remove. These Indians have already arrived in the Indian Territory.

ROUND VALLEY.

A commission was appointed under the act of March 3, 1873, to proceed to the Round Valley Indian reservation, in California, for the purpose of examining the country in that locality, and report in regard to where the northern line of the reservation should be located, and of appraising the improvements of white persons on the lands embraced within the limits of the proposed reservation, and also of all Indians on the lands proposed to be restored. Reference is made to the report of the commission, printed herewith.

FORT HALL INDIAN RESERVATION.

It being desirable that certain Bannock Indians, who by treaty stipulations were allowed to roam and hunt over certain portions of Idaho, should be induced, if possible, to relinquish this right and settle down upon the reservation provided for them, a commission was appointed to visit them for that purpose. The commission, which was also authorized to visit other Indians in Idaho for various objects, has submitted its final report, which is printed herewith.

NEW YORK INDIAN LANDS IN KANSAS.

A commission appointed under the act of Congress of February 19, 1873, to appraise these lands, have concluded their labors, and the appraisement has been approved by the Secretary of the Interior, and copies sent to the local officers of the land-office, for payment of the appraised value by the occupants of the lands.

CREEKS.

A commission appointed, under the act of Congress approved March 3, 1873, to negotiate with the Creeks in regard to their western boundary, with a view of providing more territory for the Seminole Indians, have visited that country, and a preliminary report has been received from the chairman, from which it appears that owing to circumstances, which are detailed, they failed to accomplish their object.

MIAMI INDIAN LANDS IN KANSAS.

A commission, appointed under the act of Congress of March 3, 1873, appraised these lands and reported their appraisement, which has been approved by the Department; and under direction of the Department a list of those occupied by settlers, reported to be entitled under the law by the commissioners, has been sent to the General Land-Office, to be furnished to the receiver of public moneys at Topeka, Kansas, to whom payment is to be made, for these lands so occupied, at the appraised value of the same.

Those unoccupied are, with the approval of the Department, to be advertised and sold on sealed bids.

NEZ PERCÉ INDIANS.

Superintendent Odeneal and Agent Monteith were appointed a commission, under instructions, to make an investigation and hold council with the band of Nez Percé Indians occupying Wallowa Valley in Oregon, with a view to their removal, if practicable, to the Nez Percé Indian reservation in Idaho Territory. They reported this removal to be impracticable, and the Wallowa Valley has been withdrawn from sale, and set apart for their use and occupation, by Executive order.

CROWS.

Under the provisions of the act of March 3, 1873, a commission was appointed to negotiate with the Crow Indians for the cession of a portion of their reservation in Montana Territory. The commission visited these Indians in July last, and succeeded in making an agreement with them by which they cede their entire reservation south of the Yellowstone, containing about six million two hundred and seventy-two thousand (6,272,000) acres, and accept a new one in the Judith basin, south of the Missouri, containing about three million six hundred and twenty-five thousand (3,625,000) acres.

RAWLINGS SPRINGS MASSACRE IN WYOMING.

A commission was appointed the 10th of July last to investigate the facts and circumstances attending the massacre of Indians, in June, near Rawlings Springs, in Wyoming Territory. A report has been submitted, in which the facts are recited and the whites exonerated from all blame, and recommendations made that, to avoid a repetition of similar attacks, all Indian reservations should be surveyed and boundaries designated by rivers, mountains, and other natural objects, that Indians may be enabled to understand their limits, and that they should not be allowed to leave such reservations, either to hunt or visit, (by permit or otherwise,) or for any other excuse whatever.

NORTHERN SIOUX.

A commission was appointed in May last to visit the various bands of Northern Sioux, parties to the treaty of 1868, and to negotiate with them for a relinquishment of the privileges reserved in the 11th and 16th articles of said treaty, and to effect a change in the location of the Red Cloud agency. The commission succeeded only partially in collecting the various bands in council, and as the result of the deliberation therein it was obvious that the time had not come to successfully present a proposition for the relinquishment of the unceded Indian territory of Nebraska and Wyoming, and for the surrender of the privilege of hunting buffalo on the tract of country lying north of the North Platte River and east of the Big Horn Mountains. Assurances, however, were given by the Indians that the agency would be permitted to be removed whenever the Department thought it expedient to effect it.

OTTOE AND MISSOURIA.

A commission was appointed last year, under the act of Congress approved June 10, 1872, to appraise a portion of this reserve. These Indians, on the 6th of September, 1872, withheld their assent to the proposed sale, but in open council, on the 26th of May last, reconsidered their former action, and assented to the sale of one-half their reserve, not exceeding 80,000 acres. The lands are now being surveyed, and when the survey is completed the commission will be instructed to make the appraisement.

ACTION IN REGARD TO INDIAN LANDS.

The Omaha, Pawnee, Ottoe and Missouria, and Sac and Fox of the Missouri tribes of Indians in Nebraska, having, through their respective chief and councils, expressed a desire to have portions of their reservation sold, it was recommended that Congress give the necessary authority for such action. This was done by act approved June 10, 1872, in which provision was made for the survey and sale of a portion of the following-named reserves, to the extent specified, viz: Omaha and Pawnee, not exceeding 50,000 acres each, and Ottoe and Missouria, not exceeding 80,000 acres, and the whole of the Sac and Fox of the Missouri reserve, amounting to about 16,000 acres. All of these tribes have assented to the provisions of this act, and the following exhibits a summary statement of the action had thereunder in the case of each of the reserves.

OMAHA.

The Department, in anticipation of the consent of the Indians to the provisions of the aforesaid act, under date of July 31, 1872, appointed commissioners of appraisal. The formal consent in writing of the Indians was not, however, filed in this office until the receipt of a letter from the Superintendent of Indian Affairs, bearing date September 26, 1872. Instructions for their guidance were prepared and forwarded as soon thereafter as practicable to the commissioners of appraisal, who proceeded to perform their duties and submit their report, which received the approval of the Department January 10, 1873. Thereupon the lands were advertised for sale in tracts of not exceeding 160 acres each, on sealed bids, to the highest bidder for cash. The bids were duly opened, in compliance with the terms of the advertisement, and awards were made to the highest bidders of an aggregate quantity of 300.72 acres, for a sum total of $702.19½.

In view of the small number of bids received at this sale, it was deemed inexpedient to offer the lands again before next spring.

PAWNEE.

The commissioners of appraisal were appointed in anticipation of the consent of the Indians, which consent was, however, subsequently obtained. The lands being unsurveyed, it became necessary to have a survey made before the appraisement could be proceeded with, which was done, and the number of acres ascertained to be actually subject to sale under the provisions of said act of Congress is 48,424.76.

Instructions were issued September 8, 1873, by this office to the commissioners of appraisal for their guidance in the performance of their duties, and their report, bearing date November 6, 1873, has been received, but has not yet been submitted to the Department for approval.

Should the report of the appraisers be approved, it is deemed desirable that the lands should be advertised for sale at an early day.

OTTOE AND MISSOURIA.

Provision being also made by the aforementioned act of Congress for he disposition of not exceeding 80,000 acres of this reserve, commissioners of appraisal were appointed at the same time and under the same circumstances as in the case of the Omaha and Pawnee reserves. The Indians at first declined to give their assent to the provisions of the act of Congress, they being desirous of selling either their entire reserve or none at all. At last, however, their written assent was obtained, and under date of June 2, 1873, the same was forwarded to this office by Superintendent Barclay White.

Without unnecessary delay a contract was entered into for the survey of the portion of the reserve contemplated to be sold, but as yet the plats and field-notes of such survey have not been received; consequently no further action can at present be taken looking toward the appraisement and sale thereof.

NEW YORK INDIAN LANDS IN KANSAS.

An act of Congress approved February 19, 1873, provides for the appraisement and sale of the lands allotted to certain New York Indians who removed to Kansas, for which land certificates of allotment were issued under date of September 14, 1860.

Commissioners of appraisal were appointed by the Department April 9, 1873, who received instructions through this office on the 14th of the same month to make an appraisement, &c., of said lands under the provisions of the act. The report of the commissioners was duly filed and received the approval of the Department September 30, 1873. Rules and regulations were at the same time prescribed to be observed in carrying the provisions of said act into effect. Copies of said report and rules and regulations have been furnished the Commissioner of the General Land-Office for his information and guidance in carrying into effect that portion of the provisions of said act coming under his supervision.

FOND DU LAC RESERVATION IN MINNESOTA.

Section 8 of an act of Congress approved May 29, 1872, provides for the removal, upon their consent and concurrence being obtained, of the Fond du Lac, Lac de Flambeau, and Lac Court Orielle bands of Chippewa Indians from their present reservations to the reservation set apart by the second clause of the second article of Chippewa treaty of September 30, 1854, for the La Pointe band.

The first-named band have given their written consent to such removal, and the survey of their reservation has been completed with a view to its appraisement and sale.

Appraisers were appointed by the Department April 12, 1873, but owing to incompletion of surveys they were not instructed to proceed to the execution of the duties assigned them until September 17, 1873. At a meeting of the appraisers held on the reservation November 7, 1873, it was resolved to adjourn the work of appraisal until the 20th day of March next, for two reasons: 1st. That the Indians in council earnestly requested it, claiming that their consent to the sale of their reserve was fraudulently obtained; and 2d. That the deep snow and unfrozen condition of the swamps rendered it impossible to pass over them at this season of the year.

KANSAS OR KAW RESERVATION IN KANSAS.

An act of Congress approved May 8, 1872, provides for the removal of the Kansas tribes, and the appraisal and disposition of their reservation, including both the "trust-lands" (137,658.13 acres) and "diminished reserve," (80,409.06 acres.) Commissioners of appraisal were appointed by the Department June 29, 1872, who performed their duties under the instructions given them, and submitted their report bearing date December 28, 1872. This report was approved by the Department March 3, 1873, and the lands comprising the "diminished reserve" were advertised as being subject to sale on sealed bids until June 15, 1873.

Awards were made at this sale of 2,443.94 acres, being the entire quantity bid for.

From the best information at that time attainable, the small number of bids and the lack of competition manifested was attributed to the exorbitant character of the appraisement. In consideration of these facts, which were represented to the Department in report from this office, dated June 26, 1873, the appraisement of both the "trust-lands" and "diminished reserve" (except so much of the latter as was sold at the sale of June 15, 1873) was set aside by direction of the Department in letter dated July 8, 1873, and a re-appraisement ordered. A new commission of appraisal was at the same time appointed, the chairman of which (Hon. T. C. Jones, of Ohio) reported, under date of the 8th, 13th, and 16th of September, the inutility of making a re-appraisement, stating that in his opinion the first appraisement was not too high.

Upon such representations the Department canceled the former action revoking the appraisement made by the first commission, and restored the same to full force and effect. Settlers upon the "trust-lands" have accordingly been notified to make payment of the appraised value of the tracts respectively awarded them within one year from the restoration of the appraisement, and action by Congress has been recommended relative to these lands, the details of which can be found under the head of "legislation recommended."

WINNEBAGO TRUST-LANDS IN MINNESOTA.

These lands comprised a small remnant remaining unsold of the late Winnebago Indian reservation in Minnesota, provision for the disposition of which is contained in the 2d article of the Winnebago treaty, concluded April 15, 1859, and an act of Congress approved February 21, 1863.

The recommendation of this office for an early sale of these lands was approved by the Department June 7, 1873.

The lands were duly advertised, and the day of sale fixed for August 20, 1873, but was subsequently extended thirty days. Awards were made, and received the approval of the Department October 2, 1873, for the entire residue of said lands, amounting to 4,146.43 acres, for an aggregate sum of $14,959.28.

LEGISLATION RECOMMENDED.

ISSUES OF PATENTS TO ROBERT BENT AND JACK SMITH.

By a postscript to the treaty concluded with the Arapahoe and Cheyenne Indians February 18, 1861, these Indians gave to Robert Bent and Jack Smith 640 acres of land each, and requested the Government to confirm said gifts to said parties. No provision, however, for the issue of patents to these persons is contained in the treaty; and even the postscript cannot be considered as a grant in the absence of legislation. It is therefore recommended that the gifts be confirmed and the issue of patents authorized by act of Congress, in order that the wishes of the Indians may be carried out.

KANSAS OR KAW INDIAN LANDS IN KANSAS.

These lands having been appraised under the act of May 8, 1872, and a sale of those embraced in the "diminished reserve" having been attempted, but not enough having been sold to defray the expenses of the offering, the Department decided to set aside the appraisement and have a new one made. A commission having been appointed for this purpose, after reaching the lands the chairman reported that he did not deem the first appraisement too high. It was restored, and legislation by Congress is recommended as follows: That bona-fide settlers be allowed to purchase the same at the Topeka land-office, making payment of one-fourth of the appraised value at the date of settlement, and the remainder in three equal annual installments, giving security for the deferred payments.

AGREEMENT WITH THE CROW TRIBE OF INDIANS.

An act of Congress approved March 3, 1873, authorized negotiations with the Crow Indians for the cession of their reservation, or a portion thereof, in Montana, and the establishment of a smaller reservation for them. The necessity for such negotiation was found in the fact that the recent discovery of gold on the reservation had drawn many white persons there, with whom there was likely to be trouble; also in the fact that the Northern Pacific Railroad would likely pass through a portion of the reservation; whereas the policy is to have the reservations located at a distance from the public lines of travel. An agreement was concluded with said Indians by Special Commissioner Felix R. Brunot, chairman Board of Indian Commissioners, James Wright and E. Whittlesy, on the 16th of August last, by the terms of which the Crows cede their reservation and accept a reserve in Judith Basin. This agreement is made subject to the action of Congress, and its ratification is respectfully recommended.

ALLOTMENT OF CHOCTAW AND CHICKASAW LANDS.

The 11th article of the treaty concluded with the Choctaw and Chickasaw Indians April 28, 1866, sets forth that it is believed the holding of their lands in severalty will promote their general civilization, and tend to advance their permanent welfare; and it is therefore agreed that the lands be surveyed and allotted, should the Chickasaw and Choctaw people, through their respective legislative councils, agree to the same. The lands of the Chickasaws have been surveyed at their request, and their legislative council has, through their executive authorities, requested this Department to allot their lands; besides, the Chickasaw people in public assemblages have passed resolutions petitioning the Government to the same effect. The Choctaw council, however, refuse to join the Chickasaws in making the request for allotments as contemplated by the treaty. It is deemed proper, therefore, that Congress should afford the necessary legislation to enable this Department to comply with the request of the Chickasaws, independent of the action of the Choctaws, in order that the object of the treaty may be carried out, at least so far as the Chickasaws are concerned.

PAWNEE INDIAN RESERVATIONS IN NEBRASKA.

By the treaty concluded with the Pawnee Indians September 24, 1857, a reservation was set apart for said Indians in extent 30 miles from east to west by 15 miles from north to south. Upon a re-survey of the eastern boundary-line of said reservation, it has been ascertained that the east and west lines are but 29½ miles apart in place of 30 miles, thus leaving a deficiency in the proper area of the reservation of 4,800 acres. The Pawnees insist upon indemnity for said deficiency, and it is deemed just that Congress should provide for the same, at the rate of one dollar and twenty-five cents per acre, the minimum price of Government lands.

AGREEMENT WITH CŒUR D'ALÈNE INDIANS IN IDAHO.

In 1867 an Executive order was issued setting apart a reservation for the Cœur d' Alènes, but, being dissatisfied with the location, they never located thereon, and continued to roam over the tract of country claimed by them. For the purpose of extinguishing their claim to all the tract of country claimed by them, and of locating them on a reservation suitable to their wants as an agricultural people, an agreement has been made with them by Hon. J. P. C. Shanks, Gov. Bennett, of Idaho, and Agent J. B. Montieth, subject to ratification by Congress, which is respectfully recommended. Pending such action by that body, I have deemed it prudent to have set apart by executive order the tract of country described in said agreement as a reservation for said Indians, in order that white persons may be prohibited from settling thereon and claiming compensation for improvements from the Government.

SILETZ RESERVATION IN OREGON.

By the terms of a treaty concluded with the Coo-umpqua, Sinselano, Alsea, and other Indians embraced within the Siletz agency, in Oregon, provision was made for a reservation for said Indians. The treaty, however, was never ratified, and, to secure to them the reservation, an Executive order was issued November 9, 1855, setting the same apart for Indian purposes. These Indians are well advanced in civilization, and earnestly desire allotments, with patents for the same. Congress should therefore provide for the allotment of their lands and the issue of patents to such of said Indians as desire to cultivate the soil.

OFFICIAL SEAL FOR THE BUREAU.

Much inconvenience is caused by the want of an official seal for the purpose of certifying copies of files and records frequently called for as evidence in the civil courts. As it is, the seal of the Department has to be used for the purpose of certifying to the official character of the Commissioner of Indian Affairs. I therefore recommend that Congress authorize the use of a seal by this office, and provide that papers authenticated therewith shall have the same validity as in case of the use of a seal by other bureaus.

I have the honor to be, sir, very respectfully,

Your obedient servant,

EDW. P. SMITH,

Commissioner.

The Hon. SECRETARY OF THE INTERIOR.

PAPERS

ACCOMPANYING THE

REPORT OF THE COMMISSIONER OF INDIAN AFFAIRS.

1873.

PAPERS ACCOMPANYING THE REPORT OF THE COMMISSIONER OF INDIAN AFFAIRS, 1873.

A.

REPORT OF SPECIAL AGENT JOHN G. AMES IN REGARD TO THE CONDITION OF THE MISSION INDIANS OF CALIFORNIA, WITH RECOMENDATIONS.

WASHINGTON, D. C., *October* 28, 1873.

SIR: I have the honor to submit the following report touching the "number, location, and condition of the so-called Mission Indians of Southern California," with such recommendations in their behalf as seem best adapted to meet the exigencies of their situation.

In accordance with your instructions, I proceeded in May last to Southern California, where, on the 1st of June, I fixed the headquarters of the agency at Los Angeles. At this point I was detained several weeks, in consequence of the severe illness of a member of my family. This detention, however, was rather favorable than otherwise to the investigation upon which I was about to enter. It gave me the opportunity of learning the views of many of the citizens of Los Angeles and vicinity concerning the Mission Indian question, of acquainting myself with many facts in regard to the past history and management of these Indians, tending to throw light upon their present condition, and of advising with those whom I found best informed upon the subject as to what was best to be done with and for them. It gave me, also, the opportunity of learning, from the officers of the land-office at Los Angeles, so far as the records of that office indicate, the status of land in Southern California, which will aid materially in the solution of this question. I will say in this connection that I found the sentiment of the people of Los Angeles for the most part friendly to the Indians, and in favor of the Government doing something without delay in their behalf. There is a general feeling among those who give any attention to the subject that action in the premises has already been too long neglected, increasing the grievances of which the Indians complain, and making it ever more difficult to remedy the evils to which they are subject.

During my stay at Los Angeles I had several conferences with Indians of the San Luis Rey tribe; the first on June 12, with certain Indians living in Los Angeles, who expressed their gratification that the attention of the Government was at length directed to them, and their hope that they might soon be secure in the enjoyment of their rights. They desired especially that their title to lands now occupied by them should be so confirmed that they could not be driven from them by white men, and thought if this were done the Indians could easily take care of themselves.

Information having been communicated to the Indians living at Pala and vicinity that an agent of the Government had reached Los Angeles, I was in a few days visited by Olegario, actual chief of the large majority of the San Luis Rey tribe, though not recognized as such by the late superintendent of Indian affairs for California. Olegario was accompanied by ten of his captains. With these Indians I had protracted interviews on the 23d of June and on the 3d and 5th of July. They had come to lay their grievances before me and to ask the speedy interposition of the Government in their behalf.

The burden of their complaint was to the effect that they had been gradually driven from the lands which they or their fathers once occupied, the title to which they thought justly belonged to them, until at the present time but little available land remained to them; that white men were in many cases endeavoring to take from them the lands upon which they are living, and by the cultivation of which they gain a partial support; that they were frequently annoyed by the settlers interfering with water upon which they depended for irrigation, corraling their stock, and subjecting them to fine for the same, or taking it from them altogether, threatening them with violence, and in other ways invading what they believe to be their rights; that in disposing of lands the agents of the Government have never recognized the possessory rights of the Indians, and that in consequence they have been, and are still, obliged to abandon lands which they have held in immemorial possession, and to remove from places to which they are specially attached, as the home and the burial-ground of their ancestors, and this without any provision being made for them elsewhere.

They desired the Government to interfere to prevent this being done hereafter, and to secure them in the possession of the lands now occupied by them. If this was done they could readily support themselves, and were willing to do so, without aid from the Government, except in the matter of farming implements and seed and clothing for the supply of their immediate wants.

They urged, furthermore, as a special grievance, that their right to elect their own chief had been interfered with by the late superintendent, and that the Government recognizes as chief an Indian who was repudiated by nearly all the tribe, against whom they protested at the time of his appointment, two years ago, and whose authority they had since disregarded. They wished a new election ordered, that the tribe might choose its own chief and be no longer even nominally subject to one to whom so few owed allegiance.

In reply I assured them of the sincere desire of the Government to secure their rights and promote their interests, and of its intention to do whatever might be found practicable in this direction; that I had been sent out by the Government to hear their story, to examine carefully into their condition and recommend such measures as seemed under the circumstances most desirable; that I should, as soon as possible, visit them in their homes and see with my own eyes how they were situated, so that I might be better able to advise in their behalf.

It was a matter of special gratification to me that at the conference with Olegario and his captains, held July 3, General B. R. Cowen, the Assistant Secretary of the Interior, was present to listen to their story and to give them wise counsel. General Cowen expressed himself as particularly pleased with their appearance, and hopeful of their future if they were to be regarded as specimens of the Mission Indians.

TOUR OF INVESTIGATION.

On July 7 I started on a tour of investigation among the Indian settlements of the San Luis Rey tribe, accompanied by Mr. L. E. Sleigh, who, with the approval of the Indian Office, had been appointed clerk of this agency, and by Mr. Louis Wartenberg as interpreter.

We reached San Juan Capistrano the next day, where we called upon Rev. Jos. Mutt of the Roman Catholic Church, whom we found much interested in the Indians of that locality and in possession of information of interest in regard to the pueblo lands adjacent to the mission property. He showed us copies of record matter obtained at great trouble and expense from the archives at San Francisco, from which it appears that the pueblo of San Juan Capistrano was in the year 1841 actually subdivided by the Mexican authorities among the inhabitants, the Indians sharing with the Mexicans in this distribution.

If the claim of the Indians residing there, of whom there are about forty souls, can be established, as Rev. Mr. Mutt believes, the problem as far as they are concerned will be easily solved.

On the 11th we proceeded to San Luis Rey, where are to be found half a dozen families of Indians living upon land in dispute between them and one John Somers. The condition of these Indians, as well as the facts in the case of this dispute, are ably set before the Department by the late superintendent, C. B. Whiting, in a special report under date of May 19, 1873, to which reference is respectfully made.

On the 12th we proceeded thence to the city of San Diego, remaining there until the following Monday evening for the purpose of conferring with some of the citizens of the place as to the condition of the Indians of the country and the course best to be pursued by the Government to better their condition. A diversity of opinion prevails, but all agree that the disputes between the Indians and Americans involving titles to land should be speedily settled.

Reaching Pawai on Monday evening, I was there detained by illness two days, but sent Mr. Sleigh and the interpreter forward to visit certain Indian villages with the understanding that we should meet at Pala, the headquarters of the San Luis Rey tribe. Mr. Sleigh's report of his detour is here inserted:

"LOS ANGELES, CAL., *July* 31, 1873.

"DEAR SIR: I have the honor to submit the following report of my visit to the Indian villages of San Pasqual, Santa Ysabel, and Agua Caliente, in the county of San Diego, State of California.

"I reached San Pasqual on the 15th instant, from Pawai, where you were yourself detained. I proceeded at once to the house of Panto Lion, captain of the village, and requested him to summon his people together on the following morning for a conference, at the same time explaining to him that we had been sent by the Government at Washington to inquire into their condition and to ascertain if anything could be done by the Government to aid them.

"The villagers began to assemble early. At the appointed hour the captain rose, and in a short speech in the Indian language, which seemed to be both eloquent and well appreciated, gave his hearers to understand the errand upon which I visited them. A lively interest was manifested by every one. They complained of the encroachments of their American neighbors upon their land, and pointed to a house near by, built by one of the more adventurous of his class, who claimed to have pre-empted the land upon which the larger part of the village lies. On calling upon the man afterward, I found that such was really the case, and that he had actually paid the price of the land to the register of the land-office of this district, and was daily expecting the patent from Washington. He owned it was hard to wrest from these well-disposed and industrious creatures the homes they had built up. 'But,' said he, 'if I had not done it somebody else would, for all agree that the Indian has no right to public lands.' These Indians further complain that settlers take advantage of them in every way possible; employ them to work and insist on paying them in trifles that are of no account to them; 'dock' them for imaginary neglect, or fail entirely to pay them; take up their stock on the slightest pretext and make exorbitant charges for damages and detention of the stock seized. They are in many cases unable to redeem it. They have therefore little encouragement to work or to raise stock. Nor do they care to plant fruit-trees or grape-vines as long as land thus improved may be taken from them, as has been the case in very many instances. Among the little homes included in the pre-emption claim above referred to are those adorned with trees and vines. Instead of feeling secure and happy in the possession of what little is left to them, they are continually filled with anxiety. They claim that they ought to be allowed to remain where their forefathers have lived for so long, and that they should be protected by law in the peaceful possession of the homes that have been handed down to them.

"I asked how they would like for their children to go to school, learn to speak the English language, and to live more like white people. It would be very nice, they replied, but it would do them little good if they could not have their homes protected.

"I asked them how they would like to be moved to some place where they could be better protected, have ground of their own secured to them, and more comfortable homes. The answer was, 'Our fathers lived and died here, and we would rather live here than at any other place.'

"In conclusion I assured them that I should report what I had learned about them, and that I had little doubt but that the Government at Washington would be able to do something to better their condition, charging them at the same time to strive, as I felt they had been doing, to keep the peace among themselves and with the whites.

"I proceeded thence by the most direct route to Santa Ysabel rancheria. On reaching that place, I found the captain, Augustine, absent; sent a messenger for him, and also one for the chief of the Diegenes, Pablo Pene, who lives in a neighboring rancheria. There are about one hundred and twenty-five souls at Santa Ysabel. They occupy the finest valley of the ranch of the same name, on one side of which are about twenty adobe houses for winter-quarters, while on the other side, near their fields of grain, are as many brush-houses, now occupied. At the time that I reached the village, men, women, and children were scattered over the fields harvesting their grain. Some were reaping, some thrashing, some grinding, while near the houses women were making it into bread for immediate use. It was altogether an interesting picture to look upon.

"The chief and captain arrived during the night, and as soon as possible in the morning I sought a conference with them in relation to the condition and wants of their people. I was glad to find them exempt from many of the annoyances of which the Indians of San Pasqual complain. The land which they occupy is claimed under a grant from the Mexican government by private parties, who have hesitated to undertake to eject the Indians for fear of violence on their part in resisting, as they (the Indians) dispute any ownership more sacred than their own, and insist that they should not be disturbed in their possession.

"I reached Agua Caliente on the 17th instant. From a notched stick given me by the captain of the village, José Maria Moro, it appears that there are one hundred and sixty-eight Indians at that place. The land upon which they live has been understood to be of the public domain, until a recent survey of Warner's ranch betrayed the fact that it was included within the boundary of said ranch. The owners of the ranch threaten to drive them away, and settlers have interfered with their water-privileges, and annoy them in many ways. On the whole they have little to encourage them, and begin to feel that the white man is their enemy.

"My talk with the Indians of Santa Ysabel and Agua Caliente was substantially the same as at San Pasqual. They look to the Government to relieve them of the difficulties under which they now labor. They are peaceably disposed, and for the most part industrious, and deserve better treatment than they get.

"At San Pasqual and Agua Caliente I was called upon by white settlers, the majority of whom had no good word for their dusky neighbors. 'They are thieves; they are treacherous; they are vagabonds.' It was urged that they should be taken to some one of the Territories and surrounded by soldiers to keep them at home, or to some island in the sea. I found, however, little in my journey to confirm such opinions, but was glad to note many indications of thrift. I could but wonder, indeed, that they are as reliable, honest, and peaceable as I found them to be. The sentiments entertained by very many white men in Southern California toward the Indians are well illustrated in the conclusion to which the proprietor of a small ranch near Temecula came in presenting the subject to me from his stand-point. It is well to mention that a family of Indians has occupied one corner of his ranch 'from time immemorial.' His wise and humane (?) conclusion was that the owners of large ranches should not drive 'their Indians' away, but should keep them to work for them, and set apart certain portions of the ranch for them. 'There is worthless land enough upon every ranch,' he said, 'for Indians to live on.'

"The Indians of San Pasqual and Santa Ysabel belong to the Diegenes tribe, with Pable Pene chief, while those of Agua Caliente are Coahuila Indians, under the chiefship of Manuel Largo. The two tribes speak different dialects; a few in either tribe can speak the Spanish language, but I found none able to converse in English. The aggregate number of the Diegenes is estimated at one thousand, distributed in about fifteen rancherias, which are situated in the central and southern portions of the county of San Diego.

"All of which I have the honor to submit.

"LUTHER E. SLEIGH.

"Rev. JOHN G. AMES,
"*Special Agent Mission Indians.*"

Proceeding by way of San Pasqual and Bear Valley, for the purpose of examining the country with reference to a reservation, I reached Pala on the 18th, where, on the next day, I had interviews with José Antonio Sal, chief, and with Manuelita Cota, ex-chief of the tribe; also visited the flourishing Palma rancheria on the Palma grant, reaching Rincon, the residence of Olegario, whom most of the tribe acknowledge as chief, the same evening. Here I was rejoined by Mr. Sleigh on the 20th.

It being Sunday, we held in the evening a religious service, which was attended by most of the Indians of the rancheria, who gave respectful attention to the words addressed to them. At their special request this service was concluded with the recital of a portion of the liturgy of the Catholic Church, one of their own number leading and the rest responding.

Visiting the potrero, near by, on the next day, I found an Indian family of unusual interest, because of their greater intelligence and generally recognized superiority among the tribe. The head of the family was absent, but his wife, "Margarita," known far and wide among the Indians, seemed quite competent to take the management of affairs in his absence. This Indian woman claims a half league of land which was granted by the Mexican government to her grandmother, and which she now holds by her mother's will in trust for the heirs of the same. The rancheria upon this land is composed chiefly of these heirs, who derive from the land a comfortable subsistence.

Returning to Rincon, I had the good fortune to witness in the evening one of the traditional dances in which the Indians take so much delight. It was conducted in an orderly manner, nor was it carried to excess, and could hardly be regarded by any as other than a safe and commendable amusement for them.

On the 21st, at this place, a conference was held with the San Luis Rey Indians. Runners had been sent out to inform those living in the different rancherias, and a large number had come together eager to hear the news from Washington. This tribe takes its title from the Mission of that name. It is farther advanced in civilization than any other tribe of the so-called Mission Indians. They have the reputation of being industrious, and for the most part peaceable, and but for the difficulties they labor under, in consequence of the unsettled condition of land matters and the disregard of their rights by the settlers, would be self-sustaining and make reliable citizens.

At present they are in trouble about their chief, as indicated at the conference at Los Angeles. A large majority prefer Olegario, and if an election were held now he would doubtless be chosen. He is intelligent above the average, peaceably disposed toward the whites, capable of controlling his Indians—for he is virtually chief, notwithstanding the action of the late superintendent—and is at the same time an enthusiastic defender of his people and disposed to take advanced grounds on questions of their rights. A more competent man altogether cannot be found in the tribe.

Manuelita Cota and Francisco Magla, ex-chiefs, and José Antonio Sal, chief, were also present at the conference. We were obliged to employ two interpreters, in order that all could be made to understand what we had to say. I began by reading my letter of instruction, and explained the same to them. Much satisfaction was expressed at the prospect of relief from the Government at Washington.

They complained that they were subjected to many indignities from white neighbors who covet the lands occupied by them; that the water they had long depended upon for irrigation had been turned out of its course, rendering their lands useless. Lands that they have supposed to belong to them have, on various pretexts, been wrested from them. They feel that the Government should protect them from injustice in such matters. They also expressed a desire that schools should be established among them, so that their children may learn to speak the English language and live more like Americans.

I explained to them, at length, the law in relation to the Government and grant lands upon which they live; also, the laws of the State relative to the care of stock, and trespass by the same.

In regard to the election of a chief, about which intense feeling prevails, I told them I would refer the question to the Government for instructions, as I had no authority to order an election at present.

In conclusion, addressing Olegario and his captains, and then José Antonio Sal and his captains, I charged them to see that the peace be kept and the rights of everybody's property respected; that there should be no strife among themselves, but that all should work together for the common good.

The aggregate number of the San Luis Rey tribe, as reported by the several captains, is nine hundred and seventy-five. These are distributed in ten rancherias, scattered over the northwestern portions of San Diego County and located some upon Government and some upon grant lands.

On the whole the conference resulted satisfactorily. The Indians expressed themselves as willing and anxious to live at peace with the settlers, and ready to wait patiently, yet longer, for the Government to take such action as will secure them in the enjoyment of their rights. They preferred many requests, most of which are implied in the recommendations which are to follow.

Leaving Rincon we rode over the mountains to Temecula, where is an Indian village, and from thence returned to Los Angeles.

On the 1st of August I set out to visit the Coahuila Indians. This tribe is divided into two sections, one under Cobezon as chief, living in San Gorgonio Pass, and in the desert beyond; the other, under Manuel Largo, located principally in the San Jacinto and Coahuila Valleys south of the San Jacinto Mountains. The existence of the first-mentioned section of this tribe has seldom, if ever, been recognized in any official report concerning the Indians of Southern California.

Proceeding by way of San Bernardino, I visited Mr. M. H. Crafts, residing near San Gorgonio Pass, whose letters to the Indian Office in regard to these Indians had been referred to me by the honorable Commissioner. I found Mr. Crafts thoroughly interested in their welfare, and well qualified, through twelve years' acquaintance and friendly intercourse with them, to render me efficient service. He accompanied me in my visit to the desert, where, in our conference with the Indians, I saw in their manifest regard for him how readily their confidence and good-will are awakened by kindly treatment and sympathy.

A messenger was dispatched to summon Cabezon and his captains to meet me at the potrero in the San Gorgonio Pass, on the following Wednesday. Proceeded through the pass as far as Warm Spring Station for the purpose of visiting a rancheria there located, and of ascertaining from actual observation the condition of the desert Indians, returning to the potrero to meet Cabezon according to appointment.

The venerable old man, supposed to be upwards of ninety years of age, arrived about noon of the day designated, at the head of a company of horsemen in single file, heralded by a marshal in uniform, who announced the approach of the chief and captains with much pomp and noise. The company seemed much exhausted from the fatigue of their hot ride through the desert, while the condition of their horses indicated great destitution in the matter of pasturage. Cabezon had the previous day sent an urgent request that meat and flour should be furnished them on their arrival, as they were not able to supply themselves with food at the conference. I could not do otherwise than comply with this request, purchasing the necessary provision of a white settler in the pass. This aged chief is in many respects a remarkable man. He is venerated by all his people, over whom he has long exercised a powerful influence and always in the interest of peace and good-will toward the whites. Even when their rights have been disregarded and their enmity excited, he has withheld them from acts of hostility, persuading them to wait until the Government should come to their aid. Through his influence, also, the tribe has been kept from allying itself with the tribes on the Colorado River for the purpose of making war upon the whites. His efforts seem from the first to have been devoted to the preservation of the peace between the two races.

The mind shudders at the contemplation of what would probably have been the results to the inhabitants of San Bernardino County had Cabezon and his tribe assumed a different attitude. More than this, the whites of that section of California have been largely dependent upon these Indians in the care of their farms, much of the labor in all departments of farm-work being performed by them. Many of the land-owners would have been subject to great inconvenience had not this Indian labor been available. In the mean time the Indians have reaped no permanent advantage from their labors; they have only become demoralized by their contact with the whites.

After resting a while and partaking of some refreshments, Cabezon announced himself ready to proceed with the conference. This took about the same direction as that at Rincon, detailed above.

The Indians dwelt at length upon the encroachments of the whites, depriving them of lands to which they asserted their sole ownership, and driving them back into the desert, where they must soon perish. They were very reluctant to proceed to the consideration of any other questions until they should be assured of the restoration of lands wrested from them, or, at least, of the peaceable retention of what they now occupy. They were very much disposed to eject by force one or two trespassers who were just then annoying them, and were induced to defer such action only on my assuring them that their grievances would be made known at Washington, and that I felt confident the Government would protect them in their rights.

They complained also of being overlooked in the distribution of presents, saying they had received only the merest pittance, while other Indians, who were not more deserving than they, had been liberally supplied. To this I replied by assuring them that the Government would endeavor to prevent any unjust discrimination hereafter, and that in any future distribution of goods among the Indians of Southern California they should receive their proper share.

They requested that schools might be established among them, and expressed a willingness to co-operate with the Government in any effort it should make for their benefit.

In conclusion, Cabezon said he was growing very old and must soon die, but he wished before he passed away to see his Indians settled upon lands which they could call their own, and where they and their children could live unmolested. At a subsequent interview with Cabezon and a few of his tribe at the residence of Mr. Crafts, the same topics were still further discussed, with the additional request that the Government regard his wish concerning his son, then present, whom he had appointed his successor as chief of the Coahuilas.

The aggregate number of this section of the tribe, as reported by the several captains, is one thousand and eighty, distributed in about twelve rancherias. Most of these rancherias are located in the desert or among the mountains bordering the same, where but limited opportunities for procuring a livelihood are afforded.

At the potrero, however, where the conference was held, there are, I should judge, eight hundred acres of irrigable land. This land has been occupied from time immemorial by these Indians, and has, I was told, been regarded as a kind of retreat for the squaws and the aged of the tribe, whenever they have been driven back from the now more settled portions of San Bernardino County. The potrero has been supposed to be well fortified against American settlers by the situation of their village at its entrance; but within a few months an adventurous white man, coming over the mountain, has taken up his abode in the upper part of their domain, where he constructed a rude dwelling before his presence was known to the villagers. They demanded that he be made to give up to them again their former pasture-grounds, and said they would have expelled him by force, had they not heard of my coming. They, however, reluctantly, consented to wait still longer to enable me to present the facts in the case to the Government at Washington.

We proceeded thence by way of San Bernardino and Riverside, the nearest available route, to visit that portion of the tribe which recognizes Manuel Largo as chief, residing principally in the San Jacinto and Coahuila Valleys. I found the Indians of San Jacinto involved in the usual difficulties with the whites. This rancheria is located partly upon a grant, and in close proximity to the principal spring of water in the valley. Bitter disputes have sprung up between the two races, which threatened at one time to result in acts of violence. The whites accuse the Indians of running off and killing their stock. This, I have no doubt, is sometimes done, though by no means to the extent alleged.

The Indians on the other hand accuse the whites of driving them from their lands and of wresting from them their homes, in violation of every principle of justice, protesting their unwillingness to submit longer to such treatment, and their purpose to take matters into their own hands unless the whites desist from their encroachments or the Government protects them in their rights.

Those living in the Coahuila Valley are more isolated and so less subject to annoyance from settlers. They have, however, driven off one or two whites who have attempted to squat upon their lands, and declare their intention to pursue the same course in the future if like attempts are made.

This section of the Coahuila tribe is less peaceably disposed—more inclined to resort to force in the maintenance of what they believe to be their rights—than any other Mission Indians. They have, during the past summer, been very much excited by the presence among them of the United States marshal, who came for the purpose of arresting certain parties accused of stealing stock. The state of feeling is such that I deem it very important that adequate measures be taken to preserve the peace and to secure the rights of both parties at the earliest practicable moment.

A conference was held with Manuel Largo and his principal captains, in the Coahuila Valley. This conference, in its main features, so clearly resembled those already held, hat I deem it unnecessary to give a detailed account of it.

The Indians under Manuel Largo, who was appointed chief by the late Superintendent Whiting, number, as reported by their captains, eight hundred and fifty-seven. They own more stock and are less given to agriculture than their fellow Indians; this is owing, in part, to the fact that much of their land is situated at such an elevation that grain or vegetables cannot be grown because of frost.

Returning to Los Angeles we proceeded thence to San Diego for the purpose of examining into the condition of Indians residing in the southern part of San Diego County. Having heard that there were quite a number in the vicinity of Julian, a mining town situated some seventy miles in the interior, we visited that locality. Julian is a resort to which many Indians flock for the purpose of procuring liquor, or for purposes still more reprehensible. No Indian village, however, is located there, nor could I learn of more than two or three rancherias along the southern border of the county. It was impracticable to hold any conference with them from their being so much scattered. Their condition very closely resembles that of the other Diegenes above referred to in Mr. Sleigh's report. Quite a number of this tribe are always to be found in the neighborhood of San Diego, and always in a demoralized state. The facilities which towns afford for vicious and debasing indulgences prove to no class more disastrous than to the Indians.

My tour of investigation among the Mission Indians has made me more hopeful than I had anticipated in regard to their future, provided the Government is ready to do what ought to be done for their relief.

In connection with many characteristics which belong to them in common with the rest of their race, they exhibit others more closely allying them to the whites, of which efficient use may be made in efforts which the Government shall undertake in their behalf. Their contact with the whites, while in many respects it has wrought harm, has in others operated to their advantage, especially as it will facilitate their future acquisition of the arts of civilized life. While they complain of the manner in which they have been treated by the whites, I discovered very little of the spirit of revenge among them. So far from this, I think no other race would have borne so patiently and with so little effort at retaliation the indignities and wrongs to which they have been subject. They are generally indolent, which, under the circumstances, is not a matter of surprise. I believe, however, they can be persuaded to labor if those inducements are presented to them that are most influential with other men. They are thriftless and wasteful, but there have been, in their case, small encouragements toward the cultivation of better habits. They take little thought of the morrow, satisfied if their present necessities are supplied. This fault, however, can be gradually remedied by establishing among them that individual relation to property which subsists among the whites, and by fostering a desire for its acquisition.

The sanctity of the marital relation is sometimes disregarded by them, but the law of chastity is most frequently violated through the persuasions of corrupt white men, who look upon the Indian as the defenseless victim of their lusts. The evils resulting from this are so serious as to demand the enactment of the most stringent laws tending to the suppression of this vice. Guilty white men should be made to feel severely the consequences of their acts. The infliction of punishment will operate more efficiently than any effort to keep the two races separate.

The worst habit on the whole, in its results, to which they are addicted is intemperance. This works fearful demoralization among them. The law forbidding the sale of liquor to Indians is violated with impunity. Notice has seldom been taken of such violation by those charged with the execution of the laws, partly because there has been no agent to interest himself in the matter, and partly because public sentiment has too often regarded the Indian as lawful prey even for whisky-sellers. Very unsatisfactory results have for the most part followed attempts to secure conviction under the law. The attention of the Government is earnestly called to this subject. It is probable that some change in the law itself, or in the provisions for its execution, may be made by which it shall be rendered more efficient in the suppression of this evil.

As for other evils incident to their situation, and other faults of character, these, I think, can, in large measure, be gradually remedied by the judicious management and good example of the agent who shall be put in charge of them, and of his subordinates, and especially by bringing them under the wholesome influence of law—both State and national—whose protection and restraint will serve to promote order and peace, to check individual license and self-will, and to foster a spirit of subordination and a just regard for each other's rights. I deem it of great importance that these Indians should be treated as standing in the same relation to the laws of the land as white men, and should be taught that violations of law would subject them to punishment by the civil authorities.

THE RELATION OF THE MISSION INDIANS TO THE UNITED STATES GOVERNMENT.

The Mission Indians became subject to the jurisdiction of the United States Government in virtue of the treaty of Guadalupe Hidalgo. By its stipulations they were to occupy a relation to this Government analogous to that sustained by them to the government of Mexico, and were to be protected in the enjoyment of the rights appertaining to this relation. I shall not here enter upon the discussion of the question of their citizenship under the Mexican Republic. This question has been recently discussed in a report of the late superintendent, Mr. Whiting, bearing date May 19, 1873, to which attention is herewith called. In this report Mr. Whiting asserts the fact that they were recognized as citizens by the government of Mexico and as entitled to the privilege of voting. In accordance with this view it has been decided by the United States court for the Territory of New Mexico, that the Indians within the territory acquired by the United States from Mexico are, by virtue of the provisions of the eighth article of the treaty of Guadalupe Hidalgo of 1848, citizens of the United States. If this position is well taken it would seem that, on their becoming subject to the jurisdiction of the United States, they could not justly be denied all the special rights of citizenship, or be treated as the Government has been accustomed to treat the wild and uncivilized tribes with whom it has had principally to deal. As a matter of fact, however, they have never been recognized as citizens by our Government, nor as entitled to any rights which a citizen is bound to respect.

They occupy an anomalous position. No treaty has ever been made with them by which they could be recognized as *imperium in imperio*. They have never assumed a hostile attitude toward the Government or the settlers, requiring the employment of force for their control. They never urged their claims upon the attention of the Government until recently, when it has become evident to them that they will soon be deprived of everything they had thought their own unless the Government interfere to prevent it.

They maintain their tribal relationship and self-government only in a modified form, holding themselves amenable to the laws of the United States and of the State of California. Tribal bonds are becoming gradually weaker, and at no distant day it is probable they may be readily persuaded to dissolve this relationship altogether. It would not, in my view, be wise to attempt this dissolution at present. Nor would it be wise to admit them as a whole to the privileges of the franchise, unless justice requires this—unless it can be clearly shown that this right was guaranteed by the treaty of Guadalupe Hidalgo. It is very desirable, however, that they should be admitted to all the rights of citizenship as soon as practicable, and that they should as far as possible be encouraged and helped to fit themselves for the intelligent exercise of these rights. There are a few who are already well qualified and ready to become citizens, and who are willing, if necessary to this end, to renounce all tribal jurisdiction.

Three Indians at least have recently made application to be registered as citizens in Los Angeles County. Their petition was refused by the clerk of the county court, acting under the advice of the district attorney, on the sole ground of their being Indians. They then referred the matter, through their attorney, C. N. Wilson, esq., to the United States commissioner at Los Angeles, asking him to take such action in the premises as would fully test their rights in this regard under the Constitution. He refused to have anything to do with the case, further than to transmit the affidavits of the Indians to the district attorney at San Francisco. Here the matter rests for the present, with little prospect that anything in their interest will be done by the officers of justice, to whom they have made appeal. Should this claim continue to be disregarded, the attention of the Government will again be called to their case, in the hope that some provision will be made, if not already existing, by which they, and such as they, can readily secure their recognition as citizens of the United States.

I deem it important that whatever hinders this should, so far as possible, be removed, and that in the management of these Indians the Government should always keep in view their incorporation with the body-politic at the earliest practicable moment.

THE RELATION OF THE MISSION INDIANS TO THE LANDS.

It will be observed one claim which these Indians urge with much feeling is their right and title to the lands upon which they and their fathers have lived from time immemorial. They assert their former ownership of all this country, and say that no purchase of any portion of it by white men has ever been made. Much of it, however, has been forcibly taken from them without their consent. They ask that this be no longer permitted, and that the Government secure them in the possession of the few acres now occupied by them.

However valid this claim might have been under the Spanish government, and with whatever show of justice it may now be urged, it has, I take it, no real validity in law as applied to lands in general. Since the acquisition of this territory the United States have never acknowledged any Indian title to the land. With other tribes treaties have been entered into, with a view to the extinguishment of their title, involving often large expenditures of the public money. As regards these Indians, however, a committee of the United States Senate, to whom the matter was referred, reported that no such treaty was necessary; "that the United States, acquiring possession of the territory from Mexico, succeeded to its rights in the soil; and as that government regarded itself as the absolute and unqualified owner of it, and held that the Indian had no usufructuary or other rights therein which were to be in any manner respected, they, the United States, were under no obligations to treat with the Indians occupying the same for the extinguishment of their title."

In accordance with this view, the assumed Indian title has always been disregarded by the land-officers of the Government in this district and by settlers. As expressed by the present register of the land-office, the location of an Indian family or families on land upon which a white man desires to settle is, in law, no more a bar to such settlement than would be the presence of a stray sheep or cow. And so, like sheep or cattle, they have been too often driven from their homes and their cultivated fields, the Government, through its officers, refusing to hear their protests, as though in equity as well as in law they had no rights in the least deserving consideration. Such, however, having been, and still being, the theory and practice of the Government, I cannot think it possible that it will now turn a deaf ear to the complaints and to the petitions of these Indians. Every consideration of justice and humanity, and a regard for their continued peace and good will, unite to urge the Government to make immediate provision for the few that remain of these once populous tribes, to secure them in the enjoyment of their rights and in the possession of homes which they can truly call their own.

The question of the equitable title of the Mission Indians to lands in California is discussed in the report of Superintendent Whiting, above alluded to, to which attention is again called.

The policy of the Spanish, and subsequently of the Mexican government, was to intrust the care of the Indians to the priests of the Catholic Church. These priests were authorized to establish missions wherever required, and to gather the Indians of the vicinity into communities about the missions. Lands to the amount of from four to eleven leagues were assigned for the use of each mission. The success which attended the efforts of these missionaries is attested by the interesting, and in some cases remarkable, ruins of the mission buildings erected by the Indians under their supervision; by the degree of civilization to which the Indians were raised through their influence and instruction, by the fact that at some of these missions as many as five thousand Indians were gathered; that upon the lands of the mission as many as seventy-five thousand head of cattle were kept, besides large flocks of sheep and other stock, while corn and other articles of food were grown sufficient for their support.

I am led to believe that it was the design of the Spanish government to erect these missions into pueblos, and to distribute the lands among the Indians, giving to each family a certain number of acres as soon as they were sufficiently civilized to warrant such a step. This distribution of lands, however, was never made under the Spanish rule, and, so far as I am informed, in only one instance under the Mexican rule. I refer to the mission lands of San Juan Capistrano, which, according to documents now in the archives at San Francisco, were so distributed by order of the Mexican government. Upon some of these lands Indian families are still living, claiming possession, and justly, I think, in virtue of this action.

A large portion of these mission lands is now included in grants claimed to have been made previous to the cession of this country to the United States. Nearly all the rest has been taken up under the pre-emption and homestead laws, so that of the many leagues once set apart for the special benefit of these Indians, and designed as their perpetual possession, not one now remains to them.

Many Indians are at present living upon grants which have been confirmed by the United States. Whether they are entitled to remain there and to enjoy the use of the land, or are to be regarded as trespassers, is a question which must soon be decided.

I have been frequently told that whenever grants were made under the Mexican government the right of any Indians then located upon the grant to a continual residence thereon was reserved, and the grantee was forbidden to eject or disturb them. I have not been able to verify this assertion. The Indians have assumed its correctness, and many of the grant owners have hitherto seemed to acquiesce; at least they have suffered the Indians to remain and enjoy the use often of the best portion of the grant, that, namely, whose proximity to streams or springs of water makes it available for agricultural purposes. The time will soon come, however, when they will demand, and, I think on general principles, with justice, the removal of these Indians. But, irrespective of such demand, the interest of the Indians will, in my view, be best promoted by removing them from grant-lands at the earliest practicable moment, and settling them upon lands to which the Government can give them title, and where all improvements shall redound to their own and their children's benefit.

MEASURES OF RELIEF DISCUSSED.

In view of these facts to which attention has now been called; in view especially of the peaceable and friendly attitude which they have always maintained toward the Government; of the general indifference with which their interests have been hitherto regarded by the Government; of the supposed injustice and wrong of which they believe themselves to be the subjects; of their helplessness in the presence of an increasing immigration, which, with the sanction of the law, is driving them from their homes, and seizing, without remuneration, upon possessions which they claim as their own; of the extremity to which they are reduced, now that nearly all the land available for their use has been taken up, an appeal is made to the Government that it will at length interpose its offices in their behalf, and take such action as will secure them in the undisturbed enjoyment of their rights and in the possession of homes which settlers shall not be permitted to take from them. When this appeal is made to an administration which has signalized itself by the just and humane policy it has adopted toward the Indians, I cannot think that it will be in vain. If other arguments or voices are needed to induce action on the part of the Government in this matter, I would refer to the reports of former agents who have had to do with the Mission Indians, nearly all of whom have earnestly recommended that provision should be made for them without needless delay.

What can be done?

Many suggestions have been made looking to a solution of this perplexing question. Some urge the policy of declaring them citizens, and then letting them take their chances with white men in securing lands under the homestead act. To say nothing, however, of their general want of qualification for citizenship, nor of the improbability of their soon attempting to avail themselves of the provisions of this act, there is little or no land in Southern California from which they could gain a livelihood open to them. Almost all the land fit for agricultural purposes has been taken up by settlers, or is claimed under Mexican grants. The case would probably be very different were all spurious grant-claims disallowed, and the boundaries of all genuine claims accurately defined, and the owners compelled to observe these limits. The Government would undoubtedly then find itself to be the possessor of many thousands of acres now claimed by private parties. There might then be good land enough for the Indians and to spare. There is not now. And to adopt the policy suggested would be only prejudicial to the Indians' true interests.

Some advise that they be let alone, and left as heretofore to take care of themselves, a policy which has already borne poisonous fruit, and which would result in the still greater demoralization of both Indians and whites, to say nothing of the bitter and hostile feelings which such a course would engender among the former. It is not improbable that even the Mission Indians might then be provoked to acts of hostility, insane as such conduct might appear to us.

Others recommend that they be removed to a distance from their present location, and be established on a reservation to be set apart for them either in Arizona or in some part of California remote from white settlements, where there will be least liability of trouble between them and settlers. This course is advised by the press of San Diego, and would without doubt be satisfactory to a large portion of the white population of San Diego County. The arguments advanced in its support are chiefly to the effect that the area of agricultural lands in San Diego County is so limited that it ought all to be reserved for white men; that the presence of the Indian operates, and will continue to operate, as a hinderance to the development of the resources of the country, and that only increasing demoralization can be expected from the continued contact of the Indians with the whites.

This would certainly be a simple solution of the problem if it were practicable and just, neither of which can I think it to be.

The recommendation does not contemplate, except in a most indirect way, the welfare of the Indian. It ignores all rights he may be supposed to have in the land he now occupies, and disregards any preference he may cherish in regard to his future location. It is suggested simply by a desire that that section of country may be rid of a population regarded by many as an obstacle in the way of their own prosperity, requiring for their support some portion of the good land whose possession is coveted for white settlers. It would, if undertaken, be a purely arbitrary measure, and could only be executed by force, as the Indians would not voluntarily relinquish their present homes to be transferred to some distant and unknown region.

Nor am I disposed to think that their being permitted to remain in the country and to occupy arable lands will retard agricultural development. On the contrary, I believe that if subject to judicious oversight and direction, and made secure in the possession of lands, such lands would soon yield under their management as large returns as would result if they were in the hands of white men. I see no reason to doubt but that in a few years many of them would become skillful farmers, whose peaceful labors would tend to increase from year to year the aggregate wealth of the community. But even if this were altogether doubtful, I think the dictates of justice and wisdom would forbid the approval of the plan above suggested on the part of the Government

MEASURES OF RELIEF RECOMMENDED.

It remains for me to indicate the measures that commend themselves to my judgment as most judicious in the premises.

I recommend—

In regard to the San Luis Rey Indians—That, wherever they are now found located upon Government lands, such lands be set aside for their use, to the amount of not exceeding forty acres to every head of a family and to every unmarried adult male Indian; that for such of the tribe as are now settled upon land owned by private parties, the unappropriated land in Pala and the adjacent township 9 south, ranges 1 and 2 west, San Bernardino meridian, be reserved to be distributed in portions not to exceed forty acres to each head of a family and to each unmarried adult male Indian. The undivided portion to be held in common for purposes of pasturage. These townships formed a part of the reservation set apart for the Mission Indians in A. D. 1870, but subsequently restored to the public domain.

Pala is the site of one of the old Catholic mission churches, and a place to which many of the Indians are still attached. Some of the best lands of these townships have been taken by settlers, but there remains enough, I think, to provide adequately for such of the tribe as are not otherwise provided for. There is water in the San Luis Rey River, which flows through the valley, sufficient for purposes of irrigation if the Indians be properly located and the water equitably distributed. Considerable expense will attend such distribution, as the water must be conducted long distances in ditches in order to be available for any large extent of territory. The land, however, cannot otherwise be made productive, and I think the result will justify all necessary expenditure.

The Indians who own lands in their own rights should be strongly urged to retain them in their position and to transmit them to posterity.

Concerning the question of the chieftainship of this tribe above referred to, I recommend that a new election be allowed, as the large majority desire, to be held at such time as the agent deems best, with the distinct understanding that if any portion of the tribe should object to being put under the chief then elected, they would be held as exempt from his jurisdiction on the condition of their renouncing their tribal relation and registering themselves as citizens of the United States.

I advise this course the more readily from a persuasion that if any avail themselves of this provision it will be a few of the more intelligent of the tribe.

In regard to the Diegenes—I recommend that townships 12 south, range 1 north and 1 east, and 13 south, range 1 north and 1 east, San Bernardino meridian, be set aside as a reservation for their use. This will involve an expenditure of several thousand dollars in the purchase of improvements made by settlers, which improvements, however, would then redound to the benefit of the Indians.

These townships constituted a part of the reservation above alluded to, and include lands by far the most available in San Diego County for the purposes in view. I regard it as most unfortunate that the order designating Pala and San Pasqual as an Indian reservation was ever revoked, and am convinced that this step would never have been taken had not utterly false representations been made to the authorities in Washington.

The expense and difficulty of satisfactorily settling this Mission Indian question have, in my judgment, been very much increased by such action.

If it be deemed inexpedient by the Department to purchase the improvements referred to above, I then suggest that the lands of these townships, not already taken up, be withdrawn from sale and reserved for these Indians.

The only alternative provision that presents itself to my mind is the purchase of some private grant. This would be attended with large expense, and in my view no grant-lands can be found which will meet the requirements of the case as fully as the San Pasqual Valley, included in the townships above mentioned. For further testimony concerning Pala and San Pasqual, I would respectfully refer to reports as follows, viz: Special report of B. C. Whiting, superintendent for California, under date of December 6, 1867, and special report of General J. B. McIntosh, superintendent for California, under date of August 25, 1869.

For the Coahuila Indians—I recommend the purchase of from five thousand to ten thousand acres of land in San Bernardino County, upon which the now scattered members of the tribe shall be located. Available land can, I think, be found near the base of the San Bernardino Mountains, which can be secured at a not unreasonable rate. Should this be regarded as impracticable, I then recommend that the Government lands upon which these Indians are now living be reserved for their use, viz, the Coahuila Valley, in San Diego County; the potrero, near San Gorgonio Pass, San Bernardino County, and such other smaller portions of land as they now occupy and cultivate, and that such of the tribe as are now settled upon lands owned by private parties be removed to said reserved lands. If this course be adopted all white settlers upon these lands should at once be required to vacate them.

The chief objections to this policy are, first, that it will leave the tribe very much scattered, and greatly hinder the cultivation of such knowledge and habits as will tend to render them intelligent and useful citizens of the republic; and, secondly, the fact that the Coahuila Valley is not available for agricultural purposes, being subject to frost every month of the year, and that the lands bordering the desert beyond the San Gorgonio Pass afford but an insufficient and precarious subsistence.

In regard to the settlement of Indians upon reserved lands, I think it very important that, while the grazing lands may be held in common, the agricultural lands should be distributed in clearly-defined portions among the individual families of the tribe, and that each family should be held responsible for the cultivation of its assigned portions. I suggest furthermore that each family be assured of the possession of all the proceeds of the lands thus cultivated, and the ultimate possession in fee-simple of the land itself, provided they continue to reside upon and to improve it for the space of twelve years.

It is for many reasons very desirable to break up the communistic customs which have prevailed among them, and to cultivate, as far as possible, a sense and pride of ownership and an ambition for the accumulation of property.

The Government should give the Indians clearly to understand that they must support themselves after such provision shall have been made for them as their present necessities require. I see no reason for thinking that they will not do this if they shall be made secure in the possession of land, and shall be put under judicious supervision. I should decidedly oppose the issuing of rations, or any other action which would lead them to suppose that they would be taken care of without effort on their part, but should encourage the idea that they would fare best who were most industrious. The Indians assert their willingness to labor, and say they neither intend nor wish to be a burden to the Government.

I feel confident that, if the opportunities above suggested are afforded them, they will themselves soon defray all the expenses of the agency charged with their care. More than this, I cherish the hope that they will at no distant day become prosperous and independent agricultural communities.

Some may think it would be better to locate all the Mission Indians on a single reservation, and for many reasons this would be preferable. The great difficulty, however, in finding a sufficiently large tract of land suited for the purposes of a reservation is a very serious obstacle to such a course. This difficulty arises not from any lack of unoccupied land, of which there are large areas in Southern California, but from lack of well-watered land. Water is an absolutely indispensable requisite for an Indian settlement, large or small. It would be worse than folly to attempt to locate them on land destitute of water, and that in sufficient quantity for the purposes of irrigation, if crops cannot be grown without irrigation. Moreover, I think their progress toward civilization and citizenship will be best promoted by the tribes being separately located, while the expense incurred will not be largely increased thereby.

In the plan above suggested another difficulty is obviated, viz, that of persuading the Indians to remove to a distance from the places they now occupy. They prefer, as is natural, to be left where they are, and will doubtless object in some instances to moving to any reservation. I think, however, there will, for the most part, be a readiness to comply with the wishes of the Government, if it shall be seen that the Government is disposed to regard their wishes in locating them as near as possible to the places to which from association they are attached, and also in keeping the tribes distinct from each other.

Should it be found practicable thus to locate these Indians, I would earnestly recommend that schools be established among them as soon as possible, regarding it as very much to be desired that the children should learn to speak the English language, and be taught at least the rudiments of education. It was one of their special requests that this should be done, showing some appreciation of the advantages which education gives, and of the changed circumstances under which their children are to live.

I furthermore recommend that for the supply of their present wants there be provided—

For the San Luis Rey Indians:

150 blankets.	1,000 yards of calico.	10 plows.
100 suits of clothes.	1,000 yards of muslin.	10 sets of plow-harness.
100 hats.	500 yards of jean.	50 hoes.
100 pairs of shoes.	250 yards of flannel.	10 spades.
100 pairs of socks.	250 handkerchiefs.	20 shovels.

For the Digenes:

150 blankets,	1,000 yards of calico.	10 plows.
100 suits of clothes.	1,000 yards of muslin.	10 sets of plow-harness.
100 hats.	500 yards of jean.	10 spades.
100 pairs of shoes.	250 yards of flannel.	50 hoes.
100 pairs of socks.	250 handkerchiefs.	20 shovels.

For the Coahuilas:

300 blankets.	1,500 yards of calico.	10 plows.
200 suits of clothes.	1,500 yards of muslin.	10 sets plow-harness.
200 hats.	1,000 yards of jean.	50 hoes.
200 pair of shoes.	500 handkerchiefs.	20 spades.
200 pair of socks.	500 yards of flannel.	20 shovels.

Also for each tribe a sufficient amount of grain and seed for sowing and planting the coming year.

Such present provision being made for them, it is my hope that very little aid of this kind will be required in the future.

The adoption of the policy above suggested will necessitate the appointment of a permanent agent for these Indians. Upon his practical wisdom, honesty, and fidelity, the results of this effort in their behalf will largely depend. If the effort be judiciously prosecuted under the direction of an agent who is fully in sympathy with the Indians, and who regards their good rather than his own pecuniary gains, I cannot but feel that it will greatly redound to the credit of the Government, and to the increasing welfare of these, its wards, who now appeal to it for aid and protection.

In conclusion I beg to say that these recommendations are submitted the more confidently, whatever expenditure their adoption may involve, from the conviction that the Government has been very remiss in its care of the Mission Indians hitherto; that their claims and their rights have been already too long disregarded; that they deserve generous treatment because of their fidelity to the Government; standing, as some of them have done, as a defense to the settlers of Southern California, against the fiercer tribes of Arizona, with whom they have steadily refused to unite for purposes of plunder, that they ought not to suffer in comparison with others of their race, in consequence of their more peaceable conduct and disposition; and finally, that nothing less will suffice as a satisfactory and adequate provision in their behalf.

In the hope that these recommendations will meet with your hearty approval, and whatever legislation may be necessary to enable the Department to carry them into execution may be readily secured,

I have the honor to be, very respectfully, your obedient servant,

JOHN G. AMES,
Special Agent.

Hon. E. P. SMITH,
Commissioner of Indian Affairs, Washington, D. C.

B.

REPORT OF J. W. POWELL AND G. W. INGALLS.

WASHINGTON, D. C., *December* 18, 1873.

SIR: The Special Commission appointed for examining into the condition of the Utes of Utah; Pai-Utes of Utah, Northern Arizona, Southern Nevada, and Southeastern California; the Go-si Utes of Utah and Nevada; the Northwestern Shoshonees of Idaho and Utah; and the Western Shoshonees of Nevada; and for the purpose of consulting with them concerning the propriety of their removal to reservations, would respectfully submit the following report:

The commission was delayed a number of days by snows that blockaded the railroads over the mountains, but arrived in Salt Lake City early in May.

At that time there was much excitement in the country, consequent on the disastrous conflict with the Modocs.

The commission found that the feelings of the white people inhabiting the territory under consideration were wrought to a high state of resentment, which frequently found vent in indignities on the Indians, while the latter were terrified, and many of them had fled to the mountains for refuge.

Immediately on our arrival at the city, delegations from various parts of the country met us, representing that the Indians of their several neighborhoods were preparing to commence a war of extermination against the whites; and several petitions from the citizens of different places, to the military authorities of that department, the governor of Utah, and the Commissioner of Indian Affairs, representing that the people were in immediate peril, and calling for military protection, were referred to the Commission.

Under these circumstances, the Commiss oners proceeded to investigate the state of affairs in the Sanpete Valley, Curlew Valley, Caché Valley, and on Deep Creek.

It was soon found that the fears of the white settlers were groundless, and that the Indians themselves were much more terrified than the whites.

In the mean time the Commission sent for delegations of Indians representing the tribes of Utes, Go-si Utes, Northwestern Shoshonees, and Western Shoshonees; and after meeting a number of these delegations at its camp near Salt Lake City, such information was obtained as led to a request for further conference with the Department concerning the best course to be pursued with these Indians in the light of the facts thus obtained.

In consequence of such request, one of the special commissioners, Mr. J. W. Powell, was instructed to report to the Department at Washington.

On his arrival, the following statement to the Commissioner of Indian Affairs was made:

WASHINGTON, D. C., *June* 18, 1873.

To the honorable Commissioner of Indian Affairs:

SIR: Your attention is respectfully called to the following statement of the condition of the Indians inhabiting Utah, Nevada, Southern Idaho, Northern Arizona, and Southeastern California, who are not yet collected on reservations.

These Indians are Utes, Pai-Utes, Go-si Utes, Northwestern Shoshonees, Western Shoshonees, and Pa-vi-ó-tsoes, (designated in the Indian reports as Pah-Utes.)

Of the Utes not on reservation there are two principal tribes, the Pah-vants and Seuv-a-rits. The Pah-vants are on Corn Creek, near Fillmore, in Utah Territory, and in the report of the Commissioner of Indian Affairs for 1872 are estimated to number 1,200. These Indians are under a chief named Ka-nosh; they subsist by cultivating the soil to a limited extent, by gathering seeds, fruit, and roots, and also by hunting; but chiefly by begging from the white settlers of the country.

Their condition is better than that of any other of the Indians under consideration. The chief, Ka-nosh, is an Indian of great ability and wisdom, and is doing all he can to induce his people to cultivate the soil.

He not only raises grain enough for himself and family, but usually has a quantity to sell, from which he derives a respectable revenue. His influence is not confined to the tribe over which he has immediate command, but extends to a greater or less extent over most of the Indians of Central Utah.

The Seuv-a-rits inhabit the country between the Sanpete and Sevier Valleys, on the west, and the Green and Colorado Rivers on the east.

No definite information has been obtained concerning the number of this tribe.

In the fall of 1871, one of your Commissioners met a party of them on the banks of the Sevier, and counted thirty-one lodges.

These people live by hunting and fishing, and collect seeds and fruits. They are well mounted, are a wild, daring people, and very skillful in border warfare. It may be safely stated that for the last ten years they have subsisted chiefly on the spoils of war. In their raids they have been associated with the Nav-a-jos and Utes, who inhabit the country to the east of the Colorado River.

The Pai-Utes inhabit Southern Utah, Southern Nevada, Northern Arizona, and Southeastern California.

There is a small tribe in the vicinity of Beaver, and another at Parawan, whose numbers are unknown.

A third tribe is usually found encamped somewhere in the vicinity of Cedar.

The principal chief of the Pai-Utes of Utah, Tau-gu, usually remains with this tribe.

In the winter of 1871–'2 the tribe was visited by one of your Commissioners, and forty-three lodges were counted.

There is a tribe in Long Valley, numbering about 125 persons, and one in Kanab Valley, numbering 107. There are a few Indians on the Paria River, whose numbers are unknown, and there is a small tribe on the eastern side of the Colorado, near the line between Utah and Arizona, numbering 47.

The U-in-kar-ets, dwelling among the U-in-kar-et Mountains in Northern Arizona, number about 60.

The Sheav-wits inhabit the Sheav-wit plateau in Northern Arizona, and number about 180.

The tribes of Pai-Utes thus enumerated are such as have not been heretofore included in the report of the Pioche Agency. Of the remainder who properly belong to that agency, and who inhabit Southwestern Utah, Southern Nevada, Southeastern California, and Northern Arizona, your Commissioners have but little more knowledge than is already before the Department. It is sufficient to state that they are scattered in small tribes, and hold allegiance to many petty chiefs.

All the Pai-Utes subsist in part by cultivating the soil, some of them raising the grain and vegetables introduced by white men, others cultivating native seeds.

They also collect uncultivated seeds, fruits, and roots. A few of them occasionally work for white men, and they also depend very largely on begging, and are a serious burden to white settlers.

The Go-si Utes live in the vicinity of Salt Lake and the valleys extending to the west as far as the Nevada line. They probably number four hundred persons.

Some of them are cultivating small patches of ground; one band in Skull Valley, one at Deep Creek, another at Warm Springs, and another at Salt Marsh, near the Nevada line.

They also gather seeds and fruits, dig roots and hunt a little, but chiefly subsist by begging. A few of them are occasionally employed by white men.

The western band of Shoshonees, in the reports heretofore made to the Department, have been overestimated for Utah and underestimated for Nevada, with regard to their number and distribution. Your attention is called to the accompanying statement made by Mr. Gheen, and marked A.

After carefully examining the paper and conferring with a number of the principal chiefs and leading men of the Western Shoshonees, the statement is believed to be substantially correct.

These Indians are cultivating the soil to a very limited extent. Some of them are employed by white men as herders and in other labors. They gather seeds and fruits, dig roots, hunt and fish, and eke out a miserable subsistence by begging.

Of the number of the Northwestern bands of Shoshonees, your Commission have no trustworthy information. Their condition does not differ materially from the Western Shoshonees. They are also divided into small tribes, several of which we have visited.

Of the Pa-vi-o-tsoes, or Pah-Utes, of Western Nevada, we have obtained information of three or four hundred who do not report to either of the reservations on Walker River or Pyramid Lake. Their condition is substantially the same as that of the Shoshonees.

Of the Wash-oes, mentioned in the report of the Department, we have no definite information.

The Indians mentioned in the foregoing statement appreciate that they can no longer live by hunting, fishing, and gathering the native products of the soil.

They fully understand that the settlement of the country by white men is inevitable, and know the folly of contending against it; and they earnestly ask that they may have lands of their own and be assisted to become farmers and stock-raisers, but especially do they ask that they may have cattle.

During the last few weeks that the Commission has been among these Indians, it has conferred with many of their chiefs and principal men. One of your Commissioners, as agent for the Pai-Utes, for the past year has traveled among a number of the tribes, and the other Commissioner, having been in charge of an exploring expedition for several years, has met and conferred with numbers of these Indians from time to time, and invariably they have expressed the sentiments given above. Their hunting-grounds have been spoiled, their favorite valleys are occupied by white men, and they are compelled to scatter in small bands in order to obtain subsistence. Formerly they were organized into nations, or confederacies, under the influence of great chiefs, but such men have lost their power in the presence of white men, and it is no longer possible to treat with these people as nations, but each little tribe must be dealt with separately. The broad territory over which they are scattered has been parcelled out among the tribes by common consent, usually determined at general councils, so that each tribe holds a certain district of country as its own.

Now the most important difficulty in the way of collecting these people on reservations, is the fact that each small tribe desires to have a reservation somewhere within the limits of its own territory, which is manifestly impracticable, as the Indians could not thus be protected in their rights, except at a great expense.

In the instructions furnished your commissioners for the collection of these Indians, two methods were given, the one to take the Indians on reservations already established, and, failing in this, the other was to set apart new reservations for them.

After a careful examination of the facts, it is found that the last-mentioned method is entirely impracticable, as, within the bounds of the territory over which these tribes roam, there is no district of country with sufficient water and other natural facilities for a reservation, not already occupied by white men. In fact, the lands along the streams and almost every important spring has either been entered or claimed, and should the Government attempt to purchase such lands for the benefit of the Indians, it would be found to involve a great outlay of money, as water rights and improvements are justly held at very high prices.

Nothing then remains but to remove them from the country, or let them stay in their present condition, to be finally extinguished by want, loathsome disease, and the disasters consequent upon incessant conflict with white men.

In view of the removal and distribution of these Indians to the old reservations, four important questions were presented to the commission, namely:

First. Are the reservations for the adjacent tribes capable of properly supporting an increased number of Indians?

---

* This statement has been omitted, as a more correct enumeration has been made.

Second. Would the treaty stipulations with the Indians thus located permit an addition to their numbers, and would they consent to it?

Third. Would the treaty stipulations with the Indians under consideration permit of their removal?

Fourth. What division of the roaming tribes do their linguistic and other affinities dictate?

The facts in answer to these questions, so far as they are known to the commission, are as follows:

The reservation on the Muddy is well known to both of the commissioners. There is some good land and plenty of water; there are no valuable hunting grounds on the reservation, or in the vicinity, but there are streams from which a greater or less supply of fish can be taken; and the natural products of the soil, which are somewhat abundant, would be of value as a source of partial subsistence until they could learn to farm for themselves. The timber is distant from the district where the farms must necessarily be made, but the climate is good for southern Indians, and the reservation will always be isolated from other settlements. Altogether the situation is good and sufficient.

The reservation on the Uintah is well known to one of your commissioners. There is an abundance of good soil, plenty of water, and convenient timber. The climate is good for the growth of smaller grains and vegetables, but not favorable to the raising of corn. Good range for cattle is practically unlimited—in fact, there is room enough for all the Indians of Utah.

Perhaps there is no finer valley than the Uintah in the territory of the United States west of the hundredth meridian.

The commission having no knowledge of the capabilities of the Fort Hall reservation, one of the commissioners, Mr. G. W. Ingalls, made a special trip for the purpose of examining it. It was found that there was abundance of good land, plenty of water, good and extensive range for grazing, and an ample supply of timber for the Indians already located there, and all of the Shoshonees of Utah and Nevada in addition.

But little is known by the commission of the resources of the reservations at Walker River and Pyramid Lake, but from such information as has been received it is believed they are inadequate to the wants of the Indians already collected there.

The facts relating to the second question are these: No treaties have been made with the Indians concerning the reservation on the Muddy. The treaty made with the Utes concerning the Uintah reservation provided for the gathering of all the tribes of Utah in that valley, but it was never ratified by the Senate, and although the Indians are there as they suppose under the stipulations of the treaty, it is not recognized as binding by the Government of the United States. The principal chiefs on the reservation state their willingness and desire that the other Utes should be united with them.

By the treaties made with the Shoshonees and Bannocks concerning the reservation at Wind River and Fort Hall, it is stipulated that they are made not only for these Indians but "For such other friendly tribes or individual Indians as from time to time they may be willing, with the consent of the United States, to admit amongst them."

With regard to the third question, "Would the treaty stipulations with the Indians under consideration permit of their removal?" It appears that there are no recognized treaty stipulations existing with the Utes and Pah-Utes.

A treaty was concluded October 12, 1863, with the Go-si Utes in which it was especially provided as follows:

Article 6th. "The said band agree that whenever the President of the United States shall deem it expedient for them to abandon the roaming life which they now lead, and become settled as herdsmen or agriculturists, he is hereby authorized to make such reservations for their use as he may deem necessary; and they do also agree to remove their camps to such reservations as he may indicate, and to reside and remain thereon." So that the Go-si Utes may be required to go on a reservation wherever and whenever the President directs.

A treaty was concluded October 1, 1863, with the western bands of Shoshones from which we extract article 6th, viz:

"The said bands agree that whenever the President of the United States shall deem it expedient for them to abandon the roaming life which they now lead, and become herdsmen and agriculturists, he is hereby authorized to make such reservations for their use as he may deem necessary, within the country above described; and they do also hereby agree to remove their camps to such reservations as he may indicate and to reside or remain thereon."

It is thus seen that they can also be called to a reservation by the will of the President, but such reservation must be within certain boundaries, as described in article 5th, viz:

"It is understood that the boundaries of the country claimed and occupied by said bands are defined and described by them as follows: On the north by the Wong-go-gada Mountains and Shoshone River Valley; on the west by the Sei-non-to-yah Mountains or Smith Creek Mountains; on the south by Wi-co-bah and the Colorada Desert; on the east by Pa-ha-no-be Valley or Step-toe Valley, and Great Salt Lake Valley."

Your commissioners are in some doubt as to where these boundaries are situated, but believe they include the Fort Hall Indian reservation.

By the treaty concluded with the northwestern bands of Shoshones at Box Elder, in the Territory of Utah, on the 13th day of July, 1863, it is stipulated as follows:

"Article 2d. The treaty concluded at Fort Bridger on the second day of July, 1863, between the United States and the Shoshone nation being read and fully interpreted and explained to the said chiefs and warriors, they do hereby give their full and free assent to all of the provisions of said treaty, and the same are hereby adopted as a part of this agreement, and the same shall be binding on the parties hereto."

In the treaty made at Fort Bridger, to which this article alludes, the following provisions are found.

"Article 2. The United States further agrees that the following district of country, to wit: commencing at the mouth of Owl Creek and running due south to the crest of the divide between the Sweet Water and Pa-po-a-gie Rivers; thence along the west of said divide and the summit of Wind River Mountain to the longitude of North Fork of Wind River; thence due north to mouth of said North Fork and up its channel to a point twenty miles above its mouth; thence in a straight line to headwaters of Owl Creek, and along middle channel of Owl Creek to place of beginning, shall be, and the same is, set apart for the absolute and undisturbed use and occupation of Shoshone Indians herein named, and for such other friendly tribes or individual Indians as from time to time they may be willing, with the consent of the United States, to admit amongst them."

The boundaries of this reservation have been contracted by a subsequent treaty.

It will thus be seen that the Northwestern Shoshones are under treaty obligations to settle on the Wind River reservation, but as a part of the Shoshones are already at Fort Hall, it might possibly be more agreeable to the bands under consideration to go there.

From the information which your commissioners have received it is believed that it will be necessary to remove the Pah-Utes or Pa-vi-o-tsoes from the Walker River and Pyramid Lake reservations to some better point, as the resources of the territory they now occupy are inadequate to their want.

The United States Indian agent, in charge of the reservation at Fort Hall, informs your commission that he believes that the Indians now at that place would raise no serious objection to the removal of the uncollected Shoshones to that place.

The rights and obligations of the Indians under consideration have been thus carefully examined that no unjust cause of complaint might arise.

With regard to the fourth question, "What division of the roaming tribes do their linguistic and other affinities indicate?" much has yet to be learned.

The names by which the tribes are known to white men and the Department give no clue to the relationship of the Indians; for example, the Indians in the vicinity of the reservation on the Muddy and the Indians on the Walker River and Pyramid Lake reservations are called Pai or Pah Utes, but the Indians know only those on the Muddy by that name, while those on the other two reservations are known as Pa-vi-o-tsoes, and speak a very different language, but closely allied to, if not identical with, that of the Bannocks.

The Indians of Utah and Nevada, known as Shoshones by the whites, are known by very different names by the Indians.

The two tribes mentioned above, Pah-vants and Seuv-a-rits, speak the same language, and are intermarried with the Indians on the Uintah reservations, and should be taken there.

The Go-si Utes speak a language more nearly like that of the Indians at Fort Hall, but they are intermarried and affiliate with the Indians at the Uintah reservation, and it is believed they would prefer to go there also.

The tribes of Pai-Utes, mentioned in the former part, should be taken to the Muddy.

Of the Western Shoshones, Northwestern Shoshones, Pa-vi-o-tsoes, and Washoes, sufficient is not yet known to reach a conclusion on this matter.

Whenever these Indians are gathered on reservations it will be necessary to make provision for their subsistence, until such time as they can take care of themselves, as it would be impossible for them to live upon the native products found on the reservations.

To take them there and have them scatter again would be to put them in a condition worse than they are now in, and it would probably be more difficult to induce them to return.

The appropriations made by the last Congress for the support of the present reservations, to which these people should be taken, are entirely insufficient for the support of the Indians who are already on them, and they are compelled to leave their reservations during a part of the year to obtain a living.

Under these circumstances, your commissioners did not deem that it would be wise to remove any of the Indians at present, and they submit this statement of the condition of affairs for your consideration.

Having in view the ultimate removal of all the foregoing Indians to reservations already established, the following recommendations are made:

First. That the Pah-vants and Seuv-a-rits be visited and informed that the Government of the United States has decided that they shall make their homes on the Uintah reservation, and that hereafter no goods will be issued to them at any other place.

Second. That the tribes of Pai-Utes shall be visited, and, if possible, a number of the chiefs and principal men be induced to visit the Uintah reservation, with a view to their final settlement at that place.

Should the commission find it impossible to induce them to look upon such a removal with favor, it should then make a thorough examination into the condition of affairs on the Muddy reservation, and report the results to the Department.

The agent for that reservation should immediately commence work and prepare to raise a crop the coming year to such an extent as the appropriation and circumstances on the reservation will permit.

In the mean time two or three reliable men should be employed by the commission to collect the Western Shoshones at three or more points, where they could be visited by the commission and their annuities distributed to them, and they be informed of the decision of the Department, that they are to go on reservations, and that hereafter no annuities will be distributed to them except at the designated reservation or reservations.

The same course should be taken with the Go-si Utes.

The Northwestern Shoshones should be assembled to meet the commission at Fort Hall, and, when there, their annuities should be given them, and they should be informed that the Fort Hall reservation is to be their future home, and that hereafter no annuities will be given them at any other place.

One of your commissioners can communicate with a part of the Indians in their own tongue, and Mr. Gheen, who is already in the service of the United States in Nevada, speaks the Shoshone language, but it will still be necessary to have one more interpreter, as the commission must necessarily be divided, and three or four parties organized to reach all the tribes in one season.

It is therefore recommended that Richard Komas, a native Ute, now a student in Lincoln University in Pennsylvania, be employed for this purpose.

Should these suggestions meet with your approval, it would be necessary to have the annuities for the Western Shoshones, Northwestern Shoshones, and Go-si Utes placed to the order of the commission.

Very respectfully,

J. W. POWELL,
G. W. INGALLS,
U. S. Special Commission.

On June 26 the following instructions were received:

DEPARTMENT OF THE INTERIOR,
OFFICE OF INDIAN AFFAIRS,
Washington, D. C., June 25, 1873.

SIR: I acknowledge the receipt of your letter of the 18th instant, with a statement in detail of the present condition of the Indians in Utah, Nevada, and Southern Idaho, who have not yet been collected on reservations.

With a view to the ultimate removal of said Indians to such reservations as have already been established, you recommend as follows:

1st. That the Pah-vants and Seuv-a-rits be visited and informed that the Government has decided that they shall make their homes on the Uintah reservation, and that hereafter no goods will be issued to them at any other place.

2d. That some of the chiefs and principal men of the Pai-Ute tribe be induced to visit the Uintah reservation and encouraged to make their homes at that place; and in case it should be found impossible to induce them to look with favor upon a removal to that point, then to make a thorough examination as to the condition of affairs on the Muddy reservation and report the result to the Department, preparations in the mean time being made for raising a crop the coming year to such an extent as circumstances will permit.

3d. That two or three reliable men be employed by the commission to collect the Western Shoshones at three or more points, where they can be visited by the commission and their annuities distributed to them, and that they be informed of the decision of the Department that they must go on reservations, and that hereafter no annuities will be distributed to them except at the reservation assigned to them; the same course to be taken with the Go-ship Utes.

4th. That the Northwestern Shoshones be assembled to meet the commission at Fort Hall, Idaho, to receive their annuities, and that they be informed that Fort Hall reservation is to be their future home, and that no annuities will be given them at any other place.

5th. That Richard Komas, of Pennsylvania, be employed as interpreter to the commission; and

6th. That the annuities of the Western Shoshones, Northwestern Shoshones, and Go-ship band of Utes be placed at the disposal of the commission.

The above recommendations meet with the approval of the Department, and you are hereby authorized to carry the same into effect.

Instructions will be issued to Colonel Morrow, at Salt Lake City, Utah, to transfer to you the annuity goods referred to in your letter.

Very respectfully, your obedient servant,

EDW. P. SMITH,
Commissioner.

J. W. POWELL, Esq.,
Special Commissioner, &c., Present.

While Special Commissioner Powell was thus engaged at Washington, Special Commissioner Ingalls visited a part of the Northwestern Shoshonees in Coche Valley, and, returning from this expedition, made a trip to the Pai-Ute reservation in Southern Nevada. The special commission met again in Salt Lake City.

In obedience to the instructions received, the commission then proceeded through the Territory of Utah to its southern line, visiting a number of tribes on the way, taking with them a quantity of goods to be distributed to the several tribes as they should be met from time to time.

Sometimes the commissioners traveled in company, at other times they separated for the purpose of facilitating their operations.

On this trip many of the Indians belonging to the Uintah agency were visited, especially the Seu-a-rits, as some anxiety had been entertained lest these Indians should again commence their depredations on the settlements. It was found that they had of their own accord given up their marauding life, and they signified their willingness to go on a reservation and adopt the habits of civilized men. The reasons which they assigned for so doing were very interesting.

They stated that their people had been dying very fast of late years, so that their numbers were greatly reduced, and they were specially terrified on account of some disease which had carried off more than twenty of their number in less than a week, only a short time before the commission met them.

Some of their people attributed this to sorcery practiced by other Indians, others to sorcery practiced by the white inhabitants of Utah, but the great majority seemed to consider it a punishment for the petty wars which they had waged of late years. Whatever the cause, they had determined to abandon the country, and part of them were about to join the Utes of the Uintah reservation, another to join the Pah-vants, another the Pai-Utes near the head of the Sevier, and a fourth the Utes of Colorado.

They were informed that the Government of the United States expected them to go on the reservation at Uintah.

The Pah-vants were next visited at Corn Creek, near Fillmore. This tribe was found to be much smaller, and the people in a much more destitute condition than had been represented to the commission.

Ka-nosh, the principal chief, is an elder brother of Pi-an-ump, principal chief of the Go-si Utes, and the Pah-vants and Go-si Utes, although speaking different languages, affiliate socially, and often go on their hunting excursions in company.

From this point an Indian runner was sent to bring Pi-an-ump and a number of Go-si Ute chiefs to confer with Ka-nosh and such other Indians as might be collected here, in regard to the propriety of their all going to the reservation at Uintah.

This runner was successful in bringing in the desired Indians, so that the Go-si Utes were well represented at the consultation held at Ka-nosh's camp.

They remained with the commissioners several days, and great pains were taken to explain to them the intention of the Government in collecting Indians on reservations. The result of this talk was very satisfactory.

In obedience to the first part of the second clause of their instructions, viz: "That some of the chiefs and principal men of Pai-Utes be induced to visit Uintah reservation, and encouraged to make their homes at that place," the commission sent for Tau-gu, the principal chief of the Pai-Utes, of Utah and Northern Arizona, and a number of subordinate chiefs. The only ones who could be induced to meet it were Tau-gu and Mo-ak-Shin-au-av, chief of the U-ai-Nu-ints, who live in the vicinity of Saint George.

They informed the commission that, induced by considerations presented to them in former conversations, they had held a general council for the purpose of consulting about the propriety of going to Uintah, and the suggestion had been repelled by all the people, and there was no voice raised in favor of their going. They averred that the Utes of Uintah had been their enemies from time immemorial; had stolen their women and children; had killed their grandfathers, their fathers, their brothers and sons, and, worse than all, were profoundly skilled in sorcery, and that under no consideration would the Pai-Utes live with them.

It was found that it was impossible, without using force, to induce the Pai-Utes to join the Utes, and it was determined to adopt the course indicated in the alternative presented in your instruction, viz: "And in case it should be found impossible to induce them to look with favor upon a removal to that point, then to make a thorough examination as to the condition of affairs in the Muddy reservation, and report the result to the Department."

The commission then proceeded to visit in detail all the Pai-Ute tribes of Utah and Northern Arizona, viz, Kwi-um-pus, Pa-ru-guns, Un-ka-pa, Nu-kwints, Pa-spi-kai-vats, Un-ka-ka-ni-guts, Pa-gu-its, Kai-vwav-uai Nu-ints, U-in-ka-reis, and Shi-vwits.

There is a small tribe of Pai-Utes in Northern Arizona, on the east side of the Colorado River, known as Kwai-an-ti-kwok-ets, which was not visited by the commission. This little band lives in a district so far away from the route of travel that your commission did not think it wise to occupy the time and incur the expense necessary to visit them in their homes.

Finally, delegations of all these tribes were collected at Saint George for general consultation, concerning the reservation for the Pai-Utes in Southern Nevada. The result of this talk was, in the main, satisfactory, and a delegation was sent by them to go with the commission to see the country.

From Saint George the commission proceeded to the reservation on the Mo-a-pa, (Muddy,) arriving there September 10, and here met about 400 Pai-Utes who had previously been collected in the valley. It remained eleven days for the purpose of conferring with the Indians already here, and with such delegations from other tribes as could be induced to meet here. Quite a number of conferences were held with the Indians, both by day and by night, for more than a week. The conclusion of all was, that the Indians on the reservation were willing that the other tribes should unite with them, and the delegations representing the tribes away were favorably impressed with the country, and promised that the Indians would all come to the reservation another year, on condition that the Government would provide temporarily for their maintenance, and give them such aid as might be necessary to establish them as agriculturists.

Arrangements were then made by which the Indians on the reservation were enabled to plant a fall crop.

Your commission had also another duty to perform here, viz, to inquire into the nature and amount of the claims of the present white settlers on the reservation.

This duty they performed with a desire to protect the Government against unjust claims, and at the same time to do no injustice to the claimants themselves.

The result of their investigations into these matters are given in a subjoined report.

The commission remained on the reservation fourteen days, busily employed in the duties above mentioned.

In the meantime, it provided that the annuity goods for the Go-si Utes, Western Shoshones, and Northwestern Shoshones, should be distributed and stored at a number of points in Utah and Nevada, and that information should be carried to the several tribes that the commission would meet them at designated points.

In view of the extent of country yet to be traversed, and the number of Indians yet to be met, it was thought best for the commission to divide here, and Special Commissioner Powell proceeded to carry on the work with the Pai-Utes in Southwestern Nevada and Southeastern California, and Special Commissioner Ingalls to the Western Shoshones of Western Nevada.

The work to the southwest was continued until all the Pai-Utes had been seen. Special Commissioner Powell returned by way of the Mo-a-pa reservation, Saint George, and Fillmore to Salt Lake City. On his way, in the vicinity of Beaver, the Pah-vants, who were out on a hunting excursion, were again met, and another long consultation was held with their chief, Ka-nosh.

Special Commissioner Ingalls proceeded by way of Pah-ran-a-gat Valley to Hot Creek, meeting there a number of Western Shoshones, and from thence to Belmont, where a number of other tribes were met. From Belmont he returned to Hot Creek, and from thence proceeded to Hamilton, Egan Cañon, Spring Valley, and Deep Creek, to Salt Lake City, meeting a number of tribes at each place. On this hurried trip the work was not completed. All of the annuity goods to be distributed to the Shoshones had not arrived at the points at which they were to have been distributed, and some of the Indians of the vicinity of Hamilton had not assembled. It was therefore necessary for Special Commissioner Ingalls to return to Hamilton and Egan Cañon, which he did, and on the completion of the work at those places proceeded to Corinne, Utah, where he was met by Commissioner Powell.

Under their instructions the commission should have met the Northwestern Shoshones at Fort Hall, but a number of circumstances conspired to prevent this. It was found that a part of them, under a chief named Po-ka-tel-lo, had already gone to Fort Hall, and had signified their intention of remaining and taking part with the Shoshones and Bannocks on that reservation; and another chief named Tav-i-wun-she-a, with a small band had gone to the Shoshone reservation on Wind River, and they had determined to cast their lot with Wash-i-ki and his men. Each of these chiefs sent word that they had taken this course, governed by representations made by the commission in the spring, and they desired that it should so represent the matter to the agents on those reservations that these people might meet with proper consideration. Two other bands, one under San-pits, the other under Sai-gwits, had refused to go to Fort Hall, and were encamped near Corinne, and had sent a delegation to request the commission to meet them at that point. The lateness of the season, and the limited amount of funds at the command of the commission, caused it to decide that it was impracticable to send the goods to Fort Hall and to collect the Indians there for the distribution, and the two last mentioned tribes were met near Corinne.

Leaving Special Commissioner Powell at that place to complete the distribution and to talk with the Indians, Special Commissioner Ingalls proceeded to Elko to meet the remainder of the Western Shoshones, who had, in the mean time, been collected at that point by assistants of the commission.

A delegation of the Western Shoshones, representing the tribes that assembled at Elko, another delegation of the Northwestern Shoshones assembled at Corinne, and a delegation of the Go-si Utes were brought to Salt Lake City for the purpose of conferring with another special commission composed of Hon. J. P. C. Shanks, Governor T. W. Bennett, and H. W. Reed, concerning the reservation at Fort Hall. The result of this conference was very favorable. The commissioners then returned to Washington, arriving here December 1.

This brief history of the operations of the commission will be followed by a statement of the general results obtained.

ORGANIZATION, ENUMERATION, AND DISTRIBUTION OF THE TRIBES.

Your commission deemed it a matter of prime importance to make a complete enumeration of the tribes visited, and to obtain a thorough knowledge of their organization and condition. Of the Utes, Pah-vants, Go-si Utes, and Northwestern Shoshones they are enabled to make what they believe to be an accurate statement of their numbers.

The census of the Western Shoshones is believed to be a fair approximation. The latter tribes are more or less disorganized, and in some places their tribal relations are entirely broken up, and they are scattered over a large district of country, and it would have required at least an additional month, and a corresponding expenditure, to have made the work as thorough with them as with the other tribes.

The original political organization of the tribes under consideration had a territorial basis; that is, the country was divided into districts, and each district was inhabited by a small tribe, which took the name of the land, and had one principal chief. These tribes, or "land-nameds," as they are called in the Indian idiom, were the only permanent organizations, but sometimes two or more of them would unite in a confederacy under some great chief.

The following table exhibits the names of these tribes, the number of men, women, and children, severally and in total, and also the land-name of the tribe, its locality, chief, and, wherever a confederacy exists, the principal chief of such organization. The numbers in the left-hand column refer to corresponding numbers on the accompanying map, the latter numbers indicating the region of country severally claimed by the tribes.

Tabular statement of Indians visited by special Indian commissioners J. W. Powell and G. W. Ingalls.

PAI-UTES OF UTAH.

	Tribe.	Locality.	Chief.	Chief of alliance.	Men.	Women.	Children 10 years and under.	Total.	Grand total.
1	Kwi-um'-pus	Vicinity of Beaver	Pi-vi'-ats	Tau-gu	12	8	9	29	
2	Pa-ru'-guns	Vicinity of Parawau	Tah-hun-kwi	do	14	8	5	27	
3	Un-ka'-pa-Nu-kuints'	Vicinity of Cedar	Tau'-gu	do	39	28	10	97	
4	Pa-spi'-kai-vats	Vicinity of Toquerville	Na'-guts	do	14	14	12	40	
5	Un-ka-ka'-ni-guts	Long Valley	Choog	do	14	10	12	36	
6	Pa-gu'-its	Pa-gu Lake	Un-ka'-ta-si-ats	do	31	22	15	68	
7	Kai'-vav-wits	Vicinity of Kanab	Chu-ar'-ru-um-peak	do	75	69	27	171	
8	U'-ai-Nu-ints	Vicinity of Saint George	Moak-Shin-au'-av	do	34	29	17	80	
									528

PAI-UTES OF NORTHERN ARIZONA.

	Tribe.	Locality.	Chief.	Chief of alliance.	Men.	Women.	Children 10 years and under.	Total.	Grand total.
9	U-in-ka'-rets	U-in-ka'-ret Mountains	To-mo'-ro-un-ti-kai	Taú-gu	17	13	10	40	
10	Shi'-vwits	Shi'-vwits Plateau	Kwi-toos'	do	73	66	43	182	
11	Kwai-an'-ti-kwok-ets	East of Colorado River		do	23	17	22	62	
									284

PAI-UTES OF SOUTHERN NEVADA.

	Tribe.	Locality.	Chief.	Chief of alliance.	Men.	Women.	Children 10 years and under.	Total.	Grand total.
12	Sau-won'-ti-ats	Mo-a-pa Valley	Tau-um'-pu-gaip	To-Shoap	44	34	14	92	
13	Mo-a-pa-ri'-ats	Mo-a-pa Valley	Mau-wi'-ta	do	30	22	12	64	
14	Nau-wan'-a-tats	Mo-a-pa Valley	Ai'-at-tau'-a	do	21	23	16	60	
15	Pin'-ti-ats	Mo-a-pa Valley	Kwi'-vu-a	do	20	17	10	47	
16	Pa-room'-pai-ats	Mo-a-pa Valley	Mo-wi'-un-kits	do	15	10	10	35	
17	I' chu-ar'-rum-pats	Mo-a-pa Valley	To'-shoap	do	13	16	6	35	
18	U-tum'-pai-ats	Mo-a-pa Valley	Tau'-ko-its	do	12	20	14	46	
19	Pa-ran-i-guts	Pa-ran-i-gut Valley	An-ti-av		65	58	48	171	
20	Tsou-wa'-ra-its	Meadow Valley	Pa-gwum'-pai-ats		68	52	35	155	
21	Nu-a'-gun-tits	Las Vegas	Ku-ni'-kai'-vets	Ku-ni-kai-vets	69	49	43	161	
22	Pa-ga'-its	Vicinity of Colville	Un-kom'-a-to-a-kwi-a-gunt	do	12	15	7	34	
23	Kwi-en'-go-mats	Indian Spring	Pats-a'-gu-ruke	do	7	6	5	18	
24	Mo-vwi'-ats	Cottonwood Island	Ha-va'-rum-up	do	24	19	14	57	
25	No-gwats	Vicinity of Potosi	To-ko'-pur	To-ko'-pur	} 22	24	10	56	
26	Pa-room'-pats	Pa-room-Spring	Ho-wi'-a-gunt	do					
									1,031

	PAI-UTES OF SOUTH-EAST CALIFORNIA.								
27	Mo-quats	Kingston Mountain	Hu-nu′-na-wa	To-ko′-pur	34	34	17	85	
28	Ho-kwaits	Vicinity of Ivanspaw	Ko-tsi′-an	do					
29	Tim-pa-shau′-wa-got-sits	Providence Mountain	Wa-gu′-up	do	10	12	9	31	
30	Kau-yai′-chits	Ash Meadows	Nu-a′-rung	do					
31	Ya′-gats	Armagoza	Ni-a-pa′-ga-rats	do	31	23	14	68	184
	UTES OF UTAH.								
32	U′-in-tats	Uinta Reservation	An′-te-ro	Tav′-wi	58	63	73	194	
33	Seuv′-a-rits	do	Mer′-i-ka-hats	do	48	40	56	144	
34	San′-pits	do	Pi-na-si′-a	do	10	8	18	36	
35	Ko′-sun-ats	do	Mo′-a-puts	do	24	25	27	76	
36	Tim-pa-na′-gats	do	Pi-ki′-chi	do	15	13	21	49	
37	Tim-pai′-a-vats	do	Won′-sits	do	8	8	9	25	
38	Pi-ka-kwa′-na-rats	do	Won′-ro-an	do	11	10	11	32	556
	PAH-VANTS OF UTAH.								
39	Pah-vants	Corn Creek	Ka-nosh		57	42	32	134	134
	GO-SI UTES OF UTAH.								
40	Un′-ka-gar-its	Skull Valley	Si′-pu-rus	Pi-an′-nump	56	58	45	149	
41	Pi-er′-ru-i-ats	Deep Creek	Tu-gu′-vi	do	39	33	35	107	
42	Pa-ga′-yu-ats	Otter Creek	Pi-av′ um-pi-a	do					
43	Tu-wur-ints	Snake Creek	Tat′-si-nup	do					256
	GO-SI UTES OF NEVADA.								
44	To-ro-un-to-go-ats	Egan Cañon	To-go′-mun-tso	Pi-an′ nump	72	68	64	204	204
	NORTH-WESTERN SHOSHONEES OF SOUTHERN IDAHO.								
45		Cache Valley	San′-pits	San′-pits	49	43	32	124	
46		Cache Valley	Sai′-gwits	do	47	64	47	158	
47		Goose Creek	Po′-ka-tel-lo	do	34	36	31	101	
48		Bear Lake	Tav-i-wun-shear	do	5	6	6	17	400

Tabular statement of Indians visited by special Indian commissioners, &c.—Continued.

WESTERN SHOSHONES OF NEVADA.

	Tribe.	Locality.	Chief.	Chief of alliance.	Men.	Women.	Children 10 years and under.	Total.	Grand total.
49	Pa′-gan-tso	Ruby Valley	Tim-oak	Tim-oak					
50		do	To-sho-win′-tso-go	do	83	48	44	172	
51		do	"Mose"	do					
52	Kai-da-toi-ab-ie	Vicinity of Hamilton	Que-ta′-pat-so		49	37	15	101	
54		Vicinity of Halleck	"Capt. Sam"	Tim-oak	19	12	5	36	
55		Vicinity of Elko	do	do	40	33	17	90	
56		Vicinity of Mineral Hill	Tu′-ka-yan-na		24	21	15	60	
57		Vicinity of Palisade	Pit si-nain		19	22	15	56	
58		Vicinity of Carlin	do		23	29	30	82	
59	No-ga′-ie	Robison District		Tim-oak	24	25	11	60	
60		Spring Valley							
61		Vicinity of Duckwater	Mo-tso′-gaunt		25	24	11	60	
62		White River Valley			33	32	15	80	
63	Pi-at-tui′-ab-be	Belmont and vicinity	Kai′-wits	Kai′-wits	45	39	32	116	
64		Hot Creek	Wet-sai-go-om′-beom′	do	7	8	7	22	
65		Big Smoky Valley	"Brigham"	do	10	9	6	25	
66		Vicinity of Morey District	To-po-go-om′-bi	do	8	9	7	24	
67		Vicinity of Fish Lake	Wau-go-vwi	do	25	26	11	62	
68	Na-haé-go	Reese River Valley	To-to′-a	To-to′-a					
69		do	Koo-soo-be-ta-gwi	do					
70		do	Behr-ha-naugh	do					
71		do	Uhr-wa-pits	do	186	190	159	530	
72		Vicinity of Austin	Weg-a′-whan	do					
73		do	Wedg-a′-gan	do					
74		do	Kush-sho-way	do					
75	To-na-wits′-o-wa	Vicinity of Battle Mountain	Pie-a-ra-poo′-na	Pie-a-rai-poo-na′					
76		do	Se-no-wets-o	do					
77		do	No-wits-ie	do	69	71	54	194	
78		do	Pié-á-nang-gau	do					
79		do	"Sam"	do					
80		do	Tim-pits	do					
81		Vicinity of Unionville	Ber-roo-na′	Ber-roo-na′					
82		do	Do-ro-cho	do	92	51	32	175	
83		do	Gas-shi-ma′	do					1,945

RECAPITULATION.

The Pai-Utes of Utah number	528	
The Utes of Utah number	556	
The Pah-vants of Utah number	134	
The Go-si Utes of Utah number	256	
Total number of Indians in Utah	——	1,474
The Pai-Utes of Arizona number		284
The Pai-Utes of Southern Nevada number	1,031	
The Go-si Utes of Nevada number	204	
The Western Shoshonees of Nevada number	1,945	
Total number of Indians in Nevada met by the commission	——	3,180
The Northwestern Shoshonees of Idaho number		400
The Pai-Utes of Southeastern California number		184
Total number of Indians visited by the commission		5,522

There is another confederacy, known as Chem-a-hue-vis, that inhabit the Chem-a-hue-vis Valley on the Lower Colorado. Their country is separated from that of the Pai-Utes, in the above table by the region inhabited by the Mojave Indians. These Chem-a-hue-vis speak the same language as the Pai-Utes, and claim that they formerly lived among them. They still associate with the Pai-Utes farther north in California and at Cottonwood Island, and are intermarried with them.

A delegation of these Indians met the commission at the Vegas, in Nevada. They estimate the whole number of Indians belonging to the confederacy at about 300, and this is believed to be approximately correct.

The Indians of Western Nevada belonging to the Pyramid Lake and Walker River reservations are known as Pah-Utes and Pai-Utes in the records of the Indian Department. They should be known as Pa-vi-o-tsoes, as this is the name by which they know themselves, and by which they are known throughout the surrounding tribes. They are properly a branch of the Bannocks.

In Western Nevada, and on the eastern slope of the Sierra Nevadas in California, there are a number of Indians known as Ko-eats, Pan′-a-mints, &c. They are known to speak languages of the same stock as the Pai-Utes, Shoshones, and Pa-vi-o-tsoes.

PAI-UTES.

CONDITION AND WANTS.

Of the Indians known as Pai-Utes there are thirty-one tribes. Ten of these are united in a confederacy, having for their principal chief, Tau-gu′.

The Kwa-an′-ti-kwok-ets, who live on the eastern side of the Colorado River, are nearly isolated from the other tribes, and affiliate to a greater or less extent with the Navajos.

Seven other tribes of Pai-Utes are organized into a confederacy under the chieftaincy of To′-Shoap.

The Pah-ran-i-gats were formerly three separate tribes, but their lands having been taken from them by white men, they have united in one tribe under An′-ti-av.

In the same way the Indians of Meadow Valley were formerly four separate tribes, but now one, under Pa-gwum′-pai-ats.

Four other tribes are organized into a confederacy under the chieftaincy of Ku′-ni-kai′-vets, and seven under the chieftaincy of To-ko′-pur.

The country inhabited by these Indians no longer affords game in sufficient quantities worthy to be mentioned as a part of their subsistance. A very few deer and mountain-sheep are killed, and a greater number of rabbits. The principal part of their food is obtained by gathering seeds and digging roots. All of the tribes cultivate the soil to a limited extent, raising wheat, corn, beans, melons, and squashes. Some food and the greater part of their clothing is obtained by begging, the skins of such animals as they kill being entirely inadequate to their wants for this purpose. Some of them have, for a few years, received a small supply of clothing from the Government, through the agencies at Salt Lake City and Pioche.

A few of the people occasionally work for white men, and a great many of them are learning to speak the English language; especially is this true of the children.

Prior to the settlement of the country by the white men they all cultivated the soil, and would do so now to an extent sufficient to obtain a living, if they had the lands in the districts of country which they severally occupy. In fact all these tribes, when met by the commission, asked for lands and cattle that they might become farmers; but each tribe desires to have some part of its original territory set apart for its use.

After much talk with the commission and much consultation among themselves, they all agreed to come together on the reservation set apart for them by Executive order in the valley of the Mo'-a-pa on these conditions—that the Government will remove the white settlers therefrom, and will assist them to remove their old people and children from their present to their prospective home on the reservation, and will assist them to become agriculturalists, and provide for their maintenance until such time as they can take care of themselves.

These conditions are reasonable and just. There is no game on the reservation, and the native products are few, and it would be impossible for the Indians to live on the reservation without assistance. It would be useless to take them there without at the same time providing for their support, as in such a case they would be compelled at once to scatter again over the very country from whence they had been taken.

RESERVATION ON THE MO'-A-PA.

The reservation, though large in territory, is composed chiefly of arid, barren mountains and deserts of drifting sands. The only part of the valley fit for agricultural purposes is the few acres—not more than 6,000—which can be redeemed by the use of the waters of the Mo'-a-pa, and some grass-lands of no greater extent, for the climate is so arid that agricultural operations cannot be carried on without artificial irrigation.

The reservation is between the 36th and 37th parallels of latitude; the climate is very warm, snow is never seen in the valley, and frost rarely. The part of the land which can be brought into cultivation by irrigation produces bountifully, and two crops can be raised in one season. Wheat, oats, barley, corn, sweet potatoes, cotton, and all the fruits of sub-tropical countries can be successfully raised, as has been demonstrated by the present white settlers.

The census taken shows that there are 2,027 Pai-Utes. Adding to this number the Chem-a-hue-vis of Southern California, about 300, and we have 2,327.

It is the opinion of the commission that there is enough water in the Mo'-a-pa Creek to irrigate lands to an extent sufficient to support that number of people for the present, but it would not be wise to take any greater number of Indians there. The Rio Virgen, in its lower course, runs through the reservation, but the waters of this river are salt, and its whole course is over quicksands, and altogether the nature o the country is such that the stream cannot be controlled for purposes of irrigation, except to a very limited extent on the eastern margin of the reservation, and the expense attending the management of the water would be very great.

The boundaries of the reservation should be extended to the east to a point where the river emerges from the mountains through a cañon. By this means the land available for cultivation on the reservation could be increased to the extent of two or three thousand acres. (See general recommendations, page 29.)

SALT.

In the bluffs on the banks of the Rio Virgen, a short distance below the mouth of the Mo'-a-pa, there are extensive deposits of salt, in many places very pure and easily accessible. It is probable that these salt-beds can be worked to some extent, and the products thereof made a source of revenue to the Indians.

CATTLE-RAISING.

In the upper part of the valley of the Mo'-a-pa are the grass-lands above mentioned. In addition to these, along the dry benches on either side, and in a few places along the valley of the Virgen, there is a scant supply of bunch-grass. The reservation does not afford extensive facilities for cattle-raising, though a few cows can be kept with advantage.

BUILDINGS.

The buildings occupied by the present white settlers are of adobe covered with tules, a species of reed-like plants. They would be of great value for the immediate use of the employés and a part of the Indians.

TIMBER.

Within the present boundaries of the reservation there is no timber, but a short distance beyond the western line a small amount of timber can be procured on the side of a mountain known as Gass Mountain. To prevent speculators from seizing this for the purpose of selling it to the Government, the boundaries of the reservation should be extended so as to include the timber-tract.

Hundreds of thousands of cottonwoods have been planted on the reservation, in part by the present settlers, but chiefly by others who preceded them. These are making vigorous and healthy growth, and will, in a few years, furnish an abundance of wood for fuel, and some for building purposes.

In the mean time fuel can be procured by using the few mesquite bushes that grow in the vicinity of the farms.

MILL.

There is a dam, a mill-race, and mill-building, but no machinery in the mill. This should at once be properly supplied and worked, as the distance to settlements where a mill is situated is very great.

ROADS.

There are three roads by which the settlement on the reservation is approached—one from the Hualapai mining district on the south, crossing the Colorado River at the mouth of the Rio Virgen, another from Saint George on the east, and another from Pioche on the north. All these roads are very bad, making it expensive to transport the necessary supplies and material for the reservation from the settlements where they can be procured. One of the roads, probably the one from the agency to Pioche, should be put in good order at once.

WHITE SETTLERS.

At the time this reservation was set apart by Executive order there were a number of families settled in the valley, and they still remain for the purpose of holding their claims. They occupy the best lands and control much of the water which is needed for the reservation, and it was only by their sufferance that the Indians were able to plant a crop this fall. It will not be possible for the Indians to proceed with any extensive farming until these people are removed.

There is danger of other troubles arising also, from their presence on the reservation, as there is a constant conflict between them and the Indians, which becomes more bitter daily, and, as the number of Indians is increased, it is liable to result in disastrous consequences.

IMPROVEMENTS MADE BY FORMER SETTLERS.

Early in the year 1865 a number of people from Utah settled in the valley of the Mo'-a-pa. Others followed rapidly and four towns were established, Saint Thomas, Saint Joseph, Overton, and West Point; and the number increased until it was claimed that there were more than two thousand people in the valley. These people made extensive and valuable improvements. An extensive system of irrigating-canals was constructed so as to utilize all the water of the Mo'-a-pa.

As the country was destitute of timber, cottonwoods were planted along these water-courses. Much labor was also expended on the opening of roads.

When these people came into the valley it was supposed by them that they were settling in the Territory of Arizona, but when the lines separating Utah, Arizona, and Nevada were run by Government surveyors the valley was found to be within the jurisdiction of the State of Nevada. Thereupon the inhabitants of the valley abandoned their homes and returned to Utah.

When they left, other settlers came in and located claims in the most valuable parts of the valley, under the laws of Nevada enacted for the purpose of securing possessory rights.

The houses erected by the original settlers were built of adobes, usually covered with tules or earth, and being of perishable material, they, with some exceptions, have gone to ruin. These exceptions are the few houses which the present inhabitants have occupied and preserved. These people have also kept up only a part of the original canals, constructing some new water-ways, and adapting them to their present wants.

To utilize the valley as a reservation for the number of Indians which it is proposed to assemble here, it will be necessary to repair the original canals and drain certain swamps which were only partially drained by the first inhabitants. This can be done with a saving to the Government of probably more than a hundred thousand dollars, in comparison with the original cost of the work.

The land has never been surveyed by the Government, and the original owners lost their possessory rights by abandonment. The present settlers have acquired possessory rights, not to the whole valley with all its original improvements, but only to such parts as are covered by their several claims. It would be impossible for the original owners to acquire possession of the valley again without purchasing the rights of the present owners. They could yet obtain possession of the unoccupied portions of the valley, but this would not be suited to their communal organization, and it is believed that they do not desire to return, under any circumstances.

SPECIAL REPORT.

The rights of the present settlers are more fully set forth in the special report, of which mention has been made.

THE PAI UTES SHOULD BE MADE FARMERS.

From the foregoing it will be seen that the valley of the Mo'-a-pa is well adapted to agriculture, and that a system of canals is already constructed. The Indians themselves are willing to work and anxious to cultivate the soil. Altogether the circumstances are very favorable to the project of making farmers of the Pai Utes, and thus enabling them to become self-sustaining, and converting them from vicious, dangerous savages to civilized people.

UTES.

There are seven tribes constituting the Utes of Utah, organized into a confederacy under the chieftaincy of Tav′-wi, (Tab-bi.) The total number of these Indians is 556.

By official construction they are on the reservation in the valley of the Uintah, while in fact but a small part of them remain there, the greater number assembling there from time to time to receive supplies of clothing, &c.

For a number of years the Seuv′-a-rits, numbering 144, have refused to go to the reservation as a tribe; but occasionally individuals have appeared there, allured by the annual distributions. Late in the past summer the entire tribe went to the reservation and signified their intention of remaining there and becoming farmers, if they could receive the necessary assistance. Since the installment of a chief named Nu′-ints, known to the white man as Black Hawk, this tribe has been the terror of the settlers. Sometimes they have been joined in their depredations by Utes from beyond the Colorado River, but oftener by the Navajoes. Great numbers of horses and cattle have been driven away from the settlements, often in droves of hundreds, and at one time, when they were in league with the Navajoes, all of the settlements in the Sevier Valley and many in the San Pete Valley were broken up, and eight or ten thousand white people were driven from their homes. But their great chief, Nu′-ints, is dead, and his lieutenant and successor, Un-ka′-na-vo′-run, died in great distress early in the winter of 1872–'73. Early in the last summer a terrible scourge swept off great numbers of this tribe, until but 144 remain, and these, terrified and humble, sue for peace and promise to work.

THE UTE AGENCY REMOVED FROM SPANISH FORK TO UINTAH VALLEY.

Soon after the organization of the Territory of Utah, the Ute Indians inhabiting that part of the country embraced within the Territory were assigned by the superintendent of Indian affairs on duty there, and the agents acting under him, to small reservations or farms, and were encouraged to cultivate the soil, some at the valley of the Uintah, others at Arrapene, in the valley of the San Pete, others at Corn Creek, near Fillmore, but the greater number at Spanish Fork, on the shore of Utah Lake. At this last place agency-buildings were erected and farming was conducted on an extensive scale. Subsequently these Indians were more or less neglected, and the improvements made at Spanish Fork were destroyed. In the year 1865 a treaty was made with these Indians, under which it was stipulated that they should all go to the reservation in the valley of the Uintah and give up their right to the other little farms of which mention is made above.

On the part of the United States it was agreed that they should be established as herdsmen and farmers, with mills and schools, and many other provisions for their benefit. This treaty was never ratified by the Senate, but the Indians themselves supposing it to be a valid agreement from the time it was signed by them, have, so far as it has been possible for them, conformed to its provisions. The Government, on its part, through not recognizing the treaty, still give the Indians a liberal supply of clothing, and other articles for domestic use, but it has never made any adequate provision for their support and establishment as agriculturists.

CANNOT BE KEPT ON THE RESERVATION.

In their association with the white settlers in the valleys of Utah, many difficulties have arisen from time to time, and frequent complaints have come up to the Indian Department at Washington against these Indians, on the ground that they would not remain on the reservation. But it has not been possible for them to remain; they have been compelled to go elsewhere to obtain a living.

In the summer of 1872 the greater number of these Indians appeared in the settlements about the shore of Utah Lake and in San Pete Valley, causing some alarm to the people. A special Indian agent and a number of Army officers met them in council soon after for the purpose of inducing them to return to the reservation. When told that they would be forced to go back, they openly defied the authorities, and challenged some of the officers who were present to fight. When afterward informed that they would be furnished with food on the agency, that herds of cattle and loads of flour should be immediately taken there, they agreed to go, and some of these Indians have this summer told the commission that, at that time, they had determined to fight rather than stay on the reservation and starve, for they feared hunger more than they did the soldiers. Under the existing state of facts, it is unreasonable to expect these Indians to remain on the reservation.

WHAT MUST BE DONE TO KEEP THEM ON THE RESERVATION.

They must be taught to farm, and, in the mean time, supported, to enable them to abandon their nomadic habits.

Already a number of the Indians have been induced to cultivate little patches of ground, and if a proper provision could be made to carry on this work for a very few years, they would become self-supporting.

They should also have houses built. As long as an Indian has a tent he can move his home from time to time at will, but induce him to live in a cabin and his home is fixed. A number of these Utes informed your commissioners that they desired to have houses, and their agent, Mr. Critchelow, confirms this.

Many of the better class of Indians are accumulating some property in cattle. Two or three have as many as fifty head each, and it is very noticeable that those who have property appreciate the rights of property and are advocates of peace and honesty. The valley of the Uintah is admirably adapted to stock-raising. The change from hunters to stock-raisers is not a violent step, and would be in the right direction.

NEED OF A GOOD ROAD TO THE UINTAH VALLEY.

One of the serious difficulties on this agency is the want of a good road by which to reach the settlements. Supplies are now hauled over the Uintah Mountains, crossing difficult and rapid streams again and again, and the road is traveled with much labor and great expense. A road can be made from the agency to Green River Station, or to some point farther to the east, at less cost than to build a road over the Wasatch Mountains to Salt Lake City, the road now traveled. And there would be other advantages, in that the road to the northeast could be used in winter and the distance to the railroad shorter.

PAH-VANTS.

The Pah-vants, under the chieftaincy of Kanosh, number 134. They speak the same language as the Utes of Uintah Valley, socially affiliate with them, are intermarried with them, and sometimes join them in their hunting excursions. They should be taken to the reservation at Uintah, their number being too small to warrant the establishment of a separate reservation for their benefit.

They have shown themselves somewhat averse to removing to that place, but through Kanosh, their chief, have finally agreed that if the President of the United States insists on their going, and will assist them to become farmers, they are willing to try what can be done.

Kanosh is a man of ability. He lives in a house which was built for him by a former superintendent of Indian affairs for Utah, and, in part, adopts the habits of civilized life; but his people live chiefly by gathering seeds, hunting, and begging, though they raise a little wheat and corn.

This year they cultivated about thirty acres of wheat, which yielded a very poor harvest.

No Indians in all the territory visited by your commission have, in past years, received one-quarter of the amount of goods, in proportion to their numbers, as the Pah-vants, and this generous treatment on the part of the Government has added to the influence of Kanosh, for he has thus proved to the surrounding tribes his ability to influence the Government officials, and he is their admiration and envy; and they have learned to consult him, to a great extent, concerning all their dealings with the officers of the Indian Department.

There are circumstances connected with his relation to the Mormon Church that may lead him to refuse to go. In such a case he should be compelled with any force that may be necessary.

Before such a course is taken, the Government should provide the means by which such removal would accrue to the benefit of him and his people.

GO-SI UTES.

The Go-si Utes number 460. They inhabit a district of country west of Utah Lake and Great Salt Lake, on the line between Utah and Nevada, a part being in the Territory and a part in the State.

These Indians are organized into a confederacy, under the chieftaincy of Pi-an′-nump.

More than any other Indians visited by the commission, these Go-si Utes are cultivating the soil and working for white men. Pi-an′-nump, who is a brother of Kanosh, chief of the Pah-vants, is proud to claim that he earns his own living. Scorning to beg, he is willing to work, and while he is not able to induce all his Indians to take the same course, yet his influence is entirely for good.

His people are scattered in very small bands, cultivating the soil about little springs here and there, and from year to year compelled to give up their farms as they are seized by white men. They are all anxious to obtain permanent homes, and are willing to go wherever the President will direct, if they can only thus secure land and make a start as farmers.

The Go-si Utes speak a language much more nearly allied to the Northwestern Shoshones than the Utes, though the greater number of them affiliate with the Utes, and are intermarried with them.

The greater part of them would prefer to go to Uintah, but a few, on account of marriage-ties, desire to go with the Shoshones. It would probably be well to give them this choice.

The Utes of Utah number 556, the Pah-vants 134, and the Go-si Utes of Utah and Nevada, 460, making a total of 1,150 Indians, who should be collected on the reservation at Uintah.

THE SMALL RESERVATIONS AT SAN PETE, CORN CREEK, SPANISH FORK AND DEEP CREEK.

Previous to the advent of white men in Utah, the Indians were raising corn, squashes, and other grains, and vegetables. Among the tracts of land thus cultivated, there were four remarkable for their extent, one in a little valley along a stream, tributary to the San Pete, now known as Twelve-mile Creek, another at Corn Creek, near Fillmore, a third at Spanish Fork, on the shore of Utah Lake, and a fourth at Deep Creek, near the Nevada line. At the time when Brigham Young was governor of the Territory and *ex-officio* superintendent of Indian Affairs, the Indians were encouraged to continue their farming at these places, and were told that the lands would not be taken from them. But communal towns were planted near by, and the Indians engaged on the farms were put under the charge of the bishops of these towns. During the administration of subsequent officials, buildings were erected at Spanish Fork and a proper agency established there by authority of Congress. For a number of years no definite boundaries were given to the Indian farms, or reservations as they came to be styled, but in order to prevent white persons from diverting the water to other lands, at last, certain natural boundaries were designated in such a manner as to secure the water-rights.

The number of Indians at the so-called reservations was always very small, and when the matter was more thoroughly understood by the Department at Washington, it was not deemed wise to encourage the Indians to remain on them, but a treaty was made by which they agreed to unite in the valley of the Uintah, on the eastern side of the Wasatch Mountains. (Mention of this treaty has been made above.)

Some time after the signing of this treaty by the Indians the superintendent of Indian affairs for Utah recommended the sale of the old Indian farms, and that the proceeds of such sale should accrue to the benefit of the Indians. It is necessary to a proper understanding of the matter to remember that these reservations were never established by law, or by Executive order, so that up to this time they had no legal status as reservations, but an act of Congress approved May 5, 1864, entitled "An act to vacate and sell the present Indian reservations in Utah, and to settle the Indians of said Territory in Uintah Valley," provides. "* * That the Secretary of the Interior be, and is hereby, authorized and required to cause the several Indian reservations heretofore made, or occupied as such, in the Territory of Utah to be surveyed and sold." And it still further provides that the proceeds of the sales should be used for the benefit of the Indians. (*Vide* U. S. Statutes at Large, vol. 13, p. 63.)

This is the first legal recognition of said reservations, but when the surveyor-general of Colorado Territory was instructed by the Secretary of the Interior to cause the survey of said reservations, neither the Land-Office nor the Indian Department could determine where such reservations were situated, as no plat or record of any such reservations could be found. Thereupon the Secretary of the Interior issued the following instructions:

"DEPARTMENT OF THE INTERIOR,
"*Washington, D. C., February* 6, 1865.

"SIR: I return herewith the papers submitted with your letter of the 16th ultimo, concerning the sale of Indian reservations in Utah. I also inclose letter of the Commissioner of the Land-Office of the 24th ultimo, and copy of a correspondence with that Office on the subject, and have to state, in relation to the abandoned reservations, that instructions be given to the superintendent of Indian Affairs to designate, as far as he can ascertain, the extent of the tracts of country occupied by the Indians and recognized as their reservations; and in so doing that Office may be directed to include all the arable lands of the valleys in which the reservations are situated, together a proper quantity of adjacent timber-lands, for the convenience of the farming-lands, all to be laid off in small lots, and in such form for irrigation and settlement as to be the most attractive and convenient for settlers. If it shall be found that the lands are of an unreasonable extent for the reservation, a portion can be withheld from sale upon an inspection of the plots of survey.

"Very respectfully, your obedient servant,

"A. P. USHER,
'*Secretary*.

"WM. P. DOLE, Esq.,
"*Commissioner of Indian Affairs*."

Under these instructions four tracts of land were surveyed and divided into lots. The Indian farm at San Pete was but a small tract of land at a point where a little stream issues from the mountain on which is situated the Indian town known as Arrapene. The survey of the reservation here was made to include not only the original Indian farm, but was extended over a district of country twelve miles square, so as to include the town of Gunnison, with several hundred inhabitants and extensive improvements. There is a map of this survey on file in the Land Department. The Indian farm is there properly laid down on Twelve-Mile Creek, between the main range and an outlying mountain. The town of Gunnison is not laid down on the map, but its situation is indicated by the ditch, mill-race, and saw-mill on the north bank of the San Pete River, a few miles above its junction with the Sevier.

At Corn Creek also, not only the part of country embraced within the natural boundaries indicated by the superintendent of Indian affairs, as heretofore stated, was included in the survey, but it, also, was extended over a district of country twelve miles square, so as to include within its boundaries the towns of Petersburg, Meadow Creek and Corn Creek, and a number of outlying farms.

On the map of the Corn Creek reservation, on file in the Land Department, the situation of the Indian farm does not appear, and properly, for the surveyed land did not include it. The town of Petersburg is called on that map "Corn Creek settlement," and Meadow Creek settlement is indicated.

At Spanish Fork the survey was made to include the original Indian farm, and also the farm of one white man. The interests of no other settlers were interfered with.

Whether the survey at Deep Creek was made to include any lands pre-occupied by white men, is not known to the commission.

The commission made as thorough an examination into the facts concerning these reservations as it was possible for it to do without examining witnesses by legal methods, but evidence of the correctness of the above statement can be found in the official records of the Indian Bureau, and such records have been carefully examined by the commission.

In executing the provisions of the law these tracts of land were valued by special commissions appointed by the then Secretary of the Interior, but the owners of the improvements which had been included in the surveys protested against the sale of their property without just compensation to themselves.

Thereupon the Secretary of the Interior caused an appraisal to be made of their improvements.

It has before been stated that these reservations had no legal status until the enactment of the law of 1864. The wording of that law, which recognizes certain reservations in Utah, is as follows:

"The several reservations heretofore made or occupied as such in the Territory of Utah." It would seem a forced construction of this phraseology to hold that, under it, authority was given to survey and sell tracts of land which had never been used as such Indian reservations, but which had been settled upon by white men anterior to the passage of the law. It would seem that the law under consideration contemplated the sale of certain lands which had previously been reserved for the use of the Indians by the officers of the Indian Department on duty in Utah; that is, the farms which had been cultivated by the Indians, and such adjacent lands, within certain natural boundaries indicated above, as these officials had told the Indians would be kept for their use; but lands which had been occupied by these white settlers prior to and during the administration of such officials could not properly be included under the provisions of this law. It would certainly be an injustice to sell these lands without compensating the owners for their improvements. But there are great areas of land adjacent to these, equally as good, yet unsold and unoccupied, which these same settlers could obtain by occupation under the homestead laws, and the lands in question have no other value in the market than that given to them by the improvements. In the condition of affairs in Utah, where the towns have a communal organization virtually excluding non-communal people, these improvements could be sold to none other than the people by whom they were made.

If, then, an interpretation is given to this law to the effect that the Secretary of the Interior shall cause the sale of the lands occupied by these people, it simply amounts to this, that certain improvements shall be seized by the Government, and sold to the parties from whom they have been seized, and that the proceeds of such sales shall be used to indemnify the people for the loss of the improvements seized by the Government. Such a course is manifestly absurd.

In the meantime the people of the town of Gunnison, not having been removed from the lands, have steadily increased the value of their improvements, and other settlements have been made on San Pete River. The same statement would be true in respect to Corn Creek. No settlements proper have been made on the Spanish Fork reservation. Mines have been discovered in the vicinity of Deep Creek, and non-communal people have settled on all the best of the lands within the boundaries of the so-called reservation.

The several tribes of Indians to whom the farms at one time belonged now claim their original farms, and also these communal towns, thus greatly complicating the administration of Indian affairs in the Territory. It is greatly to be desired that the question should be settled at the earliest practicable day. The commission would therefore recommend the repeal of the law of 1864, which would place these tracts on the same footing as other Government lands—subject to "homestead entry."

NORTHWESTERN SHOSHONES.

A part of the Northwestern Shoshones under Pó-ka-tel-lo and Tav′-i-wun-she′-a have already removed to reservations. Their wants will doubtless be properly represented by their respective agents.

There are yet two tribes united in a confederacy under the chieftancy of San-pits for whom provision should be made. At the last conference held with them this fall they signified their willingness to go on the reservation at Fort Hall provided its area be extended so as to include a certain valley to the southwest.

One or two days before the Commission left the field on its return to Washington an assistant was sent to accompany the chiefs of these tribes to the Fort Hall Reservation for the purpose of examining the country. Mr. Reed, the agent for that reservation, kindly consented to go with them, and to do all in his power to satisfy them of the good intention of the Government, and the desirability of that district of country for a reservation. Since the return of the Commission to Washington the following letter has been received.

"FORT HALL INDIAN AGENCY, *December* 1, 1873.

"DEAR SIR: I have the pleasure to say the Indians we saw as delegates reached here in due time, and after a day or two's rest we sent them on their journey except ——, who, with his wife, concluded to stop here over the winter. I was sick and sent head-farmer Baker, a man every way reliable and well acquainted with the country. They found a place which pleased them a few miles south of this, and up Bannock Creek found enough good land to satisfy them, all of which is on the reservation. They were so well pleased as of their own accord to abandon the journey to Goose Creek altogether. They say in the spring they will come in force prepared to have their houses and fixtures, and go to farming, &c.

Respectfully yours,

"HENRY W. REED,
"*United States Indian Agent.*

"G. W. INGALLS, Esq."

It will thus be seen that all the Northwestern Shoshones have agreed to go on the reservation at Fort Hall, instigated by their desire to obtain land and under representation that the Government would secure to them a permanent title to the same; and also provide for their immediate wants and aid them in learning to farm. These Indians have not of late years cultivated the soil, are good hunters, well mounted and nomadic in their habits, but they state their desire to become farmers and herdsmen.

WESTERN SHOSHONES.

The Western Shoshones number 1,945 and are divided into thirty-one tribes. They inhabit Southeastern Oregon, Southwestern Idaho, and Central Nevada. Of these tribes not more than one-fourth took part in the treaty of October 1, 1863, made at Ruby Valley in Nevada. The tribes living to the south and west were not present or represented in any manner. Under that treaty it was stipulated that the Western Shoshones could be called to a reservation at the will of the Pesident, and that these tribes should receive annuities to the amount of $5,000 for a term of twenty years. Only the northern tribes, who took part in the treaty, have received the benefit of this stipulation. The southern and western tribes, having taken no part in the treaty, have received no part of the annuities, and consider that they are under no obligations to the General Government, and exhibit some reluctance to their proposed removal to a reservation. The northern tribes, who did take part in the treaty, would prefer to remain where they now are, if lands could be given them in the several districts, but when informed that such a course could not be taken and explanations were given to them of the reason therefor, they expressed a willingness to settle on the Shoshone River, to the north, within the limits or adjacent to the reservation at Fort Hall, provided it should be found, on examination, to contain sufficient agricultural lands to meet their wants.

Delegates from some of the northern tribes visited the Fort Hall Reservation at the suggestion of the commission, and expressed their entire satisfaction with that district of country, but a part of these northern tribes and all of the southern tribes were unrepresented in this delegation. It is believed that there will be no difficulty in inducing all the northern tribes of Indians to remove. A little more time and more thorough explanation is needed to induce the southern tribes to consent to a removal, but it is believed that eventually their consent can be obtained.

The condition of these Indians does not differ materially from that of the Pai-Utes and Go-si Utes which have been heretofore mentioned, though it should be stated that the more southern tribes are in an exceedingly demoralized state; they prowl about the mining-camps, begging and pilfering, the women prostituting themselves to the lust of the lower class of men. There are no Indians in all the territory visited by your commission, whose removal is so imperatively demanded by considerations of justice and humanity, as these Shoshones of Nevada.

THE FORT HALL RESERVATION.

In a communication to the Department, made by the commission in June last, and which is embodied in this report, a general statement was made concerning the value of the district of country within the boundaries of this reservation. It is necessary only to repeat the statement that the reservation is quite sufficient and the country well adapted for the purposes for which it was set apart. On the reservation there are some good buildings, a saw-mill, grist-mill, and shingle-machine. Some farming has been carried on, chiefly by the employment of Indian labor. It is reported that there are 1,037 Indians on the reservation at least a part of the year. To the northwest, on the Salmon River, there are a number of tribes, numbering altogether about 500. These tribes were visited during the past year by the special commission, of which the Hon. J. P. C. Shanks was chairman, and it is proposed by that commission that these Indians also be brought to the reservation at Fort Hall. The total number of Indians thus to be collected on the reservation is 3,882, viz: 1,037 already on the reservation, 500 of the Salmon River tribes, 400 of the Northwestern Shoshones, and 1,945 of the Western Shoshones.

THE PA-VI-O′-TSOES OR PAH-UTES.

In the report of the agent of the Pa-vi-o′-tsoes belonging to the Walker River and Pyramid Lake reservations, these Indians are estimated to number 800. They seem to be making substantial progress in civilization, cultivating the soil to the extent of the facilities afforded on the reservations, and support themselves largely by fishing, selling the surplus products of the fisheries at good rates to the people of the railroad towns adjacent. There appears to be no reason to change the opinion expressed in the statement made last June that the Indians should be removed to some other place where they can become agriculturalists. Since that communication was made additional reasons for such a removal have appeared. It is probable that the Central Pacific Railroad Company is entitled to a part of the land embraced within the reservation, under the grant made to it by Congress. If this should prove true, it would be necessary to purchase such lands in order to secure these reservations for the use of the Indians, and when so purchased they would be entirely inadequate to their wants. Doubtless the Indians themselves would raise very serious objections to the removal, but they are industrious, intelligent, manageable people, and it is believed that if the necessities for the removal were properly represented to them, and, in addition to this, they are given substantial evidence that good lands will be secured to them, and that they will receive valuable aid by being supplied with farming-implements, seeds, cattle, &c., they will eventually consent to the removal. From the best information at the command of the commission, and after making diligent inquiries, it is believed that there are about 1,000 Indians allied in language to these Pa-vi-o′-tsoes, yet distributed about Western Nevada and Northeastern California.

During the past season the commission met many of the chiefs and principal men of these tribes. They, like the other Indians of Utah and Nevada, are anxious to obtain lands. Doubtless no great difficulty would be met in inducing them to go on a reservation; but within the territory inhabited by them there are no unoccupied lands which could be secured for their use. To the north, on the Malheur River, there is a reservation of what is represented to be good land, well watered, and with abundance of timber. On this reservation there are about 500 Indians allied to these of Nevada and California. The commission deem it wise that an effort should be made to consolidate all these Indians, namely, the Indians already on the Malheur Reservation, the uncollected tribes in Western Nevada and Northeastern California, and the Indians who belong to the Walker River and Pyramid Lake reservations.

The total number of such Indians would be about 2,300.

RECAPITULATION.

The tribes whose condition has been thus briefly discussed, and for whose disposition recommendations have been made, are scattered over a great extent of territory, embracing the greater part of the region between the Rocky Mountains and the Sierras. The boundaries of this region may be indicated in a general way as follows: Beginning on the north line of Oregon where that line crosses the Sierras, and continuing south along the crest of this range of mountains to Walker's Pass in Southern California, and from thence east to the southeast corner of Nevada; and from thence northeast to the point where San Juan River crosses the northern line of Arizona; and from thence east along this line to the southeast corner of Utah; and from thence north along the eastern line of Utah and beyond the line of Utah to the Wind River Mountains; and from thence in a northwesterly direction along the Wind River Mountains and the mountains which separate Montana from Idaho to a point directly east of the northern line of Oregon, and from that point to the place of beginning. The region of country thus described embraces the greater part of Idaho, nearly two-thirds of Oregon, nearly one-fourth of California, the entire State of Nevada, and the Territory of Utah, one-fifth of Arizona, and one-sixth of Wyoming, and contains about 420,000 square miles.

Within the territory thus described there are two small reservations, of which no mention has been made in this report, on the eastern slope of the Sierras in Oregon. The Indians who belong to these reservations originally occupied the country west of the Sierras, and do not belong to the great family of tribes we have been discussing. The Shoshones and Bannocks, of the Wind River Reservation, are without the boundaries of the country described, but they belong to the same family of tribes.

The same is true with regard to the tribes of Utes which belong to the great reservation in Western Colorado; and the Comanches of Texas are also a branch of this people. The Indians who inhabit this great district of country are estimated to number nearly 27,000, in the last annual report of the Bureau of Indian Affairs. The facts which we have collected show that there are not more than 9,359; and adding to this 300 Chem-a-hue-vis, belonging to the same race that live to the south of the district described, we have 9,659.

It is proposed to collect all the Pai-Utes of Southern Nevada, Southeastern California, Northwestern Arizona, and Southern Utah, together with the Chem-a-hue-vis of Southeastern California, on the Mo'-a-pa reservation, in Southern Nevada. The total number of these Indians is 2,327.

It is proposed to collect the Utes of Utah, the Pah-vants of Utah, and the Go-si Utes of Utah and Northeastern Nevada on the Uintah reservation. The total number of these Indians is 1,150.

It is proposed to collect the Bannocks and Shoshones at Fort Hall; the Shoshone tribes of Salmon River, the Northwestern Shoshones of Southern Idaho and Northern Utah, and the Western Shoshones of Central Nevada, Southwestern Idaho, and Southeastern Oregon, on the reservation at Fort Hall. The total number of these Indians is 3,882.

It is proposed to collect the Pah-Utes, Shoshones, &c., who are already on the Malheur reservation, the Pah-Utes or Pa-vi-o'-tsoes, who are now on the reservation at Pyramid Lake and Walker River, and the uncollected tribes of Western Nevada and Northeastern California on the reservation at Malheur River. The total number of these Indians is 2,300.

On the accompanying map, being a part of the map of the United States and Territories compiled in the General Land-Office, the several districts of country inhabited by the tribes included in this report are indicated by colors numbered to correspond with a tabular statement. The Indians inhabiting the districts colored with carmine are Pai-Utes, and the reservation recommended for them is of the same color, bordered with black. The brown colors indicate the tribes which should be collected at the Uintah reservation. This reservation is also colored brown, bordered with black.

The yellow colors indicate tribes which should go to the Fort Hall reservation, which is also colored yellow, bordered with black.

The Indians that should be collected at the Malheur reservation inhabit the region of country included within green lines, and the Malheur reservation is colored green, with black border.

Embraced within the boundaries of the four reservations there are about ten thousand square miles of land. Only a small portion of this land is fit for agricultural purposes, much of it being sandy desert and mountain waste.

The district of country relieved of the presence of the Indians is about four hundred and ten thousand square miles.

GENERAL REMARKS.

All of the Indians who have been visited by the commission fully appreciate the hopelessness of contending against the Government of the United States and the tide of civilization.

They are broken into many small tribes, and their homes so interspersed among the settlements of white men, that their power is entirely broken and no fear should be entertained of a general war with them. The time has passed when it was necessary to buy peace. It only remains to decide what should be done with them for the relief of the white people from their petty depredations, and from the demoralizing influences accompanying the presence of savages in civilized communities, and also for the best interests of the Indians themselves. To give them a partial supply of clothing and a small amount of food annually, while they yet remain among the settlements, is to encourage them in idleness, and directly tends to establish them as a class of wandering beggars. If they are not to be collected on reservations they should no longer receive aid from the General Government, for every dollar given them in their present condition is an injury. This must be understood in the light that it is no longer necessary to buy peace. Perhaps the Utes of the Uintah Valley should be excepted from this statement, as they might thus be induced to join the Utes of Western Colorado who are yet unsubdued.

Again, they cannot be collected on reservations and kept there without provision being made for their maintenance. To have them nominally on a reservation and actually, the greater part of the year, wandering among the settlements, is of no advantage, but rather an injury, as the people, believing that they should remain on their reservations, and considering that they are violating their agreements with the Government in wandering away, refuse to employ them and treat them with many indignities. And this consolidation of a number of tribes of Indians in one body makes them stronger, more independent, and more defiant than they would be if scattered about the country as small tribes. If, then, they are to be collected on reservations and held there by furnishing them with an adequate support, it is evident wisdom that they should be provided with the necessary means and taught to work, that they may become self-supporting at the earliest possible day; and it is urgently recommended that steps be taken to secure this end, or that they be given over to their own resources and left to fight the battle of life for themselves. It is not pleasant to contemplate the effect and final result of this last-mentioned course. The Indian in his relations with the white man rarely associates with the better class, but finds his companions in the lowest and vilest of society—men whose object is to corrupt or plunder. He thus learns from the superior race everything that is bad, nothing that is good. His presence in the settlement is a source of irritation and a cause of fear, especially among the better class of people.

Such persons will not employ him, for they do not desire the presence of a half-naked, vicious savage in their families.

Nor are the people of these communities willing to assume the trouble or expense of controlling the Indians by the ordinary agencies of local government, but are always ready to punish either real or supposed crimes by resort to arms.

Such a course, together with the effects of crime and loathsome disease, must finally result in the annihilation of the race.

By the other alternative, putting them on reservations and teaching them to labor, they must for a number of years be a heavy expense to the General Government, but it is believed that the burden would not be as great as that on the local governments if the Indians were left to themselves. It is very probable, also, that in the sequel it will be found cheaper for the General Government to collect them on reservations, for there is always serious danger of petty conflicts arising between the Indians and white men which will demand the interference of the General Government and entail some expense. The commission does not consider that a reservation should be looked upon in the light of a pen where a horde of savages are to be fed with flour and beef, to be supplied with blankets from the Government bounty, and to be furnished with paint and gew-gaws by the greed of traders, but that a reservation should be a school of industry and a home for these unfortunate people. In council with the Indians great care was taken not to implant in their minds the idea that the Government was willing to pay them for yielding lands which white men needed, and that as a recompense for such lands they would be furnished with clothing and food, and thus enabled to live in idleness. The question was presented to the Indian something in this light: The white men take these lands and use them, and from the earth secure to themselves food, clothing, and many other desirable things. Why should not the Indian do the same? The Government of the United States is anxious for you to try. If you will unite and agree to become farmers, it will secure to you permanent titles to such lands as you need, and will give you the necessary assistance to begin such a life, expecting that you will soon be able to take care of yourselves, as do white men and civilized Indians.

All the tribes mentioned in this census table, and many others, have been visited by the commission, and frequent consultations held with them concerning the importance of their removing to reservations, and they have discussed it among themselves very fully.

Care has been taken to secure common consultation among those tribes which should be united as represented in the plans above, and we doubt not that these questions will form the subject of many a night's council during the present winter; and if the suggestions made by the commission should be acted upon, it is to be hoped that next summer will find the great majority of these Indians prepared to move.

SUGGESTIONS IN REGARD TO THE MANAGEMENT OF THESE RESERVATIONS.

With a view of ultimately civilizing these Indians, the commission beg leave to make some suggestions concerning the management of reservations.

First. All bounties given to the Indians should, so far as possible, be used to induce them to work. No able-bodied Indian should be either fed or clothed except in payment for labor, even though such labor is expended in providing for his own future wants. Of course these remarks apply only to those who form the subject of our report—those with whom it is no longer necessary to deal as public enemies, and with the understanding that they must be conciliated to prevent war. It has already been stated that such a course is unnecessary with these Indians.

Second. They should not be provided with ready-made clothing. Substantial fabrics should be given them from which they can manufacture their own garments. Such a course was taken during the past year with the Pi-Utes, under the direction of the commission, and the result was very satisfactory. For illustration, on the Pi-Ute reservation four hundred Indians received uncut cloth sufficient to make each man, woman, and child a suit of clothes. With these fabrics thread, needles, buttons, &c., were issued. The services of an intelligent, painstaking woman were secured to teach the woman how to cut and make garments for themselves and their families. Three weeks after the issue of this material the commission revisited the reservation and found these Indians well clothed in garments of their own make. At first they complained bitterly that ready-made clothing was not furnished to them as it had been previously, but when we returned to the reservation it was found that they fully appreciated that the same money had been much more advantageously spent than on previous occasions.

Where the Indians have received ready-made clothing for a number of years, the change should not be made too violently, but a wise and firm agent could soon have all his Indians making their own clothing.

Third. The Indians should not be furnished with tents; as long as they have tents they move about with great facility, and are thus encouraged to continue their nomadic life. As fast as possible houses should be built for them. Some of the Indians are already prepared for such a change, and greatly desire to live in houses. A few, especially the older people, are prejudiced against such a course, and perhaps at first could not be induced to live in them; but such a change could be made gradually to the great advantage of the Indian, both for his health and comfort and for its civilizing influence.

Fourth. Each Indian family should be supplied with a cow, to enable them to start in the accumulation of property. The Indians now understand the value of domestic cattle, and are anxious to acquire this class of property, and a few of them have already made a beginning in this direction. Some have ten, twenty, thirty, and even fifty head, though these are exceptional cases, and it is interesting to notice that, as soon as an Indian acquires property, he more thoroughly appreciates the rights of property, and becomes an advocate of law and order.

Fifth. In all this country the soil cannot be cultivated without artificial irrigation, and under these conditions agricultural operations are too complicated for the Indian without careful superintendence. It will be impossible also to find a sufficient body of land in any one place for the necessary farms; they must be scattered many miles apart. There will, therefore, be needed on each reservation a number of farmers to give general direction to all such labor.

Sixth. On each reservation there should be a blacksmith, carpenter, and a saddle and harness maker, and each of these mechanics should employ several Indian apprentices, and should consider that the most important part of his duty was to instruct such apprentices, and from time to time a shoemaker and other mechanics should be added to this number.

Seventh. An efficient medical department should be organized on each reservation. A great number of the diseases with which the Indian is plagued yield readily to medical treatment, and by such a course many lives can be saved and much suffering prevented. But there is another very important reason for the establishment of a medical department. The magician or "medicine-man" wields much influence, and such influence is always bad; but in the presence of an intelligent physician it is soon lost.

Eighth. It is unnecessary to mention the power which schools would have over the rising generation of Indians. Next to teaching them to work, the most important thing is to teach them the English language. Into their own language there is woven so much mythology and sorcery that a new one is needed in order to aid them in advancing beyond their baneful superstitions; and the ideas and thoughts of civilized life cannot be communicated to them in their own tongues.

THE RELATION OF THE ARMY TO THESE INDIANS.

Your commission cannot refrain from expressing its opinion concerning the effect of the presence of soldiers among these Indians where they are no longer needed to keep them under subjection. They regard the presence of a soldier as a standing menace, and to them the very name of soldier is synonymous with all that is offensive and evil. To the soldier they attribute their social demoralization and the unmentionable diseases with which they are infested. Everywhere, as we traveled among these Indians, the question would be asked us, "If we go to a reservation will the Government place soldiers there?" And to such a removal two objections were invariably urged; the first was, "We do not wish to desert the graves of our fathers," and the second, "We do not wish to give our women to the embrace of the soldiers."

If the troops are not absolutely necessary in the country for the purpose of overawing these Indians, or protecting them in their rights against the encroachments of white men, it will be conceded that they should be removed.

We have already expressed the opinion that they are not needed to prevent a general war, and we believe that they are not useful in securing justice between white men and Indians and between Indians and Indians. In war we deal with people as organized into nationalities, not as individuals. Some hungry Indian steals a beef, some tired Indian steals a horse, a vicious Indian commits a depredation, and flies to the mountains. No effort is made to punish the real offender, but the first Indian met is shot at sight. Then, perhaps, the Indians retaliate, and the news is spread through the country that war has broken out with the Indians. Troops are sent to the district and wander around among the mountains and return. Perhaps a few Indians are killed, and perhaps a few white men. Usually in all such cases the white man is the chief sufferer, for he has property which can be spoiled, and the Indian has none that he cannot easily hide in the rocks. His methods of warfare are such that we cannot cope with him without resorting to means which are repugnant to civilized people; and, after spending thousands, or even millions of dollars, on an affair which, at its inception, was but a petty larceny, we make a peace with the Indians, and enter into an agreement to secure him lands, which we cannot fulfill, and to give him annuities, the expense of which are a burden on the public Treasury.

This treatment of the Indians as nations or tribes is in every way bad. Now, the most vicious Indian in any tribe has it in his power, at any moment that he may desire, to practically declare war between his own tribe, and perhaps a dozen surrounding tribes, and the Government of the United States.

What now is needed with all these subdued Indians is, some method by which individual criminals can be arrested and brought to justice. This cannot be done by the methods of war. As long as the Indians are scattered among the settlements the facts show that this cannot be done. The Indian has no knowledge of legal methods, and avenges his own wrongs by ways which are traditional with him, while the prejudices against savages which has grown through centuries of treacherous and bloody warfare, and the prejudices of race, which are always greatly exaggerated among the lower class of people, with whom the Indian is most liable to associate, are such that the Indian cannot secure justice through the intervention of the local authorities.

There is now no great uninhabited and unknown region to which the Indian can be sent. He is among us, and we must either protect him or destroy him. The only course left by which these Indians can be saved is to gather them on reservations, which shall be schools of industry and civilization, and the superintendents of which shall be the proper officers to secure justice between the two races, and between individuals of the Indian race. For this purpose on each reservation there should be a number of wise, firm men, who, as judges and police officers, would be able in all ordinary cases to secure substantial justice. In extraordinary cases no hasty steps should be taken. Surprises and massacres need no longer be feared, and if a larger force is needed than that wielded by the employés on the reservations, it would be easy to increase it by civil methods.

For this purpose laws should be enacted clearly defining the rights of the Indians and white men in their mutual relations, and the power of the officers of the Indian Department, and the methods of procedure to secure justice. It might possibly be unwise to withdraw all the troops at once. It might be better to remove them *pari passu* with the establishment of the Indians on reservations.

Permit the remark just here, that the expense of the military and civil methods stand in very glaring contrast. Within the territory which has heretofore been described it is probable that about two million dollars will be expended in the support of troops during the present fiscal year, and much less than two hundred thousand dollars through the Indian Department for feeding, clothing, and civilizing the Indians.

We beg leave again to mention that these remarks apply only to conquered tribes. There are some Indians in other portions of the United States, whom it is necessary to manage by other methods, who yet have the pride and insolence and treachery of savages. But by far the greater part of the Indians scattered throughout the territory from the Rocky Mountains to the Pacific coast are in a condition substantially the same as those who form the subject of this report.

APPROPRIATIONS.

ESTIMATES FOR APPROPRIATIONS SUBMITTED BY THE INDIAN BUREAU, THROUGH THE SECRETARY OF THE TREASURY, FOR THE SUPPORT, ETC., OF THE INDIANS HERETOFORE DESCRIBED, FOR THE FISCAL YEAR ENDING JUNE 30, 1875. (See letter from the Secretary of the Treasury, transmitting estimates of appropriations on pages indicated.)

Page	Item	Amount
91.	One agent for the Malheur reservation	$1,500
91.	Two agents for the tribes in Nevada, viz: the Pi-Utes and Walker River and Pyramid Lake reservations, $1,500 each	3,000
91.	One agent at Fort Hall reservation	1,500
91.	One agent for the tribes in Utah, viz: Uintah Valley agency	1,500
92.	One interpreter, Malheur agency	500
92.	One interpreter, Fort Hall agency	500
92.	Three interpreters for the tribes in Nevada, viz: Pi-Utes, Walker River, and Pyramid Lake agencies, at $500 each	1,500
92.	One interpreter for the tribes in Utah	500
104.	Fulfilling treaties with Shoshonees, Eastern, Western, Northwestern, and Goship bands	
104.	Eastern bands	
104.	Eleventh of twenty installments, to be expended under the direction of the President in the purchase of such articles as he may deem suitable to their wants, either as hunters or herdsmen, per fifth article treaty of July 2, 1863	10,000
104.	Western bands	
104.	Eleventh of twenty installments, to be expended under the direction of the President in the purchase of such articles as he may deem suitable to their wants, either as hunters or herdsmen, per seventh article treaty of October 1, 1863	5,000
105.	Northwestern bands	
105.	Eleventh of twenty installments, to be expended under the direction of the President in the purchase of such articles as he may deem suitable to their wants, either as hunters or herdsmen, per third article treaty of July 30, 1863	5,000
105.	Goship bands	
105.	Eleventh of twenty installments, to be expended under the direction of the President in the purchase of such articles, including cattle for herding or other purposes, as he may deem suitable to their wants and condition as hunters and herdsmen	1,000

105 *Fulfilling treaties with Shoshonees and Bannocks.*

Bannocks:	
Fifth of thirty installments, to purchase four hundred suits of clothing for males over fourteen years of age, the flannel, hose, calico, and domestics for four hundred females over twelve years of age, and such flannel and cotton goods as may be needed to make suits for four hundred boys and girls under the ages named	6,937
Fifth of ten installments, for purchase of such articles as may be considered proper by the Secretary of the Interior, for eight hundred persons roaming, at ten dollars each, and four hundred persons engaged in agriculture, at twenty dollars each	16,000
Pay of physician, teacher, carpenter, miller, engineer, farmer, and blacksmith, as per tenth article treaty of July third, eighteen hundred and sixty-eight	6,800
First of three installments, for the purchase of seeds and farming implements, as per eighth article same treaty	2,500
Transportation of goods that may be purchased for the Shoshonees and Bannocks	5,000

105 *Settlement, subsistence, and support of Shoshonees and Bannocks and other bands of Idaho and Southeastern Oregon.*

This amount to be expended in such goods, provisions, or other articles as the President may from time to time determine, including transportation; in instructing in agricultural pursuits; in providing employés, educating children, procuring medicine and medical attendance; care for and support of the aged, sick, and infirm, for the helpless orphans of said Indians, and in any other respect to promote their civilization, comfort, and improvement... $40,000

109 *Incidental expenses of the Indian service in Idaho Territory.*

General incidental expenses of the Indian service in Idaho Territory: presents of goods, agricultural implements, and other useful articles; and to assist them to locate in permanent abodes and sustain themselves by the pursuits of civilized life, to be expended under the direction of the Secretary of the Interior, $20,000, one-half........ 10,000

109 *Incidental expenses of the Indian service in Nevada.*

General incidental expenses of the Indian service in Nevada; presents of goods, agricultural implements, and other useful articles; and to assist them to locate in permanent abodes and sustain themselves by the pursuits of civilized life, to be expended under the direction of the Secretary of the Interior.... 50,000

110 *Incidental expenses of the Indian service in Oregon.*

General incidental expenses of the Indian service in Oregon, including transportation of annuity goods and presents, (where no special provision is made therefor by treaty,) and for paying the expenses of the removal and subsistence of Indians in Oregon, (not parties to any treaties,) and for the pay of necessary employés, $75,000; of this amount........ 10,000

110 *Incidental expenses of the Indian service in Utah Territory.*

General incidental expenses of the Indian service in Utah Territory: presents of goods, agricultural implements, and other useful articles, and to assist them to locate in permanent abodes and sustain themselves by the pursuits of civilized life, including transportation and necessary expenses of delivering provisions to the Indians within the Utah superintendency; and for subsistence and clothing for Indians located upon the Uintah Valley reservation, Utah, to be expended under the direction of the Secretary of the Interior.... 50,000

110 *Civilization and subsistence of Indians on the Malheur reservation.*

This amount, or so much thereof as may be necessary, in the purchase of goods, subsistence stores, &c., for the Indians collected on the Malheur reservation, Oregon, and in instructing them in agricultural and mechanical pursuits, providing employés, educating children, procuring medicine and medical attendance, care for and support of the aged, sick, and infirm; for the helpless orphans of said Indians, or in any other respect to promote their civilization, comfort, and improvement........ 40,000

Total amount of these estimates........ 268,737

RECOMMENDATIONS FOR APPROPRIATIONS.

In lieu of the foregoing the following are submitted:

For the Pai Ute reservation.

For the employment of one agent, three farmers, one blacksmith, one carpenter, one saddle and harness maker, one miller, one teacher, and three general assistants........ $12,900

For the purchase of teams, wagons, agricultural implements, seeds and tools, and supplies for the shops of the mechanics........ 8,000

For the purchase of lumber and other material for the agency buildings	$3,000
For subsistence supplies	10,000
For the purchase of a sufficient number of cows to give one to each Indian family	10,000
For the purchase of fabrics for clothing and other necessary articles for the Indians	15,000
For machinery and repairs on mill	5,000
For salary of surgeon, hospital steward, and medical supplies for hospital	5,000
For constructing wagon-road from the agency to such point as the Secretary of the Interior may direct	5,000
For the payment of freighting and traveling expenses	10,000
For collecting the Indians on the reservation and incidental expenses	12,000
For one interpreter	500
Total amount of appropriation recommended for the Pai Ute reservation	96,400

For the Uintah reservation.

For the employment of one agent, one farmer, one blacksmith, one carpenter, one saddle and harness maker, one miller, one engineer, one teacher, and three general assistants	$11,750
For the purchase of teams, wagons, agricultural implements, seeds, tools, and supplies for the shops of the mechanics	10,000
For the erection of houses for the Indians	5,000
For subsistence supplies	10,000
For the purchase of a sufficient number of cows to give one to each Indian family	6,000
For the purchase of ready-made clothing, and for fabrics for clothing, and other articles necessary for the Indians	8,000
For the salary of surgeon, hospital steward, and medical supplies for the hospital	5,000
For constructing a wagon road from the agency to the railroad	10,000
For the payment of freighting and traveling expenses	5,000
For collecting the Indians on the reservation and incidental expenses	5,000
For one interpreter	500
Total amount of appropriation recommended for the Uintah reservation	76,250

For the Fort Hall reservation.

For the employment of one agent, three farmers, one blacksmith, one carpenter, one saddle and harness maker, one engineer, one teacher, and three general assistants	$14,100
For the purchase of teams, wagons, agricultural implements, seeds, tools, and supplies for the shops of the mechanics	8,000
For the erection of buildings for the Indians	12,000
For subsistence supplies	12,000
For the purchase of a sufficient number of cows to give one to each Indian family	16,000
For the purchase of ready-made clothing, and fabrics for clothing, and articles necessary for the Indians	18,000
For the salary of surgeon, hospital steward, and medical supplies for the hospital	5,000
For the payment of freighting and traveling expenses	8,000
For collecting the Indians on the reservation and incidental expenses	12,000
For one interpreter	500
Total amount of appropriation recommended for Fort Hall reservation	105,600

For the Malheur reservation.

For continuing the agency for the reservations at Pyramid Lake and Walker River until the crops now planted shall be harvested, and for removing these Indians to the Malheur reservation	$12,000
For the employment of one agent, three farmers, one blacksmith, one carpenter, one saddle and harness maker, one teacher, and three general assistants	11,700
For the purchase of teams, wagons, agricultural implements, seeds and tools, and supplies for the shops of the mechanics	10,000
For the erection of buildings	10,000
For subsistence supplies	12,000

For the purchase of a sufficient number of cows to give one to each Indian family	$12,000
For the purchase of ready-made clothing, and fabrics for clothing, and other necessary articles for the Indians	15,000
For salary of surgeon, hospital steward, and medical supplies for the hospital.	5,000
For the payment of freighting and traveling expenses	8,000
For collecting the Indians on the reservation and incidental expenses	8,000
For one interpreter	500
Total amount of appropriations recommended for the Malheur reservation	104,200

ESTIMATED VALUE OF THE CLAIMS OF CERTAIN SETTLERS ON THE MO'-A-PA RESERVATION.

Isaac Jennings, J. S. Moffett	$7,500
Thomas Belding, Chandler Belding, Lewis Seabright	4,250
Daniel Bonelli	5,700
Robert G. Patterson, J. L. Lessell	6,200
William Anderson	750
Augustus James	750
Abraham James	1,500
Robert Logan	2,200
John Bennett, J. H. Ratcliff, G. R. A. Percival	1,400
Volney Rector, Peter L. Johnson	1,800
Total	32,050

It is recommended that appropriations be asked to pay the above claims.

These people already occupy much of the available land on this reservation, and have control of the water. It is absolutely necessary that they should be removed if the Indians are to be established as agriculturalists.

A special report, giving in detail the character of these improvements, viz, the buildings, trees, orchards, vineyards, water-ways, &c., together with certified copies of the surveys which were made under the State laws of Nevada to secure these settlers in their possessory rights, and a map of the reservation showing the situation of each claim, will be submitted on the completion of the map.

GENERAL RECOMMENDATIONS.

It is recommended—

First. That the act entitled "An act to vacate and sell the present Indian reservation in Utah Territory, and to settle the Indians of said Territory in the Uintah Valley," approved May 5, 1864, (see U. S. Stats. at Large, vol. 13, p. 63,) be repealed, and that the lands to which it refers be thrown open to settlement in the usual way. (See previous remarks on "The small reservations at San Pete, Corn Creek, Spanish Fork, and Deep Creek.")

Second. That the boundaries of the Pai-Ute reservation be established as follows: Beginning at a point on the Colorado River of the West eight miles east of the one hundred and fourteenth meridian, and continuing from thence due north to the thirty-seventh parallel of latitude; and continuing from thence due west along said thirty-seventh parallel of latitude to a point twenty miles west of the one hundred and fifteenth meridian; and continuing from thence due south thirty-five miles; and continuing from thence due east thirty-six miles; and continuing from thence due south to the center of the channel of the Colorado River of the West; and continuing from thence along said center of the channel of the Colorado River of the West to the point of beginning. (See previous remarks under the headings of "Reservations on the Mo'-a-pa" and "Timber.")

Third. That an inspector, together with a competent engineer, employed for this purpose from the incidental funds of the several reservations, shall visit the reservations at Uintah, Fort Hall, and on the Malheur reservation, and, in company with the agent and some of the chiefs and principal men of the tribes belonging on such reservations, shall make a careful examination of the territory embraced within the reservations and designate certain natural, or if need be artificial, boundaries for the same, and report such action to the Department, to be submitted to Congress for final approval, so that the boundaries of such reservations may be accurately established by law. When the boundaries have been thus surveyed it would be well to have the reservations surveyed and divided into small tracts and topographical maps made of them.

Fourth. That the agents for these reservations be authorized to promise the Indians that one cow will be given to each Indian family settling on these reservations annually for a term of two years subsequent to that in which the first issue of cattle is made.

Fifth. Also that the agents for these reservations be authorized to promise the Indians that $10,000 will be expended annually on the Mo'-a-pa reservation, $6,000 annually on the Uintah reservation, $15,000 annually on the Fort Hall reservation, and $10,000 annually on the Malheur reservation for such a term of years as may be necessary to give each Indian family a house, to exceed in cost not more than $200; but that such cost shall not include the labor bestowed upon the same by the Indian himself.

Sixth. That should any of these Indians prefer to go to any other of these reservations than that to which they have been assigned in the foregoing report, or to the reservation at Wind River, the Secretary of the Interior shall have the authority to transfer the proper proportion of these appropriations from the account of the reservation to which it has been specially appropriated, to such reservation as the Indians may elect—provided the Secretary of the Interior shall approve of such election.

PAPERS ACCOMPANYING THIS REPORT.

First. A map of the Pi-Ute reservation in Southeastern Nevada.

Second. A section of the "Map of the United States and Territories prepared in the General Land-Office," with the districts inhabited by the various tribes embraced in this report, colored so as to indicate the geographical distribution of the several tribes which should be collected on the reservations.

Third. Report concerning the claims of settlers in the Mo-a-pa Valley, with copies of surveys, &c., marked A, B, C, and D, and photographs numbered 1, 2, 3.

In our letter of instruction, we were directed to consult with Col. H. A. Morrow, commandant at Camp Douglas, in Utah Territory.

While we were at Salt Lake City, completing plans for the operations of the summer, Colonel Morrow was confined to his room by severe sickness, and his physician thought it unwise for us to hold any consultation with him, but we availed ourselves of his wise counsel to the limit of our opportunities.

To many of the citizens of Utah and Nevada we are indebted for information, advice, and assistance, and we are pleased here to state that we met everywhere with the most hearty co-operation from the better class of people.

Invoking your attention to the facts herein set forth, and your consideration of the recommendations made,

We are, with much respect, your obedient servants,

J. W. POWELL,
G. W. INGALLS,
Special Commissioners.

The Hon. COMMISSIONER OF INDIAN AFFAIRS,
Washington, D. C.

REPORT CONCERNING CLAIMS OF SETTLERS IN THE MO-A-PA VALLEY, (S. E. NEVADA,) BY SPECIAL COMMISSIONERS J. W. POWELL AND G. W. INGALLS.

WASHINGTON, D. C., *December* 18, 1873.

Hon. COMMISSIONER OF INDIAN AFFAIRS, *Washington, D. C.:*

SIR: The following is a statement of the character and estimated value of the claims of certain settlers in the valley of the Mo-a-pa or Muddy Creek within the territory set apart by Executive order, dated March 12, 1873, as a reservation for the Pi-Utes of Southern Utah, Southern Nevada, Southeastern California, and Northwestern Arizona.

CLAIM OF ISAAC JENNINGS AND J. S. MOFFETT.

Land.—Amount of land claimed three hundred and twenty acres. The land originally claimed by these parties was in two tracts, of one hundred and sixty acres each, but a copartnership was formed by the said Isaac Jennings and J. S. Moffett, and they now lay claim to three hundred and twenty acres as a company.

Claim surveyed February 6 and 7, 1872, by C. W. Wandell, deputy surveyor of Lincoln County, State of Nevada, in accordance with the laws of Nevada, enacted for the purpose of securing possessory rights to Government land not having been surveyed by the General Government.

(See accompanying paper marked A, "certified copy of surveys of Isaac Jennings.")

Water-ways.—The greater part of these lands are covered by irrigating canals, but only a portion of said canals have been kept in good order; in some places they are partially destroyed, in others totally. More than nine-tenths of this land has been under cultivation, but one-half of it has been neglected; the other half is still in good order, and the ditches for irrigating the same are in repair.

Trees.—Several thousand cottonwood-trees have been planted beside the ditches, being from one to eight years old, and from twenty to sixty feet high; thrifty. A small amount of garden shrubbery; a small amount of hedging set for the purpose of subdividing a part of the land into lots.

Vineyards.—Seven plats planted in vineyard, on which are two thousand good grape-vines from four to eight years old; fifteen hundred second class of the same age, and one thousand third class, or nearly worthless, of the same age.

Meadow.—Eighteen acres set in lucern, and eight acres partly set.

Buildings.—Adobe house on stone foundation, covered with tules and earth. Rooms all without ceilings. Rooms have been papered; paper now damaged. Room used as post-office, 10 by 14; parlor, 14 by 15; large bed-room, 14 by 15; low bed-room, 12 by 15; dining-room, 16 by 20; kitchen, 16 by 16; pantry, 8 by 14; wash-room, 8 by 14; room for store, (not covered,) 16 by 18; blacksmith-shop, 16 by 40; the walls are 13 feet high; substantial floors are common; casings to doors and windows plain; doors plain; outside cellar, 12 by 14; stone walls. Hen-house, 18 by 20, rudely built of adobes and covered with tules. Granary, with two rooms, each 12 by 16, covered with tules; without floor. Three small adobe stables. Large adobe corral. Sufficient stone hauled for a second corral.

(See photograph "No. 1."

Estimated value of this claim, $7,500.

CLAIM OF THOS. BELDING, CHANDLER BELDING, AND LEWIS SEABRIGHT

The amount of land within this claim is considerably less than one hundred and sixty (160) acres to each person, but the value of the claim, in the estimation of the commissioners, is in no way affected by the amount of land, as the adjacent lands are still unoccupied and as the General Government has never yielded the title to any of the said lands. The value of the improvements and water-rights only are considered.

The lands included within this claim were surveyed by the same officer and at the same time as those in the claims above, at least such information has been received by the commission, but no copy of such surveys has been received.

About one hundred (100) acres has been under cultivation; now there are forty (40) acres under cultivation in good order and with irrigating canals in good repair.

Trees.—Several hundred cottonwood and other trees are set along the canals; they are from twenty to sixty feet high, good and thrifty. Small amount of well-cultivated garden-shrubbery. A small amount of hedging set for the purpose of subdividing a part of the land into lots.

Vineyard.—Twelve hundred grape-vines, four to six years old, in good order; eight hundred second-rate grape-vines; five hundred third-rate, or nearly worthless.

Buildings.—Adobe house on stone foundation, covered with tules; common floor window and door frames and doors; rooms without ceilings; walls twelve feet high, three rooms each, 16 by 16; small low back room used as kitchen. Hen-house. Small stable. Small corral made of poles.

(See photograph "No. 2.")

Fence.—Thirty-nine panels of two-pole fence. Estimated value of this claim $4,250.

CLAIM OF DANIEL BONELLI.

Land.—One hundred and sixty (160) acres. Surveyed by C. W. Wandell, deputy county surveyor of Lincoln County, State of Nevada, February 1 and 2, 1872. (See accompanying paper marked B.)

About one-fourth of the land has been prepared for cultivation, and is covered with irrigating canals. Canals not in good repair.

Trees.—A small amount of orchard-trees and garden-shrubbery. A good hedge, inclosing ten (10) acres, on two sides of osage orange; on one side of osage orange and cottonwood trees intervening, and on the fourth side of mesquite. Water-ways for ten (10) acres in good repair.

Vineyard.—Four thousand grape-vines, in good order, from two to eight years old. Two thousand second-rate grape-vines of the same age, and two thousand three hundred and fifty third-rate grape-vines of the same age.

The number of these grape-vines was determined by counting what were believed to be average rows. A greater number were claimed. (See accompanying paper marked C.)

Meadow.—Three and one-half acres well set with lucern.

Buildings.—Adobe house, stone foundation, covered with tules; no ceilings; walls thick; twelve feet high; in good order. Front part of house, outside measurement, 15 by 32; divided into two rooms; double fire-place in partition.

Back building, outside measurement, 17 by 27, divided into two rooms; one fire-place; floors, doors, and casings for doors and windows, common cellar 12 by 14, seven feet high, with stone walls.

House said to have cost $1,000.

Small adobe hen-house.

(See Photograph No. 3.)

Estimated value of claim $5,700.

CLAIM OF R. G. PATTERSON AND J. L. LASSELL.

Land.—Two tracts of land, each of one hundred and sixty acres, claimed by these parties; one known as the Mill ranch, the other as the Island ranch; not surveyed.

The parties themselves live at the Mill ranch, and the Island ranch is occupied by a tenant.

Mill ranch.—The greater part of this land has at one time been under cultivation, and is covered with irrigating canals; but the greater part of these water-ways are not in good repair.

About one-half of the land was cultivated during the past year.

Trees.—Trees have been planted extensively along the water-ways, and a grove of three or four acres has been started.

Altogether there are from ten to fifteen thousand trees, from two to six years old, good and thrifty, chiefly cottonwood, but also several hundred small ash trees.

A few orchard trees, not in good condition.

A small amount of hedging, in bad order.

Vineyard.—Two thousand grape-vines in fair order; fifteen hundred in second-rate order, and ten thousand, third-rate or nearly worthless.

Meadow.—Six acres well set with lucern; four acres partly set.

Island ranch.—The greater part of this land has been under cultivation at one time, and was covered by irrigating canals; but these have been neglected, and are in bad order.

More than half of the land has grown up with brush-wood and weeds.

Trees.—About two thousand cottonwood trees, from two to five years old; thrifty.

Vineyard.—One hundred and fifty grape-vines in second-rate order. Three hundred in third-rate order; nearly worthless.

Meadow.—Two acres set in lucern.

Buildings.—Mill-house 20 by 24; common frame, inclosed with rough boards; two floors; common basement; room for cleaner; first floor 11-foot posts; low upper floor for bolt; frame-work for bolt at present in chamber; building covered with thatched tules; family living in mill-house.

Adobe store-room attached to frame-building 20 by 45; stone foundation; walls heavy, but low; no floor; tule and dirt roof; mill-race, with small flume, in fair order.

Estimated value of this claim, including both ranches, $6,200.

CLAIM OF WILLIAM ANDERSON.

Land.—One hundred and sixty acres not surveyed. Fifteen acres under plow, in good order; twenty-five acres covered with irrigating canals; purchased of R. G. Patterson. Prior to the erection of the house, said to have cost $200.

Buildings.—Small adobe house, two rooms; no floor; roof of tules covered with dirt; house nearly new, but very cheaply built.

Estimated value of this claim, $750.

CLAIM OF AUGUSTUS JAMES.

Land.—One hundred and sixty (160) acres, not surveyed. Twenty-five acres under plow and ditches.

Trees.—A few cottonwood trees; nursery of several thousand small cottonwood and ash trees.

Vineyard.—Three hundred second-rate grape-vines.

Buildings.—Four small adobe buildings, in second-rate repair.

Estimated value of this claim, $750.

CLAIM OF ABRAHAM JAMES.

Land.—One hundred and sixty (160) acres, said to have been surveyed. No copy of survey received. Purchased from Philander Bell.

(See accompanying paper marked "D", copy of deed in possession of said Abraham James.)

Twenty acres under plow and ditches, which are slightly out of order; about one half of the land has been cultivated at some time.

Trees.—Three hundred cottonwood trees, thrifty; a few small orchard trees and garden shrubbery.

Buildings.—Adobe house, 18 by 24; stone foundation, tule roof; floor, doors, and casings poor.

First adobe granary, 12 by 26; stone foundation, tule roof; adobe bins, good repair.

Second adobe granary, 12 by 14; stone foundation, tule roof; lumber floor; adobe bins; in fair order.

Adobe stable, 18 by 18, tule roof. Small adobe hen-house. Adobe building used as a threshing-room, 18 by 20; stone foundation, tule roof; adobe floor; good order.

Estimated value of claim, $1,500.

CLAIM OF ROBERT LOGAN.

Land.—One hundred and sixty (160) acres; farm surveyed in the name of William Stewart, from whom said Robert Logan purchased the claim prior to the date of the executive order establishing the reservation.

Thirty-five acres cultivated the past year, now in good order; water-ways for the same in good condition; one hundred and ten acres originally under cultivation, but irrigating canals, for the additional amount above thirty-five acres, need much repair.

Trees.—A few cottonwood trees; small amount of garden shrubbery.

Vineyard.—Two hundred and twenty-five grape-vines, two years old, in fair order.

Meadow.—One and a half acres, well set with lucern.

Buildings.—House consists of two adobe buildings, 20 by 20, each separated by a passage-way ten feet wide; buildings and passage-way covered with good roof of tule-thatch; good stone foundation; common board floors, window and door-frames and doors; all in fair order.

Store-room, adobe, 20 by 20; very thick walls; adobe floor; well-built stone foundation; tule roof, new.

Cow-stable and granary, 18 by 40, adobe, covered with tules; stone foundation; well preserved.

Two other buildings, each 20 by 20, adobe, covered with tules; stone foundation; in a fair state of preservation.

Estimated value of claim, $2,200.

CLAIM OF JOHN BENNETT, J. H. RATLIFF, AND G. R. A. PERCIVAL.

Land.—There are four hundred and eighty (480) acres claimed by these parties, who live together in one house. Not surveyed; fifty-five acres cultivated the past year, the same covered by water-ways in good repair; a larger amount of land was cultivated prior to the abandonment of it by the former settlers.

Trees.—Eight thousand cottonwood-trees, having one year's growth from setting, planted along the water-ways; all thrifty; two hundred larger cottonwoods, three to four years old.

Vineyard.—Two hundred grape-vines, one and two years old, in fair order.

Meadow.—Two acres well set with lucern.

Buildings.—Small adobe house, 14 by 16, not in good order.

This claim was purchased of Bell & Stewart prior to the issue of the Executive order establishing the reservation.

Estimated value of claim, $1,400.

CLAIM OF VOLNEY RECTOR AND PETER L. JOHNSON.

Land.—One hundred and sixty (160) acres claimed. Both parties live in one house; seven acres under plow and ditch, but main ditch sufficient for a much larger amount of land; the greater part of the land has at one time been under cultivation, but the original ditches have been abandoned, and are in a great part destroyed.

Nearly one-half of the land is a natural meadow.

Trees.—From two to three thousand cottonwood-trees, planted last spring along the water-ways; good and thrifty. Overgrown nursery of many hundred cottonwood trees.

Vineyard.—A few hundred grape-cuttings planted last spring.

Buildings.—House of adobe, 14 by 20, stone foundation, tule roof; second-rate order.

Granary, 10 by 12, rough stone. A quantity of stone sufficient for the erection of a small house hauled on the ground.

Estimated value of this claim, $1,800.

The commissioners after careful inquiry are satisfied that the improvements on the above claims were made prior to the establishment of the reservation by Executive order, and with the expectation, on the part of those who made them, of remaining as settlers in the valley.

Claims considered of no value.

CLAIM OF JOSEPH A. PARRISH.

One hundred and sixty (160) acres claimed; has plowed seven acres; no other improvements of value. Came into the valley December 27, 1872; was notified by one of the employés of the agency, when on his way to the valley, that it would probably be set apart as a reservation.

CLAIM OF JACOB MOON.

One hundred and sixty (160) acres claimed. No improvements. Came into the valley February 8, 1873. He also was notified that the valley was intended for a reservation.

CLAIM OF MARTHA C. TUCKER.

(Daughter of Jacob Moon. See above.)

One hundred and sixty acres claimed. Ten acres plowed; improvements of no value

CLAIM OF W. A. EARLES.

One hundred and sixty (160) acres claimed; no improvements. Settled in the valley during the month of January, 1873. States that he paid the Indians $30 for the land. Remained on the reservation three weeks, then abandoned his claim.

These claims are considered by the commission to be of no value.

With great respect, your obedient servants,

J. W. POWELL,
G. W. INGALLS,
Special Commissioners.

C.

REPORT OF A. B. MEACHAM, SPECIAL COMMISSIONER TO THE MODOCS, UPON THE LATE MODOC WAR.

SAN FRANCISCO, CAL., *October* 5, 1872.

SIR: In compliance with your instructions I herewith submit report of the late Modoc war, and in the absence of other members of the special commission to the Modocs, report individually and as chairman of said commission.

Receiving letter of instructions dated February 5, 1873, I proceeded under said instructions to arrange for a consultation with Gen. E. R. S. Canby at Fairchild's ranch. The commission was organized February 18, consisting of Jesse Applegate, Samuel Case, acting agent at Alsear, Oreg., A. B. Meacham, chairman, and Gen. E. R. S. Canby as advisor.

Referring to letter of instructions, you will discover that the duties of the commission were, "The objects to be obtained by the commission are these: first, to ascertain the causes which have led to the difficulties and hostilities between the United States troops and the Modocs;" and, secondly, "to devise the most effective and judicious measures for preventing the continuance of these hostilities, and for the restoration of peace."

Hostilities being suspended, the commission deemed it advisable to change the order of proceeding, and accordingly sought first to devise means to prevent the renewal of war. Messengers were employed to visit the Modocs and arrange for a meeting: first, Bob Whittle and wife, Matilda, (an Indian woman,) were sent, February 19, with instructions to announce to them the presence of and desire of the commission to arrange for a council meeting with the view of adjusting the difficulties that existed, and to prevent a re-opening of hostilities; also to ascertain with whom the Modocs would prefer to arrange the contemplated council.

Whittle and wife returned on the 20th, and reported the Modocs willing and anxious to "meet Riddle and Fairchilds to conclude details" for the proposed meeting. Fairchilds was intrusted with the message, and accompanied by Riddle and Artina (a Modoc woman,) visited the Modoc camp, a distance of twenty miles from headquarters, with a "message to Modocs," as follows: "Fairchilds will talk for the commission, what he agrees to we will stand by. He cannot tell you any terms, but will fix a time and place for a council talk, and that no act of war will be allowed while peace talks are being had, no movements of troops will be made. We come in good faith to make peace. Our hearts are all for peace." This message was signed by Meacham, Applegate, and Case, with the approval of General Canby.

Fairchilds and party returned on the 23d, and reported the Modocs as willing and anxious for peace, but had not arranged for a meeting, because they were "unwilling to come out of the lava-beds."

FAIRCHILDS' PROPOSED MEETING BETWEEN THE LAVA-BEDS AND HEADQUARTERS.

This proposition was not agreed to, but a request for Judge Steele, of Yreka, to visit them was made, and in compliance he was sent for, with the hope on our part that, from his intimate acquaintance with these people, he might secure the meeting. Judge Steele arrived at headquarters of commission on the 4th of March, and the board of commissioners were called together, now consisting of Applegate, Case, Meacham, and Judge Roseborough, who had been added at the request of General Canby. Steele being present, accepted the mission as messenger to arrange for the meeting of commission and the Modocs, but unwisely was authorized to offer terms of peace, which was "a general amnesty to all Modocs on condition of their full and complete surrender and consent to remove to a distant reservation within the limits of Oregon or California."

Messrs. Roseborough, Case, and Applegate voting in the affirmative, and Meacham in the negative.

He was further instructed to say to them that "General Canby would make peace and conclude terms."

Messrs. Roseborough, Case and Applegate voting in the affirmative, and Meacham in the negative.

On the 5th of March, in company with Riddle and Toby, Fairchilds, and R. H. Atwell as reporter, Judge Steele visited the Modoc camp.

Failing to secure a meeting of the commission and Modocs, made then, under instruction, the proposition above referred to, also stating that General Canby was authorized to conclude the arrangement for the surrender and removal. The propositions were not well understood, and created some discussion among the Modocs.

Captain Jack, speaking for the people, accepted the terms offered, though protests and evidences of dissatisfaction were evidently made. Steele had not, however, seemed to have been aware of this fact, for on his return to headquarters he reported that "peace was made; they accept." A general feeling of relief followed, couriers were summoned to bear dispatches, when Fairchilds, who had been with Steele, declared that "there was some mistake, the Modocs have not agreed to surrender and removal." The Modoc messengers who had accompanied Steele and party to headquarters were questioned, when it was discovered that some misunderstanding existed. Steele, however, confident that he was correct, proposed to return to the Modoc camp and settle the matter beyond question. On Steele's second visit Fairchilds declined going, fearing, as he said, "that the Modocs would feel outraged by Steele's report." Atwell again accompanied Steele, who, on arrival, or soon thereafter, discovered that a great mistake had been made in reporting the first visit. The demonstrations were almost of hostile character. He was accused of reporting them falsely and working against their interests. His long acquaintance with Captain Jack and Scar-Faced Charlie, and consequent friendship, saved him and party from assassination; these two men, and one or two others, standing guard over him throughout the night. The following morning he averted the peril by proposing to return and bring the commission with him, and on this promise he was allowed to depart. On his return to headquarters he made a full report of the visit, stating the facts above referred to, and warning the commission of the danger of meeting the Modocs, except on equal terms and on neutral ground, and expressing the opinion "that no meeting could be had, no peace could be made."

The substance of these reports and conclusions were forwarded to the honorable Secretary of the Interior, who replied as follows:

"WASHINGTON, D. C.,
"*March* 5, 1873.

"I do not believe the Modocs mean treachery. The mission should not be a failure. I think I understand their unwillingness to confide in you. Continue negotiations. Will consult the President, and have the War Department confer with General Canby to-morrow.

"C. DELANO.

"*To A. B. Meacham, Fairchilds' Ranch, via Yreka, Cal.*"

On the day following Steele's return from the second visit a delegation of Indians from the Modoc camp arrived. Mary, (sister of Captain Jack,) acting as messenger, proposed that, if General Canby would send wagons to meet them, the Modocs would all come out and surrender on the terms proposed by Steele on the first visit. General Canby, then acting under the authority of the vote of the commissioners transferring the whole matter to his care, accepted the proposition and named a day on which the final surrender should be consummated. However, before the time appointed, messengers arrived from the lava-beds, asking for further time to arrange for leaving camp, alleging that they were then burying their dead and could not come at the time appointed, but would comply at a subsequent period.

General Canby appointed another day, and assured the messengers that unless they were faithful to the compact he would take steps to compel compliance.

The day before the appointed time, Toby Riddle informed General Canby of intended treachery on the part of the Modocs, saying "no Modocs come; may be come to steal teams; they no give up." Her warning was not accredited.

The wagons were sent. Applegate, sanguine of the surrender, resigned and returned to his home, believing that "peace was made." Mr. Case, who had been relieved at his own request, had also left headquarters. Messages had been sent to the Department at Washington announcing the anticipated result, and the whole country was rejoicing, when, late on the evening of the appointed day, the wagons sent out by General Canby returned without the Indians. All of which was made known to the Department. Further negotiations seemed to be hopeless; nevertheless, knowing the anxiety for a peaceable solution of the troubles, we continued to seek a meeting. Instructions were received from headquarters from the honorable Secretary of the Interior, "to continue negotiations," and further continuing the commission, General Canby moved headquarters to "Van Bremens," and with him the commission moved. Soon after Doctor Thomas was added to the commission, also, L. S. Dyar, United States Indian agent, of Klamath. Meanwhile a herd of Indian horses had been captured by Major Biddle, notwithstanding the commission had informed the Modocs, through messengers, that no act of war would be permitted. Failing to arrange on satisfactory terms for a council meeting, the commission was notified by General Canby of the intended movement of troops nearer the Modoc camp. The movement was made and headquarters again changed, this time to the foot of the bluff, and within two miles of the Modoc stronghold. On the 2d of April the commission, including General Canby, met the Modocs for the first time, about midway between the Modoc camp and headquarters. No conclusions were arrived at, a severe storm coming up compelling adjournment, not, however, until an agreement had been made for the erection of a council-tent.

Riddle and his wife, Toby, expressed the opinion, on our return to camp, that treachery was intended; but the warning was not respected. On the 4th of April a request was made by Captain Jack for me to meet him and a few men at the council-tent. After a consultation with the board I went, accompanied by Judge Roseborough and J. A. Fairchilds, Riddle and his wife, Toby, as interpreters.

The Modoc chief was accompanied by six warriors and the women of his own family. He (Jack) remarked that he felt afraid in presence of General Canby and Doctor Thomas, saying "but now I can talk." He reviewed the whole question from the beginning, mentioning the Ben Wright treachery; the insults of the Klamath Indians while his people were on the reservation; the failure of Captain Knapp, acting agent of Klamath, to protect him, and his several removals while there, but made no complaint of want of subsistence; denied ever killing horses for food, but insisting that Agent Knapp "had no heart for him;" complained that Superintendent Odeneal had not visited him, and that Odeneal's messengers had promised to come again before bringing soldiers; that Major Jackson had attacked him before he was up in the morning of November 29, 1872; complained also of the citizens taking part in the battle at that time, declaring that had "no citizens been in the fight, no Indian women and children would have been killed, no citizens would have been murdered;" saying his young men had done a great wrong while in hot blood, but that he could not control them any more than bad white men were controlled by American law; and feeling that he could never live in peace with the Klamaths, but wanted a home, "just the same as a white man on Lost River, the soldiers taken away and the war would stop."

On being assured that, since blood had been spilled on Lost River, he could never have it in peace, unless the Lost River murderers were given up for trial, he abandoned the request so far as his old home was concerned, saying, "I give up home; give me this lava-bed; no white man will ever want it." Again assured that no peace could be made or soldiers removed while his people remained in the lava-bed, but was informed that a new home would be given him, and provision made for clothing and subsistence. He was unwilling to surrender his men who killed the citizens, saying that the "governor of Oregon had demanded their blood, and that the law of Jackson County would kill them;" remarking, that the "law was all on one side, was made by the white man, for white men, leaving the Indian all out," finally, declaring that he could not control his people, and that he would die with them if no peace was made.

No terms were agreed to or further meetings arranged for at that time.

On the day following, Toby Riddle was sent with a proposition to Captain Jack to surrender with such others as might elect to do so. He declined the terms. On her return the messenger was warned of the intended treachery, which she reported to the commissioners and General Canby. This warning was not treated with the respect due the informer. Dr. Thomas questioned a Modoc afterward as to the truth of the report, which being denied, and the name of the author demanded, he replied, "Toby Riddle." The same party, of whom Dr. Thomas had made inquiry, was informed by General Gillem, "that unless peace was made very soon the troops would be moved up nearer the Modoc stronghold, and that one hundred Warm Spring Indians would be added to the Army within a few days." All of which was reported in the Modoc camp.

On the 8th of April a messenger visited the commission, asking for a "peace talk," saying that six unarmed Modocs were at the council-tent in the lava-bed anxious to make peace, and asking the commission to meet them.

The signal-officer at the station overlooking the lava-beds reported the "six Indians, and also in the rocks behind them twenty other Indians, all armed." Treachery was evident, and no meeting was had; further negotiations appeared useless and unsafe.

On the morning of the 10th of April a delegation from the Modoc camp arrived with renewed propositions for a meeting. The terms proposed were that, if the "commission, including General Canby and General Gillem, would come next day to the council-tent, *unarmed*, to meet a like number of *unarmed* Modocs, thus proving the confidence of the commission in the Modocs, "that they (the Modocs) would all come to headquarters and surrender on the day following." Dr. Thomas, who was then acting as (temporary) chairman, submitted the propositions to General Canby. After consultation, they decided to accept.

On the fatal morning of Friday, April 11, the commission held a meeting, and the propriety of keeping the appointment was discussed; Dr. Thomas insisting that it was a duty that must be performed; General Canby saying "that the importance of the object in view justified taking some risk;" Commissioners Dyar and Meacham recounting the evidences of premeditated treachery, and giving opinions adverse to the meeting. The interpreter, Frank Riddle, appeared before the board, and repeated the warning given by "Toby," his wife, and saying further, "that if the meeting must be had, he wanted to be free from responsibility; that he had lived with 'Toby' for twelve years, and she had never deceived him; that if the commission went, it should be *armed*." However, General Canby and Dr. Thomas insisted that the compact should be kept, the General remarking that from the signal-station a strict watch had been kept, and "only *five* Indians, unarmed, were at the council-tent;" and further, that a "watch would be kept on the council-tent, and in the event of an attack the Army would come to the rescue." Preparations were made to keep the compact; General Canby and Dr. Thomas starting in advance, and on foot, accompanied by Boston Charlie.

Before leaving the camp, as chairman of the commission, I again sought to avert the peril, calling to them, and stating again the warnings and proof of danger, and proposing to take with us a force sufficient for protection. Both the General and Doctor objected, saying it would be a "breach of faith."

To the proposition to make *any promise* necessary to avert danger, they each refused assent to "any promise that could not be kept." They proceeded to the council-tent, followed by Commissioner Dyar, interpreters Riddle and wife, and myself. On arrival it was evident that we were entrapped, and would be betrayed. *Eight armed*, instead of six unarmed Modocs, were present: Captain Jack, Schonchin, Shacknasty Jim, Ellen's Man, Hooker Jim, Boston Charlie, Bogus Charlie, and Black Jim. Any attempt to signal for assistance, or to retreat, would have precipitated the assassination.

The council was opened, on the part of the commission, by referring to the proposition made by the Modoc messengers the day before, when the meeting was agreed on. Captain Jack replied "that he wanted the soldiers taken away, and then the war would stop. He did not want the President to give him anything." About that time an incident occurred that removed all doubt as to the intention of the Modocs: Hooker Jim securing a horse belonging to the commission, by tying him to a sage-brush, and removing from the saddle an overcoat, and putting it on, remarking, "I am *Meacham now;*" intending it as an insult, that would be resented, thus making an excuse for a quarrel. Understanding his design, I simply said, "take my hat, too." He replied, in Modoc language, "I will very soon." Without further noticing him, as chairman, I replied to Captain Jack: The President sent the soldiers here, we did not bring them; we cannot take them away without his consent; they will not harm you if you are peaceable; we want peace, we do not want war; we will find a new home for you; you cannot live in this lava-bed always; there are many good places for you, and we will together look out a new home. General Canby is the soldier chief, and he is your friend; he will talk now.

The General, seeing the danger, as declared by Hooker Jim's actions in taking possession of the overcoat, arose and said: "The President sent the soldiers here, to see that everything was done right; they are your friends, and will not harm you. I have had much experience with Indians. When a young man, I was sent to remove a tribe from Florida to a new home west of the Mississippi River, and although they did not like me well at first, they did after they became acquainted, and they elected me a chief and gave me a name which meant 'The Indian's Friend.' I was sent to remove another tribe to a new home, and they also elected me a chief, calling me the 'Tall Man.' I visited both these tribes years afterward, and they received me, in a friendly way. I have no doubt that *some time* you Modoc people will receive me as kindly."

Dr. Thomas spoke next, standing on his knees, and saying, in substance, "I believe the Great Spirit put in the heart of the President to send us here to make peace. I have known General Canby fourteen years, Mr. Meacham eighteen years, Mr. Dyar four years. I know all their hearts are good, and I know my own heart. We want no more war. The Great Spririt made all men. He made the red men and white men. He sees all our hearts and knows all we do. We are all brothers, and must live in peace together."

Schonchin *said*, "Take away your soldiers, and then we will go and look for a new place. We want Hot Creek for a home; take away the soldiers; *give us Hot Creek for a home*; take away the soldiers; give us Hot Creek."

Chairman. Hot Creek belongs to white men now; perhaps we cannot get it for you.

Schonchin. I have been told we could have it.

Chairman. Who told you so? Did Fairchilds or Dorris say you could have it?

Schonchin.. No; they did not, but Nate Beswick says we can have it.

Chairman. We can see Fairchilds and Dorris about it, and if we cannot buy it for you we will find another home.

Schonchin, (very much excited:) Take away the soldiers, and give us Hot Creek, or stop talking.

Captain Jack had risen and stepped behind Schonchin and nearly facing General Canby, who was nearest the council-tent, with Commissioner Dyar on his right, and about fifteen feet distant. I was on General Canby's left, within three feet, with Schonchin about the same distance in front of me. Dr. Thomas was on the left, within three feet, and Boston Charlie facing him, with Toby Riddle reclining on the ground between them. Riddle was still on the left of Dr. Thomas, and near him Black Jim, while Shacknasty Jim, Hooker Jim, and Bogus Charlie were behind Boston Charlie and Schonchin, and facing the commission. While Riddle was translating Schonchin's angry speech, two Modoc warriors, Barncho and Slolax, suddenly advanced (from ambush about fifty yards distant and a little to the left of the *front*, with rifles under their arms) rapidly toward us. We all arose and inquired, "Captain Jack, what does this mean?" who, turning suddenly, facing General Canby and within three or four feet, exclaimed in a very excited tone, "Ot we kautux-e," meaning "*all ready*," and drawing from under his coat a revolver, pointed it at General Canby's head. The first attempt only exploded the cap; he, however, quickly renewed the assault, the ball striking him below his left eye. He retreated, followed by Jack and Ellen's Man, a distance of forty yards, when, falling on the rocks, he was finally killed by a stab from Captain Jack and a rifle-shot from Ellen's Man. Dr. Thomas was attacked by Boston Charlie, and received the first shot in the left breast, but was allowed to retreat a short distance, followed by Boston and Bogus Charlie, and finally killed by a rifle-shot by Bogus Charlie. Commissioner Dyar fled, pursued by Hooker Jim, but escaped unhurt. Riddle also ran, followed by Black Jim, but he also escaped unhurt Schonchin failed in his attempt to assassinate me, though several pistol-shots took effect, but not proving mortal. I fell back a distance of fifty yards, pursued by Schonchin, Shacknasty Jim, Barncho, and Slolax, they leaving, supposing me to be dead, when Boston Charlie returned and made an attempt to scalp me, but was frustrated by the strategy of Toby Riddle, shouting soldiers, soldiers.

The officer at the signal-station overlooking the scene at the council-tent gave the alarm. General Gillem ordered the several companies to the rescue on double-quick. They arrived too late to save General Canby and Dr. Thomas.

To the officers of the Army at Tule Lake Camp South, and especially to those of the medical corps, I am indebted for my recovery.

In reporting under article 1st of letter of instruction of February 5, to ascertain the causes which have led to the difficulties and hostilities between the Modocs and United States troops, I regret very much that no other member of the special commission has made an investigation or report thereon. This failure to investigate arises from the fact, that the letter of instructions and appointment of commissioners did not empower them to compel attendance, administer oaths, and otherwise do such acts as were indispensably necessary to accomplish a full, comprehensive, and authenticated report. Hence, as chairman of special commission to the Modocs, I shall submit such facts only as I believe can be substantiated by necessary proofs when required.

The Modoc tribe are an offshoot of the Klamaths. They have occupied the country known as "Lost River Basin," and covering portions of the old Government road to Oregon and California.

The first difficulty with the emigrants, as they (the Modocs) reported, grew out of the efforts of the emigrants to recapture horses found in their possession, which they claimed they had purchased from the Snake and Pitt River Indians.

After hostilities began, continued at intervals, during which time many Modocs were killed and many emigrants were cruelly butchered. Perhaps the most revolting among the many scenes was that of the killing of seventy-five white persons in 1852.

This terrible tragedy called out a company of volunteers "for the protection of emigrants," who, under command of Ben Wright, of Yreka, Cal., arrived on Tule Lake, at Bloody Point, the scene of the wholesale butchery above referred to. Failing to engage the Modocs in a fair battle, proposed a "peace talk," which was finally accepted, and forty-six Modoc warriors responded, and were by him and his company attacked, and forty-one of them slain. This act of treachery has always been remembered by the Modoc people, and had much to do in perpetuating the bitter feelings that have since existed, and doubtless had influence in the late assassination. Ben Wright was received at Yreka with great demonstrations, bonfires and banquets, and was afterward appointed an Indian agent as a reward for this heroic act of treachery to a trusting people, and a violation of the sacred rights of a flag of truce. Had he been held to account for this unauthorized act, it would have done much to secure the confidence of the Modocs, and other tribes as well. Hostilities continued until 1864, when ex-Superintendent Steele, of California, made a temporary treaty with the several tribes in the vicinity of Yreka, including the Modocs. In October following, Superintendent Huntington, of Oregon, under authority of the General Government, held a treaty-council at Council Grove, near Fort Klamath, with the Modocs and Klamath Indians, when all the country claimed by these tribes was ceded to the Government, except so much as may be embraced within the boundaries of what is known as Klamath reservation, and described in the second article of said treaty. (See Statutes at Large, vol. 16, page 707.) Schonchin, as head chief, (a brother of the Schonchin who was executed,) Captain Jack, (as Kient-poos,) and other members of the Modoc tribe, signed the treaty in the presence of witnesses. It is in evidence that the Modocs, including Captain Jack, (or Kient-poos,) in conformity of said treaty, accepted goods and subsistence, and remained on the new reservation several months, and finally left, returning to the Modoc country, and ignored the treaty, and refused to return to the reservation until December, 1869, at which time he accepted annuity goods and subsistence; and, under promise of protection from the taunts and insults of the Klamaths, he again took his abode on the Klamath reservation, together with the remainder of the tribe, selecting Modoc Point as the site for a home. They began to make arrangements for a permanent settlement, and no doubt with *bona-fide* intentions to remain. All this was agreed to, and fairly understood by all parties interested, Klamath and Modoc Indians included. The former, however, began soon thereafter to taunt the latter with being "strangers, orphans, poor men, &c.," claiming the timber, fish, grass, and water, and in various ways annoying them. Captain Jack appealed to Captain Knapp, then acting agent, for protection from their insults. Agent Knapp, not fully comprehending how much was involved in his action, removed Captain Jack's band of Modocs to a new location, where they began again to make rails, and prepare logs for building, when the Klamaths, emboldened by the success of their first interference, and being in no wise punished, or reprimanded, repeated the insults. Captain Jack again appealed for protection to Agent Knapp, who proposed still another home for the Modocs. Captain Jack again sought a resting-place for his people, and not finding one to his satisfaction he called them together, and declared his intention to leave the reservation, which he did, returning to the Lost River country, where he remained several months, and until persuaded to return to Klamath reservation, at Yainax station. Unfortunately he here employed an Indian doctor to act as a physician, and, under an old Indian law, when the patient died, he killed, or caused to be killed, the Indian doctor. The reservation Indians demanded his arrest and punishment. He fled to the Modoc country, was pursued, but, eluding arrest, he sent messengers proposing a conference. Commissions were sent to meet him, and a temporary peace secured, on the condition that he would keep his people away from the settlements, and submit to arrest, if demand should be made. He insisted then, as he had previously done, for a home on Lost River. The commissioner, under instructions from superintendent of Indian affairs, promised to lay the request before the Commissioner at Washington, which was done, together with the reasons for so doing, also recommending that a small reservation of six miles square be allowed them at the mouth of Lost River.

No action was ever taken. In the mean time the young men of Captain Jack's band became a source of much annoyance to the citizens of the Lost River country, who petitioned for their removal. Captain Jack and his men sought advice of Judges Roseborough and Steele, of Yreka. Both these gentlemen advised them not to resist the authority of the Government, but also promised, as attorneys, to assist them in getting lands, provided they would dissolve tribal relations. I have sought diligently as a commissioner for information on this subject, and conclude that nothing further was ever promised by either Roseborough or Steele. The hope thus begotten may have caused the Modocs to treat with less respect the officers of the Government, and made them more insolent toward settlers, but nothing of willful intent can be charged to Steele or Roseborough.

Renewed petitions for their removal called the attention of Superintendent Odeneal to the subject, who, laying the matter before the Commissioner of Indian Affairs at Washington, was instructed, under date of April 11, 1872, to have the Modocs removed, if practicable, to the same reservation, (meaning Klamath,) and to protect them from the Klamaths, but that if they could not be removed or kept on the reservation, to select and report the boundaries of a new reserve for them.

Of further official correspondence on this subject the commission has not been officially advised. Superintendent Odeneal was respectfully requested to attend the meeting of the commission, but declined doing so. It is in evidence that Superintendent Odeneal sent messengers to the Modoc camp on the 26th of November, 1872, to order them to return to the reservation, and in event of refusal on their part to arrange for a meeting with them at Link River, twenty-five miles from the Modoc camp.

They refused compliance with the order, and also refused to meet Superintendent Odeneal, at Link River, saying substantially, "that they did not want to see him or talk with him; that they did not want any white man to tell them what to do; that their friends and advisers were in Yreka, Cal.; they tell us to stay here, and we intend to do it; and will not go on the reservation, (meaning Klamath;) that they were tired of talk, and were done talking." If credit be given to these declarations it would appear that some parties at Yreka were culpable. Careful investigation discloses nothing more than already recited, so far as Roseborough and Steele was concerned, but would seem to implicate one or two other parties, both of whom are now deceased; but even then no evidence has been brought forth declaring more than sympathy for the Modocs, which might easily be accounted for on the ground of personal interest, dictating friendship toward them as the best safeguard for life and property, but nothing that could be construed as advising resistance to legal authority, and their statement in regard to advisers in Yreka should not be entitled to more credit than Captain Jack's subsequent assertions that "no white man had ever advised him to stay off the reservation." This latter declaration was made during the late trials at Klamath by the "military commission," at a time when the first proposition made to Superintendent Odeneal's messengers in regard to Yreka advices would have secured the Modocs then on trial some consideration.

The only thing said or done by any parties in Yreka, that has come well authenticated that could have had any influence with the Modocs, in their replies to Odeneal's message, is the proposition above referred to as coming from Roseborough and Steele, to assist them as attorneys to secure homes when they should have abandoned tribal relations, paid taxes, and made application to become citizens. The high character both these gentlemen possess for loyalty to the Government and for integrity, would preclude the idea that any wrong was intended.

On receiving Captain Jack's insolent reply to his message, Superintendent Odeneal made application to the military commander at Fort Klamath for a force to "compel said Indians (Modocs) to go upon the Klamath reservation;" reciting the following words from the honorable Commissioner of Indian Affairs: "You are hereby directed to remove the Modoc Indians to Klamath reservation, peacably if you possibly can, but forcibly if you must," and saying: "I transfer the whole matter to your department without assuming to dictate the course you shall pursue in executing the order aforesaid, trusting, however, that you may accomplish the object desired without the shedding of blood if possible to avoid it."

He received the following reply:

"HEADQUARTERS FORT KLAMATH, *November* 28, 1872.

"SIR: In compliance with your written request of yesterday, I will state that Captain Jackson will leave this post about noon to-day, with about thirty men; will be at Link River to-night, and I hope before morning at Captain Jack's camp.

"I am, sir, very respectfully, your obedient servant,

"JOHN GREEN,
"*Major First Cavalry, Commanding Post.*

"Mr. T. B. ODENEAL,
"*Superintendent Indian Affairs.*"

Major Jackson arrived at the Modoc camp on the morning of the 29th and obtained an interview, during which he used every argument in his power to induce them to go on to Klamath reservation at Yainax, informing them that ample provision had been made for clothing and subsistence, assuring them of the folly of resistance to the orders of the Government. Finding his efforts unavailing, he ordered them to "lay down their arms." This order had been partially obeyed and prospects were that no serious trouble would ensue, until the demand was made of "Scarfaced Charlie" to surrender, who refused compliance, and Major Jackson ordered an officer to disarm him, who advanced to perform the duty with pistol drawn, when both the officer and Scarfaced Charlie discharged their arms, but so nearly simultaneous that it is a matter of doubt who really fired the first shot. A general engagement ensued between Major Jackson's forces and the Modocs in the camp on the west side of Lost River, composed of Captain Jack, Schonchin John, Scarfaced Charlie, and eleven or twelve other warriors with families.

It should be understood that Lost River, at this point, is a deep stream three hundred feet wide, dividing the Modoc camp.

While Captain Jack and other warriors occupied the west bank, Curlyheaded Doctor, Hooker Jim, and nine other warriors, with their families, occupied the east side. While Major Jackson was taking position around Captain Jack's camp a number of citizens had also taken a position commanding the camp on the east side, and when the former became engaged in battle with Captain Jack's band on the west side, the latter soon engaged in battle with the Curlyheaded Doctor's band on the east side. The commission has been unable to learn by what authority the citizens referred to were assembled on the east side of Lost River, on the morning of the 29th of November. It is, however, safe to declare that had no citizens taken part in the battle, none would have been subsequently murdered.

In reporting the causes that led to the difficulties between the United States troops and the Modoc Indians, I submit—

1st. That Captain Jack, being a lineal descendant of "Old Modocus," was ambitious to be recognized as "head chief," and Schonchin being acknowledged his superior in office, the former preferred a roving life free from restraint, where his ambition could be gratified. Hence, he was dissatisfied with the treaty of 1864, and left the reservation agreed on in said treaty council. That through the desire for peace the settlers occupying the "Modoc country" and the citizens of the adjacent towns had extended sympathy to him, which he misconstrued into indorsement of his cause and justification of his resistance to Federal authority; and that another cause for the friendship of white citizens for the Modocs grew out of the fact that the Modoc country was divided by the State line of Oregon and California, and since Indian agencies are supposed to create business, both States were desirous of securing the patronage thereof. A review of official correspondence between Commissioner of Indian Affairs and the officers and citizens of these two States will develop the fact that unusual friendship and sympathy was shown the Modocs, prior to the treaty of 1864, and continuously thereafter. But there is no evidence that any responsible party has counseled resistance, though it is certain that the sympathy of citizens and settlers, together with the ambition to obtain homes as "white men" under the proposition of Steele and Roseborough, had more or less influence with them. They left the reservation first in 1864, and refused to return. The "humane policy" then pursued in the several efforts to restore them was also misunderstood, and construed into fear and cowardice on the part of the Government. The same demonstration of force made by Major Jackson on the 29th of last November, would have secured success in 1865, without shedding blood. In 1869, satisfied that force would be employed if they resisted, they went on to Klamath reservation under promises of protection.

2d. Had they been thus protected in their rights as against the insults of the Klamath Indians they would have remained, and no second stampede would have followed; that the failure to keep the promise of protection impaired the confidence of the Modocs in subsequent promises.

3d. That in 1870 an understanding was had that an effort would be made to obtain a small reservation for them on Lost River, on condition that they kept the peace. No action was taken by the Department on this matter. The Modocs, discouraged by the delay and emboldened thereby, became an unbearable annoyance to the settlers, and removal or location could not be deferred.

4th. A small reservation, as recommended, would have averted all trouble with these people, and the failure to notify them that no action would be had on the matter was a blunder.

5th. Had they been fully apprised of the fact in a way to give them confidence that no home would be allowed them on Lost River, and an appeal been properly made by some officer of the Indian Department, they might not have resisted.

6th. Superstitious Indian religion had much to do in causing them to resist.

7th. Want of adaptability of Government agents produces confusion and sometimes war.

Finally, this war was the result of changing agents and policies too often, and the absence of well-defined regulations regarding the relative duties and powers of the Indian and military Departments, the citizens, and Indians. While the "humane policy" is the correct one, it ought to be well defined, and then intrusted to men selected on account of fitness for the work. No branch of public service more imperatively demands observance of this rule, and when it shall have been fully recognized and adhered to by appointing men to the care of our Indian population whose hearts are in the work, and who understand the duties assigned, and whose term of office depends on faithfully achieved success, we may hope to hear of Indian wars *no more*.

Very respectfully, your obedient servant,

A. B. MEACHAM,
Chairman Special Commission to Modocs.

HON. COMMISSIONER OF INDIAN AFFAIRS,
Washington, D. C.

C 2.

REPORT OF CAPT. M. C. WILKINSON, UNITED STATES ARMY, SPECIAL COMMISSIONER FOR REMOVING THE MODOCS INTO THE INDIAN TERRITORY.

WASHINGTON, D. C., *December* 12, 1873.

SIR: In accordance with orders from the Secretary of War and your instructions under date of November 4, 1873, I have the honor to report that I have removed the Modoc Indians from Fort McPherson, Nebraska, to the Indian Territory.

Upon arrival at Baxter Springs, Kansas, and consulting with Agent H. W. Jones, it was considered the wisest plan to locate these Indians, for the winter, at Seneca Station, upon Shawnee land, instead of with the Quapaws.

I. Because the Quapaws are indolent, their influence not being such as should be had upon the Modocs, whose only hope is in work.

II. It was not thought wise to locate these Indians so near to the town of Baxter Springs, a notorious place for corrupting Indians.

III. It was very much to be desired that the Modocs should have the personal supervision of some reliable man until permanently settled upon their own land.

These were, in the main, the reasons why it was decided to build temporary barracks for them at Seneca Station. These barracks are within two hundred yards of Agent Jones's house, are of the simplest kind, and so constructed as not to injure the lumber for future use.

In this connection I would earnestly recommend that, in view of this additional responsibility upon Agent Jones who has the care of seven other tribes, his son, Endley Jones, be appointed at a salary of at least fifty dollars per month, as special agent to the Modocs until they are permanently located. When Agent Jones consented to place this tribe at his own door that he might shield them from certain whites, care for their aged, and at the earliest possible moment place their children in school, I promised to request that he might have this assistance in the extra labor so undertaken. I am assured this appointment will receive the cheerful indorsement of Superitnendent Hoag.

There was no other way than to build the barracks already referred to, the total cost of which, including the expense of hauling building material twenty miles, and purchasing a large cook-stove, was but $524.40. Only three white men were employed, and they for but one day, as it was ascertained that the Indians worked to better advantage without them. Arriving at Baxter Springs on the Sabbath, the next found the Indians in quarters of their own construction.

At Agent Jones's desire, I respectfully urge that land be purchased of the Shawnees, rather than of the Quapaws, for the Modocs, thus securing great advantages as to location, quality of land, proximity to schools, and greater impulse to work, Agent Jones fearing that the lazy habits of the Quapaws would seriously influence the Modocs. If the honorable Commissioner of Indian Affairs would approve of the purchase of land from the Shawnees and so inform them, there is but little doubt of their cheerful consent, and perhaps they would adopt the Modocs, which might be better still.

I arrived at Fort McPherson November 13; left evening of the 14th with Indians, arriving at Baxter Springs, Kansas, on the 16th; held them, excepting the working party, one week at that place.

On the cars, in the old hotel-building used for them at Baxter, I found them uniformly obedient, ready to work, cheerful in compliance with police regulations, each day proving over and over again that these Modocs only require *just* treatment, executed with firmness and kindness, to make them a singularly reliable people.

I have the honor to be, very respectfully, your obedient servant,

M. C. WILKINSON,
U. S. A., U. S. Special Commissioner.

HON. E. P. SMITH,
Commissioner of Indian Affairs, Washington, D. C.

D.

REPORT OF THE COMMISSION TO NEGOTIATE WITH THE UTE TRIBE OF INDIANS.

PITTSBURGH, *October* 15, 1873.

SIR: As chairman and acting member of the commission to negotiate with the Ute Indians, I have the honor to make the following report in addition to the brief telegram sent from Denver on the 22d ultimo, and to transmit herewith the original of the agreement made with them.

A duplicate of the contract was left with Ouray, the head chief, to receive additional signatures, and when signed will be taken by him to Washington.

Under the appointment of your letter of June 20, 1873, as follows:

"DEPARTMENT OF THE INTERIOR,
" *Washington, D. C., June* 20, 1873.

"SIR: I have the honor to inform you that I deem it advisable to renew negotiations with the Ute Indians for the cession of a portion of their reservation lying in the southwestern part of Colorado Territory.

"To carry out this purpose I have concluded to appoint the Hon. Felix R. Brunot and the Hon. Nathan Bishop, members of the board of Indian commissioners, to conduct the intended negotiations, the authority for which action will be found in the act of Congress, approved April 23, 1872, "authorizing the Secretary of the Interior to make certain negotiations with the Ute Indians in Colorado." (See Stat. at L., 2d sess. 42d Con., p. 55.)

"You will please prepare instructions for the guidance of said commissioners in the duties hereby devolved upon them; and in doing so I suggest that you consult the instructions delivered to the commissioners last year for a similar purpose.

"The commissioners herein named will be paid their necessary expenses.

"I have already notified the War Department of their contemplated appointment, and have requested that Department to furnish the commissioners, through the proper officer in command, any needed transportation.

"Very respectfully, your obedient servant,

"C. DELANO, *Secretary*.

"To the COMMISSIONER OF INDIAN AFFAIRS."

and the letter of the honorable Commissioner of Indian Affairs, as follows:

"DEPARTMENT OF THE INTERIOR, OFFICE OF INDIAN AFFAIRS,
" *Washington, D. C., July* 2, 1873.

"GENTLEMEN: An act of Congress approved April 23, 1872, (Stat. at Large, 2d sess. 42d Cong., p. 55,) authorizes and empowers the Secretary of the Interior 'to enter into negotiations with the Ute Indians in Colorado Territory for the extinguishment of their right to the southern part of a certain reservation made in pursuance of a treaty concluded March 2, 1868, situate in the southwest portion of the said Territory of Colorado, and report his proceedings under this act of Congress for its consideration. The expense of such negotiation to be paid by the United States, and to be hereafter appropriated.'

"Pursuant to the provisions of the foregoing act, and in compliance with the directions of the honorable Secretary of the Interior, contained in his letter addressed to this office July 1, 1872, a commission was appointed, consisting of Governor Edward M. McCook, of Colorado; John D. Lang, of Maine; and John McDonald, of Missouri, to visit said Indians and hold a council with them for the purpose indicated. A copy of their report is inclosed herewith, from which you will observe that the negotiations failed through the influence of outside parties who had prejudiced the minds of the Indians to defeat the object of the commission.

"Recent advices, however, received at this office from Agent Adams, indicate a more favorable disposition on the part of the Indians, and have determined the honorable Secretary of the Interior to send out a new commission, and he has accordingly designated you as such commission by his letter addressed to this Office under date of the 20th ultimo.

"You will therefore proceed to the Los Pinos agency and fix a time and place for holding the new council. Agents Charles Adams at the Los Pinos agency, and J. S. Littlefield at the White River agency have been notified of your appointment and directed to afford you all the assistance in their power in order to secure a full attendance of the different bands of Utes interested in the negotiations. Agent Adams has also been instructed to provide the necessary subsistence for the Indians during the council. The acting agent at the Abiquiu agency in New Mexico has also been instructed in the premises.

"The objects of your negotiations may be more specifically defined, for your information and guidance, as follows:

"1. The reservation of the Utes referred to in the act of Congress is unnecessarily large, comprising within its limit upward of fourteen millions of acres of the best agricultural and mineral lands in Colorado.

"2. The number of Indians occupying the same is comparatively small, not exceeding, according to the most reliable data obtainable, more than four or five thousand souls.

"3. The people of Colorado are anxious to have that portion of the reserve not needed for Indian purposes thrown open to entry and settlement as public lands of the United States, in order that the agricultural and mineral resources thereof may be more thoroughly and rapidly developed.

"It was with these objects in view, and with the hope of their early accomplishment, that Congress afforded the aforementioned legislation; and you are therefore instructed, in conducting your negotiations with the Utes, to use your most earnest endeavors to induce them to relinquish to the United States the southern portion of their reservation as at present constituted, to embrace, if possible, the tract lying between the south boundary thereof and the thirty-eighth degree of north latitude.

"Any arrangement or agreement entered into with the Indians must have the assent and concurrence of at least a majority of each and every band participating in the council; otherwise it will be futile in its results.

"Some of the provisions of the treaty of 1868 with those Indians cannot be carried out, for the reason that several of the bands claimed to have been parties thereto deny any connection with the making of the treaty, and refuse to be governed by its stipulations. To avoid this difficulty in the future every effort should be made and every reasonable inducement held out to the Indians to secure unanimity on their part of approval of any agreement that may be made.

"In conducting your negotiations for the cession of a portion of the reservation to the United States weight should be given to two considerations, viz, the actual value of the lands ceded, and the necessities of the Indians.

"The agreement entered into should clearly describe the portion of the reservation ceded and the consideration to be paid therefor, expressed in such form as to admit of the largest discretion being exercised by the Department in relation to the manner of investing or expending such consideration for the welfare of the Indians.

"You will endeavor to thoroughly impress upon their minds the fact that any agreement thus entered into will be binding only upon its ratification by Congress.

"I inclose herewith a copy of the treaty of 1868, by the terms of which said reservation was created.

"You will submit a detailed report of your action in the premises, together with such recommendations upon the subject as you may deem fit and proper.

"The War Department has been notified of your appointment and requested to furnish you, through the proper officers in command, any needed transportation.

"You will be allowed your necessary expenses while engaged upon this duty.

"Very respectfully, your obedient servant,

"EDW. P. SMITH,
"*Commissioner.*

"Hon. FELIX R. BRUNOT,
"*President Board Indian Commissioners, Cheyenne, Wyo.*
"Hon. NATHAN BISHOP,
"*Board Indian Commissioners, New York City.*"

I went to Denver, en route to the Los Pinos Ute agency, as soon as my duties as a member of the commission to treat with the Crow tribe of Indians were completed. At Denver I learned that Hon. Nathan Bishop, my colleague, would not be able to join me. Owing to the unavoidable detention at the Crow agency, the time appointed for the Ute council had passed, and further delay seemed inexpedient. I therefore went on to Los Pinos as soon as possible, accompanied only by Mr. Thomas K. Cree, secretary, and Dr. J. Phillips, who had been engaged as Spanish interpreter.

We arrived at Los Pinos on the 6th of September, going via South Park and the Poncho Pass. The Department letter informing me that transportation for the commission would be provided at Fort Garland, was only received on arrival at Los Pinos. Ouray, the head chief, the principal chiefs of the seven bands of Utes, and a large number of the people were encamped in the vicinity of the agency, and the council was assembled on the morning of the 6th. Mr. John Lawrence acted as Spanish interpreter, Mr. James Fullerton being also present at the request of Ouray. It soon became apparent that the Utes had miapprehended the wishes of the Government, and were mistaken in regard to their own interests. They had received the impression that the commission was appointed to purchase from them only the mines already discovered, and these they were willing to sell with the right of way by one road to reach them. They also claimed that the commissioner who made with them the treaty of 1868, pointed out the Cochitopa Mountains as the eastern line of their reservation, but that now the surveyors said the line was twelve miles west of the agency buildings instead of the same distance east of the agency, as had been promised at the treaty. They also claimed that the commissioners told them the southern line of the reservation was upon the highland south of the San Juan River, but that now surveyors had marked a line (the southern line of Colorado) north of the river which they were told was the limit of their reservation. Both of these lines they desired to have re-instated in the proposed sub-treaty. The Muaches and Capotes wanted to have their agency continued at Cimarron, in New Mexico, and to make its continuance there a condition of even the sale they proposed. None of them were willing to sell any part of the agricultural lands of the reservation.

Believing that to purchase the existing mines only, would but postpone for a few months the apprehended collision between the whites and the Indians, and, consequently, be of little benefit either to them or to the Government, I declined to enter into such negotiations.

Having no authority on the subject of the lines of the reservation, that question was withdrawn from the council by the promise that the chiefs should visit Washington to make their representations to the Government in person.

The New Mexico Utes were told that their agency would be removed, but that I would not say that it should be done at once, and they could send a delegation to Washington to state their case to the President, and if the President thought it best to do so, he would perhaps allow them to remain longer at Cimarron.

The council continued four days, with two days intervening. Such arguments were used as seemed proper to lead the minds of the Indians to an understanding of the importance of an early adjustment of the differences between the people of Colorado and themselves, the fairness of the proposition made on the part of the Government, and its accordance with their own best interests. No presents were given to influence them, and no promises were made other than those mentioned in this report and such as are named in the agreement. Every part of the articles of agreement was carefully explained, and seemed to be fully discussed and understood by all the Indians.

After I had left the agency, Ouray dictated a letter expressing his satisfaction with the result.

To satisfy some of the Weeminuche band, who feared that their agricultural and grazing land on the San Miguel might be included within the lines of the ceded country, Messrs. Cree, Adams, and Dolan, accompanied by six of the chiefs, went through the mountains, occupying a week in the journey. It will be seen by examining the boundaries of the country ceded that it does not include the agricultural and grass lands in the southern part of the reservation. A portion of the Utes have always lived in New Mexico; to remove them to the comparatively inhospitable climate of the higher latitude and greater altitude of the northern part of the reservation would be unjust, and a needless cruelty.

In conclusion, I respectfully make the following recommendations:

1st. That to prevent intrusion of settlers or herders upon the agency, until such time as it shall be removed to the Gunnison River or elsewhere—a tract of land extending from the Cochitopa Mountains on the east to a line six miles west of the agency buildings, and in width, from north to south, twelve miles—the agency buildings being in the center—be added to the Ute reservation.

2d. That the action of Congress upon the contract be solicited as early as possible, and that, until such action can be had, no persons other than the miners shall be permitted to go upon the Ute reservation as it now exists.

3d. That should Congress ratify the contract, the lines should at once be surveyed and distinctly marked, so that both whites and Indians may know them, and that in any case, special measures should be adopted to prevent the encroachment of whites upon the unceded portions of the reservation.

I respectfully submit herewith:

1st The contract with the Ute Indians in Colorado, which cedes to the United States a portion of their reservation.

2d. Letter of Ouray, head chief of the Utes, and letter inclosing a copy of the same to the Governor of Colorado.

3d. Narrative of the proceedings of the commission by T. K. Cree, secretary.

4th. Minutes of the council with the Utes.

5th Interview with Ouray at Cheyenne.

I desire to express the utmost confidence in the friendly disposition of the Ute Indians, and commend their head chief, Ouray, for his devotion to both the interests of the Government and of his people.

To T. K. Cree, secretary; Charles Adams, agent at Los Pinos; Thomas Dolan, agent from Cimarron, and to the interpreters, my thanks are due for the most cordial and efficient co-operation.

Very respectfully, your obedient servant,

FELIX R. BURNOT,
Special Commissioner.

Hon. C. DELANO,
Secretary of the Interior.

LOS PINOS AGENCY,
September 13, 1873.

DEAR SIR: You have been to see us, and we have had a good time. We want you should tell Governor Elbert and the people in the Territory that we are well pleased and perfectly satisfied with everything that has been done. Perhaps some of the people will not like it because we did not wish to sell some of our valleys and farming-land. We think we had good reasons for not doing so. We expect to occupy it ourselves before long for farming and stock-raising. About eighty of our tribe are raising corn and wheat now, and we know not how soon we shall all have to depend on ourselves for our bread. We do not want to sell our valley and farming-land for another reason. We know if we should the whites would go on it right off, build their cabins, drive in their stock, which would of course stray on our lands, and then the whites themselves would crowd upon us till there would be trouble.

We have many friends among the people of this Territory, and want to live at peace and on good terms with them, and we feel it would be better for all parties for a mountain-range to be between us. We are perfectly willing to sell our mountain-land, and hope the miners will find heaps of gold and silver; and we have no wish to molest them or make them any trouble. We do not want they should go down into our valleys, however, and kill or scare away our game.

We expect there will be much talk among the people and in the papers about what we have done, and we hope you will let the people know how we feel about it.

Truly your friend,

OURAY.

Mr. BRUNOT.

This letter was forwarded to the governor of the Territory, with the following letter, both of which were published by the Territorial press:

"MANITOU, COL., *September* 18, 1873.

"DEAR SIR: I left the Los Pinos agency on Saturday the 13th instant, stopping over Sunday at Saguache. On Monday morning I received a letter dictated by Ouray, the head chief of the Utes, after my departure, in which he requests me to communicate certain things to the governor and people of Colorado.

"I regret that pressing engagements prevent me from remaining in Denver long enough to confer with you in person on the subject.

"I inclose a copy of the letter and suggest its publication.

"The desire of the Utes to retain the agricultural portion of their country seems reasonable, and the friendly feelings expressed by Ouray toward the miners and the people of Colorado I have reason to believe, are shared not only by all the Utes who were present at the council, but by the whole tribe. I sincerely hope this friendly feeling will be reciprocated by the whites, and that the sensational reports of 'threatened outbreaks of the Utes' will cease, or will be treated by the authorities, and all good citizens, with the contempt and discredit they deserve.

"The late negotiations were surrounded by many embarrassments, but I am happy to state that, notwithstanding these, a result has been reached which is beneficial both to the Territory of Colorado and to the Indians. A contract has been made for the cession to the United States of all the mountain-country supposed to contain metals, embraced in an area of over 60 by 100 miles.

"The Uncompagre Park, the Gunnison and San Miguel Rivers, and the agricultural and grazing lands on the south end of the present reservation are reserved to the Indians, the latter being intended for the future occupancy of the Muache, Capote, and other Utes now in New Mexico.

"The commission of last summer, after failing in its object, proposed to the Utes 'to sell the mines,' and they, supposing this to mean only the mines already discovered and worked, it was difficult for many of the Indians to comprehend why the present commission would not consent to negotiate for these alone.

"Very respectfully, your obedient servant,

"FELIX R. BRUNOT,
"*Special Commissioner*.

"GOV. S. H. ELBERT,
"*Denver City, Colo.*"

ARTICLES OF CONVENTION.

Articles of a convention made and entered into at the Los Pinos agency for the Ute Indians, on the 13th day of September, 1873, by and between Felix R. Brunot, commissioner in behalf of the United States, and the chiefs, head-men, and men of the Tabequache, Muache, Capote, Weeminuche, Yampa, Grand River, and Uintah bands of Ute Indians, witnesseth: That whereas a treaty was made with the confederated band of the Ute nation, on the second day of March, A. D. 1868, and proclaimed by the President of the United States on the sixth day of November, 1868, the second article of which defines by certain lines the limits of a reservation to be owned and occupied by the Ute Indians; and whereas, by act of Congress approved April 23, 1872, the Secretary of the Interior was "authorized and empowered to enter into negotiations with the Ute Indians in Colorado for the extinguishment of their right" to a certain portion of said reservation, and a commission was appointed on the 1st day of July, 1872, to conduct said negotiations; and whereas, said negotiation having failed, owing to the refusal of said Indians to relinquish their right to any portion of said reservation, a new commission was appointed by the Secretary of the Interior by letter of June 2, 1873, to conduct said negotiation:

Now, therefore, Felix R. Brunot, commissioner in behalf of the United States, and the chiefs and people of the Tabequache, Muache, Capote, Weeminuche, Yampa, and Grand River, and Uintah, the confederated bands of the Ute nation, do enter into the following agreement:

ARTICLE I.

The confederated bands of the Ute nation hereby relinquish to the United States all right, title, interest, and claim in and to the following-described portion of the reservation heretofore conveyed to them by the United States, viz: Beginning at a point on the eastern boundary of said reservation fifteen miles due north from the southern boundary of the Territory of Colorado, and running thence west on a line parallel with the said southern boundary to a point on said line twenty miles due east of the western boundary of Colorado Territory; thence north by a line parallel with the said western boundary to a point ten miles north of the point where said line intersects the thirty-eighth parallel of north latitude; thence east to the eastern boundary of the reservation; and thence south along said boundary to the place of beginning: *Provided*, That if any part of the Uncompagre Park shall be found to extend south of the north line of said described country, the same is not intended to be included therein, and is hereby reserved and retained as a portion of the Ute reservation.

ARTICLE II.

The United States shall permit the Ute Indians to hunt upon said lands so long as the game lasts, and the Indians are at peace with the white people.

ARTICLE III.

The United States agree to set apart and hold as a perpetual trust for the Ute Indians a sum of money, or its equivalent in bonds, which shall be sufficient to produce the sum of twenty-five thousand dollars ($25,000) per annum, which sum of twenty-five thousand dollars per annum shall be disbursed or invested at the discretion of the President, or as he may direct, for the use and benefit of the Ute Indians annually forever.

ARTICLE IV.

The United States agree, so soon as the President may deem it necessary or expedient, to erect proper buildings and establish an agency for the Weeminuche, Muache, and Capote bands of Ute Indians, at some suitable point to be hereafter selected on the southern part of the Ute reservation.

ARTICLE V.

All the provisions of the treaty of 1868, not altered by this agreement, shall continue in force; and the following words from Article II of said treaty, viz: "The United States now solemnly agree that no person except those herein authorized to do so, and except such officers, agents, and employés of the Government as may be authorized to enter upon Indian reservations in discharge of duties enjoined by law, shall ever be permitted to pass over, settle upon, or reside in the territory" described in the article, "except as herein otherwise provided," are hereby expressly re-affirmed, except so far as they applied to the country herein relinquished.

ARTICLE VI.

In consideration of the services of Ouray, head chief of the Ute Nation, he shall receive a salary of one thousand dollars per annum for the term of ten years, or so long as he shall remain head chief of the Utes and at peace with the United States.

ARTICLE VII.

This agreement is subject to ratification or rejection by the Congress of the United States and the President.

FELIX R. BRUNOT, [SEAL.]
Commissioner.

Attest: THOMAS K. CREE,
Secretary.

JAMES PHILLIPS, M. D.,
JOHN LAWRENCE,
Interpreters.

Ouray, his x mark, principal chief.
Sapivaneri, his x mark, chief of Tabequaches.
Guero, his x mark, chief of Tabequaches.
Chavanaux, his x mark, chief of Tabequaches.
To-sah, his x mark, chief of Tabequaches.
Chavis, his x mark, chief of Capotes.
Coronea, his x mark, chief of Capotes.
Kuchumpias, his x mark, chief of Capotes.
Topaaz, his x mark, chief of Weeminuches.
Maatchick, his x mark, chief of Muaches.
Tavanaserika, his x mark, Weeminuche warrior.
Vicente, his x mark, Muache warrior.
Peoch, his x mark, Capote warrior.
Acavut, his x mark, Capote warrior.
Sium, his x mark, Tabequache warrior.
Pasiz, his x mark, Weeminuche warrior.
José Maria, his x mark, chief of Muaches.
Ancatosh, his x mark, chief of Muaches.
Juan, his x mark, chief of Muaches.
John, his x mark, Muache, (son of Kaneatche.)
Chavez, his x mark, chief of Tabequaches.
Curecante, his x mark, chief of Muaches.
Parisio, his x mark, Muache warrior.
Yanko, his x mark, chief of Grand River Utes.
Quatunucutz, his x mark, Capote warrior.
McCook, his x mark, Tabequache warrior.
Buffalo, his x mark, Tabequache warrior.
Paziuts, his x mark, Capote warrior.
Valupe, his x mark, Muache warrior.
Juan Antonio, his x mark, Muache warrior.
Kiko, his x mark, Capote warrior.
Sapaya, his x mark, Tabequache warrior.
Satchuva, his x mark, Weeminuche warrior.
Artz, his x mark, Tabequache warrior.
Pasquah, his x mark, Yampah warrior.
Brunot, his x mark, Tabequache warrior.
Arop, his x mark, Weeminuche warrior.
Corutz, his x mark, Muache warrior.
Teramtup, his x mark, Muache warrior.
Acomuwep, his x mark, Capote warrior.
Washington, his x mark, chief of Capotes.
Pero, his x mark, Weeminuche warrior.
Pazio, his x mark, Capote warrior.
Jonejo, his x mark, Capote warrior.
Azumpitz, his x mark, Capote warrior.
Antelope, his x mark, Tabequache warrior.
Aiguillar, his x mark, chief of Muaches.
Alamon, his x mark, chief of Muaches.
Cocho, his x mark, chief of Tabequaches.
Quanusutz, his x mark, Tabequache warrior.

Tesaquent, his x mark, Muache warrior.
Tavaune, his x mark, Tabequache warrior.
Muus, his x mark, Muache warrior.
Patchuvuntz, his x mark, Tabequache warrior.
Ochos Blancos, his x mark, Muache warrior.
Kiratz, his x mark, Tabequache warrior.
Wapanas, his x mark, Tabequache warrior.
Martine, his x mark, Muache warrior.
Manuel, his x mark, Muache warrior.
Samora, his x mark, Muache subchief.
Penaritz, his x mark, Tabequache warrior.
Waiazitz, his x mark, Taqequache warrior.
Josié Rapier, his x mark, Muache warrior.
Tesaquitz, his x mark, Muache warrior.
Taos, his x mark, Muache warrior.
Cuchatoaz, his x mark, Tabequache warrior.
Wanazitziaskitz, his x mark, Tabequache warrior.
Kewukpo, his x mark, Muache warrior.
Christiano, his x mark, Muache warrior.
Anacksiz, his x mark, Tabequache warrior.
Sapuutz, his x mark, Tabequache warrior.
Japarka, his x mark, Tabequache warrior.
Waukoro, his x mark, Tabequache warrior.
Beture, his x mark, Tabequache warrior.
Cimarron, his x mark, Muache warrior.
Wanuponika, his x mark, Tabequache warrior.
Lovo, his x mark, chief of Tabequaches.
Colorado, his x mark, chief of Tabequaches.
Cabresa Negro, his x mark, Muache warrior.
Weutz, his x mark, Tabequache warrior.
Trucha, his x mark, Tabequache warrior.
Ator, his x mark, Tabequache warrior.
Sapitoawick, his x mark, Tabequache warrior.
Joe, his x mark, Muache warrior.
Tug; his x mark, Tabequache warrior.
Nehantro, his x mark, Tabequache warrior.
Juan Martine, his x mark, Muache subchief.
Ripis, his x mark, Muache warrior.
Zigah, his x mark, Tabequache warrior.
Wetoyora, his x mark, Tabequache warrior.
Kamoev, his x mark, Tabequache warrior.
Avoa, his x mark, Tabequache warrior.
Shavanakovaut, his mark, Tabequache warrior.
Zanovarap, his x mark, Tabequache wrrrior.
Noawakit, his x mark, Tabequache warrior.
Zariwap, his x mark, Tabequache warrior.
Ucanar, his x mark, Tabequache warrior.
Comanche, his x mark, Tabequache warrior.
Otois, his x mark, Tabequache warrior.
Katzupin, his x mark, Tabequache warrior.
Tamawitchi, his x mark, Tabequache warrior.
Kutzaporutz, his x mark, Tabequache warrior.
Wais, his x mark, Tabequache warrior.
Sepeis, his x mark, Muache warrior.
Waponikatz, his x mark, Tabequache warrior.
Zaparitzas, his x mark, Tabequache warrior.
Kutza Comanche, Tabequache warrior.
Nijeatz, his x mark, Tabequache warrior.
Izazah, his x mark, Tabequache.
Charley, his x mark, Tabequache.
Apantoa, his x mark, Tabequache.
Natnao, his x mark, Tabequache.
Aka, his x mark, Tabequache.
Tamajo, his x mark, Tabequache.
Koapuitz, his x mark, Tabequache.
Onarupe, his x mark, Tabequache.
Ziah, his x mark, Tabequache.
Guatanar, his x mark, Tabequache.
Poenika, his x mark, Tabequache.
Akaiock, his x mark, Tabequache.

Regis, his x mark, Tabequache.
Poevis, his x mark, Tabequache.
Povociat, his x mark, Tabequache.
Tabeguacheut, his x mark, Tabequache.
Urso, his x mark, Tabequache.
Kerenomes, his x mark, Tabequache.
Acatewich, his x mark, Tabequache.
Ancatara, his x mark, Tabequache.
Bapter, his x mark, Tabequache.
Atzcavi, his x mark, Tabequache.
Atzu, his x mark, Tabequache.
Panais, his x mark, Tabequache.
Capotavet, his x mark, Tabequache.

We, the undersigned, were present at the signing of the articles of agreement with the Ute Indians, and are hereby witnesses to their marks.

THOMAS K. CREE,
Secretary Special Ute Commission.
CHARLES ADAMS,
United States Indian Agent.
OTTO MEARS.
THOMAS A. DOLAN,
STEPHEN A. DOLE.

Kamuck, his x mark.
Liok, his x mark, Muache.
Teputzeit, his x mark.
Lupuget, his x mark.
Ponitz, his x mark.
Lagavavuner, his x mark.
Waziap, his x mark.
Povva, his x mark.
Tamserik, his x mark.
Moupitiz, his x mark.
Acavit, his x mark.
Larewich, his x mark.
Uncanante, his x mark, chief of Uncompagre-Tabequache.
Wap-sop, his x mark, of Uncompagre-Tabequache.
Paganachuckchuck, his mark, C. Tabequache.
No-art, his x mark, Tabequache.
Kane-atche, his x mark, chief of Muache.
To-mo-aset, his x mark, Muache.
One-a-ra-nich, his x mark, Muache.
Siarch-a-kitz, his x mark, Tabequache.
So-a-miugen-qua-a-boa, his x mark, Tabequache.
To-sa-set-to-be-qua, his x mark, Tabequache.
We-suc, his x mark, Tabequache.
Te-sen-par-kin-a-quet, his x mark, Tabequache.
Tuc-a-wa-be-quet, his x mark, Tabequache.
Sah-ach-choue, his x mark, Tabequache.
Ka-ton-a-wac, his x mark, Tabequache.
Move-ga-ritz, his x mark, Tabequache.
Tup-a-so-a, his x mark, Tabequache.
So-wa-wick, his x mark, Tabequache.
Mur-a-to, his x mark, Tabequache.
Pal-ma-cuch, his x mark, Tabequache.
Tu-up-o-na-ritz, his x mark, Tabequache.
Ma-ve-to, his x mark, Tabequache.
Tabere, his x mark, Tabequache.
Po-ka-ne-te, his x mark, Tabequache.
Pe-er-gue-it, his x mark, Tabequache.
Tu-gu-op, his x mark, Tabequache.
Sapio, his x mark, Tabequache.
Po-wa-ra, his x mark, chief of Weeminuches.
Wach-cup, his x mark, Weeminuches.
Oua-su-ach, his x mark, Weeminuches.
Ca-ve-son-ach, his x mark, Weeminuches.
Per-ca-pe-se-ach, his x mark, Weeminuches.
A-wa-re-otz, his x mark, Weeminuches.
E-ta-qu-oo-am, his x mark, Weeminuches.
Sa-o-artz, his x mark, Weeminuches.

Mo-ar-ta-witz, his x mark, Weeminuches.
Wa-wa-ta-ey, his x mark, Weeminuches.
Su-aph, his x mark, Weeminuches subchief.
José-Marie, Weeminuches subchief.
Ou-a-sent, Uncompagre-Tabequache.
Si-vich, Uncompagre-Tabequache.
Si-vich-arch, Uncompagre-Tabequache.
Aua-ra-u, his x mark, Muache.
Marromara, his x mark, Muache.
Su-er-up, his x mark, Muache.
To-coo, his x mark, Muache.
Na-co-varts, his x mark.
U-par-ca-ra-ritz, his x mark.
Opo-par-its, his x mark.
Ou-a-siz, his x mark, Tabequache.
Pe-ro-re, his x mark, Tabequache.
Et-o-oke, his x mark, Tabequache.
Ta-be-roner, his x mark, Tabequache.
Pah-sone, his x mark, Tabequache.
Te-ra-ma-tu-ke, his x mark, Tabequache.
To-si-ach, his x mark, Tabequache.
Ca-va-rup, his x mark, Tabequache.
Tu-vah, his x mark, Tabequache.
Oue-a-zarts, his x mark, Tabequache.
Sach-e-wee, his x mark, Tabequache.
Ar-rach, his x mark, Tabequache.
Ar-rup, his x mark, Tabequache.
Peach-sup, his x mark, Tabequache.
Sa-a-wip, his x mark, Tabequache.
Ou-a-curitz, his x mark, Tabequache.
Ava-su-ip, his x mark, Tabequache.
Na-na-witz, his x mark, Tabequache.
Wa-ri-ti-zi, his x mark, Tabequache.
Le-ap-ou-au-en, his x mark, Tabequache.
Wap-pah-pi, his x mark, Tabequache.
We-na-quts, his x mark, Tabequache.
No-ach-a-itz, his x mark, Tabequache.
Con-a-ra-kuch, his x mark, Tabequache.
So-va-ner, his x mark, Tabequache.
Oui-nach-e-vi-ach, his x mark, Tabequache.
Archue, his x mark, Tabequache.
Armacos, his x mark, Tabequache.
Oa-ra-ech, his x mark, Tabequache.
Cap-chu-ma-char-kitz, his x mark, Tabequache.
Ki-itz, his x mark, Tabequache.
Per-e-que, his x mark, Tabequache.
U-ch-ca-mir, his x mark, Tabequache.
U-ch-ca-poo-ritz, his x mark, Tabequache.
Uch-a-litb, his x mark, Tabequache.
To-ko-mantz, his x mark, Tabequache, subchief.
Ko-chup-a-sitz, his x mark, Tabequache, subchief.
Ar-ca-va-requa, his x mark, Tabequache, subchief.
We-ga-va-requa, his x mark, Tabequache, subchief.
Sha-va-qua-to-ark, his x mark, Tabequache, subchief.
We-ga-va, his x mark, Tabequache, subchief.
Sea-rach, his x mark, Tabequache, subchief.
So-o-mo-quitz, his x mark, Tabequache, subchief.
Pearch, his x mark, Tabequache, subchief.
Co-pah-rum, his x mark, Tabequache, subchief.
Tar-tach, his x mark, Tabequache, subchief.
Woh-chich-a-ark, his x mark, Tabequache, subchief.
Gueco-mu-chick, his x mark, Tabequache, subchief.
Ar-pa-chitz, his x mark, Tabequache, subchief.
Yer-putz, his x mark, Tabequache.
Un-no-wart, his x mark.
Sute-qu-ertz, his x mark, Tabequache, subchief.
Pas-ques, his x mark, Tabequache, subchief.
José-Raphael, his x mark, Tabequache, subchief.
Raphael, his x mark, Tabequache, subchief.
Spur-ce, his x mark, Tabequache, subchief.

Ta-r-ah-wah, his x mark, Tabequache, subchief.
Ka-qua-nah, his x mark, Tabequache, subchief.
Oe-bo-atz, his x mark, Tabequache, subchief.
Aca-une, his x mark, Tabequache, subchief.

We, the undersigned, were present at the signing of the articles of agreement with the Ute Indians, and are hereby witnesses to their marks.

THOMAS K. CREE,
Secretary Special Ute Commission.
CHARLES ADAMS,
United States Indian Agent.
OTTO MEARS.
THOMAS A. DOLAN.
STEPHEN A DOLE.

Carwarneo, his x mark.
Obatah, his x mark.
Martine, his x mark.
José, his x mark.
Nacosebu, his x mark.
Canhear, his x mark.
Mopuch, his x mark.
Warwadah, his x mark.
Yahtanah, his x mark.
Mocatacher, his x mark.
Cenponough, his x mark.
Couchewatak, his x mark.
Tahpowata, his x mark.
Pun-go-se, his x mark.
Sevaro, his x mark.
Terreon, his x mark.
Ignaceo, his x mark.
Juan-Ancho, his x mark.
Cunaspeche, his x mark.
Powincha, his x mark.
Towiar, his x mark.
Cabazon, his x mark.
Waehoup, his x mark.
Arvaoch, his x mark.
Otocora, his x mark.
Pecquough, his x mark.
Ouiceager, his x mark.
Ojos-blancos, his x mark.
Muecete, his x mark.
Caehapuro, his x mark.
Navacartia, his x mark.
Maroon, his x mark.
Sarvoweava, his x mark.
Caeeta, his x mark.
Ouaveroeh, his x mark.
Sevalho, his x mark.
Petoboun, his x mark.
Weeha, his x mark.
Swopia, his x mark.
Quinch, his x mark.
Oveto, his x mark.
Yeaneer, his x mark.
Parewich, his x mark.
Sera-bu-tom, his x mark.

We, the undersigned, were present at the signing of the articles of agreement with the Ute Indians, and are hereby witnesses to their marks.

THOMAS A. DOLAN.
T. D. BURNS.
M. V. STEVENS.

Narrative of the proceedings of the Commission to negotiate with the Ute Indians in Colorado.

☞At the conclusion of the successful negotiation with the Crow Indians, in Montana, Hon. Felix R. Brunot, special commissioner to negotiate with the Ute Indians, accompanied by Thomas K. Cree, as secretary, arrived at Cheyenne, Wyo., August 25. We were here met by James Phillips, M. D., of Washington, who had been engaged as Spanish interpreter.

We had expected to be met at this place by some employé of the central superintendency, having in charge "Friday," the son of Ouray, head chief of the Ute Indians, who has been a captive among the Arapahoes for some ten years. The importance of his return to the tribe by the commission at this time is shown by the accompanying report of the interview with Ouray, at Cheyenne, which had been fowarded by us to the Interior Department, under date of June 24th. Instructions had been sent by the Commissioner of Indian Affairs "to spare no trouble or reasonable expense in securing the young man," and we had requested by letter that he be held in readiness to send to Denver early in August. We learned on arriving there, August 27, that the agent of the Arapahoes had started from the Arapahoe camp on the 18th of August, expecting to reach Fort Scott, the nearest railroad station, on the 26th. We waited till the 1st of September, when, receiving no further intelligence in regard to him, we started for the Ute agency, at Los Pinos.

After a drive of two hundred miles we reached the agency, on the evening of the 5th of September.

It had been contemplated to hold the council about the 20th of August, and instructions had been sent to the agents at White River and Denver and the superintendent in New Mexico to have the Indians from the several Ute agencies assemble at Los Pinos prior to that date, but the negotiations with the Crow Indians having been more protracted than we had anticipated, the Indians were detained some three weeks waiting for us.

On our arrival we found about one thousand Indians at the agency, including all the representative men of the Ta-be-quache band, all the Muache and Capote bands, in charge of Thomas Dolan, subagent at Cimarron, seven representatives of the Weeminuche, and one each from the Denver and White River bands.

From information received prior to reaching the agency, we were led to suppose the negotiations would be attended with but little serious difficulty, but on arriving we found little to encourage us in hoping for a successful termination.

We found the Indians had been much dissatisfied at our long delay. The telegram changing the date of the council, and accounting for our non-arrival, having failed to reach the agency.

Ouray was greatly disappointed at the failure to bring his son Friday with us. He had said in the interview at Cheyenne, "The Government is strong enough to get my boy if it wished to do so, and if it shows an interest in me, and a desire to do what I wish, I will do what I can in carrying out the wishes of the Government in regard to the negotiations."

We met one surveying party, acting under the authority of the surveyor-general of the Territory, sectionizing for settlement the country within a short distance of the agency buildings, on which the Indians were camped waiting for the council, and which the Indians claim is a portion of their reservation.

A military surveying party, acting under instruction from the military authorities of the Department, had been engaged in surveying and making observations upon the reservation, much to the annoyance of the Indians, who could not understand the object of such survey. The officer in charge had informed the Indians that the eastern line of their reservation was some twenty miles west of the Cochitopa range, which they have always claimed as their eastern boundary, and that the agency buildings (which at the time of their location were supposed to be upon the reservation) were some twelve miles east of the reservation line.

One division of Professor Hayden's exploring party had spent some time upon their reservation, making surveys and taking observations, which excited the suspicions of the Indians; and the substance of letters from the newspaper correspondents accompanying the expedition, expressing views very offensive to the Indians, was known to them.

Parties of miners had repeatedly endeavored to pass by the agency and enter the reservation at places where the Indians were not willing they should go; and some of the miners with whom the Indians came into contact said "the Government was away east in the States, and had no power in the mines; it could not protect the Indians; and that they did not care whether they sold the mines or not, they were going to stay."

The President had issued an order to eject the miners and other unauthorized persons from the reservation under the following article of the treaty of 1868:

"The United States now solemnly agree that no person except these herein authorized so to do, and except such officers, agents, and employés of the Government as may be authorized to enter upon Indian reservations in discharge of duties enjoined by law, shall ever be permitted to pass over, settle upon, or reside in the territory described in this article, except as herein otherwise provided."

The execution of this order had been suspended; and this gave color to the statement of the miners, and led them to believe that the Government would take no action in regard to their presence upon the reservation if the Indians persisted in their refusal to sell. The fact that for two years the presence of miners upon the reservation in considerable numbers was well known, and that the frequent complaints of the Indians were disregarded, led them to distrust the promises of the Government.

The southern boundary line of the reservation was also a considerable distance north of the natural boundary line which the Indians assert was given them at the time of the treaty of 1868; and that the mistake was not theirs is probable, from the fact that an actual survey located in New Mexico, some distance below the northern doundary line, towns that had been, prior to it, claimed as being in Colorado.

The annuity goods which the commission had hoped to have distributed during the council, which had been shipped from New York June 1, and which they had specially requested should be at the agency, two hundred miles from the railroad, by August 1, had not arrived. Ten thousand dollars' worth of presents bought for distribution by the commission of 1872, and which had failed to reach the agency until after that commission had left, had all been distributed, except such articles as were useless and not valued by the Indians.

The commission have reason to think that persons in New Mexico, whose interest it was to retain a portion of the Utes in that Territory, and whose influence was used against the success of the negotiation last year, endeavored to prejudice the Indians, prior to their coming to the council, against it this year, and induced them to insist, as a condition of any agreement made, upon provisions which it would be impossible for the commission to concede, or, if granted, would inure to the benefit of the parties interested.

The negotiations of 1872 had brought prominently before the minds of the Indians all the objections to a sale, and they failed to realize any advantage it would be to them.

After their refusal last year to negotiate for the region sought to be purchased, the commission asked them to sell *only* the mines. The Indians understood this as referring to the mines that were then actually worked, and to include none of the surrounding country. These only they were now willing to sell. The Indians seem to have kept their own counsel in regard to the matter, and no one knew what they proposed to do. Mr. Adams, the agent, while inferring they were willing to make some arrangement, informed us that he did not know what they proposed to do, and was much surprised at their proposal when made in council. Letters had been received from various influential gentlemen recommending different parties as desirable ones to be present during the council, but profiting by the experience of the council of last year, and a knowledge of the usual manner of conducting Indian negotiations, the commission had requested that all unauthorized persons should be excluded from the agency during the council.

The only advantages we had in the negotiation were the oft-tested friendship of the Utes for the whites and their earnest desire to do all that would, in their opinion, tend to perpetuate and strengthen a reciprocal feeling by the whites for them, and the fact that not a single white person was present during the council except those connected with the commission or the agency.

The council convened on Saturday, September 6, and was continued on Monday. The real business of the commission received but little attention on these days, as the Indians insisted upon bringing up questions in which they felt a more direct interest, such as their eastern and southern boundary-lines, in regard to both of which they persistently asserted the Government had not kept faith with them. The bands at Terra Maria and Cimarron, in New Mexico, insisted upon remaining there for the present, expressing, however, a willingness to come upon the reservation at some future period, when the lands they now occupy shall be needed by the whites, and wished some promise before they would even consider the business proposed by the commission. With these, and other outside questions, we could only assure them that we had nothing to do, but would carry their words to the Great Father, and he could do what he thought was right about them.

On Tuesday, owing to the absence of an interpreter selected by the Indians, no council was held; but the subject was fully discussed in all its bearings by the Indians among themselves.

Wednesday the council again assembled, and a clear and explicit statement was made of the wishes of the Government, and the advantages to be derived by the Indians from an acceptance of the proposition of the commission were fully stated. The Indians replied with a distinct counter proposition, which had been foreshadowed in the first interview with them, declaring their intentions and willingness to sell only the mines then being worked, selling nothing but the tops of the mountains, and including none of the valleys. The miners were to build no houses, and not to make the mining region a permanent place of residence; but to come out each fall, returning again in the spring. For this purpose they would permit the use of a single road in entering and leaving the mines. This arrangement they thought, and urged upon the commission, was in accord with the proposition of the commission of 1872, and were much surprised on being informed that their proposition could not even be entertained by the present commission.

Thursday the proposition of the commission was again made in detail, giving them the boundaries of the proposed purchases, the price to be paid for it, and manner of payment, proposing a new agency upon the southern part of the reservation for the southern Utes, and re-affirming the treaty of 1868, including the section in which the Government agreed to prevent the intrusion of unauthorized whites upon the reservation. It was also proposed that if this negotiation was successful a party of the Indians might visit Washington and lay before the Commissioner of Indian Affairs the subjects they had brought up in council, and which the commission could not decide for them. They listened to all with great attention, and earnestly discussed the subject for several hours among themselves.

It was soon apparent that a large majority of the Indians really favored the proposition; but a small minority were very persistent in opposing it; and finding they were not likely to reach an early conclusion the formal council was adjourned.

The Indians continued to discuss the matter fully in council among themselves.

On Friday morning many of the chiefs came expressing a willingness to sign the paper containing the proposition made to them.

On Saturday morning, September 13, Ouray, the head chief, and all the principal men came and expressed their desire to sign the articles of agreement, provided, after doing so, a delegation of chiefs, representing the various bands, should visit the country sold, and if they found it was all mountains and mining country, and contained no farming land then the agreement should stand and be signed by the others; if not, then the agreement would fail as lacking the assent of the necessary three-fourths of the tribe.

This question with regard to the farming country was one of ths most serious the commission had to meet. It had been asserted by one of the Weeminuche delegates that some forty of the band he represented were farming upon the part which it was proposed that they should sell, and the chiefs said, "We will soon need all the farming land on our reservation, as the time is not far distant when the Utes will have to give up hunting, and take to farming and stock-raising as the whites do."

That they should want a large territory is not to be wondered at. It is claimed by intelligent stock-men that it requires of average Colorado land five acres to support one sheep, and fifty acres for a horse or cow, and every large stock-raiser in the Territory holds to the necessity for and his right to from five to ten thousand acres of public land as a stock-range. The Utes have already about six thousand horses and many cattle and sheep.

The only portion of their reservation fit for farming land is along the southern boundary, below the mountain-ranges; a strip along the San Miguel River, on the southwestern boundary; and the Uncompagre Park, and a small portion of the Gunnison, the central part being all a mass of mountains, containing no valleys of any size, and the western central part, as we are informed, being rocky, with the river-courses through deep cañons. The northern part is largely volcanic *debris*, producing neither grass, vegetation, nor game, and lying at such an altitude as to be shut in from intercourse with the outside world by ice and snow most of the year. Even the present agency at Los Pinos lies at so high an altitude as to be visited by frost every month in the year, effectually preventing the raising of any kind of produce. During the winter months intercourse is kept up with Saguache, the nearest post-office, with uncertainty and danger.

In accordance with the agreement made with the Indians, the secretary of the commission, accompanied by Mr. Charles Adams, agent at Los Pinos, Mr. Thomas Dolan, subagent at Tierra Maria, and Sapivaneri and Guaro, chiefs of the Tabequaches, Curecante and Corutz, chiefs of the Muaches, Asumpitz, subchief, and Conejo, son of Sobeta, principal chief of the Capotes, and Antelope, an Indian boy, started to inspect the country ceded. Leaving the agency we traveled in a southwestern direction. After crossing a range of the Uncompagre Mountains, twelve thousand five hundred feet above sea-level at the point of crossing, the party camped on the south fork of the Gunnison River, in what is known as the Lake mining region. There is no farming and very little grazing land in this section; but there is a fine chain of high mountains which are said to be rich in minerals, and in which several leads have been located. Crossing another range equally high, we struck a fork of the Rio Grande, following it to the head of Antelope Park, where, turning off to the north, we crossed a high divide, and struck the main body of the Rio Grande, which we followed to its head, crossing the range, at an altitude of thirteen thousand feet, to the head-waters of the Animas, along which, with its tributaries, is situated the celebrated San Juan mining country. We visited all the mines that have been at all developed. The Indians evinced much interest in the examination of their value. We saw but one mine that has been tested sufficiently to get much return from it. This one, it is stated, was stocked by a company at $500,000, although a legal title could not be made to the land on which it was located. The company have erected a mill, and spent in it, and in developing their mine, some $75,000, and it is said the yield is about $1,000 in gold per day. The agent of this company informed us that they had now en route for the mines a fifteen-stamp mill, with which they could produce $25,000 per week in gold. The vein is eighteen inches thick, and it yields, it is claimed, from one to four thousand dollars per ton. One of the Indians, while in this mine, broke off a piece of rock, weighing about a pound, which he crushed in a hand-mortar, getting from it, with his indifferent handling, about one dollar's worth of gold.

Since the purchase of the mining country the owners of the mine claim it to be worth double what it was worth before. At another vein, which has only been prospected, we found among the *debris* indications of free gold in every piece of rock. Other veins are said to yield as high as $8,000 in gold per ton. It is claimed the silver-veins are much more valuable than the gold leads. We were informed that one lead is six feet wide, and that another yields pay-ore in a vein forty feet wide, and indication of the precious metal sufficient to justify a claim for three hundred feet wide. Some five hundred to six hundred leads have been located, and about two hundred and fifty to three hundred miners were in the country at the time of our visit. The country is not only rich in gold and silver, but there are large deposits of copper, iron, lead, and coal.

On a rumor that the country had been bought, fifty persons started to locate town-lots, in what they claim will be the great smelting and refining center of the mining region.

This region is the greatest aggregation of high mountain peaks and ranges in the country, and, after visiting it, all other mountain scenery is completely dwarfed.

Having gone as far as the Indians desired, and having ascertained, as far as we could, that very little, if any, farming country was in the land sold, we returned to the agency. After hearing the report of the chiefs, the remainder of the Indians at the agency all signed the articles of convention, and a copy was sent to the White River, Denver, Cimarron, and Tierra Maria agencies, to be signed by all the Indians at those places. But one Indian, the Weeminuche before alluded to, opposed the sale and refused to sign the articles of convention. Subsequently he desired to sign it, but the band to which he belonged would not permit him to do so.

The country ceded contains about four million acres, and is unquestionably rich in mineral deposits.

On the conclusion of the present successful negotiation, the commission authorized Ouray and a delegation of his people to carry the articles of convention to the Great Father, at Washington.

The southern portion of the reservation, which is well watered and fertile, was retained more particularly as a reservation for the Weeminuche, Capote, and Muache Indians, with the view of having an agency located there for them, and in the expectation of having them settle upon it at an early day, their present temporary agencies in New Mexico being equally disadvantageous to the Indians and the Government.

Some of these Indians being averse to leaving their present place of living, permission was given each band to send a delegation to Washington to present the matter to the Commissioner of Indian Affairs.

At the council with the Utes, representatives of two branches of the Apaches, living and intermarried with the Utes, presented their case to the commission, and it was deemed expedient to permit them to accompany their friends to Washington. They have been ordered to join other branches of the Apaches, which they are averse to doing.

The following letter of General Alexander, commandant at Fort Garland, who is conversant with the facts, fully states the case, and is corroborated by the statements of the Indians:

"FORT GARLAND, COLO., *September* 5, 1872.

"SIR: In compliance with your request, I have the honor to furnish you with the following memoranda:

"Wherro-Mondo, chief of one band of the Jicarilla Apaches, wants the Government to set apart a reservation in Northwestern New Mexico, on a stream called the Rio Pusoco, for himself and his band, consisting of one hundred lodges, or about six hundred souls, in order that they may settle there permanently and till the soil. This tract is not occupied by any one else, and is contiguous to the present Ute reservation. Wherro is an uncle of Ouray, the principal chief of the Utes, and his band are intermarried with the Utes, and have many of their habits and customs. They therefore desire to live within visiting distance of the Utes. Wherro has always been perfectly peaceable, and has always, with a few of his people, cultivated little farms. They also are expert in the manufacture of earthenware, and get what necessaries they want by the sale of their articles to the Mexicans. They have never had any annuities from the Government. Wherro says that all his band are anxious to give up their roving life and settle down to agriculture. Wherro also suggests that the reservation be made large enough to accommodate the band of Jicarilla Apaches now living with the Muache

Utes at the Cimarron, whenever they choose to change their mode of life. These Jicarilla Apaches should not be confounded with the Southern Apaches, as their habits and mode of life are entirely different. The former have property, horses, mules, lodges, blankets, sheep, &c., while the latter have nothing, living upon grass-seed, wild fruits, and hunting. I am informed that the Jicarilla Apaches at the Cimarron are ordered to be sent to the Apache reservation at Fort Stanton. I think this would be a great mistake, as they are really not the same people as the Coyotero and other bands of Apaches on that reservation.

"It appears to me that forming this settlement of industrious Indians, so closely connected with the Utes, in the immediate vicinity, would gradually induce them to adopt these peaceful occupations in preference to their present nomadic life, particularly as game gets scarce. It is the first instance in my knowledge of wild Indians in a state of peace asking such a favor of the Government, and it is certainly encouraging, in view of a peaceful solution of this question.

"I have made these statements as brief as possible. Should you desire more particular information, I will be glad to furnish any in my power.

"I am, sir, very respectfully, your obedient servant,

"A. J. ALEXANDER,
"*Major and Bvt. Brig. General U. S. A.*

"Hon. FELIX R. BRUNOT,
"*Chairman of the Board of Indian Commissioners.*"

Respectfully submitted.

THOMAS K. CREE,
Secretary.

Hon. FELIX R. BRUNOT,
Chairman Special Ute Commission.

Minutes of the council held with the Ute Indians, at Los Pinos Agency, Colorado, September 6–12, 1873.

The special commissioner, under appointment by the honorable Secretary of the Interior, to negotiate with the Ute Indians, in accordance with the act of Congress approved April 23, 1872, accompanied by Thomas K. Cree, as secretary of the commission, and Dr. James Phillips, as Spanish interpreter, arrived at Los Pinos agency September 5, 1873.

On Saturday, September 6, Mr. Brunot had a conversation with Ouray in regard to the time for holding the council. It was decided to meet at 2 p. m. the same afternoon. He explained the reason for his delay at arriving at the agency, it having been understood that the council would be held about the middle of August, at which time the Indians had gathered at the agency. He then told Ouray of the effort he had been making to secure the return of Ouray's son, and read the letter of Superintendent Hoag, stating that Agent Miles had gone to the Arapahoe camp the 18th of August to get the boy, and word was expected from him every day in regard to him. He told him that he had waited at Colorado Springs four days, expecting to hear that the boy had arrived at the railroad, in which case he would have waited for him and brought him along; that he had left word at the station that if the agent arrived there with the boy, he should bring him right over, and he hoped he would be here in a few days. But if the boy would not come with the agent, then he would stop as we went back, and see him, and that Ouray should also go with us if he wished.

Ouray then detailed the particulars of the boy's capture, the facts in the main corresponding with the information gotten by Agent Daniels from the Arapahoe chief, Friday, and establishing the fact that the Ute boy called Friday, now with the Southern Arapahoes, and whom he had endeavored to bring with him, was the son of Ouray.

First day.

SEPTEMBER 6, 1873.

Council convened at 2 p. m.

There were present Hon. Felix R. Brunot, commissioner to negotiate with the Utes, and Thomas K. Cree, secretary; Dr. James Phillips, of Washington, as Spanish interpreter on the part of the commission, and John Lawrence and James Fullerton, as Spanish interpreters on the part of the Indians, and Ouray, the chief, as Ute interpreter, and Charles Adams, agent at Los Pinos, and Thomas Dolan, subagent at Tierra Maria, and the following Indian chiefs:

TABEQUACHES.—Ouray, Lovo, Sapiovaneri, Cocho, Chavanaux, Guero, Colorado, Tosah, Chaves.

MUACHES.—Aucatosh, Samora, Curecante, Aiguillar, José Maria, Mautchick.

CAPOTES.—Pesinte, Aigua, Chinne, Kanea, Chavis, Tapoat, (son of Sobeta,) Coronea, Topaatz, Acumpaziah.

WEEMINUCHES.—Purasitz, Venao, Prazit, Pa-si-ut, Panadnip, Terreapton.

DENVER.—Yanko.

APACHES.—Guero Modo, Aijove.

The White River band had been represented by Douglas, Sac-wioch Uugachief, Laritz, Ancatoras, but prior to the council the delegation returned to their agency, leaving one of their number to represent them.

In opening the council, Mr. Brunot said:

Whenever we hold a council with the Indians, we know the Great Spirit sees us and knows our hearts, and we want to ask him to make our hearts all right, and direct us in this council. We usually do so when we hold a great council among the whites. I want you all to stand up while I talk to the Great Spirit.

Mr. Brunot then led in prayer, all reverently standing. Ouray interpreted the substance of the prayer to his people.

Mr. Brunot then said:

When I came last year to see the Utes, there was a commission here from the President to talk to you about some business. You were very busy with that commission and had a long talk with them. You did not agree with the commission. I did not then come to talk about the business of the commission, but came from the President to talk about some other matters. You did not know I was coming, and did not understand my business, so I thought it best not to hold a council and talk with you about the business on which I had come. After the council I had a little talk with Ouray, and I told him one thing that I wanted—that the President had been told the Utes had killed a man. I said I did not think the Utes, who were the friends of the whites, had done it, and I wanted Ouray to find out who it was. Ouray did find out, and sent me word who it was. He said the Utes were all opposed to the men who committed the crime. I was glad to find the Utes were always to be the friends of the whites, and were to be depended on. I told the President that no one must feel bad because the Utes did not agree with the commission, and I thought the President ought to send away from the reservation the whites who were upon it, and the President made an order to send the miners off the reservation. After the order was issued, the President heard that the Utes were willing to sell the part of the reservation on which the miners were. He thought if he sent the soldiers and put the miners off the reservation, it might make trouble between them and the Utes; and if the Utes wanted to sell that piece of country on which the miners were, it was better to hear what the Utes had to say before driving the miners off. If the Utes wanted to sell that place, it was of no use to make trouble between them and the miners. The Secretary of the Interior has sent me the following letter. It is the same as if the President had written it:

"DEPARTMENT OF THE INTERIOR,
"*Washington, July* 14, 1873.

"DEAR SIR: During your negotiations with the Utes for the relinquishment of a portion of their reservation, I have the honor to request that you explain to them fully the reasons which induced the Government to suspend its order issued last spring for the expulsion of white settlers now within their reservation. The order for this expulsion was issued at the instance of this Department, and would have been executed at once but for the following circumstances: The President was informed that their chief, Ouray, had expressed a willingness to negotiate for the sale of a portion of the reservation, and he deemed it best to await the result of the council in regard to such negotiation, because if the Utes shall conclude to sell a portion of their reservation, it would be a needless hardship to drive out the whites, who would at once desire to return to their former occupations. To drive them out thus, would needlessly increase their enmity to the Utes. The President, therefore, in suspending the order, had the welfare and best interests of the Utes before him, as well as that of the settlers. The suspension of the order of removal only awaits the result of the negotiations, and should they fail, I have no doubt the President will renew the order for the removal of the whites.

"With my congratulations to Ouray and other chiefs of the Utes, and with the hope that your negotiations may result favorably and be productive of peace and the prosperity of the Utes, as well as of the white citizens, I have the honor to be, with great respect,

"Your obedient servant,

"C. DELANO,
"*Secretary of the Interior.*

"Hon. FELIX R. BRUNOT,
"*President of the Special Commission to negotiate with the Utes of Colorado, &c.*"

He sent and asked me to come and see the Utes and talk with you. He asked me because he knew I did not want your land for myself, and that I was a friend of the

Indians, and he thought you knew that I was your friend. I said to him I would come and see Ouray and the Utes, and talk to them about what I thought was for their good. Then he sent word to Ouray and the agents that I would come. He sent this letter to me ordering me to come.

The letter of the honorable Commissioner of Indian Affairs was then read to them.

Now, I have come to talk to you about that business. I want to tell you, as your friend, that I think you are wise, because you have thought about the matter since last summer. It is not for me to tell you what to do, but for you to say what you would like to do about this matter. You see the condition of affairs just as well as I do. You have many wise men among you, and you have a wise chief. You know a wise man looks ahead and knows the future. It is much better sometimes to do what does not please us just now, if we think it will be best for our children. I think that is what you have been thinking about, and that is why you sent word you would like me to come and see you. Before I say anything more on the subject I want to hear from the Utes.

CHAVANAUX. Those lines the surveyors are running on the reservation are not according to the treaty. The mountains were the boundary of our reservation, (on the east,) and we want to know what treaty has been made that gave them the privilege of coming in and running these lines in our lands.

Mr. BRUNOT. So you want me to tell you about it.

CHAVANAUX. We would like to know.

Mr. BRUNOT. The treaty tells the lines of the reservation. I had nothing to do with making the treaty. The way the whites have of telling lines by the compass, you cannot understand, and when the treaty was made the lines were named, but it was not put on the land; when they came to locate the agency they thought it was on the reservation.

OURAY. It was on the reservation. I was interpreter and knew what the boundary-lines were.

Mr. BRUNOT. The lines they are running is only to see whether the lines are where you thought they were or not. I do not know anything about these surveyors.

OURAY. They are measuring, and whenever they find a mine they take a little piece more of our country. They are running new lines all the time.

Mr. BRUNOT. I am sorry to hear it, and if I make any agreement I want the lines to be well understood. I think the people of the Territory are running some of these lines, and if they are not right the President will not have them for the lines.

OURAY. The line they have run they say is twelve miles west from here, and it is not right. The line is not correct as they make it.

Mr. BRUNOT. I have nothing to do with these men, and I am sorry they are here.

CHAVANAUX. How is it you do not know about this?

Mr. BRUNOT. I left Washington more than three months ago, and have not heard much from there since. I do not think this survey came from Washington. I think it came from Denver. When I go to Washington I will find out all about it, and I will tell the President what the Utes say. Mr. Adams tells me they did not make any lines; they only made observations, and when the line is run it may be very different.

OURAY. If they made observations the line will probably be where they say. I interpreted it to the Utes when the treaty was made, that the line would be from the Rio Grande to the head of the mountain. We understood it so until the present time. The rivers that run to the east from the mountain-range we understood were off the reservation; those that run west were on it. In regard to Washington Gulch and others, where they are mining, they are on the reservation as we understand it. The miners have come in and have not been disturbed by the Utes. The mines in the mountains are very important; they are surrounded by the Utes, and the miners will gradually settle down upon the Ute lands in the valley.

Mr. BRUNOT. Do the mines extend on both sides of the mountains?

OURAY. All the rivers have very fine farming-lands along them, on the Rio Platte and Animas, and San Miguel Rivers. The Indians farm and have crops now; and on all the rivers that come out on this side of the mountains the Utes farm; they have corn there that is ripe now.

Mr. BRUNOT. I see the difficulty about the matter. I saw it before I came here, and I saw it last summer—the difficulty of separating the mineral from the farming land. I see the difficulty as well as you do, and I feel the importance of it more than you do. The reason is, I see the time will come when the Utes will have to raise herds of horses and cattle, and will have to farm, and do just as the whites do. It may be a good while and it may not be so long—we cannot tell—but when the time comes to raise crops and cattle, you can only use a certain amount of the land. If you were to say to me to-day that you would sell all the land that was good for farming, I would say it was not right, you ought not to do it; but if, in order to get a line that takes in the mountains, you have to put in a piece that has some good farming-lands on it, if enough is left for you, I would think it was good. If I had been all through your country as you have, I would know what was a good line; but as I have not, I do not know exactly about the lines. I want you to say what would be a good line; if you do not know just at once, you can think about it. There may be some land across the line that you do not want to sell, but to keep that might spoil all, and it might be better to let it go. Sometimes, in order to do a great thing that we want to do, it is necessary to do a little thing we do not want to do. It is for you to decide. In order to sell a piece of your land to the Government that you want to sell, it may be necessary to sell a little piece you would rather keep; that is for you to think about.

OURAY. What have you to say in regard to the Apaches? Some of their chiefs are present, and want to hear what you have to say to them. The governor wants to take them down south with the Mescalero Apaches; they do not want to go. This one spoke last year.

GUERO MUDO, (Apache.) Some years ago some of the governors of New Mexico gave us a reservation on Muddy River, about Abiquiu: We want to keep it, and not go down with the Jicarilla Apaches. We want the land that was given us. We know how to farm, and only want land to farm on. We do not ask for anything else. After the land was given to us, some Mexicans came and took the land. We told them that was our land, but they said they would keep it, and they did.

Mr. BRUNOT. An inspector has gone down there, and I think he will inquire about your lands, and when I go to Washington I will hear about it. I have no instructions about it.

GUERO MUDO. We wanted you to know what we had to say and to inquire into it.

Mr. BRUNOT. I am glad to hear your words; they are all put down, and I will inquire into it, and it will be attended to.

GUERO MUDO. We only ask for our land. We can work. We are not friends of those Apaches in the south. We do not like any people that fight, and do not want to go with them.

Mr. BRUNOT. Would you like to come with the Utes, and would the Utes like the Apaches to come?

GUERO MUDO. We like to visit the Utes, but would rather stay where we are. We spoke to Governor McCook about it last year, and he said he would tell the President about it. He probably never told the President what we said about the matter. It was wrong if Governor McCook did not tell it. And we want you to promise us you will tell it, and to give me a promise in writing that I may show when I go back to my people.

Mr. BRUNOT. If I tell a man I will do a thing, and he does not believe it, I do not care; when I say it, it is the same as if I wrote it.

GUERO MUDO. In regard to the agents in New Mexico, they have no power; they are changing all the time, and the agents are of little account, and I want your letter to show the people that I am trying to do somtehing.

Mr. BRUNOT. You will hear about it from Washington.

OURAY. The other one is an Apache of another band from Cimarron; he wants to know what the Government intends to do about them.

Mr. BRUNOT. The inspector that went down a few days ago will report in Washington, and I will not know till I get there. We will send a letter from Washington to Guero Mudo.

GUERO MUDO. Are you certain a letter will come; will they not steal it on the road?

Mr. BRUNOT. I do not know; maybe they will.

GUERO MUDO. It may be like some things that are sent to Ouray; he never gets them. It might be so with my letter; it might never get to me.

Mr. BRUNOT. If I had come to the Utes in the old way, wanting to get your lands, I would have had a lot of people all about talking in your ears. Maybe I would have had a man to give one a horse, another a gun, to get them to talk the way I wanted. Sometimes treaties are made that way; when they want you to do what is good for the white man, but bad for the Indian, that is the way they come. I do not come that way. I tell you I am your friend, and if I could help it I would not have the Government do anything that was not good for you. When I talk to the white men or the red men, I want to talk in such a way that I will never be ashamed to meet them. Whatever I say the "Great Spirit" hears, and if it is not right I will be punished hereafter for it. I have said this because I want you to understand that I come as your friend, and I want you to do what I think is for your good, and want you to tell me just what you think about it, and we will try and fix it up in a way that will be good for all. In this way I think we will come to an agreement that will be good for all. I was to see another tribe of Indians this summer, and I saw that white men had gone upon their lands, and had found mines and were mining on their land, and other men were camped ready to go on. If I had been strong enough I would have been willing to drive them all into the river, for they had no business there; but I saw so many wanted to go upon the land, that if the President was to send the soldiers and drive them off, some of them would do things against the Indians and bring on a war with them. I saw bad men were there who would do that, and what would have been the consequence? I saw some of those men were bad men, and would bring on this trouble to get back upon the Indian's land. I knew if they did this, the consequence would be that tribe of Indians would be driven on the bad lands above the Missouri River, and they would not get anything for their good land. The war would be made an excuse to get the land for nothing. I was sure it was good for these Indians before any trouble came to get paid for their land, so I told them the President knew these people were there taking their minerals, and he was willing to pay them for their land, and as their friend I told them to take pay for it, keeping enough to live upon. At first they did not like to sell their land, and see the whites go on it; they said they and their children were born there, and they did not want to leave it. I thought I would feel the same way, but I knew it was better to let that piece of land go and get paid for it, than to have trouble come and get nothing for it. They thought about it some time, and saw it was best, and they agreed to sell it and take a large sum of money, the interest to be used for their benefit forever, and they still have enough of land to live on and hunt on.

OURAY. I do not like the interest part of that agreement. I would rather have the money in a bank.

Mr. BRUNOT. About thirty years ago the Cherokees sold their land and came west of the Mississippi, and the Government agreed to make a note and give them the interest every year; and now they have the interest paid them every year. With part of the interest they keep up their schools and their government. The same was done with some other Indians nearly one hundred years ago, and they get money every year for the interest. A nation might lose its lands, but if the Government promised to pay them interest, they would always get it. These Indians I made the agreement with have plenty of land for themselves and their children, and, besides, the interest every year will be paid them in things they need. Your case is a little like that. It may be there are none of those bad men upon your land who would make trouble; you know better than I do about that. Still, it looks to me as if the very best thing that can be done, if you can spare these mountains, is to sell them, and to have something coming in every year. If you do not think so now, some day you will remember what I told you about it, and I think you will make up your minds some day, whether you sell it or not, that what I told you was right. Last summer the commission asked me to say something. I told you I did not come about their business, but as they asked me if I would say something, I said then just what I thought, just as I am saying now. I did not go round about it at all. I said just what I thought. Perhaps you did not understand me at that time.

OURAY. We understood you then and we understand you now.

Mr. BRUNOT. I was told I had offended you because I talked so plain. You must not be offended at plain talk, for I say what I mean.

OURAY. There are many that understand what you say, and we are not offended at plain talk.

Mr. BRUNOT. If you have any thing to say, I will hear you now, or we can meet Monday morning at 10 o'clock.

CHAVANAUX. All you say about what you done with the other Indians is all right. When I was in Washington the treaty put the line on the top of the mountains and not where the line is put now. The President heard it, and knows where it was. That is what I cannot understand—why the line is put where they now say it is. That is why it is hard to make this contract; the lines have been changed and it is bad faith on the part of the Government.

OURAY. All the Utes understand the lines, and it is as we say. The lines in regard to the mines do not amount to anything; it is changing them all the time—taking a little now and a little again—that makes trouble. You said you do not know anything in regard to these lines and it may be the same in regard to lines you make. There are many men talk about it to us; they say they are going to have the lines as they want, whether the Utes like it or not. It is common talk; everybody tells it to the Utes. The miners care very little about the Government, and do not obey the laws. They say they do not care about the Government. It is a long way off in the States, and they say the man who comes to make the treaty will go off to the States, and it will all be as they want it. With you it is different; you talk in the name of the Great Spirit; we understand that, and think it right and ought to have great weight. Some people do not work on one side or the other, but so they can fill their pockets with money, it does not make any difference what they say. If I could talk just as I see fit, it might be different, but I talk for the Indians as you do for the commission. I must talk for both sides, (as interpreter,) and give the matter consideration. We are not prepared to talk now, but day after to-morrow you will hear from us.

Second day.—Monday, September 8, 1873.

Council convened at 12 o'clock. Opened with prayer by Mr. Brunot.

Mr. BRUNOT said: I do not think I need say the same things over that I said Saturday. I think you all remember them. But there are other things I ought to say, so that some of the Indians from New Mexico will learn how they are situated. You see everywhere how the whites are spreading over the country. In New Mexico there are getting to be many Americans and Mexicans where the Indians live. Some people down there want the Indians to stay at Tierra Maria and Cimarron, but many want them to go away. Perhaps there are some people there who sell things to the Government for the Indians, and some who trade with the Indians and make money out of them. That kind of people who make money out of the Indians want them to stay there. I do not know but the Indians know about it, but I know there are many people coming in, and many more wishing to come. They think the land belongs to the whites; everywhere the whites are taking up the good land there. There are so many there now that there is not much land left for the Indians, and it is getting worse and worse all the time, and soon all the land will be taken up, and there will be none left for the Indians to live upon. The President knows all this, and that is why he wants the Utes from New Mexico to come upon their reservation, where there is a good place for them to stay. I want the Utes from New Mexico to understand this. Very soon the President will have to make an order to put them on some place for themselves, and there is no good place there now that the whites do not claim. I want to tell them this as their friend—that they ought to join with the other Utes, and select some place on the reservation as their home. Perhaps they do not like to hear this. I do not like to say anything to any of the Indians that is disagreeable for them to hear. It makes my heart feel sorry to say anything that they do not wish to hear, but the Great Spirit tells me I must always speak the truth when I am talking to the Utes, or the whites, or anybody; whether they like it or not, I must speak the truth. Sometimes when a man hears anything he does not like, he thinks about it, and, if it is true, after a while he comes to like it. That is the way I think it will be with the Utes from New Mexico. They will think about it and find it is good, and I hope they will take my advice. We have met here to-day to settle up the matter we talked about Saturday, in regard to these mountains. Let us talk about that and nothing else till it is settled.

OURAY. It is better to settle in regard to moving the Muaches. They do not want to leave where they are in New Mexico.

Mr. BRUNOT. I have told them what comes to me from Washington, and I have told them what I think would be good for them; that it would be good for them to have a place for themselves on the lower part of the reservation, where they would be away from the whites and have a place for themselves. If they pick out a good place where they can raise corn and where they would like to live, I will ask the President to give them an agency there. I think the President will do it. I think the best way would be, if we make a bargain with all the Utes in regard to the mountains, that we put in the same paper that the Southern Utes, the Capotes, Muaches, and Weeminuches shall have an agency on the reservation there. I think it would be good to put in the paper that there shall be an agency on the lower part of the reservation, another one here or on the Gunnison, or the Uncompagre, or where the Indians say, not on the Uncompagre or the Gunnison, if the Indians do not want it, but where they want it.

OURAY. There is no difficulty in regard to us; we want the agency below somewhere. Mr. Adams knows where, but the difficulty is with the Southern Utes.

Mr. BRUNOT. I presume the Southern Utes want to be on the lower part of the reservation. I have told them what I think would be good for them. I know it is good for them, and I want them to have a home where they cannot be disturbed. If they would rather come here, it is good, but if they would rather have an agency in the southern part of the reservation, I think the President would establish one there for them. It is very important for them to make up their minds in regard to it, and I want them to have a place which they can always have for their children and their children's children. They know, themselves, that where they are now the whites claim and say it is their land, and after a little while there will be so many whites there that they cannot stay. I think they know very well that when a man sees the storm coming it is better to get fixed ready for it, and the sooner he gets protected against it the better. So, now, when there is a good chance to get a good home it is better to settle it. I think I have said all I need say about it. You have sense, and know what is best. One thing more, I forgot; perhaps the Utes from New Mexico think if they come on the reservation that they cannot hunt the buffalo; that is a mistake. I think the President will let them go to hunt the buffalo while they behave themselves, and while there are buffalo to hunt.

CURECANTE. We want our agency on the Dry Cimarron.

OURAY. The southern Indians say there are but few whites about the Dry Cimarron, and for a little while their agency should be located there, and when the whites get settled about them, then they will come upon the reservation. You heard them talk last year, and they say the same now. Part of the Cimarron is bought; they don't want to stay on it, but further off.

Mr. BRUNOT. I do not think the President will allow them to stay in New Mexico long. All the time, when there are white people about, when anything bad is done, whether it is done by whites or Indians, the Indians are blamed with it. Suppose there are some farmers living about where the Indians are; suppose they are good men, and a bad white man comes along, and takes some horses and gets off with them; if nobody sees him, then the people all think the Indians took them. Suppose a Mexican does something bad, the whites think it is the Indians. If a Cheyenne or Arapahoe comes and takes stock, the whites think it is the Indians who live near them. That is why, when Indians and whites live together, there is trouble among them. The President knows that the Utes are the white man's friends, and he is the friend of the Utes, and he wants to have the Utes so situated that these troubles will not come. With some Indians, when the President thinks it is best for them to do anything he wishes, he sends his soldiers and makes them do it, but with some Indians, instead of sending the soldiers to make them do it, he sends some one whom he knows is their friend to tell them what he wants, and so he has sent me to tell the Utes what is best for them, and what he wants them to do. I have told the New Mexican Utes what I am sure would be good for them, and I think it would be good to put it in the paper, if we make a paper, about the mountains. But if they think they know better, and do not want to put it in the paper, I think they had better pick one or two good men, and let them go with Ouray to Washington, and tell the President what they think about it; but that need not interfere with the bargain about these mountains, and this matter about the mountains had better be settled now.

JOSÉ MARIA. I think, as Curecante said, our agency had better be on the Dry Cimarron.

Mr. BRUNOT. I want to remind the New Mexico Utes of the treaty of 1868. I had nothing to do with making it, but it is put into my hands with the names of the Indians signed to it. The third article in it says——

OURAY. I understand it, but they are cutting off our lines, and they are not according to our agreement.

Mr. BRUNOT. Do the New Mexican Utes understand what I say? I want them to see their treaty. It was made in 1868, five years ago, and according to this, the Utes in New Mexico agreed to give up all claim to any land outside of the reservation. What I want them to know is, that all these five years the President has been kind in permitting them to stay just where they wanted to, and it seems to me the President has been kind in not making them do what the treaty says. That is the way it looks to a friend who did not make the treaty; and now, when the President thinks it is good for them to come on the reservation, they ought to listen to him. The names that are signed to the treaty I will get Mr. Adams to read, so that we will know what chiefs signed the treaty. Do you wish to hear them?

[A protracted discussion followed; those who signed the treaty objected to the reading of their names; Ouray insisting on having the names read; the Southern Utes specially objecting, the Tabequaches taking the part of Ouray; the southern Indians saying the treaty was a bad paper for them, and wanting to throw it out and make a new one.]

Mr. BRUNOT. You men are all brothers. You belong to the same people. What is good for one is good for all. You should all try and help each other, and when a friend talks to you about what he thinks is good for all of you, you should all listen and all think about it, and see what is best for all. There may be some things that some of you do not like, but then if it is good for all the rest they ought to give it up for the general good. Perhaps there is something I think is not good for me, but if it is good for everybody else I submit to it. I know I cannot have everything my way, if everybody else thinks differently. So it is all over the world; each must give up a little for what is good for all. Sometimes, when men are all trying to come to one mind, it is difficult, and takes a little time, but if they try to agree, and when they see what is good for the greatest numbers, then they agree to it. Now, we have talked about this treaty. I told you the President was kind in permitting a portion of the Utes to do what they had agreed not to do. They agreed to come on the reservation, and he permitted them to remain in New Mexico. Perhaps some of the Utes did not like that treaty, but if the chiefs agreed to it and signed their names to it, they ought to submit to it. I want to know which of the chiefs signed that paper; it does not make much difference now, because the paper is all there; but I want to know the names, and am going to have them read, and if we make another paper, it will have some things in it I will want everybody to understand; and if we make it we will have the chiefs and everybody else sign it, and that is why I want all the bands to agree to do the same thing.

Mr. Adams then read all the names signed to the treaty.

Mr. BRUNOT. Before the treaty of 1868 was made, in 1863, five years before, there was another treaty with the Tabequaches. That treaty said there was to be money given for ten years; that ten years is done this year; this is the last year for paying the money that was in that treaty; but the money and goods promised in this treaty (1868) is for twenty-five years more. Because the first treaty runs out with this year is another good reason why I think it is good for the Utes to sell the mountains and have something come to them for them. The New Mexican Utes do not come much into these mountains and do not care much about them; the other Utes that live up here care much about them; but I think if both kinds of Utes do what is good for all, they will agree to sell the mountains, and the New Mexican Utes, and those that live here will all get the benefit, and that is the most important matter for you to think about now. You know that it makes no difference to me about these mountains. I do not want anything that is in them; I have all I want a long way off. It is not for me or any white friends of mine that I am talking to you about this matter. It is because I know it is good for the Utes to do this; and that it will be good for your children after you, and now is the best time for you to do it. Suppose we talk about little things instead of this great matter, until the time is passed and I have to go away; and then, if trouble comes between the Utes and the miners, if it begins before the year ends, what will happen—where will it end? It will be too late then to settle it so that the Utes and their children will have goods and such things as they need come from it forever. There are many whites in this country with whom I have talked who are friends of the Utes; they tell me they like the Utes; but there are bad people who have no interest in the country, who try to make trouble with them. I know what those bad people think about it. If they could get trouble up with the Utes, and soldiers had to be sent in to settle the trouble, the Utes would be killed, and they could then get both the mountains and the farms that belong to you. That is what bad people think; perhaps it may be so, perhaps not; but what is the use of taking any chances like those, when, if you sell the mountains, you can have something for yourselves and your children for all time. This treaty gives the Utes $30,000 per year for twenty-five years longer. Now, in twenty-five years, perhaps Ouray, Curicante, and the older chiefs may be dead and gone. I may be dead and gone, but still some of these young men and the children will be living, and some of them will have little children; but when the twenty-five years have passed the money will be gone, and they will have none. Suppose we let that treaty stand just as it is for twenty-five years, and you agree to sell a piece of this reservation, taking in all these mountains where the miners are going, and the President agrees to pay for that land $25,000 every year; not for ten years or twenty-five years only, but forever, as long as the country lasts, so that your children and all the Utes that come after them will have something after this treaty is ended, and forever after. It would begin after the treaty was approved by Congress, and would go on forever. I want to know if there is a single Ute here who does not know in his heart that it would be good for you; I am sure it would; I know that would be good for the Utes. If I did not think it would be good for you, I would not be here to talk about it. I do not want you to sell the lands at the lower part of the reservation, the farming-lands. I want you to keep those lands, so that the Indians who like to be in a warm country in the south, can have a good place. I do not want you to sell the good lands on the Gunnison; I want those who live there to have a good place. I do not want you to sell the farming-land in the Uncompagre Park. I want the Indians who go there to have a good place. But what I think it is good for you to sell, is the land that lies between the good land on the south and the Uncompagre Park. If you are afraid some day somebody might say you have no right to go through their land, you can keep a strip of say ten miles wide on the west side, leading from one part to the other, or may be twenty miles. I think you understand what I think is good for you; but I know I am not telling you what many white people want me to tell you. Many white people would want me to say to you, you ought to sell the good farming-lands on the south, and some would want me to ask you to sell the Gunnison, and some would want me to ask you to sell the Uncompagre. I would not ask you to do any of these things, because I know a time will come when the Utes will want land to raise stock, as the white people do, and you must have that country for it. But I do advise you to sell the mountain country; it will be better for you to do so, and you will never be sorry for it.

CURICANTE. It would be well for us to have our agency on the Dry Cimarron. I am talking for the southern Indians, and I can talk to the President about it. What wrong can we do, or what wrong have we done, that we should not stay there?

Mr. BRUNOT. You must understand that I want to do what is good for the Utes, and if I make any agreement I want it also to be one that Congress will agree to. Suppose I was to put into the agreement what Curicante wants, and some little thing somebody else wants. I could put it in—it would not make any difference to me; but Congress would not agree to it, and the agreement would be at an end. For this reason I must make an agreement as good as I can for the Utes, but it must be one that I think Congress will approve. When I know myself that the Government at Washington wants the Indians to leave a place in which they want to stay, if I put it in a paper that they were to stay, Congress might not agree to it. But this I can agree to, and I think it will suit Curicante, the New Mexico Utes, and all the Utes: If we make a bargain for the mountain country, I will agree to say in the paper the Southern Utes shall have an agency on the southern part of the reservation as soon as the President shall say for them to go there. Then, if we make that agreement, Curicante can go with Ouray to see the President. He can ask the President to let them stay in New Mexico a little longer, and the President can do as he wants about it.

SAMORA. In the Cimarron there are but few settlers, and it is not necessary to have a contract to permit us to stay there, but only permission to remain there while it is sparsely settled.

Mr. BRUNOT. What Samora says is very good; but if we put in the contract that when they come away from there they shall have an agency on the reservation, it will be better. But we will say nothing about Cimarron in the contract; but when you go to Washington and tell the President what you tell me, if he says you can stay there a little while longer, it is all right.

OURAY. I tell Curicante that you cannot make an agreement to give an agency at Cimarron, for Congress might not approve of it; but if he thinks they ought to stay there, that he should go to Washington and tell this to the President, and he can let them stay if he wishes.

Mr. BRUNOT. Yes, that is best; but it must not interfere with the bargain we make. Here is Mautchick; I would like to know what he thinks of it. Does he not think my plan is a good one?

OURAY. They are talking about the business of the Muaches, and we tell Curicante that he had better go to Washington and have it attended to.

Mr. BRUNOT. I suppose the Utes have been talking the matter over, the Muaches and all the rest. It is just the same as it is in Congress. When a matter comes up they talk about it. Each says what he thinks about it, and then they take a vote; and when they take a vote, perhaps it shows a great many agree to the proposition; and if there are more in favor of it than are opposed to it, the smaller side gives it up, and all agree to it, and it becomes a law; and even if some do not like it, they agree to it because the majority want it. That is the way it ought to be among the Utes. You all have the same interest; you are all brothers; ten or a dozen ought not to stop what is good for all the rest. After it has been talked over, all ought to agree to the same thing. I hope the Utes will come to the same mind, just as they do in Congress, and the few who do not like it will give up to the greater number; that is the sensible and true way to do. I think you all understand the matter. But you have not told me what is the opinion of the majority. I want to know what the large number think, as well as what the few think.

OURAY. The business with the Muaches is what is stopping it.

Mr. BRUNOT. I have told the Utes what I think is right about that, in order that the future may be taken care of, and that they may have an agency at a future time. I will put in the paper that they may have another agency on the lower portion of the reservation. I will not put it in the paper that that agency is to be made to-day, or next year; but I will say that the agency shall be made whenever the President thinks it best to put it there. The New Mexico Utes will send their men to Washington, and they will tell the President they want to stay a while at Cimarron. They will tell the President there are few whites there; that they are doing no harm, and would like to stay there a few years longer. If the President says they can stay there longer, it is all right. There will be nothing in the paper to interfere with it; but if he will not let them stay there, I cannot help it. I want to tell you now very seriously, if you go to Washington to ask the President to let you stay at the Cimarron, and you say to him, "We prevented the Utes doing what is good for them," he will say to you, "Go to the reservation, or I will send my soldiers and make you go." But look at the other side, and see how much better, if the New Mexico Utes join with the other Utes, and do what is good for all the tribe, and then go and tell the President, "We have done what is good for all the Utes, and we would like to stay in New Mexico for a while longer," would he not be more likely to grant your request? Everybody knows that would be the best way. Curicante knows that would be the best way. If we can all agree about this, that would be for the good of the whole Ute tribe. Then, whoever goes to Washington can say, "We are trying to do what the President wants; but we want to stay on the Cimarron; there are but few whites there; but when the whites come there, then we will go to the reservation." The President would be more likely to grant the request. I want to tell what happened to me before I came here. The President asked me to go and tell some of the Sioux Indians that they must move their agency. When I went there we had a council. I told them they ought to move their agency, because it was by the river, and bad whites brought whisky to them, and did them harm. The first thing they said was, "If you give us so many guns, and flour, and things the white men have, we will move the agency; but we will not do it without you do." What did I say to them? I said the President has plenty of guns; but they have bullets in them for those who do wrong. When the President and Congress want their white friends to do what is right, they tell them, and they do it, because Congress knows what is best for them; and it is the same way with you. I said to the Sioux, "You pretend to be the friends of the President, and if you do not move the agency he will send his soldiers and make you do it; and now the council is adjourned." The next morning they came and said, "We will do what you say; we will move up there, and will trust to the President to do what is best for us." And in two or three days they were moving, and they have gone now. It was very short work. But I do not come and talk that way to you. I do not say anything about guns and soldiers. I talk to you as one friend talks to another. I do not talk to you like I do to men who will not listen to reason. I know you listen, and I think you will decide it is all right. I talk to you as I would to my best white friends, because I know you are my friends; and all good white people know the Utes are their friends, and they want to do what is good for the Utes. I think you see what is the best. I think the Southern Utes will see it is best to settle this matter, and then go to the President and tell him about the Cimarron, and maybe he will do what they wish; and whatever a majority of the Utes agree upon, that will be right. If you want to talk about it among yourselves, talk; if you want to talk to me about it, I will hear what you have to say; but do not let this question about a few Utes staying a few years on the Cimarron interfere with this question, that is for the good of all the Utes for all time. I would like every Ute man that wanted to do what was not bad to have his own way. I would be glad if I could do just what I wanted to all the time; but I cannot. Often I have to give up what I think is best, on account of the opinion of other people. So it is with every man, whether a white man or a red man. So it is with some of the men here. They do not like to give up their opinion; but they think it best to give up for the good of all. I have not yet found out what you all think; perhaps I will find out that more of the Utes will say, as they did last year, "We do not want to sell this country." May-be not; but I want to know what a majority think about it.

OURAY. This is what all say: Curicante and all the camp will go to Cimarron; then they will go and see the President, and if the President allows them to stay, then it is all right, and if the President orders them to come to the reservation, it is all right. This is the opinion of all.

Mr. BRUNOT. Do I understand that they drop the question, and after the council they will go and see the President, and do as he decides?

OURAY. The Indians that belong there will go back, but Curicante will go from here to Washington to see the President.

Mr. BRUNOT. It is important that I understand it. I do not want to make a mistake. Shall I understand the New Mexico Utes agree to what the other Utes do, and then Curicante and the others will go to see the President; or do they mean to go away and leave the matter of the land unsettled?

OURAY. Show us on the map where the mines are.

(Mr. Brunot then showed them on the map the lines of the reservation and the new lines he proposed to make.)

OURAY. The southern line is not as we agreed to. We agree to let the mines go.

Mr. BRUNOT. We had better say nothing about the southern line. That is one of the things you have to tell the President about.

OURAY. The New Mexico Indians claim the part in New Mexico—all below the river San Juan.

Mr. BRUNOT. I propose to leave fifteen or twenty miles above the Colorado line, so there will still be a country there for them. (He then explained, with the map, fully what he proposed to do.)

OURAY. We are willing to sell only the mountains where the miners are, and not to sell any of the valleys. (A full discussion over the map followed, the Indians freely expressing their opinion.)

Mr. BRUNOT. Maybe these mountains are not just right on the map; the white men were not there.

OURAY. The mines we will sell, but the Weeminuches want the southern boundary-line fixed. The mountains are large and the Rio Grande rises in them. Are there any mines on the side near the San Miguel River?

Mr. BRUNOT. The reason I want to put that part in is, there may be mines there, and then there would be the same trouble again. I do not know anything about the country.

OURAY. The mountains with mines we will sell, but those where the mines are not in we will not sell.

Mr. BRUNOT. I did not come to please the miners; but what I want is to save the Utes from all trouble with the miners.

OURAY. Take the head of the Rio Grande and its tributaries, and the stream that runs on the other side of the mountains, we will not sell.

Mr. BRUNOT. You will have to decide on some line that will show where the miners can go.

OURAY. The heads of the stream that run into the Rio Grande will be the bounds. The contract we make, a copy of it must be in the hands of the agent, one in the hands of the chief, and one you take to the President. We will not sell on the San Miguel. There must be posts put in that the miners cannot pass.

Mr. BRUNOT. We must understand each other better or our talk will be for nothing.

If the Utes sell a portion of their country, the price is regulated by the quantity they sell.

OURAY. We have no interest in selling any of it.

Mr. BRUNOT. If you think it is not your interest to sell it, you must not sell any of it.

OURAY. We want to sell the portion around the head of the Rio Grande, and we want security that the miners will not go any further.

Mr. BRUNOT. I could not make any agreement for a little piece of country where the miners only are now.

OURAY. The piece of land we offer to sell is not so small; it is large. The mountains are long, and where the miners are we will sell to the edge of the mountains, and none of the bottom-lands.

Mr. BRUNOT. The difficulty in such a contract is, there will always be quarreling as to where the lines are, and there will be more trouble than there is now.

OURAY. It must be measured, and the lines all marked so all can see them.

Mr. BRUNOT. It would take five years and one hundred men to do that. What I think is, that the Utes had better sell all the mountain country. Suppose I were to make a contract for where the miners are now, it would take all the Utes and one thousand soldiers to stand around it to see that the miners did not go to the other mountains, and instead of stopping the trouble it would make it worse. The mountains west of it, the miners would be hunting mines in. Suppose there are no mines in the part west, and suppose the Utes make a bargain for it.

OURAY. We cannot do what you want.

Mr. BRUNOT. But I want you to hear what I have to say. Suppose you sell the mountains, and if there is no gold in them, then it would be a benefit to you. The Utes get the pay for them and the Americans would stay away. But suppose there are mines there, it will not stop the trouble; we could not keep the people away.

OURAY. Why cannot you stop them; is not the Government strong enough to keep its agreements with us?

Mr. BRUNOT. What Ouray says is reasonable. I would like to stop them; but Ouray knows it is hard to do.

OURAY. In regard to the mountains around the mines, we do not say anything, but to take in so much land we will not agree to it. We know what the Government has to do by the treaty, and we know how you are talking about the trouble. You are a commissioner on the part of the Government; we are on our own part. If you do not want to buy or we do not want to sell, it is all right. The whites can go and take the gold and come out again. We do not want them to build houses there.

Mr. BRUNOT. I told you I would not have come if I had not wanted to benefit the Utes. I wanted to befriend you. I do not think I would be doing what was good for the Utes if I did what Ouray wants. It need not prevent the contract from being made, but I will not make it. I will tell the President, and he may send somebody else, and they may buy just what the Utes want to sell now, and in another year they will find the miners as bad somewhere else, and then they may send somebody else. You understand why I will not agree to it. But it is all right if you do not make an agreement with me; it will not make any difference; I will try and have you protected as well as I can. I will do as I did before. I will ask the President to drive the miners away as I did last fall, but a thousand other men will tell the President to let them alone. Perhaps he will do as I say, perhaps not.

OURAY. That is all impossible. The whites are not my brothers; they can do as they please.

Mr. BRUNOT. I want you to think about this a little more. Last fall you said you would not sell any of your land. I thought you were right in not wanting to sell the farming-lands, but you have now decided you ought to sell some of it. If you think a little longer, you may see the mountains are of no use to you, and you may decide it is best to provide for your children and sell them.

The council here adjourned.

Third day—Tuesday, September 9.

Owing to the absence of both interpreters, no council was held to-day.

Fourth day—Wednesday, September 10.

After waiting till two o'clock for the return of either of the interpreters, council convened, with Doctor Phillips as Spanish interpreter.

Prior to opening the council, the Indians spent two hours in consultation among themselves, Ouray explaining by the map the proposed lines.

At four o'clock p. m., in opening the council,

Mr. BRUNOT said: There were some Indians traveling once with their tents and all they had. They came to a river; it looked high and dangerous; some thought it was dangerous to cross, others thought not. They did not know what they had better do about it. Then they decided to call upon the Great Spirit to help them. They put their praying men on the bank of the river, and they all went over safely. That is what the Indians said; they crossed over and all was right with them. I am going to ask the Great Spirit to help us, and perhaps we may all come to one mind about this.

Mr. Brunot then led in prayer.

Mr. Brunot then said this letter of the Commissioner told me to come and make a bargain with the Utes for all the country south of the thirty-eighth degree, (showing it on the map.) When I come and know how things are, I would rather the Utes should keep some of the country on the south, (showing it on the map,) because I think it is good for them. As the friend of the Utes, I have made some marks to show the best thing I can do for them that I think Congress will approve. If I thought Congress would agree to it, and I thought it was good for you, I would mark the lines just where you want them. If I were to do that it would not be of any use. Congress would not agree to it, and it would be just as it was before I came here. I have made the lines in the very best place that I can for the Utes that Congress will agree to. If you agree to that, I will be glad, because I think it will be good for you and good for everybody. It is for you to say what we shall do. If you agree to that, I think it will be all right; if you do not agree to it, it will be all right so far as I am concerned, for it will not be my fault. I came and did the best I could for you. It is your country, and you can do just as you please about it. I am sure that if you agree to make the contract I have offered, it will be good for you; and whether you do it or not I am all the same your friend, and I hope you and the whites will always be friends. Whatever happens hereafter, I am willing to stand by the words I have said, and if you let me go away in a day or two, you cannot blame me or the President, for he has done all that he could. He has sent me to do what is right, and to settle the question about these mountains. If the spring comes, and the miners come in crowds and want to go into all parts of the reservation, it may then be too late to settle the question in a friendly way. Sometimes war begins when nobody wants it, because some bad people do something they ought not. When the war began between the people in the North and in the South, nobody wanted it, but bad people brought it on; good people did not want it, but bad people brought it on, and good people had to suffer. It was the same way with the poor fellows on the western coast; some bad people began the trouble, and see where it ended with the Modocs. After the trouble began, good people everywhere tried to stop it, but it was then too late, and it could not be stopped until now all of them are gone. Captain Jack was not a bad man at the beginning, but bad men brought the trouble on, and good men could not stop it.

OURAY. We believe that.

Mr. BRUNOT. I am talking about this because I am sorry in my heart that such things come, but there are bad men and they bring about such things, and men must be as careful as they can, and make every effort to prevent such things. You all know how careful you are to do no harm, that these bad men cannot have any reason to do wrong to you. Although you do that which is right, your agent and your friends have to defend you against these men. In spite of all the friends of the Indians in this country can do, and they say the Indians are good, bad men are trying to bring about trouble with you. Some men say, Let this matter go on; let it alone and it will fix itself; there will be trouble with the Utes and then we will get all their country for nothing. Perhaps it may be so and perhaps not, but this I know, it is better to make a good bargain, of which your children will get the benefit, than to take any risk. I think that is good sense, and that is the talk of one friend to another. If the white people go into these mountains it is right that you should get pay for them. If you sell the mountains the way I point out, and the Government agrees to pay you $25,000 per year as long as you and your descendants live, it will always be good. When that bargain is made, and if there is no gold there, and the white people do not want to stay there, you have the use of the mountains just the same, and the pay for them too. In some parts of the mountains, I do not know whether the white people would stay or not, but I fear they will want to go there; but if they do not stay there you get paid for it all the same. If you sell a big piece of country, I can pay more for it than if you sell a little piece. Some places they will go in and scrape the ground; they will not find any gold, and then they will go away.

OURAY. For that reason you require a large piece, and if they do not want it they will go away.

Mr. BRUNOT. For the large piece I can offer a large sum. Last year the commission that was here told me they were going to offer for all below the line of 38, (shown on the map,) and would pay you for ten years but little more each year than I now offer to pay each year forever. The Government did not tell me what to offer to the Utes.

I know what the commission last year proposed to offer, but because the Government did not tell me, I offer you the largest amount that I think the Government will agree to pay. That would be $25,000 per year, every year, forever. Besides that, I say that when the President thinks it is time, he will put an agency on the southern part of the reservation, and that will cost more money. The building of houses and what is wanted for an agency will not come out of the $25,000; that is the offer; that is the best I think Congress will agree to; if you agree to it, I will be very glad, and we will make out a paper with it all in it. We will make three copies; one for me to take to the President, one for Ouray, and one for the agent to keep, and all who agree to it will put their names to the paper. Ouray or some other chiefs would have to go and see the Indians who are not here, and get their names to the paper. Then Ouray will bring that paper to Washington, and one each of the Mauches, Capotes, and Weeminuches are to go with him, and they can tell the President that they want to stay on the Cimarron, and one of the Apaches could go, too, and tell the President what they want. I think you can understand that is all that I can offer, and I want you to say yes or no to-day. I want you to tell me this evening what you will do. We have talked it all over. You want to go to your camps, and I want to go to my home, a long way off, as soon as I can.

(Ouray here talked to his people for some time. A discussion followed as to the lines, the Indians saying some were farming inside the proposed lines.)

Mr. BRUNOT. If any Indians are now cultivating the soil in any part of the reservation, I will put it in the paper if you wish that they shall not be disturbed. I know very well that this arrangement will put you to some inconvenience, but that is why we offer a large sum of money. We have to look at things as they are and we must give up little things to accomplish great ones. You sell the country, and get a good price for it. The privilege of going across the country will not be taken from you. You can travel by all the roads.

OURAY. It is a large piece of country. We want the lines smaller, (making lines on the map taking in only where the miners now are.)

Mr. BRUNOT. As I said before, I would like to fix it. I see and understand what you would like, and I would like to fix it that way if I thought it would be agreed to by Congress. I want to do all I can for you. If I would do that, I will tell you what would happen. The report would go out, and everybody would say the Utes have sold their country, and the white people would come in crowds. Next winter the paper would go before Congress, and Congress would say no. That is not what he should have done; he should have bought all of these mountains. Congress would not agree to it, and the country would be so full of people we would never put them out, and the result would be, instead of helping the Utes, I would be only bringing on trouble, and rather than hurt you by what I do, I would prefer to go home and do nothing.

OURAY. There is plenty of game in the mountains. The majority are opposed to it. I am in favor of it, but it does not amount to anything.

Mr. BRUNOT. I understand Ouray to say the Utes are not willing to make the bargain with the lines I have pointed out. I could make a paper showing the lines you seem to be in favor of. Then the miners would come in there; not only those who break the laws, but those who do right; all would come in and the mountains would be filled with miners. Congress would not decide about the paper till next spring, and by that time the miners would be saying, "We want to go farther;" and a thousand people in Colorado would say I did not do right; and Congress would say the law they passed told me about buying all this country; and Congress would not agree to what I did; and when they look at the paper they would say they did not agree to it; and it would turn out, instead of having done something good for the Utes, the country would be full of miners and no bargain at all. Now, the way the matter stands, I have made the best offer that I can for the good of the Utes that Congress will agree to. I will have to shake hands and go home, and leave the bargain with the Utes, or somebody else to make.

OURAY. We do not wish to sell the part below, and we want the line farther east.

Mr. BRUNOT. I have done the best I can for you; it is all over, and we part good friends; and we may as well adjourn the council. I understand what you want. I have done what I think is best for you; it does not suit you, and I think we had better adjourn the council. We have had a long talk for nothing, but I guess it is all right. Perhaps there is something you do not know. I would say in the paper you could hunt in the part sold as long as there is any game in it. But I see you do not wish to agree to my proposition, and we will now close the council.

The council here adjourned.

Fifth day—Thursday, September 11.

There was no council held to-day, but the commission waited, expecting the Indians would decide to enter into the articles of convention, it being their opinion that a large proportion of the Utes were in favor of so doing, the principal men of the Tabequaches (Ouray's men) having expressed themselves as favorable to it. During the day the following articles of convention were prepared as embodying the views of the commission as to what ought to be done:

ARTICLES OF CONVENTION.

Articles of a convention made and entered into at the Los Pinos agency for the Ute Indians, on the 13th day of September, 1873, by and between Felix R. Brunot, commissioner in behalf of the United States, and the chiefs, head-men, and men of the Tabequache, Muache, Capote, Weeminuche, Yampa, Grand River, and Uintah bands of the Ute Indians, witnesseth: That whereas a treaty was made with the confederated bands of the Ute Nation on the second day of March, A. D. 1868, and proclaimed by the President of the United States on the sixth day of November, 1868, the second article of which defines by certain lines the limits of a reservation to be owned and occupied by the Ute Indians; and whereas, by act of Congress approved April 23, 1872, the Secretary of the Interior was "authorized and empowered to enter into negotiations with the Ute Indians in Colorado for the extinguishment of their right" to a certain portion of said reservation, and a commission was appointed on the first day of July, 1872, to conduct said negotiations; and whereas said negotiations having failed, owing to the refusal of said Indians to relinquish their right to any portion of said reservation, a new commission was appointed by the Secretary of the Interior by letter of June 2, 1873, to conduct said negotiation:

Now, therefore, Felix R. Brunot, commissioner in behalf of the United States, and the chiefs and people of the Tabequache, Muache, Capote, Weeminuche, Yampa, Grand River, and Uintah, the confederated bands of the Ute Nation, do enter into the following agreement:

ARTICLE I.

The confederated bands of the Ute Nation hereby relinquish to the United States all right, title, interest, and claim in and to the following-described portion of the reservation heretofore conveyed to them by the United States, viz: Beginning at a point on the eastern boundary of said reservation, fifteen miles due north from the southern boundary of the Territory of Colorado, and running thence west on a line parallel with the said southern boundary to a point on said line twenty miles due east of the western boundary of Colorado Territory; thence north by a line parallel with the said western boundary to a point ten miles north of the point where said line intersects the 38th parallel of north latitude; thence east to the eastern boundary of the reservation, and thence south along said boundary to the place of beginning: *Provided*, That if any part of the Uncompagre Park shall be found to extend south of the north line of said described country, the same is not intended to be included therein, and is hereby reserved and retained as a portion of the Ute reservation.

ARTICLE II.

The United States shall permit the Ute Indians to hunt upon said lands so long as the game lasts and the Indians are at peace with the white people.

ARTICLE III.

The United States agree to set apart and hold as a perpetual trust for the Ute Indians, a sum of money, or its equivalent in bonds, which shall be sufficient to produce the sum of twenty-five thousand dollars ($25,000) per annum; which sum of twenty-five thousand dollars per annum shall be disbursed or invested at the discretion of the President, or as he may direct, for the use and benefit of the Ute Indians, annually forever.

ARTICLE IV.

The United States agree, so soon as the President may deem it necessary or expedient, to erect proper buildings and establish an agency for the Weeminuche, Muache, and Capote bands of the Ute Indians, at some suitable point to be hereafter selected on the southern part of the reservation.

ARTICLE V.

All the provisions of the treaty of 1868 not altered by this agreement shall continue in force; and the following words from article two of said treaty, viz: "The United States now solemnly agree that no persons except those herein authorized to do so, and except such officers, agents, and employés of the Government as may be authorized to enter upon Indian reservations in discharge of duties enjoined by law, shall ever be permitted to pass over, settle upon, or reside in the territory" described in the article, "except as herein otherwise provided," are hereby expressly re-affirmed, except so far as they applied to the country herein relinquished.

ARTICLE VI.

In consideration of the services of Ouray, head chief of the Ute Nation, he shall receive a salary of one thousand dollars per annum for the term of ten years, or so long as he shall remain head chief of the Utes and at peace with the United States.

ARTICLE VII.

This agreement is subject to ratification or rejection by the Congress of the United States and the President.

Sixth day—Friday, September 12.

Many of the chiefs expressed themselves as willing to sign the articles of agreement, but it was thought best to wait until the head chief signed it. The Indians counseled in regard to it all day.

Seventh day—Saturday, September 13.

Ouray and all the principal men came and expressed a willingness to sign the articles of convention, provided after doing so some of the representative men of the different bands, accompanied by the secretary of the commission, should visit the country sold, and, if it proved to be mining and not farming land, then all the Indians should sign it; if the reverse was the case, then the agreement should be inoperative as lacking the assent of the necessary three-fourths of the tribe. The articles of convention were then signed by all the Indians present—being the chiefs and head-men of all the bands who had been represented in the council.

THOMAS K. CREE,
Secretary Special Ute Commission.

INTERVIEW WITH OURAY, CHIEF OF THE UTES.

CHEYENNE, WYO., *June* 24.

A dispatch was received from Charles Adams, agent of the Ute Indians at Los Pinos reservation, Colorado, saying that Ouray, head chief of the Utes, was at Denver and desired to see Mr. Brunot. We telegraphed him to come up.

JUNE 25.

Agent Adams and Ouray arrived at noon. The object of Ouray's visit was to hear what prospect there was of the recovery of his son, a young man who had been captured by the Sioux in a battle between them and the Utes on the Republican River, in Kansas, some ten years ago; since when he had not been able to hear anything of the boy, except that he learned from a Mexican woman, who had lived among the Sioux, that the captive boy was still alive.

On the visit of Mr. Brunot to the Ute agency, in 1872, Ouray had asked that an effort should be made to find him and restore him to his tribe. Subsequently we ascertained that the boy had been captured or passed into the hands of the Northern Arapahoes on the North Platte, and after several years had gotten among the Southern Arapahoes.

Before introducing the object of the visit, Mr. Brunot referred to a conversation he had had with Ouray at his agency, in which Ouray promised that he would find out the murderers of Miller—agent of the Navajoes—who had been killed by his Indians some months previously.

Mr. BRUNOT said. I am glad you found out about the men who killed Agent Miller.

OURAY. We killed one, the other escaped to the Moquis Pueblo village. They were Weeminuche Utes; the main band were up in Utah; these two had strayed behind; they followed Agent Miller and killed him to get his mules. They were out all summer, and were afraid to come in, and were almost starved. They eat up both the mules before we found them. I was sorry the one was killed; I wanted to bring him in and give him up to the agent to be punished. We followed the other one but could not catch him. If he ever comes back we will get him and bring him to the agent.

Mr. BRUNOT then explained to Ouray that when he was at the agency an officer with soldiers was then hunting the murderers; and after Ouray had promised to find them, the officer agreed, if Mr. Brunot would write him a letter and ask him to do so, to go back and let Ouray find the Indians who had committed the murder.

OURAY said at that time none of the Utes knew who had killed Mr. Miller.

Mr. BRUNOT then told him of the efforts he had been making to find his boy; told him he had been among the Sioux and had heard where the boy was, and hoped that he would be able to get him and take him to the Utes.

OURAY said the Government is strong, and can do what it wants; if the Government will do what it can for me and get my boy, I will do what I can for the Government in regard to our lands.

Mr. BRUNOT. We are trying to do what we can about the boy. If the Utes had a boy among them that we wanted, the Utes would hide him away. We have to be very careful. The Arapahoes may run him away; we must be careful. We want to get your boy home; and whatever can be done to get him we will do. It matters not how much money it costs, or how much trouble it is, we will do all we can to get him, and we want to do what is right and kind for the Indians. When I saw you some of the Indians talked bad, but I knew they did not know any better, and I thought some day they would find out what was right, and they will find out that the President is their friend and wants to do right. How soon do you want to have a council about your land?

Mr. ADAMS. Ouray said it would be best for you to come and talk with them, and he proposed we should come to Cheyenne and talk with you. Last fall they opposed the removal of their agency; now they want it moved fifty miles west. I have to run two establishments; one for our cattle and one for the agency. By putting the agency at Gunnison River, we could do away with one of them. It is a lower and warmer country, and could be cultivated. We are farming at the herding camp now. The Indian camp is only one day's ride from the proposed new agency site. Now the Indians cannot come to the agency in winter at all.

Mr. BRUNOT. I think if the agency is moved it ought to be put where it will not have to be moved again.

OURAY. We do not care about the mountains, but the Uncompagre country we will not sell. If we sell the mountains we fear the whites will bring stock into the Uncompagre country, and then trouble will begin again. If a line could be made, and all the whites kept inside of it, we would sell the mining region. At present, the Colorado people only want the mines. We want to know that our country will be kept for us.

Mr. BRUNOT. Personally I do not care about your selling, and would not have gone last year, only I went to see that no injustice was done the Indians. I thought when I was there you had better listen to the commissioners, and thus save trouble. I have no fancy for the miners who go where they have no right to go. Have there been more miners going in?

Mr. ADAMS. Yes. Ouray keeps his people away from them.

Mr. BRUNOT. I asked the President to make an order to drive the miners out. The President heard Ouray had changed his mind and would sell the mines, so it was thought best to stop the execution of the order for a while.

Mr. ADAMS. Ouray does not know the order was countermanded.

Mr. BRUNOT. We went to the Shoshones last year; they have mines in their country. They said the country was of no use to them, and they sold it, and now the miners are their friends. They wanted to be paid in cattle; they are to get them, so many each year. They are all very much pleased about it. I was to see the Sioux two years ago, and they had their agency on the bank of the river. I told them it was a bad place—they would have trouble with the whites. I wanted them to be put it in a good place where the Government would protect them. They would not do so then, but I went this time to them and they said they would put it where I wanted, as they now saw what I told them was true. I want the Sioux to promise not to come over the railroad. I do not want them to fight with the Utes, or anybody else.

OURAY. I would like to see you come down there, but no one from the Territory to come with you. Everybody from the Territory is interested in buying my country. It is best you come down and keep the matter quiet, and not let the people of the Territory know of it.

Mr. BRUNOT. They wrote me a letter from Washington, and asked who I wanted to go. I wrote and told them if they sent anybody there they had better send those who do not live in the Territory. I told them if I was to go and hold a council I did not want any of the whites who were there before to be permitted to come. They sent me a letter and told me there was a man named Powell, who, they thought, was a good man to go—what do you think of him?

OURAY. I would not object if Mr. Powell suits you, but I do not wish any one who lives in the Territory to come.

Mr. BRUNOT. He is the explorer, and does not belong to the Territory.

OURAY. I would not object to him.

Mr. BRUNOT. Do you think a council could be held and the whites kept away?

Mr. ADAMS. I think so. Ouray has given orders to his men to keep away from the miners. I heard some of the parties who were at the council last year would be back again.

Mr. BRUNOT. I asked that none should come unless invited by the commission. I said that if Ouray wanted me to go, and the President asked me, if I could do any good to Ouray's people I would go. I said I would not go unless Ouray sent word that it would be of some use for me to come.

Mr. ADAMS. You would want to see all the Ute Indians we can get to attend?

Mr. BRUNOT. I would want to see all the Indians who can be got together.

OURAY. Where are you going now?

Mr. BRUNOT. To see the Crows. How long before you could get your people together, and when would be the best time for me to come?

OURAY. How long will you be at the Crows? You know how soon you could get to the Ute agency. In August the Utes will be hunting, but the captains can come in.

Mr. BRUNOT. If a treaty is made it is necessary three-fourths of the people agree to it.

OURAY. I will talk with them and do what I can.

Mr. BRUNOT. It used to be just what the chief said; but this treaty is different; it says three-fourths of the adult male Indians, and I want the treaty carried out. From now till August we will try and get Ouray's boy; and, if we can, we will take him with us. If we cannot get him, then Ouray must not be too sorry; we will still try and get him. I hope we will get him then.

OURAY. Bring the boy if you can; if you cannot I will be sorry.

Mr. BRUNOT. We will do the best we can. Your boy talks English.

OURAY. A brother of Friday's captured the boy; he died, and Friday took the boy.

Mr. BRUNOT. The boy's name is Friday?

OURAY. Several years ago, when the Arapahoes came to Denver, I heard there was a Ute boy called Friday; but I never could see him.

Mr. BRUNOT. They kept him away?

OURAY. I heard two or three years ago from a Mexican woman that the boy was alive. I would not know him.

Mr. BRUNOT. When Ouray looked for the boy at Denver the Arapahoes kept him away, and we want to get him before they hide him now. I think you had better not tell your people the boy is coming, for if he does not, they will think something is wrong.

OURAY. I understand. I want to see the boy. The Utes understand you now. They have learned that you have worked good for other Indians before, and we think you will work good for us. I will tell them what you say, and they will know you are our friend.

Respectfully submitted.

THOMAS K. CREE,
Secretary.

E.

REPORT OF THE COMMISSION TO NEGOTIATE WITH THE CROW TRIBE OF INDIANS.

SIR: We have the honor to report that under our appointment as special commissioners to negotiate with the Crow tribe of Indians, contained in your letter of May 1, 1873, viz:

Letter of the honorable Secretary of the Interior.

"DEPARTMENT OF THE INTERIOR,
"*Washington, D. C., May* 14, 1873,

"SIR: I have received your letter of the 21st ultimo, recommending the appointment of a special commission to visit the Crow tribe of Indians with a view of negotiating an agreement with the chiefs and head-men of said tribe of Indians in the Territory of Montana for the surrender of their reservation in said Territory, or of such part thereof as may be consistent with the welfare of said Indians, as provided by the act of March 3, 1873.

"In compliance with said recommendation, I hereby appoint Hon. F. R. Brunot, of the board of Indian commissioners, *Col. E. C. Kemble, of New York, and H. E. Alvord, of Virginia, to constitute said commission, for the purpose named by you.

"Messrs. Kemble and Alvord will be allowed compensation at the rate of $8 per day, in addition to their actual and necessary expenses, while engaged in the performance of this duty. Mr. Brunot will be allowed only his actual expenses.

"You will be pleased to prepare instructions for the guidance of said commission, a draught of which you will submit to this Department for its approval.

"Very respectfully, your obedient servant,

"C. DELANO,
"*Secretary.*

"The COMMISSIONER OF INDIAN AFFAIRS."

and the instructions of the honorable Commissioner of Indian Affairs contained in the following letter:

Letter of the honorable Commissioner of Indian Affairs.

"DEPARTMENT OF THE INTERIOR,
"OFFICE OF INDIAN AFFAIRS,
"*Washington, D. C., May* 31, 1873.

"SIR: By the terms of an act of Congress approved March 3, 1873, it is provided: 'That the Secretary of the Interior be, and he is hereby, authorized to negotiate with the chiefs and head-men of the Crow tribe of Indians in the Territory of Montana for the surrender of their reservation in said Territory, or of such part thereof as may be consistent with the welfare of said Indians: *Provided,* That any such negotiation shall leave the remainder of said reservation in compact form and in good locality for farming purposes, having within it a sufficiency of good land for farming, and a sufficiency for water and timber; and if there is upon such reservation a locality where fishing could be valuable to the Indians, to include the same, if practicable; and the Secretary shall report his action, in pursuance of this act, to Congress, at the next session thereof, for its confirmation or rejection.'

"Pursuant to the provisions of the foregoing act, and in compliance with the directions contained in letter of the honorable Secretary of the Interior, under date of the 14th instant, you are informed that a special commission has been appointed, consisting of yourself, as chairman, in conjunction with *Col. E. C. Kemble, of New York, and H. E. Alvord, of Virginia, to visit the Crow tribe of Indians and negotiate an agreement with them to the end that the objects of said act may be affected.

"You will proceed to the Crow agency, and, after consultation with the United States agent for the tribe, will assemble the Indians in open council, at some point on the reservation deemed most desirable for the purpose, and explain to them the purport and objects of the act of March 3, 1873, and of your visit.

"The Crow reserve was established pursuant to the treaty with them concluded May 7, 1868, and is bounded as follows: 'Commencing where the 107th degree of longitude west of Greenwich crosses the south boundary of Montana Territory; thence north along said 107th meridian to the mid-channel of the Yellowstone River; thence up said mid-channel of the Yellowstone, to the point where it crosses the said southern boundary of Montana, being the 45th degree of north latitude; and thence east along said parallel of latitude to the place of beginning.'

"Such an extent of territory being greatly in excess of the quantity required for the necessities of the Indians, and the northern boundary thereof, throughout its entire length, being in close proximity to the proposed line of the Northern Pacific Railroad, it is desirable that the Indians should relinquish to the Government at least a portion thereof, and consent to confine themselves within more circumscribed limits.

"It is with this end primarily in view that you should conduct your negotiations under the foregoing appointment.

"You will explain to the Indians that it is the desire of the Government that they should adopt agricultural and pastoral pursuits to the end that they may in time become self-sustaining and prosperous, and that in order to encourage them in the cultivation of such pursuits all possible aid will be afforded them in the way of stock and agricultural implements.

"Should you find them willing to relinquish upon rasonable terms any portion of their reservation to the United States, you will cause written articles of agreement to that effect to be prepared and duly signed by the chiefs and head-men of the tribe, and by each member of the commission. Such agreement must clearly describe the portion of the reservation ceded and the consideration to be paid therefor, expressed in such form as to admit of the largest discretion being exercised by the Department in relation to the manner of investing or expending such consideration for the welfare of the Indians.

* Changed to Gen. E. Whittlesey, of Washington, and James Wright, M. D., of Montana.

"Portions of the reservation are very mountainous, and undoubtedly rich in minerals of different kinds. Many mining claims are now being worked by white settlers on the reserve, and, as reported by the agent, some of them were located before the country was set apart as a reserve for the Crows, and the miners in consequence claim priority of right. In view of these facts the agent has also heretofore recommended that the Crows should be induced to cede that portion of their reservation lying between the waters of the Big Horn and Yellowstone Rivers, as the only way in which satisfactory adjustment can be made of the difficulties that will otherwise inevitably arise between the miners and the Indians. You will, however, in negotiating with the Indians, be governed by your own judgment as to the portion most desirable for them to cede, taking due care that the portion retained by them shall be of a character best adapted to their necessities, with the end in view of their eventually becoming an agricultural and pastoral people.

"Care should also be exercised, in negotiating any agreement, that the portion of the reservation retained by the Indians for their use and occupancy shall be in compact form and in good locality for agricultural purposes, due regard being paid to the quantity of tillable land within its limits, as well as the sufficiency of the supply of water and timber. Also, if practicable, to include such fisheries as may be of value to the Indians as a means of furnishing them with supplies of food.

"It must also be clearly understood that any agreement made with the Indians will be of validity only upon its ratification by Congress, and this fact should be impressed at every opportunity thoroughly and forcibly upon the minds of the Indians, in order that no misunderstanding relative thereto may exist on their part.

"Another matter to which you will give your attention is the contemplated change in the location of the Crow agency. The present location thereof is understood to be highly unfavorable and unsatisfactory to the Indians, being remote from timber, and having an insufficient quantity of good agricultural land in its vicinity, as well as being greatly exposed to high winds.

"You will consult with Superintendent Wright and Agent Pease in relation to this matter, and will obtain all the information in your power as to the most suitable point for locating such agency, and report your views concerning the same to this office.

"The duties enjoined upon you in the foregoing instructions will be entered upon immediately after the completion of the duties assigned you as chairman of the special commission to visit and negotiate with the Northern Sioux, parties to the treaty of 1868.

"You will be allowed your actual necessary expenses while engaged in the performance of the duties assigned you, vouchers for which, when practicable, should be obtained and submitted to this office with your account.

"You will submit a detailed report of your proceedings at the earliest day practicable, accompanied by such form of written agreement as may have been entered into with the Indians.

"Very respectfully, your obedient servant,

"EDW'D P. SMITH,
"*Commissioner.*

"Hon. FELIX R. BRUNOT,
"*Chairman Special Commission, Pittsburgh, Pa.*"

the special commission to negotiate a treaty with the Crow Indians have the honor to make the following report:

In accordance with the instructions of the honorable Commissioner of Indian Affairs, Felix R. Brunot, chairman of the commission, accompanied by Thomas K. Cree, secretary, arrived at Bozeman, July 7, 1873. Arrangements were at once made to gather all the Crow Indians at the agency for a council.

On the 29th of July, General E. Whittlesey and Dr. James Wright, members of the commission, arrived at Bozeman. The next day a conference of the commission was held. The chairman read to the commission the letter of the honorable Secretary of the Interior, of date May 14; the letter of the honorable Commissioner of Indian Affairs, of date May 31; report of Agent Pease, of date April 30; and the treaty made with the Crows at Fort Laramie, May 7, 1868.

July 31 we drove to the Crow agency, found that the main body of Indians had not yet arrived, but some thirty chiefs and head-men, representing the Mountain and River Crows, had been sent forward to meet the commission.

The next morning we had a conference with them, Blackfoot, the second chief of the Mountain Crows, being the spokesman. He informed us that the main body of the Indians were encamped some distance from the agency, and could not arrive before the 8th or 10th of August. He accounted for their delay in getting to the agency, after the arrival of the messenger in their camp, by the fact that they had been fighting a large war-party of the Sioux, who were following them, necessitating great care in the moving of the women, children, and camp-equipage; to the prevalence of sickness from which many had died, and to the high stage of water, which delayed them considerably, as there was great danger in crossing the swollen streams. He told the commission that the party would return to the camp the following day, and would come back with it to the agency as expeditiously as possible. A full report of this conference will be found in the accompanying documents.

The main body of the River Crows left Benton in good season to reach the agency, but, as we were informed, when some four days on their journey were stopped by parties interested in keeping them in the vicinity of the trading-posts on the Missouri River.

The main camp arrived at the agency August 8. The erysipelas was prevailing among them in a contagious form; many had died from it, and Iron Bull and Blackfoot, the two principal chiefs, were both sick. Long Horse, the third chief and most prominent warrior, was in mourning for the death of his brother, who had been killed a few days before in the encounter with the Sioux.

The issue of provisions prevented the holding of a council the next day, the Indians giving as a reason for not wishing to come into council the sickness of Iron Bull and Blackfoot.

The council convened on the 11th of August. There were present, in addition to the members of the commission, General Sweitzer, commandant of Fort Ellis, Dr. Lightfoot, U. S. A., Captain Tyler and Lieutenant Rowe, of Company F, Second Cavalry, Major Pease, agent for the Crows, Nelson Story, esq., of Bozeman, Charles Hoffman, trader, several of the employés of the agency; and, of the Indians, Iron Bull, Blackfoot, and all the principal chiefs, and a large number of Indians representing both branches of the Crow tribe.

In opening the council the chairman expressed the regret he had felt at not meeting the Crows on a former visit, and the pleasure it gave himself and the other members of the commission to meet them at the present time. We then read and explained to the Indians the treaty made by them at Fort Laramie in 1868, the act of Congress of March 3, 1873, under which the commission was appointed, and the letter of instructions of the honorable Commissioner of Indian Affairs.

We dwelt upon the fact of the miners in large numbers being on the reservation; of the recent discovery of gold and silver mines; and of the danger of trouble unless the Indians were willing to sell a portion of their reservation, which was of little use to them, and accepting in payment a satisfactory sum of money that should be expended for their benefit.

We referred to the probability of the Northern Pacific Railroad coming along the Yellowstone, and that it might come upon their reservation; and we explained the necessity for a new location for the agency buildings, and offered to go with the agent and the Indians and select a new location for it. The council lasted four days. A full report of it will be found in the accompanying documents.

On the fifth day of the council, finding the Indians were not likely soon to come to an agreement, for the purpose of inducing an immediate decision, we formally closed the council.

Early the next morning all the chiefs and head-men came and expressed a desire to sign the agreement. After ascertaining that they fully understood the articles of convention, the chairman said, "You have come to tell us that you agree to the exchange of your present reservation on the Yellowstone for Judith's Basin, and wish to agree to the paper."

Iron Bull, Blackfoot, and all the chiefs said, "Yes, we all agree to it."

The Indians having expressed an unwillingness to touch the pen in making their mark, thinking it was "bad luck" to do so, the chairman said, "We wish you all to come, one at a time, and say 'yes' or 'no' to the paper. We wish you to bring in all the others, and they will say 'yes' or 'no,' and then none who say 'yes' can afterward say 'we did not agree to it.'"

The chiefs thought if they agreed to it, it was sufficient, as all the tribe would abide by their decision, but we insisted that all should approve or disapprove of it.

They then came forward, and as each said "yes," his name was signed to the articles of convention.

All agreed to it, except one head-man named "Crazy," who refused to express an opinion either way.

Each, as he said "yes," asked that they might be permitted to eat buffalo for a long time, to which the commissioners responded "yes," as the Indians shook hands with them, respectively. Others asked for guns and horses; many asked that Agent Pease might be retained. To all of their requests the commissioners answered that there was nothing in the paper about these things, and that they only said "yes" to what was in the agreement, but told them when the young men went to Washington they could talk to the "Great Father" about giving them what they wished.

The necessity for the ratification by Congress of the articles of convention it was difficult to have them understand; but it was explained to them as fully as possible during the council. We made no promises to the Indians other than those contained in the articles of convention, and no conference in regard to it was held by us with the chiefs, or other Indians, except in public council.

The sessions of the council were all well attended, all the chiefs and head-men, and many Indian men and women, being present at every session; and we have every reason to think the action of the council meets with the almost unanimous approval of the Indians party to it.

The River Crows will, we doubt not, approve of the action of those representing them, as they have always lived in the section of country now set apart as their reservation.

In accordance with the desire expressed by all the Indians in council and elsewhere, we authorized Agent Pease to take to Washington eight Indians, chiefs and others, representing both the Mountain and River Crows, to be accompanied by one interpreter. We were the more willing to take this action, for the reason that no member of the Crow tribe has ever been East, and their idea of "the white man's" power and civilization is very meager. Their steady friendship for the whites, whom they have always had every reason to suppose inferior to them in number and power, we thought also merited some return. The trip to the East will, we doubt not, prove of lasting benefit to the tribe.

The request made during and after the council, for a present of horses, we did not feel at liberty to accede to. yet we have no hesitation in recommending that such a present be made. At the time of making their former treaties, they have always been given horses, a present they prize above all others. In view of the advantages that will accrue to the Government from the arrangement entered into, and the fact that, while attending upon the sessions of the council, a large number of their horses were stolen, as well as in return for the friendship they have always exhibited for the whites, we would respectfully recommend that they be presented with one horse for each lodge or family. It is presumed that funds appropriated for beneficial purposes for the Crow tribe of Indians are available for this purpose.

We would call special attention to the last clause of the articles of convention, in which it is agreed upon the part of the commissioners that, "pending action by Congress, the United States shall prevent all further encroachment upon the present reservation of the Crow tribe," and respectfully recommend that instructions be sent the agent to prevent all whites from passing over, settling upon, or residing in said territory, except such as are specially exempted by the treaty of 1868, and such others as are now engaged in mining in Emigrant Gulch; that he be directed to prevent all exploring parties or individuals from entering upon the reservation, and that any one engaged in hunting or trapping for game be arrested and turned over to the civil authorities.

We also respectfully recommend that, pending the action of Congress, the section of country described in the first article of the articles of convention be, by order of the President, withdrawn from market, and that it be declared not to be open for, or subject to, entry under the homestead or pre-emption laws. There are at present no settlers in any portion of this country, and this recommendation is made to prevent any such entering upon it, pending action by Congress. In case Congress should ratify the action of this commission, we would further respectfully recommend that agents of tribes, other than the Crows, be directed, as far as possible, to prevent them from hunting in Judith's Basin.

That Congress be requested to define the penalty for wolfing or killing game by means of poison in the section of country contiguous to the proposed reservation, as described in article fourth of the articles of convention.

That an appropriation be asked for the erection of agency buildings, in accordance with the provisions of the treaty of 1868, and that a commission be appointed by the honorable Secretary of the Interior to locate the agency at a suitable place in the Judith Basin, as far south as is practicable, keeping in view the necessity for wood, water, grass, and a sufficient body of tillable land susceptible of easy irrigation, and not so elevated as to render crops uncertain.

Very respectfully submitted.

FELIX R. BRUNOT,
R. WHITTLESEY,
JAMES WRIGHT,
Commissioners.

THOMAS K. CREE, *Secretary.*

Supplementary report by the chairman of the commission.

PITTSBURGH, *November* 19, 1873.

SIR: In addition to the report of the Crow commission, prepared by the secretary under the direction of my colleagues when *en route* from the agency, and already in your hands, I have the honor to submit a brief explanation of the reasons influencing the commission in their negotiations.

The official instructions seemed to contemplate mainly the purchase of the western portion of the reserve, but your letter to the chairman was understood to leave a wider discretion with the commission.

We found that the principal region already occupied by the miners was along Emigrant Gulch, extending thirty or forty miles eastwardly into the mountains from the western border of the reserve, and upon Clarke's Fork of the Yellowstone River, and that the prospectors were gradually extending their operations, and could not long be prevented from overrunning the entire mountain region bounded by Clarke's Fork and the Yellowstone River. The Indians claimed the country around the heads of Clarke's Fork and the east branches of the Yellowstone in Wyoming Territory; and, although not upon the reserve, it was impossible to convince them that it had not been originally included. We also found that the topographical features of the country were such as to admit of no dividing-line, west of Pryor's Creek, which would be satisfactory either to the commission or the Indians; or which would not, if adopted, become, very soon, the cause of serious misunderstanding and contention between the whites and Indians.

The portion of the reserve which lies east of Clarke's Fork, and includes Pryor's Creek, is within the limits of the country claimed by the Sioux as their hunting-grounds. It is constantly frequented by them in large bands for the purpose of fighting the Crows, and is the battle-ground upon which the two tribes often meet.

The Sioux largely outnumber the Crows, and have even extended their raids against them to the present agency. To remove this friendly tribe to so close a proximity to their powerful enemies would be wrong, and would involve the necessity of a military fort, and a considerable force for their protection, which would be costly and inexpedient.

The commission further considered that the Northern Pacific Railroad would be located for three hundred miles along the present reservation, and one or more roads already projected from the southward would pass through it, and that the valley of the Yellowstone, and the valleys of the many fine streams emptying into the south side of that river, affording some of the choicest lands in the West for cultivation and stock, would, when thus rendered accessible to the whites, be irrepressibly demanded for their use, and make the removal of the Crow Indians a necessity.

To anticipate this necessity while there yet remained unoccupied a more retired district of country suitable to their needs, and which could be given to them, seemed of incalculable importance to the future welfare of the Indians. Postponement of the selection of a proper location for a few years would probably leave no place for them but the cold and arid region north of the Missouri River. On the other side, it was considered that the peaceable release of the fine body of land included in the Crow reserve, already partially occupied, and the possession of which must soon seem a necessity, and the avoidance of future possible controversy and bloodshed between the whites and its proper owners, was of the greatest importance to the Government.

The Judith Basin, lying out of the present and prospective line of migration, surrounded by a belt of mountains and barren lands destitute of valuable ores to attract their cupidity, and relatively inaccessible to the whites, yet possessing within itself the necessary requisites for farming—land, grass, wood, and water—and not too large for the future needs of the Indians, seemed peculiarly adapted for the purpose of a reservation.

The sum of money agreed to be invested for the Indians is a very moderate price for the quantity of land they relinquish. Probably a larger sum than the interest of the capital funded would in any event be required to be expended annually for their maintenance until they become self-supporting. Hence the ratification of the contract would involve no additional expenditure on the part of the Government.

I desire, in behalf of myself and colleagues, to express our obligations to Col. N. B. Sweitzer, commanding Fort Ellis, for facilities furnished and efficient co-operation; and to himself and to all the officers of the fort for many personal courtesies and attentions; also to Agent F. D. Pease and the employés of the agency, for their zealous co-operation.

Respectfully submitted.

FELIX R. BRUNOT,
Chairman of Commission.

HON. C. DELANO,
Secretary of the Interior.

Articles of convention made and concluded on the sixteenth day of August, in the year of our Lord one thousand eight hundred and seventy-three, at the Crow agency, in the Territory of Montana, by and between Felix R. Brunot, E. Whittlesey, and James Wright, commissioners in behalf of the United States, and the chiefs, head-men, and men representing the tribe of Crow Indians, and constituting a majority of the adult male Indians belonging to said tribe.

Whereas a treaty was made and concluded at Fort Laramie, Dak., on the seventh day of May, in the year of our Lord one thousand eight hundred and sixty-eight, by and between commissioners, on the part of the United States, and the chiefs and head-men of and representing the Crow Indians, they being duly authorized to act in the premises;

And whereas by an act of Congress, approved March 3, 1873, it is provided, "That the Secretary of the Interior be, and he is hereby, authorized to negotiate with the chiefs and head-men of the Crow tribe of Indians in the Territory of Montana for the surrender of their reservation in said Territory, or of such part thereof as may be consistent with the welfare of said Indians: *Provided*, That any such negotiation shall leave the remainder of said reservation in compact form, and in good locality for farming purposes, having within it a sufficiency of good land for farming, and a sufficiency for water and timber; and if there is upon said reservation a locality where fishing could be valuable to the Indians, to include the same if practicable; and the Secretary shall report his action, in pursuance of this act, to Congress at the next session thereof, for its confirmation or rejection;"

And whereas, in pursuance of said act of Congress, commissioners were appointed by the Secretary of the Interior to conduct the negotiation therein contemplated:

The said commissioners on the part of the United States, and the chiefs, head-men, and men, constituting a majority of the adult males of the Crow tribe of Indians, in behalf of their tribe, do solemnly make and enter into the following agreement, subject to the confirmation or rejection of the Congress of the United States, at the next session thereof:

ARTICLE I.

The United States agrees that the following district of country, to wit: commencing at a point on the Missouri River opposite to the mouth of Shankin Creek; thence up said creek to its head, and thence along the summit of the divide between the waters of Arrow and Judith Rivers, and the waters entering the Missouri River, to a point opposite to the divide between the head-waters of the Judith River and the waters of the Muscle-Shell River; thence along said divide to the Snowy Mountains, and along the summit of said Snowy Mountains, in a northeasterly direction, to a point nearest to the divide between the waters which run easterly to the Muscle-Shell River and the waters running to the Judith River; thence northwardly along said divide to the divide between the head-waters of Arnell's Creek and the head-waters of Dog River, and along said divide to the Missouri River; thence up the middle of said river to the place of beginning, (the said boundaries being intended to include all the country drained by the Judith River, Arrow River, and Dog River,) shall be, and the same is, set apart for the absolute and undisturbed use and occupation of the Indians herein named, and for such other friendly tribes, or individual Indians, as, from time to time, they may be willing, with the consent of the United States, to admit among them. And the United States now solemnly agrees that no person, except those herein designated and authorized so to do, and except such officers, agents, and employés of the Government as may be authorized to enter upon Indian reservations in discharge of duties enjoined by law, shall ever be permitted to pass over, settle upon, or reside in the territory described in this article for the use of said Indians; and the United States agrees to erect the agency and other buildings, and execute all the stipulations of the treaty of Fort Laramie, (the said stipulations being hereby re-affirmed,) within the limits herein described, in lieu of upon the south side of the Yellowstone River.

ARTICLE II.

The United States agrees to set apart the sum of one million of dollars, and to hold the same in trust for the sole use and benefit of the Crow tribe of Indians, the principal to be held in perpetuity, and the interest thereof to be expended, or re-invested at the discretion of the President of the United States, annually, for the benefit of said tribe.

ARTICLE III.

It is mutually agreed between the United States and the Crow Indians that the second article of the treaty made at Fort Laramie, between the commissioners of the United States and the Crow tribe of Indians, be, and the same is, abrogated by this agreement; and the said Indians hereby cede to the United States all their right, title, and claim to the tract of country described in the said second article, to wit: "Commencing where the 107th degree of longitude west of Greenwich crosses the south boundary of Montana Territory; thence north along said 107th meridian to the mid-channel of the Yellowstone River; thence up said mid-channel of the Yellowstone to the point where it crosses the said southern boundary of Montana, being the 45th degree of north latitude; and thence east along said parallel of latitude to the place of beginning," and which is conveyed to them therein, except the right to hunt upon said lands so long as they may remain unoccupied, and as game may be found thereon and peace continues between the whites and Indians.

ARTICLE IV.

The United States agrees to suppress, so far as possible, by the imposition of pains and penalties, the practice of wolfing, or killing game by means of poison, within the limits of the following district of country, viz: Beginning at the mouth of the Muscle-Shell; thence up the said river to the North Fork, and up the North Fork to its source; thence northward along the summit of the Little Belt and Highwood Mountains to the head of Deep Creek; thence down said creek to the Missouri River, and along the margin of said river to the place of beginning.

It is expressly understood between the commissioners and the Indians, parties thereto, that this agreement is subject to the ratification or rejection of the Congress of the United States at its next session, and that, pending the action of Congress, the United States shall prevent all further encroachments upon the present reservation of the Crow tribe.

FELIX R. BRUNOT,
E. WHITTLESEY,
JAMES S. WRIGHT,
Commissioners in behalf of the United States.

Attest:
THOMAS K. CREE, *Secretary.*

PIERRE his + mark SHANE,
MITCH his + mark BOYER,
Interpreters.

Iron Bull, Che-ve-te-pu-ma-ta.
Black Foot, Kam-ne-but-se.
Long Horse, E-che-te-hats-ke.
Show-his-face, In-tee-us.
Bear Wolf, Isa-auchbe-te-se.
Thin Belly, Ella-causs-se.
Good Heart, Uss-pit-ta-watse.
Old Onion, Mit-hu-a.
Red Sides, Si-ta-pa-ruse.
Crazy Head, A-su-ma-ratz.
Bull chief, Ise-la-mats-etts.
Shot-in-the-jaw, Esa-woor.
Lone Tree, Money-a-mut-eats.
In-the-morning, A-a-Seitz.
Boy-that-grabs, Seeateots.
White Forehead, E-seha-ehire.
Small Waist, E-hene-pea-carts.
Flat Side, Oos-tsoo-ch-seots.
Old Dog, Bis-ca-carriers.
The nest, Ish-shis-she-ess.
Crazy-sister-in-law, Ou-at-ma-ra-sach.
The Spider-that-Creeps, Ah-spe-di-ess.
Crazy Pon dé Orai, Minne-hu-ma-ra-ebac.
Bull-goes-a-hunting, Ce-da-nu-ta-cass.
Crane-in-the-Sky, A-pil-Mouse.
Coon-Elk, Chin-ka-shee-araehe.
The Old Crow, Perits-har-sts.
White Otter, Ma-pu-ku-he-te-te-suish.
Long-Snake, Bi-ka-che-hats-ki.
White Mouth, Te-de-sil-se.
Pock-Mark, Te-spu-ke-he-te.
The White Bull, Te-shu-net.
The No Hand, Te-si-closst-so-ish.
The little Antelope, Uk-ha-nak-ish.

Curley, Ash-ish-ish-e.
The Ridge, E. Nak-he-sash.
Big Horse, Te-le-si-cle-is-ash.
Calf in the mouth, Nak-pak-a-e.
Old Mountain Tail, A-mak-ha-viss-ish.
Bear in the water, Me-mum-ak-hiss-is-e-ish.
One Feather, Mash-u-a-mo-te.
The Mix, Ma-ish-ish.
Bell Rock, Mit-a-wosh.
New Lodge, As-hi-hash.
The Rings, She-da-nat-sik.
Well Bull, Te-si do-po-mo.
The Shaven, Bish-i-ish.
The one who hunts his debt, Ash-e-te-si-Oish.
One who hears good, Ma-in-ke-ku-te-sit-sine.
The Burnt, Osh-Nish.
Bear Robe, Ach-je it-se-is.
The River, A-ash-ish.
Big Forehead, Ak-hi-es-ash.
The one who knows the bull, Te-se-do-pe-e-a-te-sa.
Big Kettle, Bi-re-ke-hi-tash.
Chief Wolf, No-it-a-ma-te-sets.
The Leg, Te-tu-se-pe.
The man who sits in the middle of the ground, A-ive-ku-a-ta-mish.
Blinkey, Bish-te-ha-mo-te-te.
One who sees all over the land, A-we-ko-to-e-ka.
Bull all the time, Te-si-doss-ko-te-so-te.
Plenty of bear, A-che-pil-se-a-hush.
Rides behind a man on horseback, Ma-me-ri-ke-ish.
Bird off the ground, Ma-pe-she-ri.
Charge through the camp, Ash-e-ri-i-a-was-sash.
The old Bear, Ak-hi-pit-se-u-ke-hi-ke-ish.
Crazy Wolf, Te-se-te-man-ache.
The Plume, Te-se-do-pie-shu.she-ish.
Old Alligator, Bo-ru-ke-he-sa-cha-ri-ish.
Bob-tail Bear, Ak-hi-pilse-u-ke-hi-ke-ish.
Pole Cat Look behind, Te-spit-te-sash.
Wolf Bow, Te-sets-sha-tak-he.
The Sioux that runs fast, Ak-man-ash-u-pe-yeu-hu she.
Little Soldier. The one who hunts his enemy.
Bull Rock. Pretty Lodge. Herd the Horses.
Three Wolf. Stray Horse.

We, the undersigned, were present at and witnessed the assent of the Crow chiefs, head-men, and men of the Crow tribe of Indians, whose names are attached thereto.

THOMAS K. CREE,
Secretary Special Crow Commission.
C. W. HOFFMAN.
R. W. CROSS.
I. M. CASTNER.
F. GIESDORF.
F. D. PEASE,
Agent for Crow Indians.

The undersigned were present at the council with the Crow Indians, and witnessed the proceedings. The agreement was carefully explained, and was fully understood and assented to by the Indians.

GEO. L. TYLER,
Captain, Second United States Cavalry.
CHARLES F. ROE,
Lieutenant, Second United States Cavalry.

We, the undersigned, members of the Crow tribe of Indians, were not at the agency at the time of the council, but, after having the articles of convention fully explained to us, do hereby give our assent to the same.

The Deaf.
Crooked Face.
Little Face.
Split Ear.
Kill the Chief.
Plenty Elkhorses.
Boy Chief, Taboo.
The Buffalo.
Burnt Arm.
Buffalo Calf.
Brown Beaver.
Small Pony.

Small Boy.
White Bull.
The Sergeant.
The Blind.
Chief Bull.
The Bravo.
Eats a horse.
Medicine Chicken.
Long Hour.
Crow Head.
Arm in his neck.
Small Bear.
White Otter.
School Teacher.
White Calf.
Bull on top of the mountain.
Big Pond.
The Magpie.
Pretty Bird.
The Gooseberry.
Musk Rat.
Shoots well.
Young one in the mouth.
Sitting Weasel.
Pretty Robe.
Four Chiefs.
Sharp blade sword.
The Deer.
Cloudy Forehead.
The Knife.
Black Face.
Long Fingers.
Blind Horse.
Flying Eagle.
Calf Woman.
Pretty Bull.
Black Dog.
The Winking Eye.
Young Horse.
Sewed side.
Pretty prisoner.
Kill the Chief.
Plenty Elkhorses.
Boy Chief, Taboo.
The Buffalo.
Bad Snow.
Old Cloud.
Yellow Fender.
The Swan.
Pretty Side.
Yellow Bull.
Sharp Nose.
Crooked Nose.
The Coat.
Bear From Below.
The Hair.
The Weasel.
Two Tails.
Pounded Meat.
Sister to Crazy.
The Dumb.
The Pipe.
Yellow Horse.
Tiger Woman.
Iron Neck.
Medicine Rock.
The Shell.
Splendid Leg.
White Head.
Old Saddle.
The River Bull Woman.
Shell-in-the-Year.
Good Beard.
Little Whetstone.
Otter that knows.
Bird Woman.
Old Blackbird.
White Dog.
Pretty Gun.
Plenty head gear.
Two Lances.
Small Bull.
The Black Bird.
Fat Elk.
Green Meadow.
Old Kettle.
Tall Pine.
Diving Otter.
Friendly Beaver.
Jack Sheppard.
The Throat.
Flat Back.
Black Foot's Son.
The Red.
The Twin.
Yellow Top.
Raw-Hide.
Plenty Head.
Little Wolf.
Rotten Tail.
Red Fox.
The Onion.
Half Yellow Face.
Dog Eye.
Afraid-of-his Eyes.
Little Son.
Yellow Tobacco.
Iron Necklace.
Small Wolf.
Gray Head.
Yellow Head.
Pretty Eagle.
No Heart.
Red Beard.
Blue Moccasin.
Young Wolf.
No Hand.
The Otter.
Show his Face.
Dirty Head.
Takes the Shield.
Two Hours.
The Blind Bull.
White Swan.
Hides-his-Face.

We, the undersigned, members of the Crow tribe of Indians, who were at the agency during the sitting of the council, but were not present when the articles of convention were assented to, hereby give our assent to them.

Bad Hand, Blue Leggings.
Ugly Face.
Back Bone.
The Panther.
Sitting Bull.
Little Iron.
Fish Catcher.
Horse Guard.
Scabbed Bull.
The Chicken.
Strong-by-Himself.
The Tail.
Long Neck.
Spotted Tail.
Yellow Top.
Crane in the Sky.
Big Nose.
Yellow Leggings.
Mauntain Pocket.
Old Cloud.
Old Kettle.
Red Face.
Bear Head.
Black Head.
Shake-his-Tail.
Poor Elk.
Big Ball.
Old Tiger.
The Island.
Old Man.
Picket Pin.
Old Tobacco.
Hole-in-the-Forehead.
Crazy Head.
Iron Feather.
Red Fox.
Bird in the Neck.
The Buffalo.
Medicine Rock.
Crooked Eye.
Pretty Bear.
Old Liar.
Kills Quick.
Smart Boy, Great Hunter.

Witness: PIERRE his + mark SHANE, *Interpreter*.

I certify on honor that the above names were appended as stated.

F. D. PEASE.

Narrative of the proceedings of the special commission.

Hon. Felix R. Brunot, chairman of the special commission to negotiate with the Crow tribe of Indians, under act of Congress of March 3, 1873, accompanied by Thomas K. Cree, as secretary, arrived at Bozeman, July 7.

Arranged with Agent Pease to have the Mountain and River Crows brought to the agency as soon as possible.

July 28.—General E. Whittlesey, of Washington, and Dr. James Wright, late superintendent of Indian affairs for Montana, members of the commission, arrived at Bozeman.

August 30. A conference of the commission was held at Fort Ellis. The chairman read the letter of the honorable Secretary of the Interior, dated May 14, authorizing the commission, and the letter of the honorable Commissioner of Indian Affairs, of May 29, giving instructions for the guidance of the commission in its negotiation with the Crows. Also, the treaty at Fort Laramie, made with the Crows May 7, 1868. The commission had a free conference in regard to the objects sought to be attained.

Having learned that the parties sent out for the Mountain Crow Indians, after thirty-three days' absence, had found them, and had reported that they were *en route* for the agency, and that a portion of the River Crows had already arrived, the commission decided to leave for the agency the next day.

July 30.—Left for the Crow agency. Arrived at 9.30 p. m. Blackfoot and a few of the principal men who had come in from the camp were waiting to see the commission.

Aug. 1.—This morning some twenty of the prominent chiefs, under Blackfoot, called to pay a formal visit to the commissioners. They came in singing a song of welcome "to the commissioners from the Great Father," and, after shaking hands and embracing the great white chiefs, the following conversation occurred:

Mr. BRUNOT. We are very glad to see you. We have been waiting for some time at Bozeman. We want to see all the Crows. The Great Father sent us and told us to talk with all of you. We want to know where your camp is, and when all will be in.

BLACKFOOT. They are camped on the Yellowstone, at the mouth of Alder Creek, about forty miles away.

Mr. BRUNOT. How many days is that away?

BLACKFOOT. We can't tell how many nights; six or seven, perhaps.

Mr. BRUNOT. That is a long time for us to wait.

BLACKFOOT. Our horses are poor; it is warm weather, and the horses have given out; all the streams are high and hard to cross; they sent us men ahead to meet you. Last summer you came and sent to see the tribe, but before we got here you had gone. This time I came ahead because I wanted to see you.

Mr. BRUNOT. If they come as soon as they can we will wait. Can the camp be here in five nights?

BLACKFOOT. I do not think they can get here so soon. Do not be in a hurry; we want to see you. The streams are high, and our horses poor, but we will come as soon as possible.

Mr. BRUNOT. I waited a long time for you last summer, and the Great Father was sorry you did not come. It is a long journey from Washington; it would take six months on a horse to go there, and now that we are here we want to see you, and if the camp comes as fast as it can we will wait.

BLACKFOOT. To-morrow I will go to the camp, and bring them as soon as I can. We do not know how long it will take, but we will bring them as soon as we can; we did tell them that you were in a hurry.

Mr. BRUNOT. That is well.

BLACKFOOT. You have sent for us; we had not gotten skins enough, and were not through our hunt, but we came at once.

Mr. BRUNOT. How many lodges have you?

BLACKFOOT. We do not know how many; there are about 400 lodges, but some are River Crows, Bannocks, and Nez Percés.

Mr. BRUNOT. Where did you meet the Sioux?

BLACKFOOT. Across Prior's Creek, about twenty miles, at the foot of Prior's Mountain, we met the Cheyennes and Sioux. They were coming this way; they were a big party. The most of them did not come to fight, but a small party met and fought us, and we killed one of the Sioux. From there we went after them. We had plenty of ammunition and were friends of the white men, and we followed them down the Big Horn. There is a large party at Fort Smith; when they found we were coming they went back. The Big Horn was too high for us to cross, or we would have followed them and driven them from the country. On Warm Spring Creek, across the Big Horn, we fought and whipped them, but could not get over the river after them. The Crow soldiers wanted to cross, but the camp could not go without danger of drowning some of our people and ponies, but we sent scouts, and they brought back horses taken from the Sioux camp. The Sioux camp was between the Big Horn and Little Horn; we sent six of our men; they brought twelve Sioux horses. When they came back we sent two more. They found a Sioux out hunting; they killed and scalped him and got his horse; when they came back they found us camped at Pompey's Pillar.

Three Nez Percés went out from there and took five horses and mules from the Sioux. We sent two more men; the Sioux camp was at the mouth of the Little Horn; it was a big camp; five rows of tepees. They got some horses, and shot into the Sioux tents. From Pompey's Pillar we came to Prior Creek, and there Boyer (the messenger) found us. He came through near the Sioux camp, and just afterward we had the fight with the Sioux—just at the mouth of Prior Creek. The party was so large they came right up to our camp and attacked us. The big valley on Prior's Creek was full of Sioux Indians. Boyer will tell you the same. The white men who were with us took their guns and went out with us to fight the Sioux. Another party went from Prior Creek after the Sioux. When we came to the Stinking Water three of them had been killed. We knew you great white men who were coming from the "Great Father" to see us would hear whether we whipped or not. We began to fight when the sun got up; we fought them till noon, when the Sioux began to run; we followed them to Fly Creek, nearly sixty miles.

The Sioux must have good white-men friends on the Platte and Missouri. They get guns and ammunition; they are better armed than we are; they have Winchester, Henry, and Spencer rifles and needle-guns. We took some of these guns from those we killed; we took two Henry rifles and one needle-gun; they threw away their blankets and saddles, and we got a number of them; they threw away their ammunition. Their outfit was better than ours. We got needle, Spencer, and Winchester catridges, and powder and balls from them. The Great Father does not know that the Sioux get these arms and ammunition, and then they kill white men with them. The Crows do not kill white men; the arms and ammunition we get is to hunt with, and defend ourselves and our white friends with.

When the fight was over we intended to go to Heart Mountain, where buffalo were plenty, and get skins for our lodges, but we did not go then.

We came here to shake hands with you; and we want you to think well of the Crows. We mean to do right, and we will listen to what you say to us. We want you to know how the Sioux trouble us. There are many Sioux, but we are not afraid of them. They want to come on our land, but we intend to keep them off. I love you and hold on to your hand, but the Sioux we want to fight. We will stay here to-day, and to-morrow we will go to the camp. Too many of us cannot leave the camp at one time for fear of the Sioux. Even at the agency we watch for the Sioux. We brought a good many guns with us, and the camp is short that many. The Sioux want to get our country, but we will not let them have it.

Mr. BRUNOT. The Great Father does not give the Sioux any guns. I do not know where they get them. We know the Crows are our friends; that is the reason we come here; and we want you always to continue our friends; what we say is for your good. I have to go to see the Utes after I leave here. The Ute chief met me on the way. He heard what the Great Father wanted them to do, and they are going to do it; and so with nearly all the Indians, they are going to do as the President wishes them.

After awhile, if the Sioux do not do as the President wants, he will make them do it. Since the President's war is over he has plenty of soldiers, and he intends to make everybody—red men, white men, and black men—do what is right. He is going to make them all do it, whether they want it or not; but he does not think the Crows want any soldiers, for they are his friends and will do what is right.

Is Long Horse with the camp? I saw him last year.

BLACKFOOT. Yes; his brother was killed in the fight.

Mr. BRUNOT. We came in a wagon, and could not carry any presents with us, but we want you to have dinner with us. How many chiefs are here?

BLACKFOOT. Twenty-two Mountain-Crow men, and nine River Crows.

Mr. BRUNOT. We want the Mountain Crows to-day, and the River Crows to-morrow.

BLACKFOOT. The River Crows belong to me, and I want you to treat us all alike.

Mr. BRUNOT. This is our dinner, and we want you all to come to-day.

BLACKFOOT. Are there any cattle above the cañon on the river?

Mr. BRUNOT. Yes; I saw them there. Those cattle are on the wrong side of the river.

Major PEASE. They ought all be taken off, and the miners too. I ordered the herders to move the cattle farther up, or else across on the other side of the river.

Mr. BRUNOT. Major Pease has ordered them to take the cattle away. The country up there is not good for much; there are many mountains.

BLACKFOOT. The country is good, and we like it. It is our country, and we know it is good.

Mr. BRUNOT. I know it is your country. Where is the best country you know of for Indians to live on?

BLACKFOOT, (after much discussion.) Why did you ask that question?

Mr. BRUNOT. I want the Crows to have the best country, and I want to know where it is. I do not want any of your country for myself.

BLACKFOOT. I am going to tell you, but we are not ready yet. We have land we like very much, and we will tell you about it when our people come in.

Mr. BRUNOT. Some places the white men are in already; other places they are going in; and we want to find a good place that we can keep always for the Crows.

BLACKFOOT. Do not be too fast; wait till all are here. When the rest come in we will tell you our mind.

Mr. BRUNOT. You will come for dinner, and then you will go and bring the camp.

AUG. 8.—The Indians arrived to-day. They had been detained by fights with the Sioux, and by sickness in the camp, quite a number having died while *en route* for the agency; Iron Bull and Blackfoot, the two principal chiefs being sick; and Long Horse, an important chief, being in mourning for his brother, who was killed by the Sioux.

Arrangements were made for a council to-morrow.

AUG. 9.—Provisions were issued to-day, taking from 10 o'clock till 5, after which the Indians declined to come into council on account of the chiefs being sick and the hour too late.

Respectfully submitted.

THOMAS K. CREE, *Secretary.*

To the SPECIAL CROW COMMISSION.

REPORT OF THE COUNCIL.

CROW AGENCY, MONTANA TERRITORY,
August 11, 1873.

A council was held with the Crow Indians this morning. There were present Hon. Felix R. Brunot, chairman of the board of Indian commissioners; General E. Whittlesey, of Washington, and James Wright, late superintendent of Indian affairs for Montana, as a special commission under act of Congress of March 3, 1873, to negotiate with the Crow Indians, with Thomas K. Cree as secretary. There were present, by invitation of the commission, General Sweitzer, commandant at Fort Ellis; Captain Tyler, and Lieutenant Rowe, of Company F, Second Cavalry; Dr. Lightfoot, surgeon U. S. A.; Major Pease, agent for the Crows; Nelson Story, esq., of Bozeman, Charles Hoffman, esq., and Mr. Cross, traders; several of the employés of the agency, and the following Indian chiefs and subchiefs:

Of the Mountain Crows—Iron Bull, Blackfoot, Thin Belly, Bear Wolf Show-his-face, Good Heart, Shot-in-the-jaw, Crazy, Bear-in-the-water, Bull-goes-hunting, Crane-in-the-sky, Crazy Sister-in-law, Crazy-head, Long Horse, Old Crow, White Calf, Red Side, Onion, White Mouth, Bird-in-the-neck, Spotted Tail, Poor Elk, Little Iron, Chief Bull, Old Dog, Bell-rock, Along-the-ridge.

River Crows—Little Soldier, Wolf's Bow, Hunts-his-enemy, Boiling Leggin, White Rock, Black Bull, Cranberry, Bear-head, Poor Assinaboine, and many others.

In opening the council Mr. Brunot said:

Before we talk about business I want General Whittlesey to ask the Great Spirit to look into our hearts and make them all good.

General Whittlesey led in prayer, asking that God would guide the commission and the Indians in the deliberations of the council, and lead each right.

Mr. BRUNOT said: I am glad to meet all my friends here now. I was sorry I could not see you when I came here last summer. I came then to hear what you had to say about yourselves, and to talk to you of what I thought was good for you. I have now come again, and am very glad to see you. My heart is good to you, and I hope you are all well to-day, [many had been sick.] The Great Father sent some words to you when I started to come, and he sent these two gentlemen with me to see you. He told us there was a new general at Fort Ellis, and he also has come to see you. Another man, Mr. Cree, comes with us to write down all that is said by the white men and the Indians. I want you to speak wise words, because they will go to the Great Father. These gentlemen are all glad to see you, and they wish me tell you so. The Great Father has heard many things from this country; some tell him one thing, some another. I see with my own eyes many things I will tell him when I go back. I know he thinks the Crows are all his friends, and he wishes to do what is good for you; and when he told us to come and tell the Crows what he thinks is best for you, it is because he cares for you. I want you to know that every word I say to you comes from my heart. I would not say a bad thing for my own child, nor would I for you, and all I say you will see is true. The Great Father knows that the Crow Indians made a treaty at Fort Laramie. I was not there, nor the Great Father, but he sent commissioners there, and some of your chiefs were there; but the treaty is printed, and he gave us this printed paper. It says, "This is the treaty made at Fort Laramie." I hold it in my hand; it has some chiefs' names signed to it. The names are: Pretty Bull, Wolf Bow, Mountain Tail, Blackfoot, White Horse, Poor Elk, Shot-in-the-jaw, White Forehead, Pounded

Meat, Bird-in-the-neck, and The Swan. These are the names of the chiefs that signed the paper. That treaty says where the Crow land is to be. I think it is a good country. It is along this river about seventy-five miles above the agency, and then goes toward where the sun rises until it crosses the Big Horn, and goes half way between it and the mouth of the Rose-bud River, about twelve miles this side of Porcupine Creek. This is what the treaty and the map say. That is the country that belongs to you forever, or until you wish to sell it. Now, the country across the river, where you go to hunt buffalo, the treaty says, you can go to while the buffalo are there; but when the game is gone away from there that is all to be white man's land. The Great Father has heard that the country southwest of here is not of much use to the Crows, and that the whites are going into it. I have seen some of it along the river, and I think it is very good; but some of it is very rocky and mountainous. It is good only for people who wish to hunt gold. I have seen white people going past the reservation to Clark's Fork; I am sorry to see them going there. I do not want to see white people go upon Indian land so long as it belongs to the Indians and they want to keep it. The Great Father at Washington does not want whites to go upon land that belongs to the Indians. He has heard that the whites have gone there, and he thought, to prevent any more trouble, that the best thing for the Indians to do was to sell that land. So last winter when the Great Father's council came together and heard about these white people being on the Indians' land, they passed a law to send out men to ask you whether you would sell these lands. This law says—

"That the Secretary of the Interior be, and he is hereby, authorized to negotiate with the chiefs and head-men of the Crow tribe of Indians in the Territory of Montana, for the surrender of their reservation in said Territory, or of such part thereof as may be consistent with the welfare of said Indians: *Provided*, That any such negotiation shall leave the remainder of said reservation in compact form and in good locality for farming purposes, having within it a sufficiency of good land for farming and a sufficiency for water and timber; and if there is upon such reservation a locality where fishing could be valuable to the Indians, to include the same if practicable; and the Secretary shall report his action in pursuance of this act of Congress at the next session thereof, for its confirmation or rejection."

He says the men must not buy anything from the Indians if it is not good for you to sell it. The Indians must keep plenty of land for themselves and their children to live on. The land they keep must be good for them to farm and must have a good place for an agency, and it must be good for them. That is one thing the Great Father told us to say to the Crows, and it is for you to think about. This treaty, after awhile, comes to an end. You always have the land, but in thirty years the annuity goods stop. It says all who stay upon the reservation must be fed for four years. I am sorry it is not longer, but that is what the treaty says. Suppose the white men continue to come into the mines; they get too numerous, and after awhile there may be trouble between them and the Indians. I hope the trouble will never come. I want, as long as I live, if I choose to come here, to have the Crows take me by the hand and know I am their friend. When many men think one way and many think another way, it is best to talk it over and see if all will not come to think alike. I think this is best. The Crows do not care about digging in the mines. It would not be good for you to do so. If you can sell to the Great Father the piece of land that has the mines upon it, he will put away the money and for it send useful things to you every year. That is what I want you to think about. The Great Father is making an iron road that is coming along the river. It will make it very easy to bring things to the Crows and the people who live in this country. Sometimes the Great Father sends the goods to the Indians; they start them in the spring, but they do not get here until the next spring. They ought to come before you go upon your fall hunt, that you may have everything with you. When the railroad is done the goods will come quick. Perhaps he will make the railroad on the other side of the river, perhaps on this side; I do not know which. This side is Crow land. You can say whether you want it on your land or not. You can think about that. If you sell a part of your land you must have a better place than this for an agency. We want to help you pick out the place. You will think about that too. I have said enough; now I want to hear you talk.

Several Indians here came forward and presented buffalo-robes, and two presented pledges, each representing a horse, to the members of the commission. The commissioners demurred at accepting the presents, but were assured that the Indians would be offended if they refused. The commissioners then accepted them, but afterward gave them away to needy Indians.

Mr. BRUNOT. I have been to see many tribes of Indians. I go to see them because I want to do them good. Some places the men, to show that they are my friends, bring me something which they wish to give me. I always tell them I do not come to get anything from them; that I have plenty myself, and I do not want to take anything that is of use to them; and now the Crows have come, and, to show that your hearts are good to us you have given us these robes. I have let you do so because it is your way, and I do not want to do anything but what is kind and right.

BLACKFOOT. When we see our friends we give presents to each other. My father comes and sees me; he gives me something and I take it. We give you something and you ought to take it.

Mr. BRUNOT. A long time ago, when men wanted to get anything from the Indians they brought a great many presents. It was because they wanted to get something away from them. If I come to the Crows and bring you a lot of presents you will think I want to get something away from you. (To the whites: We prefer that what is said should go to the Indians through the interpreter, and we do not want others who talk their language to talk with them about what is said.)

OLD CROW. I give you a present. We want you to take the sickness away from us.

BLACKFOOT. You call the Great Spirit Jesus in your language; we call him in the Crow language E-so-we-wat-se. I am going to light the pipe and talk to the Great Spirit. (He lighted the pipe, and, looking up reverently, said:) "The Great Spirit has made the red man and the white man, and sees all before Him to-day. Have pity upon us! May the white man and the Indian speak truth to each other to-day. The sun that looks down upon us to-day, and gives us light and heat, sees that our hearts are true, and that what we do is good for the poor red man. The moon, that shines on us in the night-time, will see us prosper and do well. The earth, on which we walk, from which we come, and which we love as our mother—which we love as our country—we ask thee to see that we do that which is good for us and our children. This tobacco comes from the whites; we mix it with bark from the Indian trees and burn it together before Thee, O Great Spirit! So may our hearts and the hearts of the white men go out together to Thee and be made good and right."

As he invoked the Great Spirit, the earth, &c., the pipe was reverently held in the direction of each, and, after this, was presented to the commissioners and then to the chiefs to smoke, after which ceremony Blackfoot said:

BLACKFOOT. I am going to have a long talk with you. My Great Father sent our friends to see us. We see each other; that is good. You came here last summer; we were sent for to see you. We were back of the mountains when we heard of you, but high waters and the mountains prevented our coming. You said you did not see us, and you were sorry for it. We could not come any faster. This summer we were on this side, near the Yellowstone, where we were getting skins to make lodges. In the fall the traders will want our robes. We will then go over the Yellowstone to Judith's Basin to hunt. Since I was a boy I recollect that is what the Crows always did. When the Crows meet a friend they always give him something; so we do with you. You say you have a book that tells about the Great Spirit. We always give the Great Spirit something. I think that is good. We see the sun, we give him something; and the moon and the earth, we give them something. We beg them to take pity on us. The sun and moon look at us, and the ground gives us food. You come and see us, and that is why we give you something. We are men like each other; our religion is different from yours.

The old folks are dying off; then who will own the land? I went to Fort Laramie; the old Indians signed the treaty. We came back to the camp and told the young men, and they said we had done wrong and they did not want to have anything to do with it. They said, "We love the Great Father, and hold on to the hands of our white friend. All the other Indian tribes fight the whites; we do not do so. We love the whites, and we want them to leave us a big country."

All the other Indians go and talk with the Great Father; you take them to Washington; they are bad; they hide their hearts; but they talk good to the Great Father, and you do more for them than for us. This I want to tell you; yesterday you spoke to us and we listened to you. If you wish to have peace with all the Indians get them all together and make peace with them. Then I will make peace with them, too.

The Great Spirit made these mountains and rivers for us, and all this land. We were told so, and when we go down the river hunting for food we come back here again. We cross over to the other river, and we think it is good. Many years ago the buffalo got sick and died, and Mr. Maldron gave us annuity goods, and since then they have given us something every year. The guns you gave us we do not point at the whites. We do not shoot our white friends. We are true when we look in your face. On our hands is no white man's blood. When you give us arms to go and fight the Sioux we fight them to keep our lands from them. When we raise our camp and go for buffalo some white men go with us; they see what we are doing; they see that we jump over the places that are bloody. On the other side of the river below, there are plenty of buffalo; on the mountains are plenty of elk and black-tail deer; and white-tail deer are plenty at the foot of the mountain. All the streams are full of beaver. In the Yellowstone River the whites catch trout; there are plenty of them. The white men give us food; we know nothing about it. Do not be in a hurry; when we are poor, we will tell you of it. At Laramie we went to see the commissioners. Now commissioners come to see us, and we listen to what you say. The commissioners told us at Laramie if we remained good friends of the whites we would be taken care of for forty years. Since we made that treaty it is only five years. You are in a hurry to quit giving us food. I am a young man yet; my teeth are all good. They told us at Laramie we would get food till we were old, and our children after us. This is not the place for the agency, on this point of rocks. We would like to know who built the agency here. They told us they would give us our food. They promised to send a good agent and good traders, and if they were not good they would be taken away. Pease never treated us wrong; the young men and the children he always treated ight; all that was sent for us he gave us; he was not a thief; he treated us well, and we do not want him to go away from us. On Sheep Mountain white men come; they are my friends; they marry Crow women, they have children with them; the men talk Crow. When we come from hunting we get off at their doors, and they give us something to eat. We like it. We raised Shane, [the interpreter;] he was a boy when he came here. You ask us what we have to say, and that is what we tell you. Here is the doctor; when our people are sick he doctors them. He has two children by a Crow woman; we like him. Here are our traders; when we go hunting they give us ammunition; they gave me a revolver to kill buffalo. We do not know anything about Cross, [a new trader;] we do not know his face. We want the soldiers at Ellis to take the part of the Crows. When they come here to see the giving of annuity goods we give them robes to take with them, and when they hear bad talk about the Crows we want them to speak well of us. When we camp here some of the whites run off with our horses into the mountains. We know about it, but we do not say anything. We have a strong heart, as firm as a rock, and we say nothing about it, but you want to hear what we have to say and I tell you. In Gallatin Valley the Cheyennes, Arapahoes, and Sioux made a raid and the people blamed the Crows with it. We want them to quit speaking bad about us. On the Missouri River the whites have married into all the different Indian tribes; their brothers-in-law, the white men, come here and steal our horses. We follow them and find who have them. Some of the Crows went to the Missouri River and got some Crow horses. The white people sent word they were their horses, and we sent them all back. We claim our horses, but they are not brought back.

When we set up our lodge-poles, one reaches to the Yellowstone; the other is on White River; another one goes to Wind River; the other lodges on the Bridger Mountains. This is our land, and so we told the commissioners at Fort Laramie; but all kinds of white people come over it, and we tell you of it, though we say nothing to them. On this side of the Yellowstone there is a lake; about it are buffalo. It is a rich country; the whites are on it; they are stealing our quartz; it is ours, but we say nothing to them. The whites steal a great deal of our money. We do not want them to go into our country. We would like needle-guns to get game and fight the Sioux; this we tell you.

Mr. Brunot. Blackfoot says he wants the soldiers to speak well of the Crows. I will tell him what took place last summer. When I came here, white men in the Gallatin Valley told me the Crows had killed two white men, and took their horses. I did not believe it, but I wanted to find out. I went to the soldiers and asked them about it; they said it was not the Crows. So the soldiers did speak for the Crows, and as long as the Crows do well the soldiers are their friends. Afterward I found out who killed the men and took the horses; it was Arapahoes and Cheyennes. I wrote a letter to tell the governor who it was. I think he will put it in the newspapers, and everybody will know that it was not the Crows. Blackfoot says the white people are digging in the mountains, taking away your gold. I know that myself; I saw them go there. I told them it was not right. The Great Father has heard about it; and he has said the Crows had better let the people have the gold, and he will pay you for the land. The Crows have done well. You have not hurt the white people who are on the reservation and in the mines, and you tell us you are the white man's friends. The Great Father does not want any of these whites to hurt the Crows. He says for us to tell the Crows that if you let the white people have the land he will give you things you need for many years. I have been looking about over your reservation. I see you do not go much where the mines are. I think it would be good for you to let the white people have the land, and the Great Father for many years will give you what you need for yourselves and your children. I do not want this on account of the people who are on your land, but I think it will be good for you and your children. It is your land, and you can do what you please with it. If you want to keep it, I have nothing to say, but I think it would be good for you to sell it.

Blackfoot said he went to Laramie, and, when he came back, the young men did not agree to what he said. I do not want that to occur again. Whatever the chiefs do, I want the young men to know all about it, and to agree to it, and then no one can say it was wrong. You must think about this, and be sure you are right. It is your business; it concerns you, and you must do what you think is best. If you decide to sell the land from Clark's Fork to the Yellowstone, we will talk about what the Great Father must give you for it. If you do not want to sell so much, you can fix some other line. That you will think about yourselves, and will tell me what you think.

BLACKFOOT. I do not want whites to go to Heart Mountain.

Mr. BRUNOT. The upper part of Clark's Fork is not on the reservation.

BLACKFOOT. I do not care so much about the part on the Yellowstone and in the mountains, but above, in the valley, it is good. I am going to tell you I treat my friends good. When you speak to me I say, yes! yes! Along the Muscle-Shell and Teton Mountains is Judith Basin. Many men go into that country wolfing; they kill game. We thought, when we saw them, that white men are giving us food; when we have to buy what we want, they will be ashamed when they see us. When we have a friend we take him to our tepes. We give him a robe to cover himself. When we meet a wolfer, if he is poor, we give him a pair of pants and moccasins, or a blanket. We shake hands with him, and send him away all right. We would like them to quit wolfing; there are getting to be too many of them, and we want them to quit. (The commissioners examined the map.) What have you decided about on the map?

Mr. BRUNOT. We were looking at the map to see where was a good line, if the Crows decided to sell the mountain part of their reservation. Some people think it would be best to sell from the mouth of Clark's Fork up to the Yellowstone; others think it would be best not to sell so much, but to take some other line this side of that; but it is for you to make up your mind how much you will sell, or whether you will sell any. It is your land; you can do as you please about it.

We have told you what the Great Father wants you to do. I have told you I think it would be good to let the miners have the mountains where they are, and where they are going, and for the Great Father to pay you. I think it would be better for you and your children; but, if you do not think as I do, it is all right.

BEAR-WOLF. These are old men, (the chiefs.) We are young men; we are just grown up; we do not want to sell any land.

IRON-BULL. You are my friends.

Here he was interrupted by the arrival of a mourning people. Long-Neck, whose brother was killed in a recent fight with the Sioux, with his squaw, came in weeping; he placed his hands on the head of each commissioner and sung a mourning song, all the Indians looking solemn, and some weeping.

LONG-NECK. My brother is killed by the Sioux; I want to revenge myself. I come to ask you to give me good luck.

After the mourning party had gone Iron-Bull said: We are tired. I will say a few words and quit talking for to-day. Look all around us! There is no white man's blood; we do not set our feet upon his blood. When you gave us flour did we ask for it? Did we ever ask for sugar or beef? What made you give it to us? We never asked you to give us pants and stockings. You have not asked me to say what I am now going to ask you. I have asked why food is given us, and I was told we were getting food because we were friends of the whites. We like the food; do not quit giving it to us when four years are up. Here is our agency; we were looking for a white man to take charge of it. We know Pease's face. All the people, old men, young men, women, and children know Pease. If you put anybody else here as agent we will not feel like living here any more. We do not want Story and Hoffman, our traders, to go away. There is a tall man in the store called Cross; he makes bad faces to us; he is a hard man; we do not know him. I am not a fool. I am the Iron Bull. I love all white men. The Sioux, Cheyennes, and Arapahoes do not like the whites; if you do not know it, I tell you so. The whites have no horses on the Sweet-Water or in the Gallatin Valley; and over to the Missouri River all their horses are in the Sioux camp. All about they have killed white men and scalped them. If you like us, do not give the Sioux any ammunition or guns. Do what I ask you. Let people keep their cattle on the other side of the Yellowstone. The whites would like to move on our land; do not be in a hurry. Here is a good place to farm, and there is wood on the mountains. You saw that man who came here and cried. The Sioux killed his brother, just as they would you or me. Have pity on us and take the sickness away from the Crow camp. When we raise camp we will go for buffalo; we will make a medicine lodge near the lake. If we come back and nothing happens, we will be glad to see you. When we raise camp we want you to give us ammunition to defend our camp. A long time ago a peace commission sent for me to the Yellowstone. I went with Shane, (the interpreter;) they gave me blankets. I could blow through them, and they went to pieces; they gave us nothing that was good. I asked them to do something for us. They said "Yes," but they have done nothing for us. There are plenty of buffalo yet. The soldiers went down the other side of the Yellowstone; we said nothing because we loved them. When there is no game for us to eat, then we will come and tell you about it.

Mr. BRUNOT. One thing I want you all to understand. You say you want Mr. Pease for agent. You know his face and like him; so do I, and I think the Great Father likes him, too. The Great Father, when he has his men, he puts them where he wants them to go; he puts them where he pleases. General Baker was over at Fort Ellis; the Great Father took him away and sent another man there. When I came here I knew Major Pease was here; these gentlemen knew Pease was here, and that is all we know about it. If the Great Father wants to take him away you must think it is all right. Major Pease is your friend and will always be so. If the Great Father sends anybody else, that is for him to do as he wishes. He did not tell me anything about it. But if the Great Father sends a new agent or trader, you must try them and see if they are good. If a man comes who does not do right, tell the Great Father, and he will send another man. We have nothing to do with it. You are all tired, and you want to talk among yourselves about what has been said, and I think we had better stop. We will meet to-morrow and have other things to say, and we want you to talk about it and tell us what you have to say.

LOW HORN, (taking Pease and putting his arms about him.) We love him, and want to keep him. We all love him, and want him to remain with the Crows.

Mr. BRUNOT. When I talk to the Crows I mean all—the River and Mountain Crows both. I think if a man has a family it is good for all of them to be together, and not divided up. I think the River Crows ought to stay with the others; you ought all to be one family. I thought all the River Crows would be here, but some have not come. I hope you will all be friends together. We are very sorry for your people who are sick, and for those who mourn. We cannot help it. The Great Spirit does everything; but we will ask the Great Spirit to take the sickness away, and I hope he will make you well. That is all we will say to-day. To-morrow morning, at nine o'clock, we will meet in council. What you have said has been put on paper, and will go to the Great Father. There are some things I do not speak of, because I do not know about them, but all I do say is true. I will take your words to the Great Father, and he will do as he pleases. I want you to talk among yourselves, and tell us to-morrow what you will do about your land. When I came away from Washington I did not bring any presents, because I thought if I came to the Crows bringing a lot of presents you would think I would take advantage of you. But now that we are here and see you, we think we would like to give you something. We have to do the best we can. We have a few blankets we wish to give you. We give them to you to show you that we are your friends, the same as you showed us when you brought the robes to us.

Fifty blankets were then distributed among the chiefs and head-men; after which the council adjourned.

Second day.

AUGUST 12, 1873.

The council convened at two o'clock. Blackfoot made a long speech to his people, telling them of the number of whites that are coming into their country and going into Judith's Basin, eating the game, and their stock eating the grass on which the buffalo and antelope, the Indian food, feed.

The council opened with prayer by General Whittlesey.

Mr. BRUNOT. I do not wish to say the same things I did yesterday. I think you heard them all, and have thought of them, and are ready to say something in regard to the business of which we talked. We have been thinking about it, and so have you. Now you have something to say about it, and we are ready to listen. The business about the land is yours more than it is anybody else's. If a man has a great thing to think about he does not mind little things; if he sees the sun, and can look at that, he does not want to look at a little camp-fire. Some other time he will look at the little things; so now we will talk of the great matter, and some other time we will talk of the little things.

BLACKFOOT. What men say one to the other is good. Look at me. I am a big man. I have a big heart, and what I say is true. The whites have been digging gold at Emigrant Gulch for ten years. Perhaps the white men think the Crows do not know it, but we do know all about it. Above Emigrant Gulch I hear the whites have found other diggings. I love the Great Father, and I love my white friends. I will talk to you. The whites have been stealing our property. We are men, and know of it, and we will some day ask for the pay for our gold that the white men took from us. We used to go up the Yellowstone, and cross to the lake, and go through to Heart Mountain on the Stinking Water. That was our country. This summer we intend to go to Heart Mountain to get skins for our lodges. One time on Big Rocky (Rosebud) our camp met a wagon and white men with it. Four chiefs went and shook hands with the white men. The white men pulled out their revolvers and shot one of the Crow chiefs and killed him, and shot another who got well. When we heard of this we cried; we thought much about it, and then tried to forget it, because the white man was our friend.

Mr. BRUNOT. When was that?

BLACKFOOT. When General Sully first came into the country to fight the Sioux, (1862.) We do not understand you about the country. We understood Heart Mountain and Stinking River were in the Crow reservation, but you say it is not. Above the cañons they have been digging gold; now the whites want to take Heart Mountain, and we do not understand it. From Emigrant Gulch on this side we do not want to sell; above it we will sell you. We go to Judith Basin in the winter and locate on the creeks. The buffalo and antelope are ours. The whites kill them and put poison on them to kill wolves; they kill our horses with their poison. We say it is all right, because we love the white man and hold on to his hands. We are now telling you what we think. Dr. Hunter went down the river to the Warm Spring and located himself down there. I want you to hear and believe what I say. When we go for buffalo we find trappers hunting all over our country and men going everywhere on it. They think we do not know of it, but we do. White men who have married our women are stopping here for the Crows. When we kill our enemy, one who is hostile to everybody, the whites ought to be glad. A long time ago young White Bear, an Indian brave, and a white man, his friend, went together to fight the Sioux. They fought side by side. The white man was killed. Did the red man run away? No; he fought by the side of his white friend; and avenged his death. They fought hand in hand; and so they died. The bones of the red man and white are now mingled together. That shows we are friends of the white man; and as the red man and white man died, hand in hand, so ought we to live.

Right close to the agency this year Dr. Frost, a white man, and two Crow women were killed by the Sioux. The white man and the red women died together. That is why we want to war against the Sioux. The white men did not avenge the death of the white man, but we avenged the death of both the white and the red people. We think, when we died together as friends, we ought to live together as friends. We say, yes, yes, to what you say, and we wish to do what is best for both whites and Indians.

What we were told at Laramie I have in my heart. They told us to look out a white man with a good heart for our agent. We have found him. Here he is in Pease. He does not drink whisky; he likes us. He does not offer us whisky, and we like him. Pease never made any Indians mad at him; the children all like him; he is kind to all of us. What we ask you to do is to permit him to stay, and then we will listen to what you say. You come to hear what we have to say. I tell you, up above, on the river, the whites are digging gold. You can buy that country for the whites. We do not hide anything; we are men. From Emigrant Gulch to the Forks you can have; below it you cannot. I am a man, and that is what I say. We do not want a railroad alongside of the river. What do you think about it? We do not want Pease to go away. We never hurt a white man, and we can always look in the white man's face and shake hands with him. The Nez Percés Indians made peace with us, and they like us. The Bannock Indians shake hands with us, but they do badly. You should talk to them. When we went to Laramie the commissioners asked us to make peace with the Snakes. We did so and love them; we know and like Wash-a-kie, and we made peace with him. If you count the Crows there are fourteen hundred men. We would like you to give us guns enough for them, and plenty of horses, and to give us food for all time, as long as there are Crows, and that is what we want for our piece of land.

CRAZY SISTER-IN-LAW, (a chief.) We do not want Pease to go away. My boy does not want him to go away. He gives you a horse (to the commission) to keep Pease here. (He gave the commissioner a stick as a pledge representing a horse.)

Mountain Chief's daughter and Crazy Sister-in-Law's little daughter presented robes, saying, "We want Pease to stay with the Crow tribe." All the children gathered about Major Pease to hold on to him.

The council here adjourned unceremoniously, after which—

WHITE MOUTH said, "Blackfoot did wrong in sending everybody away from the council. I do not feel right about it. I thought the council was going to be a good one. We cannot help it, but we do not like it."

Other Indians came forward and said they had nothing to do with breaking up the council. Plenty of others wished to talk, but Blackfoot did it all.

Council re-assembled at five o'clock. Iron Bull, head-chief, being sick, did not return.

Mr. BRUNOT. Do any of you want to talk?

BLACKFOOT. You asked us to come back and now we want to hear what you have to say.

Mr. BRUNOT. We are glad to see the chiefs back, but we would like to see more of the young men, and hope more will come. I want to talk a little about what Blackfoot said, and about some other things. I want to talk as I always do, true and straight. I don't want my words to be like the winds that go off and are never seen again. I want them to go into your ears and into your hearts, and if you do not hear them now, some day you may be sorry for it. I want you to remember all I say, and some day you will say, that white man told us the truth. When a man sees the whirlwind coming, does he tell it to stop? No! He gets out of the way; he cannot stop it. A wise man looks ahead; he sees what is coming and he gets ready for it. I see what is coming over this country. I know what is good for the Indians, and I want you to know it, too. I have been on the Platte, and on Wind River, and on the Missouri, and away to the ocean, and what do I see? You do not see it, but I do. I see the white man's towns coming further and further; they are almost here. A few years ago, where these towns now are, there were buffalo. The buffalo used to be on the Platte, as they are now on the Big Horn and Powder River. They are all gone now. Why are they so plenty here still? They have been driven from there and have come up here. The Sioux cannot find any buffalo on the Platte, so they come up north to hunt them. If the Crows went to the Platte and the Republican, they would not find any buffalo there. They have come up here. And when they are killed off here, they will be all gone everywhere. Buffalo are the Indian's bread, but they are going away, and soon will be all gone, and the friends of the Indians want them, by that time, to have something else. We want you to have lands that you can keep, so that you will have plenty to eat; we want you to teach your children so that they may live on white man's food. These Indians who have eaten white man's food know it is good. When you went to Fort Laramie you made a treaty with the white men. I was not there, but here is the paper that tells me what the treaty was. It says, "The Crows shall have a piece of land always." It is for you and your children. That piece of land was marked on these maps. Some of you think it was larger than it is. I do not know who told you that. It was wrong; it was a mistake. If the Crows think the land is not large enough, I am sorry; but I see how hard it is to keep this piece of land for you. Some of it has the gold mountains on it. I see wherever gold mountains are, there white men go. They ought not to come here for it; it is not their land. The Great Father does not want them to come on the Crow land, but he is a long way off: he cannot see with his own eyes into the gulches and mountains. He has heard about the gold mountains and the people in them. He has also heard that the Crows do not go into the mountains much, and he thinks if the whites go into the Crow mountains, the Government ought to pay you for the lands. If the land goes away from you, by men going here, there, and everywhere, after a while it is all gone and you have nothing for it, but if you sell the land and let the people go into it, and the Great Father pays you for it, year after year, you will get things you need, and have them always. You will get them after the buffalo are all gone. The Great Father is making the railroad. It is like the whirlwind. I cannot stop it; nobody can. I might as well try to stop the Yellowstone with my hand. I cannot do it. The Sioux thought they had stopped the Great Father's soldiers last summer. The Great Father told the soldiers when they went there, if they met the Sioux and they made trouble, to come back, till they could talk about it, and now there are more soldiers coming this way than all the Sioux warriors number, and they are going to put a war-house on the border of the Sioux country, at the mouth of Powder River. You have not seen many of the Great Father's soldiers here; very few. But away to the east there are many thousands of them.

Now, about this land. I told you the Great Father wants to give you pay for it, and have you sell the mountains at this end of your reservation. It belongs to the Crows, and the Great Father does not want it to be taken away without your getting pay for it. Blackfoot talked about selling a little piece at the upper end. Suppose we were to say that will do; we will pay for that little piece; it would do no good. Here are mountains that people are going into now, and the same trouble would come again. Is not that so? I want to tell you another thing about the treaty, and I want you to know that it is not I who say this, but it is what the treaty says. I am going to tell you what the paper says. The Crows have for their lands always what is marked on this map, (showing the bounds of the reservation on the map.) Here is Crazy Mountain on the River; here is Judith Basin; here the Missouri. The treaty says this is the land of the Crows forever, (marking reservation.) Then it says as long as there are any buffalo, and as long as the white men are not here (in Judith Basin) with farms, they may go there and hunt. So on Tongue River and Powder River; you can go there. Blackfoot says white people are going into Judith Basin. The treaty does not say that whites dare not go there, but the treaty says Indians and whites both can go there. I never was in Judith Basin, but I have heard of it, and I have heard that it is a better country than this; that it is good for grass, and that there is plenty of water, wood, and game. I know the railroad is not going there, but that it is coming along here. I think if the Crow Indians could have Judith Basin instead of this, so that they would own it, and could come out and hunt here, it would be good. The way it is now, the Crows, the white men, and any other Indians can go there, but other Indians cannot come here without the permission of the Crows; but if the Crows had that for a reservation, the whites dare not go there at all, and other Indians could not go there without the Crows permitted them to do so. But the Crows could come here and hunt as long as there is game. That country there is not as large as this country here, but the country all around it you could go to all the same; but, because that country is not so large, if you go there you ought to have some pay for the difference. The treaty says the Crows were to be fed four years; somebody told the Crows it was forty years; that was a mistake; it was not true. This is the last year, but I do not want it to stop. I want that they shall have plenty to eat. The Great Father at Washington wants them to have plenty to eat, but every four years they have a new Great Father at Washington; perhaps some other man may be Great Father some day, and he may not want you to have these things. I hope you will always have them until you learn to make them like the white men; but I cannot tell; a new Great Father may be a different kind of a man. Now you can fix it so that it does not make any difference who the Great Father is, but you can always have plenty. You can do it this way: if you like Judith Basin, and want it for a reservation, we can go and say to the Great Father, it is smaller than this reservation, and for that reason you ought to have something always every year, in place of the big piece of country which you sell. We can ask him to give the Crows Judith Basin, and, because you give up this reservation, to give you food and things you need, so that you will never want. We can ask him to give you this, the interest of a million dollars, and every year you would get fifty thousand dollars in food and such things as you need; that is what we would ask the Great Father to do, and we think he would do it, but we do not know whether he would do it or not; he might think it too much, but if he thinks it is too much, and does not agree to it, it would be all the same as it is now. I have told you much that I think, and what I tell you is what I think is the best thing that could be done for you. These gentlemen with me all think the same way. I do not think I am wrong, and I know that I will not be afraid to meet the Crows anywhere, here or in the spirit-land, for what I have done is for your good and all I tell you is true and comes from my heart.

BLACKFOOT. What you have said we have listened to and we think it is true. At Laramie the treaty was made. We did not feel right. We had made a long journey and were tired and sick. They gave us some horses. They thought they were doing a big thing, and making us a big present. But the horses were wild like the antelope. We caught them with the lasso. They jumped and kicked; we held on tight to them, but they got away from us; we were sick hunting them, and when we got home nearly all of them were gone. The commissioners told me that we should have plenty of food given us for forty years. They were big men who talked with us; they were not drunk when they told us. We were men and heard them, and so it ought to be written in the treaty. I told the commissioners at Laramie that I had seen the Sioux commit a great massacre; they killed many white men. But the Sioux are still there and still kill white men. When you whip the Sioux come and tell us of it. You are afraid of the Sioux. Two years ago I went with the soldiers; they were very brave; they were going through the Sioux country to Powder River and Tongue River. We got to Prior Creek, just below here in the Crow country. I wanted to go ahead into the Sioux country, but the soldiers got scared and turned back. I was there and so were others who are here; they know what I say is true. The soldiers said they were going to Tongue River, but they got frightened at the Sioux and turned back. The soldiers were the whirlwind; they went toward the Sioux country, but the whirlwind turned back. Last summer the soldiers went to Prior Creek again; again they said they were going through the Sioux country, but they saw a few Sioux; they were afraid of them; they got scared and turned up to the Muscle-Shell, and went back again: again the whirlwind was going through the Sioux country, but again the whirlwind turned back. We are not the whirlwind, but we go to the Sioux; we go into their country; we meet them and fight, but we do not turn back; but we are not the whirlwind. You say the railroad is coming up the Yellowstone; that is like the whirlwind and cannot be turned back. I do not think it will come. The Sioux are on the way and you are afraid of them; they will turn the whirlwind back. If you whip the Sioux, and get them out of its way, the railroad may come, and I will say nothing.

We were born on this side of the Yellowstone and were raised here. It is good land. There is plenty of good land here. Timber and grass and water are plenty, and there is much game in the mountains. You talk about Judith Basin, and say you are going to give us plenty to eat. We do not want to exchange our land. You are my friend. If we were to go to the white man's country and bloody it as they do our country, you would not like it. For many years I have known the whites. You have a big heart, but it is not so with the white men who come into my country. Some of them never sucked their mother's breasts. I think they were raised like the buffalo, and sucked a buffalo cow for their mother. They have no hearts. I was not raised in that way; I am a man. I was raised and sucked milk from my mother's breast. There is no white man's blood on our hands, and I am not ashamed to shake hands with you. What I say is true. I am your friend. The sun sees me and hears what I say. The Great Spirit hears me and knows it is true. Did I ask these white men to come here and crowd me? Buffalo robes are my money; we have some buffalo left yet. If I go to the buffalo country and bring no robes back, the traders will not look at me; they won't be glad to see me and shake hands with me, and say "How," "How," as they would if I had plenty. I think you had better leave Pease with us as he was before. If you put anybody else here, very soon they will kick me in the face with their foot. All the men who have Crow women, we don't want them sent away. They are my friends and I want them to live as I do.

Mr. BRUNOT. About Pease I have nothing to say. I told you I liked him; and I like other good men who do right to the Indians. The Great Father does as he pleases about these things, so I have nothing more to say about it. But as to what I said about Judith Basin. I know every man cannot think alike. Blackfoot in some things does not think just as I do. He says what he thinks; I say what I think; both are men. What difference if we do not think alike in everything? We can be friends. I am not afraid to say what I know is right; so Blackfoot says what he thinks is right, and I like it. The Great Father sent me to talk to the Sioux; they asked for guns to fight the Crows. I said they could not have them. I was not afraid of Sioux soldiers; so now I would not be afraid of my friends, the Crows. If I am not afraid to speak to enemies, I am not afraid to speak my mind to my friends. I want you to know, and you *do* know, that what I say is true, and that it is for your good, so you will think and talk about it, and, perhaps, after awhile, you will think I was right. Suppose you think I made a mistake; you are still my friends; you are the white man's friend all the same. But you must talk about these things and see if they are not good. What have I been waiting for? Because I like you and want to do something for you. I have staid a long time; we have had two days' talk; we talked of things that were in the past and of things that are now. But this matter of the land is the most important thing; if we get it fixed we can settle the little things afterward. The agency buildings were burned up; they ought to be built somewhere else very soon, and they ought to be built and in a good place where the stake will be down strong; where there is plenty of wood and water and good farming-land, and where the Indians can stay in the winter without having their heads blown off by the wind. You want it where you can stay. Suppose the question of the land is settled; then we can locate the agency. If you decide to go to Judith Basin, we will put the agency on some of the streams there in a good place. Suppose you do not want to go there; then the agency must be put on some creek here. I am afraid if the stake is put down here it will not be a strong stake in the ground, but if it were put at Judith Basin, I think it would be, but it is for you to know what is best. You need not talk till you think about it. I think I can stay till to-morrow night, and I will hear all you want to say by that time. I think you can decide about these things, so we can take your words to the Great Father; so we can put it in a paper; but I do not know; we will see.

WOLF'S BOW. We have been talking to each other a long time. You have said what you have to say. If you want my land that is over here, (above,) I tell you we will sell it to you. We asked you for fifteen hundred guns of all kinds for the mines; we want them right away in ten days. If you want to build a new agency, go to the foot of the cañon on this side of the land we give you. We will go for buffalo, and when we come back we will find the new buildings there. We told the peace commissioners at Laramie we would hold on the white man's hands always. It was put on paper there; we have a copy, and I will show it to you. We said to one another then, we would never point our guns at each other as long as we were Crows. The Sioux fight the whites; they wanted to give us mules and horses to help them fight the whites, but we would not. We have fought the Sioux, and have left many good men on the battle-fields. When I go for buffalo, the Sioux fight me for my land. I will continue to fight them. If the soldiers go to fight my enemy, the Sioux, they do not go far; they turn back close to here. We went to fight them this summer; they were as well armed as we were. We want you to tell the Great Father the Sioux have more guns than they ought to have, and he ought not to give them any more.

Mr. BRUNOT. The Great Father does not give them any guns. I am afraid the Sioux get their arms from the same kind of people who give whisky to the River Crows. I got up to say that we have been here a long time. I have talked a great deal, and so have you, and we had better think about it a little. We have some tobacco we want to give you, and we want you all to come to-morrow morning.

After distributing some tobacco the council adjourned.

Third day.

AUGUST 13, 1873.

Council convened at 1 o'clock.

Blackfoot made a long speech to his people, closing up with the request that the commissioner should explain the treaty to them. He said there was nothing in the treaty of what they had said to the commissioners at Fort Laramie, and nothing of what the commissioners had said to them. He said our country is not as large as the commissioners promised it should be, and we do not understand the treaty as you read it. We do not think you will tell us a lie. None of the chiefs would accept this treaty. Show-his-face was the only one who was willing to take a copy of it. We want you to tell us what is in it. None of the Indians who were at Laramie know what is in this treaty.

The council opened with prayer by Dr. Wright.

Mr. BRUNOT. You would like to know everything that is in the treaty. I will tell you. I do not know whether what is in it is good and pleases the Crows or not, nor does it make any difference whether it pleases me now, or whether I like it or not. All I know, and all the Crows need to know, is that this is the treaty as it was signed at

Laramie. Yesterday I told you some of the things I read in it. To-day I will tell you again, because Blackfoot asks me to do so. It reads, "This is a treaty made at Fort Laramie, on the 7th of May, 1868, between the peace commission and the chiefs and head-men of the Crow Tribe of Indians." Article first says, "There shall always be peace between the Crows and the Government. If bad men, the whites or any other people, do wrong to the Crows, they must tell the agent, and the Great Father will have them punished. If bad men among the Crows kill or harm the white men or take their property, they are to bring them to the agent and have them punished."

BLACKFOOT. Who made this treaty?

Mr. BRUNOT. I will read their names: Generals Harney, Sherman, Augur, and others. This copy that Show-his face has was made by Captain Burt at Fort Smith, and it is a copy of the one the peace commission made. The one I have is just the same.

The second article says the United States agrees that this country shall be set apart for the occupation of the Crows and other friendly Indians, whom they wish to have and whom the United States consents shall occupy it. The country begins where the one hundred and seventh degree of longitude crosses the southern boundary of Montana; then up in a straight line to the Yellowstone; then following it till it crosses the southern boundary of Montana; and thence in a straight line east to the place of beginning. This country is for the Crows and the people who are sent to live with the Crows. Then it says after that time the Crows give up all right to any part of the United States except this part embraced in the reservation.

The third article says, because the Crows gave up the other country the United States agrees to build, on Otter Creek, a warehouse, a house for an agent, doctor, carpenter, miller, blacksmith, and engineer, and when the children of the Crows are sent to school, a man shall be sent to teach them; and a school-house shall be built; and when it is time to do so, the United States is to build a saw-mill, grist-mill, and shingle-mill.

Article fourth says, the Crows agree, when a house for the agent and other buildings are built, that they will make the reservation their home always, and they shall not settle anywhere else; but as long as there is peace between the Crows and the whites they may hunt buffalo where there are any and where there are not too many whites.

Article fifth says, the agent shall live among the Crows, and listen to their complaints, and do as the treaty says. If the Crows or the whites do anything wrong, the agent is to send word to the Great Father about it; and what the Great Father decides is right, that the agent shall do.

Article sixth says, if any of the Crows, or any one whom the Government and the Crows allow to live with them, wish to farm, the agent shall help them; and if any Indian selects a piece of land for a farm it shall be entered in a book, and it shall always be his, and he can get a paper from the agent to say that is his. The Great Father may, at any time, survey the land, and mark it out in patches, to show what each one owns. The United States may make laws to show what kind of title the Indian people shall have.

BLACKFOOT. It is all lies; we do not want to hear any more. Wrap it up and throw it all away. We will not have that treaty.

Mr. BRUNOT. You had better hear it all and know what you are to get. (At this point there was much excitement among the Indians, many of them declaring they would hear no more. After waiting a few minutes Mr. Brunot insisted upon silence, and said:) You asked me to read the treaty. I am going to tell you all that is in it. It goes on to say that all treaties made before this one are gone, but from the time of this treaty, the United States agree to send to the Crows the following articles: For each male Indian over fourteen years of age, a suit of good woolen clothes; for each woman over twelve years of age a flannel skirt, or goods to make it, some calico, or twelve yards of cotton domestic; and for the boys and girls younger than fourteen and twelve years, flannel and cotton goods to make each one a suit; and it says, so that the Great Father can send these things, the agent shall each year send word how many Indians there are to get them. This is to be done for thirty years. That is your annuity goods. In addition to this, the Great Father is to send money to the agent to use for the benefit of the Indians at the agency—not to give the money to them, but to spend it for their benefit and make them comfortable and happy. If the Indians do not want the clothing, they are to tell the agent what they do want; and if the Great Father thinks it is good for them he will send them what they want, instead of the clothing, but the agent must send to the Great Father word what they want, and the Great Father must give permission to do so, before any change can be made. For fear some one might not give all their goods to the Indians, some officer must come and see that they get them. The United States agree to send an agent, physician, engineer, blacksmith, carpenter, and farmer, and to pay them while they are here. It says the Crows must have food for four years.

I did not make this treaty. I see that, although the Crows may have made a mistake about the land, the treaty is good for them. The Great Father lives a long way off; he is trying to keep his part of the treaty; but I told you he could not see into the gulches and all these places, and he cannot come from Washington with all the goods that are sent. One man cannot always tell what is being done a great way off, but he wants to do the best he can for you, and wants you to do the best you can for him. You know the goods last year and year before were better than you got before. The reason is, men are trying to get what is right for you. I want you to understand it and know that there are bad white men, just as there are bad Indians. A bad white man steals your horse; it is not the Great Father, nor is he to blame for it. If a bad Crow takes a horse I do not blame it on Blackfoot; but if a white man takes a Crow horse the agent finds it out and tries to have the man punished. Sometimes he runs away. So it is with the Indians. The chiefs do not want bad Indians to do wrong; neither does the Great Father want bad whites to do wrong to you. Now, we all understand about the treaty, and we will put it away and say nothing more about it.

After you have been thinking about it, you may decide that Judith Basin is a good place to keep always. If you do you can then come here and hunt, just as you do there now. The difference is, now you own this, and hunt and stay over there; but if you sell this, you would own over there, and could come and hunt here. I have talked a long time, but it is your fault, not mine. You asked me to tell you what was in the treaty. When I told you some of it you wanted me to stop. That is not right. If you want to know what is in a man, you want to know all about him; so it is with this paper, and when you have heard it all it is not so bad for the Crows.

BLACKFOOT. We wanted to know just what was in that treaty, and my friend has told us. I have said before that we are friends, and that we like each other; yet we have different thoughts in our hearts. The first time I went to Fort Laramie and met the peace commissioners, what each said to the other, we said "Yes, yes." The second time we went, we signed the treaty; but neither of us, my white friends nor the Indian chiefs, said "Yes, yes," to what is in that treaty. What we said to them, and what they said to us, was "Good." We said "Yes, yes," to it; but it is not in the treaty. Shane was there the first time, and what he interpreted to us are not the words that are in the treaty. The first time we went, we did not sign the treaty; we only said "Yes, yes," to each other. The Indian way of making a treaty is to light a pipe, and the Indians and their white friends smoke it. When we were in council at Laramie, we asked whether we might eat the buffalo for a long time. They said yes. That is not in the treaty. We told them we wanted a big country. They said we should have it; and that is not in the treaty. They promised us plenty of goods, and food for forty years—plenty for all the Crows to eat; but that is not in the treaty. Listen to what I say. We asked, "Shall we and our children get food for forty years?" They said "Yes;" but it is not that way in the treaty. They told us when we got a good man for agent he should stay with us; but it is not so in the treaty. We asked that the white man's road along Powder River be abandoned, and that the grass be permitted to grow in it. They said "Yes, yes;" but it is not in the treaty. The land that we used to own we do not think of taking pay for. We used to own the land in the Mud River Valley. These old Crows you see here were born there. We owned Horse Creek, the Stinking Water, and Heart's Mountains. Many of these Indians were born there. So we owned the country about Powder River and Tongue River, and many of our young men were born there. So we owned the mouth of Muscleshell, and Crazy Mountain, and Judith Basin; many of our children were born there. So we told the commissioners. They said "Yes, yes;" but there is nothing about it in the treaty. We told them there were many bad Indians, but that we would hold on to the hands of the white man, and would love each other. We told them the Piegans, the Sioux, and other tribes have killed white men. We told them the whites were afraid of them. I asked them to look at us; that we had no arms, and they should not be afraid of the Crows. They said "Yes, yes;" but it is not so written in the treaty. The treaty, you say, has bought all our land, except on this side of the river. And what do we get for it? I am ashamed about it. We sell our land, and what do we get for it? We get a pair of stockings, and when we put them on they go to pieces. They get some old shirts, and have them washed, and give them to us; we put them on, and our elbows go right through them. They send us tin kettles; we go to get water to carry to our lodges; we dip the water up, but it all runs out again. That is what we get for our land. Why do they not send us annuity goods? We go to the buffalo country and get skins; our wives dress them, and we give them to our friends. We give more presents to our white friends than all the annuity goods we get are worth. And this is what we get for our lands. What goods are given us are no better than we give the whites, and I do not see what we are getting for our lands. We told the commission at Laramie that the Sioux were in our country on Tongue River. The Sioux and the Crows are at war; yet I went into the Sioux camp alone. They offered to give us two hundred and sixty horses and mules, all taken from white men, if we would join them; but we refused to do so. They took me by the arm, and asked me to stay with them and fight the whites; but I pulled loose from them and would not do so. I told the commission that I was asked to hold the whites with my left hand and the Sioux with my right hand; but now I gave my right hand to the whites, and would hold on to them; they said "Yes, yes." But none of this is in the treaty. We told them we had plenty of fish and game; and when they got scarce we would tell them, and ask help from them.

They said, "Will you sell the Powder River country, Judith Basin, and Wind River country?" I told them no; but that is not in the treaty. When Major Camp came here as agent, we gave him a present of a large number of robes to send to the Great Father. We never heard that the Great Father got those robes; we would like to hear about them. The Crow tribe want Major Pease to remain with us as our agent. Some of the young men want him to take them to see the Great Father at Washington. You ask us to tell you what we want. We want Mexican blankets, elk-teeth, beads, eagle-feathers, and panther and otter skins. We like fine horses and needle-guns; these things are to us what money is to you.

Mr. BRUNOT. I told you last night I could not stay much longer. I would like to stay a month, and then I might want to stay longer. I would like to stay and talk to you, and hear you talk. Our hearts are close together. You know what I have said is true. Sometimes we know a thing is good, yet we want to keep it away from us; it troubles us. A man has a horse which he likes; somebody offers him something for it that is better; at first he does not want to part with the horse; he thinks of it, and finds he gets something better for it; then he will let it go. Just so about this land. The place on which we were born and raised we think is all the good place there is. Those that were born on Wind River thought that no other place was as good; those who were born down on the Yellowstone thought no place was as good as that. The same men have been here a while; now they think this is better. You have this reservation; you think it a good place to live on; and you go to Judith Basin to hunt. You are right; this is a good place, and you do not like to think about making a change. It belongs to you, and you can do as you please about it. If you listen and do as I want, I think it is good. If you do not think it is good, I will still say you can do as you please about it. It is like a man who does not want to let his horse go till he thinks about it; when he thinks about it and finds it is better to do so, he lets it go. The man thinks about it till he gets his mind made up. It ought to be the same way about this business. You should think about it and talk about it. Do not put it away out of your mind until you are sure you are going to do right. Do not put it off till you find the commission is gone and all our words are lost. When we come together again you can come and tell us what you think about this business. If you put it off till some other time it may be too late. The treaty says the white men, the Crows, and other Indians can go to Judith Basin. If the Crows wanted to live in Gallatin Valley they could not do it. The white men are there; so, if the white men are in Judith Basin, the Great Father cannot let the Crows live there; it will be too late after the white men are there. The whites are not there now; and before it is too late I would like the Crows to think about it and decide. But do not forget you can do just as you like best. You are men, and can make up your own minds; and what I tell you is because I am your friend, and want you to have good houses and plenty to live on. If a man was to tell me to come and get some of the Crow land for myself, I would want to strike him to the ground. I do not want anything you have, nor do I come to get things for other men. I come because the Great Spirit tells me it is right to do good to the red men. What I say is from the heart, and the time will come when you will remember my words. I will say nothing more now. I want you to come and talk about the matter, and I will take your words to the Great Father. After that I will tell you something in regard to what Blackfoot said about going to Washington. I want to tell you about that after the other things are settled.

BEAR-WOLF. What we say and agree to, we say "Yes, yes," to, on both sides. Blackfoot went to Fort Laramie. They talked with each other; they said "Yes, yes." But when he came back we did not agree to what had been done. We want to go to Washington and see the Great Father. The chiefs are here, and we want to hold on to our lands. You bring a treaty; it is full of lies. The words that have gone to the Great Father have always been lies. Indians that fight the whites, the whites always do what they want. If you take us to Washington we will shake hands with our friends. The Great Father will talk good to us. I want no bad luck on the way. The old men are here; you see them; so are the young men. It is us who own the land, and we will have our say about it. We want you to give us the means to go to Washington.

The council here adjourned.

Fourth day.

AUGUST 14, 1873.

Owing to the protracted rain no general council was held to-day. The chiefs, however, were gathered in council, continuing all the afternoon.

Fifth day.

AUGUST 15, 1873.

Council convened at twelve o'clock. Blackfoot made a long speech to his people being frequently interrupted by the other Indians.

Council opened with prayer by General Whittlesey; after which three hours were given the Indians in which to discuss among themselves the propositions in the articles of agreement.

Council re-assembled at three o'clock.

Mr. BRUNOT. When we ceased talking in the council it was raining, and we said we had talked a good while and now it was time to think some and make up our minds. That was what I told you, and the chiefs said it was good to think about it. I told you to make up your minds, and whatever you said, so it should be. If you decided not to sell this place, then we know the Crows do not want to sell it; but I told you what I thought was good for you to do. I asked you to think and see if you could not do that. The next day it rained so much that we did not come together again. I think the rains came so that you would have a longer time to think, and decide what you would do. The rain comes on the ground; then the sun comes and makes the ground warm, and makes the grain grow for food for your ponies and the buffalo. So to-day the sun is bright and beautiful; and I hope that the Crows' hearts are good, and that they will decide to do what is good for themselves. Whatever you do I hope it is for a long time and for your good. We talked three days, and now this is the last day to talk, and whatever is done must all be done this evening, so that we may go in the morning. What I said was put in a paper; and if you have decided to go to Judith Basin, we will put our names to the paper, and you will put your names to it, and we will take it to the Great Father at Washington. But if you have decided the other way, we will tear up the paper, shake hands, and be friends all the same. Now we want to know what you have made up your minds to do.

BLACKFOOT. We have been meeting white men before. Whenever we met them we had something to say to them. We met you, and you told us what was written down you would take to the Great Father. We have talked three days, and my tongue is not tired.

Mr. Brunot then explained the provisions of the articles of agreement in a general way, and said: If you wish, the paper will be read; then you can put your names to it or not, as you wish.

BLACKFOOT. On this side of the river and on the other side is our country. If you do not know anything about it, I will tell you about it, for I was raised here. You mark all our country, the streams and mountains, and I would like to tell you about it; and what I say I want you to take to your heart. You make us think a great deal to-day. I am a man, and am talking to you. All the Indian tribes have not strong arms and brave hearts like we have; they are not so brave. We love you and shake hands with you, (taking Mr. Brunot's hand.) We have gone to Judith Basin a great deal, and you wish us to take it for a reservation. All kinds of men go there; trappers and hunters go there poisoning game. The Sioux Indians, Crees, Santees, Mandans, Assineboines, Gros Ventres, Piegans, Pen d'Oreilles, Flatheads, the Mountain Crows, the River Crows, Bannacks, Snakes, and Nez Percé Indians and white people, all go there. You wish us to take the Judith Basin for a reservation. All these Indians will come, and we will likely quarrel; that is what we think about it. Judith Basin is a small basin; a great many people go there; we all go there to eat buffalo. I have told you about the Sioux when they come to fight us. We go a long way from our camp. All Indians are not as strong as we are; they give up and run off. If you have two dogs, if they go to fight, and you catch them and pull apart, when you let them go they fight again. So it is with the Sioux and Crows. You tell me the railroad is coming up the Yellowstone. If you move this place away from here, the Sioux will be like a whirlwind; they will come and fight the whites; that is true as I tell you. Along Prior Mountain is the Crow trail. We listen to you, and what I tell you is true. The young men do not care what they do. We want some of them to go to Washington with Major Pease, and what they say there will be all right. I will tell you what we will do; neither of us will live forever; in time both of us will die. We will sell the part of our reservation containing the mountains from Clark's Fork, below the mountains, and the valleys we will not sell. The Crow young men will go to Washington and fix it up, and come back and tell us about it. We will sell the range of mountains to Heart's Mountain and Clark's Fork. The young men will sell it at Washington, and they will say to the Great Father at Washington, that the Crows have a strong heart and are willing to sell their land. When you buy this and give us plenty for it, we will talk about the rest, if you want to buy it. Those mountains are full of mines. The whites think we don't know about the mines, but we do. We will sell you a big country, all the mountains. Now tell us what you are going to give for our mountains. We want plenty for them. Am I talking right? The young men think I am talking right. Every one here is trying to get plenty. The railroad is coming. It is not here yet. You talk about Judith Basin. I have heard about it. I want to see what you will give for the mountains; then we will talk about the rest of our land. You think you have peace with the Sioux; I do not think you have. You want to shake hands with them. We want to know whether you are going to fight the Sioux or not; we want to know. We will see what the young men will do at Washington; if they hear what is good, we will do it. The railroad will not be here for some time, and before that we will be part of the time on this side and part of the time on the other side of the river. In the Gallatin Valley, if you sell a house and a little piece of ground, you get paid for it. I know that is the white man's way of doing. The white men are all around us. On the other side of the river all those streams belong to the Crows. When the Sioux come there, we can run them off into the river. We are friends; when our friends get horses stolen, we give them some. Many of our horses are stolen here; four of my horses are gone now; last night some horses were stolen. The Sioux took them along the mountains. On the other side of the gap, there are plenty of houses full of everything. In Gallatin Valley are plenty of cartridges; the Crows have none. If the Sioux come, I do not know what we shall fight them with. See all these old women! They have no clothing; the young men have no good blankets. We would like the Nez Percés, when they raise camp, to come here; they die with the Crows; they help to fight the Sioux. The last commission told us we could eat buffalo a long time. While we are here, the Flathead Indians take our horses. I would like you to take our part and stop them.

Mr. BRUNOT. We talked about the horses this morning with Major Pease; he is going to send and get them; and the troops will take the horses if they find where they are, and they will bring them back.

BLACKFOOT. We did not know you had talked about it. We would like you to say "yes" to what we said. At Laramie we said, yes! but not to what is in the treaty.

Mr. BRUNOT. Tell Blackfoot every man is not like every other man. I was listening, and I heard all he said, and it went into my heart. If a man hears something that makes him sorry, he looks sorry; if he thinks he is going to hear what is good, and he does not hear it, he looks sorry. I heard all he said; and when he got through, it was time for me to say something. Somebody took some horses. I heard it, and talked with Major Pease, and he is going to send for them; he is going to send to Fort Shaw, and if they find the horses, they will ask the soldiers to get them back. You have an agent to look after such things, and he does the best he can. So, Major Pease is going to try and get them back. They have one of our horses, too; I guess you did not know that. (This seemed to amuse them very much.) Now we will talk about the treaty; it is far more important than a few horses. The paper that we have made about Judith's Basin, I think we had better read; then you will know what I think is good for you. Then I will tell you what I think of your proposition. The miners were at Emigrant Gulch long ago; some are on Clark's Fork. The Great Father knows that; he could send the soldiers and make them go away, but suppose he should do that, what would happen? Some of these men would get mad at the Crows about it, and would do something wrong; and perhaps they would get others to help them, and perhaps the Crows would go after them, and somebody might get killed; perhaps a white man, perhaps an Indian. If somebody got hurt, his friends would want revenge; soon we would be quarreling. I do not want it to be so, nor does the Great Father want it. The Great Father says he does not want the Indians' land taken, nor does he want trouble; so he sends us to see whether you will take money for what the white men are doing; and find a place for the Crows where there is no gold for people to run after. If Blackfoot has a good American horse, and I have a horse that is not so good, I come and say we will trade, and he will say I do not want to trade; he thinks about it and says, "my horse is better and you must give me something more;" if I say, "I will give you something more," then we make the trade. So with this country; I say to you, you have a big country, and some of these people are on it; you like the country; I show you another country; you go to it; you like it; I say if you like that country, go there, and let the white people have this country, and we will give you so much. You get all the annuity goods and all that is in the other treaty, but you get them at Judith Basin instead of here. You live in this country now and hunt over there; if you listen to me, you will live over there and come here and hunt as much as you please. Then, every year as long as you and your children live, you have money from the Great Father to buy what you want. Every year the Great Father asks the agent what do the Crows want this year? The agent asks the Crows and the Great Father sends the things; that is the way it is in the paper. That is how it will be, if we all say, "yes," and put our names to the paper. The reason why I do not think Blackfoot's proposition is good, is this: if the Crows keep the valley and sell the mountain, the whites will want all the time to go through your country; your horses will not be safe. If you want wood it is nearly all in the mountain. You sell even the water-courses with them; it would not be good to sell that and keep this; do you not see that? The white men in the mountains would be glad if I agreed to what you propose. If I cared only for them, I might agree to it, but I care for the Indians and cannot agree to it. I do not think that would be good for any of us, for trouble might come. If you cut off all above Clark's Fork, I would carry the proposition to the Great Father, and he would give money for it, but I do not think that would be so good as to sell this place and take the other; you would not get as much for it. Blackfoot asked me about the Sioux; some of them live on the Platte and on the Missouri; they are holding the white man's hand, and they do not come up to fight the Crows, but there are some who are not holding the white man's hand. But the Great Father has sent his troops, and two boats have come to the mouth of Powder River and the soldiers are building a war-house there. They are there now; you will soon hear of their being there. In regard to going to Washington, I have something to tell you about it, but it is best not to talk of that until we have settled about the land. I think some of you ought to go to see the Great Father, and I want some of you to go, and I want you to come and see me at the same time. You will see the other gentlemen who are here, and you will have a nice time and be much pleased. You can tell the Great Father what we say "yes" to, with your own mouths. I want Major Pease to go with you. All I am afraid of is when you come back, all the Crows will want to go. Now I want you to take a vote and see whether you will agree to what we offer. The sun is going down, and what we do must be done soon. If you agree to what we offer, I will go away glad, for I think it is good. I have seen you a week, and I like you, and I want nothing but good for you, and I will always think of you, and will think for your good. I will do all I can for you, and whatever is right for the Great Father to send you, I will ask him to send; these gentlemen think the same. The Crows want some horses; we will ask the Great Father to send you some, but we will not put it in the paper, for the paper is for all time. The horses would be soon gone; but what is in the paper for you to get lasts always; you get them every year. I will read what is in the paper.

The articles of convention were then read as follows:

Articles of convention made and concluded on the 16th day of August, in the year of our Lord one thousand eight hundred and seventy-three, at the Crow agency, in the Territory of Montana, by and between Felix R. Brunot, E. Whittlesey, James Wright, commissioners in behalf of the United States, and the chiefs, head-men, and men representing the tribe of Crow Indians, and constituting a majority of the adult male Indians belonging to said tribe.

Whereas a treaty was made and concluded at Fort Laramie, Dakota Territory, on the seventh day of May, in the year of our Lord one thousand eight hundred and sixty-eight, by and between commissioners on the part of the United States, and the chiefs and head-men of and representing the Crow Indians, they being duly authorized to act in the premises;

And whereas by an act of Congress, approved March 3, 1873, it is provided: "That the Secretary of the Interior be, and he is hereby authorized to negotiate with the chiefs and head-men of the Crow tribe of Indians, in the Territory of Montana, for the surrender of their reservation in said Territory, or of such part thereof as may be consistent with the welfare of said Indians: *Provided*, That any such negotiations shall leave the remainder of said reservation in compact form, and in good locality for farming purposes, having within it a sufficiency of good land for farming and a sufficiency for water and timber, and if there is upon said reservation a locality where fishing could be valuable to the Indians, to include the same if practicable; and the Secretary shall report his action, in pursuance of this act of Congress, at the next session thereof, for its confirmation or rejection;"

And whereas, in pursuance of said act of Congress, commissioners were appointed by the Secretary of the Interior to conduct the negotiations therein contemplated, the said commissioners on the part of the United States, and the chiefs, head-men, and men constituting a majority of the adult males of the Crow tribe of Indians, in behalf of their tribe, do solemnly make and enter into the following agreement, subject to the confirmation or rejection of the Congress of the United States, at the next session thereof.

ARTICLE 1. The United States agree that the following district of country, to wit: commencing at a point on the Missouri River opposite to the mouth of Shankin Creek; thence up said Creek to its head, and thence along the summit of the divide between the waters of Arrow and Judith Rivers, and the waters entering the Missouri River, to a point opposite to the divide between the head-waters of the Judith River and the waters of the Muscle-Shell River; thence along said divide to the Snowy Mountains, and along the summit of the said Snowy Mountains in a northeasterly direction, to a point nearest to the divide between the waters which run easterly to the Muscle-Shell River and the waters running to the Judith River; thence northwardly along said divide to the divide between the head-waters of Armell's Creek and the head-waters of Dog River, and along said divide to the Missouri River; thence up the middle of said River to the place of beginning—the said boundaries being intended to include all the country drained by the Judith River, Arrow River, and Dog River—shall be and the same is set apart for the absolute and undisturbed use and occupation of the Indians herein named, and for such other friendly tribes or individual Indians as from time to time they may be willing, with the consent of the United States, to admit among them; and the United States now solemnly agree that no persons except those herein designated and authorized so to do, and except such officers, agents, and employés of the Government as may be authorized to enter upon Indian reservations in discharge of duties enjoined by law, shall ever be permitted to pass over, settle upon, or reside in the territory described in this article for the use of said Indians; and the United States agree to erect the agency and other buildings, and execute all the stipulations of the treaty of Fort Laramie (the said stipulations being hereby re-affirmed) within the limits herein described, in lieu of upon the south side of the Yellowstone River.

ART. 2. The United States agree to set apart the sum of one million of dollars, and to hold the same in trust for the sole use and benefit of the Crow tribe of Indians, the principal to be held in perpetuity, and the interest thereof to be expended or re-invested, at the discretion of the President of the United States, annually, for the benefit of said tribe.

ART 3. It is mutually agreed between the United States and the Crow Indians, that the second article of the treaty made at Fort Laramie between the commissioners of the United States and the Crow tribe of Indians be, and the same is, abrogated by this agreement, and the said Indians cede to the United States all their right, and title, and claim, to the tract of country described in the said second article, to wit: "Commencing where the 107th degree of longitude west of Greenwich crosses the south boundary of Montana Territory; thence north along said 107th meridian to the mid-channel of the Yellowstone River; thence up said mid-channel of the Yellowstone to the point where it crosses the said southern boundary of Montana, being the 45th degree of north latitude; and thence east along said parallel of latitude to the place of beginning," and which is conveyed to them therein, except the right to hunt upon said lands so long as they may remain unoccupied, and as game may be found thereon, and peace continues between the whites and Indians.

ART. 4. The United States agree to suppress, so far as possible, by the imposition of pains and penalties, the practice of wolfing, or killing game by means of poison, within the limits of the following district of country, viz: beginning at the mouth of the Muscle-Shell River; thence up the said river to the North Fork, and up the North Fork to its source; thence northward along the summit of the Little Belt and Highwood Mountains to the head of Deep Creek; thence down said creek to the Missouri River, and along the margin of said river to the place of beginning.

It is expressly understood between the commissioners and the Indians, parties thereto, that this agreement is subject to the ratification or rejection of the Congress of the United States at its next session, and that, pending the action of Congress, the United States shall prevent all further encroachments upon the present reservation of the Crow tribe.

The articles were carefully explained until they were fully understood by the Indians.

THIN BELLY. I say let them have the land.

LONG HORSE. We will give you this land for what you say. This side of the river belongs to us; we will sell it. These are our chiefs. We have waited for Iron Bull and Blackfoot to say they will sell the land; they don't say so, but the young men now say to sell it. I am going to come here to hunt. Do not let wolfers come here. These young men are chiefs and want to go to Washington to see the Great Father; let them go.

IRON BULL. Take the names of those who will sell; they will not touch the pen to sign the paper; they think it is bad luck; they will come up and say "yes," "yes."

BLACKFOOT. We smoke together; we talk through the pipe. As I told you, we are friends. The young men say they will sell and we agree to it. We want all on the other side of the river away up to Judith Basin. It is a small country.

Mr. BRUNOT. The Great Father sent me; and I do what he says if I think it is good for those I am talking to. What I thought was good I put in the paper.

BLACKFOOT. You ought not to give the Sioux guns and ammunition; you should wipe them all out; you should throw a bad disease on them.

Mr. BRUNOT. The Great Father did not tell me to talk about the Sioux. I have told you what is in this paper. Now we want all who agree to this to come and say "yes," so that after it is all over, nobody can say it is the fault of somebody else. I will put my name to it and I will never be afraid to say that I think this is good for the Crows. If you don't want to agree to this paper you will say so, and there will be none of it. I want all of you to say "yes," and then we will know it is all right. We will call the names and if you don't want to say "yes," don't say it. If more say "yes" than say "no," it is good.

MANY INDIANS. It is too small a country in the Judith Basin. We want from the Yellowstone to the Missouri.

OLD CROW. If we take Judith Basin we can shoot from one line of our country to the other line.

IRON BULL. We want to move over there, but we want all the other side of the river; that is what we want, and we tell you so.

Mr. BRUNOT. I don't say "yes." I want to talk to the young men. You say you want all the country the other side of the river; that is a bigger country than this. If I would give it, I would have to say, "What will you give for the difference?" Some people will talk that way. Most of the country over the river white people cannot live on, and never will live on. Why did I not put that in with the Judith Basin? That would make your land as big as this. If I went to the Great Father and said, "I gave the Crows all the other side of the river for this," he would say, "Why did you do that?" If I said "I promised to give the Crows, every year, food and clothing besides," he would say, "That will not do." It is no use to tell him that. But if I say, "I gave the Crows a smaller piece of land and they give you a bigger piece of land, you must give them goods every year," he will say, "That is all right." If I put in the bad land, that will make it as big as this reservation, and it would do you no good except to hunt on, and you can hunt there anyhow.

BLACKFOOT. The Crow country is a big country, and we will give it for the country on the other side of the river. What I tell you is good for both sides; and we want, besides, what you told us you would give us. This is our country, and what we give is worth more than all the other side of the river. You want to give us a little hole; we want a big country; you gave the Sioux a big country, and the Crows are a big tribe and want a big country. While Blackfoot was speaking a woman came forward to speak.

THE ONE WHO GOES RIGHT STRAIGHT ALONG. I am a woman and ought not to speak in council, but I want to speak of the first council on Horse Creek. My brother went to the States and never came back. You want to give us a little territory, and we don't want it. The whites killed my brother, for he never came back, and you never paid me anything for him. Another time we were on the Little Horn; we lived in a big grass lodge, and a white man poisoned my other brother, and he died. You bought our land before, and gave us kettles that would not hold water. We want all the other side of the river from the mouth of the Yellowstone. I want my son to have a big country; you offered us a little country and I don't want it.

OLD CROW. Tongue River, Rosebud, Powder River, and Big Horn are full of wood. In Judith Basin is no wood for a camp.

MR. BRUNOT. I am afraid some one has been talking to you who is not a Crow, and you have his ideas. If I were a Nez Percé, I might say to you do not take Judith Basin; if I were a Blackfoot, I would say do not take it; if I were an Assineboine, Piegan, or Bannock, I would say to you do not take Judith Basin; if I were a Wolfer, I would say do not take Judith Basin; and what is the reason? All these people can now go in there; if it belonged to the Crows, they could not. May be some of this kind of people have been talking to you; if any of these people advise you not to take it, you can see the reason. I told you the second day why I wanted you to have Judith Basin. Now, I tell you according to the treaty, the white men, the Wolfers, and other Indian tribes can go there the same as the Crows. These men are going in there, more and more of them, every day. If you put off, for a year or two, getting it, so many whites will be there, that you can not get it. That was one reason I was desirous you should have it now. It is not a big country; I know that is a small country. The time was when all the country from the Missouri River to the mountains had no white people; now there are a great many. Blackfoot spoke about the Sioux; there were a great many Sioux; they roamed on the plains, on the Platte, and the Republican, as they pleased. They went and fought the Utes, they went as far as they pleased. The Kiowas and Comanches were all over that country once. The whites said they were going to make a railroad, and all these Indians said as a few Sioux do now, they would not have it. If you go down there now you will see not one railroad only, but many railroads, and when your young men go to Washington, they will go ten times as fast as a horse can go. That railroad was made; the Sioux could not stop it; what could they do? They could go to the white man's cabin, where he slept, and kill him, but they do not go there to do it now, and the reason was they did not take the white man's hand then; the Great Father sent them away to the barren lands on the Arkansas, and the Sioux will be pushed I do not know where. The Great Father does not want to serve his friends so. The Great Spirit tells us we are of one blood, and must do what is good for the red men who hold our hands, as we would for our children, and that is the way I feel to the Crows. And that is why I come here. Now I have come and said what I think is right. I have given the Great Father's message. The Great Father wants to save trouble. He is willing to pay you for the mountains the white people have been going into. I told you there was a good place where you can stay forever, and it is a good place for you to go to. I have told you how the buffalo have left other countries and how they will go from this. When the buffalo is gone, if you stay here till then, you can only live on a piece of this country. You can only hunt on the other side as long as there are any buffalo. Your ponies can range on the Yellowstone, and they can range up to the Judith, but you cannot cover it all over with your villages; because your lodges don't cover it all over is no reason why you cannot hunt on it. This place is your home; it does not keep you from hunting where you please. If you take Judith Basin for your home, it is the same thing, only that is your home. You know that is a better place than this to stay both summer and winter; you stay there now longer than anywhere else. If your agency was there it would be better and you could come to this country to hunt. You say you want all the other side of the river for your reservation; that is not what the Great Father tells me to say. I cannot give you that, because the Great Father will say the paper is not good. I thought you had made up your minds to say yes to what we offered, but you say you want something else. I have said all I have to say about that proposition. We offer land, and we offer money every year for food and for the goods you need. I am going away, and that is the end of it now. But I will always think about the Crows as friends, and I hope whatever you do will be good for you. I do not know that I will ever see you again. You will remember my words, and some day you will know what I said was good for you, and all I said was true. I want some of the chiefs to go and see the Great Father. Suppose I was to die as I go to the Great Father; nobody would think the Crows killed me. Because there was a Crow man went a long way and died on his way home, that is not because the white men did bad; it was because they gave him so many good things to eat; but these young men must not eat so much. Now we will shake hands and stop the council, and it is all over, but we are better friends than when we first saw each other. But if the chiefs want to come yet and agree to the paper, they can come.

BEAR-WOLF. We want you to hold on a while. I want to go with Pease and see the Great Father and talk with him. We want to go and see how it is. You claim all on the other side of the river and give us a small piece of land. We want to go and see about it; we want Bravo and Shirley and Major Pease to go with us. We offer to give you a big country and a rich country; we love our Great Father, that is why we offer to give it to him. You want to give us a little country where there are no mines.

The council here adjourned. After the council, Iron Bull, Long Horse, and Shot-in-the-jaw, expressed themselves as favorable to making the exchange, Thin Belly having expressed the same desire in the council. Iron Bull, Long Horse, and Thin Belly are three of the principal chiefs, Blackfoot being the only principal chief not expressing a willingness to agree to it.

Sixth day.

AUGUST 16, 1873.

In the morning all the chiefs and young head-men came and expressed a desire to sign the agreement.

Mr. BRUNOT, after ascertaining that they fully understood it, said: You wish to tell me that you agree to the exchange for Judith Basin, as it is in the paper.

ALL THE CHIEFS. Yes; we all agree to it.

Mr. BRUNOT. I want you all to come, one at a time, and say "yes." Bring all the others, and they will say "yes;" and then none can say we did not do it.

IRON BULL. If all the chiefs say "yes," that is enough.

Mr. BRUNOT. It is better the others should say so too.

They then came forward, one at a time, and said "yes." In signing, all expressed the wish that they might be permitted to eat buffalo as long as there was any; others asked that they should have horses; others asked for guns; and many asked that Agent Pease should be retained. To all of these the explanation was fully given that the paper did not promise any of these things; but they were told that when they went to see the Great Father they could talk to him about giving them what they wanted.

All who were present, being all the chiefs and head-men, (except one,) came forward, and, fully understanding the articles of convention, assented to them, each saying "yes."

At twelve o'clock we left the agency for Bozeman.

Respectfully submitted,

THOMAS K. CREE,
Secretary.

To the SPECIAL CROW COMMISSION.

F.

REPORT OF T. C. JONES AND JOHN M. MILIKIN, SPECIAL COMMISSIONERS TO NEGOTIATE WITH THE CREEK INDIANS FOR THE CESSION OF A PORTION OF THEIR RESERVATION.

To the Hon. COLUMBUS DELANO,
Secretary of the Department of the Interior:

SIR: The undersigned, commissioners appointed by you to negotiate with the Creek Indians for the cession of a portion of their reservation, occupied by friendly Indians, under the act of Congress approved March 3, 1873, beg leave respectfully to submit the following report of their proceedings:

In pursuance of an agreement as to the time of meeting, the undersigned met at the office of Central Superintendent Enoch Hoag, in the city of Lawrence, in the State of Kansas, on Monday, the 20th of October, ultimo. On the following day we left for Okmulkee, in the Creek territory, where we arrived on Wednesday, the 22d.

The national council of the Muskokee Nation had been in session some weeks, and was making preparations for an early adjournment. Having been advised that the council had appointed a commission composed of nine members to confer with us in reference to the subject-matter of our mission, we availed ourselves of the earliest moment practicable to meet said commission. Accordingly, on the morning of the 23d, we met the committee appointed by the Creek council.

After our commission had fully stated the purpose of our visit and had expressed what we understood to be the wishes of our Government as to the desirableness and importance of an early and satisfactory adjustment of the question involved in the case before us, and had made special inquiry as to the character and extent of the territory occupied by the Seminoles within the limits of the Creek country, the committee on the part of the Muskokee Nation informed us that the powers delegated to them were restricted; that they were acting under special instructions from the council, and thereupon proceeded to read to us the resolution under which said commission was constituted. The resolutions are as follows:

"*Be it resolved by the national council of the Muskokee Nation*, That the said commission of nine be, and are hereby, prohibited from the sale of the strip of land in the Creek country, now occupied by the Seminoles and Sacs-Foxes.

"*And be it further resolved*, That in the event that the Seminoles residing on said strip of land desire to remain and become a part of the Creek people, according to the provisions of the treaty of August 7, 1856, that the said commissioners on the part of the Creek Nation are fully authorized to make such arrangements as will secure this end with the commissioners on the part of the United States."

Having no authority to act in the contingency named in the second resolution, we did not enter into any discussion upon the question of the Seminoles becoming citizens of the Creek Nation, under the provisions of said treaty; as the positive prohibitory terms of the first resolution made it useless for us to present any consideration as to either the duty or expediency of the proposed cession, we informed the Creek commissioners that, unless the council could be induced to reconsider its resolution imposing the restriction, the duty intrusted to us must be regarded as at an end, and requested the committee to communicate this to the council, with such suggestions as they might see proper to add as to the propriety of a further consideration of the subject.

Our views, as expressed to the Creek committee, were very promptly communicated to the house of warriors, one branch of the national council, and we were soon invited to appear before said body. We were kindly received and invited to present the views of our Government in reference to the question concerning which we were empowered to negotiate. Your commission urged the importance of an early and equitable adjustment of the difficulty which had occurred. We expressed our belief that there had been no intentional wrong perpetrated by either the Creeks, the Seminoles, or the Government of the United States; that it was an unfortunate difficulty in which all parties were involved, and that our Government, influenced by no selfish considerations, wished to interpose, to see that substantial justice was done to all parties, so that no conflict of authority should arise, and that no disturbance might be provoked, which should lead to very disastrous results. Other points were pressingly urged, tending to show that the proposed cession could do no possible harm to either the pecuniary or other interests of the Creeks, but that, on the contrary, it would leave the Creek treasury from temporary embarrassment, and would unite the Creeks and Seminoles in the bonds of an enduring fellowship. We concluded our talk with the house of warriors by respectfully asking them to reconsider the action of their body, by which they had prohibited their committee from entering into any negotiations for the sale of a part of their territory.

The considerations which were submitted to the house of warriors were received with at least no indication of disfavor. Subsequently, in our unreserved and friendly intercourse with the chiefs of the nation, and with the members of both branches of the council, we availed ourselves of opportunities offered to urge such arguments as occurred to us, and which we regarded as conclusive, as to the duty and expediency of the proposed cession. In our frequent conversations upon the subject, and in endeavoring to ascertain clearly the influences which had induced the action of the council, we found that the principal chief of the nation, the Hon. Samuel Chicote, had discussed in his recent message to the council the question of making sale of any portion of their territory to the United States. Desirous of obtaining the fullest information upon the subject we obtained his message for perusal, a copy of which, so far as relates to this subject, we herewith return, marked A.

Having examined the message, and there being no indication of action by the council, after three days had elapsed we requested an informal meeting with the Creek committee for free consultation, which was held in the executive chamber in presence of the Chief Chicote. Here in a friendly way we referred to the points taken in the message, and replied to them with such arguments and suggestions as seemed proper under the circumstances.

On the morning of the same day Chief Chicote, with the second chief, Micco Hulkee, accompanied by an interpreter, called upon us for a friendly conference, and manifested a good deal of anxiety to maintain friendly relations with our Government. He intimated that his people were opposed to a cession of lands; stated that they had been divided and their peace disturbed by internal controversies, and that he feared, now they were becoming united, to disturb them with this question.

We inquired of him if he did not expect, in cases of breaches of the peace in the territory now claimed by the Creeks and occupied by the Seminoles, that conflicts of jurisdiction might arise endangering the peace of the tribes? He admitted that there might be such danger, and agreed with us that the sooner the controversy was settled the better. We called his attention to the fact that he was informed of the pending of the bill in Congress under which our commission was appointed, and the purpose it was hoped that it might accomplish; that his delegates were in Washington City and intimated no objections, nor did the Government learn that any opposition existed until the arrival of our commission here. To this the chief answered that the Creeks were like a sick man trying to recover, careful and timid in action. In this conversation we were strongly impressed with the conviction that the chief had become satisfied that the adjustment proposed by the Government would have to be made. While we dissent from the points made by the chief in his message, we are free to say that we believe that he was prompted by no unkind or unfriendly feelings toward our Government or its officers. We found him in all things fair and honorable, and entirely willing to afford us all the facilities we desired in seeking information, and in having unreserved communication with the national council.

Notwithstanding the honorable bearing of the principal chief and his exemption from ill-feeling in reference to this question, it is proper for us to say that several things have occurred which manifestly had an unfavorable influence upon the chief and the temper of a large number of the Creek Nation. Doubtless, no intentional disrespect to the Creek authorities was meant, and yet matters were frequently referred to in our conversations as having produced unfavorable impressions. One point referred to was the refusal of the Seminoles to meet the Creeks at Okmulkee, to negotiate a basis of settlement in regard to that portion of the Creek domain occupied by the Seminoles. Entertaining the opinion that "the question was one of such grave importance to their people, and involved, as they thought, questions which they had no power to control or determine," the Seminoles declined to accept the invitation of the Creeks. Another irritating incident was the erection of a Seminole agency building on the disputed territory, against the request of the Creek chief to have the work on said building "postponed until the question at issue between the Seminoles and the Creeks should be adjusted." A third matter of complaint was the letter of the Hon. F. A. Walker, Commissioner of Indian Affairs, dated on the 18th of April, 1872, directed to F. S. Lyon, esq., United States Indian agent. This communication, a copy of which marked B is herewith forwarded, directs the Indian agent "to inform the Creek authorities that until the question of the Seminole district shall have been settled by the Department the Seminoles must not be interfered with."

However important it was in the judgment of the Commissioner of Indian Affairs that the peremptory order referred to should be issued, it was nevertheless unfavorable in its influence upon the minds of the Creek people; and doubtless to some extent it inclined the minds of many against granting the reasonable request which the United States Government is making in behalf of the Seminoles. We refer to these topics to account in part for the very decided disinclination which we found to exist, when we first arrived at the Creek capital, to treat for the sale of any portion of the Creek territory.

Finding it difficult to ascertain with accuracy the wishes and the condition of the Seminoles, and the width of the strip of land in controversy, and the precise location of the Seminole people on the Creek soil, and also to remove the objection urged by the Creeks that the Seminoles were unwilling to meet them in consultation, we decided to send a communication to the chief of the Seminoles requesting them to come to Okmulkee, so that we might confer with them in reference to the general subject in dispute. Accordingly, on Friday, the 24th, Chief Chicote very promptly furnished a messenger to convey our communication to the Seminole chiefs.

The response of the Seminoles to our message was received on the 26th, in which the chiefs say that "it is fully understood between the Commissioner of Indian Affairs and the Seminole Nation that the matter rests wholly between the Creeks and the United States Government." They then add: "We have, however, appointed a council to meet on Monday morning, the 27th instant, to confer on the subject, and the results of its action will be immediately made known to you either by letter or delegation."

Having received no official answer from the national council to our request that they would reconsider their instructions to their committee, on Monday morning, the 27th, we determined to make to the council a written communication, which, after consultation with Chief Chicote, was presented to the council by the Hon. Pleasant Porter, one of the leading members of the house of warriors. The following is a copy of our communication:

"*To the national council of the Muskokee Nation now in session:*

"The undersigned, United States commissioners, beg leave to call the attention of your honorable body to the fact that, at our first meeting with the commission appointed by the national council, upon learning the purport of the instructions under which they acted, we informed them that the only power we had was to negotiate for a cession of the land covered by the possession of the Seminoles; and as your commission was prohibited from treating with us on that subject, our mission was at an end unless the national council would modify their instruction. We requested the commission to communicate this to the council, which was immediately done. The United States commission was afterward notified that the Creek council would hear any other observations we might see proper to submit. Accordingly, on the same day, we appeared before the council and submitted a brief statement of our views on the subject of our mission, and the importance of an early disposition of it. And we respectfully requested that the national council should take action at their earliest convenience and notify us of the result. Four days have since elapsed and we have no response. In view of the possible contingency of the failure of the negotiation we are authorized to make, we sent a message to the Seminole chiefs, requesting their presence here for consultation in regard to the wishes and views of their people in the premises. They have answered that the settlement of the matter 'rests wholly between the Creek Nation and the United States Government;' that they will, however, hold a council on the subject this morning and advise us of the result. In the mean time we beg that you will excuse us for urging upon your attention the importance of an early and satisfactory disposition of the matter we are instructed to adjust.

"We are deeply impressed with the belief that a failure is likely to result in disagreeable consequences, which may involve two friendly tribes that are closely allied in blood in serious complications. We are not willing to leave the matter in this situation, because we know the importance and the necessity of all these tribes being united for mutual protection against the machinations of those who are urging measures that are believed to be seriously prejudicial to your interests. We believe that if you decline to sell the lands now occupied by the Seminoles to be used as homes by them serious conflicts growing out of contending claims of jurisdiction must arise, unless the Seminoles will agree to give up their improvements and abandon their homes.

"You tell us that you are unable to see why they will not give up their separate tribal relation and submit to your laws. We are equally unable to understand why all the tribes that have been so long settled in this great Indian territory cannot unite under one general government. No doubt it would be greatly to your interest in all respects to form such a union and establish such a government. We are compelled, however, to take things as we find them.

"We can hardly think that you are ignorant of the fact that if adherence to your present position were possible it would end in driving the Seminoles from their homes. We repeat the question, is this desirable? If it were possible for you to force it, what would be done with the improvements made by them in good faith? Are they to be left on your soil without compensation? Although you are not responsible for their being there, as an honest people do you propose to take possession of these improvements without compensation? These are questions which must be met in the contingency which you seem to contemplate.

"Understanding that the Seminoles were placed in the possession of these lands by the United States authorities, you will appreciate the anxiety of the Government on the subject, and will understand that, while it is disposed to do justice to all parties, it is unwilling to see the Seminoles compelled to leave their homes. You will therefore see that a satisfactory and early settlement of this question is extremely desirable to preserve the cordial and friendly feeling existing between your nation and the United States authorities.

"We therefore respectfully ask that the national council without delay will carefully reconsider the question whether, under all the circumstances, it is not best for their nation and the peace of the tribes to sell for the benefit of the Seminoles the strip of land now occupied by them.

"ENOCH HOAG,
"*Central Superintendent.*
"T. C. JONES,
"JOHN M. MILLIKIN,
"*Commissioners.*

"OKMULKEE, *October* 27, 1873."

To the foregoing communication on the evening of the ensuing day we received the following answer:

"OKMULKEE, COLO., *October* 28, 1873.

"*To the honorable commissioners, Enoch Hoag, Superintendent of Indian Affairs, T. C. Jones, and John M. Millikin:*

"GENTLEMEN: Your communication of the 27th instant, relative to the adjustment of the complication engendered by the settlement of Seminoles on Creek territory, has been carefully considered, and we deem it proper to respectfully reply that we feel that we can very reasonably hope that our adherence to our present position, not to cede any land, will not impair the cordial and friendly relations now existing between the authorities of the United States and the Creek Nation. We cannot understand why our anxious desire to hold that which is our own, guaranteed to us by solemn treaty stipulations, could possibly endanger the good feeling now existing between us and the United States Government. We have complied with the demand of the United States, and ceded to her, the west half of our entire domain for the settlement of friendly tribes thereon. The Seminoles purchased of the United States a portion of this ceded territofy, and if the United States Government, contrary to her promises, located the Seminoles on our reserved territory instead of that purchased by them, and have held them there and encouraged them to make improvements thereon, we cannot clearly see, by the ordinary mode of reasoning, why we should be held accountable for the difficulties arising out of the course pursued by the United States Government. Inasmuch as we have been kept out of the use of this part of our domain for a period of seven (7) years, and taking it into consideration that the materials with which said improvements have been made were our property, these improvements would not more than compensate us therefor. We feel that these improvements can be possessed by us without the violation of any principles of honesty, and if the United States Government is unwilling to remove the Seminoles and locate them upon lands set apart by treaty stipulations for their benefit and occupancy, we have no power by which we can force the measure. The land is ours. Your own survey shows it. Your Government officially tells us that it is ours. You tell us it is ours in your communication. Our only desire is to possess that which is ours. Can you with justice withhold it? Can you, moved by a spirit of justice, intimate that we should be held accountable for your Government's wrongs to the Seminoles? We think and hope not.

"In adhering to our present position, not to cede any portion of our domain, we conscientiously believe that we are pursuing the best interest of our nation. If we are forced from our position we will be divested of a valuable portion of our domain, and (as usual in Indian land cessions) will be but poorly compensated therefor. If the Seminoles are removed to the lands set apart for them by the United States Government they lose no territory.

"You expressed fears that conflict of jurisdiction would engender disagreeable consequences and serious complications. This we doubt not, if we were to attempt to extend jurisdiction over the Seminoles now residing in our territory. But as we have been prohibited so to do by the United States authorities, we have quietly acquiesced and restricted such operations, supposing the Government of the United States desired us so to do temporarily, until she could remove the Seminoles or engraft them with the Creeks. We still have no serious desire to extend jurisdiction over that part of our domain occupied by the Seminoles, if the United States Government will within a reasonable time remove the Seminoles, thus avoiding any conflict of jurisdiction of which you seem fearful. We have ever shown an anxious desire of cultivating and preserving friendly relations among the Indian nations and tribes, fully appreciating the necessity of unity of feeling and concert of action on the part of the Indians, in order to combat the dangers which are constantly threatening them, upon which you manifest so much anxiety. In view of all the circumstances connected with the matter, we are still unwilling to cede the territory in question. Trusting that the United States Government will not set aside our claim to be justly dealt with, we claim its protection and friendship."

The foregoing was duly signed by the presiding officers of both branches of the national council.

After we had made our first communication to the council, on the 27th of October, we deemed it not improper to address an informal note to Chief Chicote. It was only intended to be suggestive to him, and was written without any expectation that it would be presented to the national council for their consideration.

The chief, however, anxious that full and free communication with the council should be enjoyed by the United States commissioners, deemed it proper to send our note to that branch of their government, that it might be duly considered. The following is a copy of our letter to the chief:

"OKMULKEE, *October* 28, 1873.

"SIR: The undersigned, commissioners for the United States under the act of Congress approved March 3, 1873, entitled 'An act to authorize the Secretary of the Interior to negotiate with the Creek Indians for the cession of a portion of their reservation occupied by friendly Indians,' beg leave respectfully to call your attention to the fact that negotiations of the character we are authorized to make are always conducted with difficulty with a body so large as your national council, especially in the latter days of a session, when so much other business is claiming special attention.

"We therefore beg the privilege of suggesting whether it would not be wise to appoint a commission, with full power for and on behalf of your nation, to negotiate with commissioners acting for the United States, for the cession of the lands in said act referred to, for the purposes therein mentioned, on the basis of an exchange for other lands to be conveyed to the Creek Nation, or other fair and adequate consideration, and for the final settlement of your reservation as provided in said act of Congress.

"The fact that little or no progress has been made in the negotiation during the many days we have labored here, and our desire to return to our families, we trust will be a sufficient apology for our troubling the chief executive with this communication.

"Very respectfully, your obedient servants,

"T. C. JONES,
"JOHN M. MILLIKIN.

"Hon. SAMUEL CHICOTE,
"*Principal Chief of the Muskokee Nation.*"

The foregoing letter to Chief Chicote having been communicated to the council and referred to the committee on foreign affairs, the council returned to us the following answer:

"OKMULKEE, CREEK NATION,
October 29, 1873.

"To the Hon. Commissioners, T. C. JONES and JOHN M. MILLIKIN:

"GENTLEMEN: Your communication of date to the executive, in which you proposed an exchange of other lands for those occupied by the Seminoles, has been carefully considered. We, after considering all the circumstances connected with the matter, cannot see that such an exchange would give a practical solution of the problem. We understand that the lands proposed for exchange are those which were set apart for the Seminoles, by the United States Government, and, as a part of the Seminoles are now residing in the territory, the same troubles that now exist must necessarily continue. If we were to exchange we could not well extend our jurisdiction over that part of our domain, as there will be another government between us and that part of our territory.

"In view of these circumstances we most respectfully decline your proposition to exchange."

The foregoing was duly authenticated by the officers of both branches of the national council.

It will readily be perceived that our letter to the chief was not clearly understood by the council. We suggested that the Creek Nation appoint a commission *with full power to negotiate for the cession of the lands*, in said act referred to, *on the basis of exchange* for other lands, *or other fair and adequate consideration.* The exchange of lands did not necessarily refer to the lands of which the above letter speaks. Neither was the basis for negotiation limited to an exchange of lands. Any *other fair and adequate consideration* could become the basis for an equitable adjustment of the pending difficulty.

On the morning of the 29th, having reluctantly come to the conclusion that we could accomplish no valuable results by remaining longer, we deemed it proper to submit the following answer to the communication received from the council on the previous evening:

"OKMULKEE, *October* 29, 1873.

"*To the national council of the Muskokee Nation:*

"We are making arrangements to leave for our homes this morning, and have only time for a brief reply to your communication received last evening.

"We regret to observe that you contemplate no solution of the matter we were appointed by the United States to adjust, but a submission of the Seminoles or their removal from their homes. You are aware that the first condition will not be complied with, and the harsh alternative of a removal will, you are fully aware, be seriously predjudicial to the advancement of this kindred tribe in civilization. We had hoped that you would aid us in avoiding it, as the Government had signified its willingness to make you an adequate compensation.

"We do not question your sincerity in asserting that the cession would be prejudicial to your interests, but we are confident nevertheless that, according to the judgment of those best informed in the American agriculture, whether stock-growing or tillage, such a cession for the purpose proposed, in view of your extensive domain and sparse population, would be regarded as highly advantageous.

"We had therefore expected, as doubtless the Government did when the act of Congress was passed, and the commissson appointed under it, you would generously agree to the method proposed to avoid driving your brethren from their homes. We need hardly tell you how deeply we deplore your refusal. Occupying the position of impartial observers and contemplating all the circumstances, we are constrained to say that we fear that the general judgment of your best friends will be that a compliance with the request of the Government would not have been an unreasonable thing to expect.

"As to your views in regard to the improvements made by these people under so many hardships, we have to say that the suggestion of loss on your part, on account of being deprived of the use of these lands, in view of the tens of thousands of acres of unoccupied and unused lands of corresponding quality in all parts of your territory, seems to us wholly untenable. And as to the materials used in the construction of improvements, when we consider the abundance of these materials and the little care taken for their protection and preservation, we can hardly believe that the Creek Nation would seriously think of basing a claim upon it.

"It would be exceedingly gratifying to us if in returning rom what now seems a fruitless mission, we could entertain the hope that your nation would reconsider its position, and would co-operate with the Government in settling an important question in which the Seminoles, the Creek Nation, and the United States are seriously involved.

"Very sincerely, your friends and well-wishers,

"T. C. JONES,
"JOHN M. MILLIKIN."

After the foregoing was forwarded to the council, and we were preparing to leave, the chief called and requested us to remain a day or two longer, intimating that a more favorable action might be anticipated, our last communication with a message from the chief urging action having been read in the council.

Deeming it wise to remain as long as there was any hope of accomplishing the object of our mission, we determined to comply with the chief's request.

On the afternoon of the same day, Thomas Cloud arrived from the council of the Seminoles, giving us the information that a committee had been appointed by the Seminoles, of which committee he was a member, to meet us on the ensuing Saturday, the 1st day of November. He had been sent forward to give us the earliest notice of the doings of the Seminoles in council. We availed ourselves of the presence of said Cloud, and of another very intelligent Seminole named Fusharjo, to learn to what extent the Seminoles were occupying territory lying east of the dividing-line, to obtaining information as to the part of the country they occupied, and to finding out the wishes of the Seminoles as to a removal, and as to their becoming subjects of Creek authority.

On Thursday, the 30th, we were advised that the house of warriors, after a very able and exciting debate, had passed by a strong majority a resolution authorizing the appointment of a committee with full power to negotiate for the cession of the contested lands.

The resolution was sent to the house of kings, where an adjournment was carried before a vote could be taken. This proved unfortunate, as it afforded the demagogues (found here, alas! as well as in the States) an opportunity to canvass their forces, and by appeal to the Indian prejudice against selling land, to organize an opposition, which, upon a final vote, on the next day defeated the resolution, thus putting an end to the negotiation.

Having, therefore, no power to accomplish the object of our mission, and having derived from Thomas Cloud and Fusharjo all the information that we had expected to obtain from an interview with the Seminole chiefs, we determined to take our departure from Okmulkee. As the council had adjourned, and the members were leaving for their homes, there seemed to be no reason why we should remain to meet the Seminole committee, which was expected to arrive on the next day. We addressed to them a letter, stating the adjournment of the council and the uselessness of our longer stay at Okmulkee, and returned our thanks to them for their compliance with our request. We forwarded our letter by Thomas Cloud, one of the members of said committee.

After making the foregoing detailed statement of our proceedings as commissioners with the Creek authorities, it will not be out of place for us to give a brief statement of such facts as come to our knowledge, having immediate connection with the question we had hoped to be able to settle in conformity with the instructions of our Government.

1st. The strip of land in dispute is between eight and nine miles in width, and about thirty miles long, and contains between 155,000 and 170,000 acres.

2. Most of the Seminoles reside east of the established line, there being only two small villages containing between one hundred and sixty and two hundred inhabitants on the west side of said line.

3. A line running east and west, dividing both tracts into two equal parts, would leave nearly all of the Seminoles in the south half.

4. There are not more than from two to four Creek families residing among the Seminoles.

5. The Seminoles are unwilling to surrender their possessions, or under any circumstances to come under Creek authority. We are reliably informed that on these points is entire unanimity of opinion.

6. The Seminoles are desirous of retaining possession of all the lands in question, as well those lying west of the line as those claimed by the Creeks. They were located on the disputed territory by Mr. George Reynolds under the superintendency of Mr. Wortham.

The position and purposes of the Creeks, aside from what is embodied in their official proceedings, are as follows:

1. While insisting that they have been patient and forbearing with the Seminoles, and submissive to the rather hard requirements of the United States authorities, they claim that they own, and are entitled to the possession of, all the land lying east of the established line, and that they have a clear right to exercise exclusive jurisdiction over the same.

2. Heretofore they have not exercised their authority over the lands occupied by the Seminoles lying east of said line. In the future the chief, in answer to an inquiry, told us he would not claim that cases arising between Seminoles shall be subject to Creek authority. Cases arising between Seminoles and Creeks, or between Creeks, he claims shall hereafter be adjudicated under Creek authority.

The Creeks are entirely willing that the Seminoles shall retain their possessions, provided they will acknowledge Creek authority, and live in submission to its requirements.

Notwithstanding our failure to accomplish the object of our mission, we are not without hope that, on the whole, the termination of the negotiation, as above detailed, may in the end prove beneficial. The effect of the discussion has certainly been most favorable. When we arrived at Okmulkee the sentiment in all quarters was unanimously against the cession. When we left, it was with the more intelligent and influential immensely the other way.

If the resolution to authorize the appointment of commissioners had passed, it is probable that, with the pressure recently so strong against the cession, that the commissioners would not have been willing to accept a price that would have been satisfactory to the Government. Time will greatly modify opinions in regard to important questions bearing upon the compensation the United States ought to pay. We think we have convinced the Creeks that the Government did not wish to interfere with their policy in regard to the cession of territory, and that the sales in question being to a branch of their own tribe, now engaged in developing the great agricultural resources of the Indian Territory upon their border, and thereby contributing to their prosperity, the adjustment proposed was not only reasonable in itself, but one that would result in decided advantage and profit to the Creek Nation.

All of which is respectfully submitted.

T. C. JONES,
JOHN M. MILLIKIN,
Commissioners.

NOVEMBER 10, 1873.

F 2.

EXTRACTS FROM THE MESSAGE OF CHIEF CHICOTE TO THE CREEK NATIONAL COUNCIL, HELD IN OCTOBER, 1873.

"In the treaty of 1866, the Muskokee Nation ceded to the United States the western half of their domain for the purpose of settlement thereon, by the United States, of other friendly tribes and freedmen. Before a survey was made setting apart the ceded territory, the Seminoles settled on the Wewoka River and commenced to make their homes, and when the legal survey by the United States was made, as provided for in the treaty, the Seminoles were found to be occupying and living on Creek soil, and even after the establishment of the boundary line by the United States survey, and according to the express terms of the treaty, and with full knowledge of the facts, the Seminoles continued to make improvements, and the United States Government, with the same knowledge of the facts and treaty stipulations, has caused the new Seminole agency buildings to be erected on Creek soil."

The national council, in October last, instructed the principal chief to communicate with the Seminole authorities and invite them to Okmulkee to negotiate a basis of settlement, in regard to that portion of our domain their people were occupying. The following is a part of the resolution passed by the last national council directly touching the Seminole question:

"*And be it further resolved*, That, in order to arrive at such a basis of settlement, the principal chief of the Creek Nation is hereby instructed and fully empowered to proceed upon negotiations with the United States authorities.

"*And be it further resolved*, That, should the principal chiefs and Seminole authorities arrive at a satisfactory basis of settlement, he is hereby authorized to instruct a delegation to adjust this question with the Government of the United States after the manner agreed upon with the Seminoles."

I appointed the 12th day of November, 1872, as a time for a conference at this place. The Seminole authorities did not see proper to meet us at the time and place proposed; but I received a communication from the chiefs that they declined "because the question at issue was one of such great importance to their people, and involved, as they believed, questions which they had no power to control or determine." Subsequently the Seminoles appointed a delegation to go to Washington City, and make known their wishes to the United States Government. Thus this important matter remains unsettled and in the same position that it did at the last session of the national council.

On the 9th of May last I addressed a communication to Major E. R. Roberts, United States agent for the Creeks, informing him of the preparations being made to erect the agency buildings for the Seminoles, on Creek soil, and requested him, as the agent of the Creeks, to have building of the agency postponed, until the question at issue between the Seminoles and Creeks should be adjusted. In reply Major Roberts states as follows, relative to the occupancy of a portion of the Creek soil by the Seminoles tribe of Indians: "I have the pleasure to state that, under act of Congress approved March 3, the honorable Secretary of the Interior has appointed a commission, consisting of three members, to visit and negotiate with the Creeks for the cession to the United States of such portion of their country as may have been set apart in accordance with treaty stipulation for the use of Seminoles, &c., found to be east of the line separating the lands from the Creek reservation."

I also received a letter from Hon. Enoch Hoag, superintendent of Indian affairs, in which he states that he was in receipt of a letter from one of the commissioners appointed to negotiate with the Creeks for the purchase of a strip cut off from the Seminole reserve by a recent survey. Mr. Hoag states that the commissioners in behalf of the United States were T. C. Jones, of Ohio, John M. Millikin, and himself, and proposed an early day in July last as the time to enter into negotiations. I replied to Hon. E. Hoag, in a communication dated June 16, last, that I could not name a day earlier than the first Tuesday in October, at which time the national council met, and which alone had jurisdiction in the matter of negotiations with the United States commissioners. Now at this time the presence of the United States commissioners is expected for the object as indicated in act of Congress approved 3d March last, and I respectfully recommend that your honorable body take action providing for a special commission to meet and confer with the United States commissioners, giving them full power to negotiate under such instructions as your wisdom and a proper regard for our honor as a nation, and the best interests of our people and their prosperity will suggest.

In connection with this subject it is not inappropriate to remind you that many years ago the Muskokees lived east of the great Mississippi River, the father of waters, and were the undisputed possessors of a vast territory, whose extent, compared with our present limited domain, makes the latter appear insignificant. But our people made treaties with the United States Government, until they became dispossessed of all those grand possessions, and then emigrated to the far West in the hope of securing peaceful and permanent homes; but since coming here they have continued to make treaties with the United States Government, and in 1856 parted with a large portion of their new domain; again, in 1866, they sold to the United States one-half of the then Creek territory, and now the United States again wishes us to sell them a considerable portion of our already too greatly reduced domain.

It is true the Creek domain as it now is may appear a considerable territory on the map, and exhibit an area larger than the needs of our population if closely farmed in cereals and other field crops; but we know a large portion of it is mountainous and swampy, unfit for any valuable purpose except as grazing ground, and for that purpose our entire territory to-day is not too large when the marked increase in stock raising is considered. If the improvement in this industry continues, and there is every reason to believe it will, in a few years our people will find their domain too small, and if we sell the country now occupied by the Seminoles, the young and rising generation of Creeks may find themselves restricted in territory, and debarred from the pursuit of a livelihood in the manner which is most agreeable to their natural instincts and habits of life. Such being my convictions I would respectfully submit that, in the negotiations with the United States commissioners, it would be unwise on our part to relinquish the strip of land sought of us to be ceded. If the Seminoles prefer to remain where they are, rather than there should be a further disintegration of our territory, let them remain in the homes they have made on Creek soil and submit themselves to the jurisdiction of the Creek government. The Creeks and Seminoles are a people of one language and the same blood. There are many Creeks living among the Seminoles, and many Seminoles among the Creeks; and if the proposed arrangement could be perfected it would be hard to discover whereby either would be injured.

DEPARTMENT OF THE INTERIOR, OFFICE OF INDIAN AFFAIRS,
Washington City, April 18, 1872.

SIR: This Office is in receipt of a communication from Agent Breiner, under date of the 2d instant, transmitting one from the chief of the Seminole Indians, setting forth that the Creeks had informed the Seminoles that, according to the recent survey, the latter are upon the lands of the former, and can only remain there by becoming subject to the Creek laws. That No-case-yau-holer Judy, of the Wewoka district, has, in obedience to instructions received from the chiefs of the Creeks, notified them that they must conform to the requirements of the Creek laws, &c., and adding that, in consequence of such interference in their affairs, they are greatly alarmed.

In view of the foregoing you are instructed to inform the Creek authorities that, until the question of the Seminole district shall have been settled by the Department, the Seminoles must not be interfered with.

Very respectfully, your obedient servant,

F. A. WALKER,
Commissioner.

F. S. LYONS, Esq., *United States Indian Agent, present.*

G.

REPORT OF E. P. GOODWIN, J. A. CAMPBELL, AND S. R. HOSMER, SPECIAL COMMISSIONERS TO INVESTIGATE FACTS CONNECTED WITH THE "RAWLINS SPRINGS MASSACRE," IN WYOMING TERRITORY, IN JUNE, 1873.

To the Hon. COMMISSIONER OF INDIAN AFFAIRS:

The special commission appointed to investigate the facts relating to the killing of a number of Indians near Rawlins Springs, Wyoming Territory, on the 28th of June last, have the honor to submit the following report:

In the absence of the Hon. N. J. Turney, and the non-arrival of his successor, Stephen R. Hosmer, esq., in accordance with the instructions of the honorable Secretary of the Interior, Gov. John A. Campbell and Rev. Edward P. Goodwin commenced the investigation at the earliest practicable moment after the notification of their appointment.

It seemed to us of first importance to secure the testimony of the parties at Rawlins as principals in the affair; accordingly we visited that place, and on the 21st and 22d of July took the sworn statements of the persons who seemed to have most connection with, and knowledge of, the matter. Following that, we proceeded to Fort Steele and took the evidence of Lieutenant Rogers, who visited the spot where the fight occurred, under the direction of General de Trobriand, and noted facts of importance connected therewith.

On the 24th of July we met Mr. Littlefield, Indian agent for the Utes, by appointment, at Laramie, and took his sworn statement respecting the non-participation of the Utes in the fight.

Returning to Cheyenne we were joined by Commissioner Hosmer, who had arrived during our absence. In view of certain reports communicated to Governor Campbell by Dr. Daniels, Indian agent for the Northern Arapahoes, Sioux, and Cheyennes, we arranged for a meeting on the 30th of July at Red Cloud agency with certain Arapahoes, said to have been in the party fired upon, as also with such of their chiefs as could be induced to be present.

On our arrival at the agency we found, much to our disappointment, that Dr. Daniels was absent; that none of the Arapahoes said to be concerned in the affair had been notified, or were within reach. We were compelled accordingly to be content with the second-hand statements made to some of the Arapaho chiefs, more particularly Plenty Bear and Black Bear's son, (known as Black Whiteman,) by members of the party on their return.

The names of the whites engaged in the affray, copies of all the evidence taken, and statements made, are herewith submitted to the Department.

Passing to the results of the investigation, it appears beyond doubt that the Indians concerned were not Utes, as at first supposed, but Arapahoes. The party of whites who did the shooting undoubtedly believed the Indians to be Utes. But the admission of the Arapahoes that they were the party, their grief for the loss of their dead, and their demand for the return of the ponies and guns lost, and for compensation to be made to the relations of the Indians killed, would seem to be decisive.

And with this agrees the statement of Agent Littlefield that the Utes knew nothing definitely of the fight; that none of their number were either killed or missing, and that no feelings of resentment or hostility had been aroused among them.

It is the conviction of the commission that the affair was very nearly what it would appear to have been from the sworn statements of the Rawlins party. The version given by the Arapahoes differs materially from these, as was to be expected. But neither their account of the movements of the Indians prior to the fight nor their explanation of the fighting was satisfactory, while their proverbial disregard for truth even in matters of trifling importance, according to their agent, makes their statements of little worth compared with the sworn and agreeing testimony of the whites.

The truth would seem to be that a party of Arapahoes, made up largely of young braves, eager to win distinction, took the war-path for a raid upon their traditional enemies, the Crows; that, hearing while on their way that there had been a recent fight with the Crows by a party of Arapahoes and Cheyennes, they concluded that it would not be wise to make the attack proposed, and decided to attack the Utes instead; that they turned their course to the south for that purpose, and crossed the railroad ten or twelve miles west of Rawlins; that some of their party captured two horses belonging in Rawlins while out at pasture; that two of their number concealed in the sage-brush near the road, the rest being in advance and on the bluffs or hills to the south, espied a young man coming with a four-mule team; that they concluded suddenly to capture the team, and accordingly fired upon and wounded the boy in the foot; that he returned the fire, and hastening back to Rawlins gave the alarm, whereupon a party of ten, headed by the sheriff of the county, started immediately in pursuit; that they supposed the Indians to be Utes and followed them, not with the intention of making an attack upon them, but of ascertaining who they were, that they might inform the agent and urge upon him the necessity of keeping the Indians in his care upon their reservation; that, on overtaking them, or rather heading them off, the next morning, the Indians claimed to be Utes; that the whites recognized and positively identified two horses as belonging to citizens of Rawlins; that they insisted on the surrender of the horses, and upon the Indians refusing to give them up they insisted upon their return with them to Rawlins to meet the agent of the Utes then expected there; that the Indians declared they would not go; that they denied also the shooting of the boy, charging it upon the Arapahoes; that while the whites were seeking to persuade them to return to Rawlins the Indians suddenly drew their pistols and firing behind them as they rode, spurred their horses into the bushes; that the whites returned the fire, killed and mortally wounded four of their number, captured eleven horses and one Winchester rifle, and came back to Rawlins; that the Indians buried two of their dead where the fight occurred, and two on their way back; that they abandoned the proposed expedition against the Utes, and immediately returned, not to the agency, but to the Indians farther north, and that they now claim the surrender of the lost horses and gun, and also that presents be given to the relatives of those killed in the fight.

As is shown by the evidence, the investigation sought to ascertain exactly how the trouble originated, and precisely who were the aggressors. The result is, in the judgment of the commission, that the whites do not appear to be blameworthy. Their evidence was positive and agreeing that no old grudges existed which they were anxious to avenge; that there had been no difficulties with either Utes or Arapahoes due to recent gambling or horse-racing; that the members of the party were not intoxicated when the fight occurred, and that there was no liquor with the party; that there was no ill will from any cause felt toward the Indians, but that, on the contrary, a consultation was held before coming up with the Indians, wherein it was agreed that they would not attack them unless themselves attacked; that the Indians fired the first shots, and they returned the fire in self-defense; and furthermore did not pursue the Indians after they took to flight.

The commission are therefore of the opinion that the trouble was wholly due to a war expedition growing out of an ancient feud between the Arapahoes and the Utes, which expedition was in direct violation of the treaty ratified by the Northern Arapahoes and Cheyennes in 1868, whereby they bound themselves not to cross the Platte nor go beyond the limits of their reservation, hunting excursions alone excepted.

It is therefore the judgment of the commission, that no just claim can be set up on the part of the Indians, either for the return of the captured property or for damages incurred by the fight. And the commission find it difficult to see how such claim can be entertained without putting a virtual premium on the very elements of willful lawlessness which it is the prime object of all Indian treaties to repress.

At the same time the commission readily perceives that, with reference to future dealings, it may be deemed politic by the Department to conciliate the Indians by the restoration of the captured horses. But it is felt that this should only be done coupled with the emphatic declaration by the Department, that the Indians had justly forfeited all claim to the property; and they should further be made to understand, that the Government cannot be expected to keep its pledges while they break theirs; and that, therefore, with every violation of their agreements, they must expect not only the censure of the Government, but the penalty which such violation entails.

As to the best means to prevent such collisions in the future, concerning which it is made the duty of the commission to report, the commission desire to express themselves with great diffidence. They feel that such a question goes to the root of the whole Indian policy, and that to have clear and decisive opinions, and to be sure that these are wisely settled, where so many and so delicate questions are involved as is the case respecting the relations of whites and Indians on our frontiers, is no easy thing.

Nevertheless the investigation made by them has developed and deepened in the minds of the commissioners certain convictions which they venture to express for the consideration of the Department.

First, then, it appears to the commission that it would be a helpful step in the management of Indian affairs to have the various reservations surveyed at the earliest practicable day, and their boundaries and limitations thoroughly and permanently established so far as may be practicable; it is greatly to be desired that such boundaries should be the natural ones of mountains, streams, divides, and the like. The Indian finds great difficulty in getting right notions of imaginary lines of latitude and longitude. The consequence is, that he is easily betrayed into violations of treaty stipulations, both as respects invasion of the territory of the whites and that of other Indians; and naturally out of such disregard of lines and boundaries, sooner or later, trouble comes.

2. Another and fruitful source of "irritation" is the practice of issuing passes or permits whereby Indians, individually or in small parties, are allowed to go beyond the limits of their reservations.

Such permits are always liable to abuse by offering temptations to thievishness, predatory forays among the whites which provoke retaliation and excite bad blood, and similar raids coupled with more hostile intent upon other Indians. And the facts go to show that in many if not in a majority of instances, Indian nature is not proof against the temptation held out, nor white nature proof against the prejudice aroused, and in consequence outbreaks occur.

The general feeling along the frontier is strongly against the system, and your commission feel certain that it is productive of more mischief than good and should be done away.

3. Your commission venture further, and raise the question whether it would not be a great gain to so shape the policy of the Department as to prohibit at an early day all going beyond the bounds of their reservations by the Indians for whatever purpose. This would interfere, we are aware, with the hunting privileges now enjoyed, and would hence be, without doubt, strenuously opposed by the various tribes enjoying such immunities. But there can be little debate as to the value of such a prohibition in preventing the collisions which under the present order of things continually occur.

Through the opening of the Pacific Railroad, with its connections, these hunting-grounds of the Indians have been thrown open to settlers and immigration is rapidly pouring in. The mining-districts also, which border the reservations, are rapidly filling up; the result is that the hunting expeditions of the Indians find, on the one hand, increasing difficulties in their path as respects the securing of game, and on the other increasing temptations to run off stock, pillage, and commit depredations generally; and the likelihood of collisions and troubles with the settlers and other whites is obviously very much enhanced by the multiplied opportunities afforded of procuring liquor, indulging in gambling, horse-racing, and other vices to which the Indian is prone, and out of which almost inevitably mischief and often bloodshed comes.

Furthermore, it is the clear policy of the Government, as witnessed in all treaties with the Indians, to induce them, at the earliest possible day, to give up their roving and predatory habits, and, instead of relying upon the always uncertain supply of game, to become cultivators of the soil with permanent homes, and thus gradually, under the influence of labor-schools and other appliances of Christianity, cease to be a savage, and become a civilized people.

Obviously, this is the only way in which, apart from utter extermination, a complete end of Indian troubles can ever be hoped for; and this involves the necessity of a surrender, at some time, by the Indians, of the present privilege of hunting beyond the limits of their reservations. It seems therefore to your commission that the true interests of both whites and Indians imperatively demand that the policy of confining the Indians to their reservations be steadily and strenuously urged; and whenever difficulties should occur in the application of such policy, as they doubtless would, especially in its initiation, it would seem to your commission better to secure its establishment by increasing the amount of annuities or of supplies granted than to take the risk of pillage and bloodshed inseparable from the present system. And if the expense of such a policy were deemed by any an objection thereto, it ought to be sufficient answer to say that by the witness of experience, it is vastly cheaper to feed the Indians than to fight them. So the honor of the Government must be maintained and the beneficent ends it proposes, as respects both whites and Indians, be realized. The avoidance of collisions is cheap at any price.

4. But the most prolific cause of trouble remains to be noted. It is the fact, attested by our conferences and witnessed to by both Indian agents and officers of the Army who have had most acquaintance with the tribes, that there is neither any organic unity among them, nor any recognized permanent and responsible headship. The Indian chiefs, certainly among the Sioux, Cheyennes, and Arapahoes, with whom we had more particularly to do, are the braves, who, by their prowess and daring, have won renown and made themselves leaders by a kind of popular acclaim. They are, however, clothed with no authority, have no control over their respective tribes other than their personal influence, and hence can only lead and act for them to the extent of their ability to persuade the Indians to accept their views. At any time a rival may arise, and, either by his eloquence or his deeds, wrest away the chieftainship and become the chosen leader of the people. The consequence is that the tribal headships are incessantly changing, and hence what has been agreed to under one chief is repudiated under another, or sometimes part of a tribe will cling to one chief and abide by his counsel, and part adhere to another, and thus two authorities come to exist, each supreme in its sphere, and yet in direct antagonism as upon such a question as that of peace or war.

Naturally enough the Indian transfers this notion of obligation into his dealings with the Government, and accordingly thinks himself freed from the compacts entered into by his chiefs whenever these change their opinions, as they so often do, or whenever other chiefs with differing views get the people's ear and usurp their place. Further, because of the lack of anything like tribal unity and hence of tribal responsibility, they deem themselves not bound by the engagements of their chiefs unless they personally concur in the desirableness of what is done.

In illustration of such notions, the commission found that the Arapahoes interviewed by them did not consider themselves bound by the treaty of 1868, mostly because they had not personally agreed thereto, and partly because another set of chiefs, who had not been parties to the treaty, had, since its ratification, come into power. And that this is the prevalent Indian notion of obligation, would appear from the fact that no demand for the surrender of Indians known to have committed depredations or outrages upon the whites can be enforced anywhere upon the frontier. Your commission have been repeatedly assured, alike by the officers of the Territory of Wyoming and those of military posts situated therein, that they are powerless to secure the apprehension of such wrong-doers, although their delivery by the Indians upon demand by the proper authorities is one of the first provisions of every treaty.

So long as such ideas obtain, it must be obviously impossible to ratify treaties that will be of any avail. Indeed, it is more than doubtful whether, among all the numerous tribes or bands throughout this region, a single treaty is to-day regarded by the Indians supposed to be obligated thereby as of binding force in all its stipulations: while they insist stoutly upon the full measure of all the pledges entered into by the Government, they seem to think themselves privileged to be their own judges of the good faith to which they are held. And thus it happens that, in the main, the only force of these compacts with the various tribes is with those who are either in sympathy with the objects they propose, or who have discernment enough to see that conformity to the treaty is their only sure means of securing the bestowals of the Government.

In this state of things, something more is needed to insure peace than a reliance on the good faith of the Indians in carrying out the provisions of the treaties made with them. As in the case of the Rawlins fight, or the more recent massacre of two white women in the Sweet Water country, in just so far as they dare, the Indians will follow their own likings, and in spite of all compacts engage in forays upon each other, or in pillaging and murdering the whites.

The remedy for this unfaith and its consequent disorders, it may not be easy to point out. But after a careful survey of the difficulties involved, and comparison of the views entertained by citizens, Indian agents, and officers of the Army, your commissioners offer a few suggestions.

1′. It is a matter of especial satisfaction that, so far as appears, whatever the difficulties of this vexed question, they are not due to any failure on the part of the Government to perform its part in the compacts made. On the contrary, while hardly an agreement has been fully observed by the Indians, and many clear provisions have been repeatedly disregarded, no invasions of Indian territory by whites have been allowed, no annuities withheld, no supplies cut off. In fact, the Government has acted throughout, not merely with scrupulous fidelity, but with marked forbearance and generosity.

2′. It is clear, however, that, in carrying out the policy of the Department, too much emphasis cannot be laid upon the necessity of having agents of unquestionable ability and integrity. Their position is, in its nature, one wielding a prodigious influence, and capable of being made potential for good or ill, according as those who occupy it are men with or without the true qualifications for the place. The men imperatively needed are those fully in sympathy with the policy of the Government, above all suspicion of dishonesty, and possessed of a good share of discretion, tact, and sound sense. For standing, as they do, close to the Indian, it is clear that, however wise and beneficent the measures proposed by the Department, they may fail utterly of success, through either the cupidity or the stupidity and blunders of the agent.

3′. It may be questioned whether the present rate of compensation is sufficient to insure men of the ability demanded for such an important trust. Too often, it would appear, the scant salary of the agent becomes a temptation to practices which cost the forfeiture of the confidence of both whites and Indians; and when this occurs, as it sometimes does, the very medium through which the Government seeks to dispense benefits becomes a source of continual mischief. One unprincipled agent can counterwork the whole Department, and foment troubles which it will require years of treasure and blood to subdue.

4′. Your commission are further persuaded that the various Indian agencies might be so used as to constitute probably the most effective of all instrumentalities in the realization of those beneficent results which it is the aim of the present Indian policy to secure. Whatever the Indian fails to understand, he understands clearly the argument of supplies. Year by year it is becoming plainer to nearly all the tribes that they are dependent upon the Government for food and clothing. Take away the supplies now furnished, and it hardly admits of doubt that a full half of the Indians of this region would be faced by starvation. They could not dispossess other tribes of their hunting-grounds, and they could not possibly support themselves on their present reservations.

If, now, the various Indian agencies were instructed to make the issue of their supplies and the payment of annuities conditioned upon the Indians keeping strictly within their reservations, and upon their prompt surrender of all perpetrators of wrong, it is evident that a most potent argument for justice and good order would be brought to bear.

So keenly felt already is the dependence upon the Government for material for tepes, for blankets, and clothing; and so urgent, especially, is the demand for food, that it is firmly believed by your commissioners that few tribes or bands can be found in these reservations which a rigid application of such a rule would not ultimately bring to terms.

Of course the enforcement of such a policy would demand the support of the military arm of the Government. But it is idle to think that any policy can be made effective without such support. And it is the opinion of military officers whose long experience among the Indians qualifies them to judge, that only a small force of soldiers would be needed to secure each agency against possible attack. It was, for example, the judgment of officers at Fort Laramie that a single regiment, with two pieces of artillery, would be ample to protect the Red Cloud agency from all uprising among the 12,000 or 14,000 Indians supplied therefrom.

5′. Finally, if, in connection with such a policy, a provision could be made whereby each tribe or each cluster of agreeing tribes could have some thoroughly competent and honest attorney appointed by the Department, whose duty it should be, in all cases of violation of treaties, or of collision or other difficulty with the whites, to conduct the case in behalf of the Indians before the territorial or other courts having jurisdiction, it is the opinion of your commissioners that great good would result.

Such an attorney would serve effectually to protect the Indians against the undue influence of prejudice and animosity so often felt upon the frontier. And, at the same time, he would avail more and more, as he secured the confidence of the Indians, to restrain their propensity to retaliation for supposed wrongs; to cultivate among them true ideas of obligation, and to establish over them the full supremacy of law.

In conclusion, your commissioners desire to express their acknowledgments to General de Trobriand, of Fort Steele; General Bumford, of Fort Russell; and General Smith, of Fort Laramie, with the officers of their respective commands, for valuable assistance rendered, and many courtesies received, while engaged in the investigation.

We have the honor to be, very respectfully,

EDWARD P. GOODWIN,
J. A. CAMPBELL,
S. R. HOSMER,
Special Commissioners.

CHEYENNE, WYO., *August* 9, 1873.

H.

REPORT OF J. P. C. SHANKS, T. W. BENNET, AND H. W. REED, SPECIAL COMMISSIONERS TO INVESTIGATE THE CONDITION OF THE INDIANS IN IDAHO AND ADJACENT TERRITORIES.

SALT LAKE CITY, UTAH,
November 17, 1873.

To the Hon. EDWARD P. SMITH, *Commissioner of Indian Affairs:*

The undersigned, special commission appointed by the inclosed letter of instructions of July 1, 1873, make this their general report touching the condition of Indian affairs in Idaho Territory, and such adjacent territory as is mainly connected therewith in considering the subject.

This general report is in addition to the special report and agreement relative to the Indians interested in and connected with the Fort Hall reservation, and agency in Idaho, of this date; and in addition to the commission's other special report, of even date herewith, touching the tribes known as Okinakanes, Lakes, Colvilles, San Poels, Spokanes, Calispells, Kootenays, Pend d'Oreilles, and Cœur d'Alenes, and their reservations.

Treating upon the general subject of the troubles between whites and Indians, the commission has, by either one or more of its members, visited the Indians at Fort Hall, Camas Prairié, Nez Percé, and the tribes named above, and also the chiefs and headmen of the mixed Shoshones, Bannacks, and Sheep-Eaters, and made diligent inquiry as to the bands under small chiefs roaming through the country.

The Indians complain of the whites because of encroachments on their farming lands, hunting and fishing grounds. Worthless white men associate with bad Indian women, prostituting them, and leaving such women and their children a burden upon the Indians. However, this is seriously condemned by the white people generally, and is not so much practiced as heretofore. It is a source of great complaint among the Colvilles of Washington Territory, and Nez Percés of Idaho. The sale to and use of intoxicating liquors by the Indians is bitterly complained of by the chiefs, and has received the severest censure from citizens at every point. The courts have, in Idaho, made it especially dangerous to violate the intercourse laws. There are four persons in the penitentiary of Boise, at this time, on sentence for this offense, and others under arrest on several similar charges. The United States courts of Washington Territory have been vigilant in this matter also, and the common practice of giving liquors to Indians to drive bargains, will be prohibited, so far as possible, there hereafter. The agents at Fort Hall, Nez Percés, and Colvilles are also active in preventing this evil. The people are demanding a prohibition of the sale of liquors to Indians.

Some misunderstandings occur between whites and Indians on account of pasturing stock. What is known as ranchmen, object to have the inferior bands of stock owned by Indians to mix with their herds and bands. This is one evidence of the necessity of putting Indians with their stock on reservations and prohibiting white men from interfering with them there. To this the people are favorably inclined.

We must not forget that [in] the political organization into States and Territories of all our western country and its settlement by white people in such numbers as to make Indian wars impossible, has had a salutary effect on Indians and on that class of bad white men who always infest and curse a frontier country, and by their bad conduct embarrass good settlers and excite hostilities among Indians. The people have power to enforce good order now, and are demanding it from all parties; this is the best security for peace, and has done much to call the attention of the Indians to the necessity of abandoning the chase and a resort to permanent homes and to agriculture.

The worst trouble between the whites and Indians in Idaho, and the one that the whites seem most unwilling to overlook, is the annoyance occasioned by roving bands of Indians, generally Shoshones and Bannacks, and who, under the provisions of the treaty of July 3, 1868, belong, and should have permanent homes upon, the Fort Hall reservation, but who go about the country, ostensibly hunting on unoccupied public lands, under a right to do so secured to them by the fourth article of the treaty referred to. The presence of these Indians near white men's homes causes distrust and fear on the part of women and children, and their universal custom being to carry all their effects with them, their horses turned upon the prairies encroach on the inclosures of the whites. These troubles, however, will be in the power of the Government, when the agreements entered into with these Indians on the seventh instant under your instructions are confirmed, and so soon as the roving bands can be sent to the reservation under orders of the Government. It is absolutely necessary to put the Indians on reservations and protect them there from encroachments, or to put them on farms diversified over the country and attempt to protect them there from a loss of title and possession. The reservation system is, in the opinion of the commission, the better course, until the Indian can be instructed further in agriculture and business life. The commission believe further that these reservations should be large and the Indians concentrated from the country joining on these, so as to relieve as much of the country as possible from their presence, and further and more particularly, [so] that the subject may receive more direct and efficient aid from the Government with less expense than from multiplied agencies. The commission would respectfully recommend the following as necessary to a successful management of the Indian question: by law or executive order directing agents to apportion lands on the reservation among the several Indian heads of families, and such young men as are willing to take homes, and put those families and persons on their respective tracts, and not permit them to remove their tents or houses from the particular grounds allotted to them, but cause them to labor on those grounds, to raise gardens, grain, &c.; and until this is done you will have nationalized pauper-houses, instead of progressive reservations. Unless this course is adopted the Indians will retrograde and will scatter over the country and become vagabonds in society. It would ruin any people to feed and maintain them in idleness at a common crib. Already, [by] the encouragement given by the agent at Fort Hall by hiring Indians to work on the reservation for wages, instead of white men, as is too commonly the case, he has over forty laboring Indians, thirty-nine of whom signed the agreement of the seventh instant as laborers; and this spirit of advancement has been so far instilled into these people by encouragement that at this agency now there are more Indians asking to become laborers than the agency is authorized to employ. This presents an encouraging view of the question on the vital point of difference between civilized and uncivilized men; the one esteeming labor honorable, and the other feeling it to be dishonorable and only to be done by women.

The people of Idaho have the general dislike to Indians that is felt to some extent all over the West, and of which it is not necessary in this report to trace the causes; yet they have punished promptly those who violate the law against them. There is a man in the penitentiary at Boise, under sentence of death, convicted before a jury of white men at Lewiston, for the murder of a Nez Percé woman.

There are some white men residing on the Nez Percés reservation—William Cadwell, who is there under an authority from a former agent, as the ostensible keeper of a stage station; but really is farming largely, cutting hay, timber, &c., on the reservation to sell to other parties. He occupies a place of importance to the Indians, and should be removed. There are some others on the reservation under various pretexts, and are in the way of a proper management of the agency. There is also a man by the name of Finney, who claims to hold [his place] under a treaty provision, made in the interest of his father-in-law, one Craig, long since dead. Congress took action in this case, and the commission recommend the importance of removing this man from the reservation. He, like Cadwell, keeps numbers of men about him, hired hands and others, injurious to the proper management of the interests of the Indians.

One of the most troublesome questions in the way of the Government controlling Indian affairs, is the contest between the Catholic and Protestant churches. The Nez Percé reservation is in the hands of Protestants; and one Catalde, a Catholic priest, who is in charge of the Cœur d'Alene mission, has procured an order from the Office of Commissioner of Indian Affairs, authorizing him to construct a church on the Nez Percé reservation. It is proper to call attention to these matters, and to say this strife between the two religious denominations is a great detriment to the Indians, as they are not well prepared to see that there is no religion in such a contest. If the Catholics are allowed to build a church on the reservation, it will measurably destroy the schools on the reservation, or compel the establishment of other schools than those provided for by treaty, as it is well known that the priests will not permit the children of Catholics to attend Protestant schools. It is well to see whether the Indian Department has authority, to authorize any church to construct its private buildings on Indian reservations, without the consent of the Indians. To further illustrate the evil effects to the Indians of this persistent and injurious contest between religious denominations, among and concerning the Indians, the commisssion quote the language of Joseph, chief of the non-treaty Nez Percé Indians, now located in the Wallowa Valley, Oregon, but who with his people held a council with the commission at the Nez Percé agency near the Clear Water River, Idaho Territory, on the 2d day of August, 1873:

"By the commission:

"Question. Do you want schools and school-houses on the Wallowa reservation?

"Answer by JOSEPH. No; we do not want schools or school-houses on the Wallowa reservation.

"Question. Why do you not want schools?

"Answer. They will teach us to have churches.

"Question. Do you not want churches?

"Answer. No; we do not want churches.

"Question. Why do you not want churches?

"Answer. They will teach us to quarrel about God, as the Catholics and Protestants do on the Nez Percés reservation, and at other places. We do not want to learn that. We may quarrel with men sometimes about things on this earth, but we never quarrel about God. We do not want to learn that."

One cause of complaint made by the Nez Percé Indians, is what they understand to be a great fraud practiced on them through their former agent, Sells, in the matter of fencing on the reservation. The commission examined the fences put up under the Sells contract, and state that it can only be characterized as a most scandalous fraud. It is a post-and-board fence. The posts are not well set. Much of the lumber is deficient in width and length. The posts are not dressed, the lumber laps at any joint where it may chance to meet, whether on the posts or between them, and the boards are not jointed on the posts where they meet; they are lapped and fastened generally with one nail, so that they are falling down rapidly. The lumber was cut on the reservation; the contract price of the fence was very high, and the fencing done in places of no value to any one, for the reason that water cannot be had for irrigation. The Government cannot be a party to such frauds on the people who intrust it with their property. These people never raised their hands against the Government, but always defended the whites against other Indians.

The commission recommend that the marital relation of Indians and the marriage or cohabitation of white men with Indian women; the liabilities of Indians for debts contracted by them; the descent of property among them; their admission in court as witnesses, and such other matters as may be necessary to their proper protection and preparation for civilized life, should be the subject for careful legislation by Congress. And the commission especially recommend that criminal law be extended over the Indians, making them liable and punishable as white citizens are for similar offenses. The murders and other crimes and misdemeanors committed by them on their own race are fearfully common, and need prompt punishment from a power that they respect and fear.

And it is further recommended that every white employé on reservations be compelled to have continually in his service one or more Indian apprentices at work in charge on the reservation, to employ only married men upon the reservation as agents, farmers, millers, &c., and to make their employment conditional upon their removing their families to, and remaining with them on the reservation. The presence of white women and white children among the Indians is necessary to the best interests of the whites and Indians. The schools on the reservations to be kept open as continually as possible. The reservation schools should be free to children of agents and their employés.

Every agent should be compelled to report officially the respective violations of the law by Indians under his charge against Indians or whites, and of whites against Indians.

All of which is most respectfully submitted.

JOHN P. C. SHANKS,
T. W. BENNET,
HENRY W. REED,
Commissioners.

J.

REPORT OF J. P. C. SHANKS, T. W. BENNET, AND H. W. REED, SPECIAL COMMISSIONERS TO INVESTIGATE AND REPORT UPON INDIAN AFFAIRS IN THE TERRITORY OF IDAHO, AND TERRITORIES ADJACENT THERETO.

SALT LAKE CITY, UTAH,
November 17, 1873.

To the Hon. COMMISSIONER OF INDIAN AFFAIRS:

The special commission, consisting of J. P. C. Shanks, T. W. Bennet, and H. W. Reed, directed by you under the attached instructions of July 1, 1873, while inspecting matters connected with the Nes Percé reservation at Lapway, on the Clear Water River,

Idaho Territory, received from General Milroy, superintendent of Indian affairs for Washington Territory, the inclosed letter bearing date July 31, 1873; and on the 3d day of August, 1873, General Milroy came in person to Lewiston, Idaho, at the mouth of the Clear Water River, to meet the commission for the purpose of securing its attendance at the Colville agency, Washington Territory. Having been instructed by you to examine the condition of Indian affairs in the Territory of Idaho, and report thereon, and believing that the Calispells, Pend d'Oreilles, Kootenays, and Spokanes, who inhabit the northern portion of Idaho, would be interested in a council to be held at or near Colville, and interested in a reservation that had been set off including the Colville Valley, and which reservation had been changed to the west side of the Columbia River, by the action of interested white men; and, insomuch as we were instructed to ascertain and report the causes of complaint by the Indians against white people, and of white people against the Indians, the commission deemed it proper to send one of its number with General Milroy to examine and report the facts, so far as he could, touching the matters of complaint, and accordingly sent J. P. C. Shanks of the commission on that duty.

The commission herewith incloses his report made to them, together with a record of the council held with the Indians interested, who were present, and make both the record of the councils and the report of Mr. J. P. C. Shanks part of this report to you, and ask your attention to both, as showing the condition of our Indian affairs along the line of British America, and to the great injustice done to these peaceable Indians by the interested action of white men; and especially to the conduct of their ex-agent, Park Winans, in procuring a change of reservation through selfish motives; and to the more important fact that the reservation, as now located, is in a frigid and high latitude, where farming is impossible, while the lines of the reservation cut the Indians off from the Columbia River, and remove them from the Spokane River, the only source from which they could procure a livelihood by fishing, game being nearly exhausted; so that [they are] without fish or game, and in a locality where farming is impossible, as proven by white men who have settled on the new reservation and abandoned the country on account of frost, &c.

The act of compelling these Indians to go to the reservation west of the Columbia River is either to annihilate them or make them a perpetual tax on the Government; while they are industrious and desire to make their own living by work.

The commission recommends to the Government that these Indians be permitted to remain where now situated, for the reasons set forth in General Shanks' report to the commission, herewith filed as stated; and that the boundaries thereof be as follows: Beginning at a point in the channel of the Columbia River, opposite the mouth of O'Kinakane River; thence up the center of the channel of the Columbia River to a point opposite the mouth of the Spokane River; thence up the center of the channel of the Spokane River to the mouth of Hangman or Lotah Creek; thence up the center of Hangman or Lotah Creek to the line dividing Washington and Idaho Territories, as recently surveyed; thence south on said line to the top of the ridge between Hangman or Lotah Creek and Pine Creek; thence easterly along the summit of said ridge to a point which is five miles in a direct line east of said territorial line; thence in a direct line north to the dividing-line between the United States and British Columbia; thence west along said line to the O'Kinakane River; thence down the center of the channel of said O'Kinakane River to the place of beginning.

That this reservation shall be a permanent reservation—a home for the following tribes and such parts of these tribes as may be proper, namely: Cœur d'Alenes, Upper and Lower Spokanes, Calispells, Pend d'Oreilles, Kootenays, Lakes, Colvilles, San Poels, Methows, and O'Kinakanes; ten in all.

A reference to General Shank's report to the commission will explain this matter more in detail.

The commission is informed of the following facts: By an order from the Commissioner of Indian Affairs, Odeneal, then superintendent of Indian affairs of Oregon, and J. B. Monteith, Indian agent at the Nez Percé reservation, were directed to negotiate with the Cœur D'Alenes, and to set off a reservation for them.

Odeneal did not go to see these Indians, but it is stated that he made a report to the Department from information received of D. P. Thompson, but without counciling with J. B. Monteith.

Under the instructions to the commission to visit the Indians in Idaho, Shanks and Bennet, in company with J. B. Monteith, agent, met in council the Cœur D'Alenes at Hangman or Lotah Creek, on the 29th day of July, 1873, and entered into a written agreement with the Cœur D'Alenes, for a reservation, conditioned that it should be approved by Congress. This agreement is in the hands of J. B. Monteith, and perhaps has been reported to you.

The commission did not desire to go beyond its authority in this matter, and only joined Mr. Monteith as there seemed to be a necessity for it at the time. But the commission, after an investigation of the whole subject, now recommends that the agreement entered into with the Cœur d'Alenes be not confirmed, but that the reservation recommended by the commission for the nine tribes, including the Cœur d'Alenes, be adopted.

All of which is most respectfully submitted.

JOHN P. C. SHANKS,
T. W. BENNET,
HENRY W. REED,
Commission.

COLVILLE, STEVENS COUNTY, WASH.,
August 14, 1873.

Hon. T. W. BENNET and H. W. REED,
Gentlemen of the Special Commission:

I left Lewiston, Idaho, at the mouth of the Clear Water River, as you are aware, on the 3d day of August, 1873, by steamer down Snake River, accompanied by General Milroy, the superintendent of Indian affairs, for Washington Territory, and landed at the mouth of the Pelluce River, where we met John A. Simms, agent at the Colville agency.

From the mouth of the Pelluce we proceeded by wagon to Fort Colville, in Stevens County, in Colville Valley, Washington Territory, where we arrived on the 7th of August, 1873, and on the following day proceeded to the Kettle Falls, on the Columbia River, and, crossing that river, passed up Kettle River and the Sue-Whock to a point near the line of British Columbia, and returning from this point by the Columbia held a council, August 12, with the following tribes in general council—held at the old British trading post, about one mile above the Kettle Falls: The Colvilles, Lakes, San Poels, O'Kinakane, upper and lower Spokanes, and Calispells. The following are the facts as I found them:

1. All these people are peaceable, quiet, and industrious, and express a loyalty to the United States Government, as simple, confiding, and faithful as children.

2. They are divided into Catholics and Protestants; the majority of the latter being Presbyterians; and are very zealous in their faith respectively. In the aggregate the Catholics largely outnumber the Protestants.

3. Their agent, John A. Simms, is a Catholic, and the Indians, irrespective of faith, have confidence in his integrity, and speak well of him.

4. They all, as irrespective of religious faith, condemn their ex-agent, who immediately preceded Simms, one Park Winans, a merchant of Colville.

5. All these Indians desire a permanent reservation, schools, churches, &c.

6. They generally labor either on farms of their own, of which there are a considerable number, or for others, which is the general rule. Many who had farms before the recent influx of whites have sold their farms to whites, and now work by the day for a living.

7. The whites have encroached on the Indians very much, and are continuing to do so.

8. In these encroachments their late agent, P. Winans, was a principal and participant, and still continues to be their exponent and principal operator. He was a partner in a trading-house dealing with the Indians, while agent, from which whisky was given to secure bargains in furs, which is the principal trade in that locality. And when the reservation was set off east of the Columbia River, he concealed that fact from the Indians, and busied himself to have it changed to the cold, dry highlands west of that river, where white men have abandoned the country after trial, and failed to farm owing to frosts and other difficulties in the way.

9. The reservation has been, by interested, and in many cases unscrupulous men, relocated from east to west of the Columbia River; and from the advantages of the salmon fisheries on the Spokane and Columbia to west of the Columbia, only coming to the west bank of that stream, and that without any privilege of fishing in that river, literally robbing the Indians of their country and their food.

10. There are numbers of white settlers in the Colville Valley, where the Indians now are, the Indians not having been removed west of the Columbia under the late unjust assignment of reservation, and I hope never will.

11. These whites are the same persons who procured the change of reservation, and are not entitled to any sympathy, as they obtained an unjust order against the Indians, knowing that the new reservation was unfit for habitation, and, avoiding it themselves, procured an order that gave them the Indians' homes, and drove the Indians where they would not reside themselves.

12. These Indian tribes are now situated adjacent to each other, and have been so since time immemorial.

13. These tribes speak the same language, the same as spoken by the Flatheads and Cœur d'Alenes.

14. The Kootenays, who were not in the council but who reside in Northeast Washington, North Idaho, and Northwest Montana, speak the same language, and should be included with these tribes.

15. These tribes desire reservations together, beginning as follows: At a point in the channel of the Columbia River opposite the mouth of the O'Kinakane River; thence up the center of the channel of the Columbia River to a point opposite the mouth of the Spokane River; thence up the center of the channel of the Spokane River to the mouth of Hangman or Lotah Creek; thence up center of Hangman or Lotah Creek to the line dividing Washington and Idaho Territories, as recently surveyed; thence south on said line to the top of the ridge between Hangman or Lotah Creek and Pine Creek; thence easterly along the summit of said ridge to a point which is five miles in a direct line east of said territorial line; thence in a direct line north to the dividing line between the United States and British Columbia; thence west along said line to the O'Kinakane River; thence down the centre of the channel of said O'Kinakane River to the place of beginning.

16. These Indian tribes propose surrendering their title to all the country south and east of the country as named. This gives the United States all that beautiful country along Pine Creek, and from the Pelluce to the proposed line which you have seen, and which is more valuable than all they desire to retain.

17. They ask no money or clothing; all they wish is that their homes be secured to them.

18. They say if the United States has money to give let it be given to the whites for their improvements. The Indians will make their living if protected in their homes.

19. The country they wish to retain is, with the exception of the Colville and Hangman's Creek Valleys, mountainous and poor, except small spots, but the fishing is good, and it is their cherished homes and much desired by them.

20. It would be expensive, troublesome, dishonorable, and wicked to drive these people away from their homes, where they have lived from time immemorial, to give place to cunning men who have supplanted them, and procured the action of the Government against them.

21. None of these Indians have been in hostility to the Government at any time, except the Spokanes and Codur d'Alenes, and they only were when they defeated Steptoe, and were in turn conquered by General Wright.

22. These people generally dress as white people do, and are anxious to improve in agricultural pursuits. They ask for nothing but their homes, and for these they plead as children.

There has been no treaty with these tribes for whom this reservation is proposed, and their title to all the country from Steptoe's Bute to the Flathead country and British line, and to the Sierra Nevada to Snake and Pelluce Rivers is theirs yet. All this is to be relinquished by them, except that included in the proposed reservation.

I left General Milroy, at Colville, on the 14th day of August, 1873, preparing to carefully examine that part of the new reservation lying west of the Kettle River, this part of it, lying between Kettle and Columbia Rivers, having been examined by Mr. Milroy, Simms, and myself, as stated above. General Milroy will make report to the Indian Department of his further investigations, to which I respectfully ask attention.

The Colville agency is one difficult to manage for the reason that it is not on a reservation. The reservation was changed from east to west of the Columbia River by Executive order, but the Indians, and consequently agency, remained east of the Columbia River, at Colville, within the limits of the reservation as just set off. This leaves the agent no controlling power over bad white men, who may wrong or intrigue with the Indians, other than such as the courts can give under the intercourse laws, leaving the agent or court no power to prevent the association of bad white men with the Indians under his charge.

The better class of white people see and feel the effect of this condition of things, and have spoken to me of it quite freely.

At the general council held near Kettle Falls, on August 12, 1873, Antoine, chief of the Colvilles, speaking for his people who reside in the Colville Valley and around Colville, and the old trading post where the council was held, said, (among other things of deep interest,) to General Milroy, Agent Simms, and myself, "We want you to take our part; the liquor is coming up to our knees; we tie our people up for drinking, but the whites do not tie up or punish their people for selling liquor to Indians. I wish you who come from Washington would take our part and stop this selling liquor to us."

Another ground of serious complaint is the prostitution of their women by bad white men under the plea of marriage. These white men take the advantage of the difference between the marriage ceremonies of white people and the simple voluntary association which is the Indian form of marriage, and while the poor Indian woman believes she is married to a white man, he treats it in the light of cohabitation only, and which he breaks off at will, often abandoning both women and children with impunity and with gross indifference. The speeches of the chiefs at the council will explain fully the condition of things in this regard around Colville during Park Winan's agency. Agent Simms is doing all he can to prevent this evil, and has done much.

Judge Lewis, United States judge of that district, has set his foot in unmistakable earnest on these offenses and those who sell and give liquor to Indians, and the good effect is very perceptible. A number have recently married their squaws (with whom they had families) to avoid prosecution. Antoine, chief of the Colvilles, when speaking at the council in presence of the Indians, and of many whites who had collected there, touching wrongs inflicted on Indian women by white men, said, "I want you to take pity on us and help us; bad white men have taken twenty of our squaws from us, and when they have borne children to them, the white men take all the property and leave the squaws and children. They leave no property or food for the squaw, mother, or children, but leave them on us, so we must maintain the mother and raise the children. When I want to get my daughter or my sister from these white men they will not let me have her, and when I then ask them to marry our women whom they took, they would refuse to marry them, but would keep them in sin; what shall we do? We want your help. I am raising plenty of white men's children, white men whom I am looking in the face now. (Then addressing himself to Winan's former agent; Sherwood, Winan's farmer, while agent, who has a squaw in adultery and two children; and Dr. Perkins, who has a deaf and dumb squaw in adultery and three children; and Smith, who wanted the agency, who has a squaw in adultery and two children, and other squaw men present, Antoine said:) "White men I am talking to you of your actions; I am raising your children on my poor food, my roots and berries and fish and rotten salmon, (rotten salmon being those found dead along the river,) and when I have raised them these white men demand them and take them. I am poor, and this is very hard."

The Indians complained that Winans permitted some bad Indian women to keep places of ill-fame at Colville, near his place of business, and that he did not try to prevent it, but that Agent Simms at once prevented it when he arrived. Numbers of white men stated to me the same facts; and Winans did not deny any of these and other charges made by these Indians, in his presence at the council, against his administration; and, though privilege was given to Winans and other whites, as will appear by the records of the council, to speak in reply to the severe charges made against them by the Indians, (and which charges were confirmed by white citizens,) they all declined. General Milroy said to the whites present, "Insomuch as the charges are made in your presence, perhaps you should answer in the presence of the Indians;" but they declined, saying they would put any statements they wished to make to the Government in writing. This will prevent the Indians from seeing or confronting them, and that is the desire of these men.

In relation to the removal of the reservation from east to west of the Columbia River, the Indians charged Park Winans—and in this they are sustained by the whites, and by his own confession—that when the order setting off the first reservation reached Winans, their agent then, he concealed the fact from them until he could and did manipulate the change.

Taking Winans's acts, surroundings, and associations, and it proves him to have been an unworthy agent and dishonorable man. He is charged by white people with having sold Indian goods from his store, and by paying his individual debts out of Indian supplies.

Some of those who, with Park Winans, labored to change the reservation, are acting in bad faith to the Government, as well as to the Indians; for instance, a Mrs. Myers wrote to the President, pleading for her home as though she had no protection, and as though she was a sufferer. This letter was referred to Commissioner of Indian Affairs, and answered to her by him. This letter I saw in the hands of her husband, (for she has a husband.) The facts are these: Myers and his wife reside on one hundred and sixty acres of land in what was the reservation, and which they aided to change, (I have been on the place;) while Myers has possession of another 160-acre tract, including the old Hudson Bay mill property; so the wife claims one, and the husband the other. Such are the fraudulent actions of these pursuers of the Indians of Colville Valley. I have seen Myers, his wife and home, and had his own explanation as to the two claims. Mrs. Myers is a white woman, and he a white man.

The records of the councils held at Kettle Falls, Stevens County, Washington Territory, and at the Spokane bridge, July 12, 13, 14, 1873, are herewith presented, and made part of this report.

All of which is respectfully submitted.

JOHN P. C. SHANKS,
Special Commissioner.

NOVEMBER 11, 1872.

NOTE.—My attention was called to the discrepancy between the laws of Great Britain and those of the United States, touching the sale of intoxicating liquors to Indians.

General Milroy, superintendent of Indian affairs for Washington Territory; Judge

Lewis, of Walla-Walla, and whose district includes Stevens County, in which lies Colville Valley; Mr. Simms, Indian agent at Colville, and other white persons, and some Indian also, request the attention of the Government to this subject.

British Indians are British subjects, and it is claimed that our restricted statutes will not reach the sale of liquor to a British subject, and, hence, sales to these have been permitted, which furnishes an excuse for selling to any who claim to be British subjects. The British law prohibits selling or giving liquor to any North American Indian, and our statutes should be made similar to it in this respect.

Respectfully submitted.

JOHN P. C. SHANKS,
Special Commissioner.

NOVEMBER 11, 1873.

K.

REPORT OF J. P. C. SHANKS, B. R. COWAN, AND CHAS. MARSH, SPECIAL COMMISSIONERS TO DETERMINE THE BOUNDARIES OF THE NEW RESERVATION AT ROUND VALLEY, CAL.

WASHINGTON, D. C., *November* 1, 1873.

Hon. E. P. SMITH, *Commissioner Indian Affairs:*

SIR: The board of commissioners appointed by the honorable Secretary of the Interior in pursuance of an act of Congress entitled "An act to restore a part of the Round Valley Indian reservation, California, to the public lands, and for other purposes," passed March 3, 1873, submit the following report:

By your instructions dated May 6, 1873, we were required—

First. To make examination of the country embraced within and adjacent to the proposed Indian reservation.

Second. To make an appraisement of all improvements of white persons north of the southern boundary of the reservation.

Third. To make an appraisement of the improvements of all Indians south of the southern boundary of said reservation.

The commission reached the Round Valley Indian agency on the 2d day of June, 1873, all the members present, and at once entered upon the discharge of their duties. A careful reconnaissance of the entire reservation was made by the members of the commission, and the mountainous country of the northern portion thoroughly explored to ascertain the most practicable northern boundary. That portion of the country being unsurveyed, we were anxious to select natural boundaries that would be so well described as to avoid misunderstanding and prevent encroachment by white settlers and herders.

The boundaries selected are of this character; being cañons and water-courses strongly defined, some of them practically impassable, and well known throughout that entire country. We recommend the following as the boundary of the reservation:

Beginning for the same at a point in section 36 of township 23, range 12 west, Mount Diablo meridian, where the township-line crosses Eel River, being at a point about eighty (80) rods west of the southeast corner of said township and section; thence following the courses of Eel River up said stream in the center thereof to a point where the same is intersected by the stream known as Williams Creek or Bland Mountain Creek; thence following up the center of said creek to its extreme northern source on the ridge dividing the waters of said creek from the waters of Hull's Cañon or Creek, a tributary of the north fork of Eel River at the foot of Bland Mountain, crossing said dividing ridge at a point on a line where a small white oak tree and a cluster of arborvitæ trees are branded with the letters U. S. R.; thence in a direct line to the center of said Hall's Cañon or Creek; thence following down the center of the same to its intersection with the north fork of Eel River; thence down the center of said north fork to its intersection with the main fork; thence following up the main fork of the Eel River in the center thereof, where the township-line between townships 22 and 23 north, range 13 west, would intersect said river, if produced; thence east along said township-line through ranges 13 and 12 to the place of beginning. We would also recommend the reservation to the Indians occupying the Round Valley reservation, of the right to fish in the middle fork of Eel River, and in Eel River up as far as Bland's Cove.

The northern position of the reservation, if our recommendation as to boundary meets the approval of the Department, is very mountainous, the highest elevation being probably five thousand feet. This portion is well timbered with pine timber of excellent size and quality for manufacturing into lumber. There is also excellent pasturage for horses, cattle, and sheep, which for several years has been used by squatters who have no legal rights thereon.

The Indians there have experience as herders, being employed by the citizens for that purpose, and it would be well to encourage them to engage in sheep and cattle raising.

The area of mountainous country embraced within the proposed boundaries will afford ample range and excellent pasturage during the entire year for at least thirty thousand head of sheep, besides all the cattle and horses which can be properly managed by the agent. If well stocked and cared for the agency could be made self-sustaining in a very few years.

We submit herewith a schedule of appraisement of the improvements owned by citizens and located upon the new reservation, marked A. Some parties have probably acquired rights to lands within the reservation by pre-emption or homestead settlement. If such rights exist, measures should be taken for their extinguishment by payment to the parties of such amounts as their claims may be worth. Still other parties have patents for lands embraced in the reservation, all of whom are willing to sell to the Government.

Our instructions were silent in reference to lands claimed in the new reservation, and also as to the lands south of the southern boundary of the reservation; but we nevertheless respectfully submit some suggestions relative to the latter class, based upon our actual examination of them.

That portion of the lands south of the reservation which lie within the valley, is, for the most part, of the very best quality of farming-lands, upon a great portion of which excellent crops were growing at the time of our visit.

They are fully equal to the average quality of the valley farming-lands of California and are for the most part claimed by settlers. The settlers have not entered upon them upon any pretended homestead or pre-emption claims, but simply have laid claims to all the lands they wanted for farms in the valley.

These claims range in extent from 45 acres up to 880 acres, the last amount being the largest claimed by any single individual. A firm of two brothers, one of whom resides in the State of Nevada, claim 1,680 acres, while a number of persons claim 640 acres each.

The possessory titles to these claims are recognized as property by the State of California, and the same are listed for taxation. We procured from the assessor of Mendocino County the official appraisement of the property in Round Valley, a copy of which is herewith submitted, marked B. It will be observed that the greater portion of these lands are appraised by the county assessor at $10 per acre, for the possessory title simply. This would not be an excessive appraisement if the parties had the fee-simple of the land, and, in fact, few of the settlers thereon would sell their claim at the price named, some of them asking $20 per acre, to our personal knowledge. Again, while settlers are restricted to 80 and 160 acres of land under the pre-emption and homestead laws, we found parties there claiming to hold 640 and even 880 acres, and threatening all persons who attempted to settle upon any portion of their claims. The schedule will show the names of all parties whose claims are above the amounts allowed to be entered. In fact this class of settlers have no more legal right to the property they claim, (and even had the valley been open to settlement they would only have been allowed to enter 160 acres each,) than the settlers upon the lands in the present reservation. But under the law the latter class of settlers must leave the lands upon which they have been living, receiving pay only for the improvements, and must remove from the valley entirely, unless some arrangement can be made for them to enter upon the excess of land improperly claimed by the former class. Under the existing law it is not at the discretion of any officer to make any discrimination; but it is respectfully suggested, if practicable, that the attention of Congress be invited to the subject, in order that the settlers who will be ousted from the lands in the reservation may be afforded the opportunity to purchase lands in the valley, without the boundaries of the reservation, before any of said lands are offered for sale to persons who were not actual residents of the valley at the date of the passage of the act of March 3, 1873.

The area of good land in the valley is ample to furnish farms to all the residents, and we deem it but equitable that some arrangement as we suggest be made. As we have before said, the lands are as good as the average of valley farming-lands in the State of California.

The law puts the minimum price for such lands at $1.25 per acre, below which they cannot be sold. Does that limitation imply the right of the Secretary of the Interior to name a higher price for these lands? We think not. We have shown that they are worth from four to eight times as much, and that they cannot be bought from the present claimants at a much higher figure. Some of this value has been created by the occupants, and consists in improvements of houses, fences, and tilled fields. For this appreciation of the property the Government does not expect to be remunerated.

Deducting, however, the proper percentage, say, from one-half to three-fourths, would reduce the lands to $5 and $2.50 per acre.

Upon this basis, and after carefully examining the quality of the land, we take the liberty to submit for your consideration the following appraisement:

Sections 4, 5, 6, 7, 8, 9, 16, 17, 18, 19, 20, 21, 29, 30, of township 22 north, range 12 west, 8,960 acres, at $5	$44,800 00
East half section 1, section 12, east half section 13, east half section 24, township 23 north, range 13 west, 1,600 acres, at $5	8,000 00
West half section 13, west half section 24, township 23 north, range 13 west, 640 acres, at $2.50	1,600 00
Amounting in all to 11,200	$54,400 00

This makes an aggregate of $54,400 of the value of the lands in the valley without the reservation, but embraced within the boundary of the old reservation. By reference to the schedule of the appraisement of improvements upon the present reservation, it will be seen that the aggregate value thereof is $32,669.78. In addition to this, certain claims by pre-emption, homestead, and purchase, will have to be extinguished, which will require at least $20,000 more, which will absorb the amount realized if the above appraisement should be authorized.

If our scaling of the lands to be sold should be adopted, the amount received from that source will be sufficient to pay for all improvements appraised, and for the claims, heretofore alluded to, of homestead and pre-emption settlers and purchasers, and for the expenses of the commission. Unless authority is given to appraise these lands at something near their true value, the proceeds of their sale will not be sufficient to pay for the improvements we have appraised, and the appropriation of at least thirty thousand dollars will be needed in addition to the proceeds of sales, to carry out the provisions of the present act.

We therefore respectfully suggest that Congress be requested to so amend the act of March 3, 1873, as to authorize the Secretary of the Interior to cause the lands south of the southern boundary of the reservation, as established by said act, to be appraised and offered for sale, giving preference to the settlers thereon at the date of the passage of said act, and allowing them a reasonable time in which to make proof and payment for their lands. With regard to the lands not so taken by present settlers, preference should be given to those who occupy lands within the boundary of the said reservation, who should also be allowed a reasonable time to make entry and payment before the residue of the lands are thrown open to general sale.

We also suggest that all persons, whether settlers or not, purchasing any of said lands, shall be restricted to 160 acres.

We respectfully submit a projet of a law, embodying the suggestions made above.

The State of California has sold a certain portion of the lands within the new reservation as swamp-lands, and the purchasers are claiming under certificates from the State land-offices. Those lands, however, have not been confirmed to the State by the United States Government as swamp-lands, and we respectfully represent that they are not in any sense of the term swamp-lands, and should not therefore be confirmed to the State as such. The references above to claims upon lands in the reservations do not allude to these swamp-lands.

JOHN P. C. SHANKS.
B. R. COWAN.

L.

REPORT OF J. P. WILLIAMSON AND J. W. DANIELS, SPECIAL COMMISSIONERS TO INVESTIGATE THE CONDITION OF THE INDIANS ALONG THE NORTH PACIFIC RAILROAD WITH REFERENCE TO THEIR PROBABLE OPPOSITION TO ITS CONSTRUCTION.

RED CLOUD AGENCY, WYO., *May* 9, 1873.

SIR: In accordance with instructions contained in your letter of March 27, we respectfully report:

On the receipt of your commission we learned that the Indians you wished us to visit were divided into a number of small camps in the neighborhood of the Black Hills and the head of White River, and that they were generally moving southward on account of the scarcity of food, a number having already reached this agency.

Agent Daniels had previously been using his best endeavors to gain their friendship and bring them under the control of the Government.

On completing our arrangements word was sent to all the camps requesting the chiefs and head-men to meet us in council at this place on the 9th.

On the day appointed we found representatives from about four or five hundred lodges in council. They were informed of the wishes of the Government as contained in your letter of instructions.

They expressed themselves very glad to hear from their Great Father, but they were not prepared to accede fully to his request. Their people did not want the Northern Pacific Railroad built, and they did not want any white men in the country. The trader was the only white man they wanted to see, and they wanted the Great Father to allow him to sell guns and ammunition. They said they would take the words of the Great Father back with them to their people, and talk it over, and when they agree to let the Great Father know.

The principal men in the council were Red Thunder, a chief; Thin Soup, Ashes, Little Chief, and Hump Rib, head soldiers of Oncpapas, Minneconjoux, and No Bow bands of Teton Sioux.

Owing to the limited time allowed one of the commissioners, Black Moon, No Neck, and Lame Antelope, chiefs in these bands, had not arrived. In closing the council your commissioners impressed upon the minds of the Indians the importance of stopping the raids of their young men upon our borders, and the great advantages they would secure by remembering the words of their Great Father. With apparent good feeling on the part of all the council then closed.

Your commission does not see the way open to prosecute the work further at present. They feel no hesitancy in assuring the Department that there will be no combined resistance to the construction of the Northern Pacific Railroad. The Indians neither have ammunition nor subsistence to undertake any general war, neither do they manifest any such spirit in council.

Small raiding parties will doubtless visit the Northern Pacific Road, and perhaps the border settlements.

It is probable that a majority of the Indians with whom we counciled will remain in the vicinity of this agency, and in view of the scarcity of buffalo in the Sioux country it is believed that all northern hostile Sioux will ultimately be compelled to come to the different agencies for subsistence.

Very respectfully, your obedient servants,

JOHN P. WILLIAMSON,
J. W. DANIELS,
Commissioners.

Hon. EDWARD P. SMITH,
Commissioner Indian Affairs, Washington, D. C.

M.

REPORT OF T. C. JONES, SPECIAL COMMISSIONER TO APPRAISE LANDS BELONGING TO THE KANSAS OR KAW RESERVATION IN KANSAS.

DELAWARE, OHIO, *September* 16, 1873.

SIR: Having sent a telegram from Emporia, Kans., announcing my purpose to return without proceeding to make the appraisement of the Kaw lands in that State, and mailed from Saint Louis a brief note, stating the reasons, I now submit a more formal report.

On the 25th ultimo, when preparing to leave for Kansas, I received a telegram from the honorable Commissioner of Indian Affairs, from Chicago, directing a stay of all proceedings until I should hear from him at Washington. After a delay of a few days I was notified to see Superintendent Hoag before proceeding with the work, in obedience to which I left on September 1st for the city of Lawrence, where, before seeing Mr. Hoag, I had conversations with several well-informed gentlemen as to the character and location of the Kaw lands, and the price at which similar lands were selling, &c. Construing the dispatches from the Department to mean that the appraisement should not be proceeded with, if I, after consultation with Mr. Hoag, should deem it inexpedient, I had a conference with that gentleman and a Mr. Mullen, who had been connected with Indian work at the Kaw mission. I became satisfied that the only complaint as to the work of the former commission was that the price fixed for the sale of the land was too high. There was, so far as I could learn, no controversy as to the claims of settlers as finally determined upon [by] the report of Government agent, so that it appeared to me nothing was necessary now to be done but to fix the price at which the land should be sold. After further reflection I became satisfied that even this was not necessary, and so telegraphed the Department, and received, September 8th, a dispatch giving the opinion of the honorable Secretary of the Interior, that as no sales could be made without new appraisement, we should proceed with the work according to instructions, which required us to go over all the work of the former commission *de novo.* This I became satisfied we should not have time to do before we should be stopped by cold weather. But deeming it best to go on the ground and look further into the matter, I wrote my associates, Robley and Campbell, to meet me at Council Grove, sending telegram to the Department as to amount of work required, and asking if we were to investigate all the claims of settlers, and what provision had been made for expenses, the answer to be sent to Council Grove. Arriving at this place, I found Mr. Edwards first named as commissioner, (in whose place Campbell had been subsequently appointed,) ready and anxious to enter upon the work. I received answer to last dispatch that the claims of settlers were to be investigated, and that no funds were available for expenses until lands were sold. The same evening, Mr. Campbell, who had been named as commissioner, arrived in accordance with the notice received from me to enter upon his duties. After examining the maps and plats of the lands, I rode out in different directions so as to get an idea of the character and locations of the lands away from the Neosho Valley, through which we had passed on the Missouri, Kansas, and Texas Railroad from east to west.

The whole tract, including the trust and diminished reserve lands, is nearly 22 miles square, of which a small portion has been deeded, leaving subject to sale, under the act of 1872, about 218,000 acres of the richest and most beautifully located lands in the State of Kansas, the whole being underlaid with an excellent quality of magnesian lime-stone, which crops out on the slopes of the elevations, reminding one strongly of the blue-grass regions of Kentucky.

The bottoms of the Neosho River on this reserve are more extensive than those of any stream I ever saw, and of the richest and best quality, there being scarcely any wet lands there. The uplands, except the small portions on the bluffs where the lime-stone is seen on the surface, are as fertile as the splendid uplands of our Miami Valley, and more uniformly so. I formed the opinion, from the appearance and characteristics of this soil, and from the crops that in some places were growing upon them, that they were equal to any uplands I had ever seen for the production of grass, grain, or fruit.

The supply of timber and water is better than upon any lands I saw in Kansas, and I believe generally admitted to be as good as any to be found there, and the natural drainage furnished by the streams and elevations renders the location not only very beautiful, but I should suppose exceedingly healthy. The village of Council Grove, with a population of over 700, where the best quality of coal is now about being mined, is situated near the center of these lands. The railway and Neosho River pass through the tract from east to west, with numerous smaller streams entering from either side, such as Big John, Rock Creek, Little John, &c. Besides these, springs issuing out of the side-hills and valleys are for this country very common. The thrifty village of America, with a population of about 500, a large cheese-factory, &c., is near the eastern border, while only eight miles further east we have the flourishing town of Emporia, with 2,500 people at last census, now eleven churches, five stores, &c., with a most excellent country population around it. Now what, under these circumstances, should this magnificent tract of land be worth? It is spoken of through the whole State as the best, or among the very best, in Kansas. It is a long way off, it is true, but the railroad facilities are good, and cattle which sell here as high now as $3.50 per 100 pounds, are shipped to Chicago at $110 per car.

The commission put the diminished reserve lands at only $3.88¾ per acre, average, and the trust lands at only $2.28 per acre, making a general average of the whole of less than $2.28 per acre.

The best of the bottom-lands along the railroad with water and timber are put at $8 to $11 per acre, and some few pieces nearly all timber, at $12 to $15 per acre, while the uplands are $1, $1.10, $1.50, &c. If these lands are not worth these prices there must be a good deal of land in Kansas that is worth absolutely nothing; and as near as I could learn, all the railway lands of anything like similar quality are held at largely higher figures.

Speculators (in which is included one or more of the railways) are anxious for a lower appraisement, under which they hope, with the system of making bids at Washington, to get control of all these lands, and it is surprising what a pressure they are able to bring to bear in favor of their interests.

It is impossible that any impartial man who is a judge of lands can fail to see, after a full examination of all the facts, that the appraisement of last year is a fair and just one. And I beg that I shall be pardoned for repeating that there is no doubt of the lands being taken up, if an agency is established on the spot for their purchase, the expense of which the Indians can well afford to pay. This plan, too, with a reasonable credit for two-thirds of the purchase-money, on interest, deeds to be made on full payment, would be exceedingly satisfactory to the people, as it would encourage sales to actual settlers. For these reasons, I was of the opinion that a re-appraisement was not only unnecessary, but would involve a large expense, which ought not, in justice, to be imposed upon these Indians.

But I should have hesitated before interposing my opinions if there had been time to make the appraisement, and we had been furnished with means to complete it. To have made an examination of each 160 of the 218,000 acres and take testimony in regard to the claims and improvements of over 200 claims of settlers, would have taken four or five months' labor, most of the time in the field, under tent at night, with two wagons, chain-carriers, surveyors, &c.

The former commissioners were engaged over four months in this way, and I am satisfied they worked most faithfully and did their work as well as men could. Mr. Edward F. Ellis, who seemed quite anxious to go on, being a member of the senate, said he could not devote so much time to the work. Under the circumstances I thought it best to return without organizing the commission, it being obvious that the work could not be completed this fall.

Of course it is to the interest of all parties to have these lands disposed of as soon as possible, and this, as suggested in my note from Saint Louis, can be best accomplished by an amendment of the law, so as to authorize the Secretary of the Interior to establish an agency for their sale in Kansas, upon the basis of the appraisement already made. This is the opinion of every man with whom I conversed in Kansas, having experience in such matters. In no other way can the Government dispose of these lands so rapidly, at fair prices, and to actual settlers; and it seems to me, an effort ought to be made to save to those who shall become occupiers of these magnificent lands the large profits which the speculators hope to realize from handling them.

All which is respectfully submitted.

T. C. JONES,
Special Commissioner.

Hon. EDWARD P. SMITH,
Commissioner Indian Affairs, Washington, D. C.

N.

REPORT OF H. M. ATKINSON AND T. G. WILLIAMS, SPECIAL COMMISSIONERS TO VISIT THE KICKAPOOS IN MEXICO, WITH THE VIEW OF INDUCING THEM TO COME AND REMAIN IN THE INDIAN TERRITORY.

WASHINGTON, D. C., *October* 8, 1873.

Hon. E. P. SMITH,
Commissioner of Indian Affairs, Washington, D. C.:

SIR: Pursuant to your instructions of March 31, 1873, we reached Fort Duncan, Tex., on the Rio Grande River, on the 30th of April. From the best information obtainable we expected that the governor of the Mexican State of Coahuila would shortly arrive at Piedras Negras, a Mexican town just opposite Fort Duncan, and as it was essential to secure his advice and co-operation in our work, we awaited his arrival; also, in order to procure and fit out such vehicles and animals as would be needed for traveling in that country, where no public means of transportation could be obtained.

On the 8th of May we crossed the Rio Grande. As the governor had not come to the frontier, we proceeded on to Saltillo, the capital of Coahuila, about three hundred and fifty miles distant. We deemed it useless to go first to where the Kickapoos, Pottawatomies, and other roving bands of Indians, Lipans and Mescaleros, were reported to be encamped, because they were all, by a recent treaty or agreement with Governor Cepeda of Coahuila, under his direct protection and supervision.

On the 15th of May we arrived at Saltillo. The next day, there being no American commercial agent or consul in that city, John C. O'Sullivan, jr., esq., a prominent merchant, kindly accompanied and introduced us to Governor Cepeda.

We presented our credentials and explained our instructions relative to the removal of the Kickapoo and other Indians from the frontier of Mexico back to their proper reservations in the United States. We requested his active co-operation in effecting the objects of our mission, and also that he would select one or more of his officers to act, on behalf of his State government, as commissioner to accompany and work with us.

In response to our requests, the governor seeming to feel and appreciate how important our mission was, and how upon its success depended the peace and quiet of the frontier, and perhaps the continuance of friendly relations between the United States and Mexico, not only appointed a commissioner, Señor Antonio Montero, but also issued a proclamation to all officials and citizens in the State, requiring them to assist us in our work; and he advised the Indians to accompany us, if they thought that their condition would be improved. Before leaving Saltillo we communicated with our minister at the city of Mexico, asking him to make such efforts as he might see fit to get the general government's indorsement upon Governor Cepeda's action. To this letter we received no reply; but as Señor Montero's commission was never revoked, and as he was permitted to continue working with us, we have inferred that Governor Cepeda's course was approved by the general government. Many influential citizens of Coahuila, and members of the State legislature, strongly opposed the governor's course toward us, and made it one of the grounds of the revolutionary proceedings now transpiring in that State.

On the 20th of May we left Saltillo and went to Monterey, the capital of Nuevo Leon, in which State some of the Indians resided. On the 21st we arrived, and, accompanied by J. Ulrich, esq., our consul, called upon Governor Gonzales, to whom we made known our business. The governor expressed his desire for the success of our mission. At our request he issued a circular-letter to all the alcaldes of the border towns, to place no obstacle in our way, and directing officials and citizens to co-operate with us. The following day, 22d, we set out for Santa Rosa, the town nearest to where the Indians were located. On the way some 30 leagues from Monterey, and before reaching Monclova, we were informed by a courier with a dispatch from Mr. O'Sullivan, of Saltillo, sent via Monterey, that Governor Cepeda had just heard that a party of Americans had crossed into Mexico, and had attacked the Kickapoos near Remolina, had killed several and taken some prisoners. On arriving at Monclova, where Señor Antonio Montero, the Mexican commissioner, joined us, we heard that it was General MacKenzie's raid. Being informed of the disturbed condition of the country, consequent upon the raid, we obtained from the alcalde of Monclova an escort, via Avosata, to Santa Rosa, which place we reached on the 28th of May. On the 29th we sent word to the Indians that we were there for the purpose of inducing them to go with us to the United States. That afternoon a few came in and we made arrangements to collect as many as possible of the chiefs and warriors so that we might have a council. This involved a few days' delay and considerable expense. We found the Indians in a very destitute condition, and, owing to the scarcity of game, much scattered; we had to provide subsistence and money to provide food for those whose families were at a distance while they were assembling to talk with us. Immediately upon our arrival at Santa Rosa, some of the most influential citizens of the town, in violation of Governor Cepeda's instructions and advice, in open disregard of his authority and that of the Mexican commissioner, went to work to prejudice the Indians against us. Through Michael Thomas, our Indian interpreter, who came with us from the Kansas reservation, and who staid at night in the Indian camps, we learned that the Indians were advised by the Mexicans to kill us forthwith, or to capture and hold us as hostages for their women and children captured by General MacKenzie. The Indians were also told by the Mexicans that our object was to poison them, (the Indians,) and advised them not to accept any provisions from us; that we wanted to get all the tribes together and that United States soldiers would be at hand to murder them; that if they went over into Texas they would all be killed. The Mexicans raised a subscription to buy provisions for the Indians and to bribe them to stay in Mexico. Day after day new lies were manufactured and told to the Indians to set them against us. Our assassination was freely advocated. For some days our lives hung by a thread. Besides Señor Montero our party consisted only of ourselves and two teamsters, and the interpreter, too weak, of course, to hope for successful resistence if attacked by the Mexicans and infuriated Indians. But, feeling the important issues involved in our mission, we ignored these personal threats and attempted intimidation and kept steadily at work. Governor Cepeda was notified of the situation and wrote cautioning his commissioner and ourselves to be most watchful and observant. At this time a report of our assassination was sent to Texas. We have also reason to believe that a few citizens of Texas, and some Americans and foreigners in Mexico, were implicated in the opposition to our mission. For all purchases we had to make, exorbitant prices in gold were charged. The Indians were urged to make raids into Texas to capture women and children, to kill male settlers, and steal cattle. These desperate efforts were made chiefly by those Mexicans who had belonged to the revolutionary party of 1872, and who opposed Governor Cepeda's administration.

Notwithstanding these obstacles, on the 1st of June we met the Indians in council and talked with them seven hours. We stated the object of our presence there, explained our commissions and instructions, and urged the advantages to them of an immediate move to their United States reservation. The Mexican commissioner indorsed our statements, and told them it was the desire of both governments that they should go, that they would be protected, and in all respects better off. The Indians, through their chiefs, said in reply that they had just been attacked by United States troops from Texas; that in passing through that State in 1864 (the party who at that time went from Kansas to Mexico,) they had been attacked undeservedly; that early in May they heard we were coming to induce them to return to the United States, and that then they had held a council, and a large number of them had decided to return with us, if their reasonable demands for supplies were complied with by our Government; but since that council their people had been killed, women and children captured by United States troops; that therefore, until the captives were restored, they would not listen to our offers; but, if they were returned they would forget about those who were killed, and would return with us, as both governments desired it. On the following day we met and again renewed our efforts. We asked the chiefs to go with us to the Texas border where they could be assured of the safety of the captives, and that if they would cross over on their way to their reservation the prisoners would be restored to them. After several talks it was finally agreed that one of the principal chiefs, Che-quan-ka-ko, should accompany us to see about the captives. Upon arriving at San Antonio, Tex., on 13th June, to which place the prisoners had been taken, we had the honor of communicating with you by telegraph, and requested that the Indian captives should be put under our charge. Our intention was not to release them, or to return them to Mexico, but with proper precautions take them back near the border, and holding them on the limits of Texas, induce the Indians to cross over, and proceed at once to their reservation. We felt assured that as soon as the Indians were convinced of the safety of their women and children, and could be made satisfied that we were acting in good faith for their good, they would consent to move. We found it difficult to answer their often repeated question as to how it was that at the very time we, as commissioners of the United States Government, were in Mexico to treat with them, that the United States soldiers should have gone into Mexico to attack, kill, and capture their people. We read to them what General MacKenzie had written to us; that he was following a trail of Lipan Indians, and that it led to the Kickapoo camp, and that they had received a blow intended more particularly for the Lipans, who had just been depredating in Texas.

That attack, so admirably executed by General MacKenzie, evidently somewhat delayed our negotiations, but doubtless its results contributed largely to our final success, by exhibiting the power of the United States even outside of our country, and proving to the Indians that Mexico could no longer afford them a safe harbor after their raids into Texas.

Our request concerning the captives not having been granted, on the 23d June we left San Antonio and returned to Zaragoza, Mexico, about thirty miles from Piedras Negras; arrived there 28th June. From that time up to the 14th July was employed in again getting together the scattered bands of Kickapoos and Pottawatomies, numbering about 800, and also in sending word to the Lipans and Mescaleros, numbering in all about 2,000, to meet us in council at Remolino, some thirty miles northwest from Zaragoza. On the 14th July a council was held. We again set forth the object of our mission, and the reasons why they should move. Only one Mescalero chief was present, and left abruptly before the council was over, and, stealing a Mexican's horse, departed. None of the Lipans or Mescaleros again appeared in council, although they had said that they would like to go with us to the United States. Future efforts with them might be more successful.

In the councils held at Remolino all of the Pottawatomies, and a large part of the Kickapoos, consented to go to their reservation. They required, however, that we should first furnish them with subsistence, clothing, and other supplies, and some pack-mules and horses for transportation on their journey, and that these things should be delivered to them at their camp at Remolino. Their objection to receiving supplies on the Texas side of the Rio Grande was because of their fear of attack from the Texans. They also asked us not to accompany them on their march, saying that their intended route would be west and north of all the settlements in Texas; that they would pass through the Comanche and Kiowa country; that if these Indians saw white men with them they would be unfriendly and might attack; that if anything should happen to us before reaching the reservation, the United States Government would hold them responsible. After careful deliberation upon all the circumstances of the case, we determined to take the risk and responsibility of complying with their conditions. The result to be attained, if they kept faith with us, was fully worth the risk. If our mission failed, feelings of revenge and desire for retaliation, encouraged by bad Mexican citizens, would have led forthwith to the devastation of the whole Texan frontier, and ultimate complications with Mexico; and, again, we had no other alternative but to abruptly break off all negotiations and return home without having accomplished anything or comply with their request, and thereby settle the question as to whether it was possible to succeed in moving them by peaceable means. Our interpreter assured us that they would act in good faith and return to the United States. We therefore concluded to concede to their demands, fully understanding the possibility of their deceiving us after they had received the supplies.

We accordingly procured the requisite supplies in Mexico and in San Antonio, Tex., and had them delivered at Remolino. We were told by the alcalde at Zaragoza that efforts would probably be made by bands of Mexican robbers to capture the supply-train *en route* for Piedras Negras to Remolino. We therefore made application, by courier and telegraph, to the Mexican government to permit us to take along a United States military escort. This was refused, but permission was given for us to have an armed escort of citizens.

The custom-house officials at Piedras Negras demanded payment of duties on the supplies for the Indians. The amount levied was over $7,000 in gold. We represented to those officers that our mission was appointed by the United States Government, at the suggestion of the Mexican government, and was one effecting the interests of both republics; that the goods taken in by us were solely for the Indians then about to move; that we felt sure the government of Mexico could not properly, and would not, levy duties upon such supplies as could not be procured in that part of Mexico. The question was referred to the city of Mexico, and a reply received that all supplies intended for consumption of the Indians, during the time occupied in reaching the frontier, and previous to crossing the Rio Grande, should pass free of duty. This reply was interpreted by the Peidras Negras officials to except only a part of what we had to deliver at Remolino, leaving a balance of over $4,000 gold to be paid by us. We refused to pay this, believing that the case was not fully understood, and again referred the matter to Mexico, and also to our Government, for future adjustment. We also refused to give the bond required, but furnished them with a list of the articles taken into Mexico by us. A permit to pass the goods was then given.

On the 26th August the goods were delivered to the Indians, only to those who had consented to start. The Indians themselves would not permit any who remained to share with them.

On the 28th August the movement was commenced toward the Rio Grande. As near as we could estimate about four hundred, including warriors, women, and children, started, consisting of all the Pottawatomies and a large part of the Kickapoos. We furnished Michael Thomas, our Indian interpreter, who went along with the Indians, with letters showing the character and object of the movement. At our request, General Auger, commanding the department of Texas, issued orders to the troops of his command not to molest the Indians on their march through his department.

At the time we have the honor to submit this report the Indians are *en route* along the eastern border of the Llano Estacado toward the western part of the Indian Territory. One band of Kickapoos, numbering all told about 280, remained in Mexico, and have since gone down near Parras, in the southwestern part of Coahuila. We believe that these, too, will rejoin their tribe as soon as they are assured of the safe arrival of those who have started to the United States. We very respectfully suggest, and request, that we may be allowed to take two or three of the chiefs after their arrival in Kansas back with us to Mexico, and get all the rest to return to their reservation. Three of the warriors accompanied us by railroad from Texas, one we left at Fort Gibson, with the captives, and the other two we took to the Kansas reservation.

Owing to the fact that our operations were in a foreign country, where only coin could be used, and where all supplies are scarce and dear, and that considerable expense had to be incurred in traveling, also in collecting together and subsisting the Indians while in consultation with us, the amount at first placed to our credit was soon exhausted.

In reply to our second requisition for funds, we received notice from you that on 11th August a requisition had been made on the Treasury for amount required; upon this notice, together with the promise contained in our instructions that funds would be promptly furnished to carry out our work, we incurred certain obligations for the supplies given to the Indians, and made promises to them of additional gifts upon their arrival in Kansas.

On the 6th September, two days after reaching San Antonio, your telegram was received informing us that the comptroller had decided not to approve said requisition, and that the unexpended balance of the appropriation for "collecting, subsisting, and removing Kickapoos, and other roving bands of Indians from Mexico," had lapsed, and that a re-appropriation by Congress would be necessary before further funds could be furnished. This information left us in a most embarrassing situation. We had made purchases of supplies and means of transportation, and not being able to meet these obligations, and more particularly the probability of not being able to keep our word to the Indians, was endangering the whole result of our mission. We are now not only in danger of losing the successful fruits of our whole summer's work, but also, what is of even graver importance, incurring the hostility for all time to come of these Kickapoo and Pottawatomie Indians, and, by not being able to keep our promise to them, cause them forever after to distrust all negotiations with our Government, and perhaps leading to a second Modoc-like war upon the frontier of Texas. These consequences can be best obviated by the prompt and faithful fulfillment of our pledges, and if, in your judgment, no funds can be furnished to us forthwith, we most earnestly request that Congress be urged to appropriate, at an early day, such an amount as you may deem requisite to complete the service we have so far advanced.

From personal observation and reliable information obtained in Mexico and on the Texas frontier, we beg leave to express the opinion that what we have already accomplished has added very largely to the wealth of the country, in the enhanced value of the vast and splendid grazing and agricultural lands of Western Texas, which, owing to the presence of these Indians on the Mexican border, were shunned by settlers and emigrants to Texas. Moreover, removing the Indians takes away the mask or pretext hitherto used by Mexican cattle-thieves and marauders. Now further raids into Texas can be charged directly to the lawless frontier-citizens of Mexico.

We would state that much kind and valuable aid was extended to us in promoting our public duties by Gen. C. C. Augur, commanding Department of Texas, and Gen. R. S. Mackenzie, commanding that district along the Rio Grande, and by Col. W. R. Shafter, commanding Fort Duncan, also by William Schuchardt, esq., United States commercial agent at Piedras Negras. Che-quan-ka-ko, the chief of the Pottawatomies, and Michael Thomas, the Indian interpreter, served most faithfully and contributed largely to our success. During the whole time Governor Victoriano Cepeda, of Coahuila, and the Mexican commissioner, Señor Antonio Montero, were unremitting in their efforts to help us, and by the judicious exercise of their authority gave us most important assistance.

For a detailed statement of all of our expenditures, please see the accompaying vouchers, abstracts, and account-current.

We have the honor to be, very respectfully, your obedient servants,

HENRY M. ATKINSON,
THOMAS G. WILLIAMS,
Special United States Indian Commissioners.

Hon. EDW. P. SMITH,
Commissioner of Indian Affairs.

1

NEW YORK INDIAN AGENCY,
Forrestville, N. Y., October 25, 1873.

SIR: In submitting my fourth annual report, I have the honor to state the present population of the Indians on the eight reservations in the New York agency at 5,141, being an increase over last year of 71; and their wealth in individual property at $341,856, not including farms and farm-buildings. Nineteen thousand seven hundred and thirty-seven acres of land are under cultivation by the Indians. There are 1,576 Indian children between the ages of 5 and 21 years residing on these reservations. Of this number 1,221 have attended school some portion of the school-year ending September 30, 1873. Twenty-eight schools have been taught on an average of 32 weeks each, and the school-registers, as kept by the several teachers, show an average daily attendance of 811 Indian children, being an increase of daily attendance over the preceding year of 103, and over the school-year ending September 30, 1871, of 179. Eleven of the teachers employed in these schools some portion of the school-year were Indians, and succeeded well. These schools, except one, are embraced under the free-school system of the State of New York, and have been sustained during the year at an expense of $8,647.47, of which the Indians have contributed $611.

I report an increase of population on all the reservations during the year except Tuscarora. On this reservation there is a decrease of thirty-nine, owing to great mortality among children by measles.

I have to report the first murder committed by Indians in this agency for several years. It recently occurred on the Tonawanda reservation, and the persons implicated in the crime were intoxicated. The Indians are quite as free from the violation of the criminal laws as any like portion of the white population of the State.

Generally the year has been a prosperous one among the Indians in this agency. At no former period has the evidence of their advancement in wealth and civilization been more satisfactory, as will appear from the statistical returns of farming and education herewith transmitted.

The Senecas of the Tonawanda band, residing on the Tonawanda reservation, appropriated $4,500 from their trust fund interest, for the construction and maintenance of a manual-labor school on such reservation; also the sum of $1,600, from the same fund, for the purchase of improvements of individual Indians on eighty acres of land, to be used in connection with the school.

The State of New York also appropriated $4,500 for the like purpose, but owing to defects in the laws making the appropriations, the comptroller of the State refused to pay over the money, and, in June last, the acts making the appropriations were amended to meet his objections. The title to this reservation is vested in such comptroller in trust for the Senecas of the Tonawanda band, and in a letter, under date of the 21st instant, he signified his willingness to convey the land for the purposes of the school, and to pay over the funds appropriated.

The trustees of the school, appointed under the law, have recently qualified, and have appointed an early day to select the eighty acres of land; and it is hoped that the work of erecting the necessary buildings will now be speedily pressed to completion.

The chiefs of this band have manifested a very commendable degree of public spirit in appropriating from the annuities of these Indians such large sums for their education and civilization. This appears quite remarkable in view of the poverty of most of the Indians of the band.

It is confidently anticipated that the proposed manual-labor school will, under judicious management, be of great and permanent benefit to these people.

In your communication to me under date of the 11th ultimo you inquire, in speaking of the Indians in this agency, "whether they are not prepared for citizenship, and whether steps should not be taken to bring them in condition with other people of New York," adding, "your long acquaintance with them and their affairs will enable you to make suggestions which will be of value to this office."

In endeavoring to answer your inquiries I respectfully state that over one-half of the Indians in this agency reside upon the Alleghany and Cattaraugus reservations. The Ogden Company, or its assigns, claim what has been termed the pre-emption right to these two reservations, together with whatever right, title, and interest the Commonwealth of Massachusetts conveyed to Robert Morris by deeds dated May 11, 1791. It is understood that the Ogden Company claim that this is an absolute title in fee simple, subject to the possessory right of the Indians so long only as they actually occupy the reservations as a tribe. On the part of the Indians it is claimed, on what seems better authority, that they own the fee to these lands by their own original title, and that the Ogden Company has only the right to purchase whenever they choose to sell. So early as 1847 the State of New York passed a judicious law, providing for the allotment of these lands among the Indians, but they have been adverse to such allotments, fearing that the same might prove an entering wedge to dispossess them, as stated in my last annual report. The claim of the Ogden Company is at least a cloud upon the title of the Senecas to these reservations, and I am satisfied it is a serious impediment to their advancement in civilization. It produces an unsettled feeling as to the title of their lands, and prevents them from making improvements. Love of property and home being with them, as with others, among the chief incentives to industry, the present state of things tends to make them shiftless and improvident, and is an obstacle in the way of their becoming citizens. With this difficulty obviated I see no reason why measures might not be properly instituted at an early day to make the Indians of New York citizens, in case provision should be made to protect them from improvidently selling or encumbering their lands for a period say of about twenty years.

I inclose the annual report of the trustees of the Thomas Asylum for orphan and destitute Indian children on the Cattaraugus reservation. This institution continues under most excellent management, and is doing a practical work of great value for the Indians in this agency. As will be seen from the inclosed report, the Society of Friends at Philadelphia continue their humane offices in aid of this asylum. I respectfully recommend the continuance of the annual appropriation by the Government for its support.

I am, very respectfully, your obedient servant,

D. SHERMAN,
Agent.

Hon. E. P. SMITH,
Commissioner of Indian Affairs.

2

OFFICE OF MICHIGAN INDIAN AGENCY,
Lansing, September 15, 1873.

SIR: I have the honor herewith to submit my second annual report of the Michigan Indian agency.

This agency embraces the care of about ten thousand Indians. They sustain treaty relations to the United States Government under four different names, viz:

The Ottawas and Chippewas of Michigan.
The Chippewas of Saginaw, Swan Creek, and Black River.
The Chippewas of Lake Superior.
The Pottawatomies of Huron.

OTTAWAS AND CHIPPEWAS OF MICHIGAN.

This is by far the most numerous tribe, numbering about six thousand, their general location being in the northern part of the lower peninsula of Michigan.

In 1855 there were set apart from the public domain about twenty-seven townships of land in different places as reservations, within which the members of this tribe were to make selection of land; those that were heads of families eighty acres, and single persons twenty-one years of age forty acres each, and for which selections the United States Government was to issue and deliver to them patents in fee simple; after which the remaining unselected land in these reservations was to be restored to market.

In 1864 Hon. D. C. Leach, then the Indian agent of this State, reported to the Department the selections of land made by the Indians, but for some reasons the report was recommitted to his successor, Maj. James W. Long, for reconsideration and perfecting. This report being made, it was supposed to contain the names and selections of all that were entitled to land under the treaty of 1855, and patents were issued and forwarded to me for delivery in 1872. Upon the delivery of these patents, which took place in July, 1872, I found a large number of the Indians holding certificates of their selections of land that had been given to them by Agent Leach in 1864, but for whom I had no corresponding patent. The number thus omitted, and for whom no patents had been issued, amounted to three hundred and seventeen, as ascertained afterward by a careful examination by myself, assisted by special commissioner Maj. John J. Knox.

These facts being brought to the notice of the Hon. Secretary of the Interior, orders were given for a careful examination of these cases, and a report of the same, at the earliest practicable period.

A large number of these persons living on the islands in Lake Michigan, and there being no means of visiting them in the winter season, I was obliged to defer my visit to them until the opening of navigation.

On the 16th of May, 1873, in connection with Special Commissioner Knox, we commenced our labors, and continued them until we had visited all their reservations and made a complete list of all such as had been previously omitted in the official report, the number amounting to three hundred and seventeen. These were duly reported, with their selections of land, and recommended for patents. This gave great satisfaction to all the tribe, as it was feared by them that they would be deprived of their selections of land upon which many of them had made their homes for years, and had some valuable improvements.

HOMESTEADS.

By an act of Congress, signed by the President June 10, 1872, entitled "An act for the restoration to market of certain lands in Michigan," it was provided that those of this tribe who had arrived at twenty-one years of age since the formation of the treaty in 1855, (and for whom no provisions had been made in the treaty in regard to land,) should, upon the certificate of the Indian agent, be allowed six months' time in which to locate homesteads on the reservations under the general homestead law. A large number availed themselves of this generous provision, entered their homesteads, have gone on to them, and have displayed commendable zeal in making improvements.

I have great hope in the final success of this generous and wise arrangement in their behalf.

CHIPPEWAS OF SAGINAW, SWAN CREEK, AND BLACK RIVER.

Of this tribe there are about fifteen hundred, and in the matter of civilization it is in advance of the others of the agency. The reasons for this, to my mind, are two: In the first place they are located in their reservation away from the waters, and are, therefore, free from the demoralization usually connected with dependence upon fishing, and obliged to procure their subsistence from husbandry. This has a tendency to cultivate in them habits of industry and frugality. In 1855 there were set apart for them as a perpetual reservation six adjoining townships of land in the county of Isabella. Some of this land was heavily timbered with pine, but the most of it is excellent farming land and favorably located, so that eventually such as have made selections of farming lands must become well off with suitable industry.

The other cause of their greater advancement in civilization is in the fact that they are better provided with moral and educational instrumentalities. Their educational fund, as provided in the treaty of 1855, still remains unexhausted, and consequently we are maintaining four schools among them; and furthermore they are almost universally Protestants in religion, and enjoy the benefit of this type of Christianity which has no fears of light and liberty. Not long since I spent a Sabbath with them, and labored and worshipped with them in two different settlements. In one neighborhood there was a respectable church well filled. In the orchestra was a choir of young singers with a cabinet organ, played by one of the young Indians. Several pieces were sung, and some were recited, all in the English language. With these natural and circumstantial advantages, therefore, enjoyed by this tribe, they have outstripped the others in progress and civilization.

THE CHIPPEWAS OF LAKE SUPERIOR.

This tribe is located in the county of Houghton, on the upper peninsula of Michigan Their reservation (three townships) is favorably located about L'Anse Bay, and furnishes them excellent fisheries and farming land. Two schools are maintained, and the Catholic and Methodist Churches each have a mission among them. The tribe numbers about thirteen hundred, and still receives annuities in goods and money. The past year has been one of marked material prosperity with them.

POTTAWATOMIES OF HURON.

This is but a small band of about 60 in number, located in Calhoun County; receive $400 annuity money, and subsist by gardening and basket-making.

AGENCY OFFICE.

In the month of April last, by permission of the Hon. Secretary of the Interior, the office of this agency was removed from the city of Detroit to the city of Lansing, the capital of the State of Michigan, it being much more central and convenient to the business of the agency.

PROGRESS IN CIVILIZATION.

The chief design of the Government in its policy toward the Indians being their elevation from a state of barbarism to that of civilization, it is a matter of profound interest as to whether or not the beneficent methods employed for this work are succeeding.

An intelligent comparison of the past and present condition of the Indians of this State, covering the time of only one generation, reveals the fact that a great advancement has been made. Now they almost universally wear the dress of citizens; they live in houses; they discard poligamy; they engage in husbandry; some become mechanics; many of them become sailors; the younger ones speak in many instances the English language. In religious matters Paganism and conjuring have been almost universally abandoned, and the Christian religion adopted; and furthermore, for the amount of labor expended upon them by the schools and churches in a language foreign to the Indians, and after making a charitable allowance for the perversity of human nature, and remembering the terrible temptations to evil thrown upon them by a class of unscrupulous whites usually found in the neighborhood of the Indian settlements, I conclude that there are no just grounds for complaint or hopelessness in the condition of the Indians of Michigan. It has been my endeavor to co-operate heartily with the religious agencies for the lifting of the Indians up into a state of intelligence, industry, and piety.

The rum traffic is the greatest source of difficulty and degradation. During the past year its influence and effects have been uncommonly disastrous, owing to the fact that new lines of railroads have brought the whites and Indians more generally together. Then, too, in cases of prosecution under the United States law against selling liquor to Indians, we have found it difficult to enforce the law on account of the plea that, as the Indians had become citizens, they are entitled to no special claims to protection.

Respectfully,

GEO. I. BETTS,
United States Indian Agent.

Hon. EDWARD P. SMITH,
Commissioner of Indian Affairs, Washington, D. C.

3

UNITED STATES INDIAN AGENCY,
Green Bay, Wis., September 30, 1873.

DEAR SIR: The annual report of this agency will be brief, as I have been here only between two and three months, most of which time has been consumed in special duties, and the last annual report of my predecessor was so full and complete that little need be added except information contained in the table of statistics herewith inclosed.

This agency includes the Stockbridge and Munsee tribes, the Oneidas and Menomonees. A few of the Menomonees, most of the Oneidas, and all of the Stockbridges and Munsees speak English, and all, except a small portion of the Menomonees, wear citizens' clothing and live in houses.

The number of Oneidas now living upon their reservation is 1,279. During the past thirty years this tribe, instead of diminishing, has increased between three and four hundred by the excess of births over deaths. Their reservation is only about ten miles from Green Bay, and contains 60,800 acres, of which a large portion is well watered and fertile. Most of the families cultivate land and keep cattle, and there are many large, well-tilled farms among them.

The past year one man has raised 500 bushels of wheat, 550 of corn, 300 of potatoes and 1,000 of oats; and owns 9 horses and 22 cattle. Another raised 148 bushels of wheat, 500 of corn, and 600 of oats; and owns 10 horses and 25 cattle. Still, many of the tribe have no enterprise or economy, and live contentedly in their huts, tilling their patches of beans and maize.

Services have been regularly held in their two churches. Rev. E. A. Goodnough, rector of the Episcopal church, has been teaching and preaching among this people for twenty years, and his experience shows that the Indian is capable of advancement in all respects, although the apparent fruits of his labors have been hardly sufficient to keep alive his enthusiasm. Rev. S. W. Ford, pastor of the Methodist church, and teacher of one of the schools, has recently returned to this charge after an absence of about twenty years.

The two schools have had a total attendance of 175 pupils, with an average of 73. There are on the reservation 608 children between the ages of six and sixteen, and I hope to be able to recommend some plan by which the work of education may be carried on more vigorously.

A mortality list inclosed herewith shows 35 deaths from such diseases as are prevalent among the whites of this climate. Seven deaths resulted from small-pox, of which there were some fifty cases. The disease was arrested by vaccinations performed by Rev. Mr. Ford, mission teacher. For medical attendance they are dependent upon the physicians of Green Bay and De Pere, at an expense of from six to eight dollars a visit. It seems to me that their community of 1,279 ought to have a physician.

Daniel Bread, for many years the leading chief of this tribe, died in July at the age of 73.

The dissensions with reference to individuals cutting and selling timber, and the status in the tribe of those called "homeless Indians," who came to the reservation later than the others, continues to exist without any apparent prospect of settlement, unless the Department takes up these questions and disposes of them.

Under the provisions of an act of Congress of 1871, relating to the Stockbridges and Munsees, two rolls were made, one containing the names of those who wish to leave the tribe and become citizens of the United States, the other the names of those who wish to continue as a tribe. Of the former there are 131, and of the latter, 110. Owing to conflicting views and wishes these rolls have not received the signature of the superintendent of the allotment, or the approval of the Commissioner of Indian Affairs. On account of questions arising under other provisions of the act referred to, the proceeds of one and a half townships of land sold in January, 1873, have not been divided, and the tribe is now in a very unsettled condition. It is to be hoped that the recommendations of the special Indian commissioner who has recently visited this tribe are such as will lead to a settlement of existing difficulties.

A school has been taught with fair success by Rev. J. Slingerland, a Presbyterian clergyman, and a member of the tribe, who has also acted as the pastor of their church. These educational and religious influences have been very much neutralized by the quarrels in the tribe.

Certain parties who had purchased the pine on a certain tract of the unsold portion of the reservation have committed trespasses to the amount of about seven hundred thousand feet, worth four or five dollars a thousand, against some of whom criminal proceedings have been commenced in the United States court. I hope that neither the social standing nor political influence of these men will shield them from deserved punishment. If white men can be taught that it is a crime to steal timber from Indians, the value of their property will be increased, the work of agents made easier, and the cause of morality promoted.

The Menomonees are the largest of the three tribes in this agency. Their last annuity-roll contains 1,480. Their reservation is about fifty miles from Green Bay, and contains 230,400 acres. During the past year these Indians have built for themselves several new block-houses, and some progress has been made in agriculture. Their houses, however, have not been located in accordance with any system. I suggest that their reservation be carefully surveyed and platted, and some plan adopted whereby each family may have a sufficient quantity of good land without interference from others.

The members of this tribe are gradually becoming accustomed to labor. During the year they have cultivated considerable more land than ever before, made fifty tons of maple-sugar, cut 550 tons of hay on their marshes, and done a large part of the work of cutting and putting into the river 2,500,000 feet of pine timber, besides working some in other lumber-camps.

The productions of the farm have been 200 bushels of potatoes, 12 tons of hay, and 450 bushels of oats. At the mill 7,280 bushels of grain have been ground, and 217,200 feet of lumber sawed. The blacksmith reports that he has shod 169 horses and 39 oxen; repaired 65 wagons, 93 guns, 27 traps, 5 stoves, 9 axes, 11 bells, 79 sleds, 84 grub-hoes, 17 pitchforks, and 13 plows; mended 59 chains; made 53 stove-rods, 140 spears, 31 clevises, 27 hinges, 31 knives, 78 needles, 73 chain-hooks, 15 wedges, 15 clasps and staples, 14 pan-handles, 10 cant-hooks, 8 swamp-hooks, 107 cold sheets, 18 sap-gauges, 39 rakes, 106 trammel-chains, 9 shovels, 3 trowels, 8 sled-raves, 11 drag-teeth, and 75 heel-wedges; ironed 26 whiffletrees, 11 neck-yokes, 19 sleds, 12 cutters, 13 wagon-tongues, 7 wagon-boxes, and 5 ox-yokes; and baled 10 kettles.

The school of Alex. Grignon has been continued without much encouragement for its teacher or the friends of the Indian. The school at Keshena having but few pupils, a school-building and a dwelling-house for teachers were built in the hard-wood timber-land where many of the tribe had settled. Since January last Mr. and Mrs. J. W. Stryker have been teaching the few pupils they could induce to attend, sometimes forty and sometimes two. The boys prefer playing ball outside of the school-house to studying inside, and Mr. Stryker's unusual enthusiasm has failed to excite in them any great desire for learning. Scarcely any in this tribe, except some of the young men, talk English, which makes the labor of study, as well as of instruction, tedious. They can learn, however, if they try. One lad in five months learned to read intelligibly in the second reader. A system of compulsory education seems to be needed. I hope the way will soon be clear for the establishment of a boarding-school. I have talked with the chiefs about it, and they appear to be in favor of using some of their pine money for this purpose.

The only purely religious work among them has been done by the Romanists, who now have a priest at Keshena.

My predecessor cut about 2,500,000 feet of pine logs last winter, and although he labored under disadvantages, because of his employing Indians, of his limited experience in lumbering, and of opposition from unfriendly outsiders, and although the price of logs is unusually low this season, yet he cleared for the tribe much more than the same class of timber has sold at on the stump.

The pine of the Menomonees would yield about a million dollars if it could be disposed of at its real value. If the interest of such a sum could be used for educational and agricultural purposes, the work of their civilization could be pushed rapidly forward.

I must add a word upon the threadbare subject of intemperance among the Indians. Every Saturday gallons of the vilest stuff are swallowed by these people. Some sellers have been punished, but the business is still brisk. I have been here long enough to see the evil, but hardly dare venture suggestions as to its remedy. I do hope, however, that the Department will give agents full opportunity to try expedients, and will be liberal in the use of funds that are available for this object.

Very respectfully,

THOS. N. CHASE,
United States Indian Agent.

Hon. E. P. SMITH,
Commissioner of Indian Affairs.

4.

WHITE EARTH, *December* 1, 1873.

SIR: I have the honor to submit herewith my annual report.

My commission bears date May 17, 1873. From my monthly report, and from letters official relating to the Otter Tails, Gull Lake, and Pembina bands of Indians, may be obtained a more minute description of their condition and of my labors than would be allowed in this document, and to such papers I would respectfully refer you.

During this year that portion of the agency known as Red Lake has been constituted a separate department, and the funds belonging thereto have, in accordance with your order, been placed to the credit of the special agent in charge at that point.

With this exception no changes of importance have been made in the general features of this charge. In the absence of a regularly appointed agent the general management of affairs became necessarily somewhat deranged; and this fact, together with the revival of the spirit of industry and self-improvement, have made my labors exceedingly onerous, and prevented me from beginning the annual distribution of goods and money before October 1. The enrollment, but just completed, gives the following result:

ENROLLMENT.

	Men.	Women.	Children.	Total.
White Earth	161	188	252	601
Otter Tail Pillagers	113	150	222	485
Gull Lake bands	20	30	22	72
White Oak Point	172	242	349	763
Mille Lac	134	169	207	510
Snake River	62	76	125	263
Leech Lake Pillagers	468	574	505	1547
Pembina	87	113	196	396
	1,217	1,542	1,878	4,637

SUMMARY.

Mississippians	2 209 against 2,139 in 1872.
Pillager and Lake Winnebagoshish	2,042 against 2,088 in 1872.
Pembina	396 against 547 in 1872.

The excess of 137 of last year is owing to my dropping 150 half-breed Pembinas from the annuity roll.

The Pillager, Otter Tails, the Gull Lakes, and 147 of the Pembina band were paid with the White Earth Indians at the agency; the Mille Lacs at Soul's Camp, on Rum River; 249 Pembinas at Pembina on the 26th ultimo. The Pillagers and White Oak Point Indians received their annuities upon their respective reservations. From a perusal of the annual report of 1871–'72, I am unable to discover any remarkable change in the condition of any of these 4,627 Indians, with the exception of such as reside upon White Earth reservation.

OTTER TAILS.

The Pillager Otter Tails, 500 in number, a powerful and most promising people, stand pleading for admission to this reservation, and for assistance from Government enabling them to adopt the habits and enjoy the blessings of civilized life. They have indicated their preference for a township 20 miles southeast of this agency, where there is abundance of water, pine and oak timber, and excellent prairie soilfor cultivation.

The paper which I had the honor of sending the Department upon this subject expresses the desirableness of removing this ill used people, who, from a clerical error in the original summons, were, it is said, not represented in the grand council in Washington, and as a consequence are to-day without any reservation or civil protection. I have listened to their earnest pleading for houses and lands, for school and church privileges, and under all the circumstances of the case I cannot but believe that an appropriation of at least $25,000 will be secured in their behalf at the present session of Congress.

GULL LAKES

This band probably numbers 300 members. One hundred of them were located by my predecessor in comfortable homes upon this reservation. The rest of them repeatedly disappointed his reasonable expectations for their removal. The houses built for them have in part stood unoccupied, exposed to destruction by fire, the responsibility resting back upon such as failed to fulfill their promise to remove hither.

Recently I have removed 75 more of them, and shall be obliged to subsist them until next spring.

PEMBINA

In accordance with a regulation made by the Department and the White Earth Indians, a township has been assigned to the Pembina band of Mississippi Indians upon the Wild Rice River on this reservation, 17 miles northwest of this agency. The entire band was duly notified that the annual payment would be made this year at this township. Their extreme poverty and destitution, the great distance which they would be obliged to travel, from 150 to 300 miles, and the evil influence of men who hope to be benefited by their being paid at Pembina, prevented them from coming, with the exceptions of such as lived at Grand Forks and at other points not distant from the proposed place of payment. The balance were paid at Pembina the 26th ultimo. The Turtle Mountain band have virtually abandoned that distant field to the Sioux, and live, as do the others, upon forbidden soil, without hope. There is neither hunting nor fishing in the vicinity of Pembina, and I would earnestly entreat the Department to secure their early removal to White Earth. By prompt action they may be saved to themselves and to the world. If neglected, their ruin is inevitable.

LEECH LAKE.

By far the larger class upon any reservation is that of the Pillager and Lake Winnebagoshish bands located about Leech Lake. They are the most restless, turbulent, and desperate of any Indians in the State. During the entire summer they have been kept in a state of excitement by representations made to them by outside parties to the effect that they were being defrauded in the sale of their timber. Disappointed politicians and envious speculators have been active in stirring up strife among them.

Whiskey-drinking frequently leads to homicide, and creates the necessity of sending troops among them several times each year, always at payment time. The reservation, except in insignificant measure, is entirely unadapted to grazing or tillage. The only natural mode of life among them is that which they have followed for generations. It is expensive caring for the few who are most given to habits of industry. The three thousand dollars ($3,000) appropriation is inadequate to meet the demands for a boarding-school. Not more than twenty pupils can be educated for that sum in a school in which everything is furnished by the Government. It is exceedingly difficult, with so small a sum, to secure the services of competent instructors for such a position. The former incumbent has recently resigned, and his place has been filled by another, both of whom are gentlemen of worth, but destined to be discouraged by the smallness of the school, which is owing almost solely to the meagerness of the appropriation.

The Government has done a most wise and beneficent deed in converting their useless timber into available funds for the improvement of the people. Already has the needed saw-mill and corn-mill been erected, and several yoke of oxen, with wagons, have been purchased by funds from this sale, to be given to the most deserving. But it is idle, even with the aid of this large annual fund, to hope for any great and permanent improvement among them, without first providing them with lands suitable for tillage and pasturage, allowing them to retain intact their present reservation for the purposes of hunting, fishing, and sugar-making. There should also be secured for them six townships located upon the eastern boundary of White Earth reservation, running eighteen (18) miles from southeastern corner of said reservation due east, and twelve (12) miles due north from the same southeast corner, and bounded in part by Meneken River, a tributary to Crow Wing River. This would furnish them with excellent water, abundance of timber and wood, and one of the finest agricultural districts in the world. Abandon Leech Lake as a center of operations and transfer the agency buildings to the agricultural home; open a communication direct with the North Pacific Railroad at Hobart or Detroit, a distance of twenty-five miles, and thus save to the Government its large transportation bills. Build for every family who will come a good house and break up and fence two acres for every householder. Thus their tribal relations would be broken up, the better part removed from the contaminating influences of the more vicious ones, an opportunity for self-improvement actually and for the first time secured for them, while they would all be brought within thirty (30) miles of the agent's home, and twenty-five miles from the mills at White Earth, and the example of the best Indians in the State.

MILLE LACS.

Nothing whatever is being done to improve the condition of that portion of Mille Lac Indians still residing in the vicinity of the lake bearing that name. No class of Indians under my charge appear more manly and noble than these. I am profoundly impressed with the moral obligations of the Government to adopt immediate measures for their education and civilization. They hold their present territory by the most feeble tenure. Their brethren upon this reservation would most cordially welcome them and they would soon take their places among the foremost in every good work. The degree of their present exposure to the evil influences of white men is yearly becoming more alarming.

The Snake River band have no reservation.

WHITE-OAK POINT.

These Mississippi bands can scarcely be said to live anywhere. More than seven hundred souls are left wholly without encouragement or aid, except the annuity goods and money. They live in winter in proximity to lumber camps, and in summer hunt and fish, and waste their lives away. No school, no missionary, not even a blacksmith to repair their guns and traps, is furnished them. Their great removal from the agency renders it impracticable to do much for them.

With proper effort they could be in large part induced to remove to White Earth, or upon a portion of the land proposed for the agricultural district of the Pillagers.

WHITE EARTH.

This is the center of operations. Here, if anywhere, is being solved the problem of Indian civilization. Seven hundred reside upon this one million of acres, exclusive of the Pembinas and Gull Lakes, who have but recently arrived.

The employés are Congregationalists, but the religious supervision is that of the Episcopal and Roman Catholic Churches. The former have a church of more than one hundred members, fifty of whom have been confirmed during the present year, with a native pastor and an English-speaking rector. The Romanists represent fifty families, the larger part of whom are of mixed blood, and will erect a house of worship next summer.

HOSPITAL.

By the munificence of a Christian woman, a friend of the Episcopal Church, a beautiful hospital is nearly ready for occupancy; an incalculable blessing to this people. The resident physician will be in attendance daily; and the Indians have already indicated their appreciation of the institution by generously contributing for its support of the products of their farms. From the report of the Government physician, which is herewith transmitted, we learn that the prevailing diseases are caused principally by ignorance of domestic industry, uncleanliness, and social vices. The year past has been one of unusual healthfulness.

SCHOOLS.

During the major part of the year there have been two schools for young children and the boarding-school, averaging forty pupils. The boys are taught agriculture by cultivating the school-farm, and the girls domestic industry by being required daily to assist in household affairs. The time has fully come for an increase of the appropriations for school purposes. The accommodations are now fully occupied, and many will be obliged to seek elsewhere for such privileges. Nothing can be more encouraging to the friends of humanity than to witness this revival of interest among the Indians of this reservation. Already have I thrown open another school-room for those most advanced in speaking English, and I look to the Government for a small appropriation of $1,000 additional to enable me to meet the growing interest in learning. An evening school has been in operation during the greater part of the year, and another will be commenced soon for the winter months.

But for the timely aid of the American Missionary Association, our boarding-school could not have been supported by the governmental appropriation. The employés are supporting a small school of their own, as they cannot properly patronize the Indian school, and the citizens of the reservation are petitioning for the organization of a school-district.

INDUSTRIAL HALL.

There has been erected an industrial hall 40 by 25 feet, for the purpose of teaching the art of weaving rushes and other material, of basket-making and other kinds of handiwork, to the women. An appropriation of $1,000 has been wisely made for our use in this department.

MILLS.

The steam saw-mill, with its planer and its shingle and lath machines, has been in full blast during the entire season, requiring twenty-four men, nearly all of whom are Indians. Six hundred and eighty-five thousand feet of lumber have been manufactured, nearly the whole of which has been used for building purposes. Thirteen hundred dollars were paid to Indians for drawing logs and lumber. Seventy-five dollars' worth of lumber has been given, upon an average, to every chief. The progress of the people in agriculture has created the necessity for a grist-mill, and one has been erected, and is now in successful operation, propelled by the engine which drives the saw-mill.

FARMING

The principal occupation upon this reserve is that of cultivating the soil. The Indians are rapidly becoming farmers. From the report of the farmer, it appears that there have been raised not less than 2,000 bushels of wheat, 6,000 bushels of oats, 500 bushels of corn, 10,000 bushels of potatoes, 13,000 bushels of turnips, and quantities of onions, beets, and other garden vegetables. One hundred gardens have been under cultivation. Eight hundred tons of hay were stacked. There are 500 head of cattle, 40 horses, 40 yoke working cattle, and as many wagons. Thirteen yoke of oxen have been issued this year, 10 ponies, 12 cows, several double wagons, yokes and chains, 12 new harrows, 11 sleds, and a large amount of farming tools, as hoes, forks, scythes, and spades.

This most absorbing of all material interests upon the reservation engages all parties and affects all relations. It greatly increases the work of the

BLACKSMITH

An estimable half-breed, married to an Indian woman, has been at work learning the trade, all the year, in the expectation of soon commencing business here upon his own responsibility. To keep 40 wagons, as many plows and harrows, a mowing-machine, a reaper, a thresher, yokes and chains for forty yoke of cattle, in a word, to make and repair for so many who are unskilled in labor, has increased the labor and the expense of this department five-fold in a single year.

CARPENTER.

Similar has been the effect upon the work of the carpenter. So urgent have been claims of the people for houses and household furniture, for farming tools, wagons, and the many necessary things made of wood, that it has been absolutely necessary to employ skilled workmen to a considerable extent.

From the report of the carpenter we learn that the number of coffins made since January, 1872, have been 36; tables, 48; bedsteads, 28; cupboards, 42; chests, 30; lounges, 7, and 40 houses.

CONCLUSION.

It is evident that the true policy of the Government should be one of concentration, to bring all the Indians under my charge, with the exception of the Leech Lake Pillagers, upon White Earth reservation, locating the Pembinas on Wild Rice River, a township 17 miles northwest of the agency; the Otter Tails upon the southeast corner township, 20 miles from the agency; the Gull Lake and Mille Lac bands into the immediate vicinity of the agency, where the first installment of those Mississippians are already located; placing the Leech Lake Indians, so manyof them as are disposed favorably, upon an agricultural district adjoining White Earth reservation on the east, (6 townships,) allowing them to retain their present reserve for fishing, hunting, and sugar-making purposes, changing the location of the agency buildings of Leech Lake to this new territory, thus bringing the people within 25 miles of the Northern Pacific railroad and within 30 miles of the central office; allowing the White Oak Point Indians to take a separate township upon the reservation or to merge their forces with those of the Pillagers and White Earth people.

Thus the expense of doing the business will be vastly diminished, the one agent can easily give his personal attention to every separate interest, and the light received by each will but reflect and intensify the light of all the rest.

I am, very respectfully, your obedient servant,

E. DOUGLASS,
United States Indian Agent, White Earth, Minnesota.

Hon. E. P. SMITH,
Commissioner of Indian Affairs, Washington, D. C.

5.

AGENCY OF THE SAC AND FOX INDIANS IN IOWA,
Toledo, Iowa, September 1, 1873.

SIR: In compliance with the requirements of the Indian Department, I have the honor herewith to submit the subjoined report of the condition of the agency of the Sac and Fox Indians in Iowa, under my care, for the year ending August 31, 1873.

I took charge of this agency, relieving Hon. L. Clark, September 19, 1872. These Indians residing in Iowa comprise nearly one-half of the remaining Sac and Fox Indians of the Mississippi. In 1846 this united tribe of Indians numbered over 2,000 souls. They then resided on large tracts of land in Wisconsin and Iowa. These lands were ceded to the United States, and they received in lieu thereof a reservation in what are now the limits of Kansas, and by treaty stipulations they were removed to Kansas, but owing to the great mortality that followed their removal, and other causes, about two hundred and seventy-five of them returned to Iowa. By the sale of some of their ponies they were enabled to purchase and pay for a tract of land located in Tama County, Iowa, containing 419 acres, and by an act of the Iowa State legislature they are permitted to remain in Iowa as long as they are peaceably disposed. It is a fact worthy of note here that while that part of the tribe remaining in Kansas and the Indian Territory have, from a variety of causes, rapidly dwindled in numbers, that part of the tribe residing in Iowa have increased in numbers at an equally rapid ratio. The Sac and Fox Indians in Iowa, according to the census just taken, number, men, 86; women, 104; boys, 75, and girls 70; total 335; an increase of 18 during last year. It may be proper, however, to state that 5 of these Indians who have had their homes in Kansas or Indian Territory, but who now persist in remaining here, by the advice of the Indian Department are put on the rolls here. The health of these Indians has been good, very few deaths having occurred during the past year.

As regards farming operations among them during the past year, I am safe in reporting some advancement. After many efforts during last spring, I succeeded in getting about fifteen familes to locate on lots of land embracing from 3 to 10 acres each, the familes agreeing to cultivate that amount of land for their own benefit. I furnished them the implements with which to till their lands, and some of the seeds to plant. In this way about 100 acres were put under cultivation, mostly in corn and beans. All seemed to be progressing satisfactorily until one warm day in the latter part of July they announced to me in the most solemn manner that they just received a revelation from the Great Spirit, telling them "that the men must not work any more, but they must hunt, trap, and fish and the squaws must do the work, as in the days of their fathers;" and in spite of all I could say or do, the greater part of them removed their wigwams over the river into their village, and soon started on a deer-hunt into the northwestern part of Iowa and into Nebraska. I have learned that the medicine-men are in the habit of pretending to receive revelations from the Great Spirit, that they may the more successfully carry out their nefarious purposes. Regarding it as proper, the agent has issued an order prohibiting the proclamation of any of these pretended revelations in future that would interfere with the industry and good order of the Indians under my care. Some few, and especially several of the young men, have labored under the direction of the farmer during the spring and summer with zeal and a good degree of regularity. Several hundred panels of post-and-rail fence have been put up during the spring and summer. We design having all their lands here put under fence by the expiration of another year.

Quite a goodly number worked in the harvest-fields of their white neighbors during both hay and wheat harvest, rendering satisfactory service. They altogether earned about $1,000 during the last harvest. This to me seems hopeful. The statistical returns of farming for the year ending August 31, 1873, which I herewith transmit, show the wealth of these Indians in individual property to be over $12,000, not including lands. They have over three hundred ponies at this time. Too many of these ponies are a detriment to the Indians. I am urging them to sell off some of their ponies and buy cattle and sheep.

With regard to their civilization and christianization, I think some perceptible progress has been made during the past year. The younger ones are gradually adopting the habits of the whites. A few have received regular instruction in reading and writing during the part of the year that they have been at home, and they have made commendable progress. The farmer has assisted when at leisure.

I have held out-door religious services for their benefit on the Lord's day, but what religious impressions are being made we must leave to future development to unfold. We greatly need a suitable building for school and religious purposes. I may here say that I am more than ever convinced that but little can be done in the way of educating and christianizing these Indians without a suitable building in which to collect them daily in order to impart instruction to them. If an appropriation sufficient to erect a suitable building could be secured, I have the means at command to carry forward missionary labors without any further cost to the Government.

The farmer erected a small board house during the summer, that answers the threefold purpose of a tool-house, shop, and office. This is the only house now on the Indian lands here.

I recently visited the Pottawatomie Indians residing at Steam-Boat Rock, Marshall County, Iowa. They are only a small band, numbering about 30 souls. They are farming lands, I believe, successfully, which they have rented of their white neighbors. They desire to locate on lands adjacent to the Indians under my care, that they may enjoy the benefits of our mission here. There are several bands of Winnebago Indians prowling around, who are almost a constant annoyance to my Indians, committing depredations on their property and stealing their ponies whenever opportunity affords. I have, therefore, thought it best to forbid them mingling with the Indians under my care in future.

In conclusion, allow me to say that although the results of my labors are not what I desired they should be, yet I am safe in saying that at least something has been done during the past year in the way of civilizing and christianizing the Indians under my care. God bless the efforts!

Yours, respectfully,

A. R. HOMBERT,
United States Indian Agent.

Hon. E. P. SMITH,
Commissioner of Indian Affairs.

6.

OFFICE OF UNITED STATES INDIAN AGENT,
Red Lake, Minn., December 2, 1873.

SIR: In compliance with your circular letter received two days since, I herewith transmit my report.

Upon my arrival at this place, August 13, 1873, I found things in rather a demoralized state, with accounts unsettled for several months, and it required a vast amount of labor to get them into good working order, but, have succeeded in making good progress with the new buildings, although nearly all the lumber was boards, and the saw-mill was out of repair and few logs in the mill-yard; but by considerable attention we have made the mill do good service, so that now we have three dwelling-houses well under way, so that we expect to occupy them this winter, and a school-house nearly finished on the outside.

The Indians seem ready and anxious to adopt the habits of civilization, and are calling for stoves and cooking utensils, and seem desirous of trying to raise wheat and other grains, offering to clear land and take care of the crop, if they can be furnished the seed.

The crops of corn and potatoes have exceeded those of any previous year, and their houses have been rendered more comfortable, the work being done mostly by themselves, the materials only furnished by the Government.

The time has come with the Indians here that with proper aid and encouragement, and with judicious expenditure of money, they can be rendered self-supporting, and a large outlay to accomplish this would be true economy.

I therefore earnestly recommend some extensive repairs on the saw and grist mill, which is at present in a very inefficient condition. A new dam is needed, as the old one is very weak and insecure. A new mill, or the present one thoroughly repaired and supplied with a good turbine wheel, would give sufficient power to do all the work required at this agency, at a total cost not to exceed five thousand dollars.

I would recommend the building of a good steam-tug on Red Lake, as it is greatly needed in transporting hay, grain, lumber, and building-material to and from the opposite side of the lake, which is inaccessible at present, and renders it very difficult to do anything for the Indians on the other side of the lake.

The educational work has been carried on apparently with good success, with an attendance of from twenty to thirty pupils, who have made fair progress. We greatly need a boarding-house for the pupils, in order to secure punctual attendance; and an appropriation for building and furnishing such a house is absolutely needed. The probable cost of building and furnishing the same for the accommodation of thirty pupils would be twenty-five hundred dollars, and one thousand dollars would be needed, in addition to the amount pledged by the Indians from their lumber-fund, (which is one thousand dollars per annum,) to pay the contingent expenses the first year.

Very respectfully, your obedient servant,

R. M. PRATT,
United States Special Indian Agent.

Hon. E. P. SMITH,
Commissioner of Indian Affairs, Washington, D. C.

7.

NORTHERN SUPERINTENDENCY,
OFFICE OF SUPERINTENDENT OF INDIAN AFFAIRS,
Omaha, Neb., Ninthmonth 27, 1873.

RESPECTED FRIEND: The Indians of the Northern Superintendency have during the past year made as satisfactory progress in civilization as the circumstances by which they were surrounded would permit, and the advancement of each tribe has been rapid or slow, in proportion as its officers could command and control the influences operating upon the tribe.

No Indian of the superintendency has been accused of the murder of a white man, and but one case of assault upon a white man during the year has officially come to my knowledge. This was of a trivial nature, and occurred on the reservation, and in defence of property about being stolen from the Indian by the white man.

SANTEE SIOUX.

The Santee Sioux have quietly and commendably given their attention to agricultural and industrial pursuits. They are yearly becoming more self-reliant and self-supporting.

During the spring a contract was let for the building of a frame house for an industrial boarding-school, planned for the accommodation of twenty scholars of each sex, their teachers and care-takers. Said building is now rapidly approaching completion, and will be ready for pupils during the first autumn month, but as yet no provision is made for its support or the salaries of its officers.

A matron, appointed and paid by the Society of Friends, has labored in this tribe during the year. Her duty has been to visit the Santee women and girls in their homes, and instruct them in household duties, and in the fitting and making of garments. Her services have been of value to the tribe.

WINNEBAGOES.

The Winnebagoes have made rapid advancement during the year. They have tilled more ground than ever before, have cultivated it skillfully and well, and reaped a bountiful harvest.

The appropriation from their invested fund, for a purpose of improvement, has been expended for an industrial boarding-school house, fifty dwelling-houses, miles of fencing, and quantities of stock, and agricultural labor-saving machinery; the latter of which, having been judiciously distributed among the most industrious and worthy members of the tribe, has produced a great interest in agricultural pursuits throughout the tribe, and these Indians are now making more extensive preparations for the agricultural labors of another year than ever before.

The Winnebagoes have unanimously assented to the removal to their reservation of that portion of the tribe still remaining in Wisconsin, but as all their timber-land is allotted in severalty, and as the Wisconsin Indians have been dwelling in timber, they ask that timber-land adjoining their reservation may be purchased of the Omahas, with Winnebago funds, and the Wisconsin Indians placed thereon, under the special care ot a sub-agent.

Their request is a proper one, and meets my approval, excepting that I would recommend that the purchase proposed should include sufficient prairie-land adjoining to make farms for the Wisconsin Winnebagoes, which should be allotted to them in severalty, when, with proper encouragement, and the example of the reservation Indians, there is little doubt that the more industrious among them will soon turn their attention to agriculture.

The Winnebago agency farmer, who is a half-blood Indian, has shown more efficiency and given better satisfaction in his department than any white man who has filled it for years. It is encouraging to be able to state that several hundred Winnebago men assisted the farmers in adjoining counties during the late harvest in gathering their grain-crops, and proved themselves efficient and satisfactory workmen.

The Winnebagoes have three flourishing day-schools, and the industrial boarding-school house, intended to accommodate forty pupils of each sex, will be ready for occupation this autumn. The situation of this school is similar to the Santee industrial school. I would respectfully suggest that ample provision be made for the payment of the salaries of proper officers for the Santee and Winnebago industrial boarding-schools, from the fund "support of schools not otherwise provided for," or other available funds, during the remainder of the present fiscal year, in order that the schools may be organized soon after the completion of the buildings, and that provision be made in the next Indian appropriation bill for a liberal support of said schools.

Under the provisions of the third article of the treaty made March 8, 1865, with the Winnebagoes, the Government agrees to break and fence one hundred acres of prairie-land for each band of the tribe, the number of bands at that time being fourteen. By reference to Agent White's report for the year 1872, it appears that the whole number of acres broken on the reservation, when he took charge of it in the spring of 1869, was but six hundred.

I therefore would respectfully urge upon the Department that an appropriation of $2,400, or $3 per acre, for breaking the remaining eight hundred acres due these Indians, and also a sufficient sum for making five miles of fencing to inclose the same, be asked for at the next session of Congress.

The Winnebagoes are a striking example of what can be accomplished in a comparatively short space of time in the way of civilizing and christianizing Indians, when a proper influence is exerted over the tribe, and a sufficiency of means are at command for the needful expenditures. By reference to Agent White's report, it will be seen that rapid improvement has been made by the tribe during the last four years.

At the time of his taking charge they were a rebellious, turbulent people, with chiefs adverse to the adoption of civilized habits and customs, and but few improvements had been made on the reservation. Now this beautiful tract of country is dotted over with substantially built cottages, which have been built upon farms that have been allotted in severalty. These farmers own their wagons, horses, harness, and furniture of their houses, dress in civilized costume, raise crops and take them to market for sale. Surely they are on the high road to civilization.

OMAHAS.

The Omahas have not made much advance in civilization during the year. This is owing in part to the failure of the proposed sale of 50,000 acres of land, the proceeds of which were to be used for purposes of improvement.

With additional legislation to complete said sale, or the sale of a portion of their land to the Winnebagoes, as desired by the latter, and the proceeds therefrom judiciously expended for purposes of agricultural advancement only, the Omahas will probably awaken to the importance of increased attention to this subject.

They are deficient in labor-saving agricultural machinery, but appear to have a desire to extend their farming labors, when proper implements are at their command.

Three day-schools have been in successful operation on this agency, and a building for a fourth day-school has been completed during the year.

The Omahas are at present absent from their reservation upon a buffalo hunt in the southern part of the State, and their schools and farms are neglected in consequence of such absence.

PAWNEES.

The Pawnees' mill-dam and race-way were ruined by an overflow in the Beaver River, during the summer. This has occurred so frequently that it is now concluded to abandon the attempt to use water as a motive-power for the mill, and apply wind-power instead. After personal inspection of windmills now in successful operation, the late agency-miller has made a report to the agent, which is so satisfactory that the agent has made an estimate for funds to apply such power to the mill. As soon as these are received the mill will be put in operation, and as it is near a well-settled country, its income will materially assist in the support of the tribe.

A village matron is now laboring among the females of this tribe, and her services are of great value As a rule, the men of the Indian tribes under my care are very much in advance of the women in point of civilization; hence the importance of sending an earnest, untiring, conscientious woman to lift the women of the tribe slowly but surely from their degraded life in the Indian village. I earnestly recommend that this appropriation for village matron be continued.

A deficiency of 4,800 acres of land has been discovered in the Pawnee reservation. As the tribe has now more land than is necessary for its wants, it is hoped that provision will be made by Congress for a proper compensation to the tribe for said land, to be expended for purposes of agricultural improvement.

A party of Pawnee buffalo-hunters, numbering about 250 men, 100 women, and 50 children, or 400 in all, with the permission of the Commissioner of Indian Affairs, superintendent of Indian affairs, and their agent, and under the special care of a white man appointed for that purpose, left the reservation on the 3d day of July, for the purpose of hunting in the valley of the Republican.

Their hunt was successful, and they were returning to the reservation with the meat and skins of about 800 buffaloes, when, on the 5th day of August, they were surprised and attacked by 600 Sioux belonging to the Ogallalla and Brulé bands, the former at the time under the charge and care of Special Subagent Antoine Janis, and the latter of Special Subagent Estis.

So complete was the surprise that Sky-Chief, in command of the Pawnees, was killed while skinning a buffalo. Most of the Pawnee men were hunting straggling buffalo, and the women were in the act of striking tents for the day's journey. While in this condition, the Pawnees were attacked and twenty men, thirty-nine women, and ten children, sixty-nine in all, were killed, eleven wounded, some of them severely, and eleven captured. The captives were afterwards delivered up at Julesburgh, Neb., and returned to their homes. In this massacre the Pawnees lost over one hundred horses, most of their saddles and arms, and all the proceeds of the hunt.

With a view of avoiding future trouble with the Sioux, seven prominent Pawnee chiefs, with the United States interpreter for the tribe, on the 17th day of July last, with the consent of their agent, called upon the military authorities at Fort McPherson, and asked them to send out and invite Sioux chiefs to meet them in council, there or at some point designated, for the purpose of arranging a permanent peace between the tribes.

Under these circumstances, I respectfully ask that measures be taken by the Department to obtain through Congress compensation to the Pawnees for all their losses sustained in the said massacre, as well as reparation for their losses by the Sioux during the past two years, and protection from them in the future.

OTTOES.

The Ottoes and Missourias have reconsidered their former action, and now accept the provisions of the act of Congress approved June 10, 1872, providing for the sale of one-half of their reservation, and the improvement of their condition upon the remaining portion. Their school has been well attended, and is now in a flourishing condition. The progress of this tribe has been much retarded for want of funds, and in consequence of their unsettled condition.

SACS AND FOXES OF MISSOURI.

The visit of the Sacs and Foxes to the Osages during last spring, with a view of purchasing land of them for a future home, having failed in its object, they have since been divided in judgment, as to which part of the Indian Territory they would prefer to go, but are now nearly united in a desire to remove to the reservation of the Sacs and Foxes of Mississippi.

Their condition in regard to civilization is nearly the same as at the time of my last report. If Congress provides for the sale of that portion of their reservation lying in Kansas, a speedy removal to the Indian Territory will be an advantage to them, as their present unsettled state prevents all improvement of their condition.

IOWAS.

The Iowas have made very satisfactory progress in civilization, and their condition is probably in advance of any tribe in the superintendency.

One great cause of this improvement is, I believe, the attention which has been given to the elevation of the women of the tribe. In my opinion this is the foundation of success in christianizing and civilizing Indians, and no tribe can be much advanced in either until the men are taught to respect the women and share their burdens, and thus relieve them from their present slavish condition, and assist them in assuming and maintaining a proper sphere in the tribe. Another cause of advancement is the proficiency they have made in acquiring the English language.

The Iowa Industrial Home building has been enlarged. This institution is very popular with the Indians, and the most promising children of the tribe are sent to it for care and education. With a continuance of its present support and management, it must necessarily become a great means of elevating the tribe.

I recommend for it that liberal support which it so justly deserves.

BUFFALO HUNTS.

Buffalo hunts or their substitute, beef-rations, are at present indispensable for the subsistence of the Pawnees and Ottoes, and nearly so for the Omahas. There are many objections to the hunt, and in my opinion if the Government will substitute for it a beef-ration, it will promote the welfare of the Indian tribes who are now allowed under treaty stipulations to continue the hunt.

The presence of Indians on the border outside of their reservations is a source of anxiety to the isolated settler, and the progress of the Indian hunters between the reservation and hunting-ground gives occasion for much difficulty between the whites and Indians. The crops of the Indians also suffer by their absence, and the schools are interfered with by their practice of taking their children with them on the hunt.

For these and other reasons I believe it will be better for the Government, white settlers, and Indians, if arrangements are made as soon as possible by which the Pawnees, Ottoes, and Omahas will receive from the Government beef-rations in lieu of any privileges they may now have under treaty stipulations of hunting buffalo outside of their reservation.

I believe it would be impossible for the Pawnees and Ottoes to subsist at present, deprived of the privilege of the hunt, without such substitute. But as a permanent beef-ration would be a hinderance to proper energy toward progress in support, such ration should be gradually reduced in quantity as the tribe becomes self-sustaining, which would soon be the case in the tribe named, with removal of present retarding causes.

ANNUITIES.

All of the tribes in this superintendency, except the Santees, receive a money annuity. This is paid to individual Indians, and is often expended in such a manner that no lasting benefit is realized by the Indian.

In my opinion the progress made by the tribes in civilization would be materially accelerated, if all the annuity money which is now paid to the Indians in this State could be placed at the disposal of the agent of the tribe, to be used as compensation for labor performed by Indians, and for the purchase of necessary stock and implements with which to cultivate the ground.

In this connection I would also suggest that there is no greater incentive to labor among these Indians than the consciousness of individual ownership of the soil. I, therefore, earnestly trust that by suitable legislative action during the next session of Congress, provision will be made for the allotment of the reservations in severalty to heads of families of each tribe, where such allotment has not already taken place, and also for the disposition of the annuity funds as above proposed. In this way the industrious would be encouraged and rewarded, and the idle compelled to labor, in order that they might procure the necessary subsistence with which to sustain life.

POPULATION.

I subjoin a table of population of the different tribes in the Northern Superintendency, showing the increase or decrease in each tribe during the last year:

Tribe.	Male.	Female.	Total.	Increase.	Decrease.
Santee Sioux	412	505	917		48
Winnebago	740	782	1,522	82	
Omahas	486	515	1,001	32	
Pawnees	1,032	1,344	2,376		71
Ottoes and Missourias	218	229	447		17
Sacs and Foxes of Missouri	46	49	95	7	
Iowas	114	107	221		4

CONCLUDING REMARKS.

My observation and experience during the past two years in this work among the Indians of Nebraska puts at rest all doubts in my mind respecting the possibility of civilizing Indians.

Three of the tribes of this State, viz, the Santees, Winnebagoes, and Iowas, have made as rapid progress in this direction as could be expected under the circumstances; and I do not hesitate to say, that if the same liberal support is granted to them in the future, and the same guarded care is extended with respect to the appointment of agents and employés who are sent among them—every one of whom should be a missionary in the true sense of the word—that the time is not far distant when these tribes will become useful, industrious, self-supporting citizens, and fitted to exercise the elective franchise with at least as much judgment as many of the whites who now enjoy that privilege.

With respect to the remaining tribes in this State, who have made less progress, I am confident that, with the necessary funds to compensate the Indians for their labor, the same good results would follow.

It is impossible in the very nature of things to change the habits and thoughts of a whole people in a year, or even in several years; the old cannot be expected to make great changes in their mode of life. It is only from the minds of the young and rising generation that we can hope to eradicate the plants of superstition and ignorance which now so darkly shadow the intellect, and to plant there instead the seeds of virtue, knowledge, and truth. Whatever is thus accomplished must be done through patience, perseverance, and forbearance, keeping in view the divine injunction, "Whatsoever ye would that men should do unto you, do ye even so unto them."

Very respectfully, thy friend,

BARCLAY WHITE,
Superintendent Indian Affairs.

Hon. EDWARD P. SMITH
Commissioner Indian Affairs, Washington, D. C.

8.

SANTEE AGENCY, NEBRASKA,
Ninthmonth 9th, 1873.

RESPECTED FRIEND: I herewith respectfully submit this my third annual report:

I think I can truthfully say that each year marks an advancement in the condition of these Indians.

The health of the tribe is improving some, but there are retarding causes which will require years to overcome, one of which is syphilis, in its varied forms, and not unfrequently terminating in scrofulous consumption.

The Indians have received a fresh impetus to engage in farming operations since the honorable Commissioner's visit here, and his officially notifying them that their subsistence would be discontinued after this present fiscal year. So far, with few exceptions, they neither complain nor seem discouraged, but accept it very cheerfully, expressing their determination to show by their efforts that they intend to make a living. I have grave doubts, however, about the propriety of discontinuing altogether their subsistence. I would suggest that the flour ration be continued for one year longer, for this reason: Many of them will not have enough ground broken to commence raising wheat the first year. It need not be issued regularly, but might be left discretionary with the agent, to be given to the able-bodied ones for actual labor performed in lieu of money, and the old, infirm, and sick to be cared for as they are now. Unless something of this kind is done, I am satisfied that there will be considerable suffering, especially among the latter class.

The past season, like the one previous, has been remarkably good; plenty of rain to keep crops growing nicely, although it was too wet early in the spring, retarding planting to some extent on the bottom-lands, and during the "June rise" of the Missouri some of these lands were so badly overflowed that in a few places the crops were entirely destroyed. The migratory grasshopper threatened the crops at two different times. They came over in the Sixthmonth, and again in the Eighthmonth, but did not alight in sufficient numbers to do any particular harm, although large clouds of them passed over at each time. For a full statistical account of the farming operations, I refer thee to the farmer's report.

The manual-labor school-building is progressing satisfactorily, with a fair prospect of its being completed within the time contracted for.

For the purpose of carrying on this institution, (manual-labor school,) including board of scholars, salary and board of employés, about the sum of $6,000 will be required. If there are no funds applicable for this purpose, I would respectfully suggest the propriety of obtaining the aforesaid amount to be used for that purpose, believing that when the Government takes into consideration that hitherto the Santees have been educated almost, if not entirely, by benevolent aid and missionary enterprise, it will become apparent that such an appropriation is but a simple act of justice.

The missionary schools are in a satisfactory condition. The accompanying reports will show the number of scholars, average attendance, number of teachers, &c.

The grist-mill has been running pretty constantly, except a brief time in midwinter and a short time in the spring, when the dam was impaired by heavy spring freshets.

The saw-mill was operated up to about the middle of Fourthmonth, when the great snow-storm came and demolished the building. It was also ascertained by inspection that the boiler could no longer be used with safety. It has been replaced with a new one, and is now in running order.

There have been thirty additional log-houses put up this summer, mostly by Indian labor.

The carpenter and his apprentices are kept busy making door and window frames, cupboards, benches, tables, and chests, repairing machinery, &c. The object is to furnish each house with a cupboard, table, and chest. There are about half of them thus furnished.

The blacksmith and his apprentices find plenty to do shoeing horses in winter and repairing machinery in summer.

The physician complains of the lack of hospital accommodations. A few hundred dollars would supply the necessity.

Hoping and trusting that the Government will continue its bountiful care over this tribe a little longer, not in a degree to spoil them, only to render material aid in completing a work which is promising so fair to produce good results,

Very respectfully, thy friend,

JOSEPH WEBSTER,
United States Indian Agent.

BARCLAY WHITE,
Superintendent Indian Affairs, Omaha.

9.

WINNEBAGO AGENCY, NEBRASKA,
Eighthmonth 21, 1873.

MY DEAR FATHER:

It is very gratifying to me, in presenting my fifth annual report of the condition of affairs on the Winnebago reservation, to be able to record the great advancement of the tribe in civilization during the past four years. In order the more readily to show what has been accomplished during that time, I have arranged the following statistical information to exhibit the relative conditions of these Indians in 1869 and 1873:

	1869.	1873.
Population	1,343	1,445
Wealth in individual property	$20,000	$100,000
Number of schools	2	3
Number of scholars enrolled	135	225
Land cultivated by Indians (acres)	300	1,500
Frame houses occupied by Indians	23	75
Log houses occupied by Indians		40
Wheat raised (number of acres)	10	600
Wheat raised (number of bushels)	200	9,000
Corn raised (number of acres)	300	800
Oats raised (number of acres)		50
Potatoes raised (number of acres)	2	50
Hogs owned		500
Chickens owned		1,000
American horses owned		40
Ponies owned	411	900
Wagons and sets of harness owned	3	100
Fencing (number of miles)	2	25

This improvement, though extending through the whole period, has been greatest during the past year, when fifty frame houses were constructed, and the Indians nearly doubled the amount of their tillage.

The general health of the tribe has been good, and there has been a small natural increase in the population during the year. There are now, according to a recent census, 1,522 Winnebagoes on the reservation. Seventy-seven of these have recently moved from Wisconsin, and expect to make this their permanent home.

FARMING.

The farming operations have been superintended the past year by Alexander Payer, an Indian, who has been more efficient and has wrought better results than any white man who has preceded him as farmer for the Winnebagoes since my acquaintance with the affairs of the tribe. It is the duty of the farmer to look after the crops cultivated by Indians, see that they farm properly, and to instruct them, when necessary, in the use of tools; also to plant and till what land has been broken on the Indian allotments, and is not needed by the owners for the use of their families. This he does for the benefit of the tribe in common; and the Indian workmen who are employed for the purpose are paid at the rate of $1.50 per day out of funds belonging to the tribe. In this way 300 acres have been farmed the present season, to wit: 220 acres in wheat, which has been harvested and stacked, and will probably yield 20 bushels to the acre; 40 acres in oats—these were injured to some extent by grasshoppers—and 40 acres in corn, which promises well.

The balance of the farming has been done by Indians, on their own account, and compares favorably with that of their white neighbors. Seed-wheat, potatoes, corn, beans, peas, and onion-sets were purchased with tribal funds, in sufficient quantities to meet all necessary demands of those Indians who wished to farm.

It has been the custom, prior to this year, for the agent to pay the Indians for breaking and fencing their own land. This was found necessary in order to induce many of them to make a beginning, they preferring to work for others where they received immediate pay, rather than for themselves and wait for returns they were uncertain about. After having the ground broken and fenced, and the seed furnished, they were willing to plant and take care of their crops, and with the exception of a few who were very late about sowing their wheat, and had it destroyed by grasshoppers, they have been rewarded with a bountiful harvest. As this is the first crop of wheat many of them have raised, the receipts will be such, we hope, as to encourage them to extend their farming operations.

ELECTIONS.

The annual election for twelve chiefs at the beginning of the second quarter passed off quietly, nearly all the Indian men on the reservation participating in it. Seven chiefs of the previous year were re-elected.

A census of the tribe was taken a few days after the election, when, as near as practicable, every member was required to be present, and to name the chief in whose band they wished to be enrolled. The chiefs were then arranged on the roll, and numbered according to the size of their bands. The first chief receives an annual salary of $150, and each of the others $100. Each chief is allowed to select a policeman from his band, who receives the same amount of salary as the chief.

FINANCES.

An error was made in the last Indian appropriation bill by which the Winnebagoes will be deprived of the use of $5,000 the present year, which amount is justly due them as interest on their trust funds; this, together with the balance of last year's appropriation on hand at the end of the fiscal year, which, according to a late decision of the First Comptroller of the Treasury, must be deposited to the credit of the United States, will greatly reduce the amount of funds to which this tribe is entitled, and which are needed in making improvements the present year.

The issue of beef-rations to the Winnebagoes, which has been continued for many years, and has cost the tribe from $10,000 to $20,000 per year, was abandoned on the first of Seventhmonth last. The funds thus saved will probably be needed to support an industrial boarding-school, for which a fine brick building, to cost $15,388.70, is now being erected. This will be ready to open about the first of Eleventhmonth next, and is intended to accommodate eighty scholars.

EDUCATIONAL.

Three day-schools have been in successful operation during most of the year. These were conducted by Howard A. Mann, Caroline Thomas, and Lucy A. Lamb, all of whom are eminently qualified as teachers. The attendance during the year averaged about 70 scholars, although there were three times that number enrolled. The greatest difficulty that the teachers have to contend with is the irregularity with which the children attend school. The advancement of the few who have attended regularly is very encouraging, and it would be well if some plan could be devised to compel a better attendance.

The principal branches taught are reading, writing, arithmetic, orthography, and geography. The scholars have all been provided throughout the year with good clothing, donated by the members of New York Yearly Meeting of Friends, who have also contributed clothing for the aged and suitable food for the sick. The market value of supplies received from this source during the year would probably amount to $2,500.

The plan of issuing crackers, at the noon recess, to each scholar in attendance at the schools, has been adopted with great satisfaction to the scholars. It was previously the custom to issue weekly rations of flour, for regular attendance, to the parents of the scholars.

WISCONSIN WINNEBAGOES.

As it seems to be the settled purpose of the Government to move the Wisconsin Winnebagoes, numbering 1,000, to this reservation, I would respectfully urge the necessity, before such a step is taken, of providing more timber-land for them adjoining the present reservation. The amount of timber owned by the tribe at present is barely sufficient for the use of the Nebraska branch of the tribe until they plant and raise timber on their farms; this they should be encouraged to do immediately, by offering them premiums for successful tree-culture.

MINNESOTA WINNEBAGOES.

When the Winnebagos were removed from Minnesota in 1863, about 160 members of the tribe, who were mostly half-breeds, remained; these have since, in accordance with an act of Congress, been naturalized, and paid their proportion of the trust-funds belonging to the tribe, amounting at that time, as the Wisconsin Winnebagoes were not considered a part of the tribe, to over $800 per head. The honorable Secretary of the Interior has recently decided that the Wisconsin branch of the tribe are entitled to and will hereafter receive their proportion of the interest on the Winnebago trust-funds.

Several of these naturalized Indians, who have disposed of all their money, have since moved to this reservation, and no doubt look forward to being again admitted into membership with the tribe. I have carefully avoided showing them favors, and have, as far as possible, discouraged their remaining here.

Very respectfully, thy son,

HOWARD WHITE,
United States Indian Agent.

BARCLAY WHITE,
Superintendent of Indian Affairs, Omaha, Nebr.

10.

OMAHA AGENCY, NEBR.,
Eighthmonth 29, 1873.

RESPECTED FRIEND: I herewith submit my fifth annual report of the affairs of the Omaha Agency, as follows:

Since my report last year an effort has been made to carry out the provisions of the act of Congress for the sale of a portion of the Omaha reservation, amounting in the aggregate to nearly 50,000 acres. Unfortunately, however, for the prosperity of these Indians, only a small portion of the tract offered for sale was disposed of, owing, it is presumed, to the minimum rate fixed by Congress ($2.50 per acre) being too high to meet the views of those desiring to make investments. The want of success in consummating this sale is more to be regretted on account of the discouraging tendency it has upon the efforts of the Indians to subsist by agricultural pursuits. Many who are disposed to be industrious among them have not the teams, plows, and other necessary appliances for prosperous farming; neither have they the means for purchasing stock, which in this country is the most profitable branch of husbandry.

As the sale of these surplus lands is the principal hope of securing means for the permanent improvement of the farms allotted to the Omahas in severalty, it seems very desirable that additional legislation by Congress should be secured so as to effect that object.

Since it has been decided by the Indian Department to remove the Wisconsin Winnebagoes to the reservation adjoining that of the Omahas, a proposition has been made by the special commissioner appointed to the duty of superintending the said removal to purchase from the Omaha tribe, for the benefit of the Winnebagoes, now being removed, a strip of land two miles in width, lying along the south boundary of the Winnebago reservation, and extending westward from the Missouri River about ten miles, to where the Winnebago reserve widens out from four to eight miles in width, embracing about 12,000 acres. This proposition has been sanctioned by the Commissioner of Indian Affairs, and the price offered for the said tract is at the rate of $2.50 per acre. The substance of this proposition has been submitted to the chiefs and head-men of the Omaha tribe, who are now out on the hunt, and a reply through the sub-agent or care-taker sent out with them has been received to the effect that they are averse to selling any more land to the Winnebagoes, for the reason that the latter have been addicted to stealing their ponies and other property, for which they have been unable to obtain suitable redress; but if these wrongs can be satisfactorily settled, and a recurrence of them prevented in future, they will consider the proposition and report their decision on their return from the hunt; but they have already decided not to sell any more of their reservation unless they are allowed to go to Washington and confer with their Great Father themselves.

EDUCATION.

A very commendable interest is still manifested by the Omahas upon the subject of the education of their children. Three schools have been well supported throughout the year until the time of vacation, which occurs while the Indians are absent on the hunt. The number of children enrolled is 110, with an average attendance of 75 at the three schools.

A new school-house and dwelling-house for a teacher have just been completed, and arrangements are now being made for opening an additional school at that place, which, with the other schools, will afford facilities for the education of all the children in the tribe. It is very gratifying to report the continued success of these day-schools, and the rapid progress of the Indian children in their studies. The establishment of an industrial school at some future time, when sufficient means are at the disposal of the tribe, would add greatly to the benefits to be secured to the rising generation.

The reports of two of the teachers are herewith submitted; but no report of the day-school at the mission has been received, the teacher of that school having left the reservation since the commencement of vacation.

FARMING OPERATIONS.

I regret to report that in this department success has not, in some respects, been so good as last year. Many of the Indians who have not teams and plows at their disposal have failed to get the usual amount of ground plowed for their corn-crop, for the reason that no funds were at the disposal of the agent to pay other Indians possessing the necessary facilities for plowing, as has been the practice heretofore.

It has been customary for a portion of the annuity money of the tribe to be set apart, with the consent of the chiefs and head-men, to meet these contingencies; but, owing to the meddlesome interference of certain designing individuals, the chiefs have been induced to object to the usual appropriations for this branch of their business, with the result as above stated. About 180 acres were sown in wheat this year, and a good crop has been harvested, notwithstanding some injury by grasshoppers. Potatoes planted by the Indians have also been depredated upon, to some extent, in the same way; but in many cases a good yield will be obtained. The season has been very favorable for grass, and a good supply of hay is now being put up for winter use.

To sum up the prospects in this department, notwithstanding some unfavorable features, there seems to be ground for hope that the coming winter may be passed without material suffering on the part of the Indians, particularly if the hunt should prove successful.

STOCK AND FARMING-IMPLEMENTS.

The cattle owned by the Omahas are now in fine condition and rapidly increasing; and it is only to be regretted that they are too poor at present to add materially to their stock of hogs, cows, &c., by purchase. In respect to wagons, plows, harness, &c., they are very deficient, and great embarrassment in agricultural pursuits necessarily results therefrom.

They own a large number of ponies, which are of little use except in the hunt; and when that is abandoned, which of necessity it soon will be, they must be disposed of, and the proceeds used to furnish them with teams adapted to the purposes of agriculture.

BUILDINGS, ETC.

The agency buildings have been kept in good repair during the past year, and a new council-house has been built by the Indian carpenters. The school-house and dwelling-house for the teacher have also been built, as before stated; but for want of means the building of cottages for the Indians has been necessarily suspended since my last report.

CONCLUDING REMARKS.

Being now about to retire from the field of my labors among these Indians, in which I have been engaged for more than four years, I leave them with the full assurance of their capacity for civilization, self-support, and the enjoyment of the rights of citizenship; and though the chief reliance must be upon the rising generation now undergoing the necessary process of intellectual training, yet much can be done to improve the condition of those now on the active stage of life, by judicious appropriation of means to stimulate them to present exertion in adapting themselves to new modes of procuring subsistence. There is also an urgent need of additional legislation to protect them from the encroachments of those of their own race, as well as occasional depredations upon their timber and other property, by white settlers contiguous to their reservation. The Omahas continue to maintain the most friendly relations with the Government, and are at peace with all the Indian tribes.

As far as heard from they have not been molested by the Sioux or other depredating bands of Indians while on the hunt, though the recent attack upon the Pawnees has led to some apprehension on their account.

The health of the Indians on the reservation is generally good. By a recent census the population of this tribe is found to be 1,001; an increase of 32 over last year.

Very respectfully, thy friend,

E. PAINTER,
United States Indian Agent.

BARCLAY WHITE,
Superintendent Indian Affairs, Omaha, Nebr.

11.

PAWNEE AGENCY, GENOA, NEBR.,
Ninthmonth 20, 1873.

RESPECTED FRIEND: In presenting my first annual report of the condition of this agency, I can only speak of my personal experience during the few months I have been in charge, viz, since the 10th of first-month last. At that time the Pawnees were just returning from their winter hunt. They had caught but few buffalo, and were attacked by the Sioux, who killed one man and captured over one hundred of their best horses. Being thus deprived of their accustomed and needful amount of subsistence, on application, $3,000 was placed at my disposal to procure provisions, nearly all of which was expended in the purchase of flour, beef, and other necessities for their relief.

In the spring, as soon as the state of the weather would permit, the new mill-race was pushed toward completion, and the prospect seemed fair of soon having our mill at work; but about the first of the Fifthmonth heavy rains and a very destructive freshet succeeded the great snow-storm which visited this region, and completely destroyed the labors of the past year, leaving the water-power of the mill in a state of hopeless ruin. A similar loss from the destructive elements was felt in a wide region of country around us, and in the view of all competent observers it was beyond the power of human skill or foresight to prevent. Wind power has since been suggested, and after considerable attention to the subject, from the successful experiments and tests of others, I feel quite favorable to its application. A safe, reliable, and inexpensive motive power to keep in repair is a desideratum, and a good mill is one of the greatest needs of the agency.

The continued spring rains in this region retarded all planting-labor, and some of the Indian fields and patches were too wet to be planted in season; but their corn has yielded an average crop, and they have cultivated various other edible plants. From the agency farm we have just threshed 1,100 bushels of oats, 312 bushels of rye, and 760 bushels of wheat. The oat crop was much injured by the grasshoppers, and the potato crop will be very light owing to the ravages of the potato bug and drought. Our heaviest crop is corn and the yield promises fair; and a stock of hay, thought to be ample to last through the season, has been securely housed or stacked. I trust by the end of the calendar year we can show that the manual-labor school depends as much upon the farm as the farm depends upon the school-fund, not excepting the expense of harvesting and threshing the crop. I see no good reason why the farm should not be self-sustaining and at the same time aid the school and other departments of the agency materially in the carting of supplies, provision, and fuel. Being twenty-two miles from the railroad and nearly eight miles from the timber-tract, much time and expense are necessarily involved in transportation.

One new day-school has been erected near the Indian villages, and this, as well as the other day-school, is now in successful operation. The whole number of scholars at these two schools is 70; and the average attendance during the past year has been 55. The manual-labor school, under the present corps of employés, is making satisfactory progress. Twenty additional pupils have recently been added thereto. The only death in the school during the year is that of one boy, who recently died of consumption. The whole number of scholars is now 70, of whom 16 are girls. The number of children in all the school is 140.

Various needful repairs have been made upon the agency buildings, within our limited means for this purpose. A wood-shed has been built at the manual-labor school, and a room has been attached to the new day-school house, which is used by the village matron for a laundry, and also for temporary hospital purposes. This does not interfere with the school, and is found to be a very convenient and useful arrangement. The census of the tribe, just completed, shows the aggregate number to be 2,376, viz, 556 men, 868 women, and 952 children, a slight decrease from last year's report, but probably without much change in numbers. Some of the Indians, I think, begin to see the necessity of depending more upon their own labor for a living and less upon the buffalo hunt, which has proved so uncertain and unreliable. Even their annuity, both of money and goods, as timely and useful as it often seems to be in providing for their immediate wants and comforts, no doubt often tends to paralyze the true incentive to labor.

The squaws are nearly all industrious and do what they can in their own way to cultivate their corn, beans, and squashes, and assist in procuring fuel and hay; but some of the men will not labor until driven to it by stern necessity, as long as the Government will feed and clothe them. Many of the young men, however, are anxious to work for compensation, and labor well under a little instruction, as I have seen in gathering our harvest and at other kinds of work, but we have no fund with which to pay them, and no means at command or plan developed to make their labor remunerative or self-sustaining to the agency. I trust this difficulty may in time be met, but they now need something more than mere kind advice to go to work for themselves. In assuming the habits of civilized life they feel helpless, and while they may see others reaping the rewards of their labors in gathering plentiful crops, they feel like initiates in a new life, and in their generosity to their friends many will allow the idlers to eat out and virtually rob them of the fruits of their hard-earned toil. There is an abundance of undeveloped muscle in the tribe, which I hope will yet be brought into active and beneficial use even though the process be gradual. The sale of their lands now about to be thrown upon the market, I hope, will also afford some means of relief to enable them to leave their present villages and erect dwellings upon their separate allotments. Some of the young men who leave the school find employment as apprentices in the different mechanical departments or as farm hands, but the entire number of this class is small, and vacancies are not frequent.

There is a great difficulty to prevent those who might make mechanics or laborers under proper incentives from relapsing into idleness and nomadic habits or re-contracting the filthy customs of their village life.

A portion of the tribe are using their agricultural implements, such as plows, wagons, mowing machines, and hay-rakes more than heretofore, and aided by their farm instructor they have gathered more hay than usual. All are now busily engaged in cooking and drying their corn for winter use. A vast room for improvement is left, and some may grow weary at the apparent tardiness of the work, but many things have to be considered to avoid hasty conclusions, and it is rather encouraging to see evidence of progress even in its rudest and most elementary forms, especially when we have to contend with superstition, and where the tendency is to view the ways of civilized life as an unwelcome innovation upon traditional and time-honored customs. The great drawback to improvement, by way of removal from their mud lodges to separate allotments, is the fear of their hereditary enemies, the Sioux. Their own intentions, as well as those of the Government, are thus thwarted, and a disposition is formed to barter away their wagons and many other useful articles, which, when discovered in time, I have succeeded in checking. We now stamp their iron and tinware, and I have forbidden all traders, by written notices, from receiving it.

About the first of Seventhmonth some 300 of the tribe were permitted to go on the summer hunt, and were placed under the charge of a white man, who had special instructions to prevent their making any annoyance to the white settlers or showing any hostile demonstrations to those of their own race.

After a successful hunt over a month on the waters of the Republican, in the southwestern part of the State, in which they caught several hundred buffalo, and had the meat and hides carefully dried and packed, and were about to return home with over three hundred horses well laden, they were suddenly attacked by a large war party of Ogallallas and Brulé Sioux. The Pawnees made a short stand to resist the attack, but the overpowering numbers of their enemies caused them to flee to avoid being surrounded, leaving all their meat, robes, saddles, and provisions strewn upon the ground. The women and children not having so good a chance to escape suffered most in the indiscriminate slaughter which ensued as they were overtaken. As near as we can learn by subsequent investigation, both here and on the ground, there were twenty men, thirty-nine women, and ten children killed, making sixty-nine in all. About a dozen were wounded, brought home, and are gradually recovering. Eleven women and children who were captured by the Sioux have since been recovered, and some children thought to be captured are yet missing. It is hoped that stringent measures will be adopted to enable this peaceable tribe, thus robbed so repeatedly, both of life and property, to be amply remunerated for all their losses from the annuities of those who have nearly always been the aggressors, without just cause, in these thieving raids and inhuman massacres. In all other respects I feel well pleased to report a favorable and harmonious state of affairs at the agency.

Very respectfully,

WM. BURGESS,
United States Indian Agent.

BARCLAY WHITE,
Superintendent Indian Affairs, Omaha, Nebr.

12.

GREAT NEMAHA AGENCY,
Nohart, Nebr., Ninthmonth 1, 1873.

RESPECTED FRIEND: I herewith submit my fifth annual report of affairs within this agency for the year ending Eighthmonth 31, 1873.

The Iowas have evinced an increased disposition to work, and since the date of my last report many of them have extended the area of their farms, and nearly all of them have diligently attended to their crops. The weather during the past summer has been very dry and unfavorable, yet their corn and other crops will compare well with those of their white neighbors generally. It is said by many that throughout this section of country corn will not average more than half a crop, and yet I think it safe to estimate that the corn-fields of the Indians will yield from thirty to forty bushels to the acre. The amount of produce raised is shown in the accompanying statistics of farming.

The stock belonging to this tribe has been well cared for during the past year. Hay and corn were plentiful through the cold weather of last winter, and spring found their oxen and horses in good order and ready for work. At present the Iowas are actively engaged in securing hay, and they have already harvested a much greater quantity than during any former year.

Perhaps no evidence of their progress is more encouraging than the almost universal desire among them to possess and live in houses. Their carpenter is kept steadily at work, and several new houses, either finished or partly finished, attest his efficiency. The school has been properly maintained during the school-year, and the attendance and progress of the pupils has been very satisfactory. The industrial home, established in connection with the school for the board and industrial training of a portion of its pupils, is an institution that deserves ample support and maintenance. It has heretofore labored under the disadvantage of inadequate buildings, but the recent erection of a frame addition, 18 by 33 feet, and a slight enlargement of the old building, have remedied that evil, and now, with increased facilities for accomplishing its purpose, its usefulness has increased proportionately.

Since my last report the sanitary condition of the Iowas has been comparatively good. The Society of Friends have continued to furnish us with the means wherewith to administer to the sick, and they have also clothed the infirm and indigent. On the whole, so far as the Iowas are concerned, there is much to encourage, although evil influences around still lead them to intemperance and its attendant evils, which is a drawback much to be regretted.

The Sacs and Foxes of Missouri have made little if any progress during the year. Drawing as they do a very large annuity in money, and having neither school nor employés among them, it is not strange that they continue as idle and intemperate as ever. They desire to remove to a new home as soon as possible, but have not yet ascertained where it shall be.

A visit on the part of their chiefs and myself to the Osage tribe, and a council with its chiefs, resulted in extinguishing all prospects of a purchase of territory from them, and they now desire to buy a home in the Indian Territory of their kindred tribe, the Sacs and Foxes of Mississippi. Unfortunately the enactment of Congress enabling the sale of their lands was made to apply only to that portion lying in the State of Nebraska, and until a supplementary act including under its provisions their lands in Kansas can be obtained, I fear there is little prospect of either a sale or their removal.

With the sanction of the Indian Department I conducted the chiefs of this tribe to Washington, D. C., shortly after they had assented to the provisions of the law touching the sale of their land, and they there formally requested that the proceeds of one-half of their entire reservation should be invested for educational and other beneficial purposes. It is hoped that this request will be complied with.

In conclusion I will only say that in the present unsettled condition of the Sacs and Foxes of Missouri, their early removal is evidently important. The urgent necessity of a supplemental act to enable the sale of their lands in Kansas demands action, and delay in the sale of their lands, and consequent delay in their removal, must continue them in an unsettled and unsatisfactory condition.

With respect, thy friend,

THOS. LIGHTFOOT,
United States Indian Agent.

BARCLAY WHITE,
Superintendent of Indian Affairs, Omaha, Nebr.

13.

OTOE AGENCY, *Ninthmonth* 4, 1873.

ESTEEMED FRIEND: In submitting this, my first annual report of the condition of Indian affairs on the Ottoe reserve, I shall not be able to make it as full and compresive of the work being done within the past year as might be desired, from the fact that my connection with the agency began only with the second quarter of the present calendar year, and hence can but commence with the condition in which I received it at that time.

After reporting at thy office, on the 19th of Fourthmonth last, I came directly to this place, and received from former agent A. L. Green all the books, papers and other articles of property then shown as belonging to this office, the reception of which was duly acknowledged. On the 23d instant was held a formal council with the Indians, in which I was presented to the leading characters of the tribe, and at the same time witnessed the closing ceremonies of my predecessor in office, taking leave of his charge.

At the time of my coming among them I found a considerable portion of the Indians in a state of perfect apathy as relates to any idea of improvement, and at the first regular council I held with them the burden of their desire, as expressed, was to sell out their entire reservation and "seek a new home." I listened to their earnest expressions with interest, but without giving an opinion, told them I had heard what they had said, would give the subject due consideration, and help them do what I thought would be to their best interest. Upon subsequent investigation I was satisfied, however, that the desire to remove was by no means a universal one; that it was entertained principally by a class who wanted a wider range of country, not circumscribed by white settlements, in which to continue the pursuit of their old Indian customs, and that it simply meant opposition to civilization.

These being ruling members in the tribe, others feared the loss of popularity by expressions, or even actions toward improvement, that showed a contrary sentiment. Hence they were, and, as I was assured, had been for some time, in an unsettled and dissatisfied condition, tending rather toward retrogression than advancement, and that this feeling was being continually fomented by a class of scheming white men, who were desirous of getting possession of the Indians' lands. I also became satisfied that the sentiment of the tribe, if numerically expressed, would be largely in favor of remaining where they are, and which sentiment has since been gaining strength to a very noticeable extent.

At a second regular council, held the 25th of Fifthmonth, I brought the subject of their situation fairly before them, and pointed out what I thought their best plan to adopt, telling them that they could not long remain as they now are, that they must do something, and that if the present officials of the tribe could not act so as to do business, we would have to have those that could. A time was given them to deliberate upon it among themselves, when the unanimous expression was to accept the provisions of an act of Congress approved June 10, 1872, providing for the sale of a portion of their land, and the proceeds to be applied to the improvement of their condition. The council closed under strong manifestations of the best of feeling, and I am gratified that truth permits me to state the same has continued to this writing.

What had formerly been fenced and cultivated as the agency farm I found neglected and the fence entirely destroyed. Owing to the lateness of the season, the unsettled condition of the tribe, the absence of agricultural appliances, and the need of funds applicable thereto, I did not deem it advisable to attempt refencing for cultivation this year, but urged the Indians to use what means they had and cultivate all they could, in order to provide as far as possible a winter's subsistence. They nearly all planted more or less of corn, beans, potatoes, and pumpkins, an aggregate of probably 200 acres, mostly in the creek bends, where they could easily protect their patches from the depredations of ponies and cattle. They are now about preparing their corn for future use. Many of them will have plenty of that kind of food, but owing to the unfavorableness of the season their crops, as a whole, are not good, and they must know a great scarcity before the return of another season.

They did not go on their summer hunt, as has heretofore been their custom, which I regard as a step gained in the right direction, that will result to their advantage; for although the hunt may have gained for them a temporary supply of meat, yet this would have been more than counterbalanced by the loss of their crops through neglect, besides the demoralizing effect of their unrestrained actions on the extreme frontier. I am led to regard the hunt as a great obstacle in the way of their civilization, and think its necessity may be effectually obviated by the establishment of a herd of cattle of sufficient size to furnish the tribe a constant supply of meat, and be within itself self-sustaining. This I believe to be entirely practicable, with no other outlay than that required to start the herd. A small portion of the grass that is annually burned on the reserve will do the rest, and allow the herd, if properly managed, to increase yearly in value.

No instance of violence of any description, nor cases of intemperance from liquor, have come under my notice, although I have learned, indirectly, that some cases have occurred in Marysville, Kans., where the Indians have gone to trade, through the instigation of unprincipled white men, in which some have been induced to drink.

I found on my arrival here but two employés on the reserve, an interpreter and blacksmith. These I have retained, on their former salaries, and have since employed a teacher for the school, which constitutes all that are at present engaged. Several more are much needed in order to advance these Indians in the customs of civilized life to a degree commensurate with public anticipation and to the satisfaction of our own desires; but there being no means applicable to the purpose none could be employed, and until these needs can be supplied, the work of improvement in many important respects must remain in a state of comparative stagnation. I nevertheless consider that to be able to strike and move in the several directions of needed improvement at the present time as highly important, inasmuch as where there is not active advancement there is actual retrocession, or at best a state of lethargy, fostering their old Indian customs, consuming their means of sustenance, exposing them to unfavorable influences, and daily rendering them poorer, less confident, and harder to reclaim. It is hoped that the sale of a portion of their land, to which they have consented, will supply the needed funds, and could a small advance on said sale be obtained it would enable the work to progress at once.

Permission having been granted for a portion of the chiefs to visit Washington, in order to arrange for the appropriation of the proceeds of their lands to be sold, that event is looked forward to with scarcely greater interest by the Indians themselves, in anticipation of the trip, than by those who have at heart the future welfare of these oft-injured wards of our Government. It will in all probability decide the question whether they shall become a self-supporting and prosperous people in this their present allotted home, or be allowed to roam on a wider domain as wild Indians still; finally, under all probabilities, to become extinct under the coercive arm of Government. A decisive policy on the part of the Commissioner and other officials that advise with the delegation that may visit Washington, favorable to their retention on this reserve, will at once settle the question that has tended so much to unsettle them for the last two years; it will relieve the great suspense under which they have labored, and be highly satisfactory to most of the tribe.

In my first council with them they objected to a continuance of school, but in the second one, above alluded to, they also reconsidered these objections, and unanimously consented for it to go on. The day-school was therefore started at once, and has been continued to this time with but little interruption, and I may say with marked improvement in most important respects, but being situated in the Indian village, it is, more or less, interrupted by tribal influences, rendering it less satisfactory than it would be if more favorably located. The school-building needs repairing in order to make it comfortable for winter, or even convenient for summer.

Most of the children have been clothed by donations from the Society of Friends, and much other clothing distributed that was furnished from the same source, but most of the men still appear clad in their characteristic Indian costume. Most of them also live in earth-cased wigwams and canvas lodges. A few frame houses are on the reserve, but they are insufficient, with but simple board-siding to keep out the winter blasts.

No prevailing epidemic has affected the health of the tribe since I came here, though there has been considerable sickness for the past two months, mostly complaints arising from malarial influences and unwholesome food. No medical attendance nor hospital accommodations are provided on the reserve. Some medicines and a few sanitary supplies have been furnished by donations from the Society of Friends, which we are called upon to administer many times daily. Several deaths have occurred, which, with one exception, were confined to quite small children.

The Ottoes have had numerous visitors from other tribes, and have largely returned their visits. A few have obtained permission, and been furnished passes to go, but they have generally gone without my knowledge, a practice that I do not consider conducive to their general good, but not seeing how to prevent it, I have not deemed it best to agitate it, except in an advisory way.

The agency-buildings, including the mill and smith-shop, I found in a poor state of repair, and as yet have made but little improvements. It will require the expenditure of several hundred dollars to make them efficient and reasonably comfortable.

Before closing this report, already more lengthy than I had intended, I wish to say that although there is much to discourage in the Indian service at this place, yet there is also much to encourage, and with sufficient means to make them comfortable, and to furnish them the necessary appliances for success in the various directions of needed improvement, I feel confidently hopeful as to the result.

Very respectfully, thy friend,

JESSE W. GRIEST,
United States Indian Agent.

BARCLAY WHITE,
Superintendent of Indian Affairs, Omaha, Nebr.

14.

LAWRENCE, KANS., *October* 1, 1873.

RESPECTED FRIEND: In transmitting my fifth annual report on the condition of the Indians under my charge, it is gratifying to be able to state that all the tribes, as such, have remained at peace during the past year, and, with the exception of the comparatively small number who roam upon the plains, are continuing to advance in industrial pursuits and in the education of their youth, and are making commendable progress toward a higher degree of civilization.

The tribes resident in the Indian Territory and Kansas number about 75,000. Four-fifths of these are considerably advanced in the habits and comforts of their Anglo-Saxon neighbors, many of them having comfortable homes, and being members of Christian churches, with liberal provisions for the education of their children. Several of the larger tribes are subject to written laws and well-organized government, and with warrantable security in the permanency of their possessions would rapidly advance in all the avenues leading to higher moral and Christian attainments.

The remaining tribes, numbering 15,000, embrace the Kiowas, Comanches, Apaches, Cheyennes, Arapahoes, Kaws, and Osages. The most of these still wear the nomadic costumes, and spend much of their time on the plains in procuring necessary supplies of food, robes and furs. None of these last-named tribes, except the Kaws and Osages, have invested funds on which to rely for support and aid in their advancement, and these two excepted tribes are beginning to turn their attention to industrial and settled pursuits.

I regard the school education of the Indian children as of the highest importance in measures adopted for their improvement, and have assiduously labored to promote this, so far as means have been provided. The schools have been prosperous, and the number of children in attendance has increased, while the interest manifested by adults in the educational work has evidently also deepened. An unremitting prosecution of this branch of the service will tend to reduce the many Indian dialects, and ultimately substitute our own language. This result alone will greatly facilitate civilization.

I would respectfully refer for detailed information of the tribes to the reports of their respective agents, and will only allude to such interests as require the attention and action of the Department.

KICKAPOOS.

The Kickapoos number about the same as in 1868, a few having become citizens. They are industrious and self-sustaining, and are well supplied with agricultural implements, which they use with skill and a fair productive return. Their educational interests are well provided for, and meetings for divine worship after Christian methods are held at two places on the reservation every Sabbath. That portion of the tribe which seceded years ago, and have lately resided in Mexico, are now on their way to the Indian Territory, and will be located contiguous to the Kaws, immediately west of the Arkansas River, and south of the southern boundary of Kansas. If the necessary encouragement be given to these Indians in subsistence, agricultural implements, and suitable care-takers, it is highly probable that their improvement will be such as to induce the removal of the Kickapoo tribe proper from their present location, and the consolidation of the two portions in the Indian Territory. Preliminary to this, legislation will be necessary to provide for the sale of their reservations in Kansas.

POTTAWATOMIES.

The reservation Pottawatomies are making commendable progress. Some of their leading men have heretofore opposed education, but their opposition has been overcome, and they now have a flourishing school in which thirty-four children are provided for. They are also well provided with agricultural implements and are self-supporting.

The Pottawatomie treaty provides for the enrollment and classification of the tribe, so as to determine the number who desired to become citizens, and the number who desired to hold their possessions in common. The report of the commissioner appointed for this service represents the entire Pottawatomie Nation to consist of 2,180 persons, of whom 1,400 elected to become citizens, and 780 to hold their possessions in common. There was, however, in the State of Wisconsin a considerable number of the Potawattomie Nation who were not included in the enrollment. They now desire to return to the tribe, and I recommend that provision be made for their removal. The reservation is ample, and the tribe is willing to receive them. In their present location in Wisconsin they have no lands and no provisions for the education of their children.

KAWS.

The improvement of this tribe has been greatly retarded by the constant expectation of being removed to the Indian Territory for three years past. They reached their new home about midsummer, and, of course, could raise no crops this season. With proper subsistence and necessary aid in other respects I hope they will be able, by next spring, to enter upon a new and progressive experience.

Their lands in Kansas were thrown upon the market at a time of financial depression, and I learn that only a small portion was sold. That these lands were not too highly appraised is evident from the fact that cash offers were made for the same by different parties aggregating about the same amount as that of the aggregate appraisals. If the appraisement should be reduced, sales would still not be affected during the present financial disturbance, and so the end would not be reached. It is exceedingly important that these Indians should secure the full value of the land, to enable them to pay for their new reservation, to satisfy their debts, to build houses, open farms, provide for the education of their children, and make them generally independent of support by the Government. It would not be wise, therefore, to force their lands into market under any circumstances. I apprehend that they will sell under the present appraisement as fast as the proceeds will be required, if provision can be made for time, with interest on one-half or two-thirds their value. If approved by the Bureau I recommend such provisions.

SACS AND FOXES.

The Sacs and Foxes are doing better than in any previous year. They have suffered severely in their farming interests by the drought the present season, although they had planted a larger area than usual. In imitation of their Creek neighbors, they are entering upon the raising of stock. The building for school purposes will soon be completed, and their children will then feel the benefit of the ample educational provision of their treaty.

A portion of the tribe numbering six or eight lodges became exiled from the tribe several years ago, and are now located in Tama County, Iowa. Since their location there some Pottawatomies, Winnebagoes, and dissolute citizens have amalgamated with them until they number upward of three hundred. They have purchased about four hundred acres of land—the title vesting in the United States—on which a few of them raise some produce, but insufficient for their support. They subsist mainly as vagrant beggars, and would be amenable to State law on this account if they were citizens. The Government long ago established a wise provision that fragments of Indian tribes should forfeit their shares of annuities while absent from their proper reservations. An unfortunate exception was inserted in the Indian appropriation bill of 1868, by which these Iowa Sacs and Foxes are allowed to receive their proportion of annuities so long as they remain peaceable and have the consent of the State of Iowa to remain within its limits. This exceptional provision has been continued from year to year, and while the money thus withdrawn might have benefited them had they been with the tribe in the Territory, its effect in their present location has been to increase their habit of vagrancy. Believing that they will not improve under their present circumstances, I recommend the suspension by Congress of their annuities while off their reservation, and that they be removed, with another remnant of the tribe in Kansas, to their proper home in the Indian Territory. I believe also that the best interests of the Sacs and Foxes of the Missouri now in Nebraska would be promoted by a union with the tribe under consideration in this paragraph. The reservation is ample for all, as they would number in the aggregate less than one thousand, and the services of two agents could be dispensed with.

I cannot too earnestly urge the provision of funds necessary to continue and render adequate the educational work among the absentee Shawnees who are attached to this agency, and whose influence over the tribes of the plains is decidedly salutary.

MIAMIES.

Under a law of the last session of Congress the Miami lands have been appraised preparatory for sale, and most of the tribe have confederated with the Peorias in the Indian Territory. The few who have elected to remain in Kansas as citizens are mostly white, or nearly so, and well qualified for citizenship. I recommend the early execution of the law concerning the sale of their lands, and the consolidation of their funds with those of the Peorias, and that congressional action be taken to transfer the funds of those applicants from the Indiana Miamies and Weas residing with the Peorias, that their homes with the latter may be legalized.

SHAWNEES.

As the Shawnees, except the Black Bob band, have become consolidated with the Cherokees, I desire to call attention to the necessity of legislation for the sale of their valuable lands near Kansas City, which are occupied by white men, none of whom have legal titles. The Indians have been crowded out of their reservation by these intruders, and, disheartened and poverty-stricken, they have sought homes as beggars, some among the Eastern Shawnees, some with the Cherokees, and others with the absentee Shawnees. If their lands were sold at a fair price the whole Black Bob band might be gathered with the Eastern Shawnees, who have sufficent land for them, speak the same language, and would welcome them to their reservation. I earnestly recommend that all illegal sales of any portion of these lands be set aside, and that provision for appraisement and sale, for cash, to the highest bidder, of the entire reservation, be made at as early a day as practicable, by a law similar in its provisions to that passed by the last Congress for the sale of the lands of the Miamies of Kansas.

CHEYENNES AND ARAPAHOES.

Great exertions have been made by Agent Miles to restrain the roving disposition of these Indians, and to prevent alliances for hostile purposes with other tribes of the plains. Peace has been preserved, and they have remained mostly on their reservation. Unfortunately they have been exposed to influences tending to produce distrust of the promises of the Government. Early in last spring a small war party of Cheyennes left their reservation, without the knowledge of the agent, and went into New Mexico to fight their enemies, the Utes. While returning they were surprised by United States soldiers and several of them killed and wounded. On the day of their return with the news of their loss to the Cheyenne camps, in the western portion of the reservation, the whole tribe was in a state of demoralization from whisky brought to them by citizens of Kansas. On the following day, while the chiefs were in council with a sub-agent, four of a surveying party, a few miles away, were killed, probably by drunken relatives of the Cheyennes who had been killed in New Mexico. The chiefs were not complicated in this unfortunate affair, and condemn it. They were, however, much displeased with the survey and subdivision of their reservation, for which there was no provision in their treaty, and of which they had no official notice. To them it foreshadowed a repetition of the old policy of forcing them from their lands and compelling them to seek new homes. In addition to the loss of their men in New Mexico, the presence of surveyors on their soil, and their demoralization by whisky, they had just received information from the Arapahoes on their return from Washington that the Government, without their knowledge and consent, had assigned to the former tribe the most desirable portion of the reservation owned by the two tribes in common. Under these adverse and irritating influences it has required much vigilance and exertion on the part of the agent to preserve friendly relations with the Government. This has only been accomplished by repeated visits to their distant camps by the agent, whose presence among them has tended to dispel their fears and dissipate their jealousies. For the first time a proper delegation has consented to visit Washington, that their reservation interests may be settled, and that a union may be made with the Northern Cheyennes and Arapahoes.

QUAPAW AGENCY.

The several tribes constituting this agency are continuing to progress in the right direction. Their schools and farming operations are successful, and a continuous use of the means now employed for their benefit offers a most hopeful prospect of permanent good results. These Indians are mostly in a condition of progress which is highly favorable to successful effort for their improvement.

OSAGES.

The evidences of industrial progress upon the Great and Little Osage reservation since last year are very decided. Besides the erection by the agent of buildings for agency and school purposes, saw-mill, &c., very many of the Indians have split rails and inclosed with their own hands plats of ground, which they have cultivated the past summer. These fences are well made and very creditable to the Indians as the result of their first efforts at farming. I deem it important that their ample funds be used to foster their industrial interests and to educate their children instead of being placed in their own hands. They are unable to direct the proper use of money to much extent, and would be greatly demoralized by receiving it, and, at the same time, become the subjects of deception by unprincipled parties. The wise guardianship of the Government during their transitionary period will be of incalculable importance to them.

WICHITAS AND AFFILIATED BANDS.

I would again call attention to the great importance of these Indians, on account of their influence upon the wild tribes. Their location is exceedingly favorable for securing their aid to the Government in its endeavors to prevent mischief on the part of the Cheyennes, Kiowas, and Comanches. This proximity to the wild tribes has sometimes resulted in the loss of the crops raised by the Wichitas, but this trouble is constantly diminishing, and I believe that a liberal policy, persistently pursued toward its wards at this agency, will greatly promote the objects of the Government in regard to the tribes in that vicinity. I therefore cordially recommend a continuance of the aid hitherto furnished, and which has already yielded such desirable results. Permanent security to their lands has been repeatedly recommended, and should be no longer postponed.

KIOWAS, COMANCHES, AND APACHES.

The interests of the Kiowas, Comanches, and Apaches have been managed under very unfavorable circumstances. The Kiowas were assured last autumn by the Government that their imprisoned chief would be returned to them in the spring, on condition that the tribe remained at peace on their reservation. The fulfillment of these conditions was acknowledged in Thirdmonth, and preliminary steps inaugurated looking to a faithful execution of Government pledges. The excited condition of the country, growing out of the massacre of General Canby by the Modocs, induced postponement of further action in their case until the 4th of the present month, when Satanta and Big Tree were returned to their tribe, and confidence measurably restored.

Although no raiding can be clearly charged against the Kiowas, and much less than that of any preceding year against the Comanches, and having the assurance that the most influential men of both tribes are pledged to loyalty and peace, yet it is necessary to employ several persons of proper qualification to remain in the camps of said Indians to restrain their roving habits, and induce their consent to settlement on permanent homes.

The most prominent obstacle to the advancement of the Indians in general civilization is the uncertainty of retaining their lands. The constant pressure of the public press, inducing emigration into the Indian Territory, the persistency of railroad interests to procure the extinguishment of Indian titles in said lands, are very discouraging to the Indians. Renewed efforts on the part of these migratory and corporate interests will be made at the approaching session of Congress, and should be as promptly met by the equitable and moral power of the people. This territory is the only resting-place for the Indians therein, and if opened for the ingress of citizens it will result in the extermination of the Indians, and the inauguration of consequent evils which cannot be countenanced by a Christian nation.

Very respectfully,

ENOCH HOAG,
Superintendent Indian Affairs.

Hon. E. P. SMITH,
Commissioner Indian Affairs, Washington, D. C.

15.

KAW INDIAN AGENCY, INDIAN TERRITORY,
Ninthmonth 1, 1873.

I submit herewith my fourth annual report for the Kansas agency.

The prosecution of the work of appraising the lands belonging to this tribe in the State of Kansas was pushed forward last fall to completion, and a report submitted to the Indian Department on the 28th of Twelfthmonth, 1872, which was accepted, and, in accordance with the bill for the disposal of the lands, they were advertised for sale the past spring, but for various reasons only a small portion was sold. Among them the depressed state of the money market; also, the short time which the lands were offered for sale did not admit of persons coming from a distance, making their selections, and getting their bids to Washington in time; and, by an order of the honorable Secretary of the Interior, that appraisement has been set aside, and a new one ordered. I regret very much that the Department believed this step necessary, as it will defer the sale of the land another year, and, consequently, retard the work of improvements on their new reservation.

The school was kept up during last fall, winter, and spring, with a larger average than any previous nine months since my connection with the tribe. The progress of the children was all we could ask, and many of them gave evidence by their daily life that they had received a knowledge of the plan of salvation, and were living up to it. The Indians had promised, on their removal, to leave their children in school in Kansas until suitable buildings could be erected for them here. But, as the time drew nigh to start, their affection for them overcame their better judgment, and they decided to take them along. Consequently the school was closed the last of Fifthmonth, 1873, except Sabbath-school, which has been kept up at this place. But few of the full-blood Indian children attend, having worn out their citizen clothes and being ashamed to come in their Indian costume. The tribe left their old reservation in Kansas on the 4th of Sixthmonth, and arrived here on the 21st without the loss of one member, and without having had any difficulty with the whites or among themselves. They have been well satisfied thus far with the change, and, if not annoyed by other and wilder tribes, and funds can be had, will make more rapid strides in civilization than they did in Kansas, but it must be in proportion to the funds received to aid them in purchasing stock, implements of husbandry, seeds, &c. Both children and adults express great anxiety to have suitable mission and school buildings erected as early as practicable, and they are certainly suffering great loss for want of them. A few temporary cabins have been erected for the use of employés of the commissary stores, blacksmith shop, &c., and about 200 acres of prairie broken on the reservation, but, unfortunately, the Indians did not arrive in time to plant but a small portion of it. About 150 tons of hay have been put up for the use of the agency stock and for the Indian horses. The health of the tribe has been better since their removal than it was in Kansas, although a few deaths have occurred, and I earnestly recommend that a physician be employed at a stipulated salary to reside among these Indians.

Very respectfully submitted.

MAHLON STUBBS,
United States Indian Agent.

ENOCH HOAG,
Superintendent of Indian Affairs.

16.

UNITED STATES AGENCY FOR CHEROKEES,
Tahlequah, Cherokee Nation, Ind. T., September 20, 1872.

SIR: In accordance with the requirements of your office, I forward the following as my report for the year 1873.

The Cherokee Nation consists of a heterogeneous population, differing from each other in language, race, and degree of advancement in civilization. For this reason they require a great variety of appliances to secure their further progress in all that pertains to civilization and religion.

The various classes may be thus enumerated:

1st. The full-blood Cherokees.

2d. The half-breed Cherokees.

3d. The Delawares, both full-blood and half-breed.

4th. The Shawnees, both full-blood and half-breed.

5th. The white men and women who have intermarried with these.

6th. A few Creeks who broke away from their own tribe, and have been citizens of the Cherokee Nation for many years.

7th. A few Creeks who are not citizens, but live here without any rights.

8th. A few Natchez Indians who are citizens.

9th. The freedmen adopted under the treaty of 1866.

10th. Freedmen not adopted, but not removed as intruders, owing to an order from the Indian Department directing agent to remove them.

These require widely differing appliances to meet their necessities with regard to education.

The half-breeds among the Cherokees, Delawares, and Shawnees, consisting of that class who speak the English language vernacularly, need no other means of education than those which prove effective in an ordinary community of English-speaking people in the States. They are able to use with success the ordinary English school-books, and avail themselves profitably of the services of teachers who speak English only. The same is true also of the freedmen. These classes, therefore, need only the continuance of the means of education hitherto used among them with such gratifying success, together with such improvements as may from time to time be suggested by the progress of the science and art of teaching.

That part of all the tribes who do not speak English vernacularly are far differently situated. They labor under difficulties very great and very hard to overcome. As the full-blood Cherokees form the most numerous class, outnumbering all other classes combined, my remark with reference to other than the ordinary means of education will be especially directed to their necessities. The means of education thus far adopted have most signally failed, so far as they are concerned. While that part of the people who speak English vernacularly have been greatly benefited by the public schools, the full-blood Cherokees have received but little benefit. Their children have learned to spell, read, and write the English words and sentences mechanically, while they know not the meaning of these words and sentences. To this great defect in the Cherokee system of education I have repeatedly called their attention and pointed out a remedy effective and entirely within the reach of the nation and easy of application. I have zealously urged its adoption, but as yet without sucess. My recommendations have not met with the approval of those in authority, and hence the old parrot-like system is continued with this large and interesting class of Cherokees. As a consequence the interest in education among them has fallen off, and the schools which have depended on them for support are very lightly attended, and the advancement made by the pupils small indeed. This is by no means owing to any inferiority in the intellects of this particular class. In natural capacity they will compare favorably with any other children, either here or elsewhere. The failure is attributable altogether to the lack of a proper method of instruction, energetically and intelligently carried into effect.

I have urged persistently a plan something like the following:

1st. Have a work prepared for the purpose of teaching the English language to Cherokees, to adults as well as to the children, through the medium of their own language as written in the Sequoyah characters. Such work should be prepared on the conversational or Ollendorff methods.

The lessons should begin with a few simple words, and be so constructed as to impress their meaning firmly on the mind of the learner, and also to give him practice in the use of these words in the structure of sentences. Other words should be added gradually, and used in such a way that their meaning and use will be thoroughly learned as the pupil progresses. The lessons should thus advance until a work is prepared, containing all the common words of the English language, and a sufficient number of exercises given to enable the pupil to attain a thorough knowledge of their use in ordinary conversation. An exercise in spelling should form a part of each lesson. A carefully prepared glossary should be appended to the work. By this the pupil could readily refer to the meaning of any word contained in the lessons.

2d. As introductory to this work, and for the use of the smaller children, I have recommended the preparation of an illustrated primer, prepared as follows:

I. To contain the English and Cherokee alphabets; also a sufficient number of exercises to familiarize the pupil with the forms and sounds of the characters.

II. Select an object, for instance a horse, make a picture of it; under that picture print in large letters its name, horse, and the same in Cherokee. Select some quality which can easily be represented to the eye, as that of blackness; make a black picture to represent it, print under it the word black, and its equivalent in Cherokee. Then make a picture of a black horse and print under it the words black horse, and their equivalent in Cherokee. Then take other colors, picture them and associate them with the object in like manner. Then make the picture of a poor horse and print under it the words poor horse, and their equivalent in Cherokee. In the same way picture a fat horse, and small horse, a large horse, &c., giving expression to the ideas in both languages. Then take objects commonly used with the horse, such as saddle, bridle, wagon, plow, &c. Use these words in carefully-prepared exercises as the lessons advance.

Take other objects; treat them in the same way; use a few verbs, pronouns, &c., as required, until a sufficient number of exercises are prepared to furnish the pupil with a small stock of English words, and familiarize him with their use through his previous knowledge of the Cherokee. The extent to which this method of illustration will be carried, and the excellency of the exercises connected with it, must depend on the skill and judgment of the party who prepares the work. It should, however, be carried only to a limited extent, and for more complete instruction the learner should depend on the more complete work already proposed.

3d. Primary lessons should be prepared on arithmetic, geography, and history, and printed in English on one page and in Cherokee on the opposite page. For primary lessons in grammar the work proposed will be ample.

4th. A limited system of normal instruction should be introduced, adapted especially to the training of teachers for the full Cherokee schools. For this purpose such teachers should be selected as already understand the Cherokee language, and have an English education. This normal instruction should continue for a short time each term. It should be directed to training the teachers in the use of the books already proposed, and to fit them to teach the English language &c., to pupils who do not speak it vernacularly.

5th. Lectures should be delivered in every part of the nation, in both English and Cherokee, to arouse the people to a sense of the fact that it is absolutely necessary that their children should learn English—should learn it *thoroughly*, correctly, and immediately. In that portion of the lectures delivered in the Cherokee language, instruction should be given as to manner of using the books above proposed, so as to secure a knowledge of the English. By this means a large number of adults who read Cherokee well would be enabled to acquire knowledge enough of the English to be of great service to them. They have great desire to learn, and without doubt would eagerly use all such means if placed within their reach. The importance of skilled labor, of industry, economy, and the value of time, and the intimate relations which education sustains to all these, should be made prominent in such lectures.

Such is an outline of the means for the promotion of education which I have urged in behalf of the full Cherokees. But my plans and suggestion do not meet with favor at the hands of those in authority, whose simple acquiescence would be sufficient to put them into efficient operation at an early day without labor or effort on their part. Owing to this fact there is but little probability of the early adoption of such reformatory measures in their educational system, although the means at command are ample, and the plan proposed is inexpensive as compared to boarding-schools and other methods. For these more expensive methods the funds are not sufficient.

For that portion of the Delawares and Shawnees, Creeks, and Natchez, who do not speak English, some special efforts should also be made to give them a knowledge of the English. As each of these classes is comparatively small in number, and as different appliances would be necessary for each class, the question as to the best means of educating them is one far more difficult of solution. A portion of the Creeks and Natchez, however, speak Cherokee and can be reached in the manner above indicated. In case some such plan as that I have proposed for the Cherokees should be adopted by the Creek authorities for their own people, the books necessary for the few Creeks we have here could be easily obtained from the Creek Nation. By the same means, also, most of the Natchez could be reached, as they also generally speak Creek. But as yet I have no plan fully matured in my own mind as specially adapted to meet the wants of these detached portions of this nation.

I recommend that the educational interests of the Indian be placed under the supervision of the Commissioner of Education; that provision be made by Congress for the appointment of such subordinates as may be necessary to inaugurate and carry into effect efficient measures to promote the work of education among the Indians. The duties of Indian agents are in some cases so diversified and arduous, that it is impossible for them to give the necessary attention to the work of education. Yet, this is without doubt the most important work connected with the civilization of the Indians. A well-devised scheme for the co-operation of the Bureau of Education with the local managers of the work in the several tribes or nations would result in giving far greater efficiency than has hitherto been attained to the educational institutions among these tribes.

There have been in operation during the past year sixty (60) common schools. These schools have been taught by 26 male teachers and 34 female. Of these, 12 have been white and 48 native Cherokees. There have been in attendance on these schools seventeen hundred and thirty-three (1;733,) 800 boys and 933 girls. Three of these schools have been for the exclusive use of the freedmen. These statistics are furnished by the kindness of Col. O. P. Brewer, superintendent of public schools.

CHEROKEE ORPHAN ASYLUM.

Besides the common schools and the seminary, the Cherokees have, during the whole year, had in operation a most excellent and efficient orphan asylum. The success with which this institution has been carried on is in the highest degree creditable to those who have had it in charge. The Cherokees have been remarkably fortunate in the selection of principal, teachers, and matron. Together they constitute a most efficient band of workers. The principal, Rev. W. A. Duncan, is a Cherokee, as is also one of the teachers, Mr. S. S. Stephens; both were educated entirely in this nation. Mr. George Mason, the other teacher, is a native of the state of Maine. Mrs. Kate A. Caleb, the matron, comes from the state of Delaware.

The funds for the support of this institution consist of 15 per cent. of the interest annually accruing on the Cherokee invested funds. This, though not as yet sufficient for all the purposes of the asylum, is increasing with every addition to the Cherokee funds. It is also the intention to connect with this asylum a large farm and some shops, that the boys may learn to be farmers and mechanics. If in doing this proper economy is used in the expenditure of funds, and the farm and shops are carried on with energy and economy, there will be ample means to support and educate all the orphans in the nation.

It is the desire of the Cherokees to make their asylum a model institution of its kind; to make it a place where the unfortunate children, whom God has deprived of their natural guardians, belonging to any and all tribes of Indians, can find a home and enjoy the care and instruction of teachers and guardians who are at once kind and sympathizing, and fully competent to discharge their duties.

I recommend that the Government render to the Cherokees every facility possible for carrying out this noble and humane purpose; that measures be taken to induce other tribes who have an orphan fund to unite their means with that of the Cherokees in building up an orphan asylum which shall afford ample accommodation and instruction for all their orphans; that where tribes have no such fund the Government take their friendless children and bring them to this asylum, and defray the expense of their instruction and support at fixed rates, to be agreed upon by the Cherokees and the Government. By this means you could gather many children from the wild tribes of the plains and the Rocky Mountains and place them here among the most intelligent Indians of the continent. In fact, you could place them here in an institution where their opportunities for improvement would be equal to those afforded by similar institutions in the States. They would still be among Indians and have their instructions from persons of their own race, and yet from persons completely civilized.

I herewith inclose the report of the superintendent. From it you will see that the asylum has now in attendance, as pupils, 43 boys and 47 girls; ninety in all. The course of study is all that can reasonably be desired in such an institution.

AGRICULTURE.

The industrial interests of the country are advancing gradually; stock-raising continues to be the chief and most remunerative occupation of the people.

The Cherokees are each year taking more and more interest in fruit culture. The number who have this year set out orchards is vastly greater than in any previous year. The desire for orchards is increasing, and the facilities for obtaining choice trees are greater than hitherto. The very low price at which the best grafted apple-trees can now be had, will most certainly soon fill the nation with this fruit.

The culture of cotton has been commenced in the southern part of the nation with very encouraging success. There are a few large cotton-growers, but most of it is being grown by small farmers. This season there is a prospect of very fine cotton crops. This will bring money into the country, as no other crop will. I look at the continued culture of cotton as a source of permanent prosperity to the people. I shall do all in my power to encourage this branch of industry, and to extend it among the people as far north as the climate will admit of its profitable culture. It furnishes that which has long been greatly needed—a commodity from which the farmers can realize in cash a quick reward for their labors. Stock-raising, with all its advantages, requires the farmer to wait too long for the reward of his toil, to be depended on as principal occupation of a people as poor as are the Cherokees.

One of the greatest necessities of the Cherokee country is a more diversified industry. There is too great a portion of the people engaged in agricultural pursuits. If by any means a great number could be induced to take up the various mechanical trades, and thereby furnish a home market for farm products, and in return furnish the farmer with improved implements, the aggregate productions would be increased, while the number of people engaged in farming would be diminished. Thus, I think, the people would be stimulated to greater industry, and far greater prosperity would result. I refer to the statistical table herewith furnished for a more particular statement of the products of the country.

BOUNTIES AND PENSIONS.

Claims for bounties and pensions for the Cherokee soldiers and their heirs are at last in a fair way to be finally disposed of, under the provisions of the late acts of Congress.

The labor of making these claims, which was thrown on the agent, has been very great, and has seriously interfered with the proper discharge of the agent's duties in other respects. They will, however, soon be completed. I beg leave to recommend that some action be taken to modify to some extent, in the case of Indian soldiers, the laws and the rulings with reference to deserters. My reasons for this recommendation are the following:

First. Many of the Indian soldiers are marked as deserters unjustly.

Second. Owing to the fact that they spoke a different language from the officers who kept the rolls, many of them were deemed guilty of a technical violation of regulations with reference to desertion, when in fact no such desertion was intended.

Third. Many when sick or wounded had ineradicable prejudices against being treated by the surgeons of the Army, and were taken away at their own request to be treated by Indian doctors, and had no idea of being regarded as deserters.

Fourth. Many of them, when broken down or taken sick on the march, fell out of ranks and were marked deserters. Some of them died of this sickness. Others, upon recovery, reported to their companies, and served faithfully to the end of the war. Yet many of both these classes are borne on the rolls as deserters.

Fifth. Some of those who, upon coming back to their companies, found that they had been dropped as deserters, went back to the hills, joined independent companies, and did effective service for the Government in scouring the country, reporting the movements of the confederate army, and in repelling marauding bands of the enemy. These independent companies acted under the general supervision of the Army officers, and received ammunition from them. Many who had unjustly been placed on the roll as deserters, together with some who had really deserted, came back at the call of the President and served to the end of the war, and very properly have received honorable discharges.

In view of these facts, I think both justice and expediency demand that they receive the benefits of the bounties and pensions provided by Congress. In further support of these recommendations I refer to the decision of the Supreme Court of the United States in the case of United States, appellants, *vs.* Thomas H. Kelly. Decision rendered at the December term of 1872.

I beg leave to call special attention to the opinion of the Judge-Advocate-General, which Chief Justice Chase, in delivering that decision, quoted as follows:

"The honorable discharge of the deserter was a formal, final judgment, passed by the Government upon the entire military record of the soldier, and an authoritative declaration by it that he had left the military service in a status of honor. That as such it dispensed altogether with the supposed necessity that the soldier must obtain bounty by removal by order of the charge of desertion from the rolls, and amounted of itself to the removal of any charge or impediment in the way of his receiving bounty."

CRIME.

It has been repeatedly charged that crime has greatly increased in the Cherokee country within the past few years. This charge, I am compelled to admit, is true. It is also true that the representations of this increase of crime have been exaggerated and distorted. The disturbance which occurred at Coody's Bluff on the election day in August has been greatly misrepresented. It was the occasion of telegraphic dispatches representing the political parties of this nation as arrayed in action and armed hostility to each other. The facts in the case are that a set of bad men made a wanton attack on one Jordan Journeycake, a Delaware citizen. Their victim fled into the room where the voting was in progress. The ruffians followed him into the room firing pistols and making other demonstrations of violence. The sheriff's force, who are the custodians of peace, did not interfere; the voting stopped; the judges and clerks' of election fled. No one, however, was killed. Journeycake escaped unhurt. The judges and clerks of election afterward got together and opened the polls, and soon after closed the election. The desperadoes then went to the houses of two peaceable citizens, destroyed furniture, broke windows, and committed other depredations. But the men are unsustained by any political party; none regret the occurrence more than the members of the party to which these men belong. They were soon after arrested by a party of citizens and turned over to the sheriff. A part of them are now awaiting trial for these crimes before the Cherokee court, while others are in jail at Fort Smith, Ark., awaiting trial before the United States district court for the western district of Arkansas, on charge of other crimes previously committed. None will defend themselves except in a legal way before the several courts where their cases are to be tried. This is about all there is of the great war among the Cherokees, reported by telegraph and published throughout the country. Although this and other cases have been exaggerated, yet the fact remains that crime has increased, that we are compelled to deplore a greater insecurity of life and property. This state of things results largely from the existence of organized cliques and parties, said to be pledged to defend each member when arraigned for the violation of law.

Instances have occurred where the basest of crimes have gone unpunished, apparently owing to the operation of such parties. Witnesses have been intimidated, others have been run off, so that their testimony could not be obtained. Truth has been suppressed on the witness-stand. Particular friends of the criminals have been placed on the juries to try them. Cases have occurred where men have been afraid to testify against, or even to charge crime on, those who are most clearly guilty. This has occurred in the midst of a people of wide-spread intelligence, where the great mass of the people read and write either in English or Cherokee, where schools fill the land and large and active churches exist. How to remedy this state of affairs, I can hardly say.

UNITED STATES COURT.

In my report of last year I recommended that Congress establish a court of the United States for the Indian Territory, in accordance with the treaties with the various tribes concluded in 1866. I then urged the following reasons in support of that recommendation:

1st. That the United States district court for the western district of Arkansas had proved itself to a great extent an instrument for the oppression of the people of this nation.

2d. That the operation of the United States deputy-marshals connected with said court were the occasion of great complaint among the Cherokees; that the Cherokees regarded them as exercising a usurped and oppressive authority; that they often arrested innocent men, and dragged them to Fort Smith, Ark., before United States district courts on the most flimsy pretext. They were required to give bail in a strange city, the language of which they did not understand, or in default of such bail were imprisoned.

3d. That the laws of the United States to regulate trade and intercourse with the Indians and the provisions of treaties with said Indians conflict with each other. I referred to cases of great wrong growing out of this state of things. I now say that this state of things exists, though during the past year there have not occurred as many cases of flagrant wrong as previously, owing probably to increased vigilance of the Department of Justice at Washington, and the constant complaints of the people, and to a change in some of the officials. But the urgent necessity still exists and is increasing daily for the creation of a court of the United States in the Indian Territory. I therefore renew my recommendation of last year, that such court be created by Congress at its next session in accordance with the Indian-treaties of 1866. I would, however, change my recommendation of its location from Fort Gibson to Tahlequah. Tahlequah I regard as a location eminently suitable for such court. The Cherokee capitol there is a building finely adapted to its use. It is a large and commodious brick building, with many rooms for offices, &c. Its use no doubt could be obtained from the council for such purpose until a building for the special use of such court could be erected.

The council at its coming session will doubtless authorize the erection of a large and strong jail. The use of this could also be obtained until one can be built for the exclusive use of the court. Tahlequah is also pre-eminently a healthful place. It is very finely watered.

In connection with this matter I again recommend that a careful revision be made of the United States laws to regulate trade and intercourse with the Indians. They were enacted mostly in 1834, have been but slightly amended since. In the mean time the five principal nations in this Territory and some other tribes have rapidly advanced in civilization. Their condition is now greatly changed, and these laws have become in many respects very unsuitable to their present condition. Other tribes are still largely uncivilized. This great diversity in the condition of the various tribes demands that corresponding distinctions be made in the laws applicable to them. It must be apparent to all reflecting persons, that laws suitable for the government of Kiowas, Comanches, and Apaches would be very unsuitable for the government of Cherokees, Choctaws, &c. Again, there is now no tribunal where civil suit can be tried between citizens of the United States and Indians, or even where citizens of the United States are the only parties, if the cause of action arises in the Indian Territory. There are also many crimes of which the United States court at present takes no cognizance. I therefore urge the establishment at Tahlequah of a court with sufficient powers to meet all the necessities of the country. The most important thing of all is to have the offices of judge, district attorney, and marshal filled by men of such high probity that they will under no circumstances prostitute their offices to oppress the people.

TERRITORIAL GOVERNMENT.

As the scheme for the organization of a territorial government for the Indian Territory still continues to be agitated by the press throughout the States, a continued anxiety exists relative thereto among the Cherokee people. Of the opposition to such territorial government I spoke at length in my last annual report. (See report of Commissioner of Indian Affairs for 1872, page 236.) During the past year there has been but little modification of that opposition. The great mass of the people of every class regard the organization of a territorial government with abhorrence. Quite a strong minority are in favor of the Ocmulgee constitution, as passed by the grand council of tribes which assembled some two years ago at Ocmulgee. But the majority are opposed to it, principally, perhaps, for fear it will lead to other innovations, and finally bring about a territorial government. Even the minority favoring the adoption of that constitution in its original form are opposed to it with the modifications and amendments recommended by the President in his message submitting said constitution to Congress for ratification. The masses are also opposed to having their lands surveyed and allotted in severalty. Their reasons for such opposition are —

1st. The fear that the transfer of title from the nation to individuals might be construed as weakening said title, and such construction might be forced upon them.

2d. That, if the title to lands were vested in individuals, the ignorant and improvident among them would soon sell their lands, consume the proceeds, and impoverish themselves and their families, and their posterity ever after be rendered landless and homeless; that, in case they were unrestricted as to parties to whom they could sell, it would prove the means of introducing a white population which would soon overrun the Cherokees; that, in case they were permitted to sell only to citizens of the Cherokee Nation, their market would be so restricted as to greatly diminish the market-value of their lands.

3d. In view of the existence of charters to railroad companies, granting them alternate sections of the Indians' lands whenever the Indian title is extinguished, so arranged that one company gets the odd sections and the other the even sections, they fear to disturb their title as at present situated, lest it be construed as involving such extinguishment of title to a part of their lands, and thus the conditional grants made to railroads be put into effect. This would entail great loss in their landed interests. They have an instinctive prejudice against sectionizing land, constantly associating it with a territorial government, and the introduction of a white population to overwhelm.

There are, however, some points on which the Cherokees desire legislation by Congress. The first and most important act which they desire is the unconditional repeal of all acts granting lands in the Indian country to railroad companies, to take effect when the Indian title is extinguished. These grants the Cherokees regard as unjust and unwarranted. They hold that the land was and is theirs, bought and paid for, and held by patent, and that the Government had neither moral nor legal right to give away, conditionally or otherwise. They, therefore, demand the immediate and unconditional repeal of the laws making such grants. Should a difficulty arise, growing out of the repeal of these conditional land-grants, the Cherokees demand that the Government settle that difficulty with the railroad companies in such a manner as in no way to jeopardize or compromise the interests of the Indians. They claim that these conditional land-grants were made without their consent, and contrary to their will, and that it is the duty of the Government to relieve them entirely of any complications that may arise out of the condition of affairs brought about by these conditional land-grants. They also desire such legislation as will secure to the Cherokees the payment at an early day of a fair price for all lands west of the 96° west longitude, upon which the Cherokees have agreed the United States may settle other Indians. The first step toward getting the Cherokees to consent to the allotment of their lands in severalty, or to the adoption of the Ocmulgee constitution, or other change in their government, is the repeal of all acts granting their lands to any parties whatever. This I regard as a necessary condition; without this they will scarcely consider the question of allotment or change in their government.

I have the honor to be, very respectfully, your obedient servant,

JOHN B. JONES,
United States Agent for Cherokees.

Hon. E. P. SMITH,
Commissioner Indian Affairs.

17.

U. S. INDIAN AGENCY FOR CHOCTAWS AND CHICKASAWS,
Boggy Depot, C. N., October 20, 1873.

SIR: In compliance with your instructions, I submit the following as the annual report of the condition of the Choctaw and Chickasaw Indians for the year 1873.

Because of the large extent of territory occupied by these nations—being about three hundred miles east and west by one hundred and twenty north and south—it has taken more time and labor than I expected to obtain the inclosed statistics. This is the reason of the late date of my report:

I have found, as my estimate shows, that the amount and kind of products are quite different from those reported last year. The growth of cotton, wheat, barley, and oats has largely increased. These nations have much more wealth and are making more progress in agriculture than they have heretofore been accredited with. They are opening new farms, building thousands of rods of fence, and preparing in every way to extend their agriculture. They are not limited, as formerly, to the crop of corn, but are now raising cotton, wheat, barley, oats, &c., with good success.

There has not been much change in their educational systems or opportunities. There are several more schools in each nation than reported last year. The progress of the pupils has been in accordance with the character of the teachers. The teachers are selected by the officers of the nations in all the schools except Spencer Academy and New Hope Female Seminary of the Choctaw Nation. A large part of the teachers of the other schools are unfit for their positions. The funds appropriated by the Chickasaw Nation are sufficient to support good schools, but through incompetency of many of the teachers less progress is made than should be. The funds of the Choctaw Nation are not so large; but much of theirs used in support of neighborhood schools does little good, because they have poor teachers. A majority of the officers appointed or elected to take charge of the schools and select the teachers are incompetent for the duties of their offices, and hence poor teachers and poor schools. If there were fewer schools, with educated teachers, selected, for instance, by some missionary board, or other competent authority, there would be much more moral, religious, and educational progress in these nations.

Much dissatisfaction has been expressed by the Choctaw Nation because the contractors with the Missouri, Kansas and Texas Railway Company have been cutting ties and timber and shipping them out of the Territory without any authority or license from the nation. Individuals of the nation would claim to own a certain tract of timber land, and sell the timber to these contractors which really belonged to the nation. A few individuals would thus receive the pay that should have gone into the treasury of the nation. The railroad company claims that it has, by its charter and the treaty of 1866, the right to purchase and use ties and timber necessary to build its road; and as the Choctaw Nation did not provide a way to purchase the same, therefore the railroad company purchased, as best it could, of individuals of the nation. Although such matters create dissatisfaction with the majority of the nation, yet they peaceably await the action of the railroad company to settle any claims for ties or timber which by mutual consent were not claimed by or paid to individuals, and which I expect the railroad company will soon settle.

The peaceable character and law abiding disposition of these people I think must excel that of most Indian tribes. They seem as ready to have their private difference adjusted by their courts as do the white people, and they treat with the utmost respect all the wishes and commands of the United States Government. Their laws are few and not generally well executed, yet in most cases they respect each other s rights.

I have been very much pleased with the religious interest manifested by them, especially by the Choctaws. They attend religious meetings, and seem anxious to know the truth, and many of them, members of churches, appear to be living Christian lives.

Some of the freedmen are improving farms and accumulating property. They seem very well satisfied in all respects, except the uncertainty of their right to vote and the want of any educational opportunities for them. The honorable Secretary of the Interior decided that they clearly had a right to vote, but the disposition of the Chickasaws and Choctaws has been to oppose it, and the freedmen have therefore not voted for fear of offending them. The freedmen seem very anxious to have school privileges, and say they will furnish school buildings if by any means teachers and books can be obtained for them.

As I stated in my last monthly report, I hope some provision will be made to meet this want. I wish the Choctaw and Chickasaw people could see that it was for their interest to educate these freedmen and thus prevent crime and secure the general welfare of society.

The subject of surveying the lands of the Choctaw Nation, and having them allotted to members of the nation, has occupied their minds more than any other subject since my arrival here. A large number of these people are in favor of this measure. I believe all the Chickasaws are in favor of it. Some of the Choctaw leaders have represented to the less enlightend part of the nation that they will lose the title to their lands if they are surveyed and allotted. They also represent that there would be no protection given them against the occupation of their lands by the whites when they are surveyed. They forget the assurances given them in the treaty of 1866, and remember only that they had to leave Mississippi against the wishes of some of them. I think the number is increasing who favor dividing their lands; and I hope it may be done very soon, and in accordance with some plan approved by themselves. Many difficulties arise because the title is in the nation, but in a certain sense claimed by individuals thereof, and (as in the matter of the ties hereinbefore mentioned) the individual takes advantage of any want of action by the nation. If the lands were owned in severalty by the members of the nations, each would jealously guard his rights, and all would unite in protecting individual interests against intruding whites. Besides each would be stimulated by the other in increasing and making his property valuable and drawing from it all the profits he could. Thus the nations would be enriched in proportion as the members were thriving, and religious and educational advantages would come to them through the means of their wealth.

Very respectfully, your obedient servant,

A. PARSONS,
United States Indian Agent.

Hon. EDWARD P. SMITH,
Commissioner Indian Affairs, Washington, D. C.

18.

CREEK AGENCY, INDIAN TERRITORY,
September 30, 1873.

SIR: In compliance with the duty imposed upon me as United States agent for the Creek Indians, I have the honor to submit herewith my report of affairs at the Creek agency for the year ending September 30, 1873.

I assumed charge of this agency on the 1st day of May, of the present year, relieving my efficient predecessor, F. S. Lyon, esq., who for more than two years had labored faithfully for the best interests of the Government and the welfare of the Creek people, even to the sacrifice of his own interests, both socially and pecuniarily.

I found the residence of the agent to consist of an old worm-eaten log-house with two rooms, neither of which were lathed or plastered, corresponding (to draw it mild) with those inhabited by the poorest farmers in Posey County, Indiana. This building is situated in the center of a corn-field, with no trees or shrubberry of any kind around it to relieve the barrenness of the prospect, or to furnish shade during the intense heat of summer.

I received very valuable assistance from Major S. G. Vore in regard to the condition of affairs at the agency. Major Vore has been in this country among the Creeks and adjoining tribes for the last twenty-seven years, and is a walking encyclopedia of Indian history, and I desire to express my thanks for information and assistance. I found the Creeks divided into two factions by reason of political differences, which had existed since the late war, and which, at one time, had nearly culminated in bloodshed and civil strife. A special commission appointed by the Hon. Secretary of the Interior having investigated the causes of these differences and made their report to the Interior Department, a decision was pending.

Discovering signs of agitation among these two parties, which was being fanned on one side by irresponsible white men, I called the attention of the Department to the fact, and urgently requested that the decision above referred to be at once promulgated, which was promptly acted on, and the Checote or administration party recognized as the ruling power, and to whom allegiance was due; which decision was widely disseminated by me, and its purport and meaning fully explained. It had a most happy effect. The disaffected or Sands party at once accepted the situation, and sent their representatives to the nation's council, and came in and took part under the regular government; thus forever setting at rest these unfortunate difficulties which have caused this people so much trouble and expense.

GENERAL CONDITION OF THE CREEKS.

The general condition of the Creeks financially is much improved since the last annual report from this agency, an increased number of acres being under cultivation, and a larger amount of stock being raised. There are now about thirty-one thousand acres of ground tilled, (out of 3,215,469 acres, the number contained in the reserve,) on which have been raised 500,000 bushels of corn, 100,000 bushels of wheat, 75,000 bushels of potatoes, and about 5,000 bushels of other vegetables. They own about 15,000 head of horses, 35,000 head of cattle, and 10,000 head of hogs.

The greatest obstacle that seems to lie in the way of a more extensive cultivation of the soil, and the raising of stock, which has and will continue to be their means of livelihood, is the want of an example for them to follow in these pursuits. If the Government could run a model farm on the section of land which it has reserved by treaty on which to erect new agency buildings, which farm could be carried on without the expenditure of one dollar by the Government, outside of the amount required to stock it with modern farm implements, the lessons taught and the example given by this enterprise would be of more material advantage to the Creeks than anything that could be thought of, and would place them in a condition to compete with the white farmer, with whom they will evidently soon have to come in contact.

EDUCATIONAL.

There are thirty-three schools in the Creek Nation, two of which are mission-boarding schools, accommodating eighty scholars each. These two schools are supported by the nation and the religious denominations.

The Tullahassee mission school, carried on under the auspices of the Presbyterian board, is situated on a high point between the Arkansas and the Verdigris Rivers, about three and one-half miles north of the agent's residence. The mission building is 125 feet long and three stories high, the lower story for dining-hall and rooms for teachers, the second for recitation-rooms, and the upper for sleeping apartments. This school is under the superintendency of Mr. Sanford Perryman, a citizen of the nation, and a graduate of this mission. The board selects the teachers and pays their salaries, and the nation pays $70 per annum for each of the eighty pupils attending.

The Asbury mission, situated near North Forktown, and near the banks of the North Fork of the Canadian River, is under the auspices of the Methodist board, and is conducted and supported in the same manner as the Tullahassee mission. Rev. Mr. Holmes is the superintendent, and with his efficient corps of teachers has made the school a source of admiration and pride to the nation.

There are five schools for colored children, which are well attended, and making commendable progress. The average attendance in these five schools is thirty.

The other schools among the Creeks, numbering twenty-four, maintained at an annual expense of nearly $10,000, are located in different parts of their country. The school-buildings are simply log hovels, without proper or even passable sittings, desks, or other furniture, and but few of them are furnished with maps, globes, blackboards, or other aids found in the poorest schools outside the Territory among whites or blacks. There is a manifest need of some system of books among these schools entirely different from those now in use, and also of a much superior class of teachers than now employed. The majority of the adult Creeks cannot speak English, and their children, with great difficulty, learn to read and write English, and even then without comprehending the meaning of it. Save a few hours in the school-room, all their association and conversation is with those who cannot speak English, and is a fatal barrier to progress in their studies.

The amount of money now expended by the Creeks for these neighborhood schools is simply a waste; and I would earnestly recommend that the Government insist on a radical change in the entire system of education among these schools. Among the most important changes made should be the establishment of a normal school, for the purpose of furnishing teachers thoroughly trained, and permitting only the graduates of such an institution to teach in their schools. In the mean time, or until the normal school could furnish these teachers, the necessity should be met by those who are intrusted with the management of the school-funds, by removing the present incompetent teachers throughout the nation, and supplying their places with efficient, capable teachers from the States.

This subject, I conceive, should receive from the Government, in its capacity as guardian, the most careful consideration, as, in my judgment, advancement in civilization by these people can be obtained only through the school-room.

TERRITORIAL GOVERNMENT.

In view of the probable erection of a territorial government over this territory, I deem it proper to give my views on this subject, and the light in which it is looked at by the great majority of the Creek people. It is apparent to every intelligent man that there is a need of some laws that will apply to all in the Territory. The establishment of United States courts is an imperative necessity. The intercourse laws should be overhauled and amended so as to meet present demands, and the question of jurisdiction clearly settled.

As the signs of the times seem to indicate the erection of a territorial government over this country, it is but right to say that the people of the nation are almost unanimously opposed to the measure, because they look upon it as only the first move to deprive them of their last resting-place; a move that will open upon their defenceless heads a flood of evil that will only cease when the last of their race have disappeared; a move that will fill their beautiful and fruitful country with white men who will be too numerous to be removed, and then the Government will pay them for their lands at the rate of thirty cents per acre. These are their fears and their reasons for opposing the measure, and no arguments or assurances can make them think differently. They claim, also, the rights guaranteed to them by treaty where they are assured that no such government shall be erected over them without their consent.

If Congress does pass these laws making this country a Territory of the United States, great care should be taken to throw around the Indian such safeguards and protections as will prevent the disposal of their lands to speculators, or the overrunning of their country by white settlers, thus realizing their worst fears. But our Government, with an almost illimitable supply of other lands, will not permit these to be realized.

With a stable government to protect them; with United States courts among them to deal out justice to all; with missionaries and schools working among them, they will soon take their stand, dignified by labor, and enobled by learning, among our free people, the peers of all.

Very respectfully, your obedient servant,

E. R. ROBERTS,
United States Indian Agent.

Hon. EDWARD P. SMITH,
Commissioner of Indian Affairs, Washington, D. C.

19.

SEMINOLE AGENCY, *September* 1, 1873.

SIR: Since my last annual report the Seminoles have uniformly sustained their former reputation for morality, steady and peaceable habits, industry, and success in their agricultural operations. There is an evident improvement among them in everything pertaining to a higher status of civilization; and with proper management there seems to be no reason why they should not, in a few years, attain that condition of civilization and moral and intellectual comprehension of duty and responsibility which would qualify them for becoming honored and worthy citizens of the United States; an end for the accomplishment of which every effort of both church and state should be steadily put forth. But the consummation of this desirable condition of this people will be retarded in the ratio of the increase of a white population among them, embracing, as it does, many individuals whose conduct is not sustained by the laws of any civilized country. Many of the whites seek a residence among the Indians, where there is no law to restrain them in the gratification of their evil passions; whose manner of living shows that they have no conception of responsibility to the Father of us all for their violation of laws, human and divine, and whose teachings, by precept and example, are demoralizing even "to the noble red man" in a state of nature.

In order to make the efforts to civilize and christianize the Indians successful in the shortest time and with the least expense, none should be permitted to live among them whose principles are not in accord with these designs. Penalties should be attached to laws of Congress, prohibiting whites from living among the Indians unless by permission, and enforced when violated. An act of prohibition without a penalty is of no practical account.

These men have produced and are still producing troubles and dissensions among the Indians, and are endeavoring, and with a measure of success, to alienate them from those who are most interested in their temporal and spiritual welfare. Their example and teachings are in direct opposition to the humane and Christian policy of the Government. It would not, I think, be considered a usurpation of authority, nor as dictating to conscience, to prohibit the entrance of such men, and their consequent practice of evil, by statutes and penalties, since it is the purpose of the Government to regain the confidence of the Indians by a generous and honorable intercourse with them, thus acquiring access to their better natures.

Notwithstanding the unsettled state of affairs connected with the present reservation, they have made some enlargement of their fields and improvements in their houses and other buildings,, and have planted a greater area in corn, potatoes, and rice, than in former years; but, on account of the cultivation of the crops being prevented in the early part of the season by the wet weather, more perhaps than of the drought in the latter part, the yield will not be more than half as large as it was last year, or not more than half a crop. The rice crop will be very small.

It is evident from the anxiety of the Seminoles to obtain work, their willingness and their adaptability to various kinds of work, that, had they the inducement of a prospect of remunerative prices for their labor, or of securing a market for the products of the soil, they would labor still more diligently and successfully as agriculturists. It is the prospect of realizing something more than is merely necessary to sustain life that creates industry, and stimulates and brings into activity the energies and inventive faculties that lie dormant in races of men who have never had any motive to labor, beyond the necessity of satisfying their present wants.

Since the agency building was commenced, the 10th of July, some dissatisfaction has been produced, because all who made application did not obtain employment, and those who did obtain it appear sorry that their labor is about ended there, the building being now nearly finished. To say that "the Indians won't work, and can't be civilized any more than the wild buffalo of the plains," is equivalent to saying that he is not made of the same blood as the rest of the human family, with hands not only designed for, but so nicely and admirably adapted to labor, and with an intellect capable of cultivation and expansion, enabling him to comprehend the benefits and blessings attending the higher attainments of civilization, and their superiority to customs and manners approaching those of the lower order of animals. Many of them have a keener perception, and a higher appreciation of the duties of civilized life and its Scriptural requirements, than some of those who would degrade them to the condition of man in his original form, as assumed in the Darwinian theory.

The sanitary condition of the Seminoles has been very good during the past year; and, although one or two valuable men died during my absence last winter, there have been fewer deaths than in previous years. Much suffering from disease and protracted illness has been prevented through the means furnished by the Department; and, although it increases the labor and care of the agent, it is still a source of pleasure to know that good is being accomplished for them through this means.

Your district schools have been in successful operation during the last year; and, although the attendance has not been as good as in former years, there has been no abatement of interest in education on the part of either parents or children; but, owing to the severity of the past winter, and other causes that could not be obviated, the number in attendance during the winter was very small. The coming session, it is to be hoped, will open with brighter prospects for the Seminole children.

The mission school was suspended on the 1st of March, on account of the resignation of the missionary, Rev. J. R. Ramsay, and will probably not be resumed the coming year, in consequence of the embarrassed state of the Presbyterian Board of Foreign

Missions, from which all the funds for defraying the expenses of the mission and school were derived. But in place of this, I hope to be able to start a school at the agency, which will answer all the purposes of a mission school; for which I have engaged a teacher possessing all the qualifications requisite to make a first-class missionary teacher, mainly through the efforts of the Seminoles, a room is now being built, 20 by 30 feet in size, as a basement to the church, for school purposes, and will be ready for occupancy in about one month. This is one of the most important enterprises ever undertaken by the Seminoles, and I trust there will be no lack of spirit and energy displayed until it is completed.

The Seminoles still protest against any form of territorial government, enacted by Congress, that would in any of its departments, legislative, executive, or judicial, include citizens of the United States. They maintain that their people are not yet prepared by education, nor by a desire to abandon their ancient form of government, to submit to any authority but that of their own people; that to force upon them any form of government with which they are wholly unacquainted would be destructive to the prospect they have of ultimately becoming fitted for citizenship of the United States; and that the result would be equally injurious to their hopes if the territory were to be opened to white settlement.

Very respectfully, your obedient servant,

HENRY BREINER,
United States Indian Agent.

Hon. EDWARD P. SMITH, *Commissioner.*

20.

QUAPAW AGENCY, IND. T., *Ninthmonth* 15, 1873.

ENOCH HOAG,
Superintendent Indian Affairs:

In accordance with instructions of the Department I present herewith my annual report of the condition of this agency. The progress of the various tribes under my care during the past year has been good, though perhaps not so rapid as I could have wished.

All the tribes have worked well in farming this season, but owing to the very dry weather and the ravages of the chinch-bugs their crops are cut short, not over half a crop on an average. Still all, except possibly the Quapaws, will have a sufficient amount of grain for home consumption, and possibly some to spare.

Considerable additions have been made to the amount of land in cultivation by all the tribes; though, owing to some extent to the limited numbers able to work in some of them, the additional amount improved has been small. The Eastern Shawnees in particular have but a very small number of able-bodied men in their tribe.

The "Black Bob" Shawnees, who are living on the reservation of the above-named tribe, are not making very rapid progress in farming; partly, I believe, in consequence of the uncertainty of their condition, not knowing whether they will ever be enabled to acquire a right to their homes, and partly owing to the shiftless and demoralized habits contracted during their wandering and homeless lives. Quite a number of their children have been induced to attend the Seneca, Shawnee, and Wyandotte mission school, where their progress and conduct has been such as to lead to the hope that the rising generation, at least, of the "Black Bobs" will be useful and honorable people.

It is important that the necessary legislation may be had to sell the reserve of this people in Kansas at an early day, so that they may be enabled to get a permanent home. The Eastern Shawnees, though not actively opposed to education, were on the first opening of their school very averse to placing their children in it; but by the exercise of much care and persuasion I have at length induced nearly all the children of proper age to attend, and many of the parents are much interested in the progress their children are making.

The Senecas from being, with a few exceptions, at the time of making my last annual report, bitterly opposed to schools, are now, except a small portion of one band, decidedly favorable, and, I believe, on the approach of winter, quite a large addition to the already respectable number of their children attending school will avail themselves of the present good opportunities for acquiring an education. They have been tolerably successful in their farming the present season.

The Wyandotts have had a year of prosperity and have made considerable improvements in their farms and buildings. They have kept the greater portion of their children in school most of the time during the past year, and they have made good progress.

The Ottawas have continued to do well. Their farms have been well cultivated. Their school has also been well attended, and has given good satisfaction. Great loss will result to the cause of education and civilization in this tribe if, for lack of means, we shall be compelled to close this school. The confederated Peorias, &c., have broken out and prepared for cultivation a large additional amount of land this season. The Miamies who are confederating with them have also done well for the first season in the country. A trip across this reservation plainly answers the question, "Is the Indian susceptible of civilization?" in the affirmative. The improvements they have made in the last three years and their continued efforts show plainly that, with proper encouragement, much can be accomplished.

The Quapaws are, I believe, gaining. Some additions were made to their area of land in cultivation this spring; and many of them show a disposition to do more than ever before. Their school is in a very encouraging condition. The greater portion of the children of a suitable age to attend school do so, although they do not yet fully appreciate the importance of regularity and punctuality. This, I think, can be overcome with care. With all our discouragement the present average is better than those best acquainted with them hoped for. They have a much larger reserve than is needed for their use, or they can ever put in cultivation. I think much greater benefit would accrue to them if at least half of their lands could be disposed of to some other tribe, and the money they would bring used in improving the remainder. The efforts and labors of A. C. and E. H. Tuttle, in charge of Quapaw mission, have been of great benefit both to the children and adults of the tribe.

I wish, as soon as practicable, to have buildings erected and a mission school opened for the benefit of the confederated Peorias and Miamies. The present day-school among the Peorias gives good satisfaction and is accomplishing a good work; but I believe that more can be reached and a more permanent impression made by means of a boarding school than in any other manner.

During the past season I have had farms opened at each of the missions in this agency. That at the Quapaw mission was fenced by money appropriated by the chiefs from funds belonging to the tribe. I paid for the plowing out of the "civilization fund." I got a portion of it plowed very early and had about sixty acres planted in corn, beans, pumpkins, and various other kinds of garden vegetables. Notwithstanding the unpropitious season and its being "sod," quite a valuable crop has been raised. The school has been supplied with vegetables all summer, and a considerable amount will be left over for winter use.

In pursuance of an agreement made with the Ottawas that they should fence forty acres for a mission farm, providing the Government would do the plowing, I had the breaking done, but the tribe failed to get the fencing completed. About five acres have been cultivated this season, and have produced quite a supply of vegetables, &c., for the use of the school. I hope to have all fenced in time for a crop next year.

The Wyandotte council donated a sufficient amount of their national funds to pay for fencing 160 acres for a mission farm at the Seneca, Shawnee, and Wyandott school. I had eighty acres plowed this summer, but owing to the dry weather and some other adverse circumstances the crop will amount to but very little. I had not expected very much from the sod crop as it seldom amounts to much except under the most favorable surroundings. Still enough has been done the present season to show that in the future much of the expense of carrying on the schools can be met by the products of the farms, if we can be furnished sufficient means to properly stock them. A good supply of milk cows in particular would be of great profit; hogs, also, will pay well.

The agency buildings at this place are very old, and afford a very inadequate protection from the weather during the winter; and, in summer, owing to their faulty construction, are uncomfortably warm. It is essential to the health and comfort of the agent and his family that an appropriation should be made for the speedy construction of more suitable buildings for the residence and office of the agent.

Although there has been considerable diminution in the amount of drunkenness among these Indians, yet the difficulties which exist in enforcing the present laws against selling whiskey to them by the citizens of the towns along the borders renders it well nigh impossible to obtain a conviction for this offense; yet I believe the public sentiment of the better class of citizens is improving rapidly. I have, after long continued efforts, succeeded in getting two of the worst cases in Baxter Springs placed under bonds for their appearance at the next term of the United States court at Topeka. I hope that their conviction will result in frightening others engaged in the nefarious traffic so that they will abandon it.

Very respectfully,

H. W. JONES,
United States Indian Agent.

21.

SAC AND FOX AGENCY, *Ninthmonth, 1st*, 1873.

I herewith submit my first annual report of the Sac and Fox Indians under my charge.

Numbering about five hundred, they are located on one of the most beautiful reservations in the Indian Territory, amply sufficient in extent to accommodate all the detached bands of the tribe in the various portions of the country. It is claimed, upon pretty good authority, that about two hundred of these Indians, under Mo-ko-ho-ko, a disaffected chief, still remain as *vagrants* in the State of Kansas, being excluded by treaty provision from participating in the annuities of the tribe while away from their reservation. Also a few lodges still remain in Iowa, confederated with straggling bands of Winnebagoes and Pottawatomies, and although the Sac and Fox portion of this confederation cannot number more than eighty souls they are allowed, under this arrangement, to draw annuities from the common tribal fund for about three hundred persons.

That portion of the tribe who have removed to the reservation, and are under my charge, are prospering in their agricultural and educational interests. A mission school and boarding-house, provided for in treaty, have been erected and are ready for use, and competent teachers have been secured to take charge of the children who manifest a disposition to avail themselves of the opportunity of education.

The number of our fields have been increased and their area enlarged during the year, and these Indians are now encouraged in the belief that they are settled upon a a permanent home, to which they invite for settlement the straggling bands of the tribe now wandering elsewhere, and particularly that portion confederated, as above stated, with the Winnebagoes and Pottawatomies in Iowa, who are, without benefit to themselves and to the detriment of the people of that State, drawing quite too large a proportion of the annuities of the tribe, and making up their scanty subsistence by a regular system of begging from door to door, among their white neighbors resident in Iowa.

The Absentee Shawnees under my charge are in a prosperous condition. They number nearly seven hundred. They all live in houses provided by themselves, and generally have cultivated farms. They subsist themselves, with the oversight of the agent and some assistance by way of agricultural implements, &c. Their educational interests require attention. A good school, established at the expense of the Government, is well supported and is flourishing; but the house and facilities are entirely insufficient to relieve their necessities. I would recommend that $7,000 be appropriated by Congress for the erection of suitable buildings for a mission school for these deserving people, and that $5,000 annually, for a brief period, be appropriated for the support of the same. The effects of an institution of this kind established among a people who appreciate the need of education and will improve every facility afforded them, who have no annuities, no assistance provided by treaty, *cannot be overestimated upon the wild tribes who surround them.* They are peaceable, loyal, and industrious, and a liberal outlay on the part of the Government for their education is but just, and is but a short avenue to the civilization of the wild tribes above mentioned, and will be found to be strict economy in the management of Indians.

Very respectfully,

JOHN H. PICKERING,
United States Indian Agent.

ENOCH HOAG,
Superintendent Indian Affairs, Lawrence, Kans.

22.

OSAGE AGENCY, I. T., *Ninthmonth*, 1873.

ESTEEMED FRIEND: My fourth annual report of the Neosha agency is herewith submitted.

My statistical account of the population of the Osages taken from the spring enrollment is 2,823. Last year the number given was 3,906, yet I believe the tribe is on the increase, the true number being about 3,500. It is almost impossible to obtain a correct census.

Early in the current year a delegation of the Kaw Indians, with commissioners Stanley and Spray, visited the Osages with a view of selecting their future home in this reservation, as provided in Osage treaty of Thirdmonth, 1872. The requisite amount of land was chosen from the northwest corner of this reservation and the boundaries determined by the commissioners.

Having been to much expense and trouble in procuring a good machine for thrashing and cleaning the crop of wheat harvested by the Osages, from the fifty acres sown in their former reservation, I was much nonplussed to find that a Cherokee named Joseph Bennett had taken possession of the crop and was threshing and wasting it. I notified him to desist and quit the premises, but he refused to do so, claiming the improvements and crop under Cherokee law, which provides that "intruders" shall loose their crops and improvements. The occupation of the Cherokee country by the Osages for a short time by mistake, yet by authority of the United States Government, certainly should not place them in position of intruders. I trust the Department will instruct the commissioners who are to appraise the Osage improvements, as provided in treaty of Thirdmonth, 1872, to ascertain the probable amount of wheat and its value taken by this Cherokee, and allow the Osages a credit for the amount on the lands purchased from the Cherokees.

Thy invitation to the governor and chiefs to visit thee at Lawrence, was regarded by those who had participated in depredations on persons and property on the plains as a trap to get them into prison. The governor and some other leading men could not be induced to go; fifteen chiefs and head-men consented. This their first ride on the cars, three days' stay in the city of Lawrence, visiting the schools, shops, and other places of interest, the plain and emphatic talk they had from their superintendent in reference to depredations on the plains, the encouragement they received for good conduct, made so deep an impression upon their minds that they are now the principal leaders in their bands in favor of civilization.

As the reservation is large and very broken, not admitting of dense settlement, I have made five divisions of it, viz:

Names of divisions.	Population.	No. of acres planted.
Agency	400	225
Bird Creek	350	345
Hominy	1,000	200
Salt Creek	1,000	300
Little Osages	750	1,120

Each division is in charge of an efficient farmer and assistants, who reside at a station most central and convenient for the Indians in his care, where are kept oxen, plows, wagons and other farming implements for general use in that division.

The agent visits each station as often as practicable to see how the work is progressing and advise with farmer and chiefs as to their necessities and future operations.

This method has worked admirably, bringing all the Indians to some extent under the influence of the agent. These divisions are being provided with necessary dwellings for the employés at the stations, none of which are nearer the agency than fifteen miles, and some of them are fifty miles from each other.

Immediately after the payment in Tenthmonth the tribe went on their winter hunt, except those who had no ponies and a few who staid on the reservation to try and acquire civilized habits. To these I agreed to pay $2.50 per hundred for rails split by them and laid up in a good staked and ridered fence inclosing prairie suitable for cultivation, I promising to break all they would thus inclose for their own use. It was necessary to pay them in order that they could obtain means to support their families, otherwise it would have been necessary to issue rations, to them, which would have destroyed all incentive to labor. Fifty-eight blanket Indians accepted and went to work on the above proposition, splitting and laying up in fence about eighty-one thousand rails, thus supporting their families and acquiring skill in labor; but what is still better, they have now a spot of ground they call "home," which they prize very highly, and have no thoughts of again returning to the chase.

It was quite late in the spring when the Indians returned from their winter hunt. Almost every family then selected a claim and desired to have prairie broken for farming purposes. Although I purchased several more breaking-teams and hired others to break and plow, I was unable to meet their urgent demands. At least eleven hundred acres have been broken and eight hundred acres plowed for them. There are about 530 families in the tribe; of these 209 have now plowed land from one up to eighty acres each; the remainder should be similarly provided for next spring. The corn and vegetable crop this season far exceeds that grown by the Osages in any former year. The governor, and some of the head-men who have been very conservative, now finding their people almost unanimously in favor of farming, are advocating the same in council and in private.

There are about twelve thousand ponies in the tribe, and a proposition to exchange some of them for stock-cattle is favorably entertained by those desiring to quit a roving life. During the extreme cold of the past winter many of the Indians suffered a great deal from pneumonia, caused by their scanty clothing and their custom of wearing moccasins, which, during the wet weather, are scarcely any protection to the feet, but, by being constantly wet, engender pulmonary diseases. I have secured the services of a good shoemaker, and a number of them are now wearing boots and shoes, the demand for which far exceeds the supply.

The large number of Osages and their scattered condition when on the reservation make it impossible for one physician to visit all the sick and administer to their wants. A young half-breed of fair education and intelligence is now studying medicine with the physician, and renders good service as assistant and interpreter. The physician furnishes his own conveyance and forage. Most of his patients are twenty miles or more from the agency in different directions, rendering his labors very onerous. The increasing demand for his practice can only be met by the erection of a hospital at the agency. I inclose his views on that subject.

The labor in the blacksmith-shop so increased that it became necessary to put up an additional forge, which has been in constant use; two of the workmen are Osages. One or more wheelwrights (Osages) have been busily employed the greater part of the season. The services of the gunsmith (an Osage) have proved indispensable.

The saw-mill was put in operation in the latter part of Thirdmonth, and has since been running almost constantly in order to supply the native lumber required in the agency buildings, and by the Osages for finishing their log houses, and making rude furniture for them. Excepting the sawyer and engineer the labor at the saw-mill is performed by blanket Osages. The machinery is of the best quality, and the building, 41 by 70 feet, is a substantial frame structure with stone foundation. The grist-mill machinery has been purchased, but the building has not yet been erected. A substantial and commodious barn with stone basement for stables has been built for agency use. The other agency buildings are being put up by contract. The agent's, physician's, and blacksmith's dwellings, the warehouse and blacksmith-shop are all inclosed, but none of them yet completed. About half of the work is done on the church and school-house. The last-named buildings are of good quality of sandstone, an inexhaustible supply of which is easily obtained at the agency.

Sabbath-schools, evening schools for spelling, and meetings for worship have been carefully fostered and attended by most of the employés and some of the Indians. Last Sabbath fifty-four persons took part in the scriptural exercises, forty-five recited texts, and about one hundred attended religious service. The moral tone at the agency will compare favorably with the most refined neighborhoods in the States. Every employé is expected to perform missionary work. Among them are found ministers, elders or deacons, and active lay members of various religious denominations. Thirty-three Osage children have been in attendance at the Catholic school at Osage Mission, Kansas. The boarding-school building at the agency will soon be in readiness for pupils.

A superstitious custom prevails among the Osages of taking the life of an enemy soon after the death of a friend or relative, founded on the belief that the spirit of the departed cannot rest until a sacrifice has been made for them. A son of one of the head-men of the tribe went in mourning on account of the death of his wife, and led a party of young men to the plains seeking for a victim. They met Es-ad-da-ua, chief of the Wichita Indians, hunting buffalo, near the salt plains. They professed to believe he was designed by the Great Spirit for them, killed and scalped him, then returned to the reservation, when the customary scalp-dance was had, then the mourning ceased.

The information soon came to this office of the murder of the distinguished chief, which was supposed by his people to have been done by the Osages. The Osages, fearing the consequence of this rash act of their young men, and apprehending an attack from the Plains Indians, collected together for defense, thus greatly impeding the operations of those who were endeavoring to put in crops. The chiefs and leading men severely condemned the act, and sent a letter to the Wichitas, offering satisfaction. A delegation of thirty-eight Wichitas visited this agency soon after, and accepted from the Osages money, ponies, blankets, guns, &c., to the amount of fifteen hundred dollars, as compensation and satisfaction. One of a similar mourning party soon after killed a white man on the plains, but was also mortally wounded himself. This custom has, with the Indians, all the sacredness of a religious duty, and I apprehend more victims have been sacrificed by them than was heretofore supposed. Information can now be had, through the employés at the different stations and confidential Indians, of the forming of those parties, which require several days' ceremony to perfect, and, by persuasion, gifts, and threats, all of them have since been broken up. The usual amount of depredations by the Osages on persons and property have not been committed on the plains this summer, which can be largely attributed to the presence of B. K. Wetherill in their camps and on their lines of travel; a part of his duties being to keep informed of the location of the different bands while they are on the hunt, and investigate any depredations they may commit, so that remuneration may be promptly paid by the guilty party, and to make them feel that the eye of the Government is constantly upon them.

The Osages returned from their summer hunt prematurely some weeks since, on account of one of their men being attacked and severely wounded by a small party of Arapahoes; his horse was killed. They are waiting to hear from the chiefs of that tribe whether the act is condemned or not, and are willing that friendly relations should still exist if satisfaction is offered; otherwise they propose to retaliate. I have no doubt the difficulty can be peacefully adjusted.

The Osages regard the recent valuation of their reservation at seventy cents per acre as a plain violation of the promises of the Government which guaranteed to them a home in the Indian Territory on lands that should not cost them more than fifty cents per acre. I presume this will not be questioned by any citizen who attended the various councils held with Osages by the Indian commissioners on that subject; but, aside from obligations plain and implied, the land would certainly not be valued above fifty cents per acre by competent persons after seeing it.

At the payment in Sixthmonth two prominent Cherokees, C. N. Vann and W. P. Adair, were in the camps of the Osages for several days, counseling them to sign an order on the honorable Secretary of the Interior for the sum of three hundred and thirty thousand dollars as payment of a claim for alleged services rendered the Osages in procuring the defeat of the treaty made by the Osages with the L. L. & G. Railroad Company; also for procuring the passage of the act whereby the Kansas Osage lands were taken in trust by the Government to sell at one dollar and twenty-five cents per acre. Those who have a right to know attribute the defeat and success of these two measures to other agencies. The treaty was withdrawn from the Senate by the President upon the report of the superintendent of the Central Superintendency after a council with the Osages on the subject. The act referred to was a part of the Indian appropriation bill, passed July 15, 1870, having the approval of the President, his board of Indian commissioners, Secretary of the Interior, Commissioner of Indian Affairs, the chairmen of the Senate and House Committees on Indian Affairs, and all of the leading men in Congress, and all the philanthropic and earnest friends of the Indians, because it was an act of justice, plain and uncovered, requiring no corrupting influence to make for it hopeful and constant supporters.

I interviewed these Cherokees to ascertain the nature of their services. Not obtaining the desired information, I requested them to desist importuning the Osages, interfering with the business of the chiefs at the agency, and give me an opportunity to investigate their claim, and, if it was just, I had no doubt the Government would authorize the payment of it. This was met with an implied threat in that if I would let them alone they would let me alone. I openly advised the chiefs in council not to sign any agreement nor commit themselves to any amount until the officers of the Government could ascertain whether these Cherokees had performed any services for them or not. Several of the chiefs refrained from counseling with them afterward; but through persuasive influences, that were generally believed in camp to be improper, several chiefs were induced to sign such an order, after the Cherokees had reduced the sum to two hundred and thirty thousand dollars. No member of the Little Osage tribe of any position signed the order, thus preventing the document having any binding force on the tribes. A half-breed of known integrity has left on file in my office an affirmation stating that fully one-half of the names affixed to the paper were not present, and many of them have since informed me, after hearing their names had been attached, that they had not authorized any one to do so, and it was done against their will.

After these Cherokees had left the agency, the half-breeds proceeded to get up a remonstrance which the masses of the tribe appear to have signed, including all the head-men of the Little Osages and most of the smaller chiefs of the Great Osages. At a subsequent council held about the 25th ultimo, Watianka, the leading spirit favoring the payment of the Cherokee claim, informed me that he understood the sum to be two thousand three hundred dollars instead of two hundred and thirty thousand dollars, and desired those who had not signed the order to sign the remonstrance and prevent the payment of the claim. At that, four out of the six principal chiefs of the bands signing, did sign a revocation of their order, and requested the Department to authorize their superintendent and agents of the Cherokees and Osages to investigate the claim of those Cherokees for services, aud pay what they deemed just and right; which request I hope will be regarded, such being the cool and unbiased wish of the tribes.

Respectfully,

I. T. GIBSON, *Agent.*

ENOCH HOAG; *Superintendent Indian Affairs.*

23.

KIOWA AND COMANCHE AGENCY, INDIAN TERRITORY,
Eighthmonth 30, 1873.

DEAR FRIEND: In accordance with the Department requirements, I submit my annual report, which is necessarily fractional, as I have only been in charge of this agency five months. I arrived here late in the Thirdmonth, and took charge the 1st of the

Fourthmonth. During the first month of my administration I had a great many visits or special calls from the Indians, anxious to become acquainted with their new father, which afforded me the opportunity of forming and cultivating their acquaintance. Many of them were also drawn hither, expecting soon to meet their kindred and friends then held as prisoners in Texas, whose release had been promised them, provided they complied with certain requirements made of them by the Department, which they professed to have fully done; hence [they] felt that they had a right to expect their friends, but had to wait far beyond the time set, the Kiowas being still waiting. The Qua-ha-da Comanche women were fortunately not under State control, being held by the military, and their detention beyond the time set for release would seem to have been unavoidable, as transportation was scarce, and just at the time of their being *en route* an abundance of rain fell, causing the streams to overflow their banks and very much impede the travel; their release was almost three months after the time promised, and though much of it could be accounted for from unavoidable causes, still the anxiety of the Indians to see their friends made them very restless, and filled them with surprise. On the 10th day of Sixthmonth, the train, in charge of Capt. Robert MacClermont, arrived at the agency, having one hundred women and children on board, who were received by me, and on the following day turned over to their friends at the close of a very pleasant and satisfactory council. Captain MacClermont deserves kind remembrance in this report for the faithful and energetic manner in which he discharged the duty imposed upon him. The Kiowas have not been as fortunate as their red brothers in receiving their friends, but through the long months of spring and summer have had to wait and quietly nurse the feelings of suspense which one disappointment after another would create, and amid it all, though as wild as the wildest, as a tribe, still, the better-disposed have been able to hold in check or perfect control the more evil, and I may truthfully inscribe here that, notwithstanding the seeming failure on the part of the Government to make good its solemn promises to its wild red children, they have not failed on their part to make good in every particular all the requirements of them, and to-day deserve the commendation of the world for their behavior in the face of so much and such gross disappointment as has been heaped upon them.

Notwithstanding the season was much advanced when I came, I had plowing and planting done for a number of Comanches and two Apaches; had their fields substantially fenced; and had not the season been so dry they would have had a very good yield of corn. Some of the Comanches went themselves into the field and worked, while others were better satisfied to send their wives to represent them. The Apaches were very attentive, working themselves with the hoe. Apache John, a chief, is especially deserving of mention; he worked hard, had all the weeds hoed out, and, in addition to his corn, has a fine crop of watermelons, some of which he has brought me as a present. It was a very nice sight to see one who a few months ago was regarded as a wild and dangerous man drive up in his wagon (I had given him one) and unload from it a number of fine melons of his own cultivation and raising. Truly his case affords encouragement for others, and gives renewed hope to the philanthropist that the day is coming when the wild red man of the plains shall become civilized and a tiller of the soil or follower of other industrious pursuits. The Delawares have very good crops; their locality has been more favored with rain; they are much further advanced in civilization than either of the other tribes of this agency; their number is but few. A large number of the Comanches, a few of the Apaches and Kiowas, have become anxious for farms or fields next year, and I feel encouraged to believe our list of farmers will be largely increased with the next year.

When I took charge, I told the Indians in council that I had come among them as their friend, and desired us to live together as friends. As a proof of my confidence in them, I had the soldiers whom I found on duty removed, and relied upon them to conduct themselves in a peaceable and friendly manner; told them with their help we could make this a peaceable country to live in. I desired them to abstain from raiding or stealing. The chiefs promised me assistance; said if their young men would not listen, but ran off and stole horses, they would bring in to me all they brought back, and I could restore them to their owners. A short time ago I reminded the Comanches of their promise—told them I had heard some of their young men had been in Texas and brought back a number of horses. Within two weeks from the time I spoke to them, fifty-two head of horses and mules were delivered to me as having been stolen from Texas since I came in charge as agent. I did not make any threats of stopping rations, or anything of the kind; simply reminded them of their promises, and appealed to their better natures with the very satisfactory result referred to.

The present condition of the Indians is very hopeful. I do not think any very large bodies have gone raiding thus far this season. Small parties of Comanches have raided into Texas, and some of them have been reported as gone to Mexico. The Kiowas, I am satisfied, have none of them raided any, but have remained on the reservation awaiting the return of their people. The Apaches, too, have remained quiet; they seem very anxious to settle down and become farmers. Their situation at present is unfortunate in being divided—part at the Cheyenne and Arapahoe agency and part at this. Being all one tribe and kindred, they should all be at one agency.

The situation and location of this agency are bad. The agency office and commissaries are on the military reservation, and one and three-fourths miles from the shops, mill, and farm. Water has to be hauled from Bluff Creek, a distance of one mile. It would be much pleasanter were all the affairs of the agency situated more together. We are also in need of many conveniences and necessaries, such as a bakery and hospital.

Our boarding-school closed the last of Sixthmonth with a very satisfactory examination, commendable alike to teachers and scholars.

Thomas C. Batty has not been very successful in keeping up a school organization among the Kiowas, though much encouraged to believe he will get them to allow a regular school this fall and winter. Though not permitted by circumstances to teach their children in regular school during the summer, he has accomplished a great deal of good among them, exerting an influence for good which is very perceptible upon those with whom he is most intimately associated. Among the many difficulties of the country on the frontier, as we are, the peddling of whisky by unprincipled men is one of the greatest. Horse-stealing also causes us a great deal of trouble; being so near the Texas border, it affords an opportunity to quickly get beyond our jurisdiction. Another great trouble we have to contend with is to get witnesses to go to Fort Smith to appear in a case; the expense is several dollars more than the fees; hence many parties who, under ordinary circumstances, would give information by which culprits might be apprehended and brought to justice, decline to do so for fear of having to go to Fort Smith as a witness. By special police I have apprehended and arrested some whisky parties, wasting upon the ground almost a barrel of very poor Texas whiskey; have also recovered a number of Indian horses, and restored them to their owners.

Altogether I may say our prospects for the future are very encouraging, and I firmly believe if good faith is kept with these people, that the day will come when they will cease to be a burden to the Government, will become self-sustaining—with the spear turned into the pruning-hook, the art of war no longer learned, and the sweet name of Jesus spoken and loved by many, the elevating and redeeming influences of civilization exert its power among them, their nomadic lives be changed to that of the settled husbandman, with pleasant associations around.

In closing this hastily-written and imperfect report, I desire to return my sincere thanks to the superintendent and his chief clerk, Cyrus Beede, for the very great assistance they have rendered me, in the trying times through which I have had to pass. Neither would I be unmindful of the debt of gratitude I owe to Him, who has kept me as in the hollow of His hand, guiding me by His Spirit, to whom be everlasting praise.

Respectfully,

J. M. HAWORTH,
United States Indian Agent, Kiowas and Comanches.

ENOCH HOAG,
Superintendent Indian Affairs, Lawrence, Kans.

24.

UPPER ARKANSAS AGENCY, INDIAN TERRITORY,
Ninthmonth 1, 1873.

RESPECTED FRIEND: In compliance with instructions and the regulations of the Indian Department, I submit the following as my second annual report of the Indians under my charge, to wit:

CHEYENNES AND ARAPAHOES.

It gives me much pleasure to state that, since the date of my last annual report to the present time, the Cheyennes and Arapahoes have remained on what I have told them is their reservation, as tribes, at peace with all men, both white and Indian, and have preserved all their treaty promises with the Government, with two single exceptions, which will be noticed under appropriate head.

I cannot, however, report as much progress in the ways of civilization, agriculture, and farming as I was sanguine of doing at this time the preceding year, but as much, perhaps, as I can reasonably expect, when the circumstances under which we have labored are all known and understood.

THE ARAPAHOES,

as formerly, still rank first in adopting the ways, manners, and customs of the white man, and have remained as a tribe peaceable and friendly, although some of their young men have shown a disposition to be impudent and saucy when mingling with employés and other white men in the vicinity of the agency.

The main villages of this tribe were located during the forepart of last winter on the Cimarron River and its branches, small streams extending up into the southern portion of Kansas, where the buffalo were plenty. Here they were visited by hordes of dissolute white men, who engaged quite extensively in the whisky traffic, and to such proportions did this trade swell that I was compelled, in early winter, to obtain assistance from Gen. Jno. R. Brooke, commanding Camp Supply, to arrest and remove not less than thirty white men; and quite a number of ranches were captured, and some four hundred gallons of whisky and other spirituous liquors were destroyed; and soon after, at my earnest solicitation, the whole tribe removed on to the reservation, and quite a profitable winter's hunt ensued.

Early in the Fourthmonth the Arapahoes began to arrive at the agency, and by the 15th the whole tribe were gathered within a mile of the agency, and began preparations for their big medicine, which was afterward held on the North Fork, three miles east of the agency, in Fifthmonth.

On the first of Fourthmonth, 1873, Jno. F. Williams, agency blacksmith, left the vicinity of Camp Supply with Powder Face, an Arapahoe chief, and seven young men of his band, as witnesses summoned to appear before the grand jury of the judicial district of Kansas, then in session at Topeka, Kans., and through his untiring efforts quite a number of the aforesaid whisky peddlers were bound over for trial at the next term of court. But as this matter was fully reported in my monthly report for Fifthmonth, 1873, I deem it unnecessary to speak of it further here.

After some time spent in endeavoring to induce the Arapahoes to select sites for farms without success, I had the large agency field, situated east of the agency, plowed up and divided up into small sections, and to each band a small lot was assigned as a corn-field and melon-patch, but with indifferent success. (For full particulars, see statistical report of farming, hereto attached.)

The Arapahoes remained at the agency until the latter part of the Seventhmonth, when the main villages, under "Left Hand" and "Powder Face," left on their fall hunt; the remainder of the tribe followed about the 10th of Eighthmonth. I visited them in camp near Supply on the 25th ultimo, and by frequent intercourse hope to avoid last year's experience in the whisky traffic.

THE CHEYENNES.

In this tribe not much change has taken place for the better except that, as a tribe, they have remained friendly and, most of the time, have remained on the reservation, having only visited the agency from time to time to obtain rations and annuity-goods.

"Big Jake," "Whirlwind," "Little Robe," "Ma-nino-ake," "Big Horse," "Red Moon," and perhaps two-thirds of the tribe, visited the agency in Sixthmonth and staid about a month, but they soon grew tired of the locality and moved off up the Canadian River.

Only one depredation can be traced to this tribe during the past year, and that relates to the killing of the four surveyors on the Cimarron River, on the 19th day of Thirdmonth last, which occurred the next day after the introduction of a barrel of whisky into their camps, and while fifteen hundred Indians were drunk, and, no doubt, was partly in revenge for the death of some Cheyennes that were killed up on the Canadian River by some United States soldiers. I apprehend that if I had been able to notify the Indians of this agency of the presence and intentions of the survey party in time, and had been furnished the police force asked for in my last annual report, so as to keep improper characters out of the country, the above killing would not have occurred.

It is much regretted by all, and by none more so than the chiefs and head-men of the Cheyenne tribe. They are at present encamped on the Wolf River, southeast of Camp Supply, in the neighborhood of the "Antelope Hills." I visited them on the 20th ultimo at their villages, and while peace and hospitality abounded I was pained to see traces of ardent spirits in camp, and was sorry to learn that whisky in considerable quantities has made its way into their camps from toward New Mexico by Mexican trading "outfits."

The nomadic habits of this tribe of Indians is an effectual bar to their civilization.

ANNUITIES.

Owing to some mismanagement in the shipment of the annuity-goods for the Cheyennes and Arapahoes, they did not reach the agency in time to do the Indians much good, many of them not receiving them until late in the spring.

They consisted of the usual articles and were issued to Arapahoes, at their urgent request, in bulk, while to the Cheyennes the same method as reported last year was adhered to. I would say in this connection that the calico was very much damaged by being so long in transit, and being stored in leaky store-houses. I also desire to acknowledge the receipt of a box of goods for our mission-school, from the Women's Aid Society, in Philadelphia, Pa., containing many articles essentially necessary for the school, which are not furnished by Government.

SCHOOLS.

The progress of our school has been very good. We have not the past year been able to secure the attendance of any Cheyenne children, so that our school is mainly composed of Arapahoes and half-breed Arapahoes. During the time when the tribe was located at the agency we were full to the utmost capacity, sometimes as high as seventy scholars being present; but as the bands leave the agency the children go with them, and having no restraining power we are compelled to abide in the patience and watch the school day by day dwindle away, until at the present time but sixteen scholars are left. Those who have attended have made commendable progress, and we have faith that in the end our efforts will be crowned with success. For further information see statistical report on education and Superintendent Trueblood's report, herewith inclosed.

INDIAN FARMING.

We have made some little progress in the way of farming. "Big Mouth," "Yellow Horse," "Tall Bear" and some minor chiefs have made a beginning—some ten small patches of ground being planted and tilled by Arapahoes, comprising about sixty acres in all. The work was but imperfectly done, and the drought and grasshoppers have materially lessened the results; but we feel encouraged to believe that the attempt, small as it is, is but the beginning of greater efforts in the future.

We have broken no new ground except about ten acres broken and fenced separately for Big Mouth, the remainder of our Indian farmers being located in the large agency field that is situated about one mile east of the agency.

We have raised about 150 acres of corn for the agency; 95 acres more were planted, but the drought and grasshoppers have effectually destroyed it. Of the 150 acres reported, we can expect but little over half a crop.

Thirty acres of oats were sown in early spring, but dry cold weather coming on, the seed rotted, and the ground was replowed and planted in corn.

IMPROVEMENTS.

We have added some improvements to agency-buildings since last report. We have finished the mission-building, and erected a commodious drug-store and a consultation-room for the physician—a building that we have needed very much heretofore. We have in addition erected a house for Big Mouth, and another for "John Chalk," an Arapahoe brave, who has taken the lead of his tribe in manual labor. Having worked faithfully at the agency the past two years, and seemed deserving of some special attention, it is my intention to fence him a small farm adjoining his house, and give him some cows in the spring, should he still hold out faithful, and evince a disposition to do for himself. We have also remodeled most of the buildings for employés, lathing and plastering the rooms, and putting in good cellars with permanent stone walls.

Our fences have been to renew the past spring, as the immense herds of ponies that are kept in the vicinity of the agency make it extremely difficut to keep good fences. In addition to the foregoing, a small farm of ten acres has been fenced for Big Mouth, and a substantial stockade corral and pig-pen built adjoining his house; also a well dug.

SANITARY.

Owing to the extreme hot, dry weather experienced in this country the past summer, considerable sickness and a number of deaths have been recorded. I would again respectfully urge the necessity there is for a substantial hospital-building at this agency.

From further acquaintance with this people, I am satisfied that much of their superstitious "medicine" practices are dying out, and giving way to faith in the white man's medicine. I inclose report of physician for further information on this subject.

CIVIL LAW.

In concluding this report, I desire to say a few words in regard to civil law among Indians. I am of the opinion that the sooner these Indians are made amenable to the civil law, and personally responsible for their acts as individuals, the better it will be for all concerned, and especially for the efforts that are being put forth to civilize and christianize them. To punish a whole tribe or community for the acts of one or two evil-minded persons is folly in the extreme, and places the better-disposed completely in the power of a few reckless individuals; but so soon as these men are made to understand that they and they alone will be punished for guilty acts committed, the sooner will a wholesome dread of consequences be engendered.

I would respectfully call the attention of the Department to this subject, and ask that proper legislation be had in the premises. I also desire to again urge the Department to furnish me in some way with a police force, to operate against Indian outlaws, white horse-thieves, and whisky-peddlers. The descent on the whisky-ranches on the frontier of Kansas last winter, elsewhere referred to in this report, has inspired the denizens of that section with a wholesome dread of consequences that is salutary in the extreme, and must be maintained.

CONCLUSION.

My further acquaintance with these Indians emboldens me to say that the progress made during the past year in the avenues of civilization are encouraging, and leads me to the expression of my firm belief of the ultimate success of the peaceful policy. Work of this nature must necessarily be very slow, and requires at times deep and abounding faith, and an entire reliance on Him who doeth all things well.

We must first gain their confidence; and, in order to do this, they must know by our acts that we are interested in their affairs, and then they will be more ready to accept good counsels. To this end, it has been my practice to visit them in their distant camps to counsel with them on various subjects, in order that they may become better acquainted with me and I with them.

Please accept my grateful acknowledgments for assistance and kind co-operation extended to me while conducting my official intercourse.

Respectfully,

JNO. D. MILES,
United States Indian Agent, Cheyennes and Arrapahoes.

ENOCH HOAG, *Superintendent Indian Affairs.*

25.

WICHITA AGENCY, INDIAN TERRITORY,
Ninthmonth 1, 1873.

DEAR FRIEND: As required by instructions from the Indian Department, I herewith submit my fourth annual report.

Although this is my fourth annual report, I have been officially connected with the agency but about three years, my commission being dated Eighthmonth 21, 1870. The autumn of that year being one of unusual rains and freshets, but little could be done during the time toward commencing business for the new agency. Some provision, however, was made of a temporary nature, during the fall and winter, for the protection of animals and property, and preparation was made for an agency-house; but our work was not fairly under way till the following spring. It will be recollected that there were no improvements of any kind on the reservation; in consequence of which my family and all the employés, when they reached the settlements of these Indians, were exposed to great hardships during a cold and unusually stormy winter.

The Caddoes, Delawares, and Ionies were all living in ordinary skin or canvass lodges or rude wigwams covered with mats or grass; the Wichitas and kindred bands having built grass houses, in their own peculiar way, were more comfortably protected.

During the three years mentioned, ending Sixthmonth 30, 1873, there has been expended by the agent, in improvements made for bettering the condition of these Indians, the sum of eighty-one thousand two hundred and eighty dollars and sixty-two cents ($81,280.62) of the appropriations made by Congress for "colonizing and supporting Wichitas," or an average of twenty-seven thousand and ninety-three dollars and fifty-four cents ($27,093.54) per annum.

It would be impracticable to enumerate all the improvements that have been made upon the reservation and exhibit the various articles purchased for carrying on the affairs of the agency here, but the mills with their fixtures, the farm implements, and tools for the use of the different mechanical branches which have been necessary for our advancement, the shops with their equipments, the stock of animals necessarily procured, and many other things, in addition to the buildings and other improvements, are in good condition and still represent the greater part of their original value.

The Indian houses now on the reservation, built of logs or lumber furnished them from the saw-mill, number over sixty, and other improvements have been extensively made in the way of fencing in pieces of land, some of which amount to large fields of ten, fifteen, and twenty acres, and, in one or two instances, fifty acres are thus inclosed and the land is under cultivation. The fields have mostly been fenced by the Indians themselves; but generally the ground has been broken at Government expense. In many cases the Indians have been assisted in building their houses, and a large amount of lumber has been furnished to them for doors, door and window-frames, floors and other purposes, and shingles have been sawed for them for roofing. Cupboards, tables, bedsteads, benches and other articles for furnishing their houses are constantly in demand, and large numbers of them have been made at our workshops.

In comparing the amount expended with what has been accomplished, I think it will appear that the sum is a small one, when we consider that our situation is so remote from railroads or other means of transportation and travel, except by road-wagons, and that we are among uncivilized people.

During the year there have been extensive additions made to the machinery at the mill, and a lathe has been introduced, by which turning can be done for bedsteads and other furniture required at the schools or for Indians, and the work can be done neatly and expeditiously. A commodious building has also been erected for a blacksmith shop and wheelwright shop, with adjoining rooms for farm-implements, &c., and also for articles needing repairs.

The boarding-school house, referred to in my last report, was ready for scholars in the early spring, having been finished in a neat and substantial manner, and has given general satisfaction to the Indians. They met in council at the time of opening, and encouraged the children and one another to make the best possible use of the advantages thus offered them for obtaining a good education. The transfer of the scholars to the new buildings occurred on the 28th of Thirdmonth, and the school continued its sessions until the 27th of Sixthmonth, when it was suspended for vacation during the hot weather. For a more detailed account of the condition of the school, and the progress made by the scholars, I would refer to the report of Alfred J. Standing, principal, herewith.

A day-school was opened on the 14th of Firstmonth, and continued without interruption until it closed for vacation, at the time mentioned for the close of the boarding-school. Meals are furnished to the scholars at this school, but they lodge at their camp. It is desirable that lodgings should be provided at this school; also, that the moral influence of a family may be thrown around the wild and uncultivated offspring of uncultivated parents, by which they may be weaned from the habits of a savage life and turned to those of virtue and usefulness. For further information in relation to this school I would refer to the report of the teacher, William J. Hinshaw, herewith.

To the children we are to look for that improvement which will prepare the Indians to take a place among civilized and Christianized communities, which may, and doubtless will be brought about, if the labor now being prosecuted should be perseveringly continued.

The Indians of this agency are not only willing but anxious to have their children educated; and the children show an eagerness to learn such branches as are taught in our schools, that will compare favorably with the children of any people. These remarks do not apply, perhaps, to all the bands in their full force, yet the disposition shown by all encourages to perseverance; and if Christian workers, workers whose hearts and sympathies are resigned to the Indians' best interest, who are qualified for the service, can be obtained, and those thus qualified, who are now in the service, can be retained, there is no doubt of the success.

From a census recently taken with great care and much labor, in which service I had the assistance of A. J. Standing, I find the Indians belonging to the reservation number as follows, to wit:

Caddoes, 401; Wichitas, 300; Wacoes, 140; Tawacanies, 125; Keechies, 106; Delawares, 61; Ionies, 50, and Penetethka Comanches, 345. Total 1,528.

The value of stock-raising is well understood by some of these bands, and the Caddoes and Delawares have been gradually introducing and raising cattle, and they now have in their herds 1,386 head; and they and the Ionies have 1,700 head of hogs. These Indians have been somewhat discouraged in their efforts to raise cattle, from the circumstance that some of the stock has been killed by those belonging to the wilder tribes, but I think this difficulty has very much diminished of late, and I have heard of no depredations of the kind for some time.

The Wichita agency, being situated immediately between those of the Kiowas and Comanches and the Cheyennes and Arapahoes, the Indians from both are frequent visitors here, especially those of the Kiowa agency, and the Arapahoes from that of the Cheyennes. I not unfrequently issue rations to these Indians, always, however, in small quantities, giving them to understand that it is to relieve their present wants. Some of them, at times, I give a meal at our tables. I have been induced to do this, partly for the purpose of cultivating friendly feelings with these savages, and at times from necessity to relieve hunger. I have always been careful to do it in such a way as to prevent visits for the purpose of being fed merely, and from the long intervals between the visits made by the same parties, and other circumstances, I am convinced that this is not the case. The wild Indians are all friendly with the affiliated bands, and there have been times when they could be approached through this agency, while it was difficult to reach them in any other way. Of late, however, they have been accessible through their own agency, but they still occasionally come in here, and I have not thought it best to discourage it. The time has not arrived for withdrawing a liberal support from the affiliated bands, who, being in a transition state, their progress for self-support is slow; but I have always taken every opportunity that has offered, since I have been connected with them, to impress upon them the importance of providing for their own support, and to inform them that it is not the intention of the Government to feed and provide for them permanently, but, that in a few years, this support would be withdrawn. Many of the Indians understand this, and are making preparations accordingly.

Hereafter I would recommend that the usual supply of "annuity goods" (clothing, &c.) be withdrawn, and the funds now used for their purchase expended in procuring farm-implements, and improving and increasing their stock of cattle.

About the 6th of Fifthmonth, Es-sad-a-wa, head-chief of the Wichita band, was murdered by a band of Osages. He had obtained a pass from the agent to hunt buffalo, and gone to the plains with some of his men for this purpose. In the chase he became separated from his men, and falling in with a small party of Osages, after exchanging salutations, apparently friendly, they killed him without any known provocation. The Wichitas were thrown into a high state of excitement when the information reached their village, and preparations were about to be made for retaliation. The sympathies of the whole affiliated bands were enlisted in a general banding together for a war against the Osages, and in a few days they had the offer of the assistance of the Kiowas and Comanches of the Kiowa agency, and the Indians of the agency for the Cheyennes and Arapahoes. But word of the murder was brought to the agency as soon as it was known, and a council was called in which a more moderate course was urged, when it was concluded to endeavor to settle the matter by negotiation, and a demand for the murderer. Shortly after, a letter was received from the Osages, speaking in strong condemnation of the murder of Es-sad-a-wa, which they alleged had been committed by a band of lawless men of the tribe, and asking for an interview with the Wichitas, by which they hoped to satisfy them, as far as possible. Thereupon, the Wichitas, after a good deal of discussion, in council, concluded to appoint a delegation to proceed to the Osage agency, and accordingly about thirty of their head and representative men were selected for this purpose. In accordance with their appointment, they met the Osages at their camp, in council, and made known the condition upon which they hoped to have the difficulty settled. Several days were occupied in counseling together, and the Osages not being willing to give up the parties guilty of the murder, but offering to pay to the Wichitas a sum of money and turn over some ponies and goods, a settlement was finally made in this way, an understanding being had that in case a similar deed should be committed the guilty men should be given up.

Although this settlement was not in accordance with what would appear justice among civilized communities, yet it shows a great change in the disposition of the Indians of the affiliated bands, which naturally demand life for life; and the great forbearance shown by them on the occasion of such an event—the unprovoked murder of a beloved and highly influential chief—leads to the remark that an Indian may become susceptible of the refined feeling which will draw him to say, "Let us have peace."

The summer has been a very dry one here, and the crops have suffered greatly, particularly the corn; all of which that was planted early will be almost an entire failure.

During the year good health has generally prevailed upon the reservation, both with the Indians and others.

That there has been some advancement in the right direction by the Indians belonging to this agency, I believe is manifest, and with the fostering care of the Government and earnest, self-sacrificing labors of those to whom their immediate care may be intrusted, with the blessing of Divine Providence, they doubtless will continue to improve and eventually become a useful people.

Very respectfully,

JONA. RICHARDS,
United States Indian Agent.

ENOCH HOAG,
Superintendent Indian Affairs, Lawrence, Kans.

26.

SISSETON SIOUX INDIAN AGENCY,
Lake Traverse Reservation, Dak., September 20, 1873.

SIR: In compliance with the regulationsof the Department, I have the honor to submit the following annual report of the affairs at this agency, and the condition of the Indians belonging thereto:

Notwithstanding the severity of the last winter season, and the general prevalence of the measles the past summer, the general health of the Sisseton and Wahpeton bands of Sioux of my charge has been good, and through a kind providence the number of deaths has been less than usual among so many so much exposed. (See report A, Dr. George H. Harves, herewith transmitted.)

It has pleased Divine Providence to bless the labors of those who have cultivated the soil, and to reward them with good crops this season, and having completed our flouring-mill and manufactured their wheat into flour for their use, a very great impetus has been given thereby to the cultivation of wheat on this reservation.

The increase of the number of milch cows with calves, and also work-oxen, wagons, and plows this season, has awakened a deep interest among this people in raising stock as well as more grain for their own use. Of the fifty cows and calves issued to them this spring, I have heard of only two or three who have killed the calves, and these were claimed to have been killed for the sick. For statisticts relative to the results of attempts at farming of these Indians, I would respectfully refer you to "statistical return of farming," herewith transmitted.

POPULATION.

There are now enrolled at this agency: males over 21 years, 339; females over 21 years, 501; males over 12 and under 21 years, 111; females over 12 and under 21 years, 112; males under 12 years, 238; females under 12 years, 239. Total population, 1,540, representing two bands of Sioux, viz, Sisseton and Wahpeton.

This increase of the number enrolled is mainly in consequence of the success had in inducing the Big Stone Lake band of Sisseton and Wahpeton Sioux, who for years past occasioned so much trouble along the border of Minnesota, to come on this reservation and settle, and conform to the conditions of the treaty of 1867, and thereby avail themselves of the benefits thereof. They number, old and young, sixty-two. They are wild, and, as yet, unaccustomed to work, and therefore are no help to those already struggling for improvement.

There is still another band, known as the Wabey Indians, with Big Eagle Feather as their chief. These are mostly Sisseton and Wahpeton Sioux, and properly belong here, but they are quite wild and shy of all our attempts to induce them to settle and cultivate farms for themselves. They annoy our working Indians very much with regular visits, dancing, feasting, and begging after the old fashion of the Dakotas forty years ago. They would like a share of the provisions of the treaty under which this people are working, but they abominate the conditions on which aid and encouragement are given. There are, also, relatives of our Indians out yet beyond the line of our northwest boundary, in the British Dominions, awaiting time and opportunity to come in and join this people in their march to civilization and labor for a competency in life

I am happy to be able to report progress on the part of a very large number of our enrolled Indians at this agency. It is true that some are yet attached to their old customs and habits, and retain many of their old notions and ideas, and probably will hold on to them—some of them until they die; but these, only like stubs of old trees drifted down and dragging along with the current, show how much faster the main current moves on.

In regard to the physical and material interests of this people, there are evidences of progress—more cleanly, neat, and respectable in their persons, dress, and in their houses; and there is a growing demand for soap, shears, combs, chairs, tubs, bedsteads, dishes, knives and forks, beds and bedding, cook-stoves and parlor-stoves, as well as better houses and homes.

EDUCATION.

There has been a marked increase of interest in the education of their children, and hence all eyes are looking to the contemplated new school-houses with hope, and especially to the manual-labor school-house, near this agency, now in process of erection, the main part of which, at least, we hope to have completed in time to occupy the coming winter.

In the schools taught by John L. Hodgman, Andrew Hunter, and Mrs. J. B. Benville at the agency, Long Hollow, and Ascension, respectively, the children have made commendable progress, and we are, from these beginnings, encouraged to renew our efforts and enlarge our plans in this department as the hope of this people. The school at Goodwill Mission has been taught by Mr. W. K. Morris, now under the patronage of the A. B. C. F. M., and has been well attended and fraught with good results. The school at Flandreau, Dak., among the Santee Sioux, taught by Philander A. Vannice, has been interesting and satisfactory to that people.

In regard to social life I am happy to be able to report advancement among this people. Polygamy and bigamy are at a very great discount. Some have recently put away the women whom they had for years unlawfully kept in their families, and have provided for their support and that of their children. Others who, only a few months since, boasted of their plurality of wives, now express their regret that they are so environed, and are looking about them to see how they may best rid themselves of this greatest of all hindrances to their progress.

Chieftainships are having a rapid downward tendency among us, and the whole people are fast ripening for self-government, and, among other things, elective franchises as among their highest privileges. Law and order are called for by a large majority of these bands, and lest they should, in the absence of some good and wholesome laws securing to them protection of life and property, fall a prey to the lawless and lazy, a code of laws from the Department of the Interior is most earnestly recommended, in accordance with the tenth article of the treaty of 1867.

Old, frequent and protracted councils are now below par with our old and wise men. Altogether we have reason for devout gratitude to God for the degree of peace, tranquility and harmony that now characterize this people. All are now working industriously, cutting and hauling their hay, repairing up their houses and barns for the winter during the week and resting on the Sabbath, and the larger majority regularly attending religious worship on the Sabbath-day, according to the Divine commandment, and all of them, now, cheerfully conceding the right of every one to worship God according to the dictates of his own, and not another's, conscience. In view of this state of things at this agency, we may well exclaim, "Behold what God hath wrought." And here I have only to add that your late visit, and that of the honorable Secretary, C. Delano, to this agency had much to do with bringing about this favorable change in the state of affairs as herein reported. Such visits from the Department, frequently made are recommended.

With regard to my outpost at Flandreau, Dak., and the Santee Sioux in that settlement, I have to report that the supply of clothing delivered to them last February, and the oxen and wagons, plows, hoes, scythes, &c., delivered in June last, were very gratefully received by that noble band of natives, who, through faith, have escaped the pollutions and thralldom of tribal and annuity arrangements, and are struggling against poverty and want with a heroism and zeal truly commendable. The school taught there by Mr. Philander A. Vannice is in a flourishing condition, and cannot fail to have a salutary effect among that people, so long as that devoted, excellent young man has charge of it and gives his advice and instruction to that people. I have to recommend that they receive aid again in the supply of oxen, wagons, and plows for the remaining half of those who have settled in that region. Such agricultural implements, with teams, will promote their interests better than food and clothing, and yet, for one or two years at least, they might be aided to great advantage to them and with honor to our great and good Government.

Such illustrations of the power of the Gospel to save man, and such examples of the influence of Christian civilization, are worth working for and looking after.

With thankfulness for the past and present evidences of the advancement of this people, we enter anew upon the toils and cares incident to the work for the new year before us, with the confident expectation that [only] with the continued Divine presence and blessing we shall not live and labor among this people in vain for their highest civilization and ultimate evangelization.

Very respecfully, your obedient servant,

M. N. ADAMS,
United States Indian Agent.

Hon. EDWARD P. SMITH,
Commissioner of Indian Affairs, Washington, D. C.

27.

DEVIL'S LAKE RESERVATION,
Fort Totten Agency, Dak., September 15, 1873.

SIR: In compliance with the requirements of the Indian Department, I have the honor to report the condition of the people under my charge.

This year has been an eventful one for them, as the first step toward permanent civilization has been taken by the building of a manual-labor school-house, with arrangements consummated to have it placed in charge of Rev. Sisters of Charity; and the receipt of thirty ox-teams complete, which have been distributed among the more industrious Indians, must tend to make their efforts in labor a success; and the school will give the start toward a better state of things for the rising generation. In connection with the school a mission will be established for religious instruction on a more permanent basis than heretofore, and must dispel the darkness of their superstitution. Although many adults have learned the necessity of labor and seem desirous of establishing farms, and in many instances their success has been remarkable, still they are wedded to their traditions and are superstitiously afraid of innovations. The "medicine dances" and "singing doctors" keep their superstition alive through fear of sickness and death if disobedient, and the belief in the power of these medicine-men to have punished backsliders from their teaching, [together] with the practice of polygamy, are deplorable obstacles in the way of Christianizing this generation. But I hope still, through the teaching of good men, good influence, and example, they will be brought to break asunder these bonds of superstitious slavery. Great allowance will have to be made for the slow progress in the accession of the population to this reservation by bringing in from the wandering hordes of the Sioux the still many Sissetons among them, who hesitate on account of the necessity of laboring for their own support and improvement; the old and infirm, of course, are taken care of, which is so different from the old system of giving in common. It seems unfortunate that the policy existing at the Sisseton Agency and here does not become general; for how much easier would then be the work; and although the majority here are in favor of it, now that it has been tested, and do give to the agent all their assistance to carry it out, still it is found difficult to have all conform. And when a trial is made, after their corn is grown and gathered, many go back to their old haunts, but often return again, with renewed promises to remain. The constant visits of the more lawless bands, by their dances and advice, destroy the result of much good example, and have demoralized those whom it was thought were permanently changed. It is known of young men who have been laboring for more than a year as white men, performing all labors required of them, to leave everything, resume their Indian costume, and disappear from the reservation under this influence. This season more than usual have been the visits of the roving bands of Yanktonais Sioux, "Cut Heads," and this reservation was made the road to the buffalo range north, and not by their usual route, probably owing to the large number of troops on duty along that way.

The Chippewas also, under the plea of peace-making, or rather cementing a peace already established, have several times visited this agency. One band of over 80 souls came from Red Lake, Minn., another came from North Pembina, beyond the national line, Dominion of Canada, all with the same ostensible object, peace; but really to get horses. They have taken from here over thirty horses—given to them—or exchanged for bead-work, and their fancy clothing, transforming many a young fellow, in coat and pantaloons, into a painted savage. They all come here in a starving conditon, and have made sad inroads on the subsistence depended upon for the use of this reservation. Referring to the Chippewas, while it is a matter of congratulation that peace is established between them and the Sioux of this reservation, still I would respectfully suggest that it would be better if these constant interchange of civilities be abolished. They have to pass through a country settled by "whites" in their goings to and fro, which always creates fear among the settlers. And as the visits are made at a time in our short summer season which interferes materially with our labors, this year it was impossible to get our usual laboring Indians to work for over two months, all on that account, and which rendered the engaging of several employés in addition, to enable us to finish the buildings commenced, making hay, harvesting grain, &c., besides the giving away of what goods had been earned.

A week ago the agent heard there was a movement on foot for a number of these people to make a return visit to these Chippewas, and at the time of the distribution of goods and money to the Chippewas. A council was called by him, and by showing these Sioux that such a visit was impracticable at this time, for dependence was placed in them to haul what flour and goods were still at the railroad to the agency, with the teams given them, ground to break, &c., and that winter would overtake them with nothing finished, he endeavored to prevent it. Finally, to stop this movement, they had to be told that a "telegram" would be sent to their "Great Father," who would doubtless order them to be sent back from the Chippewa country. The day after the council was had, and the promise given to remain at home, the commanding officer of Fort Totten received a telegram sent by express from Jamestown, Dak., on Northern Pacific Railroad, coming from Grand Forks on the road to Red Lake, stating that the people there were very much alarmed, having heard from the Chippewas on their return home that a body of Sioux would pass that place on a return visit to the Chippewas, and, in consequence, troops were had from Pembina for their protection. If these people were kept strictly on their reservation, unless these visits were made by permission and the Indians in charge of some responsible white man, I believe it would be best; for every time the Chippewas, in the last two years, have visited this agency, it has been feared that some trouble would be had by straggling Missouri Indians, more or less always here, killing some of them, and thereby rekindle the flame of war with two-fold fierceness, as the writer has known to be the case several times in days gone by.

The number of Indians on this reservation was, on the first day of August last, 1,020; there have been over 1,200 at times this summer, and most of them declared their intention of remaining here; others have left to return again. The Indians have cultivated over 100 acres of corn and 20 acres of potatoes, and all have made gardens. Seventy-five are living in houses and the larger proportion dress as white men. A good deal of damage has been done to the crops this year again by the grasshoppers, but when spared the yield has been abundant. Approximately there will be 3,000 bushels of corn and 2,400 bushels of potatoes. Turnips and garden vegetables, except squash, were destroyed by this insect pest. They, themselves, have cut and secured about 200 tons of hay. The receiving of ox-teams distributed among them has been an incentive toward better things. Eighty tons of subsistence, &c., so far have been hauled by them from railroad station, Jamestown, Dak., to agency, a distance of 85 miles. There has been harvested and secured, in seven large stacks, wheat, which will probably yield 500 bushels from the seed of 35 bushels. A portion will be kept for seed, to be distributed among the Indians who may have land prepared, and the remainder will be ground for general use. One hundred and sixty tons of hay has been secured by employés, with Indians, for the general use of agency.

The building operations were retarded this last spring by the high-water rendering transportation very difficult, and it required some time to prepare for making brick and burning lime, also making machines for moulding, &c. But the success in the quality of brick and lime compensates for the trouble and expense incurred. The manual labor school-house is 40 by 60 feet, two stories high. The brickwork is nearly all finished, and, I trust, it will be inclosed by the end of this month, and finished this fall, as well as the repairs on the old buildings at the old post, turned over permanently by order of honorable Secretary of War to Indian Department. Early next spring an agency building will there be erected, at but little cost comparatively, as the material, much of it, will be on hand. It is contemplated to get out a large lot of saw-logs at once, preparatory to making lumber and shingles for buildings now in course of erection, and to be erected, as well as for use of Indians, especially shingles, intending to cover all their log-buildings with them, instead of the ordinary ground covering now in use. Hence, it will be necessary to employ two more laborers than the regular number now employed. The employés working at buildings will be discharged as soon as their extra work is finished or winter sets in. The services of the brickmaker not being now required he has been discharged, as will be the masons, when the school-house is plastered.

The agreement made with the Sisseton and Wahpeton Sioux, last year, and amended by Congress last winter, for certain lands owned by them, as recognized by their treaty of 1867, was ratified by these Indians on May 19 last, but not without much difficulty; not on account of not wishing these amendments to be made, for they cared nothing about them, as the money to be paid had not been affected thereby, but from the opposition raised by the lazy and worthless among these people, who preferred having everything turned over in common, on the ground that the goods sent were for payment of lands, and not, as heretofore, simply a civilization fund, appropriated as Congress might deem proper. The intention was an opposition to the laboring party, and to break up, if possible, the arrangement about to be consummated. They were supported in this by a large number of "Cut-head" Yanctonai Sioux, who urged their right also to these lands from a former residence, but as they are now recipients of the national bounty on another reservation their claims are doubtless unfounded. For a time, however, the discussion was stormy and threatening. Much credit is due, however, to Messrs. Adams and Smith, my co-commissioners, for its successful termination, especially the latter, for his patience and judgment throughout the whole—surprising, as this was his first introduction to Indians; and also Mr. Faribault, whose knowledge of Indians aided us greatly in consummating this matter, he having acted as interpreter throughout. I would also add a tribute to the cool determination and fearless conduct of Teo-wash-tay, head chief, in carrying through this ratification for the benefit of his people in the face of the threats from the opposition. He determined to have this money expended to advance the interests of labor and civilization, as well as for the support of the infirm and old who are not able to work. It is difficult, often disheartening, to an agent in his work of trying to do away with the prejudices existing for ages among a people as egotistical as the American savage, brought up to know no restraint, trained to the chase for his support, and to war—oftentimes as a religious necessity, or as a duty. Under such circumstances, as I said before, the difficulty is disheartening, especially as he views his teachers as belonging to the race who brought him to this necessity of manual labor for support. Reasoning thus, it is not strange that the work is one of difficulty; but, under Providence, it can be accomplished. They can be taught that even manual labor will be a blessing to them, but it requires patience, kindness, and justice, as well as firmness, and my thirty-five years' experience among the Sioux tells me much can be accomplished. They are susceptible of moral improvement, have native intelligence, giving them quick perceptions, far above what one would suppose a wild, untutored people could possess. By kind attention, I have tried to make the many wandering bands who visited this agency understand that their "Great Father" is their true friend; and have taken occasion to explain to all the advantages which would accrue to them by settling down on a reservation and following the more certain pursuits of farmers or stock-raisers, protected by the Government, than by clinging to their present precarious mode of existence, with so often suffering, and I flatter myself with some good result.

Again, I would respectfully urge the necessity of this reservation being surveyed and divided into quarter-sections, as provided by the treaty made in Washington with these people February 19, 1867. They are settled too close to each other, and it is an evil already felt in regard to the future ownership of fields now cultivated. At first, owing to the fear from incursions made by war-parties of Chippewas and Mandans, &c., they did so for mutual security. But as that dread no longer exists, and with their present advantages, they feel the necessity of enlarging their fields; but unfortunately all wish to possess the lion's share of what has been held in common. But if once surveyed they would soon seek to take possession of the more desirable homesteads, and the wish to raise stock, pigs, chickens, &c., would assist in requiring this desirable separation of interests to be made.

In conclusion, I would also respectfully ask, at the request of the principal men of the reservation, that they be allowed to visit their "Great Father" in Washington. It was urged in council last fall, and also this spring before the commissioners, at the time these people ceded certain lands to the United States, and they were promised that an effort would be made. If the request would be granted, I think it might be productive of much good. So many parties have been lately called there, that they feel slighted, especially as they have tried to improve their people, and obey instructions.

I have the honor, sir, to be, very respectfully, your obedient servant,

WM. H. FORBES,
United States Indian Agent.

Hon. E. P. SMITH,
Commissioner of Indian Affairs, Washington, D. C.

28.

GRAND RIVER INDIAN AGENCY,
Standing Rock, Dakota, September 27, 1873.

SIR: In compliance with the requirements of the Department, I have the honor to submit the following as my annual report:

On the 9th of June last, I relieved my predecessor, J. C. O'Connor, and entered upon the discharge of my duties. I found all the warehouses to be in a dilapidated condition, and entirely unfit for the reception of supplies, and set about repairing them; but, on receipt of a dispatch from the Department, stating that the agency was to be removed to Standing Rock, I discontinued the repairs, and proceeded at once to select a new site for the agency. I selected this place as in my opinion the best adapted for an agency. It is situated on high table-land, about seventy-five miles above Grand River, by water; the river is narrow and deep, and, with a good landing, is accessible to steamboats at all stages of water. There is an abundance of cottonwood timber, suitable for building purposes, both above and below the agency, and a fine tract of land near by, sufficient to accommodate all the Indians for farming purposes. On the 18th of July all the property pertaining to the old agency was removed to this place, with the exception of the buildings, which are old log structures and not worth the cost of removal; they have, therefore, been left in charge of a watchman until such time as some disposition can be made of them.

The Indians under my charge consist of the following tribes and number, viz: Upper Yanctonai Sioux, 1,386; Lower Yanctonai Sioux, 2,534; Uncpapa Sioux, 1,512; and Blackfeet Sioux, 847. These embrace the Cut-heads and Sans-Arc Sioux, formerly reported. I am pleased to be able to state that they have behaved well, so far, and I am not aware of any hostile act being committed by these Indians since my connection with them. A great many were dissatisfied at the removal of the agency, and expressed their unwillingness to leave their old locations; but, on pointing out the great disadvantages they would be under by pursuing that course, they nearly all agreed to move to this place when the balance of their crops was gathered.

The Indians have had about six hundred and fifty acres of land under cultivation during the present year. The plan heretofore adopted has been to break as much ground as was supposed to meet the wants of the respective bands, or as time and force would permit, issue seeds and hoes to the Indians, and leave the rest to them. The Indians have then allotted the ground to families, each taking as much as would be required for a small garden-spot by a white family, and marking the boundaries of their respective possessions by rows of turf removed from their patches. The work has been mostly done by the women, but some of the men are beginning to learn that work is not dishonorable, and have labored on their farms with considerable faithfulness. Their manner of farming is very slovenly, but they are anxious to learn to farm as the whites do. The land was planted by them in corn, pumpkins, squash, and melons, but, receiving very little cultivation, was overrun by weeds, and, as a consequence, the crops have amounted to little or nothing as a means of subsistence beyond a little fresh garden-truck, which was mostly consumed before properly matured. I am, therefore, unable to give an estimate of the amount raised by them.

Although they appear to have manifested an interest in these simple and limited operations, I am of the opinion that no material advancement can be made in farming without the aid of considerable skilled labor, and the necessary appliances to render such labor of the greatest possible or practicable utility. Fields of respectable dimensions should take the place of garden-patches, and all operations should be directed and assisted by skilled and intelligent agriculturists, with the use of suitable implements, until such time as the Indians may become sufficiently skilled to manage their own farms profitably. This plan will require considerable expenditure of money, but if progress is hoped for, in the effort to render the Sioux Indians self-sustaining on a civilized basis, the outlay seems to me to be most essential.

As the Indians have abandoned their old farms, and moved to this place, with the exception of a portion of the Lower Yanctonai, who are encamped on the other side of the river, opposite the agency, and who will, no doubt, remain there until they see if their friends on this side are bettered by the change, it will be necessary to have some land broken for them here. In view of the foregoing I would strongly recommend that half an acre of land, for each family, be broken for them at once; or say five hundred acres in all. I would also recommend that a sufficient number of log-houses be built, enough to accommodate all the chiefs and head-soldiers, say about three hundred. I know of nothing that would tend more to their civilization than by getting them into houses, as it would, in a great measure, break up their roving disposition.

Although the principal Indians of this agency take no interest in the establishment of schools, I think it of the utmost importance that some steps should be taken toward the establishment of at least one school-house. There are a great number of youths here between the ages of 7 and 14 years, of whom, I have no doubt, the greater part, by a little judicious handling, could be made to attend. I would, therefore, recommend that the sum of $7,500 be placed to my credit from the general school fund, for the erection of a school-house and pay of teachers.

On the 12th and 17th of last month the Gros Ventres made two raids upon this place, and carried off 14 horses, one of which belonged to the United States Indian Department, and the others to employés and Indians. This raid, as a consequence, created great excitement among the Indians, and it was with considerable persuasion that I succeeded in preventing them from retaliating, promising to exert myself to have the stolen stock returned. On my requesting J. E. Tappan, United States Indian agent at Fort Berthold, to endeavor to secure them, he promptly responded, and the horses were returned to their proper owners, which had the effect of allaying all bitter feelings among them.

I have just finished issuing the annuity goods, with which the Indians seem well satisfied. They are also much pleased at the sight of the wagons, oxen, cows, &c., and are anxious to go into farming on a large scale next spring.

The new saw-mill, which was received on the 12th instant, has been set up, and is now in successful operation, turning out a large amount of lumber daily.

The work on the new agency buildings is progressing rapidly, but has been somewhat delayed on account of the long detention of the saw-mill at Bismarck.

Since the removal of the agency to this place I have had only a guard of 12 soldiers, and I could dispense with them, only they are required as a check against the roughs who infest this river.

On the 12th ultimo, as the Indians were ferrying their beef across the Missouri River, just above the old agency, the boat, by some accident, was overturned, and Mr. J. H. Hardie, the agency farmer, and two Indians, were drowned. It was impossible to render them any assistance, as there was no other boat at the place. The steamer "May Lowery" passing soon after the accident, I found it necessary to engage her services in ferrying the Indians and their beef across the river. The bodies of the two Indians have been recovered, but I regret to state that although every endeavor has been made to recover the body of Mr. Hardie, it has not been found.

I am, sir, very respectfully, your obedient servant,

EDMOND PALMER,
United States Indian Agent.

Hon. E. P. SMITH,
Commissioner of Indian Affairs, Washington, D. C.

29.

CHEYENNE RIVER INDIAN AGENCY, DAKOTA,
October 25, 1873.

SIR: I have the honor to submit this my first annual report as agent for the Two-Kettle, Minneconjoux, Sans Arcs, and a part of the Blackfeet bands of Sioux Indians.

I entered upon my duties as agent of the above-named Indians on the 16th day of August, 1872. The agency at that time presented a very forlorn appearance, owing to the filthy condition of the poorly constructed shacks, and the small space upon which the same were located. The warehouses in particular were utterly unfit for the storage of provisions, infested with rats, and unsafe in other respects. The flour and corn warehouses have been repaired and are now rat-proof. All of the old shacks have been taken down and used for fire-wood, the old logs being totally unfit for any other use.

One sawed-log house, 16 by 70 feet, one and a half stories high, with shingled roof, has been erected, which is occupied by the interpreter, employés of the agency, and agency mess. Two frame houses have also been erected, one 26 by 36 feet, the other 20 by 30 feet, with good shingled roofs. These buildings have been erected by the agency carpenter and employés, the only extra expense to the Department being for the pine flooring, siding, and hardware, and freight on the same. Besides these agency buildings there have been built two hundred and twenty-five Indian houses, chiefly by the Indians themselves. Most of the logs have been hauled by agency teams and agency employés. The sawed lumber required for these houses has been furnished at the agency saw-mill; the logs for this purpose have all been cut and rafted by the employés.

There is now in process of erection a building 28 by 40 feet, with an L 20 by 46 feet, to be used as a boarding-school for the Indian children; this school-building will be completed about the 1st of January, 1874, and a boarding-school will be put in operation at once, under the auspices of the Protestant Episcopal Church, with the Rev. Henry Swift as principal and Miss Mary J. Leigh as teacher; two other teachers will be added in the spring, and more if required.

Two day-schools have been in operation most of the time during the past year with good results. These schools have been under the able management of the Rev. Thomas L. Riggs, of the American Board of Foreign Missions, and the Rev. Henry Swift, of the Episcopal mission.

The Indians at this agency are divided into two classes: the friendly, who have settled at the agency, and the hostile, or those who adhere to their wandering life on the plains. The friendly or farming Indians seem to be contented and happy, and evince a desire to learn and adopt the customs of civilized life. The farming Indians have made wonderful progress during the past year. A large number have worked hard, cultivating their fields and building houses; fifty are wearing citizen-dress, and many more are very anxious to follow their example.

In comparing the prospects and general state of these people with their condition a year ago, I am encouraged to believe that the efforts which have been made for the improvement of their condition have been bountifully crowned with success. The number of acres planted and cultivated by their own labor is about six hundred. Although their crops were totally destroyed, by drought and hail, they do not seem discouraged, and are more anxious to farm than ever before. About four hundred acres have been broken during the past year, most of which was planted last spring. About five miles of wire fence has been built by the employés of the agency, which is the only fence ever built here, save the Indian brush-fence. Many of the Indians have saved their beef-hides, and purchased mowing-machines, horse-rakes, and harness.

Every Indian's house is furnished with a good cook-stove, with furniture complete. During the past year the Indians have been furnished with wagons, harness, hoes, spades, shovels, scythes and snaths, saws, augers, hammers, hatchets, axes, axe-handles, plows, harrows, hay-forks, and rakes, which were the only tools they have ever received. This is a very poor country for farming, but very good for stock-raising. I will here take the liberty of stating, that, in my judgment, these Indians will never be able on these lands to subsist without Government aid. About 3,600 Indians are permanently located in farming districts on the river about forty miles on either side of the agency, which makes the agency very difficult to manage. The morals of the Indians of this agency are very good. They are industrious and temperate; during the fourteen months that I have been here, I have not seen or heard of an Indian under the influence of liquor. The hostile or roaming Indians, who are about equal in number to the friendly, seldom visit the agency in any considerable numbers except, once a year, in the spring. Small parties come in more frequently; their stay is usually from six to ten weeks, and, as a general rule, they conduct themselves very well, and a large number have come in and located during the last year. I can safely say that four times as many Indians have farmed the past year, as any previous year.

The annuity goods were issued September 4, 1873, with perfect satisfaction to the Indians; the goods were of much better quality than the goods of last year. The subsistence stores have all been received for the present year ending July 1, 1874, and are of good quality, and in good order. I have strong faith in the ultimate success of the present Indian policy, but it will require time and patience, and still I am afraid some will yet have to be dealt with severely, before the lessons to be taught are learned. In my judgment the most objectionable object in the way of civilizing these Indians is their stronghold near the Black Hills. Some strict measures should be adopted to break up their hostile camp there, which would compel them to settle at their respective agencies. As it now is, a small party from the hostile camp can visit any of the agencies and commit murder and theft and make their escape. The total number of Indians belonging to this agency is estimated from seven to eight thousand souls. Whatever success may have been accomplished with these people under my charge, is in a great part due to Mr. Frederick W. Wright, head farmer, and the employés of the agency. They have encountered hardships and privations, and have promptly responded to every call of the service, and their energy and fidelity entitle them to special commendation.

I am, very respectfully, your obedient servant,

H. W. BINGHAM,
United States Indian Agent.

Hon. EDWARD P. SMITH,
Commissioner of Indian Affairs, Washington, D. C.

30.

UPPER MISSOURI SIOUX AGENCY,
Crow Creek, Dak., September, 1873.

SIR: In compliance with the regulations of the Indian Department, I have the honor to submit this, my annual report, as Indian agent, for the lower Brulé and lower Yanctonai Sioux.

The average number of Indians at the agency during the past year has been 3,000. The advancement of these Indians during this time has been quite perceptible compared with that of former years. Three hundred and fifty acres have been cultivated by them during the present season, and good crops realized. They have also erected for themselves, during the past six months, thirty substantial log houses, which are the first ever erected by Indians upon this reservation. Many are now providing hay for the cow and yoke of oxen promised to such as provide hay and shelter for the same.

The presence of one company of United States troops stationed at the sub-agency, at lower Brulé, has done much toward preserving order, and throwing a restraint over many young warriors, who otherwise might have caused serious disturbance. With the aid of the military the sale of intoxicating liquors to Indians has been nearly suppressed.

Since my last report two missions have been established at this agency, under the auspices of the Protestant Episcopal Church; one at the agency-proper, in charge of Rev. H. Burt, the other at the subagency, (Lower Brulé,) under charge of Rev. W. J. Cleveland. A day-school at each of these missions has been in successful operation, with an average attendance of twenty each, the past year. At Lower Brulé a substantial block warehouse, 22 by 80, and a carpenter-shop of like material, 22 by 48, have been constructed, while at the agency-proper warehouses and other buildings have undergone repairs, 100 acres of new ground broken, and 700 rods of substantial post-and-board fence erected.

I would respectfully call the attention of the Department to the fact that these Indians are now being subsisted in accordance with the 10th article of the treaty concluded April 29, 1868, between the Government and different tribes of Sioux Indians, and which expires with the close of the present fiscal year, at which time these Indians will be thrown entirely upon their own resources so far as subsisting themselves is concerned. This they are wholly incapable of doing at the present time, owing to their limited experience in agricultural pursuits, and the scarcity of game. Without farther aid they will probably make forays upon the settlers and farmers of the frontier for the necessities of life, and which would soon lead to serious trouble. I would therefore recommend that such legislation be taken as would enable the department to continue the rations of flour, beef, and bacon for the present, withholding that of sugar, coffee and tobacco from all Indians, except the aged and infirm, and those who are willing to render an equivalent to the Government. All of which is respectfully submitted.

Very truly, your obedient servant,

HENRY F. LIVINGSTON,
United States Indian Agent.

Hon. EDW. P. SMITH,
Commissioner of Indian Affairs.

31.

FORT BERTHOLD AGENCY, DAKOTA, *September* 15, 1873.

SIR: I have the honor to submit this my third annual report as agent for the Arickaree, Gros Ventre, and Mandan Indians.

* * * * * * *

LAND AND CLIMATE.

The bottoms of the Missouri have, in this neighborhood, an average width of about a mile and a half. The most elevated parts are about fifteen feet above low-water mark, but four times within the last twenty-three years they have been entirely overflowed. From side to side, in these bottom-lands, the Missouri winds cutting at each bend almost, or entirely through the first bench, and sometimes through this to the second bench. In the latter case we find the stream bounded on one side by a high and precipitous bank.

* * * * * * *

The general surface of the land is not fertile; generally sterile and sparsely timbered and watered. The deeper ravines and bottom-lands produce grass sufficiently long to be made into hay, but on the higher ground the grass is too short to be cut. Even on the better soil the second crop of hay is not as abundant as the first. For agricultural purposes only the lower lands seem to be available. In the bottom-lands of the Missouri, where they are covered with timber and undergrowth, the soil is rich and rendered tolerably moist by percolation from the river, and because the melted snow and rain and water from overflows are retained long on the surface, in consequence of the flatness and peculiar composition of the soil. Drought is one of the chief difficulties, but not the only one, for what the drought spares the grasshoppers are apt to devour. Some years when there is a pretty fair rainfall, and a scarcity of grasshoppers, careful husbandry may be rewarded by a fair crop on these bottoms. At Fort Clark, seventy-five miles below here, where the Arickarees formerly lived, at the mouth of Knife River, sixty miles below here, the site of the old Gros Ventre and Mandan Villages, and here the Indians have for many years cultivated (without irrigation) corn, squashes, and pumpkins, and been rewarded by fair success.

* * * * * * *

The cottonwood constitutes the bulk of the forest-trees in this vicinity, and is the only wood available in any quantity for fuel or building purposes. The low bottom-lands along the Missouri and Yellowstone Rivers are, for the most part, covered with cottonwood forests. The wild yellow, or red plum, is found in the ravines and on the prairie side of points of timber on the river lands. It is edible and of good flavor, being the best fruit this vicinity affords. The number of trees, however, is limited, and the supply consequently scanty. The choke-cherry is found in much the same places, and a variety of service or June-berry, somewhat similar to the huckle-berry, is abundant along the streams as a shrub. The smooth wild goose-berry is sparingly found in the ravines. The currant is more common in the same locality. The buffalo, or bull berry, an edible, acid, red fruit, ripening late in the season, is to be met with abundantly in the bottom-lands. It is very valuable to the Indians, who often subsist on it almost entirely for several weeks during the fall, at times when there happens to be great scarcity of game. The *pomme blanche*, or "Indian turnip," is abundant in the high grounds and sandy soil. It is much used for food by the Indians. The prickly pear, or cactus, is extremely abundant on the prairie, and its sharp, stiff spines are very annoying to the traveler, whether mounted or on foot. Lamb's quarter grows plentifully. The wild onion is common on the prairies, and a species of wild mint finds a place on the moist or marshy banks of streams.

CLIMATE, ETC.

The average temperature is about 43° F.; extremes, 105° F. and 40° F. The summers short and hot; winters long and cold, continuous, and severe. Wind and snow storms are of common occurrence. The atmosphere is dry, and the variations in temperature not so marked as in more humid climates. The climate is generally dry; the fall of rain is very small; the annual average for the past five years has been only ten and a quarter inches. It is generally supposed that game is plenty about here. This is an erroneous impression. There are but very few small streams, an entire absence of lakes, and an almost entire destitution of timber, the whole country being one wilderness of dry prairie for hundreds of miles around, and hence there is but a very little small game, fish, or wild fruits to be found. In former times the buffalo roamed over the country, but they have receded and are now some two or three hundred miles away.

MANUFACTURES, ETC.

These Indians are manufacturers as well as agriculturists, being very skillful in various manufactures, and display great art and ingenuity in the design of the various articles they make. Besides the usual pipes, pipe-stems, bows, arrows, &c., they make a species of matting out of the wild rushes for floors, and baskets out of the bark of the willow, dyed with various colors and woven in different and intricate patterns. Large beads are also made by the Mandans and Arickarees, an art said to have been derived some hundred years ago from some prisoners of the Snake Nation, and the knowledge of which is a secret even now confided to a few among the Mandans and Rees.

* * * * * * *

They also make earthen pots of various sizes, from a pint to three gallons; they are a familiar part of the culinary furniture of every Mandan lodge, and are manufactured by the women of this tribe in great quantities, and modeled into many different forms and shapes. They are made by the hands of the women from a tough, black clay, and baked in kilns which are made for the purpose, and are nearly equal in hardness to our own manufacture of pottery—in fact, they are so strong and serviceable that they hang them over the fire as we do our iron pots, and boil their meat in them.

VILLAGE.

Their village has a most novel appearance to the eye of a stranger; their lodges are closely grouped together, leaving but just room enough for walking or riding between them, and appear from without to be built entirely of dirt, but one is surprised on entering them to see the look of neatness and comfort, and the spacious dimensions of these earth-covered dwellings. They all have a circular form, and are from forty to sixty feet in diameter. Their foundations are prepared by digging some two feet in the ground, and forming the floor of earth by leveling the requisite size for the lodge. These floors or foundations are all perfectly circular, and varying in size and proportions to the number of inmates, or the quality or standing of the families which are to occupy them. They are made by placing forked posts about six feet high around the circumference of the circle. These are joined by poles from one fork to another, which are supported also by other forked poles slanting from the ground. In the center of the lodge are placed four higher forks, about fifteen feet in length, connected together by beams; from these to the lower poles the rafters are extended so as to leave a vacancy in the middle for the smoke. The frame of the building is then covered with willow boughs; over this hay is laid, and over this mud or clay. The doorway is about four feet wide, and before it is a sort of entry extending about ten feet from the lodge. The top of the lodge is a favorite lounging-place for the whole family—an airing-place and a lookout for all.

In the center and immediately under the skylight, is the fire-place—a hole of four or five feet in diameter, of circular form, sunk a foot below the surface and curbed with stone. The lodges hold from twenty to forty persons, and are not adapted to promote health, cleanliness, or comfort.

During the past year the Indians connected with this agency have been gradually improving their condition; although their advancement has not been rapid, it is preceptible, and I think with judicious measures will steadily improve.

The labor of these Indians has met with but poor success this year, owing to the unusual high stage of water in the river during the June rise, which covered the fields and remained so long on the land as to rot the corn that was planted, and on receding left a heavy deposit of sand over their patches. The corn on higher ground will yield but about half the usual amount, owing to the cold and wet summer, and an early and severe frost (September 3d) prevented that from fully maturing. From these causes I can but anticipate that it will be absolutely necessary for the Government to provide much more bountifully for these Indians than heretofore. You may well immagine that the prospect is indeed gloomy, and that under these circumstances the approaching winter is looked upon by all with much apprehension.

The Indians have built for themselves about ninety log-houses since my last report. The agency has made and put in the doors, floors, and windows, and furnished each house with one table, four benches, and two bedsteads, besides making one hundred doors for lodges and two hundred and forty-two bedsteads.

The work in the shops has been repairing guns, wagons and carts, making hinges and latches, sharpening plows, shoeing horses for Indians, and the general repairs for the agency and farm. I have built for the use of the agency one root-cellar, 40x20x10 feet; one flouring-mill, 40x20 feet, and about two miles of fence. I have plowed the agency-farm (two hundred and fifteen acres) and about one hundred acres for the Indians—no breaking done this year. The crops planted by the agency have done very well; they consist of wheat, 55 acres, yielding 23 bushels to the acre; oats, 65 acres, yielding 40 bushels to the acre; corn, 35 acres, yielding 40 bushels to the acre; (season not favorable for this crop, and the seed not acclimated;) potatoes, 20 acres, yielding 275 bushels to the acre; turnips, 9 acres, yielding 55 bushels to the acre. Owing to the cold and wet season, pumpkins, squash, and melons did not succeed.

The annuity-goods arrived this year during the month of July, and were issued September 3; they gave good satisfaction as to the quality and quantity, although about one-half the number of blankets were sent that were asked for, and some other articles entirely omitted that they had expected.

They especially request that they may be furnished with a few good field-glasses, and some breech-loading guns and ammunition; they prefer the United States two or three banded breech-loading gun.

I would again respectfully call your attention to the great want of proper accommodation for the agent and employés; the present buildings are too small and old, and are about falling to pieces. Should teachers be sent here, it will be necessary to build for them a school-house and dwelling-house. Two more store-houses are absolutely necessary, and a proper building ought to be built for the agent; for office, bed-room, kitchen and dining-room, I am compelled to use one large room, divided by a light board partition.

A proper building ought to be erected for a hospital, where serious cases could be treated, and where the native doctors could be kept from the patients; where proper food and medicine could be given with some degree of certainty that the sick would get the food as well as the medicine; as it is now, it seems like a waste of money and of time, of supplies and attendance. Many cases of scrofula, rheumatism, inflammation of the eyes, and venereal disease could be successfully treated, and the lives and eyes of the patients saved, could they be kept from the Indian doctors, and the relatives of the sick kept from stealing the food sent to nourish them. I have twice before called the attention of the Department to this. A new building is also required for the saw-mill; the one we now have has been standing some years, and having been built of cotton-wood, is fast falling to pieces; the sills having rotted away, the building has to be supported by props.

The three hundred head of beef-cattle received August 14 were a very fair lot of cattle, and will be of great assistance to the Indians during our long and dreary winter. In this connection, a few remarks on the subject of agency-farms, the result of three years' careful observation, may not be out of place. On my arrival here, nearly three years ago, not being familiar with the subject, I had come to the conclusion that the plan of an agency-farm attached to each reservation was a system long since adopted by the Government, and that it was the design of the Department to work a large farm in connection with each reservation, with white labor, for the purpose of giving the Indians an ocular demonstration of the benefits and comforts to be derived from continued and earnest efforts and attention to agriculture, hoping that, after their minds were convinced, they would voluntarily abandon their nomadic life, and become frugal and industrious; but observation and the experience of the past three seasons have convinced me that agency-farms, at least in this part of the country, are, I think, generally a fraud, so far as the Indians are concerned. There is not one agency-farm out of ten that is not pecuniarily a loss to the Indians. The difficulty is that the teams and employés eat up and use up in one way and another all the products of the farms, and the Indians, after paying the bills, get little or nothing. I am not prepared to say that nothing should be done, because so little good results, but I do say that it is our duty to see that the money spent for the Indians should entirely result to their benefit; and under the present system too much is expended in salaries and expense of crops. This is unavoidable, owing to the climate and the country; the season for growing is so short—hardly five months, that quite a force is required to put in the crops and care for them, to harvest and prepare for the next year's crops—that is, fall-plowing, getting the manure on the ground, &c. And the wages here are very high, as everything the men use has to be purchased from the traders, who charge the most exorbitant prices. Then the uncertainty of the seasons, and consequently the uncertainty of the success of the crops, add greatly to the expense. One year in three may be counted upon as a success; other years drought, grasshoppers, or early frosts destroy the season's work, and the result is that there is no adequate return of products to remunerate the Indians for such investment, and occasionally a total loss to them of the money expended for labor and the destruction of the crop. Would it not be better to expend the money and labor in assisting the Indians to open and cultivate large patches or fields than they now have, and adopt a judicious system of rewards for the encouragement of the industrious? And perhaps it would be well to add to this a small premium or bonus to those who would produce the largest crops, and keep the ground in best condition, according to our notion of the best agricultural system. They should be attended and encouraged by frugal and industrious men of good habits, who could, by their example and uniform kindness to them, win their respect, and thus exercise that kind of influence over them calculated to encourage them in well-doing, in industry, and economy.

I regret that I am unable to report any progress in education. The matter of furnishing teachers to these Indians has been left to the religious denomination under whose control they have been placed. Although repeated promises have been made, no teacher has yet appeared.

The Indians are very anxious to visit Washington to see their Great Father, and, until taken there, they refuse to entertain any proposition about removal to other lands in the Indian Territory.

For the detailed accounts of their respective departments, I would respectfully refer you to the accompanying reports of the physician, engineer, and farmer.

I am, sir, very respectfully, your obedient servant,

JOHN E. TAPPAN,
United States Indian Agent.

The Hon. COMMISSIONER INDIAN AFFAIRS, *Washington, D. C.*

32.

YANKTON AGENCY, DAKOTA TERRITORY,
September 20, 1873.

SIR: I have the honor to submit this my second annual report of the condition, progress, and prospects of the Indians under my charge.

GENERAL REVIEW OF THE YEAR.

It gives me pleasure to be able to say that during the past year the Indians under my care have been peaceable, and, to some extent, industrious. All, with the exception of a certain number of the young men, have been engaged during the entire year in wood-cutting and hauling (when able) timber to the mill to be sawed into house-logs and lumber. A great number of houses have been built during the year, and a large number are under way. These houses are well built, of either sawed or hewn logs. I prefer them to bring their logs to the mill and have them sawed, as it saves timber and gives them the slabs for roofing. If the Yanctons had cattle and wagons, I feel sure that within a very short time they would all have good log-houses, built by themselves. They are now anxiously looking for oxen and wagons, as they understood the Commissioner to make them a promise of these, as well as other articles, to assist them in their attempt to live like white men. I trust that these things will soon be forthcoming. During the spring and summer the people have remained quietly at home on their reservation planting and tending their corn, potatoes, and gardens. The crop this year has been for this country very large. There is scarcely any tepee or house without its frames of poles loaded with corn, thus curing for winter use. The potato-crop was not as large as could have been desired. The fields have been so long under cultivation, and so badly tended, that it is almost impossible to make them yield a good crop. New lands should be broken, and every family given their own share or homestead. As far as I have been able during the last year I have worked on this plan. It works well. During the early spring I had parcels of ground broken and allotted to such Indians as would promise to live near them, plant, and fence them. Now, as one travels through the reserve, these little homes and farms will be noticed on every hand. Besides breaking for individual families, I have also broken forty acres, in one body, on the high lands of the reserve. My object in doing this is to try if wheat cannot be successfully raised on the high lands or plateaus heretofore untried in agriculture. I believe this can be done. From the nature of the soil and climate in this part of Dakota the corn-crop will always be precarious. The wheat, on the other hand, when sown early, will mature before the great heat and drought of August comes on, and yield an abundant harvest. If this proves to be a success it will eventually be of the greatest importance to these poor people. They have several thousand acres of this land, high table-land, more than enough to give each family a farm of eighty acres. The only serious drawback to their making their houses on these high lands is the great scarcity of water and timber. The lumber, however, can be procured from the neighboring bottoms, a distance varying from two to ten miles. The water I am as yet in doubt about. I have in several places made the attempt to find water by means of bored wells, but as yet have met with no success; then again the water, when found in small quantities, is of a brackish or alkaline nature, unpleasant to the taste, and unhealthful. The Indians object doggedly to living on these high lands, and are all located on what is here called the bottom. This is a strip of land along the Missouri River, varying from one to four miles in width, and extending the entire length of the reservation. It is partially timbered, and well provided with abundant hay. Farming should be checked on these lowlands, and protection extended over hay and timber, or the time will soon come when they will be in want of both. During the early spring we were visited by a fearful three-days' snow-storm, causing great loss in cattle and horses among the Indians. The horses have, to some extent, been restored by friendly gifts from Indians above, but the cattle are a total loss. The storm, however, while it did great temporary harm, has taught these people the lesson greatly needed, viz, that if they intend to raise stock they must provide for them hay and house. In consequence we have had more hay put up this year than ever before. Houses to shelter the animals from the severity of the winter-storms are beginning to show themselves as adjuncts to their little log-houses, and these, with the hay-stack near at hand, with chicken-coop and pig-pen, make many of our Indian houses look quite farm-like.

APPRENTICES.

The department of work which gives me the most satisfaction is that performed by the apprentices. There are employed at this agency four apprentices, viz, in blacksmith's shop, tin-shop, carpenter's shop, and mill; three of these are half-breeds, one a full Indian; they are quite regular and industrious. They have been employed about nine months, and are able to do many things in their several departments; the time is not far distant when they will be able to do the entire work required. The greatest difficulty I find with them is their obstinate refusal to speak English. They can all understand what is said to them, however, and in time will overcome their prejudices. Besides these apprentices in the shops, we have several other full-blood Indian employés to do farm-work, and whatever is necessary to be done about a place so self-dependent as an Indian agency. These young men are rapidly learning to plow, plant, and cultivate the soil, to feed, care for, and drive horses and cattle, and, in short, to do all such work as is required upon a western farm. Others again are engaged as herders and butchers.

Thus it will be seen that in all things necessary to independent living, these people are being trained. It gives me pleasure to state that the white employés of the agency do all in their power to further my efforts in this behalf.

SCHOOLS.

The greatest disappointment we meet with in endeavoring to civilize the Indians is in regard to our schools. It seems impossible to induce Indian children or young people to attend school in any great numbers, or with regularity. This, I believe, is principally owing to the fact that in their homes they are without discipline of any kind; the Indian theory is to let the child have perfect freedom, no restraint, no punishment, no good example. I am well persuaded we shall never be able to succeed to any extent as long as we continue to work on our present plan of day-schools. We must first capture these children of nature and tame them to our home-life; this can only be done by something like home or boarding schools. I propose, as soon as I shall be able to undertake the work, to ask aid to this end. I am persuaded that such schools would soon be well filled, and good results would follow, if well and wisely administered. The efforts of the missionaries, both of the Episcopal and Presbyterian churches, have been wisely and perseveringly put forth. The fault is not with them; it lies in the unfitness of the day-school system for Indians.

CHURCHES.

The religious services of the several churches of this agency are remarkably well attended. The conduct of the people at these services is all that could be expected—quiet, orderly, and to a good degree attentive. Quite a number of the young men have been prepared and instructed to conduct these services in the Indian tongue where white men could not be procured. As a general thing they do it with propriety and seeming earnestness. Quite a large number have become church-members, and I believe are endeavoring to live in accordance with their solemn vows. In this connection it gives me pleasure to state that the Rt. Rev. W. H. Hare, Episcopal bishop of the Indians included in the diocese of Niobrara, has taken up his residence at this agency, making it his home and headquarters of all his efforts for Indian christianization. A portion of land has been set apart by the agent and Indians, on which he is now building a residence and theological-training school. I feel sure, with God's blessing, good results will follow the bishop's efforts for the Yanctons.

SUBSISTENCE.

There is quite a universal feeling of uneasiness among the Yanctons with regard to the prospect of future subsistence. They have been informed that with this year may end their rations. The general expression is of utter hopelessness. They say, "In that case we may as well make up our minds to die." I would here give it as my judgment, that if now all further aid in rations is withheld, very serious consequences will follow as far as the Yanctons are concerned. The greater part of the young men will leave the reservation and join the wild Indians above. Others will scatter among neighboring white settlements and towns, and become outcasts of the lowest order.

The good begun will thus be utterly overthrown, and the old state of things return, with adjuncts too fearful to contemplate, both to border white men and Indians.

SICKNESS AND MORTALITY.

During the summer and fall there has been an unusual degree of sickness among the Yanctons. Early in the spring measles broke out among the people on the lower end of the reservation, and has continued to spread over its entire extent. In many cases, both among the old and young, it has proved fatal, so that, as far as I can ascertain, over one hundred persons have died from its effects. This is owing to the fact that they could not be persuaded to take proper precautions, nor persevere in using the doctor's remedies; impatient if not cured in a day, they would call in their medicine-men, and expose themselves to wet and cold. We were also threatened later in the summer with small-pox, it having broken out on an island only fifteen miles distant. As soon as I heard of it I placed Indian guards between it and the reservation. As the dread disease has now disappeared from the island, I trust we have escaped this fearful calamity.

In conclusion I would say that, although many of the Yanctons are yet Indian in life and character, yet, if wisely and kindly treated, the time will come when all efforts for them by the Government, philanthropist, and Christian, will be well rewarded by their loyalty, civilization, and Christianity.

Very respectfully, your obedient servant,

JOHN G. GASSMANN,
United States Indian Agent.

Hon. E. P. SMITH,
Commissioner Indian Affairs, Washington, D. C.

33.

PONCA AGENCY, DAKOTA TERRITORY,
October 18, 1873.

SIR: I have the honor to forward my first annual report of the condition of the Ponca Indians at this agency, where I arrived on the 25th day of October, 1872, leaving Omaha, Nebr., immediately after receipt of my instructions from the Department, but did not meet my predecessor until I returned to the agency with my family on the 9th November, 1873, and he relinquished his charge to me November 12, 1873.

I found the Poncas numbering about 750 souls, living in three villages, (one entirely of tents or tepees,) and all within two miles of each other. The villages were:

1. Agency Town, occupied altogether by United States employés, the saw-mill, workshops, and warehouses, and an Indian population of one hundred and twenty-three "half-breed," families or lodges, often two or more in one house.

2. Hu-b-than, or Fish Town, occupied by a mixed population of full-blood Indians and half-breeds numbering twenty-four lodges.

3. Point Village, occupied altogether by full-blood Indians, with a council-house on the north bank of the Niobrara River, a distant settlement, from 6 to 8 miles from Agency Village, according to the route traveled, which is regulated by the season, or by alarms of hostile invasion; and these causes tend also to induce migratory habits in the people, who stay only a portion of the time at their village, and spend the greater part of the season under shelter of the agency guns. Population, fifty-six lodges at the time of my arrival here, living in tents or tepees among the forest-trees, two miles from the agency village.

The farming operations had not been profitable. A very little wheat and oats was the result, although a large tract of land, amounting to near 200 acres, had been cultivated. The grasshoppers and hail-storms previous to and in the harvest season had wrought irreparable damages, and I found the Poncas entirely dependent upon Government rations for support. A few families had wild beans, dug up by the women, but in very limited quantities; none had corn. At the Point Village I found about 15 bushels of potatoes set around the cook-stove, which were frozen and spoiled. Flour and beef were occasionally issued by delivery to the chiefs, who distributed at their pleasure to whom they would, regulating quantities of the viands disbursed by favor or disfavor. In the general appearance and exhibit of the Ponca tribe my first impressions were, as I have always since maintained, that it is possible by firmness and faithfulness to reach the heart of the untamed, uncivilized Indian, and to build therein a moral, social, and business capacity. * * * * * *

My earliest efforts were directed to the disabusing the minds of the Indians of the final power of brute force as pitted against the power of intelligence—which included efforts to amend—and a skillful industry which would be labor-saving, and yield a greater percentage of profit for the outlay. A few well-directed strokes of an ax would accomplish more than the manifold random blows of an ill-directed aim; a house, larger than the ordinary, full of light, chinked and plastered, warm and snug when the cold winds blow, cleanly always, well ventilated and well kept, would be a home it was sought to make appreciated; small cupboards, tables and benches, bedsteads and house-doors, with an extra window for ventilation, a pine house-door, as all to be desired in that direction, was added, and few (not one-fourth) but possess these treasures now. No filth or garbage offends the sense of smell, and shelves and clothes-hooks exchange a pendant condition for the ill-kept garments on a pile of filth and rottenness. The lessons of the past have left a few tiny ill-nurtured seeds which, with a sickly vitality, have continued to live, but are now a grateful evidence of the deep earnestness of the tillers of the soil. As the efforts of to-day clear away, in some measure, the choking weeds, these little flowers lift up their heads, shed a fragrance in the pathway, and impart a beauty to the rugged rocks around us.

The Poncas appear a strong, hearty race of people; the men much more so than the females; from reports, peacefully disposed toward whites and to other Indians, except attacked or molested in their persons or property. They are ill-provided with arms and without funds to purchase them, unless taking that money which they so much need for improvements, agricultural and civilizing aid. They cannot hunt with safety, and, except the blankets and annuity goods supplied them once a year by Government, have no clothes and are often found nearly naked, or clad in tattered blankets or old buffalo-robes, affording poor protection against cold and thrown aside as ill-adapted for summer wear. These deficiencies, in a great measure, as far as summer clothing is concerned, have been supplied by missionary benevolence. Scrofula and consumption have made dreadful ravages among the tribe, but I am hoping that cleanliness, proper food in quality and quantity, a more active life, and change of mode and materials for living, have wrought a beneficial change in these people's sanitary condition.

I found that I had to address myself to the task of changing the tribal relations—the servile submission of the commonalty to the chiefs and head-men—in other words, to attack the revenue policy of the Ponca chiefs; and on the 27th day of November, 1872, commenced the plan of "family distribution," giving to each head of a family, according to the number of persons, women and children, he was shown to have on the census-list. * * * To disarm the anticipated resentment of the chiefs, we promised and gave one extra family-ration to each of the leading chiefs, and sometimes presents for feasts. Thus the change was smoothly made, and soon became an accomplished fact without any fear of falling back. * * * *

The winter season was consumed in logging, which brought us 350 logs, cutting fire-wood for mill and shops, &c., in repairs to corrals, stables, and buildings, care and tending of stock, care and slaughtering of beef-cattle, &c., as our facilities for freezing were necessarily very limited, the weekly disbursements, work in saw-mill, &c. The winter season had several severe storms, in none of which any of the Government cattle suffered, and often to prevent suffering the Ponca cattle were taken into the agency corral and cared for. In the fearful storm of April last more than half the Indian ponies were lost and several Indian cattle. One man, one woman, and a boy perished together, buried in a snow-drift, while they were searching for fuel, and had sheltered in a ravine. * * * * * * *

As the spring opened the melting snows on the hill-sides filled the valleys with water a foot or more deep, and but few patches of high ground were above water. The Missouri River, up to the middle of June, continued to rise and fall often rapidly, and as farming progressed on the Missouri River valley chiefly, the budding crops of corn and potatoes and various edibles on the Indian allotments worked from the early morn to evening, except during the hotter mid-day, by Indian men and women exclusively, with diligence and will, instructed and encouraged by the farmer and myself, were my especial pride and gratification. So diligent were the workers, so ready for instruction, resulting in cleanly kept grounds, that my sorrow and mortification cannot be estimated when the 3d of July ultimo brought the commencement of a ruin to our prospects in the unrestrained and unrestrainable rapidly advancing overflow of the Missouri River, and for near two weeks thereafter the work of salvage from the ever-threatening destruction occupied nearly day and night our whole available labor-force. We succeeded by united efforts in carrying from the river-bank to near half a mile inland the whole of the agency buildings, mechanics' houses, stabling, and sheds, and more than twenty Indian houses and nearly every panel of fencing around the Indian field, all of which has been at this date restored with additions and improvements. The Poncas, with frequent urgings and words of encouragement, increased wages and prompt payment, worked well and long, often through the night; and the fact that the disaster did not cost us ten dollars of actual loss is to be attributed to their labor, continuous and persevering, incurring risks for the preservation of property, working sometimes over the swiftly flowing waters, terrible and turbid, on the edge of the newly formed current but a few inches below them, and into which a fall would have then been certain death, even to an Indian. Three hundred yards deep of the Missouri River frontage has been ingulfed for near a mile on the Missouri River, and the site of the old agency village is now the bed of the main channel of the river. The Indian field there of sixty acres has suffered from actual loss of ground very considerably, but was nearly all submerged and the whole crop destroyed or damaged, while the land away from the Missouri River lost almost as much of its produce from the earlier immersion of the snow-water, the late season in consequence preventing the planting a greater breadth of field, and otherwise rendering agricultural operations precarious and less profitable. The accompanying returns show that all was done that could be to insure success in that direction; and that a failure was brought about neither by negligence nor laziness is some solace to the sorrow we all feel.

Another cause, not only that of disquietude, but that it demoralizes our people and breaks in on our plans, and hinders and delays operations, cooping us up in too narrow bounds for safety's sake, and thus narrowing our area of and for improvements, is the frequent visits of the hostile Sioux. It is almost a weekly occurrence that one or more horsemen are seen by the guards stealthily approaching the working parties or the villages, and are to be chased away, at the expense of two or three hours' delay. But far worse is the record of disasters from frequent engagements with hostile Indians, who come in force to fight in disproportionate numbers these poor ill-armed, but really brave Indians, peaceably imbibing and receiving the practical lessons of civilization, and proving to their friends their evident desire to better their condition.

I found here a military force of ten men with a second-lieutenant commanding, but these were withdrawn November 19, 1872, and no military aid was nearer than Fort Randall, D. T., thirty to thirty-five miles away in a northwesterly direction, and at the Bohemian settlement of the Niobrara River Valley, fifteen miles in a southwesterly direction, both approached from here through a country indented with ravines and dotted over with trees and shrubs of stunted growth, forming an undergrowth impenetrable to the passing eyesight, and, consequently, a most excellent covert for an ambushed enemy. No soldiers were sent here until March 13, 1873; withdrawn again in May; a smaller number returned in June, and since then the detachment has consisted of five to seven men, with orders to protect no working party, nor pass in fighting hostile Indians, beyond a limit, which is about three hundred paces west of the church building; to guard no wagon train or perform other duty than to suppress internal commotion among the Poncas, and protect Government property from their outrages; and this on account of the small number which composed the detachment, the Yellowstone expedition leaving but few men in garrison at Fort Randall, D. T.

On one occasion only, ten men have been sent at my request for the protection of the Ponca village, at the Niobrara, when attacked and stock driven off, and also for the benefit of white settlers in the Niobrara Valley, sufferers from attacks of hostile Indians, in August last. During my absence from this agency, in obedience to directions of the honorable Commissioner of Indian Affairs, in September last, the following telegram was received by Agent Gassman, at Yankton agency, who has telegraphic communication with the forts above and the States below his agency:

CHEYENNE, *September* 22, 1873.

To JAMES GASSMAN, *Yankton Agency:*

Please notify the Ponca agent that a war-party of one hundred Sioux left this agency 18th instant, to attack the Poncas.

J. J. SAVILLE,
United States Indian Agent, Red Cloud Agency.

The superintendent, at the time of the receipt of the telegram, was also away, in search of stolen horses, intrusted to a white employé, who, with the team and carriage he drove, were missing and unheard of; and my wife, with two other white women, six white children, two white employés, and fifty-six Indians, and these very poorly armed, and without a leader, asked through Agent Gassman for military aid. Luckily the assistance asked was not then required for fighting the expected Indians, nor was it given, in any perceptible shape; but the mental prostration of my poor defenseless wife, which immediately followed, will long be remembered by me. We have had, as your office has been promptly informed, quite a number of attacks from hostile Indians, resulting in a loss, when the number of the marauders and the frequency of their visitations are taken into account, comparatively trifling in the aggregate. 10 Indian ponies, stolen at different times. 2 American horses, stolen at different times. 4 work-oxen—2 killed; 2 died from wounds. 1 cow killed.

The Poncas, having thus almost unaided kept the enemy at bay with little better than clubs and bows and arrows, and fought their way through a season of greater peril from hostile Indians than has ever before been encountered by them, as I am informed, ask only that guns of long range and capacity for speedy execution be put into their hands, and this application I would earnestly indorse and urge upon the attention of the Department as an act of justice to these brave men, who are struggling upward to the light, and if protected in their persons and property, and given such efficient aid as their rate of progress requires, will, as the evidences bear me out in saying, make a record that cannot but justify the benevolent intentions of the Government, and prove beyond cavil that the Indian can be and will be made to contribute to the general welfare, and can appreciate while he shares the benefits and blessings he has with others earned.

From the attacks of hostile Indians the Poncas have lost in person, three men killed, and had three others wounded, all of which have recovered, one of them with the loss of an eye. Attacks from war-parties in small or large numbers have been frequent, and made both during the day and in the night season. Every reasonable precaution which suggested itself to my best judgment has been, and will be taken for the safety and comfort of the people and their property, and I am grateful to Almighty Providence that the bloodthirsty and heathen enemy, whose errand is evident mischief, has never surprised the Poncas, or taken them at a greater disadvantage than what I have stated heretofore, always a superiority of numbers, and better guns on the side of the assailants. We have a few plain signals with the bell and the voice, which all well understand, and which evoke always a ready response. There are no cowards in camp, except it be the young women and small children; the old women, when they are not permitted to fight, urge on the lagging and make most excellent camp followers, and in the last battle, (October 15 ultimo,) when no other way was left, an old Ponca women, to contribute to the defense of the village, while brandishing a long knife she carried to quiet opposition, caught and made ready for the affray, the Indian ponies of the village, and riding around until she found a footman, gave him the horse, if his face were toward the fighting ground.

Two battles, one of June 9 ultimo, over 100 of the enemy, (from the Brulé, lower, chiefly,) were confronted and routed with no loss in men, and but two horses on the Ponca side, but the pathway of the retreating enemy was marked by a continuous line of blood from the wounded ponies and persons for near fifteen miles, where the pursuit ended. The second battle of October 15 ultimo, in which over 200 hostile Indians were counted, was the most formidable in numbers and destructive elements.

On the 8th day of August, ultimo, the Hon. Edward P. Smith, Commissioner of Indian Affairs, on a tour of inspection visited this agency, and on the 9th day of August, ultimo, after a conference with the agent, who furnished such information, in response to the inquiry as would seem to justify that course, the honorable Commissioner directed the agent to commence a system of universal labor wherein the able-bodied Indians of the Ponca tribe should work for a living, and for those things that they had come to regard as necessary to their personal comfort, and essential to their welfare. The free "ration system" should be abolished, and, except to the old and infirm, the orphan children and family of deceased Poncas, and the temporarily disabled, no free ration should be given, but all should buy with the proceeds of their labor. It was hoped and believed that among the Ponca tribe could be found sufficient good material for fully testing the long mooted question as to whether an Indian is, or would be, with fair advantages, capable of self-sustenance, and the problem fairly presented.

To the Indian nature the question of labor presents itself as a degradation, and to overcome this distaste for labor is a work of itself harder to perform than any task or trial ever presented to him. I had not only to contend with this contempt within, but as the matter had been talked of by the Commissioner as to other Indians, at their different agencies he had visited, it had become a subject of deep thought and of vexatious disquiet to the Indians above and below this agency. Three delegations of Yanktons and others came down to talk the Poncas into a combination disfavoring and condemning the labor movement. My abilities as a debater were severely tested, and I was at last brought to see that a dictator was the proper person to cope with the situation. * * * During the year past [we] have, (with the exception of an average of six white mechanics and machinists, &c.,) almost exclusively with Indian labor, cut 350 logs, burned a large quantity of charcoal, chopped and handled fire-wood, [cut] near 1,000 fence-posts, which have all, (with many others, [used] in straightening fences, &c.) been employed in new fences around new fields; grubbed new lands of superfluous roots and tree-stumps; plowed (broken) for the next year's crop, in amount about 100 acres; cultivated lands plowed, dragged, cleaned, or attempted to be, and cultivated seeds drilled in, and drill driven and controlled by Indian labor, weeding and farm labor, done by men and boys, (Poncas,) two of four reapers and mowers, guided and altogether controlled by Indian labor; cut and gathered three hundred and fifty tons of hay, (Indian labor nearly exclusively;) [built] seven large bridges; opened new and shorter routes between villages, timber lands, and tracts, now or proposed to be occupied for farming or agricultural purposes. Over two and a half miles of new road with bridge-drains have been made, including cutting around hills, and moving dirt by wagons and wheelbarrows—some carried in blankets—the road-bed through a portion formed by trees cut down, and with wood-brush and dirt surface forming a road-bed. No white labor [was] employed on roads. [The other improvements are:] hay corrals; stock-sheds in three corrals, large, with large hay-racks; leveling, scraping, ditching on streets and grades by Indian labor; stables 70 feet long; two large warehouses, corn-house, and granary; tool-house and armory; council-house; Fairbanks's scale-house; soldiers' quarters; over thirty Indian houses rebuilt and new;

repairs and additions to agent's house and office. We have an Indian engaged in making ox-yokes, ox-bows, and helves for axes and hatchets; an Indian carpenter, who can put up houses with doors, windows, &c.; put on locks, and glaze windows, &c.; we have two drive-wells, made this summer, and now in operation. The greater part of this has been done by the increased labor force of August 9, ultimo. It is a pleasant view where an Indian has his house, stable, and yard, with hay-stack adjoining; and at the Point Village, (Niobrara,) the full-bloods excel the half-breeds in providing for the winter, while the Hu-b-than Village has scarcely a house where the stable and sometimes a plow and wagon shed does not form part of the homestead.

* * * * * * *

White Eagle, the head-chief of the full-blood Indians, lives at the Point Village, and was the last to "fall into line" on the labor scheme, but has since guided a mower for grass and a reaper for hay. I have provided him with a large dinner-bell, which he rings just after breakfast and dinner to go to work, and at the quitting times. So much is won from barbarism. Eagle is a young man, not thirty years old, but not physically strong, though broad-shouldered and of commanding presence. Latterly his conduct and manner have been cordial, and have been shaped to aid, instead of, as in the past, to hinder and perplex.

The assets of the tribe, individual property, are about 40 wagons, and about 60 yoke of oxen, which will be increased by 15 other wagons, on the way now, thrasher, 2 drills, large and small, 27 cows, quite a number of cook-stoves and household furniture, chiefly made on the agency. Four have clocks in their houses, beside the usual agricultural tools, 40 hay-forks, 4 horse-rakes, several plows, harrows and drag, hay and wood racks, shovels, spades, grubbing-hoes and garden-hoes, with several ponies, and near twenty sets of harness; and I am very much gratified to be able to report that many, nearly all, are very careful as to the condition and keeping of their goods, and speak with pride of their possessions. The feeling is growing that an idle man *is* as much to be scorned as the worker *was*, and the Poncas exclaim of a non-worker, "no work—no flour;" and they have now ceased to threaten to break down the doors to procure what the lazy man could not get, food without work.

I am inclined to the belief that there is a very perceptible improvement in the moral, social, and physical condition of the Poncas. They are learning habits of obedience, and gaining confidence in the superior knowledge of their instructors; they are often petulant, like spoiled children, and though not as easily rebuked, yet a stern glance, or a sharply spoken word, generally quiets the most obstreperous. I think it is right, and best for their interests, to gain daily, as much as safely may be, an influence and authority, which can substitute new ideas for their old notions, and command a confidence which insures obedience, not from servile fear, but that their reasoning powers are aroused to action, and can easily perceive the personal benefit to accrue to them from the source of former favors, now estimated at a value, which to lose would not be desirable. Regulations are made and kept, and the "morning rule" of the "get-ready bell," rung 20 minutes before 8 o'clock a. m., arouses the village, while the sharp sound of the "labor-bell" gives a view of the hurrying Poncas at the superintendent's office, where each worker must be at roll-call to get his mark, and allotment for labor, or return disconsolate, with a half day's loss and a short notch on his own record.

Respectfully submitted.

CHARLES P. BIRKETT,
United States Indian Agent, Poncas.

Hon. EDW. P. SMITH,
Commissioner Indian Affairs, Washington, D. C.

34.

RED CLOUD AGENCY, WASHINGTON TERRITORY,
August 18, 1873.

SIR: In compliance with the requirements of the Department, I have the honor to make the following report of the Indians at the Red Cloud agency the past year:

At the old agency on the Platte farming was not commenced, owing to the uncertain time of their removal to the new place that was selected last season for their home. The removal of these Sioux away from the Platte could not be effected last season, owing to the opposition of Red Cloud and his particular friends, the "Bad Faces." Red Cloud proved recreant to his promises made to the Government by opposing the removal and all the chiefs that favored it.

The agency was removed the first of this month, after much trouble with these same "Bad Faces." It is now located on White River, about eighty miles east of north, in a very pretty valley with good water and all the farming land they will require for the next ten years. Building material can be had within ten miles of the agency, and good hay-land in about fifteen.

They should be furnished with Ree corn, for seed, as early in the spring as possible. This is best for the altitude, as it is hardy, productive, and is ready for roasting-ears within six weeks after it is put in the ground.

The disposition of these Indians and those of the north toward the whites has changed much for the better within the past year. They show more feeling of dependence, and more anxiety to be at peace; all of which they try to cover up with a greater amount of bravado talk by the soldiers, while the chiefs say very little. Those Indians from the north that spent the winter here were quite well disposed, and spoke well. They were not disposed to dictate or complain as those who had been a long time at the agency. This marked improvement among all of these Sioux is greatly owing to the generous course pursued by the Department in feeding them the past winter.

The northern Indians came to these agencies starving and enemies, and received the same kind care that was given to those who had been here for years, though the chiefs were loth to come to the agency. When they first came in they sent their soldiers to get rations that they might taste white man's food without his knowing of it; but after a few issues they came to acknowledge their dependence.

Those Indians that committed the depredations on this frontier the past year were composed of Bad Face Sioux of the Ogallala band, numbering about forty lodges, and have not been fed at this agency. The head-men of these outlaws are Crazy Horse, Little Big Man, and Little Hawk. It is reported these have headed the war parties that killed the whites. Red Cloud is called the chief of all the Bad Faces by the Indians, and most of his relatives belong to the outlaws. His son-in-law was one of the principals in killing the two women in the Sweetwater country in July.

For the good of the Indians, as well as the peace of the frontier, it is important that these murderers be summarily dealt with. By education the Indian is incapable of appreciating leniency, and to prevent a border war it requires more firmness in their management. To do this the agent must have force to enforce his demands.

The Cheyenne and Arapahoes, for the first time since their treaty with the Government, have all been at the agency the greater part of the year. They behaved themselves well and avoided all bad talk in their councils. These Indians are anxious for an agency by themselves, which is considered advisable if selected on the reservation, as their going south to join their people is impracticable, and they should be away from the Sioux in drawing their rations.

Very respectfully, your obedient servant,

J. W. DANIELS,
Acting United States Indian Agent.

The COMMISSIONER OF INDIAN AFFAIRS,
Washington, D. C.

35.

SHOSHONE AND BANNACK AGENCY,
Wyoming Territory, September 17, 1873.

SIR: I have the honor to submit the following annual report relative to the progress of the service at this agency.

The Shoshone Indians have, since my last report, deliberately resolved in council to settle down on their reservation and cease their migratory habits. The number at that time on the reservation was 791 men, women, and children, numbering 126 lodges. Nearly all of the families wanted implements, seed, and land to commence farming last spring. There was about 200 acres of land broke in a field of 320 acres, all of which they plowed over with their ponies, assisted with the Government work-cattle, and sowed with wheat, or planted with potatoes and garden-vegetables. Though pretty well prepared for a small beginning, I had not anticipated so many new farmers requiring more plows, harness, and other implements, than I was able to supply. All worked, men and women, old and young, with great good humor and perseverance. It has been necessary to employ additional white men to assist in instructing them, irrigating their crops, &c.

Each family worked a piece of ground separately. It is believed they will cultivate a large amount of land next year, and a new field of about 300 acres has been fenced in this summer by the employés, and a frame building 20 × 40 feet is being erected to store Indian grain and protect farming implements. The aggregate amount of the crop raised by the Indians this year will be from ten to twelve hundred bushels of wheat, from two and a half to three thousand bushels of potatoes, and a considerable amount of carrots, beets, onions, and other vegetables for winter use.

There is a growing interest felt in schools, though some difficulties still to overcome; superstition and want of parental authority are perhaps the greatest. The teacher is laboring with commendable zeal, and about forty boys have been instructed during the past year. Those that attended with some degree of regularity have advanced rapidly.

Houses for the Indians to live in would not only conduce to more regular attendance at school, but would have a civilizing influence over them in many ways. They speak of houses and cattle as their greatest want not yet provided for. They have been comfortably subsisted during the past year. This has been dealt to them by a regular system, by which every man, woman, and child get their exact rations, and the tally-paper of each issue, giving the number of Indians and the amount issued, is filed away for reference.

Treaty stipulations on the part of the Government have in the last three years been strictly complied with at this agency; perhaps the only exception is the continued and persistent effort of white men to crowd upon the reservation, the bad result of which may be severely felt at some future time.

The general appearance of the Indians has very much improved. Instead of the dirty, squalid, sickly people they once were, they are now becoming much more tidy in their dress and cleanly in their persons and habits; they are cheerful and healthy, and say that there are about two births for one death in the tribe, whereas they were heretofore rapidly decreasing.

Neighboring tribes of Indians have sent runners to this agency to see if it was true that the Shoshones had settled quietly down on their reservation and commenced farming. The Crow Nation has sent, congratulating the Shoshones on the favorable change in their affairs. Shoshones who left the tribe long ago, and other Shoshones, mixed bloods, numbering 46 lodges and 216 souls, have lately come into the agency, and ask that they may be permitted to stay and learn to farm; and it is reported among the Indians that many more desire to come, and I have no doubt will be here in due time.

Many difficulties have to be met and overcome, yet there is no reason known to me why these Indians shall not be self-subsisting in a very few years, and a secure foundation laid for civilization.

I am, very respectfully, your obedient servant,

JAMES IRWIN,
United States Special Indian Agent.

Hon. EDWARD P. SMITH,
Commissioner of Indian Affairs, Washington, D. C.

36.

OFFICE INDIAN AGENT, NEZ PERCÉ INDIANS,
Lapwai, Idaho, September 9, 1873.

SIR: In compliance with the requirements of the Department I respectfully submit the following as my annual report:

THE TRIBE.

During the past year the Indians have been unusually quiet; those living on the reserve having engaged largely in farming, manifesting greater interest than ever before, and the results of their labors showing greater progress in the art of husbandry; and if they continue to progress as rapidly as appearances now indicate they will, it will not be long before they will be in reality a civilized people and worthy of becoming citizens.

Those living outside the reserve are mostly non-treaties, and do not make much progress or advancement. They have given no trouble during the past season, and seem to have made up their minds to get along as easily as possible with all.

Joseph and band have spent the greater part of the summer in the Wallowa Valley and will remain there until snow falls.

FARMING.

The crops are much better this season than last, and those Indians who cultivated their fields will have plenty and to spare. Many such will find a good market for their surplus, having from fifty to one hundred bushels of grain for sale. The products of lands cultivated for the agency is in excess of that of last year. Will have an abundance of vegetables for the schools and nearly enough wheat for one year. The table of statistics will give details of farming.

There are many old Indians that have been cast off who will have to be cared for during the coming winter; a part of their subsistence will come from that raised at the agency.

SCHOOLS.

The boarding school has been in successful operation until the first of July, when a vacation was given. Many of the boys were getting tired of being kept in school so long, and I thought it best to let them go home and help their parents through harvest, and by such means prevent them from getting dissatisfied and running away.

The scholars have made marked progress in their studies the past year; one is capable of carrying on a correspondence with friends living in adjacent Territories, and is now as good an interpreter as can be found among the Indians. The school will commence again the 15th of September with renewed vigor, and we hope to have many new scholars to look after. The schools will be divided; the one at Kamiah for the girls and the one at Lapwai for the boys, which will prevent some trouble we have had heretofore by keeping the two sexes together.

IMPROVEMENTS.

There has not been the amount of building among the Indians I hoped for this season. As soon as our mill is repaired I believe the Indians will bring along their logs, and we may yet be able to do something in getting out lumber and building for them this season. During the summer and fall I have caused to be erected at Lapwai one church and one hospital and dispensary, and at Kamiah one church and one boarding and lodging house for the school, all of which make a great improvement to the Government buildings.

In this connection I would call attention to an estimate forwarded some time ago, and which now accompanies this report, for buildings for employés. We need two new buildings at Lapwai and two at Kamiah. I have six employés at Kamiah outside the school, and only two very uncomfortable and small log-houses for them to live in. Here at the agency there are but three buildings that are fit to be occupied as dwellings, the balance are continually needing repairs. United States inspector of Indian affairs, E. C. Kemble, said they ought to be condemned, and said he would recommend that the new buildings be allowed. The repairing of the Lapwai mills will be commenced next week and completed as soon as possible.

INDIANS LIVING OUTSIDE THE RESERVE.

The Department cannot too soon take the necessary steps toward those living outside the reserve. It should be decided who are to come on the reserve and occupy the suitable lands that can be found, so far as such lands will go, allowing each head of the family twenty acres, and the remainder allowed to take the same amount of land in the localities decided upon, and the same attached or considered a part of this reserve, that protection may be theirs, and prevent settlers from crowding the Indians off or interfering with their rights as now is the case. The treaty of 1863, as also the treaty of 1868, provides for the locating of all the Indians, and it should be done at as early a day as possible.

Some measures ought to be adopted whereby the Indians can be prevented from going to the buffalo country. A party has just come in with great stories of how they whipped a party of Sioux and captured mules, horses, &c., creating quite a desire on the part of many to go back next spring and try their hand at it. When they go they stay one year, consequently nothing can be done toward civilizing such, and by their example they keep others from settling down. If orders could be given to the military to turn back all Indians from this side of the mountains next summer, I think it would have the desired effect, and end all trouble in the future from that source. Many of the old Indians would rejoice at such a move.

During August Hon. J. P. C. Shanks visited this agency, spending one week. He seemed much pleased with what he saw here and the appearance of the Indians. He met most of the leading men of the treaty and non-treaties.

The last of August E. C. Kemble, esq., United States inspector Indian affairs, made this agency a visit, remaining eight days, during which time he examined accounts, papers, buildings, &c., also visited Kamiah, leaving here for Colville, September 3, 1873.

Estimated cost of four new buildings required for use of the employés on the Nez Percé Indian reservation, Idaho.

Two dwellings at Lapwai, at $1,500	$3,000
Two dwellings at Kamiah, at $1,500	3,000
	6,000

All of which is respectfully submitted.

Very respectfully, your obedient servant,

JNO. B. MONTEITH,
United States Indian Agent.

Hon. EDWARD P. SMITH,
Commissioner of Indian Affairs, Washington, D. C.

37.

FORT HALL INDIAN AGENCY, *Idaho, October* 8, 1873.

SIR: I have the honor to submit the following as my annual report of the condition of affairs in this agency:

RESERVATION.

The reservation is ample, both as to size and capacity, not only to subsist the Indians now occupying it, but with suitable arrangements could be made to accommodate several thousand. The size, embracing as it does about fifty miles square, is all that could be desired. It is a matter of doubt whether Indians in the near future, with their lack of experience in agricultural pursuits, with the labor of irrigation, and the liability of grasshoppers and crickets destroying the most promising crops, should be expected to subsist themselves; yet there is no doubt but with herds of cattle and sheep, with such ample means to subsist them as this reservation affords, especially if there could be added manufacturing and mechanical pursuits even in their most simple forms, they could soon become entirely self-supporting.

THE FARM.

Farming in this country seems to be an experiment, *i. e.*, the raising of grain, and I have no idea that any judicious man would like to depend on it exclusively for a living; yet with such facilities as this country and especially this reservation afford, there should be little apprehension of failure. The land of this farm is as good as almost any land in any part of this sage-bush country. We have reported some 200 or more acres in cultivation, to which we have added some fifty or more this season. Our crops are mostly fair, though nothing very extraordinary. The potato yield would have been much larger but for the raid of crickets on them when they had reached near the period of bloom; as it is, most of our grain and vegetables are a fair yield. There can be added to the farm some 50 or 75 acres more, with the present means of irrigation, *i. e.*, with our present amount of water and the dam already built; then, by building new dams on other streams there could be put in cultivation several thousand acres of land in addition to what we have.

STOCK.

We have a small herd of cattle, *i. e.*, small for this country, amounting, as they do, to only 150 or such a matter, including our work-cattle. This seems small, especially when thousands of cattle might be kept with ease on the reservation, and the expense only increased a small amount. Any number of Indians could be secured as herders, as they are fond of the occupation, and I have no doubt but this in the end will be the chief occupation of both whites and Indians all over this country.

MILLS.

Our mills are now in a good condition for business, except that the bolt for the flouring-mill is not yet finished; we hope, however, to have that done before spring. The saw-mill has been run during the summer and several thousand feet of logs made into lumber, and quite a portion of it is already in improvements on the place. We have about finished the house built for the physician, now occupied by the agent, and are finishing the house by the mill (built I suppose for the miller) for the physician to occupy, at least for the present. We have already built a meat-house as well as also a flour-house, each 22 by 24 feet. They will answer an excellent purpose, especially as we will have a corral sufficient to keep all Indians away while we butcher, so that the scenes heretofore occurring during the operation, making them appear a good deal more like swine than human beings, will be prevented.

INDIANS.

The Indians on the reservation are about equally divided between the Bannacks and Shoshones. The Shoshones are generally the most docile and easily managed; their reputation, at least, is the best by far. This season quite a number of Bannacks, young men, have been employed on the farm, and have done excellent service. I have no doubt, with the exception of a very few, they can be managed as easily as other Indians.

All of the Indians on the reservation have behaved far better than the same number of whites could be expected to do under similar circumstances. We have had from 30 to 40 Indians employed on the farm, and herding cattle, and more earnest and cheerful employés I have never seen. With proper men to superintend, and with facilities, and inducements to encourage, I have no doubt any number could be employed, not only on the farm, but also at mechanical labor. They seem to be ready to do almost anything that will yield the slightest income. It seems indeed a sad pity to see hundreds of men and women ready to labor even for the smallest income, and yet have to remain from year to year with nothing to do.

SCHOOLS.

We have none, nor indeed has there ever been anything like one, on the reservation; there have been, indeed, no buildings nor arrangements for a school. We however have the material now prepared, and in a few days expect to start the building and finish it before winter sets in. I secured a few days since books to start a school, and expect as soon as possible to get things in shape for proper tuition of those who may be induced to attend.

I judge from what I can learn that the Indians here were never more quiet, and things connected with them in a more hopeful shape, and yet apparently everything almost to make these men such as they can be, and ought to be, is to be done. We have, with some little change in the form of the treaty which is now hoped for soon, and with proper outlay of means and example, labor and patience on the part of those employed to look after them, as well as the same solicitude and evident willingness on the part of the Department that has already been shown since our labor here, the most cheerful hope for the future.

Respectfully, yours,

HENRY W. REED,
United States Indian Agent.

Hon. EDWARD P. SMITH,
Commissioner of Indian Affairs.

38.

CROW AGENCY, MONTANA, *September* 28, 1873.

SIR: I have the honor to submit herein my third annual report in regard to the Crow Agency, and the Indians under my charge.

The Mountain Crows now number about thirty-two hundred souls, including half-breeds and remnants of other tribes, who have become incorporated in the Crow Nation. They still continue to conform in all respects, as nearly as practicable, to their treaty stipulations. About fifty lodges of River Crows have remained with the Mountain Crows during the past year, and have been mostly subsisted and clothed out of the Mountain Crow fund. Twenty lodges more have lately joined the Mountain Crows, and the balance (twenty lodges) have notified me that they would soon come to this agency, and remain permanently with the Mountain Crows, thereby making but one tribe. The River Crows, in all, number about twelve hundred souls.

On the 21st of September, 1872, a large war party of Sioux and Arapahoe Indians made a raid upon this agency, running off a large amount of stock, killing one white man, (Dr. Frost,) two Crow squaws, and one Crow infant. Again, this season, on the 3d of the present month, they made their appearance, and tried to run off the agency stock; but being discovered in time by the employés of the agency, they received such a warm reception that they failed to accomplish their undertaking, further than killing Charles Noyes and Joseph Hosea, who were at the time about one mile from the agency buildings, and in getting away with a few head of cows and oxen belonging to the agency.

About two o'clock a. m. of the 30th of October, 1872, a fire was discovered by the watchman in the bastion and laborers' quarters, and although the alarm was promptly given and every endeavor was made to save the buildings composing the stockade, owing to a high gale of wind prevailing at the time, the buildings were all destroyed, together with most of their contents. For further information upon this subject I respectfully refer you to my special report of the fire, soon after its occurrence.

From what material I could use from Indian houses, I succeeded in erecting temporary houses and quarters, sufficient, barely, to prevent freezing during the winter.

On the 10th day of February last I issued to the Mountain Crows their annuities for 1872, in the presence of Capt. L. C. Forsyth, who was detailed from Fort Ellis, Montana, to witness the same.

In regard to the farming operations at this agency for the present season, I have to report almost an entire failure. Owing to the farm being situated in the low bottom-land, near the river, the extreme high flood inundated nearly the whole of the farm for some two months, thereby almost utterly destroying the entire crop. A portion of the cereals would however have matured had it not been that a large and destructive army of grasshoppers made its appearance just before the grain was ripe. For further particulars on this subject, see farming statistics.

In regard to the progress of the schools, I have to report the same old story; the constant warfare between the Crows and Sioux, and the unsettled condition of this agency, being the excuse as usual. But the real fact is, that the Crows have not yet been agency Indians long enough to see and understand the necessity of an English education, or the benefits derived therefrom. In my opinion, the only way to accomplish anything in the way of educating these Indians, is by having a series of books published in their own language.

On the 31st of July last, Hon. F. R. Brunot, Gen. E. Whittlesey, and Dr. James Wright, arrived at this agency with instructions from the Hon. Secretary of the Interior to negotiate with the Crows for their present reservation. After fully understanding their business and instructions, and the wishes of the Government in regard to them, the commissioners, on the 16th of August, completed an agreement with them to cede all their present reservation, and to take in lieu thereof what is known as the Judith Basin, comprising about one-third the extent of territory as that of the present reservation, and lying on the south side of the Missouri River. In connection with this matter, I beg leave to state that the supplies not yet having arrived from the East, I have been compelled to purchase sugar, coffee, &c., from N. Story, in order to subsist these Indians in accordance with treaty stipulations. I have also been compelled to purchase supplies for hospital use, on requisition of physician, and by recommendation of the special commission, such as tea, rice, hominy, fruit, and corn meal, to be issued to sick Indians; and hope my action in the matter will meet the approval of the Department.

Having received orders, I accordingly turned over the Crow agency and all property and appurtenances thereto belonging, on the 17th instant, to my successor, James Wright.

Respectfully submitted,

F. D. PEASE,
Agent for Crow Indians.

Hon. COMMISSIONER INDIAN AFFAIRS,
Washington, D. C.

39.

FLATHEAD INDIAN AGENCY, MONTANA,
September 8, 1873.

SIR: I have the honor to submit this my first annual report of the condition and management of this agency. I also inclose herewith statistics of farming and education.

On the 1st of January last I relieved my predecessor, Mr. C. S. Jones, and on the same day assumed the duties of agent. The condition in which I found the agency was as poor as could be described; the work-cattle were worthless, three of them having since died, and the balance of the band are not expected to survive the coming winter. There was only one serviceable wagon, no serviceable plow, and the harrow consisted of a few pieces of iron driven through some bars of rotten wood. The only property which could at all be utilized (except the mills) was a span of horses and the wagon, neither of which were first class.

There was not subsistence and forage enough to keep life in employés and stock for one week. The buildings were dilapidated and few, and everything wore an appearance of gloom and decay; even the Indians appeared to have no confidence in any statements made to them.

Of the twenty Indian houses ordered built by General Garfield, August 27, 1872, not one had been finished, nor did the work on the four which had been commenced amount to as much as the completion of one; neither was there any timber on hand or cut for the purpose; and this was used as an argument by the Flatheads in justification of their non-compliance with the terms of the contract made between General Garfield and themselves, (August 27, 1872.)

After a full review of the situation I deemed it advisable to change the condition of things as soon as possible. I therefore immediately commenced breaking and fencing land preparatory to putting in crops, in order that I may thereby infuse the Indians with a spirit of industry and self-sustenance. In order to facilitate the building of the Flathead houses, on the 20th of March I employed additional men and teams and continued to employ additional means according to the exigencies of the service, until their completion, which was effected on the 30th of June last. These houses are 16 by 18 feet, one and a half stories high, well lined and ceiled, with good shingle roofs and adobe chimneys, and one door and two windows each. Six are frames and fourteen sawed logs, (the latter being preferred by the Indians.) Two are for the second and third chiefs, and are double the size described. In addition to those, I have built one large four-room house for use and occupancy by the resident physician, and repaired the shops for present use.

Thus I have built 21 houses, repaired others, erected 1,480 rods of fencing, broken and seeded 140 acres of land, made about 6 miles of irrigating and other ditches, cut about 60 tons of hay, 40 tons of it a distance of 10 miles from the agency and the balance about four; built an excellent roller, and have now on hand a good stock of tools, agricultural implements, and machinery. I have also secured the entire agency-crop and am making preparation for the erection of a school-house, barn, shops, employés' quarters, &c., all of which can be erected by next spring. As soon as the shops are completed and in operation I would recommend that Indian boys be taken from the agency-school and instructed in the different branches of mechanism. With this object in view, I have directed the teachers in charge to nominate those that appear most capable of acquiring and utilizing a knowledge of the different trades, in order that they be placed under instructions as soon as practicable after the approval of this recommendation by the honorable Commissioner.

I am endeavoring to induce these people to abandon war and the chase and adopt the ways of civilization and industry. With this object in view I have offered to fence, break, and seed a piece of land for each family that remain at home from war and hunting, and also prepare a sufficient quantity of lumber to build a home for each. Promising these Indians nothing but what I give, and always giving when I can, I have thereby gained their confidence and respect.

As there is nothing could tend more to the elevation and civilization of these people than education, and as the boarding-school system is the only one by which it can successfully be attained, I would earnestly recommend that an annual appropriation of $3,000 be made for the extension and maintenance of the one conducted by the Sisters of Charity at Saint Ignatius Mission on this reservation. With this additional appropriation educational facilities can be afforded in the boarding-school to all the children who can be induced to avail themselves of its advantages. The yearly cost of schools on the reservation exceeds $4,000; of this amount the Government has been paying only $1.800, and the balance has been provided by the Sisters of Charity and the labors of the Missionary Fathers. The schools are now in successful operation. There are 27 pupils in the boarding-school and 50 on the roll of the day-school. They are taught spelling, reading, writing, arithmetic, geography, grammar, and history; the girls are also instructed in sewing and other needle-work and house-work generally. The boarding scholars are making good progress; but the day, very little.

The sanitary condition of the tribes will compare favorably with that of neighboring ones. The establishment of a hospital, as recommended in my letter of the 27th ult., is anxiously looked for by them.

The substitution of agricultural implements for blankets as annuities is agreeable to them, and though not yet having an opportunity of practically testing the matter, I believe the result will be beneficial and satisfactory.

The Flatheads and Pend d'Oreilles are more industrious than the Kootenays, the Flatheads having 52 farms under cultivation and the Pend d'Oreilles 55, averaging 15 acres each, making 1,155 acres, while the Kootenays have but 4 farms, or about 60 acres.

The extension of the boarding-school, establishment of a hospital, and introduction of agricultural implements will be productive of the most satisfactory results. These Indians are well and peaceably disposed to the Government and the whites, and there need be no apprehension of any hostile demonstration from them. I take pleasure in stating that I have never seen an Indian of this confederation under the influence of liquor or evince a spirit of hostility to the whites. Although no danger need be apprehended from the confederated tribes of this agency, yet there is a large and uncontrolled band of Nez Percés which camp in and around Missoula every spring, and the law in relation to the sale of liquors to Indians being defective, some mercenary whites engage in the whisky-traffic with them to such an extent as to cause them to indulge in its excessive use, and when under its influence they are perfectly furious and dangerous to the lives and property of the people of Missoula and vicinity, and in my opinion the establishment of a military post at the latter place is the only protection its people have for life or property.

Sharing in the desire of the Government and a majority of the people of this Territory to effect the removal of the Flatheads from the Bitter Root Valley to this reservation, (as well as endeavoring to do my duty as an officer,) I gave the matter my earliest attention, and on the 19th of April last, I had so far succeeded as to secure the hearty co-operation of the missionaries, and thereby gain the entire confidence of those Indians; and on the 20th of that month 14 families had promised me that they would remove as soon as their houses were built, and desired my interpreter and myself to select locations for them. Subsequently nearly all of them expressed themselves in favor of accepting such locations as I may select; but, on the 5th of May, I accompanied the then Superintendent Wright to the Bitter Root Valley, and, agreeably to his wishes, I called the Indians to council on the 6th, when, to my utter astonishment, all those people most positively refused to remove, and expressed an entire want of confidence in his statements. Many of them made speeches in opposition to their removal, and based the strength of their arguments on the non-fulfillment by the Government of treaty-stipulations and other contracts. On this occasion they frequently interrupted Mr. Wright by asking him if he was speaking the truth in the presence of his God. Having never abandoned the hope of effecting the peaceful removal of this tribe, I have never ceased to work for the accomplishment of that purpose, and there is now no reasonable doubt of the removal of a large portion of it within the next sixty days. When the tribe becomes thus divided the balance will soon follow to the reservation, and there being no pressing necessity for their immediate removal it would be impolitic to resort to coercion.

I have visited most of the Indian lodges and houses in the Bitter Root Valley, and talked as much as possible with the white settlers, and notwithstanding the desire of the latter to see troops brought into requisition, yet some of them don't wish to part with the Indians; nor can they state more than one case in which a Flathead has committed a crime against a white person, and this was the shooting of a cow by one who received one hundred and fifty lashes for the offense by order of the chief Charlos.

In reference to the act of January 5, 1873, I have spent from the 1st to the 6th instant in the Bitter Root Valley, with the view of directing the Flathead Indians in the selection of their lands; but I have found none who wish to avail themselves of the benefits of that act. Those refusing to remove to the Jocko reservation state that they will remain in the Bitter Root Valley as Indians, not as citizens, and we may survey their lands as much as we please, but they will neither recognize survey boundaries or pay taxes.

Arley and Adolph, second and third chiefs, have on this occasion again promised me that they and twelve or fourteen families would remove to this reservation in two weeks time, and others would follow from time to time until none but Charlos, first chief, and one or two others be left in the Bitter Root Valley. In order to secure the active co-operation of the second chief, I promised to recommend him as head chief of the tribe in place of Charlos, who forfeits his right by refusing to remove or be a citizen. And in consideration of the services he has rendered, I therefore recommend that Arley be made head-chief of the Flathead tribe.

Very respectfully, your obedient servant,

D. SHANAHAN,
United States Indian Agent.

Hon. EDWARD P. SMITH,
Commissioner of Indian Affairs, Washington, D. C.

40.

BLACKFOOT AGENCY, MONTANA,
September 1, 1873.

SIR: In accordance with instructions from the Department, I have the honor to submit herewith my annual report.

DISPOSITION OF INDIANS.

I arrived here and took charge of the agency September 15, 1872, and from that time up to the present writing, with one exception, which was reported at the time of the occurrence, I have not learned of any depredations upon white men, by Indians under my charge. Their desire, expressed and acted upon, has been not only to sustain peaceable but friendly relations with their "white neighbor," and I am pleased to report, as a general rule, an equally kind feeling existing on the part of the better class of settlers on the borders of the reservation.

Quite a number of the Piegan tribe have expressed a willingness to settle, live in houses and cultivate the soil, and were it not for the infamous whisky-traffic, (of which I shall make more extended mention hereafter,) I have not the slightest doubt but that I might have been able to report a fair representation of the Indians as cultivating farms.

NUMBERS.

As nearly as I have been able to ascertain from positive data, and such reliable information as has been furnished me by the principal chiefs, I find the estimate made last year of the different tribes belonging to this agency about correct, to wit:

	No. of lodges.	No. of Indians.
Blackfeet	600	3,000
Bloods	300	1,750
Piegans	350	2,750
Total	1,250	7,500

Of these, the Piegans are the only Indians who, as a tribe, come to the agency for supplies. One band of the Bloods, under the chief Running Rabbit, also come regularly for their rations; but every effort on my part to induce the Blackfeet and the main camp of Bloods to visit the agency has thus far proved abortive. These tribes range north of the British line, from two hundred and fifty to four hundred miles from the agency, and are kept from coming in by illicit traders, who stop at nothing to accomplish their purposes, thus securing the very profitable trade of the Indians.

RESERVATION ESTABLISHED.

The recent executive order, setting aside a large portion of territory, viz, from the Missouri River on the south to the northern boundary of Montana, and from Sun River on the west, extending eastward to Dakota Territory, for the benefit of the Blackfeet Nation, including Blackfeet, Blood, and Piegan tribes, and other Indians, is an action long needed and will prove of incalculable importance and benefit to the Indians and to the Department. Heretofore, with no defined reservation limits, a great portion of the work of the agent has necessarily proved futile in its results. Official orders have been quite ignored, and when any objective ends were attained, their accomplishment has been under disadvantage of which the fact of no regularly defined reservation having been established was the sole cause. This laudable change will at once work radical cures for a great many existing evils.

THE WHISKY-TRAFFIC.

The most stubborn opposition with which I have had to contend, and the one great evil with which I have been constantly fighting, is the infamous business of trading liquor to Indians. It has been estimated that, during the past six years, no less than six hundred barrels of liquor, and that of the most poisonous quality, have been yearly traded to the Blackfeet Nation, and during that time no less than *twenty-five per cent.* of the three tribes have died from the effects of liquor alone.

I have fought this monster with varying success during the past year; but, with the limited resources at my disposal, it has been impossible to entirely stop it. Upon my return from a short stay in the East, during my recent leave of absence, I find that no less than thirty-two Piegan Indians, including two prominent chiefs, were killed through the agency of liquor; and to any question which might be asked concerning progress of the Indians, and why they are not rapidly improving in industry, civilization and religion, the answer " whisky " might be truthfully given in every instance.

I have recently, with the approval of the Department, appointed an efficient detective force, to act under the direction of Mr. Charles D. Hard, who, by cool determination, and a complete knowledge of the country and of the class of individuals with whom he has to deal, has proven himself eminently fitted for the position; and with the reservation lines clearly established, and the active co-operation of this force, I have every encouragement to hope for a speedy and thorough check to the whisky business.

EDUCATIONAL INTERESTS.

Until my arrival, last September, there had never been any school at this agency, and it was with the greatest difficulty that any of the children could be induced to attend school regularly. At the first opening of the school-house the room was crowded, but, just as soon as the curiosity of the children had been satisfied, they would leave, and their places would be filled by as many more, when they in turn would take their departure, until (according to the estimate of the teachers) nearly five hundred children had visited the school-room, solely from curiosity, none of them returning more than three or four times. And although the school, to all appearances, was in a flourishing condition, there was really nothing accomplished until some little white children, families of agency employés, commenced attending regularly, when a few Indian children, following their example, became more regular in attendance, and around this little nucleus others have been gathering, until at present there are twenty-eight or thirty regular scholars; and the white and Indian children are pleasantly contending together for the honors of their various classes. Suitable buildings are now in course of preparation, and will soon be occupied as dormitories and kitchen for a boarding-school, when I shall be able to largely increase the number of regular scholars and make the school one of the principal features of the agency. For further particulars concerning school I respectfully refer you to statistics of education accompanying this report.

FARMING AND AGRICULTURAL INTERESTS.

Potatoes, of which there will be harvested about 3,000 bushels, is the only crop of which I can speak favorably, the cereals having been nearly, if not quite, destroyed by grasshoppers. These pests, in perfect myriads, visited the farm during the latter part of July and first of August, sweeping everything in the shape of grain. Turnips, and cabbage were so badly damaged as to entirely stop their growth. Potatoes, however, resisted, and will yield a handsome crop. As soon as haying and harvesting shall have been completed, I shall put teams at work breaking up new ground, preparatory to putting in a much larger seeding of vegetables next year. Ten thousand bushels of potatoes and turnips could be advantageously issued to Indians; and, as a sanitary measure, it is important that they should have a proportion of vegetable diet. I shall also break up several garden plats and build several additional houses, and expect, with the abolition of the liquor trade, to induce a like number of Indian families to settle down and cultivate the soil.

MISSION WORK.

It is a fact to be regretted that there has never been a mission-school established, neither any missionary labor on the reservation. The Blackfeet Nation of Indians affords a large field for work of this kind, and I earnestly hope that something will be done in this direction during the coming year.

I am, sir, very respectfully, your obedient servant,

WM. T. ENSIGN,
U. S. Indian Agent for Blackfeet and others.

Hon. EDWARD P. SMITH,
Commissioner Indian Affairs, Washington, D. C.

41.

OFFICE OF NEVADA INDIAN AGENCY,
PRYAMID LAKE RESERVATION,
Nevada, September 30, 1873.

SIR: According to the regulations of the Indian Department, I have the honor to submit the following as my third annual report as United States Indian agent in Nevada.

One year ago, when I submitted my second annual report, I was full of hope, and only looked forward with bright prospects to an early and continued success. And now, as I retrospect the year that is past, I am constrained to believe that while disappointments have had their place, and not as much of success as anticipated has attended our efforts, yet much has been gained for which we have cause to be grateful.

One thing is apparent to all conversant with our work: An increased interest on the part of a largely increased number of Indians in the measures put forth by the Government for their improvement. At first it was not often you could see Indians at work unless a superintendent was with them continually, but now at almost any time you can see Indians working, improving their ranches, building fences, hauling stone for dams, digging ditches, clearing lands, and, in fact, doing any and all kinds of work known to the farmer.

In passing an Indian ranch, a few days ago, I discovered a building going up, the mechanism of which was so novel that I got out of my wagon to inspect it. It was about 14x18 feet in size, and was constructed by cutting timber about 6 inches in diameter and 10 or 12 feet long, squaring both ends and then setting one end in a trench in the ground, and bringing the top ends to a line; hewing each row so that they would fit closely together; and thus the building was complete. I interrogated the leader as to what he was building, and he said it was for a chicken-house. I pronounced it royal, and who knows but some wayfaring divine may yet have occasion to thank him for his industry in this department of civilization?

But this was not all; the same Indian desired that I should leave my team in care of "one of the boys," and go with him. I went, and, to my surprise, he brought me to a corral where I was shown a fine young cow, with a calf by her side, that he had purchased a short time previous. What could I say? One year ago I recommended to the Department the stocking of the reservations with cattle for breeding, as one of the most important measures that could be adopted. The appropriation was not made; but here, an Indian, of his own accord, and with his own appropriation, had made the beginning. It was good to see the sparkle in his eye while he was thus showing me around. But this was not all. The same Indian and his band of associates have raised their second crop, and the past year received from the Government not to exceed twenty-five dollars. They have broken their own horses, and have plowed, sown, and reaped enough to give them a good support.

It affords me the greatest pleasure to be able to state that, as the Indians improve, a growing sympathy toward them is apparent on the part of the citizens of this commonwealth.

I have not been visited, as I have often desired and many times expressed, by commissioners during my service in Nevada; but now and then visitors have favored me with their presence, and, after a brief sojourn, have gone from our field of labors with advanced views of the work, and to present the workings of the policy to others in a way to bring sympathy and interest.

Much is due to the press for the hearty support given to the efforts put forth to ameliorate the condition of the Indians. * * * But you may say that the Indians cannot read, and how can they be thus inspired? Very true; but scarcely a report is made through the press that they do not learn about. They cannot read, but their hearing is acute.

I said, in the beginning of this report, that one year ago I was full of hope of a speedy success; and so I was. We had raised a fine crop for the number of acres cultivated and the meager means we had for irrigating the lands; the season had been in our favor; an abundance of snow on the mountains had kept the streams up, and the seepage had aided materially in making up for any lack on the part of the ditches. And it being in reality the first crop raised upon the reservations of Nevada, by the Indians, increased numbers were enlisted to work the past season, and there was no reluctance manifested by them in opening their bins and sacks of last year's growing and sending forth their grain for sowing the larger and more perfectly prepared fields. This year, at least twice the number of acres were sowed as the year before. No one could have witnessed the industry of the Indians in clearing off the lands, fencing, cutting cross-ditches, &c., without feeling that they were worthy of great efforts and appliances in their behalf. To me it was an incentive to present large claims, and press them with more than common earnestness. This I tried to do by showing to the Department, and all concerned, the necessity of flumes and improved means for irrigation. * * * * * * ** * * * *

I now see that, could we have had the works complete that are now being completed, a much more favorable report at this time might have been presented. The past season proved unpropitious; but little snow fell in the mountains; the rivers on both reservations have been remarkably low during nearly the whole season, and therefore, though we had fully twice the number of acres under cultivation the present that we had the previous year, yet the aggregate of crops was not equal to the previous harvest.

The Walker River reservation has suffered more in this respect than that of the Pyramid Lake, from the fact that a rain on the mountains of the head-waters of the Walker River caused a sudden rise of such force as to break the irrigating ditch, and before the same could be repaired the water was so low that almost an entire failure of crops was the result. But assured of success, the undaunted *savages*, as they are called, went to work, and with our assistance in constructing waste-weirs, flumes, and head-gates, they have not only repaired the breach, but have made it what it should have been at first. And though they failed the past year, they are sanguine that a better future awaits them.

"Better late than never" is an old adage, but most of us prefer not to wait. In due time the Department was favored by Congress, and though too late to help us the past season, the instructions came, and with the same the collateral for the long-desired flumes. And while I am writing this report, a good, strong force of experienced workmen are engaged in building a flume for the irrigation of this reserve, which will be, when complete, twelve hundred feet long, three feet wide in the clear, and twelve inches deep. to take the water from the hard bank on the west side, carry it across the whole of the sand-flat, across the Truckee River, and thence to the hard banks of the east side.

At the same time a good, strong force of Indians are at work on a canal commencing two miles and a half up the river from head of flume, all of which, in all probability, will be completed within the next four weeks. The ditch of itself is a wonderful undertaking for Indians, but, assured of its importance, the work goes on. And when it is complete, I trust my antiquated Baptist cry for *much water* will cease, for I am assured there will be enough for all practical purposes.

Other useful and important improvements have been made during the year. I need mention only one or two. Ever since I entered the service I have seen the imperative want of two bridges; one to cross the slough or inlet of Mud or Winnemucca Lake, which puts out of the Truckee River near its terminus in Pyramid Lake. This was a great barrier to the fishing interests, especially as it deprived any and all parties from reaching the Pyramid Lake with teams. A good and substantial wagon-bridge has been completed. There was also a like want on the Walker River, near the reservation-house. At times the river was above all fording, and at such times great difficulty was found in carrying on the works on both sides of the river, as in the case just above mentioned; with the approval and consent of the Department, I have had erected a strong, substantial frame wagon-bridge, worth to the service and in real value four times what it cost to build.

Store-houses have been built, and also, without cost to the Government, a nice log-house, hewn inside, for Interpreter Qeep. Including the hay-ranches, there have been added to the number of ranches of last year six new ones on Pyramid Lake and eight others upon the Walker-River reservation, and all these are ready for successful cultivation the coming year.

I regard as second to none the importance of bringing the Indians individually to care for themselves. Co-operative systems, as a general rule, are failures; and to attempt the concert of any considerable number of Indians upon a certain work is attended with untold difficulties, as they are naturally inclined to jealousy. It has been my rule to encourage single Indians with their families, or, at most, only small companies, to concert their efforts upon parcels of land cultivated, thus inspiring them to make their work permanent, to have and to hold the same, undisturbed by others.

And I suggest that some legislation might be well in the premises, to make their right secure, that Indians may not be in perpetual *qui vive* relative to changes that are at present a drawback, in this, as well as the Indian service elsewhere. An order to survey and apportion to such as may avail themselves of a permanent home, might obviate all further difficulties in this direction. The above is sustained by Mr. Frazier, my efficient foreman, whose judgment I regard of much value in these matters, as his work brings him into contact with all the difficulties connected with bringing the Indians upon a sphere of independency.

I desire now to call the attention of the Department to the fact that there is an area, according to the report of Commissioner of 1872, and sustained by surveys, of 320,000 acres in the Walker River and Pyramid Lake reservations, each, and yet it is an indisputable fact that there are not more than 1,200 acres upon the Pyramid Lake, and 1,500 acres upon the Walker River Reservation, susceptible of cultivation within this area. Upon each reserve there is a large lake, and on both sides of either lake there is scarcely any land that can be made suitable for farming purposes. Most of it, in fact, is rugged, rocky mountain peaks and ravines. Now, a portion of each lake near the mouths of the rivers that flow through the reservations is important to the Indians for fishing purposes, but the larger portion is entirely worthless for the Indian service; in fact, it is a burden, as it only requires an expenditure of time to guard.

I respectfully recommend that all that portion of Pyramid Lake reservation north of a due east and west line from the north side of the island be cut off. It is of no use whatever, as I have said, to this service. This will give to the Indians and this service, after said reduction, more than twelve miles of the Pyramid Lake—all that can ever be made available for fishing purposes. I also recommend that a like reduction be made on the Walker River reservation, by cutting off all that part; in a direct line east and west, south of what is known as the Wellington Pass, giving fully six miles of the Walker Lake to the Indian service, and every foot that can be cultivated. Now, I should never recommend these reductions could I see the least benefit to be derived to the Government or Indian service. The question then may arise, if all that portion is no benefit, what harm will it be to let it remain, and what can be the object in the reduction? In answer, I have to say, strange as it may appear, anything that is forbidden seems to be always coveted. Though there are millions of acres of good lands in the territory of the United States that can be had by simply occupying them, yet the disposition to encroach upon reserves seems to be a mania. And lands never so rugged or remote from civilization are not exempt from those of the class above mentioned.

* * * * * * * * *

I pass now to notice the sanitary condition of the Indians, which, as a general rule, has continued good; still, there have been quite a number of deaths, especially upon the Walker River reservation, and among the children. Sore eyes still predominate as the most general difficulty. In another report I have given this subject thorough notice, and this will suffice, while I turn to notice, as in last annual report, the educational interest.

To make a report I will not attempt, for there is none to make, though I lament the fact; but did I know what course to pursue to bring about the desired end, I would try to pursue it. The time has come to establish schools upon these reserves. Good, faithful teachers are ready to enter the work, but who can make brick without straw? A friend in Boston wrote me some time ago, that all our cause needed was a visit from me to the East, when the denomination to which was given the direction of these Indian interests would respond to our call, and success would follow. I feel that it ought to be enough for one man to laden himself with the responsibility of preparing the way and superintending the enterprise when established; but if it is necessary, and the Department so approve and direct, I will consent; anything in the way of work for me, that the end may be gained.

The trout fisheries, the past season, resulted in a larger revenue than ever before in a single year. By careful estimate it is judged that the Pah-Ute Indians, from the Pyramid Lake and Truckee River, caught and sold to the amount of ten thousand dollars' worth of fish. Upon the Walker River reservation, large quantities were caught, but there being no near market, they could not be sold. However, a great benefit was derived from the fishery for home consumption.

Just at this time, the large portion of the Indians from both reservations are absent in the mountains gathering pine-nuts, and from reports of this yield the present year, it will be impossible to even approximate the amount that will be gathered. No doubt hundreds of tons will be secured by the Indians, which will make up, in a large measure, for the failure of crops.

I must not close this report without a record of the course of my Indians during the unhappy war with the Modocs last winter. For some time it was apprehended that the roving bands of Pah-Utes were in concert with the Modocs. Our Indians were apparently conversant with all the movements of Captain Jack and his followers.

Three days' ride from this agency, for an Indian, would bring him to the lava-beds. It was a time of watchfulness with me, for I meant to detect, if possible, any connection, if there was any, with the belligerents.

One day, I think in February, Captain Joe, one of the faithful leaders on this reserve, brought me a letter to read for him, just received. I opened it and found it signed by the name of Winnemucca, the old war-chief of the Pah-Utes, known to be unfriendly toward the whites. The contents of the letter were as follows:

"Captain Joe: Some Indians have been killed over on Stein River, and I you want to come and bring some of your best men and go see about it."

This seemed to indicate a movement in alliance with the Modocs. As soon as I read the letter to the captain, he asked me if I would write a letter for him. I answered in the affirmative, assuring him I would write what he desired. "Then, agent," dictated the captain, "you write old Winnemucca that I haint lost any Indians and shall not come." With this brief letter terminated all communications relative to the war, on the part of those with whom I have to do; and nothing would produce more anxiety in their minds than the utterance that the Government believed them in any way associated with the war. * * * * * *

One fact I think worthy of note. When I entered this office, in the superintendency of the Walker River and Pyramid Lake reservations, the Indian service was in debt between seven and eight thousand dollars. To-day I have satisfaction to say that, so far as I am aware, the Indian service in this superintendency does not owe one dime.

With gratitude for the generous forbearance of the Department, and humbly urging that sufficient means will be granted to carry forward this enterprise to the desired end,

I am, very respectfully, your obedient servant,

C. A. BATEMAN,
United States Indian Agent, Nevada.

Hon. EDWARD P. SMITH,
Commissioner of Indian Affairs.

42.

WHITE RIVER, COLORADO, *September* 30, 1873.

SIR: Agreeably to instructions, I have the honor to submit my annual report of the agency and the Indians under my charge. The five dwelling-houses at the agency have been put in a comparatively good condition for the winter. Dr. J. D. Bevier, Indian inspector, after making a thorough examination of their condition for permanent use, recommended as slight repairs as possible. He also recommended, and I approve the same, that the new buildings to be erected for the agent and the employés be put up two miles below, down the river, adjoining the best arable land in the valley. I have erected one frame house 22 by 40 feet, 8 feet high, to be used by the Utes as a reception-house, and for the purpose of holding council. It is so constructed that it can be removed without injury to the spot designed for the other buildings.

The mill is again in successful operation, the belting and frame-work having been destroyed by the fire of July 3, 1873, which caught from the furnace.

Dr. Bevier recommended, and I approve the same, that the timber necessary for the erection of the new buildings be got out and thoroughly seasoned the coming year. The pine timber, the most desirable and difficult to be obtained here, will have to be cut fifteen miles up the river and rafted down at high water in the spring. Cottonwood, which must form the principal part of the lumber, is plentiful and near the mill, and will be sawed into lumber this winter. We also require miles of fencing for a pasture and for the farming land.

The year has been a very unpropitious one for agricultural pursuits. From fifteen to twenty acres were put under cultivation in the spring, of wheat, oats, potatoes, and garden vegetables. The extreme drought, no rain having fallen from May to September of any account, prevented the crops from maturing on the irrigated lands. The wheat and oats were well irrigated in the early part of the season, and gave for a time better promise than last year, but the extreme drought caused the creek to dry up, and the countless number of grasshoppers that darkened the sky for three weeks in July, eating up every blade of grain and almost every green thing, completed the work of destruction. We succeeded, however, in putting up 100 tons of hay that grew in the low-lands and springy places, where the ravages of the grasshoppers did not prevail to so great an extent. The herd of cattle has increased from 571 to 704 during the past year; al though they are not in so fine condition as last year, owing to the scanty pasturage of the summer; yet they are in a fair condition.

The Indians, to the number of 800, have been uniformly on the reservation the entire year, with the exception of small parties, who have received passes, who have, from time to time, gone to Denver. None of them have gone farther north than

Snake River, where a trader by the name of Charles Perkins succeeded in decoying away a small party of them by trading to them whisky, causing much trouble at the agency for the first time since I have been in charge. Chief Jack narrowly escaped with his life, having been shot at three times by Peah, head chief of the tribe, whose special agency is at Denver. During the excitement succeeding the attack of the Rawlins men on a band of Arapahoes, at Pine Grove Meadows, and the Indians having been mistaken for Utes, they remained perfectly passive and quiet. They were guilty of no acts of violence upon the employés, and have maintained a quiet, orderly demeanor when the excitement along the border of the Territories of Colorado and Wyoming was at a fever heat. When I reached Rawlins, July 11, 1873, I found the people of both Territories excited to an extraordinary degree with apprehensions of a general Ute war; and the various conflicting stories and irreconcilable reports that had been put forth by the press were fully credited, which made, for the time being, matters very critical with us here. Douglass and his chiefs knew nothing of the events at Pine Grove Meadows to a certainty, but were told, on what was regarded as the most reliable authority, that they had been the sufferers in the killed and wounded in this affair; yet for at least two weeks they preserved a quiet and calm demeanor; and when he, with thirty of his warriors, went to Snake River, and Mr. James Baker, the old pioneer of the mountains, gave his opinion to them that it must have been Arapahoes and not Utes, without any positive knowledge on his part, they quietly returned to the agency to await further developments. Since that time the Utes have declared to me their gratitude to the Rawlins men for intercepting and driving back this band of Arapahoes, their most inveterate enemies, and when at the time they were attacked by the Rawlins men [they] were on the trail to White River to murder and scalp the squaws and children and steal their stock, as the Sioux did to the Pawnees this summer. At the time they were camped at Pine Grove Meadows the larger portion of the Ute women and children were camped near William's Fork, on the reservation, the warriors away hunting, and they would have fallen an easy prey to these murderous Arapahoes, armed with their Sharp's and Winchester rifles. If these predatory bands of Arapahoes, Sioux, and Cheyennes are to be allowed to make these raids on the friendly Indians, I would suggest that a fort be erected near the northern limit of the reservation; it would serve to protect the friendly and well-disposed Indians from molestation, and likewise cause the Utes to remain within the limits of their reservation.

The sanitary condition of the Indians has been very good, in comparison with last year. Our chief, Sawachewicket, an Indian doctor, and four others are all that have died that I have any knowledge of; and in comparison with last year the mortality has been light. They have been better supplied with clothing, and seem to desire to have things more in accordance with the usages of civilized life. Chief Uncachief asked to have his squaw buried according to our Christian custom, and she was so interred, the employés assisting at the burial.

No complaints or disturbances of any kind have occurred at any time during the past year, with the one exception mentioned above, caused by whisky. I am not aware of a single instance of crime having been perpetrated during the past year within the limits of the reservation. One instance of suicide, which I mentioned in a former report, having occurred, caused by depression and consequent derangement of mind.

In educational matters I have nothing to report. There was some interest manifested during the winter by a few young men; but owing to the fact of not having school-buildings suitable, and the want of interest on the part of the Indians generally, I felt it my duty to discontinue the school for the present, trusting that after we shall have erected suitable buildings it will be re-opened, and some good accomplished through the agency of a school. Only a boarding-school of an industrial character is practicable in the present stage of Ute development.

I have the honor to be, very respectfully, your obedient servant,

J. S. LITTLEFIELD,

United States Indian Agent, White River Ute Indian Agency, Colorado Territory.

Hon. E. P. SMITH,
Commissioner of Indian Affairs.

43.

LOS PINOS AGENCY, COL.,
September 26, 1873.

SIR: I have the honor to submit herewith my second annual report of the condition of affairs at this agency.

This report was necessarily delayed a few weeks on account of the pending negotiations with the Indians under my charge for a portion of their reservation, during which I had to make a trip of inspection to the territory about to be ceded. I returned from this trip on the 21st instant, and all the Utes then at the agency signed the treaty. I am in hopes, and have made the necessary arrangements, to have the requisite number of males sign before Congress meets, so that the treaty can go into effect at the commencement of the next fiscal year. It is unnecessary for me to go into details in regard to the treaty just concluded, as Mr. Brunot, commissioner, will report upon this. The country ceded by the Utes, including, as it does, probably the most extensive and richest mining district in the United States, embraces about four million acres of land, of very little value to Indians, being unfit for agricultural purposes and devoid of game, but of almost incalculable value to Colorado and the nation. A strip, fifteen miles in width, along the line of New Mexico, embracing agricultural land only, has been reserved for the southern bands, and I would respectfully recommend that at an early date, as contemplated in the new treaty, an agency be established for these southern bands upon this strip of reservation, which would obviate the necessity of continuing the agencies at Terra Amarilla and Cimarron, New Mexico. The Utes are rather inclined to agricultural pursuits, while the Tabequaches prefer to hunt and probably engage in pastoral pursuits.

During my presence upon the land just ceded, I found that quite a number of persons, in anticipation of a favorable result of the pending negotiations, had gone beyond the mountains to locate farming-claims and town-sites. As it will be necessary to survey the line dividing the strip of farming-lands from the mountainous portion just ceded, and as the whole agreement has to be ratified by both houses of Congress, before even upon the ceded lands pre-emptors can establish title, I promptly ordered all persons away from the southern portion until the line is clearly established. Upon the movements of the miners, however, in the mountainous portion I placed no restrictions.

There are several other matters connected with this agreement for the early settlement of which it has been found desirable, almost necessary, that some of the representatives of the Ute people should see the authorities at the seat of Government. I have, therefore, received instructions from Commissioner Brunot to take a delegation to Washington. These matters are of great importance to the Utes, and will permanently settle all misunderstandings. Among others, the establishment of a military fort, at least during summer, upon the portion of the territory just ceded is desired by the Utes. The question whether this agency should be removed to a place further west had better be discussed at Washington, and the question of the right of the Cimarron or Muache Utes to absent themselves from the reservation must be settled at once. I shall leave therefore all these matters in *statu quo* without recommendations until after the visit of this delegation, which will take place next month.

I am enabled this year to report approximately the number of Indians belonging to this agency. By noting and counting all fresh arrivals during this summer, I find that the following number of Utes of the different bands have actually visited the agency for the purpose of obtaining supplies, and to attend the council with United States commissioners, viz:

Tabequaches, 423 men, 557 women, 1,024 children; Muaches, 78 men, 113 women, 256 children; Capotes, 26 men, 31 women, 72 children; Weminuches, 23 men, 19 women, 41 children. Total, 550 men, 720 women, 1,393 children.

Of this number, the Weminuches were only represented by a small portion of their tribe, and their number may be estimated by the best and most authentic advices as 250 in all; but of the other three tribes it is fair to surmise, by actual knowledge and information from the chiefs, that seven-eighths of the whole have visited the agency; and so by adding one-eighth to the above figures (see statistical tables) I arrive at a result which I think is correct.

During the year no act of the Indians prejudicial to their known friendship has come to my knowledge; on the contrary, any collision with the whites has been studiously avoided by them. The first act of Ouray, the principal chief, this spring, when miners began to overrun their reservation, and the military authorities rather assisted these intruders, was to give strict orders to all his people not to interfere with any person whom they might meet, but to keep away from that part of the reservation where the mines are located. This order was issued by him in anticipation of a satisfactory arrangement with the Government in regard to this land, and it was strictly obeyed by his people. None of the many prospecting and mining, none of the scientific, military, and territorial surveying parties were molested, but, on the contrary, were sheltered and fed by the Indians in time of need.

The majority of the Indians remained on the reservation during the year, subsisting themselves six months of this period. The only band which was absent for some time was Kaneatache's of Muache Utes. On their return from the buffalo country, last spring, they stopped at the Cucharas River, about 120 miles east of this agency. Quite an excitement was created by the settlers in that neighborhood; many rumors were set afloat in the local newspapers of depredations committed and preparations for war made by them, so that it was thought necessary by the War Department to arm the settlers and send troops from Leavenworth, Kansas, to the locality mentioned The whole thing was a farce, and it exploded as soon as troops arrived; a few Utes (ten lodges) were found on the Cucharas, not enough to make war upon a single rancho. Still the object looked for by the complainants was attained; the soldiers afforded them a market for their spare provisions; each man had a nice breech-loading rifle, and immigration for another season was kept away from this section of Colorado, where the residing settlers want to keep as large an area of public lands as possible as a range for their herds.

So ended the great Cucharas war; but it teaches the lesson that as long as whiskey is sold in that neighborhood to the Indians, so long will these Indians go there. The only way to stop future complications of this kind is to give the agent power to remove such Indians as go buffalo-hunting during winter to the reservation, as soon as they return in the spring.

The Department has previously been notified that one of the murderers of Agent Miller has been killed by the Utes themselves and it is desired by them that his partner in the crime may be punished by the authorities in like manner. The Indians have certainly proved in this instance that confidence may be placed in their word, and that they will not allow the acts of individuals to bring the name of the tribe in disrepute.

Of the Rawlins affair, in which several Utes were reported murdered in cold blood, by rowdies and outlaws, who frequent the line of the Union Pacific Railway, it is unnecessary in this report to speak, as no Utes were killed after all. The conduct of the Indians, when everybody supposed the outrage to have been committed upon them, and when even the western newspapers for once denounced the act, was most commendable, as in solemn council they repudiated any idea on their part of retaliation, and left the punishment of these men to the Government. All these acts tend to show an increasing friendship on the part of the Utes for their white neighbors, and an increasing desire to comply with the wishes of the Government. I wish I could speak likewise of their desire to be civilized and become self-supporting by labor. My efforts in this regard have been persistent, and tending to encourage beginners; still the progress is slow, and it will take several years before their old prejudices can be eradicated.

The school established at this agency a year ago as an experiment, upon a very infirm basis, has been quite successful. During the early summer months, when the Indians had their camp in close proximity to the agency, great interest was manifested, and as many as twenty children attended the day-school at one time, while about forty scholars were enrolled. The small-pox appearing at the agency forced me to order the camp away several miles, and, in consequence, the attendance afterward was rather limited; the boarding scholars have made excellent progress, especially in the English language, and from their progress I expect favorable results in influencing other children to attend the day-school.

Agriculture in the neighborhood of this agency, on account of the altitude, is a decided failure. On the Uncompagre, Dolores, and La Plata streams, good crops have been raised by the few Indians living there, and several besides those who farmed last year have been induced to settle down; still, the abundance of game offers such great attraction to the majority of this people that necessity only will drive them to be tillers of the soil. They all understand that they will be obliged to do so at no very distant day, and they become more and more accustomed to this idea, and for this very reason they positively refused to sell their farming and grass lands at the late council.

Of the stock-herd belonging to the Indians in common I can report very favorably. A year ago I received from my predecessor 440 head of cattle and 69 calves, showing about 25 per cent. increase; the increase for the year past is somewhat more than 80 per cent., as I have 232 calves in a herd of 305 cows. The herd, as counted on August the 5th, consists of 305 cows, 135 bulls, steers, and two-year olds, 69 yearlings and 232 calves—a total of 741 head against 509 a year ago. I would recommend that next spring this herd be gleaned in such a manner that all bulls, stags, and steers over a year old be issued to the Indians in lieu of beef, and the money saved to them in this manner be expended in purchasing cows for them; also, that the money now on hand to purchase sheep be likewise expended for cows, as experience teaches me that neat-cattle will do much better here than sheep. I had advertised, as authorized, for proposals for sheep; the bids received, however, were above the regular market-price, so I rejected all, and would now recommend, as indicated above, that only cows and good bulls be purchased for these Indians.

I am very much disappointed in not receiving the annuity-goods for the Indians up to date. Cold weather may, in this region, be expected at any time, and upon the advent of the first snow the Indians will go west without waiting any longer. The majority have gone, and the rest will follow, as they have a dread of snow, and are very anxious to hunt the deer, which is now in its prime, and very plentiful in the valleys west of here. I have to let them go without their blankets, shirts or tents, and cloth for women's dresses; I fear great suffering will necessarily follow. They will take the goods next spring, but will never forget that once more the Government has failed to keep its promises. These goods have been on the road since June 8, but have not been heard from by me; and I would respectfully call your attention to the fact that some way should be devised in the future so that the Indians may receive the goods on or before September 1 of each year.

In conclusion, I desire to acknowledge the promptness of your Department during the year in acting upon my requisitions and recommendations, whereby I was enabled to transact the business of this office in a like prompt manner.

I have the honor to be, very respectfully, your obedient servant,

CHARLES ADAMS,
United States Indian Agent.

Hon. E. P. SMITH,
Commissioner of Indian Affairs, Washington, D. C.

44.

UINTAH VALLEY AGENCY, UTAH, *September* 25, 1873.

SIR: In accordance with the instructions of the Department, I submit this my third annual report of the service under my charge. The past year has been much more quiet and satisfactory than the preceding one, so far as the temper and achievements of our Indians are concerned. The policy of treating them liberally has been abundantly shown to be both economical and wise. After the excitements of the so-called Indian war were passed, and our Indians saw and realized that their wants and necessities were comparatively well provided for, they settled down quietly upon the reservation and seemed to be well satisfied with the annuity goods forwarded by the Department, and the beef, flour, and other supplies we were enabled to issue. There were about five hundred Indians on the reservation most of the winter. A greater number than usual; still they were comparatively contented. As the season for agricultural labor approached they held many "talks" among themselves, and finally got up quite an enthusiasm. The result was that about fifty lodges, or about two hundred adult Indians, were directly or indirectly engaged in farming operations. So great was the zeal for farming in the spring that there was great difficulty in supplying all with the necessary teams and implements, as they all wanted to work at the same time. Wheat was the principal crop with all. They seemed to think there could be no farm without it. According to the estimate of my head farmer they had, in wheat alone, from one hundred and fifty to two hundred acres, beside about fifty acres in other crops. Much of this land was cleared of sage brush, and the greater part of it plowed by the Indians themselves. Some of them were so ambitious that they sowed their own grain, preferring to do *all* the work themselves. Of course, their farming was not done in the most approved manner; still there was much hard labor performed. Work is a civilizer, and though the products were comparatively small, yet the aggregated beneficent results to the Indians themselves cannot be easily estimated. The products were not commensurate with the amount of ground cultivated, or with the work actually done. Many, after putting in their crops, when the time for visiting the mountains and settlements came, could not resist the temptation. Though they promised, and I doubt not intended, to return and attend to their crops, most of those who went failed to do so, and thus lost the result of their earlier labors. But those who remained or returned in season are now rejoicing in what to them seems a bountiful harvest. Among those specially worthy of commendation for their persevering efforts and success in farming I would mention Chief Tabby, whose example and counsels have been most salutary. There were also several sub-chiefs and other prominent Indians whose efforts are worthy of special praise. As the Indians take entire charge of their crops it is almost, if not quite, impossible to tell what was produced, but it is estimated that their wheat crop alone must have been about twelve hundred bushels. Had it not been for the cold, backward spring, and neglect on the part of many, the yield would have been very much greater. But, as before intimated, the full benefits of the year's labors are not to be estimated by the amount of products, but very largely by the moral and encouraging influence of those labors upon the Indians themselves, which is shown by their commencing even now to prepare ground for next year's crop. During my intercourse with these Indians I have never known them to be in better temper or have so much ambition to help themselves; and with judicious encouragement and aid this agency might, in a few years, be brought nearly, if not quite, to a self-sustaining condition.

As one means to this end, I would recommend that rewards be given for special excellence or efficiency in any department of agricultural work. A small fund placed at the disposal of each agent, under judicious regulations, might be productive of most happy results. From our isolated and unprotected position, and the comparatively small amount of beef required for the use of this agency, it is almost impossible to secure a supply at reasonable rates. I would therefore renew my former recommendation that this agency be stocked with cattle sufficient to yield supplies of beef for the wants of the agency. Also, when thought advisable by the Department and the agent, to furnish a cow to each lodge, none but the male issue to be used. This matter commends itself to my judgment for two reasons. First, its economy. I believe that fifteen thousand dollars, judiciously expended, would, with proper management, yield a constant and increasing supply of stock for all the demands of this agency. It is true there is some liability to loss, but in my judgment not so much as though they belonged to outside parties; and they claim and, in my opinion, should receive protection and indemnity for losses sustained when the property is legally on the reservation. In the second place, the moral and civilizing effect of ownership is not inconsiderable. I have been led to observe the conservative character of those of our Indians who own stock. They are more localized in their habits, and a sense of ownership makes them more careful of the rights of others.

We have not had our saw-mill in operation since last fall, at which time, and during my absence on leave, from some cause the saw was sprung and rendered practically useless, so that it became necessary to purchase another, which was done, and when we came to start the mill it was found that a check-valve belonging to the engine was broken. A new one had to be obtained in Salt Lake City. These various mishaps and delays have prevented the manufacture of lumber, and as a consequence the completion of our mill-building and the erection of a school-house, which we had hoped to do, and to have had a school in operation long ere this. But a small matter or mishap with us in our isolated position causes the consumption of much time and labor. Our greatest difficulty is to secure and retain a mechanic competent to put in order and run our mill successfully. Such a one we must have. I have not felt at liberty to pay heretofore the wages demanded, but economy in our situation is to secure the necessary skill.

Though we have not yet had either school or mission nominally established, still, I think, there is evidently a softening and civilizing influence at work, gradually leavening the masses and preparing them for more rapid advancement when those more efficient means are brought into operation. Altogether it is believed there is a noticeable advance in the right direction, but it must be admitted to be slow. I sometimes feel discouraged at the little progress made in view of the means and efforts expended, but I apprehend I am not the only one in the service who has been compelled to modify his views with regard to what can be accomplished in a given time.

The Indian farms are so scattered and the timber for fencing so scarce and inaccessible that much time and labor have been expended, altogether by the employés, in fencing, as the Indians have not, thus far, been willing to take part in labor of that kind. Some few would if they were paid wages in money as other employés, which is done elsewhere. I have, and would still recommend the payment of small wages to those Indians who are capable and willing to do general work. A small amount of money would be a powerful stimulant, and would ultimately supersede the necessity for the employment of so many whites.

We have a large number of logs ready for the manufacture of lumber. We have cultivated about thirty acres for the agency, but, owing to the extremely late and cold spring, the yield has not been good. It was further materially injured by some breachy oxen which no fence could restrain. For the estimated amount of products of both Indian and agency farms I refer you to my statistical report. The general health at this agency has been good. Still three deaths have occurred, which were chronic cases of diseases arising from their peculiar habits and mode of life. I would still urge the employment of a physician for both Indians and whites. Without any sufficient data upon which to warrant a change in the estimated number of our Indians I shall continue my former one of 800, though only about 500 have been on the agency at any one time. I have found it very difficult and almost impossible to get an accurate enumeration of the Indians beloning to this agency. Richard Koneas, one of this tribe, but who has been for some time at Lincoln University, Pennsylvania, visited his friends during my absence in Salt Lake City, and has, at my request by letter, taken as complete a census as possible. I have not yet seen him to ascertain the result, and, if possible, correct my own estimate. Most of our Indians are now out on their annual visit and hunt. Upon their return, about the first of November, the annuity goods will be distributed.

I have the honor to be, very respectfully, your obedient servant,

J. J. CRITCHLOW,
United States Indian Agent.

Hon. E. P. SMITH,
Commissioner of Indian Affairs, Washington, D. C.

45.

DENVER, COLO., *September* 1, 1873.

SIR: In obedience to your instructions contained in circular of date June 30, 1873, I have the honor to submit, for your information, the following report of the administration of affairs at this agency during the year just past.

Instead of entering into any details I desire to call the attention of the Department to the uniform good behavior of "Pi-ah's" band during the time above referred to, and to their comparative freedom from the vices which almost invariably characterize the Indian when brought as closely and constantly in contact with whites as these Utes have been. But few complaints of anything like even misdemeanors on their part have been brought to my notice; and not a single case of drunkenness has occurred among them while they have been in or near Denver. The same good reports of their behavior come to me from the plains and the parks, the only irregularity of which they have been guilty of late having been the attack (July 7, 1873) upon a small band of Arapahoes on the Little Republican, in which affair the Utes report having secured twenty-eight ponies and one scalp. I wrote you of this occurrence July 10, 1873, a telegram having been received by me from the K. P. R. R. agent at Deer Trail, relating the facts as nearly as he could learn them from "Pi-ah." In my letter I stated that the Arapahoes were the aggressors, but I have since learned from the Utes themselves that the latter made the attack.

Immediately upon the receipt of the telegram above mentioned I ordered Pi-ah and his followers to come at once to Denver, reporting to you the fact of their arrival.

The subsequent difficulties in Denver, growing out of the efforts of certain parties here to usurp the agent's powers, create dissatisfaction among the Indians, and to induce them to indulge in a barbarous and disgusting spectacle in the streets of the city, have been fully explained to you in a letter from this office dated July 16, 1873. On this occasion the Indians behaved exceedingly well, and dispersed quietly as soon as they understood it to be the wish of the agent that they should not make any public display; their quiet demeanor and ready obedience to the proper authority being in decided contrast to the action of the parties who inaugurated, and swore they would carry out, the "Ute procession and scalp-dance" scheme. The latter persons tore up the ground in their wrath, cursing the agent, the administration, and the Department for what they seemed to think was an unwarranted interference with their sacred and inalienable rights.

Immediately after the squelching of their circus, petitions were put in circulation, addressed to the Secretary of the Interior, asking (or demanding) the immediate removal of the agent, and from the reports of saloon caucuses and sidewalk conferences of these injured patriots that reached me, I really feared that they would undermine, blow up, and utterly eliminate the beneficent institution known as the Indian Bureau. I presume, however, that the dawn of the succeeding morning brought (along with much headache) some sober thoughts, as I have never since heard of their petitions; and, so far as I am informed, the Indian Bureau still exists. In concluding my remarks upon this subject, I merely wish to say that I deprecate any such excitement as that which grew out of this affair, but at the same time I intend to exercise my authority, within legal limits, whether it suits the half-savage and more than barbarous white element of this community, or not. In other words, I will "have peace" even though I have to fight for it.

In returning to your Department and to the board of commissioners the statistical tables furnished me, it has not been possible for me to give as full information on many points as you or they may desire. The reasons for this are given at length upon the blanks which I have already forwarded. I believe the number stated thereon is not exaggerated, taking the statement as an average the year round. Although Pi-ah's band proper will not number over 350, yet they are always accompanied to Denver by more or less delegates from the bands belonging to the other agencies in Colorado, who come for the purpose of trading in the city, and to join Pi-ah and his fellows in their regular spring and fall buffalo-hunts. On account of the deadly enmity existing between the Utes and the Plains Indians, (Cheyennes, Arapahoes, Sioux, and Kiowas,) it is the custom of the former to muster as many effective warriors as possible for these campaigns, so that it is not unusual for Pi-ah to be accompanied by the Chiefs Sha-na-no, Gurso, An-ka-tosh, and Cu-ra-can-ti, from the southern agency, and by such northern representatives as Sac-ne-och, (son of Ne-va-va,) Pah-aut, Tab-ou-cha-ken, An-thro, and others, each with a few chosen warriors. I believe that every Indian of note in the seven bands of Utes has visited Denver and shaken hands with me within the last nine months—if I except Sac-ne-och, Sap-o-wa-we-re, and Kan-e-a-che. The latter gentleman I warned, through an Indian runner, not to come here at all, as he is notoriously mischievous; and the other Utes informed me that they did not wish to be blamed for the disturbances which the presence of himself and band were sure to create. Of course it is not my province to relate his amusements in the southern counties during the past spring and early summer. Suffice it to say that I should not have tolerated anything of the sort near here.

The sanitary condition of these Indians is not what it should be, nor, I am satisfied, from conversations with members of the Board of Commissioners, what the Department desires it should be. I presume there is no remedy for this state of things so long as this band refuse to avail themselves of the ample provision made at the agencies on the reservation for their wants in the way of shelter, clothing, and medical attendance; yet, for humanity's sake, I regret that the Government cannot stretch a point and minister to all the needs of this inoffensive people, even though they be "off the reservation."

I have no further suggestions to offer in regard to the future management of this "roving band of Utes;" but I trust that the peaceful relations which have existed between them and the whites for the past three years may continue while the tribe exists.

I desire to acknowledge the courtesy and attention of all the Department officers during the past year, and am, very respectfully, your obedient servant,

JAMES B. THOMPSON,
United States Special Agent.

The COMMISSIONER OF INDIAN AFFAIRS,
Washington, D. C.

46.

OFFICE SUPERINTENDENT OF INDIAN AFFAIRS,
Santa Fé, N. Mex., November 15, 1873.

SIR: I have the honor to submit my annual report, together with those of the several agents connected with this superintendency.

I assumed the duties of my position on the 14th of December, 1872, and since that time have visited all the agencies, and, with two exceptions, all of them at least twice. In every instance where there seemed to be the least probability of an outbreak by the Indians, I have endeavored to reconcile them by visiting them in person, hearing statements of their grievances, and where it lay in my power I have remedied any mismanagement of which they complained.

So far as this superintendency is concerned, the friends of the present Christian and humanitarian policy have reason for congratulation. During the past year but few serious depredations have been committed by the Indians, and during the entire year I have learned of but two murders of white persons by savages.

Your attention is invited to the condition of affairs at the several agencies, brief notices of which will be found in the following remarks:

MESCALERO APACHES.

This agency is located at Fort Stanton, about 200 miles southeast from this place. The Indians are among the most wild and savage under my charge. For some years they lived with the Comanches and participated in their depredations; but they have been gradually collected about the agency, although the communication between them and the Comanches seems to be only partially interrupted.

When I became superintendent these Indians were very much excited about the murder of their principal chief, Cadette, who was killed, it is supposed, by Mexicans, against whom he had recently given evidence on a trial of them for selling whisky to Indians. Fears were entertained by the settlers that they might break out and devastate the surrounding country. Twelve days after assuming charge of this office, I started to visit them. I found that affairs at this agency required the presence of some officer determined to protect the interests of the Government. The firm which held the appointment of Indian traders, and acted as military traders, seemed to have taken entire possession of Indian affairs at that place. The agent appeared to have very little business except to approve vouchers made for him by these men. The Government had no buildings, and there were none in the neighborhood that could be rented. The agent was, in consequence, compelled to accept such hospitalities as they felt inclined to bestow on the Government and its officers.

I remained at this agency several days, and held three councils with the Indians, visited them in their ranchos, and saw much of the country they claimed as theirs, and desired to have set apart as a reservation. The chiefs told me that this country was their home, that they were anxious to have it set apart as a reservation, and were not only willing but anxious to remain at peace. They were very desirous that the murderers of their chief should be punished, but assured me that they would refrain from taking the matter into their own hands. I promised that the murderers should be dealt with by the law, if discovered, and asked them to advise the agent if any new facts were ascertained. Up to the present nothing is known of the murderers.

The chiefs assured me that if supplied with implements, they would engage in planting; I am not sanguine that they will do much for some years, but believe it expedient to make a beginning. On the 18th of February I submitted a report of my visit to these Indians, and urged that buildings be provided for the agency, in order that the Government might conduct its business through its own officer instead of private citizens interested more in the success of their own affairs than those of the Government. I also recommended the setting apart of a reservation for these Indians. Authority was given me on the 24th of May, either to purchase the buildings of Murphy & Co., or to erect new ones, as I should think best. After receiving estimates for the erection of new buildings, and considering the subject in all its bearings, I concluded to buy the buildings of Murphy & Co.

The new agent, Mr. S. B. Bushnell, reported for duty on the 29th March, and at once undertook to assume charge of the affairs of his agency; he, however, found so much opposition on the part of those who had formerly managed affairs there, that he only secured full charge of his agency when I visited there on the 2d of September. Although the buildings had been purchased by the Government, the former owners had upon one pretext and another retained possession of the buildings, and Agent Bushnell had very little more to say about the conduct of Indian affairs there than had Agent Curtis at the time of my first visit. I at once demanded possession, and promised to take the trouble of vacating the premises upon myself unless the agent received possession within twenty-four hours. The buildings were vacated. I directed Agent Bushnell to make immediate preparations for the issue of beef from the block, instead of upon the hoof as it had formerly been done. I also directed him to establish regular weekly issues, instead of issuing to the bands separately whenever they chose to come, as had been the custom. I have always believed that the number of these Indians was considerably exaggerated, but under the past system of issues it has been impossible to ascertain the facts. I have now directed Agent Bushnell to place the Indians in a corral on each issue-day, and furnish tickets to them previous to his issue of rations; by this means I hope to prevent fraud, and to secure the Government against paying for rations that are neither supplied by the contractors nor received by the Indians.

Upon my arrival at this agency on the 1st day of September, I found there Major W. R. Price, Eighth United States Cavalry, commanding troops in Southern New Mexico, in command of six troops of cavalry. Major Price had received sworn complaints from a large number of citizens charging that the Mescalero Apaches had stolen stock (mostly horses) from the complainants. Major Price was very anxious to take immediate and energetic action in the premises. I doubted the propriety of assailing these Indians, even for offenses committed, at that particular moment, because the Indians had not yet become familiar with the boundaries of their new reservation; nor did I think they had been sufficiently instructed as to their duties towards the settlers. According to their views, they own all the surrounding country, and honestly believe that white men settling there should pay them tribute. I believed the best course to pursue was to inform them that they were to remain upon their reservation, and when found off from it they would be driven back by troops, and where depredations were committed they would be held responsible; but Major Price urged that he had moved his command a long distance; that it would be difficult for him to have them in this locality again during the year; that the disposition of his troops was such that he could prevent the Indians leaving their reservation, and compel the return of stolen property in their hands. I therefore addressed him the following letter:

OFFICE SUPERINTENDENT OF INDIAN AFFAIRS,
Fort Stanton, N. Mex., September 3, 1873.

GENERAL: I have the honor to inform you that I have learned from the affidavits of several citizens living in this vicinity, that the Mescalero Apache Indians have been stealing horses and other stock from the settlers, and bringing the same upon this reservation. From the same source I learn that some portion of the stolen property has been identified in the hands of Indians visiting this agency. I therefore respectfully request that you will take such means as you think proper, to recover property previously stolen, and to prevent further depredations.

Very respectfully, your obedient servant,

L. EDWIN DUDLEY,
Superintendent of Indian Affairs.

Gen. W. R. PRICE,
Commanding Troops in Southern New Mexico, Fort Stanton, N. Mex.

Major Price immediately arrested Santa Ana, and a younger brother of the principal chief, Roman, and notified the Indians that they would be held as hostages for the return of stolen horses. The Indians became alarmed, expressed great dissatisfaction, and with the exception of about 200 immediately left the reservation. Advices since received, inform me that a portion of them have gone to old Mexico; some have returned to the Comanches, and others are in the mountains near the reservation, and so far have been able to skirt about the troops without meeting them. One officer, in command of about 60 cavalrymen, succeeded a few days since in attacking a single rancheria and killing all its inhabitants, seven persons, men, women, and children. Owing to the peculiar state of feeling in this Territory this is regarded as a very important military achievement. I expect to secure the return of these Indians to their reservation within a short time, and shall endeavor to keep them there by peaceable means.

On the 6th of October I made a recommendation for an amendment of the boundaries of this reservation. The proposed change will add some arable land, and the lines can be more easily ascertained by a surveyor. I would respectfully recommend that an appropriation be made for surveying this reservation and marking its boundaries in some way that shall be perfectly intelligible to the Indians.

I believe that a school can be established at this agency, and I shall endeavor to do so as soon as a suitable person can be found as teacher. I would also recommend an appropriation of $2,000 for supplying these Indians with agricultural implements and seeds for planting.

SOUTHERN APACHES.

This agency is situated about 300 miles southwest from this place. These Indians are the most difficult to manage of all in this superintendency. They were never satisfied to go upon this reservation, and were determined to compel the Government to allow them to return to Cañada Alamosa, where they had formerly lived. They endeavored to bring this about by threatening the agent, shooting at him and his employés, and a general system of bullying which was very difficult for either the agent or myself to endure. I visited them in February, and remained long enough to become fully acquainted with the policy which they were pursuing. I then told them that they would not be allowed to go to Cañada Alamosa, and that means would be adopted to prevent their movement in that direction. I gave them presents and made concessions to them, but did neither until they had first conceded some point to myself or the agent. They complained that the reservation was too cold to mature any crops; and cited the fact that in the season of 1872 the corn planted by the soldiers stationed there was killed early in September by the frost. I first reminded them of the fact that they had made no effort to raise corn, and then assured them that it was an unusual season; that probably the corn planted was not a variety which ripened as early as it ought, and that in all probability other varieties of crops would succeed. I promised to furnish a variety of seeds to the agent, and they consented to remain during this season and await the result. I accordingly supplied the agent with seed-wheat, three varieties of seed-corn, potatoes, oats, and seeds of garden-vegetables. To make the experiment a success, I promised the agent and his emyloyés that if they would work the agency farm they might supply themselves with vegetables therefrom. They were directed to make every effort in their power to secure the aid of the Indians, but failed to do so; but by their own unaided exertions they raised about 200 bushels of wheat, 150 bushels of potatoes, three acres of oats cut green for feeding agency animals, and a very considerable quantity of cabbages, beets, onions, turnips, and other garden-vegetables. I believe this experiment has been attended with very good effects upon the Indians, and have no doubt that a considerable number of them can be induced to join in their farming operations next year. I again visited these Indians on the 13th of September, and all excepting about 200 hundred of them, were absent from the reservation. They have been in the habit of leaving it upon stealing expeditions, and during the month of July Maj. W. R. Price, Eighth United States Cavalry, commanding troops in Southern New Mexico, came upon the reservation at the head of three troops of cavalry, and, at the request of the agent, endeavored to compel the Indians to surrender stolen stock in their possession. He succeeded in alarming them so much that all immediately fled to the mountains. By a very energetic and active movement of his command, Major Price succeeded in intercepting about 200 of them, and brought them back to the agency, where they have since remained. The remainder of these Indians have during the summer made the Chiricahua reservation headquarters, and, as nearly as I can learn, occupied themselves in depredations in Southern New Mexico and Arizona, and the State of Sonora in Old Mexico. Some have lately returned, and I hope that this entire band will be upon the reservation in a few weeks.

No effort will be spared to impress upon them the fact that willful depredations by them will be punished, and that if they wish to be safe they had best remain upon the land provided for them by the Government. Agent Thomas is a very firm disciplinarian, and has instituted many reforms in the management of this agency. He is thoroughly practical, and firmly believes that his Indians should be forced to refrain from hostile acts toward himself, his employés, and the settlers of the country, while they are receiving the liberal bounty of the Government. I believe his administration has already done much to improve these Indians, and I am confident that he will soon succeed in establishing schools among them, and ultimately bring them to adopt habits of industry.

One of the principal troubles of these Indians is an intoxicating liquor called "Tiswin," which they manufacture from the corn issued to them as rations. By your direction the issue of corn has been greatly decreased, and will entirely cease as soon as the supply on hand is exhausted. This will increase the discontent of these Indians, and cause many of them to go to other agencies unless the abolition of the corn-ration is made universal. I therefore recommend that the flour or beef ration be increased, and the corn abolished at all Apache agencies, both in this Territory and Arizona.

At my last visit, these Indians consented to the establishment of a school, and I have authorized Agent Thomas to erect a log school-house, at a cost not exceeding $150. The school will be commenced as soon as the building is completed and a suitable teacher can be found. The buildings of this agency are utterly worthless; they have been chiefly erected by the employés when not otherwise engaged. Agent Thomas and his wife are obliged to live in quarters that are uncomfortable, and totally unfit for the occupation of a gentleman and lady. Material is abundant, and good buildings can be erected at a small cost, say not exceeding $5,000, and I therefore recommend an appropriation of that amount.

I believe that if these Indians had property to care for it would detain them at home and aid very materially in preventing their depredations. I would, therefore, recommend an appropriation of $2,000 to be used in purchase of sheep. This amount, at present prices, would purchase at least 1,000. The increase of this number of sheep would in a few years occupy the time of most of these Indians, and I believe it would lead them to the adoption of some of the manufacturing arts.

In closing my remarks relative to this agency, I desire to say that in my judgment no better place can be found for these Indians. I believe that they are gradually becoming satisfied with the location, as they now talk but little about removal to Cañada Alamoso, and admit some of the advantages of this location, and I therefore recommend the erection of permanent buildings, and that the reservation be surveyed and permanently located.

NAVAJO AGENCY.

This agency is located about 240 miles northwest from this place. The tribe numbers over nine thousand. The Indians are the best among those who have heretofore been wild in this superintendency. They plant a variety of crops, and are familiar with several mechanical arts. They have been perfectly peaceable and well-disposed toward the whites since I have been in office. The only depredations charged upon these Indians have been occasional stealing expeditions by a few of their wild, bad young men, but in most instances stock stolen by them has been recovered by the native police force which has been maintained upon the reservation.

These Indians are rapidly acquiring property, and I have no doubt that when the provisions of the treaty of 1868, for supplying them with annuity goods expires, they will be able to maintain themselves without Governmental aid. They have at present a very large number of sheep and horses, generally estimated at about 250,000 of the former, and 10,000 of the latter. The sheep do not profit them as much as they might, because of their very primitive way of saving the wool; they scrape it off instead of shearing.

The location of this agency is over 8,000 feet above the sea-level, and consequently crops, which require a long season in which to mature, are often destroyed by late frosts in the spring or early frosts in the autumn. It has been proposed to establish a subagency in the San Juan Valley at the northern end of the reservation, and many of the Indians are anxious that this shall be done. The altitude of that valley is much less than that of their present location. The land is described as more fertile, and most persons who are familiar with the country deem it very important to colonize some portion of the Navajoes there at an early day. If this subagency is established, it will be necessary to have a small military force encamped in the vicinity for a year or two to protect these Indians from incursions by the Utes, the southern boundary of whose reservation is but a few miles distant. It will be necessary to erect temporary buildings and acequias, (irrigating ditches,) and to construct a road over which supplies can be transported for the subagency. I have heretofore recommended that the Secretary of War be requested to detail an engineer officer to decide upon the most feasible route for a road, and determine what ditches are necessary to irrigate the valley. I am now of opinion that buildings for this subagency, irrigating ditches, and a road can be constructed at a cost not exceeding $15,000. I am certain that after the first season the Indians placed there would need no subsistence from the Government, and that a very considerable saving would be the result; and that the Indians would be advanced toward civilization much more rapidly than if they remain at their present location.

These Indians seem to have reached a point where it is entirely feasible to begin the work of educating and christianizing them. Schools have already been established, and the teachers have met with fair success; but at present there is no teacher at this agency. I know of no better missionary field, and feel confident that two or three really first-class teachers could find all the scholars they could teach, and that they would soon bring the Indian children sufficiently under their influence to advance them rapidly both in letters and the useful arts, while they could at the same time disseminate among them knowledge of religion. I think them a people peculiarly adapted to receive religious instruction, and to practice its teachings. I am of the opinion that other things besides a mere knowledge of letters should be inculcated by teachers. I would have the men taught the use of agricultural implements, and how to preserve their crops. Some ought to acquire knowledge of carpentering, blacksmithing, and other mechanical arts. They should be brought to prefer permanent abodes instead of their hogans, and be taught how to construct them. The women ought to be instructed in the domestic arts; a great saving in their food could be made if they understood approved methods of cooking. The wool of their sheep would have a much greater value if they understood how to preserve and manufacture it. My ideas of the duties of a teacher for these Indians calls for a more able person than the small salary allowed is likely to procure, especially when we consider the isolated position of the agency, and the great cost of living there. I shall endeavor to secure the services of two competent persons, and make an effort to have my views practically tested. The treaty with the Navajoes provides for the erection of a school-house and chapel, and I most urgently recommend that the erection of such building be provided for at once. I would not expend more than one-half the amount named in the treaty, ($5,000,) but would reserve the remainder for the construction of another building for the same purpose in the San Juan Valley, in the event of the subagency being established there.

Agent Arny recommends the establishment of a boarding-school, with a corps of teachers and officers which would do credit to a first-class institution in a thickly populated community. I am of opinion that an institution would be out of place at the present time, and should much prefer the more simple method until the children have been somewhat advanced.

The agent recommends an enlargement of the reservation by the addition of a strip along the southern end six miles in width. The reasons given for this increase of the reservation strikes me as good. At present, settlers can locate within two hundred yards of the agency, and keep the agents and Indians in constant trouble if so disposed. The addition to the reservation proposed will embrace all the water within twenty miles of the agency, and thereby prevent any settlements near enough to interfere with the agency or the Indians. I therefore respectfully recommend that the President set apart the following-described tract of land as an addition to this reservation: Beginning at the southeast corner of the present reservation, running thence due south six statute miles, and thence due west to a point due south of the southwestern corner of said reservation, and thence due north to said southwest corner.

The Navajoes have raised less corn and other crops during the present summer than usual, owing to the shortness of the season, and it will be necessary to provide them with supplies until their crops can mature next year. I have the less hesitation in recommending that these Indians be subsisted during a time like the present, because I am aware that they have the means of devastating a large portion of this Territory, and I know that they will have but little hesitation in doing so if they are in a starving condition. The expense of subsisting them for a year would probably cost less money than fighting them for a week, and would of course save much human life. The agent estimates that it will require $70,000 to subsist these Indians until their crops mature next year. I am of opinion that, in addition to supplies now on hand, $50,000 will be ample.

The native police force, under the command of Manuelito, the war chief, has accomplished great good during the year. This force has recovered a large number of stolen animals, which have been returned to the owners by the agent; and it has now become so unprofitable to steal that the depredations have nearly ceased. I recommended the disbandonment of this force, because their time of usefulness seemed to have passed. Should the settlers again be troubled by the Navajoes, no better means could be employed than the re-institution of this police force, and I shall so recommend if any occasion occurs where it seems to be necessary.

THE ABIQUIU AGENCY.

This agency is located at Tierra Amarilla, about one hundred miles northwest from this place. The Weeminuche and Capote Utes and a portion of the Jicarilla Apaches make this agency their home. The two bands of Utes were parties to the Ute treaty of 1868, and should live upon the reservation in Colorado, but have never been willing to go there. I have desired to see them removed because the land they now occupy belongs to private parties, and no permanent provision can be made for them there. They attended the council held at the Los Pinos agency in August, and their representatives accompanied the delegation to Washington. I have not been advised what understanding, if any, has been reached about their future residence, but most earnestly recommend that they be required to go and stay upon the reservation in Colorado, and believe they will go if peremptory orders are given from your Office. These Indians are peaceable and quiet, and will refrain from committing depredations so long as they are fed and clothed, but will make no advancement toward civilization or a position to provide for themselves so long as they remain at Tierra Amarilla. If put upon a reservation they could be brought in contact with civilizing influences.

The portion of the Jicarilla Apaches who make this agency their home are, like all other Apaches, restless, thieving vagabonds, quick to learn all the vices of civilization, but seemingly determined to know nothing of its virtues and benefits. No good will come of them until they can be gathered upon a reservation and kept there. I have endeavored to remove them to the reservation at Fort Stanton and Tularosa, but without effect. I am of the opinion that you should decide where you wish them located. Command them to be there by a certain day, and tell them that after that time they will be attacked by troops if found elsewhere.

They are the worst beggars the world affords, and seem to have no idea of doing anything except to eat and wear what the Government gives them, and stealing from the settlers when their supplies fail. I have nothing to recommend regarding these Indians except their removal to some reservation and proper provisions for them until that is accomplished. I have reduced their supplies of food to one pound of beef and the same quantity of unbolted flour per day. If the Utes remove and the Apaches remain it will cost about $15,000 per annum to subsist them, and I recommend an appropriation of that amount. Heretofore these Indians, including the Utes, have been provided for out of the incidental fund, and in consequence that fund has been inadequate to the demands made upon it.

While writing about this agency, I ought to refer to the fact that in March last I found that the agent was guilty of so many improper and disgraceful acts that I took the responsibility to suspend him, subject to your approval, and appointed a person temporarily in charge of the agency. Mr. W. D. Crothers, the new agent, took charge of the agency, July 10, and has given entire satisfaction to the Indians and myself since that time.

CIMARRON AGENCY.

This agency is located in the town of Cimarron, about 160 miles northeast from this place. The Indians who make their home here are the Muache Utes, and a portion of the Jicarilla Apaches. Like the Abiquiu agency, these Indians are located upon lands belonging to private parties, and, as at that agency, the Utes were parties to the treaty of 1868, and belong upon the reservation in Colorado. No regular appointment of an agent for these Indians has been made since the resignation of late Agent Roedel, in the summer of 1872, and the agency has since that time been in charge of an employé of the superintendent. If these Indians are to remain at this place it would be much better to appoint a regular agent.

The Muache Utes left their agency in the early spring and went to Colorado, where they annoyed the settlers in the Arkansas and Cucharas Valleys. In April, under your direction, I sent Mr. Gould, then in charge of the agency, to confer with them and endeavor to secure their return. He failed. I went to see them in June, and held a council with Kaneatche and ten other men, and after a long debate succeeded in securing their promise to go to the Ute reservation. They started before I left, and I supposed would keep their promise; but I had been but three days at home before I learned that they had returned with greatly increased numbers. I took the stage and proceeded there at once. Having previously asked the commanding-general of this military department to station troops in the valley of the Cucharas, I found one company of infantry on the ground and one troop of cavalry within a day's march. In accordance with instructions from you, I labored earnestly to secure their removal by peaceable means. Failing in that I told them they must go to their reservation within three days, and that if found in their present locality after that time they would be driven there by troops. They understood that the power against them excelled their own, and they went at once. Of late a large number of these Utes have returned to Cimarron. I believe they will move to their reservation if positively required by you. Of course I am not aware what decision was reached by the recent conference with them at the Los Pinos agency and at Washington. I have made four trips to Cimarron during the year to endeavor to remove the Jicarilla Apaches from there, but have been prevented from accomplishing the desired result in great part by the interference of a few bad white men, who find their interests furthered by keeping the Indians there.

The Indians are in the midst of the settlements, and annoy the better class excessively, and on every account it is desirable that they shall be removed. The only rations now issued these Indians are one-half pound of beef and the same quantity of shorts—the least possible amount which will keep them from levying their supplies upon the settlers. There are no schools among them, and it will be impossible to institute any while they remain where they now are. I see no hope of their ever making any advancement until they are placed upon a reservation. I have favored the establishment of a new reservation on the Dry Cimarron, in the northeast corner of this Territory, and placing all the Weeminuche, Capote, and Muache Utes and Jicarilla Apaches upon it, in the event of failing to remove them elsewhere. This would require the establishment of a new military post. The execution of this plan would place these Indians in a location where they would be a barrier against the incursions of the plain Indians into this Territory and Colorado. It would also be an obstacle in the way of the traffic in stolen Texan cattle, now so extensively carried on by Mexicans and Comanche Indians. I believe it best to consolidate the Indians where possible, as it saves great expense; but if it be found impossible to place these Indians on any reservation now established, I would recommend that a new one be created.

THE PUEBLO AGENCY.

This agency is situated at Santa Fé, and the Indians are located in nineteen villages, one of which is within nine miles of this place, and the most distant of which is about two hundred miles away. These Indians are entirely self-sustaining. They have a rude knowledge of some of the mechanical arts, and an equally rude acquaintance with agriculture and its implements. However, they succeed in feeding and clothing themselves in a manner which satisfies them, even though it might not be satisfactory to civilized people. They possess a very considerable amount of property, consisting of lands, houses, horses, cattle, sheep, goats, &c. This people appear to be midway between barbarism and civilization; and although the Roman Catholic priesthood claim to have civilized them two hundred years ago, yet I believe it would be difficult for the most shrewd observer to discover any difference between their manners, customs, and condition at that early time and the present period. They live in the same manner, practice the same rites of a heathenish religion, (albeit now slightly changed by the forms of the Romish Church,) and are as great worshippers of the sun, Montezuma, and idols as at any period in their history. The Government has for several years endeavored to establish schools among this people, and its efforts have been attended with but slight success, but from one cause alone—the opposition of the Roman Catholic priests. This priesthood oppose teaching the Pueblo Indians the English language, apparently because it will prevent their having in the future, as they have now, the close monopoly of missionary efforts among them. I am not a bigoted follower of any religious denomination. I certainly never could be of one which finds it necessary to keep the people in ignorance in order to maintain its control over them. The action of the Romish priests of this Territory reminds one very forcibly of the nursery story of "the dog in the manger." They will neither teach these Indians themselves nor allow others to do so. I have a single instance to relate which exemplifies their power and purpose in this matter. For more than two years constant, persistent efforts have been made by my predecessor, the different Pueblo agents, and myself to establish a school at Tesuque Pueblo, nine miles from this place. All these efforts, however persistently made, were unavailing. In August last a young man came to me, stated that he was a Mexican, a Roman Catholic, and had been a teacher. He said that he was out of employment; that his family were suffering; that he could teach the common English branches, and that he desired the appointment of teacher at this pueblo. It was my wish to have these Indians taught to read and write in the English language, and having failed with all the appliances at my command, I thought it best to make an effort in another direction. I therefore told this young man that if he would procure a letter from the resident bishop of the Romish Church directing these Indians to furnish him a room and send their children to his school, I would at once give him employment. What representations he made to the bishop I am not advised, but he obtained the letter, and has succeeded without difficulty in establishing a school.

The education of these Indians, both in letters and the arts, seems to be of the first importance, and to be the principal duty of the agent. I am happy to be able to say that their present agent, Mr. E. C. Lewis, has succeeded in establishing several schools, and if he continues the same ardent efforts he has heretofore made, I am sure we can soon chronicle great improvement in the mental condition of the Pueblo Indians of New Mexico.

The subject of encroachment of Mexicans upon the lands belonging to these Indians is of great importance to them, and I believe should receive your favorable consideration. Most of the grants of land they occupy have been surveyed, but no marks now exist which they understand, and settlements are constantly made upon lands which undoubtedly belong to the Indians. I would recommend an appropriation of $5,000 for a resurvey of these grants, and the establishment of suitable corner monuments. If this were done the rights of these Indians could be protected by the courts and the agent.

The question whether the Pueblo Indians are citizens has been raised, and more than once have the courts decided in the affirmative, and that they were entitled to vote, (they have often been solicited by aspiring candidates to exercise the right of suffrage, but in every instance they have refused, preferring to remain as wards of the Government,) and exercise all the rights and privileges of citizens of the United States. On general principles I should be glad to have this decision sustained, but I am aware that with the present simple manners and customs, the slight business knowledge they possess, and the prejudice which exists against them on the part of the Mexicans, their condition would be rendered much worse if deprived of the care of an agent and the special protection of the Government. I am therefore opposed to any effort to secure any decision by the Supreme Court of the United States upon this question.

Agent Lewis recommends that a provision be made for supplying the wants of destitute Pueblo Indians during the coming year on account of the general failure of their crops during the past season. I believe that it would be proper to make an appropriation of $5,000 for this purpose, otherwise there will be great suffering and perhaps starvation among a portion of them.

For other matters relative to these Indians, I respectfully refer you to the very interesting report of Agent Lewis.

GENERAL REMARKS.

I desire to call your attention to the fact that it is impossible, in nearly every instance, to procure the services of competent men as agents at the salary allowed, fifteen hundred dollars per annum. It is no economy to employ incompetent men because they can be obtained for a small salary. The cost of living in this Territory is fully double that in the States, and an agent who has a family must of necessity be strongly tempted to engage in transactions of questionable character, in order to eke out a living, however miserable. I would recommend that agents be paid two thousand dollars a year, and then require the nomination of men of business experience and capacity. I know the Government would save money by such a course. I would earnestly request you to require the missionary board making nomination of agents to look into other matters than mere piety of the persons selected for nomination. A competent bad man will in the long run cost the Government less than an incompetent good man. There are here plenty of unscrupulous men who are entirely willing to do the work of Indian agencies, and relieve the agent from all trouble. A man may be perfectly honest himself, and yet allow dishonest men of more ability than himself to do his work for him, and rob the Government continually. Please give us good men if you can, but do let us have men of ability who can manage their own business.

Of course I have nothing to say about the pay of superintendents; but you will allow me, I trust, to suggest that a better man for the position might be obtained if the salary were increased.

The sum allowed for the salary of interpreters, five hundred dollars per annum, is entirely inadequate to secure the services of men who can speak *any* language with even the slightest degree of accuracy. I believe more troubles have arisen from misinterpretation of the language of officers than from any other cause. When General O. O. Howard was at Tularosa, the Indians received an impression through the interpreter of which General Howard was entirely ignorant, and which has caused much of the trouble at that agency from then until the present. I would recommend that interpreters be paid one thousand dollars per annum, and that all agents be required to employ only such men as can read and write both languages correctly, saving in instances where interpreters of Indian languages are required.

I believe that the Government will save much money by making appropriations sufficient to meet all expenses with promptness. I find it difficult to make purchases at low prices, because the persons selling expect to wait a long time for their pay.

I am, very respectfully, your obedient servant,

L. EDWIN DUDLEY,
Superintendent of Indian Affairs.

Hon. EDW. P. SMITH,
Commissioner of Indian Affairs, Washington, D. C.

47.

NAVAJO INDIAN AGENCY,
Fort Defiance, N. Mex., September 4, 1873.

SIR: In compliance with your instructions, it becomes my duty to make a report of the condition and wants of the Indians of this agency.

Were it not for my former knowledge of the agency, and my long acquaintance with the Navajoes and their history, it would be impossible for me to comply with the requirements of the Department, and furnish an annual report, as I have only had charge of this agency for three days. I arrived here on the 12th of August, but was not permitted to assume charge until September 1.

SPECIAL AGENCY, ETC.

Special Agent J. L. Gould has submitted and furnished me a copy of his report on the practicability of establishing an agency on the San Juan River. In that report he recommends the establishment of this agency at that place, and the discontinuance of a special agent, and an appropriation of $47,500 for the erection of buildings &c., to which I have added in my indorsement of his report the sum of $10,000, making in all $57,500, and this I think is a very low estimate. I am of the opinion, however, after a careful and thorough examination, that an appropriation of $20,000 to repair the buildings, corrals &c., at Fort Defiance (the present agency) and an additional appropriation of $5,000 to erect a chapel council-room, and a boarding-house for Indian children attending school at this agency, would be of much greater benefit to the Indians than the expenditure of $57,500 necessary to remove the agency to the San Juan.

The establishment of a summer camp on the San Juan, under the direction of the agent and farmer, would obviate the necessity of the removal of this agency, save thousands of dollars to the Government, and at the same time avoid any difficulty between the Navajoes and Utes, provided a small summer military camp be established in the immediate vicinity. This would render it unnecessary to establish a permanent military post, which would be a great expense, and would be imperatively required if an agency were established there.

NUMBER OF INDIANS.

Since taking charge of this agency it has been impossible to obtain the number of Indians belonging to it; but I am satisfied that there is at least the following, as ascertained by the latest count, viz, 2,912 men, 3,300 women, 2,902 children under 16—total, 9,114.

In addition to the above, there are a number of Indians under a sub-chief named Agua Grande, who live off the reservation, in the valley at the foot of the "Mesa Calabasa," and another considerable number who live near "Cubero" and "Cebolleta," many of whom do not visit this agency, as they raise sufficient for their support, and need only to be supplied with facilities for their education and civilization, which can be done under the direction of the agent, and by the employment of an additional farmer and school-teacher, and the erection of dwellings for them, and a school-house in the valley of the "Mesa Calabasa."

NAVAJO LANDS.

The Navajo Indians have a reservation containing 3,328,000 acres of land; but a very large portion of it is not fit for agricultural purposes, and cannot be cultivated so as to raise cereals or vegetables. One-half the reservation is adapted to pastoral purposes, and there is a tract of land south of the reservation on which the Indians have for several years raised corn, wheat, &c., which land, in my judgment, should belong to this reservation, and by attaching it, would tend materially to the moral improvement of the Indians, furnish them much subsistence, and be a decided aid toward their improvement and advancement. I therefore very respectfully request that the attention of his excellency the President be called to this subject, and that by a proclamation the following-described lands be declared an addition to the Navajo reservation, viz:

Commencing at the southwest corner of the present reservation; running thence south, six miles; thence east, sixty miles; thence north, six miles, to the southeast corner of the present reservation; thence west along the south line of said reservation to the place of beginning.

There are now only two white persons who claim each one hundred and sixty acres of land within the above-named limits, neither or whom have any right or title to it. One is not a citizen of the United States, and both, in my opinion, are unfit to be on or contiguous to reservation. By making the proposed addition to the reservation it will make it impossible for any white person to locate nearer to this agency than twenty miles; and will enable the agent to control his agency and keep from it persons who now encourage gambling and other vices which tend to debase the Indians.

FARMING, ETC.

The corn, wheat, &c., raised by these Indians will nearly all be consumed by them before the 1st of December, and from that period they must be fed. Owing to the dry weather during the spring months, they have not raised as much as usual, and, in my opinion, they will require an appropriation of at least $70,000 to purchase beef and corn for them till they can raise another crop.

They have had no farmer employed for some time, and as it is important to begin properly, I respectfully ask to be authorized to employ one at a salary of $100 per month. A proper person for this position will, under the direction of the agent, save thousands of dollars to the Government, and be of vast benefit to the Indians.

Large quantities of seed-corn, wheat, pumpkins, &c., have been formerly furnished to the Indians here, at much expense to the Government and with but little profit, as they were not furnished in time for planting. After another year this expense can be saved by the cultivation of these articles for the seed, by the farmer at the agency, and the seeds would be better than those purchased, as they would be acclimated.

For next spring I estimate that three thousand dollars' worth of seed will be required, which, in my judgment, should be purchased from seed raised in New Mexico, if possible, and delivered at the agency on or before the 1st of March, 1874. Many of the seeds heretofore furnished have been of no benefit in consequence of the fact that they reached here too late in the season for planting, and in some instances not till the crop from them should have been cultivated and gathered. As soon as possible I will furnish a list of the seeds and quantity which will be required for next spring's planting.

HORSES, SHEEP, ETC.

The Indians of this agency now own over 10,000 horses and about 175,000 sheep and goats. It was estimated when Colonel Donophan conquered them, that they had over a million sheep and goats, most of which were lost during the war. They value the sheep very highly for the wool, which they manufacture into a superior article of blankets.

QUANTITY OF GRAIN, ETC., RAISED.

It is impossible to estimate the amount of grain they raise annually, as they have no idea of our measures, and begin to use their products before it is ripe, take no care to save what they raise, and usually have it all consumed before the 1st of December of each year, as will be the case the present year.

CARPENTER'S AND BLACKSMITH'S TOOLS.

The tools in the carpenter's and blacksmith's shops have been so long in use that they are worthless, and new ones are required. Herewith I have the honor to submit the report of the late carpenter and present blacksmith, with estimates of what is necessary.

EDUCATION, ETC.

On taking charge of this agency I find no teacher employed, and consequently no schools. It is now about twenty-five years since Colonel Donophan found and conquered the Navajo Indians, and our Government acquired them with the Territory of New Mexico. It is five years since they were removed here again, under the treaty made by General Sherman and Colonel Tappan, and to-day I firmly believe there is not an Indian on the reservation who can read, and not one who can speak a dozen words of English; hence all the effort for twenty-five years to civilize, Christianize, and make self-sustaining these Indians has been a failure, and the money expended a loss to the Government and the Missionary Board.

These Indians are as apt to learn as any that I have ever known. What, then, is the cause of the failure? My experience with Indians, and my knowledge of the Navajoes after an acquaintance of many years, has impressed me with the conviction that the defect lies in the fact that industrial and boarding schools have not been established; day-schools are of no account. This week a party of Indians may come to the agency, remain five or six days, and while here their children are sent to school and learn a portion of the alphabet; when the parents leave, no provision being made to feed and clothe the children at the school, they leave with the parents, and are not seen again for weeks. In the mean time they have forgotten what they did learn.

There are two thousand nine hundred and two children on the reservation, scarcely twenty of whom know the alphabet, although thousands of dollars have been expended to educate them. The defect in the education of these Indians can undoubtedly be corrected by the establishment of an industrial boarding-school at this agency, with provisions for the clothing and feeding of two hundred children, boys and girls, under two teachers to begin with, and a superintendent of labor, whose duty it will be to see that the boys labor a couple of hours each day on the model and experimental farm near the agency, and a matron to teach the girls housework. With two teachers, a superintendent of labor, a patron and matron for the boarding-house, at a salary of one thousand dollars each per annum, and an appropriation of five thousand dollars ($5,000) for the erection of the necessary buildings, as provided for in article three of the treaty of 1868, and two thousand dollars ($2,000) for furniture, stationery, &c., for the boarding house and school, and the rations and annuity goods to which the children would be entitled under the treaty, the agent could establish such a school, which in four years could turn out two hundred native teachers to teach other children on the reservation, and thus in a few years' time the children would be possessed of a primary education, and an influence for good exerted over the parents. I therefore respectfully ask that I be authorized to employ, and that the Missionary Board be requested to recommend, two teachers, a patron and matron, and a superintendent of labor, at one thousand dollars each per annum, and that I be furnished with seven thousand dollars ($7,000) to erect the necessary buildings and furnish them, and be instructed to establish an industrial boarding-school, such as I have here indicated.

HEALTH.

There are a considerable number of Indians suffering from disease contracted by their association with white men, and their own loose habits. Time, and the moral and industrial education, with the medical assistance of the physician, who should be fully supplied with remedies, will correct this to a great extent. For full information on this subject I respectfully refer to the report of Dr. J. Menaul, herewith, and urge that the medicines, &c., for which he has estimated, a list of which is herewith, be furnished as soon as possible, in addition to what I have purchased, which will be exhausted in a short time after they reach here. Dr. Menaul is certainly doing a good work, and can do much more if he is supplied with the necessary remedies.

NAVAJO POLICE.

About one year ago, under the authority of Gen. O. O. Howard, a Navajo police was organized of over one hundred Indians, and I concur with my predecessor in what he says in regard to this organization, on page 302 of the report of the honorable Commissioner of Indian Affairs for 1872: "Though this force has been in service but a short time, it has proved conclusively in this brief period to be the best feature ever inaugurated in this direction. The custom of branding stock with the initials, or some other mark of ownership, by the holders of stock in this and other adjoining Territories, renders it an easy task to detect stolen animals brought upon the reservation. * * *

"The effect produced by the Navajo cavalry in seizing stock from the (Indian) thieves and returning it to its owners, is most salutary in proving their hearty and determined co-operation with the Government to prevent this wrong, while the moral influence exerted in discouraging a repetition, by its almost certain detection, will be, if possible, still more beneficial."

I regret that my instructions, just received, require me to disband this organization. The order of General Howard was a good one, if properly carried out, and was given after personal observation by him, and has resulted in good. Its discontinuance now will tend to favor depredations upon the stock of citizens by the Indians, and afford no assistance to the agent to prevent it.

As the treaty holds the chiefs responsible for all depredations, and as they cannot, and I know will not, devote their time and attention to this matter without compensation, and as I am fully convinced that the disbanding of this organization, at this time, will be very disastrous, I earnestly ask that I be instructed to continue the organization, with Mannelito at $25 per month, and thirty others at $5 per month each; this will give to the chiefs and Indians an inducement to perform all the duties required of them under the treaty, especially as the police force embraces some of the principal chiefs, and the relations of others, who are proud of their position, and very energetic and determined in the discharge of their duties, which they would not be if their pay was to cease.

THE EMPLOYÉS OF THIS AGENCY

have heretofore been of two classes, viz, Americans and Indians, who were engaged for two objects First, to conduct the education and civilization of the Indians; second, to furnish labor to carry on the affairs of the agency. According to the instructions I have received, it appears to be the desire of the Government if possible to have moral and religious persons employed here. With this view I submit herewith a report of the employés, with suggestions for changes, which I am fully convinced will tend to the advancement of the moral and religious improvement of the Indians under my charge, and to that end I respectfully ask its approval, so that I may be able to have the co-operation of the employés in the work of educating, civilizing, and christianizing this interesting nation of red men.

In conclusion I must apologize for the length of this report, it being my first in regard to the Navajoes, and desiring to vindicate the course and policy I wish to carry out, it is more lengthy than it otherwise would have been. I promise more brevity in the future, and will only add that if the course and policy I have vindicated are vigorously carried out, the Indians of this reservation will speedily be civilized and made self-sustaining, and become intelligent and useful citizens; otherwise they will continue in ignorance, crime, and degradation.

I have the honor to be, very respectfully, your obedient servant,

W. F. M. ARNY,
United States Agent for Navajo Indians.

Hon. EDWARD P. SMITH,
Commissioner of Indian Affairs.

(Through Col. L. E. Dudley, superintendent of Indian affairs for New Mexico.)

48.

UNITED STATES NAVAJO INDIAN AGENCY,
Fort Defiance, N. Mex., September 3, 1873.

SIR: In compliance with the requirements of the Indian Department, I have the honor to present my annual report of the condition and advancement of the Navajo Indians, of New Mexico, for the year 1873. I arrived at this place, for duty in connection with the Navajo agency, August 5, 1873, and, as soon as the necessary arrangements could be made, proceeded to the San Juan River, to make an examination and report of the country belonging to the reservation in that vicinity for purposes of agriculture, as directed by you. A copy of that report was forwarded to your office, August 31. The Indians of this tribe are advancing rapidly in material wealth, year by year, and side by side with the white settlers of this country. They have now in their possession several hundred thousand head of sheep, over ten thousand head of horses, and a large number of cattle. Sheep are their favorite stock, owing to their rapid increase, the ease with which they are kept, and the benefit of their wool.

The manufacture of the well-known Navajo blankets is a source of considerable profit to them, by providing them with the main portion of their clothing, by sale, and by trade among the Mormons of Utah Territory and other tribes of Indians. They also make their own saddles, bridles, bridle-bits, moccasins, belts, leggins, and a variety of other articles for comfort and convenience, with a degree of skill that is surprising when their limited facilities for these purposes are considered.

Their conduct for a number of years past (since their complete subjugation in the late Navajo war) has been a source of great trouble, by their propensity for stealing live-stock. This custom, however, has been gradually discontinued, and I am happy to say that not a single depredation of this kind has come to the knowledge of their late agent, Mr. Hall, for the past year. Persevering efforts have been made to educate these Indians, and induce them to adopt a civilized mode of life, but, owing to their being thinly scattered over an immense extent of territory, it has been impossible to make such progress as had been hoped for.

If my report of the San Juan country is favorably considered, it is believed that most of the disadvantages in this respect may be overcome. A statement of the general management and condition of the agency will be forwarded in the agent's annual report.

Very respectfully, your obedient servant,

J. D. GOULD,
Special Agent for Navajoes.

Col. L. EDWIN DUDLEY,
Superintendent of Indian Affairs, Santa Fé, N. M.

49.

OFFICE MESCALERO APACHE AGENCY,
Fort Stanton, N. Mex., September 1, 1873.

SIR: I have the honor to submit the following annual report of the affairs and condition of this agency. On assuming charge, April 2, 1873, I found no designated reservation, no buildings belonging to the agency, no accommodations of any sort or kind, but the agent was dependent upon outside parties for every necessary for himself and for supplies of whatsoever kind. The Mescalero Apaches are savages, having no inclination to civilization in any respect. Their government is patriarchal; dwelling in bands or families, with one principal chief for each band; remaining but a short time in one place and having no fixed abode; traveling a large extent of country, seldom or never appearing in full numbers at the agency, but receiving rations by representation. Although at peace, frequent depredations were charged to these Indians as having been committed in Texas and along the valley of the Pecos River, the great cattle-trail from Texas to New Mexico and Colorado; and learning that one drover had been attacked and severely wounded near Pope's Crossing, about the 1st of August, I visited Seven Rivers, distant one hundred and fifty miles, to ascertain the truth of these reports. I found the wounded man at Seven Rivers, (since dead,) and found all the facts and evidence obtained, and from the finding of stolen stock and property in their possession near the agency, and from the apparent fact that the number of horses and mules was very great and constantly increasing, the conclusion was fair that these Indians were guilty of complicity, at least, and shared in the profits of the thefts, if not entirely responsible for all.

The presence of any other tribe has not been at any other time proven, and it is well known that these Indians were accustomed to visit that region, having a rendezvous in the Guadalupe Mountains, in which direction all trails of stolen stock led. The custom of issuing passes to them to visit Texas, Seven Rivers, and the plains east or any point remote from the agency, was discontinued as being improper, and no pass has been issued since I assumed charge of this agency. I have insisted that they should remain in this immediate vicinity. It has been impossible, from various causes, to establish a regular issue-day, or to effect a regular attendance. A reservation has been set apart and designated for these Indians, but has not been surveyed or its boundaries indicated to them; neither has an official copy been furnished this office. The buildings on the military reservation of Fort Stanton, and belonging to the former post trader, I am informed, verbally, were purchased in June by the superintendent of Indian affairs for the use of the agency. The buildings are ample for all the necessities of the agency, and would afford suitable rooms for schools if it was deemed expedient to establish such. There is no other way of civilizing these Indians than to compel them to remain upon their own reservation by a military force, restore the property they have stolen, dismount and disarm them, and teach them to respect the rights of citizens. Were they disposed or inclined to labor by cultivating the soil in the valleys along the streams, raising stock upon the mountains, they might become rich in flocks and herds, and would soon be self-supporting.

Respectfully, your obedient servant,

S. B. BUSHNELL,
Agent Mescalero Apaches.

L. E. DUDLEY, *Superintendent Indian Affairs.*

50.

SOUTHERN APACHE INDIAN AGENCY,
Tulerosa, N. Mex., September 4, 1873.

SIR: I have the honor to submit hereby my first annual report of the Southern Apache agency.

I assumed charge of the agency on the 11th of January, of this year. At that time there was no appearance of order in the management of the agency, but in a few weeks I succeeded, against strong opposition from the chiefs, in establishing a uniform ration and a regular day for issuing rations. The beef had been issued "on the hoof," and there were always quite a number who failed to get a share

The Southern Apaches have never known the power of the Government, and since they have been upon a reservation have accepted Government bounty in a spirit far different from what was intended and expected. Their idea of the reservation system a few months ago was that they were to be furnished with a home where they would have every bodily want supplied by right; that the agent and his employés were among them to act as their menials, and to await their pleasure in all things; that during the pleasant season they would be allowed to leave their women and children to be fed and protected on the reservation, while they visited the settlers on the Rio Grande to steal stock and bring it home with them and claim the protection of the agency. It is only occasionally that such stolen stock can be proven and returned to the owners. I tried hard for nearly five months to stop this practice of stealing horses, telling them that it would soon bring trouble upon them, but without effect.

Early in the summer Col. William Redwood Price, of the Eighth Cavalry, took command of the troops in Southern New Mexico, and since then I have had his earnest and efficient aid in controlling these Indians. In July, Colonel Price came to the agency with a force of three companies of cavalry, and, at my request, arrested a number of Indians. This frightened the tribe so that they fled to the hills, and, at my request, Colonel Price pursued them with such persistence and rapidity as to overtake them in two days and compel a council, which they had refused to hold at the agency. They saw that they were overpowered, and came back to the agency very penitent. I appointed a new principal chief, who exercises a good deal of wholesome authority over the tribe.

The issue of corn as a ration to these Indians has been the cause of a great deal of trouble until a month ago, when that ration was ordered to be very much reduced. They manufacture an intoxicating drink of the corn, and, under the influence of this drink, they do a great deal of fighting among themselves. Since January, seven have been killed in these fights and about twenty wounded.

There has been no farming done by these Indians. Although they are very fond of nearly every variety of vegetable, they are too averse to work to make any effort to cultivate any of them. The employés have raised a garden and about five acres of spring wheat. The reservation is not well adapted to the cultivation of corn, but wheat and all varieties of vegetables do excellently well. The cultivation of potatoes alone would be very profitable. If the Indians would pay any attention to raising stock, they would soon be rich from that source alone.

The population varies from six hundred in winter to two hundred in summer. It is hoped that the Indians will be under better control by next spring, and that it will be possible to keep them on the reservation during the summer. Their property consists of horses, mules, and burros, and of these there are generally about one hundred on the reservation.

The establishment of a school has not been attempted, because I knew that, under the existing state of affairs, a school could not be made to do any good, but would only result in failure and the expenditure of a large sum of money. Now, however, the drunkenness will be nearly done away by reducing the corn ration, and the Indians will become *tamer* in all respects, I hope, and it is proposed to secure a good teacher and make a strong effort to establish a school among them as soon as possible. There will be many superstitions to overcome, but the old chiefs must *see* a school and know what it is before they will withdraw their opposition. At present they seem to have the idea that *a school* is an institution wherein knowledge is propagated by a sort of clubbing process.

There are not any worse Indians in the whole country to bring under the influence of the policy of the Government for civilizing and Christianizing them; still there has been progress made—enough for encouragement. It has not been long since they wore but *very little* clothing; now the women sew excellently, and all the grown Indians wear clothing of some sort or other. Three months ago, the lives of the agent and employés were threatened almost every week; sometimes shot at with arrows and sometimes threatened with fire-arms. Now the Indians are pretty well convinced that such demonstrations are neither for their profit nor pleasure. There is gradual improvement noticeable and I think that next year's report will notice a very decided improvement.

If this reservation is to be considered the permanent home of these Indians, new agency buildings should be constructed at once, because the temporary buildings now in use will not last longer than six months.

Most respectfully, your obedient servant,

B. M. THOMAS,
United States Agent for Southern Apaches.

Col. L. EDWIN DUDLEY,
Superintendent of Indian Affairs, Santa Fé, N. Mex.

51.

ABIQUIU INDIAN AGENCY,
Tierra Amarilla, N. Mex., September 15, 1873.

SIR; I have the honor to submit to you my first annual report relative to the condition of the Capote and Weeminuche Utes and the Jicarilla Apache Indians connected with the Abiquiu agency.

I relieved Capt. W. S. Defrees, acting agent for the Abiquiu Indians, July 10, 1873.

Owing to the short time I have been connected with the agency my report must necessarily be brief, and not as satisfactory to the Department as would be desired. I regret that circumstances have been such that it has been impossible for me to take the census of the Indians connected with my agency during the short time I have been in charge. I observe that Lieutenant Hanson, who was in charge of the agency in 1870, reports, at that time, as follows; Capote Utes, 250; Weeminuche Utes, 650. I have reason to believe that the Weeminuche Utes have a much larger number at this time, and would not estimate their number at less than nine hundred. There has been in the vicinity of my agency, since I have been in charge, some four hundred Jicarilla Apache Indians; a portion of whom do not belong to my agency, but have been drawing rations for the last two months.

Most of the Indians are well disposed, and no depredation of any kind has been committed by them since I have been in charge. Most of them are destitute of clothing; but few have blankets. This is an article which will be indispensable to them when cold weather sets in. As regards location of the agency, I would regard it as favorable as any other, unless the Indians could be placed on a reservation by themselves. This I would recommend to be done at an early day as practicable. The establishment of an Indian agency at or near any of our Mexican towns has a tendency to demoralize the Indians, and is suicidal to their progress in civilization and Christianity. There are a class of men, I may say, about all Mexican towns, whose highest ambition in life is to sell whisky to the Indians. This is the only trouble I have had in connection with my agency, and the only suggestion I have to make to remedy this evil would be to place the Indians on a reservation by themselves, and locate the agency as near the center of the reservation as practicable, so as to prevent outside parties from locating near the agency.

There is some dissatisfaction among the Utes of my agency relative to their annuities. They complain because their annuities are not issued to them at the Abiquiu agency. The Los Pinos agency is so far from them that but few ever receive their annuities. I would respectfully suggest, if it is the pleasure of the Department to continue the agency, that provision be made by which the Utes of my agency may receive the amount of goods due them from the Government, in accordance with the treaty of 1868, at the Abiquiu agency. This will be more satisfactory to them than five times the amount given in any other way.

In regard to the establishment of schools among the Indians, I cannot represent matters as being encouraging. There are, however, many orphan children among the Utes, and it is to be hoped that, by proper influences, they may eventually be placed in schools.

No attention is given to agriculture by the Indians of this agency, and, owing to the great scarcity of game, their dependence for subsistence is on the Government. This dependence will be protracted until the Indians are placed on a reservation and taught to cultivate the soil; which I trust will be done at an early day.

I have the honor to be, very respectfully, your obedient servant,

W. D. CROTHERS,
United States Indian Agent, Abiquiu, N. Mex.

Col. L. EDWIN DUDLEY,
Superintendent of Indian Affairs, Sante Fé, N. Mex.

52.

PUEBLO INDIAN AGENCY, SANTA FÉ, N. MEX., *September* 25, 1873.

SIR: In compliance with instructions from the Department, I have the honor to submit the following annual report of the condition of the Pueblo Indians:

I assumed charge of this agency July 1, and have endeavored to make as complete an annual report as the limited time permits. No adequate means of transportation was at my disposal when I entered upon the duties of this office. I therefore called a meeting, at Santa Fé, of the governors of all the pueblos, (villages,) in order to learn as quickly as possible, from the Indians themselves, (pending a personal inspection,) their condition and wants. The information derived from them regarding population, individual wealth, number of horses and cattle, value of crops, &c., afforded little more than basis for estimates. Since the above meeting, I have visited thirteen out of the nineteen pueblos, and although the statistics of education and return of farming are not claimed as being strictly correct, they nevertheless afford an approximate idea of the present condition of these Indians. To prevent a too flattering estimate being made of the wealth of this people in lands, it would be proper to state that by far the larger portion is unproductive, either by reason of rocky formations or absence of water for irrigating purposes; the latter condition being an all-important one in this Territory. With regard to individual wealth, also, the general rule of consolidation applies, and the condition of any particular pueblo depends altogether upon its water-privilege. All the pueblos contiguous to the Rio Grande are comparatively independent, and are but slightly affected by lack of rain. The pueblos remote from this river depend upon small streams and rainfalls, and lead from year to year a precarious existence. Many of them are very poor, and their condition is made worse by church-taxations and the oppressions of their unscrupulous Mexican neighbors. Owing to the light rainfall of this year, (less than known for many years,) considerable suffering will be experienced in quite a number of these pueblos ere another harvest can be gathered. Neither the wheat nor corn crop will amount to half the average yield.

No appropriation has been made for these Indians for some years, but in view of the very poor harvests of the present season, I would most earnestly recommend that a reasonable sum be appropriated for distribution among the really destitute. These Indians are very industrious, and are simple in their habits. They are inoffensive, and crimes are almost unknown. They are by no means addicted to whisky-drinking, and no cases of drunkenness occur during their visits, for trade or other purposes, at Santa Fé. During the time of their "feasts," held in spring, early autumn, and Christmas holidays, they are visited by Mexicans liberally supplied with whisky, and a small number of their young men sometimes patronize these pocket-merchants. An habitual drunkard cannot be found among them.

I have elsewhere referred to their oppression by Mexican neighbors. The greatest source of complaint is the encroachment of Mexicans upon their lands; and in most cases of this nature their agent is powerless and cannot, by reason of absence of any well-defined boundaries, afford them any relief. This trouble continually increases, and unless decided action is soon taken, years of litigation will not suffice to establish the rights of the Indians. No justice can be had in the Mexican courts. The native alcaldes (justices of the peace) are elected by the Mexicans, Indians not being allowed to vote, and almost invariably decide cases in favor of the Mexicans and against the Indians, no matter how clear the evidence may be in favor of the latter. In this city I recently caused the arrest of a Mexican who had seriously wounded and robbed an Indian of the pueblo of Nambe. The Indian pointed out his assailant from among a large number of Mexicans in the court-room and produced the strongest corroborative evidence of the assault and robbery. The Mexican was acquitted, notwithstanding. Had I allowed the case to end here it would have resulted in the Indian receiving a bad wound, losing his money, and paying costs of prosecution. With such justice (?) at the agency, the result is far worse when the alcalde is under no restraining influence whatever. In isolated localities the most petty cases are invented by the Mexicans and entertained by the alcalde. So well do the Indians themselves understand their probable treatment at the hands of the alcalde and his court, that they hasten to compromise all suits brought against them. To prevent such gross injustice, I would respectfully recommend that Congress enact that all suits in which these Indians are made parties shall only be brought before the United States district court. To prevent encroachments upon Pueblo lands, I would respectfully recommend that Congress repeal the act of May 30, 1862, relating to survey of private land-grants in New Mexico, of which these necessarily form a part.

The status of these Indians is by no means clearly defined. The action of the territorial courts in recognizing these Indians as citizens has not lessened, but rather increased, their many injuries. By reason of this decision the agent cannot afford them the relief that is justly their due as wards of the nation. So long as they maintain their present relations to the General Government they are entitled to protection and to all the benefits derived by any tribe of Indians. Whatever may have been their position under Spanish rule, or however essentially different from their nomadic brethren their mode of living, they are Indians in every sense of the word.

One of the peculiar institions of these Indians—rather anomalous for "citizens"—is their domestic government, a word regarding which may not be inappropriate. They annually elect a "governor" and assistant officers; the latter usually consisting of two "lieutenant-governors;" "sheriff," and two deputies;" "captain of war," and two lieutenants. The "governor" selects from among the old men of the Pueblo, three "principals," who constitute a court (of which the "governor" is chief justice) for the trial of all offenses and misdemeanors. This mode of settling disputes is very simple and effective, and an appeal from its decisions to the agent is rarely made.

In regard to the the religious belief of the Pueblo Indians, they are nominally Roman Catholics, but their relations with this church are of the slightest possible nature. In two or three pueblos ministers of this church are located, but in the majority services are only held twice or thrice during the year, and in some instances only once. I have carefully studied their habits, and am convinced that their ancient customs and superstitions (as followers of Montezuma) have full sway. At this season many "feasts are held, and having spent several nights in their midst I have had opportunities for observing their practices on these occasions. I have been admitted into their "estufas," (buildings originally used by the fire-worshipers, and in which even at this day Indians only have permission to enter,) and in one instance obtained a glimpse of a house (more properly hovel) of a "cacique," (medicine-man and Montezuma priest.) A slight view of one of these hovels is sufficient—'twould be a strong constitution that could endure, for any length of time, the stench arising from bodies of decaying animals, and other accumulated filth therein.

In former reports much has been very properly written regarding the education of these Indians. The importance of this subject cannot be overestimated. Since the charge of this agency has devolved upon me, I have given attention almost wholly to this matter. My success has not been as great as I could desire, although at this date the number of English teachers is greater than at any former period. The Indians generally desire schools, and whenever a sufficient number of families in any pueblo guarantee the attendance of their children, I send them a teacher.

Although there is no interference whatever on the part of the agent with their choice of a religion, I meet with very great opposition from their present religious teachers, (Roman Catholic,) who constantly advise them against obedience to the wishes of the Government and its agent. These men tell the Indians that the Government of the United States has no power in this Territory, and its agent cannot exercise any control over them whatever.

During the time of my visits I find no difficulty in persuading the Indians that great benefits will result by reason of schools, but the presence among them of Mexicans, who are in collusion with their religious teachers, (who purposely keep the Indians in ignorance,) continually operates against the best efforts of their agent. After close study and serious consideration of the subject of education, I would most respectfully and earnestly recommend the establishment of an experimental school at Santa Fé, or some other convenient and healthy location, where direct supervision can be exercised over the Indians by the agent.

The building erected for this purpose should be of size sufficient to accommodate from fifty to one hundred pupils. Three young men should be selected from each pueblo, preference being given to the most intelligent, and provisions made for clothing and boarding them at the expense of the Government. In connection with the school there should be land enough for gardening purposes, in order that lessons might be given in this (to them) very essential branch of education, and also that the school might be made in a measure self-supporting. It would be advisable to connect with the institution a carpenter or wheelwright and blacksmith shop, in order that such of their number as might elect could receive instructions in these branches of mechanics. Enough work would be given by the different pueblos to make the shops self-supporting. In the course of a year, or little more, members of the school would receive a good rudimentary knowledge of English, and be competent to open school in their respective pueblos, where they would make more rapid progress with the people than any English teacher, and be employed at a much lower salary.

To conduct such a school there would be required a principal, assistant, (who should also be a practical farmer,) two practical mechanics, and a matron, the whole under the immediate supervision of the agent. The establishment of this school may be deemed too expensive, but a little careful consideration will correct such an impression. Schools are now sought to be established at the respective pueblos; total number, nineteen. Should a teacher be sent each, the salaries alone would amount to $11,400. For school-houses and repairs add $8,000; for school-books, fuel, &c., $2,500; total, $21,900; by no means a liberal estimate. The experimental school-building and lands would cost $10,000, salaries $5,500, incidentals, (provisions and all other expenses,) $15,000, total, $30,500; a very liberal estimate.

After a careful review of the efforts that have been made from time to time to Christianize these Indians, I am convinced that the recommendation herewith submitted will, if adopted, prove to be the most practicable and economical solution of this difficulty. The maximum number of pupils could be maintained, and thus from one to three young men, possessing an elementary knowledge of English language and customs, would be returned to each pueblo every year. The influence exerted by them would be marked, indeed, and far greater than any resulting from missionary labor in their midst. For the accomplishment of the recommendations set forth in this report, I would respectfully ask that the following special appropriations be made:

Re-survey of Indian lands, the sum of	$10,000
Civilization of Indians, the sum of	25,000
Agricultural implements, food and clothing, in cases of extreme necessity, the sum of	10,000
Total	45,000

Believing that these simple and industrious Indians are entitled to much consideration at the hands of a Government they have occasioned but slight trouble and expense, I have submitted an estimate of their wants. The merely nominal sum required for their education will be returned in revenue to the Government a thousand-fold when they shall have become intelligent citizens.

With the hope that the suggestions in this report will receive the careful consideration of yourself and the honorable Commissioner of Indian Affairs,

I am, very respectfully, your obedient servant,

EDWIN C. LEWIS,
United States Indian Agent.

L. EDWIN DUDLEY, Esq.,
Superintendent of Indian Affairs, Santa Fé, New Mexico.

53.

INDIAN AGENCY, CIMARRON, N. MEX., *December* 22, 1873.

SIR: In compliance with your letter to Superintendent Dudley, dated December 4, 1873, asking for the annual report from the agency, I have the honor to submit the following:

I assumed charge of the agency on the 1st day of August last, under appointment from Superintendent Dudley. Most of my time since my appointment I have been absent on other duty, and for that reason I am unable to make as full and complete a report as I would like to make.

The employés at this agency are one interpreter, at a salary of $500 per annum, and one commissary, at a compensation of $40 per month.

INDIANS.

There are under my charge one band of Utes, (the Muaches,) and two bands of Jicarilla Apaches; I have no means of knowing their exact number, as they have never all been at the agency at any one time since I have been in charge, but from the best information which I have been able to obtain, and from my observation, I believe they number, men, women, and children, nearly twelve hundred, in about the following proportions, to wit:

Muache Utes:		
Men	180	
Women	210	
Children	240	
		610
Jicarilla Apaches:		
Men	140	
Women	180	
Children	240	
		560
Total		1,170

SUBSISTENCE.

Their subsistence is furnished under contract, and consists of fresh beef and shorts, and is issued to them three times a month, at the rate of half a pound of beef and one pound of shorts per day to each; occasionally sugar, coffee, and tobacco are purchased for them (in open market) in very small quantities. All such purchases are paid for at the office of the superintendent at Sante Fé, N. Mex., on certified vouchers.

LOCATION.

The agency is located on a private land-claim, belonging to the Maxwell Land Grant and Railroad Company.

UTES.

The Utes spend most of their time on the plains or in the mountains hunting, and only come to the agency when game is too scarce to furnish them subsistence, or to obtain a supply of powder, lead, &c. A few of them, however, stay in and about the Mexican settlements in this vicinity, which does not at all tend to improve their morals. The Utes, as a general thing, are very peaceable, and I hear very few reports of any thefts or other depredations committed by them, but very few of them have acquired any habits of industry aside from those pertaining to the chase.

JICARILLA APACHES.

The Jicarilla Apaches spend most of their time in an and about the Mexican settlements; some of them have acquired habits of industry; not a few of them have acquired all the vices and none of the virtues of the Mexicans; most of them will get drunk whenever they are able to purchase intoxicating liquor in sufficient quantity to produce that state, which, I regret to state, is only too often. Their petty depredations on the property of the white settlers in this vicinity and the surrounding country are, to say the least of them, very annoying.

UTES AND APACHES.

These people are entirely without education, and, so far as I can learn, there never has been any effort made to establish schools among them, and I feel convinced that any effort in that direction, surrounded by their present influences, would be almost useless and a waste of time and money. If it were the intention of the Government to allow them to remain in this locality, I should feel that any attempt to improve their morals, establish schools among them, or in any way better their condition, would be almost a fruitless undertaking. But as the Utes agreed in the late treaty at Los Pinos to remove onto their reservation, as soon as an agency should be established for them, and as the Jicarilla Apaches have just accepted a proposition from the Government for their removal to, and location upon a reservation in every way adapted to their wants, there is good reason to believe that these Indians will, with care and good management, become, in a few years, sober, industrious, and self-supporting.

I would earnestly recommend that the "Southern Ute Agency," where these Indians are to be located, be established as soon as practicable, and the Indians themselves removed thereto as soon as possible. I would suggest the first of April next as a very good time for their removal. This would enable those of them who desire so to do, to commence farming as soon as they occupy their new homes.

Very respectfully, your obedient servant,

THOMAS A. DOLAN,
In charge of Indian Agency, Cimarron, N. Mex.

The Hon. COMMISSIONER OF INDIAN AFFAIRS, *Washington, D. C.*

54.

UNITED STATES INDIAN AGENCY,
Gila River Reservation, Arizona, August 31, 1873.

SIR: Obedient to circular instructions from the honorable Commissioner of Indian Affairs at Washington, I have the honor to submit this my third annual report of the condition of affairs among the Pima and Maricopa Indians of Arizona.

A careful review of the year ending to-day, fails to show any particular improvement on the part of these Indians.

In my second annual report, I alluded to several of the principal causes then combined to prevent the advancement of this people into a higher moral and physical standard, and prominent among them were the lack of proper means for educating them, the limited facilities to enable them to remain self-sustaining, and the evil influences with which they are compelled to associate. These same causes exist to-day, and the latter two named augment from year to year, in a degree that threatens the most serious consequences to all concerned.

The lack of good land, plenty of water, and a sufficient number of schools for the children, has long been felt here, and in consequence of which there exists, on the other hand, a certain degree of idleness, intemperance, and prostitution. The future welfare of these Indians demands a sufficiency of the one and an immunity from the other, and until these are secured them, it is folly to expect them to improve.

The water question is with us an almost threadbare subject. The Department has several times during my stay here been informed of the condition of affairs relative to that element, the want of which has been more severely felt this year than ever before. Nor have these Indians been the only sufferers, for the settlers living above this reserve on the Gila River are all complaining of the lack of water. On the western part of the reservation the river has been entirely dry for nearly three months, in consequence of which there will be no fall crops of any kind. In many fields the small grain harvest was almost a failure from a want of water. The settlements above the reservation are still increasing, and in a few years the farmers there will need and appropriate all the water that the river affords during the warm season preceding harvest. The reservation does not afford a sufficient quantity of water for the support of all the Indians belonging to it, and some of them in consequence have left it in order to get a living. About thirteen hundred members of these tribes are thus living outside the lines of their reserve—about one thousand just above it on the Gila, and some three hundred have moved to the Salt River Valley.

Their close proximity to the whites is continually begetting troubles of more or less importance between them, and, in the opinion of many people in the Territory, it will at an early day lead to a war between the two races. The condition of affairs in this respect is illustrated in the following occurrences, both of recent date:

On the 24th of last June, known and celebrated as San Juan's day by the Mexican population of the Territory, quite a number of that nation gathered at the town of Adamsville, some ten miles above this reserve, and spent the day in the usual manner, riding, feasting, &c., and a few of them getting drunk. In the evening they had a dance, which they continued through the night. A number of Pima Indians were in and about Adamsville during the day watching the Mexicans in their sports, and several of them remained at night to witness the dance.

Among these Indians was the son of Antonio Azul, head chief of the Pimas. During the night they were in and out of the dancing-room, behaving themselves properly, and, as far as I can learn, were all sober.

About an hour before daylight the next morning, one of the Mexicans, without any provocation whatever, struck the chief's son with a knife to the heart.

Later on in the day the Mexican was arrested, and it being shown by some Mexican witnesses that he was the guilty party, he was kept until the morrow for a preliminary trial. The next day came and with it several hundred Pimas, who in the mean time had been advised of the murder of their chief's son. About 10 o'clock the prisoner was taken into the court-room, and the trial commenced. While one of the witnesses was being examined, or about to be examined, three or four Pimas entered the room, and, approaching the prisoner, motioned for him to stand up. He paying no attention to this command was suddenly lifted to his feet by the Indians, and his hands secured with a rope. He was then led out of the court-room to the edge of the town, about a hundred yards distant, and was there surrounded by the other Pimas, who joined the party. They then formed a circle around the prisoner and with little or no ceremony they killed him with their war-clubs. The Indians then quietly returned to their homes. In the mean time, anticipating some such trouble, troops were sent for, and a small detachment arrived from Camp McDowell, about an hour after the death of the Mexican. A few hours later, another small command came in from Camp Lowell, but by this time matters had become so quiet that the troops soon returned to their respective posts. It was a high-handed affair for these Indians thus to take the prisoner from the court-room, and I trust its parallel will never occur again. The Indians defend their action by saying that the murderer would never have been punished, but would have escaped, or would have been discharged. They also reminded me that last year one of their tribe was killed by a Mexican who was arrested, and afterward escaped to Sonora.

The settlers on the Gila have been very anxious to have a company of troops stationed in the vicinity of Adamsville, and I applied to the commander of the department, Gen. George Crook, and requested that troops be sent there, until I could hear from your office, to which I had referred the matter. Gen. Crook seemed to think that the troops should be stationed at this agency, and declined to send any to any other point on the river. As the trouble did not occur at this agency, but at Adamsville, some twenty miles from here, it seems to me that if troops were needed at all they should have been sent there.

About two weeks ago, one of the Pima chiefs, who, with his family, was living in the Salt River Valley, lost a child by death, and, as is the custom on the decease of a member of the family, the chief proceeded to burn one of his huts. It appears that the hut in question was built on a portion of land owned and occupied by one of the settlers in that valley, who objected to having it burned. The Indian insisted, and, in the attempt to fire the hut, was shot and seriously wounded by the settler. The Indians were much excited by the occurrence, and for a while it was feared that some further trouble would ensue, but they have since assured me that no retaliation would be attempted. The hut had not been used by the Indians for some time previous to the affair, and I understand that the settler in question claims to have bought it, and was using it as a store-room for grain. The Indians say there was nothing in it at the time they wanted to burn it.

The above occurrences are as yet almost exceptional cases, but the time is not far distant when such things will become more common. The Indians are by no means blameless for the state of feeling between themselves and the settlers. There are some of them, principally the young men, who, having nothing to occupy their time on the reserve, leave it, and a part of these usually gather about the settlements, where they earn their living by begging, pilfering, and sometimes by working when they can get anything to do. These are the men who bring reproach on the tribe, and by them the whole tribe is judged by many of the citizens of the Territory.

The liquor traffic is still being carried on, and since my last report has increased in a degree that will soon make intemperance a general evil among this people. It had become so notorious that it attracted the attention of the United States grand jury some months since, and an effort was made to find out who were the parties engaged in selling liquor to the Indians; and though many witnesses were summoned before that body, nothing definite was elicited to lead to the prosecution of a single case. A few years ago to see a drunken Indian about the reserve was an unheard-of thing; but now, not to see one or more in the vicinity of the settlements near here, would be equally strange. If something is not soon done to check the rapid growth of this evil, it will prove a powerful auxiliary to the ruin of the tribes. Our proximity to Mexico affords those who are so disposed ample opportunity to engage in the liquor trade with the Indians, as they can bring the liquor within a few miles of the reservation, dispose of it, and return within the Mexican lines before any of the officers of the law can be made aware of it.

Prostitution, the companion of intemperance, is also doing its work among these tribes, and little can be done to prevent it, so long as the Indians are obliged to leave their reserve in order to obtain a living, or so long as the liquor traffic prevails. Only a few years ago such a thing was unknown among these people, and to-day the monthly report of the resident physician shows more than twenty cases on the sick-list as the result of this evil. Like intemperance, the only remedy lies in the early exodus of these tribes to some point beyond the reach of such influence.

Several scouting expeditions have been organized by these Indians against the Apaches since my last report, but of late they have not been very successful, and frequently report no Apaches to be seen. This is accounted for from the fact that General Crook, by a series of vigorous campaigns during the last year, has compelled many of the hitherto roving bands of those Indians to remain on their reservations. Occasionally, however, a few of them visit the vicinity of this reserve, and usually signal their presence by taking from it a horse or two.

The question of illicit trading is not yet settled, though I understand the case has been pending before the United States Supreme Court for more than a year.

About the time of completing my last report, I received from Dr. H. Bendell, the then superintendent of Indian affairs for Arizona, and who was on a visit at Washington at the time, a letter advising me that he had succeeded in securing from your Department an appropriation of $5,000 for educational purposes among these Indians, and stating that that sum would immediately be placed at my disposal for the uses mentioned. On his return to Prescott we were very much surprised and disappointed by a communication from him informing me that the appropriation was made partly for the purposes of building a school-house and partly for paying for the erection of some additional rooms at this agency, which were needed, and which he had authorized me to build. The payment for the rooms left me but little over half the original appropriation to devote to educational purposes, but with that remainder I have built two comfortable and convenient school-houses, one at San-tan, a Pima village, two and a half miles from the agency, and the other at Hol-che-dum, a Maricopa village, some four and a half miles distant. These houses are not large, but they will meet the wants of the two villages for the present. Should these tribes not be removed to the Indian Territory, there should be a school-house erected in each village on the reserve, and all of them supplied with teachers as early as practicable. If, as is generally conceded, "the hope of the Indians lies in the children," every facility should be afforded them for obtaining an education and otherwise fitting them for the future, which, from their present general ignorant condition, seems each year more and more uncertain. Having two school-houses, we shall need two more teachers when school re-opens, which will be about the middle of next month, and it is to be hoped that the Department will immediately authorize their engagement at a salary allowed the male teachers now here. In our schools we have the only means of improving the condition of the Indians, and while we may be and are accomplishing some good among the few children that our facilities enable us to reach, the remainder are growing up in ignorance. There are nearly sixteen hundred children of the right age to attend school living on this reserve, and at the utmost, with our present means, we can only reach about one hundred and twenty-five.

Much interest has been shown by the Indians in the question of their removal to the Indian Territory, and it is with pleasure that I acknowledge the receipt from your office of a communication authorizing me to prospect that country with a delegation of these tribes, with a view to their removal should they be satisfied with the appearance of the territory and the terms of removal. The Indians cannot remain here much longer and continue self-sustaining. Should they remain, it will be but a few years until they will become so reduced that in order to live they will have to be fed, or they will steal. If they are fed, it will cost the Government immense sums of money annually, while the Indians, who have always been self-supporting heretofore, will degenerate into a lazy, shiftless people, and a life of utter worthlessness, from which it will be almost impossible ever to reclaim them. If, on the other hand, they steal, it will involve them in a war with the Government, which, while it will cost still more than to feed them, will prove more disastrous to them in other respects. It is the desire of the Government that all her Indians should support themselves, and it is far better that these tribes be removed to some locality where they can continue self-supporting than for them to remain here, where, in a few years, they must become dependent. The Indian Territory offers the best inducements for them, and I recommend their removal there as their only salvation.

The Reformed Church, which your agent represents, manifests a deep interest in these Indians, and is fully alive to the necessity of early education and christianization. For the past two years since this reservation was assigned to that body, it has kept a lady-teacher here, and has rendered us valuable assistance in various other ways.

We also feel indebted to the Ladies' Union Missionary Association, of New York, for its kindly assistance in supplying us with many articles useful for school purposes.

I enclose herewith statistics of education and farming, marked respectively A and B, which are based on the best information at my command.

Hoping I may be able to make my next annual report of these Indians to you from the Indian Territory,

I remain, sir, very respectfully, your obedient servant,

J. H. STOUT,
United States Indian Agent.

Hon. E. P. SMITH,
Commissioner of Indian Affairs, Washington, D. C.

55.

AGENCY PAPAGO INDIANS,
Tucson, Ariz. Ter., September 1, 1873.

SIR: I have the honor to submit this my third annual report showing the condition of the agency under my charge.

The peace made during the past year between the Papagos and the Aribaipa and the Pinal Apaches, has been kept to the satisfaction of all concerned, and has been the means of doing much good.

It is the first time in the recollection of the Papagos that they have been at peace with these Indians, and the fact that they are not only safe in person, but can now keep and raise stock in security, is a consolation and advantage that they seem fully to appreciate, and, should this condition of affairs continue, it will be but a few years before these Indians will possess considerable wealth, and be self-sustaining and independent.

These Indians have always been celebrated for virtue, industry, and integrity, and no doubt their good conduct is, to a great extent, due to the labors of the Catholic fathers who built a mission for their instruction at San Xavier del Bac, over a century ago. Through the hostility of other Indians, and internal strifes among the people of Mexico, the mission has for many years been going to decay; but the Papagos still linger around it, fondly cherishing the memory of the past, and adhering to a great extent to the precepts that were taught them.

I have received $2,500 to be devoted to educational purposes, and with this sum I have erected a school-house. The building is over one hundred feet long, surrounded by a good wall, and is conveniently divided into rooms for the accommodation of classes and teachers, and is in every way admirably arranged for the comfort and convenience of both pupils and teachers.

I have engaged two Sisters from Saint Joseph's Academy to teach the school. This selection gives great satisfaction to the Indians, and it being with the sisters a labor of love, I have great hopes that the school will be the means of promoting much good.

I believe it to be highly necessary to teach some of the boys mechanical trades, and a number have expressed a strong desire to have their boys so instructed. I have noticed that many display considerable ingenuity in the use of tools. It is necessary for them to have a considerable amount of mechanical work done, such as making and repairing plows, carts, &c., and as they progress their necessity will increase. I would, therefore, recommend the building of a blacksmith and wagon shop, and the employment of two good mechanics to perform the work for the agency, and to teach such of the boys trades as desire to learn and show a faculty for it; by this means in two or three years they could do their own mechanical labor; besides, it would serve to stimulate them to a higher order of civilization.

Their agricultural pursuits have been fairly rewarded this year; the yield has been very satisfactory, and they have cultivated, in addition to the old lands that they have so long used, a considerable portion of new land. This, in connection with many natural products they gather, and the proceeds of labor they perform for others, will be sufficient for all their wants and afford them the means of living more comfortably than at any period for years before.

In accordance with instructions from the Department, I have ordered a map made, which will soon be completed, of that portion of country which they desire set apart for a reservation, and I would most earnestly recommend that either this or some other locality suitable to their wants be set apart for them, so that they may, without molestation, enjoy and have security in their homes.

The health of the Indians during the past year has been good, and at no period since the acquisition of the Territory by the United States have they appeared so contented and happy.

Very respectfully, your obedient servant,

R. A. WILBUR,
United States Indian Agent.

Hon. COMMISSIONER OF INDIAN AFFAIRS.

56.

COLORADO RIVER RESERVATION,
Parker, Ariz. Ter., August 30, 1873.

SIR: I have the honor to submit the following as my annual report for the year ending this date:

Since my last annual report the Hualpais have been placed under my charge. This people range through the country north and east of the Mojaves. Their strength has been variously estimated at from 1,200 to 1,600, but the number fed at Camp Beales Springs, where they have been collected during the year past, has not averaged more than 600. It is my intention to remove them to this reservation in October next, where they can be fed with less expense to the Government.

The Chimehuevis and Yumas, who have never been on this reservation, will also be removed hither, as soon as the irrigating canal is finished, which will probably be during the coming winter.

Continual trouble is being experienced by the squatting of Mexicans near the boundary-line of the reservation, who tamper with the Indians, and attempt to introduce liquor among them. The only remedy I can suggest is to extend the reserve to the south to take in the abandoned town of La Paz, and to the east to include in its limits all the bottom-land between the river and the edge of the mesa. The proposed increase would take in all the land which has any value, and would inclose the reservation within natural boundaries. By this extension no rights would be interfered with, as no claims are recorded; consequently no difficulty will result from taking in this land.

The Chimehuevis and Yumas have not been regularly fed, as I consider it impolitic to give anything to Indians who are not on reservations, except to prevent absolute suffering. They have been accustomed to raise their own crops; and, as soon as the irrigating canal is finished, I shall remove them to the reservation, and assign them sufficient ground for their support.

The canal by which it is intended to irrigate this reservation has been pushed forward since my last report. A tunnel has been cut for 430 feet through the solid rock; another tunnel, of 320 feet, has been got under way, but no work has been done since the commencement of the summer, on account of the rise in the river. The water will, however, shortly fall, and work will be resumed, with a prospect of being finished this winter.

The Indians object to labor, except for money. They should not, I think, be indulged in their idle habits, and I desire to have a sufficient force stationed on the reserve to compel them to work for their own benefit without compensation, save rations. My opinion is that the Indian must be made self-sustaining before he becomes susceptible to the influences of missionaries or teachers.

The crops of all the river Indians will be much smaller than usual this year, owing to the lateness of the river in rising, and the small overflow.

The Hualpai Indians, at Camp Beales Springs, object to coming upon this reservation; but they are now settled directly upon one of the principal lines of travel; settlements and mining-camps are springing up all around them, and I agree with the Department commander (General Crook) that the only way to avoid serious complications with this tribe will be to remove them to this place, or to the Rio Verde reservation; and of the two places I consider this one preferable, for the reason that with the Mojaves the Hualpais have always had kindred ties and intercourse, while with the Indians on the Rio Verde reservation, Apache-Mojaves and Apaches, they have been more or less hostile, and have lately fought against them as soldiers under General Crook. I have requested the Department commander to furnish a sufficient force to coerce them to move, and to remain with them for a time until they become thoroughly submissive.

I would desire to call the attention of the Commissioner to the necessity of increasing the salaries allowed employés; the compensation offered by the Department is usually so much lower than that given by the other bureaus of the Government in Arizona that it is very difficult to secure good employés.

Good, reliable interpreters are also difficult to obtain, and I would suggest the sending of one or two boys from each tribe to the Howard University, to be fitted for positions as interpreters and school-teachers; absolute separation from their parents and people is necessary to education and elevation.

We had a school in operation for six months, but had to close it in April last, on account of the inadequate salary allowed the teacher. While it continued, such children as attended made very good progress; but they were not many, as the parents are prejudiced against learning, and, besides, exercise no control over their children.

Lately, when acting as superintendent of Indian affairs, I discontinued feeding the Mojaves who live about Camp Mojave. This section of the tribe have never come upon the reservation. They number about 800, and I expect them during the coming winter, as I hear their crops have failed.

I am, sir, very respectfully, your obedient servant,

J. A. TORMER,
United States Indian Agent.

The COMMISSIONER OF INDIAN AFFAIRS, *Washington, D. C.*

57.

MOQUI PUEBLO INDIAN AGENCY, ARIZ. TER.,
December 30, 1873.

SIR: I have the honor herewith to submit my first annual report, in compliance with copy of circular of June 30, 1873.

W. D. Crothers, my predecessor, and myself exchanged papers on the 9th of July, he relieving me at the Sierra Amarilla agency, New Mexico, and I taking charge of the Moqui Pueblo Indians of Arizona Territory. As soon thereafter as possible I visited the Indians under my care, and met with more than an ordinary cordial reception from them, owing to the fact that the night preceding the morning of my arrival, and the night following, we had quite a good deal of rain, much needed by their growing crops. They being an extremely superstitious people received it as a very propitious omen. Their new Tata agent and the rain coming together they expressed it as evidence of the Great Father's pleasure; that He had been angry with them for some time, but now a brighter day was dawning for them. I found them very superstitious. I have endeavored to disabuse them of their superstition, but find it is a part of their existence;

that it will take time, a civilizing and Christianizing influence thrown around them to free them from it.

From reports I had concerning their houses I was prepared to see desolation and barrenness, but I am free to acknowledge I had not, in the worst pictures I had formed, imagined anything *nearly* so desolate as it appeared when there, and as it was in fact. Their condition as to locality and surroundings you are fully advised of in previous reports.

I am pleased to advise the Department that there is, on the part of the Indians of the different villages, a growing disposition to harmonize one with the other. There is at present a better feeling existing than for some years back. As I advised you in my former reports, the Oreybes, those Indians affected with a bad feeling toward the other villages, and toward the agent, are now inclined to be friendly, and seem very anxious that I should go among them to live.

In previous reports I strongly recommended the removal of the Moquis to a more suitable place for farming and grazing. I also sent in an estimate for funds to build agency-house, school-house, mill, to open asequias, &c. I have received $1,500 for the purpose of erecting agency building and one school-house; I have also received permission from the honorable Commissioner to build at the place to which I will remove the Moquis; I have already commenced operations preparatory to building.

I would earnestly recommend that the Department aid these Indians to the extent of my estimate in opening up this place and in building a mill, &c. I believe that if the Government would assist them in establishing themselves in this new place that it will prove the most economical plan; for by helping them *now*, in this way, you will enable them to help themselves, and can sooner withdraw the aid the Department so kindly furnishes them now. At the expiration of from three to five years, at the furthest, they would not require help from the Government, and be in a better condition than they are at present with assistance. I base my belief upon the fact that they are an industrious people, and if they are assisted with a start in a good place, where their labor will be rewarded by good crops, they would have abundance for home consumption and plenty to dispose of; while the little assistance rendered them by the Government, although thankfully received by them, does not in reality do them much good.

Their crop, promising so fair in the early part of the season resulted in little better than a failure. I fear there will be some suffering among them this winter and spring. I shall employ the Moquis in the erection of buildings, which will greatly relieve their sufferings.

They are much pleased that they are to receive sheep this year. I would heartily recommend that as long as it is the pleasure of the Department to aid these people that it be in this way. Aside from a little brown muslin, let them have stock, as it tends to a more substantial good than anything else.

These Indians should have more schools. There is one in operation with a good average attendance. The children have made excellent progress in their studies. I have just purchased a blackboard for use in the school, an article long needed. I hope in a short time to report more favorable on my school as soon as we get into our new school-house. Three other schools could be started, with a good attendance, one at each of the other pueblos.

The health of the Moquis is good. They live lives of virtue; consequently they are free from disease. It is impossible for me at this time to estimate the amount of land farmed by the Moquis, as it is in patches and scattered over a great deal of territory. I hope soon to make an improvement, as soon as I can get them to move to their new place, where I will give to each family a little farm, adjoining one another; have all the land farmed in a body, so we can know just what they are doing.

Regretting my report has been so long delayed, I am, sir, very respectfully, your obedient servant,

W. S. DEFREES,
United States Indian Agent for Moqui Pueblo Indians.

Hon. E. P. SMITH,
Commissioner of Indian Affairs, Washington, D. C.

58.

OFFICE OF AGENCY RIO VERDE INDIAN RESERVATION, ARIZ. TER.,
September 1, 1873.

Hon. E. P. SMITH,
Commissioner of Indian Affairs, Washington, D. C.

SIR: I have the honor to submit the following report of the condition of affairs at this agency during the past year:

Shortly after my last annual report, it having been attempted by General Crook to arrest some Indians at Date Creek who were supposed to have been concerned in the Loring stage massacre, there was a general stampede of the Indians to the mountains, where they remained for several weeks. Ultimately, after sending out runners to them with friendly assurances, the greater portion of them returned to the agency. Nothing of unusual importance occurred after their return until they were informed in April that it had been decided to remove them to their permanent home at the Rio Verde. At this many of them expressed great dissatisfaction, and Jemaspie, head-chief of the Apache Yumas, positively refused to go there, stating that he was at present living in his own country, and contented to remain where he was. A few days before the time for their removal to the Verde, Jemaspie and a number of his Indians left during the night, making their way to the Colorado River, and afterward going on to the Indian reservation there. This band were soon afterward brought over to the Verde by the military. The remainder of the Indians, numbering about 360, under charge of Lieutenant Schuyler, United States Army, started on Thursday, May 1, for the Rio Verde reservation, where they arrived on May 12. Meanwhile, General Cook having declared peace with the Indians, the Apache and Apach Mohave Indians in the vicinity of the Rio Verde came into Camp Verde in large numbers, and it became necessary for me to leave Date Creek for that place, in order to assume charge of them and to remove them to this reservation. This, in compliance with instructions from the superintendent, I did, arriving at Camp Verde on April 27.

As soon as I could procure the necessary transportation for supplies, May 8, I removed the Indians, numbering 1,120, from the military reservation to this reserve. The agency-camp I located in a suitable place about eighteen miles from the military post. The Indians I camped at points within five miles of the agency. The superintendent failing to supply implements, tools, &c., for which I had made requisition, and which were much needed at this time, the formation of the camp, building corral, &c., was necessarily very up-hill work. The military loaned me a few axes, picks, and spades, and these, with a small supply afterward purchased, composed the main part of the tools with which to employ the Indians, and do the needed work at the agency.

Owing to the small supply of implements and the lack of an irrigating-canal to supply the needed moisture, together with the lateness of the season, only a few small patches of land have been brought under cultivation by the Indians. Many of them appeared willing to work, and, under more favorable circumstances, will no doubt raise considerable crops.

The Apache Indians, numbering about 900, left the reserve for the mountains on the 12th of August. This movement was induced by a renegade Apache, named Chapo, from Camp Apache, who reported to them that a number of soldiers and Indian scouts were coming from the lower country to massacre them. A runner was sent out from Camp Verde to bring in Eschetleepan, their head chief, and, after his arrival, in a conference with General Crook, having been convinced of the falsehood of the report, and of the good intention of the whites toward them, he expressed himself ashamed and sorry that he had left the reserve, and promised to return to the reserve, and to endeavor to induce the others to do so, too. Up to this date about 586 have returned. On the 4th of August Delché arrived at this agency with a few of his warriors. This Indian has the reputation of being one of the worst and most inveterate enemies of the whites in the Territory. He had gone on to the Camp Apache reservation after the proclamation of peace by General Crook in the spring, having been severely handled during the winter campaign. It was reported that his life had been threatened by Indians at Camp Apache, and that consequently he had left that agency. General Crook, believing the report to be true, requested me to receive him on to this reserve, in case he came here. In accordance with this request I told Delché that he might bring his people on to the reserve, providing he would behave himself, which he promised to do. I also told him that this was the last opportunity that would be given him to live on a reservation.

The Apache Yumas and Apache Mohaves from Date Creek have, since their arrival here, behaved well, and seem desirous of remaining upon good terms with the agent and with the white population generally. They are also more ready to learn and to adopt the customs of civilization than the others, many of them wearing ordinary clothing, using improved cooking-utensils, building superior cabins, keeping their camps or villages policed, &c.

The Apaches are in a more untamed state, and it is likely that there will be considerable trouble in reducing them to such a contented state of mind as will be favorable to their rapid advancement in civilization.

The aggregated number of the Indians on this reserve increased at one time to over 2,000. About 40 Indians belonging to the various tribes here are enlisted in the United States service as scouts, and they have proved very efficient in the discharge of their duties. There is a detachment of 15 United States soldiers, under charge of Lieutenant Schuyler, stationed near the agency. A few arrests of Indians have been made for absence from the reserve without pass, for stealing, misinterpreting, and attempting to kill a squaw. This latter case was a result of a system which the Indians follow of killing women of their tribes whom they believe to be witches. There has been a very large amount of sickness, principally intermittent fever, whooping-cough and ophthalmia, among the Indians. There has been quite a number of deaths from these causes. The Indians superstitiously lay the blame upon a number of the women; believing them to be witches, and believing that by killing them they will be rid of the diseases, they have been accustomed to do so. This being the case, I found it necessary to take prompt measures for the suppression of this evil; but I expect to be able only partially to do away with it, while the older men of the present generation are living. Owing to the sickness there have been a number of desertions from the reserve; small bands of Indians have gone into the mountains, where it is healthier. I do not think that those who have gone in this way intend to commit depredations.

For a time it will be necessary to have the co-operation of the military in keeping the Indians on their reserves. They are yet, to a large extent, wild and untamed, and there will be parties who will go off from time to time, and the aid of the military is necessary to insure their return. A small military force is also required to keep in awe and insure the good behavior of those who are on the reserves. This aid has been, as far as this agency is concerned, promptly rendered, and I have found General Crook to be ready at all times to co-operate with me in the management of the Indians, and in seeking to make the present Indian policy of the Government a success. I am much indebted to him for said co-operation, and for his valuable counsels.

This reserve is comprised of that section of country for 10 miles on each side of the Rio Verde, commencing at the northwest boundary of the millitary reservation of Camp Verde, and extending to where the old wagon-road to New Mexico crosses the river at a point supposed to be about 45 miles up the river. In order to cultivate the soil with a reasonable prospect of success, it is very necessary that an irrigating canal be made to supply moisture during the period of drought in the spring and early summer. There is a considerable quantity of land that can be cultivated if irrigated. A ditch about 10 miles in length would irrigate from 1,500 to 2,000 acres of fine tillable soil. I would strongly recommend that an appropriation of $25,000, the amount estimated as requisite for this purpose, be made, so that work may be commenced at an early date. Should this quantity of land be insufficient, there are other tracts that can be irrigated in like manner and cultivated to great advantage. The expense of feeding the large number of Indians here is, of course, very great, and if they are to be rendered self-supporting, I deem the construction of the irrigating canal to be of the greatest importance, and almost absolutely necessary to this end.

It is also important that the Indians be employed at an early date, as while lying idle there is greater likelihood of their becoming discontented and leaving the reserve.

A very large portion of the reserve is particularly suitable for grazing purposes, and I would recommend that a small number of sheep and cattle be purchased for each band, that they may be enabled to commence stock-raising. I deem it very advisable to encourage and to aid them to possess stock, as such ownership would be great inducement for them to remain upon the reserve, and would probably in time aid materially in rendering them self-supporting.

The agency garden of about two acres, watered by a small mountain spring, is in good order and yielding its acceptable fruits for the use of the agent and employés. The small patches cultivated by the Indians, although comparatively useless as a means of subsistence, have given some employment and apparent pleasure to the owners.

No permanent buildings have yet been erected, no funds for that purpose having been appropriated. The agent and employés are living in tents loaned by the military. The temporary structure in present use as a storehouse is made mainly of raw-hide and paulins furnished by the military. The site of the present camp has proved very unhealthy. It is intended to locate the permanent buildings about two miles from here on a mesa above this level and near to the spring of water used for irrigating the agency garden. It is believed that the location is very healthful. For the purpose of erecting the necessary buildings, agency, store-house, quarters for employés, blacksmith and carpenter's shops, school-house, stables, and corral, I respectfully ask that an appropriation of $50,000 be secured, this sum being the estimated cost of the same, as unless the permanent buildings are commenced at an early date it will be necessary to put up some temporary buildings. I would urge the advisability of action in this matter at once in order to make the expense to the Government as little as possible.

Before closing this report I respectfully make the following statement with regard to stores furnished the department at Date Creek:

Six months supplies for that feeding-station were purchased by the superintendent in San Francisco last fall, and invoiced by him to me. A portion of the supplies arrived during the winter. The quality of some of the articles was fair, but the sugar was of so inferior a quality that I declined to receive it, and informed the superintendent of the fact. The coffee was also of an inferior quality, but not having been supplied with data in regard to the quality purchased, I receipted for it.

Upon comparison I find that the Indian Department have been paying a very much higher price for supplies than the military pay. This I believe to be owing to the fact that they were purchased in San Francisco without the advantage of competition. In future, I respectfully suggest that all stores required and that are produced in this section of the country, such as beef, flour, corn, beans, &c., be purchased here, and that a fair competition for the contracts be allowed to all responsible merchants. This I am satisfied, from certain data in my possession, would very materially diminish the cost of feeding the tribes on the different reservations. Here I would suggest that such articles as are not produced here, and that may be purchased by the commissioner in San Francisco or the Eastern States, be inspected before their shipment, or that samples be furnished me, so that the faithful filling of the contract may be insured.

I am, sir, very respectfully, your obedient servant,

J. WILLIAMS,
United States Special Indian Agent.

Hon. E. P. SMITH,
Commissioner of Indian Affairs, Washington, D. C.

59.

SAN CARLOS DIVISION WHITE MOUNTAIN RESERVATION, ARIZ.,
August 31, 1873.

SIR: I have the honor to report that during the past year the Indians upon this reservation, composed of Pinal and Aravaipa Apaches and Tontos, have been removed from the old Camp Grant reservation, upon the San Pedro River, to their present location, at the junction of the San Carlos and Gila Rivers, which removal was delayed by the frequent change of agents.

Upon September 13, 1872, Mr. George H. Stevens relieved Mr. Jacobs, and took charge at the Camp Grant agency. During his administration the Indians behaved extremely well, the only outbreak being the murder of a Mexican boy by an outlawed Indian named Charley.

In December, 1872, the Indians were counted daily, by order of the department commander, and, after thoroughly understanding what was required of them, were very seldom absent from the muster.

Upon February 9, 1873, Dr H. R. Wilbur relieved Mr. Stevens, and immediately proceeded to remove the Indians to the present agency, arriving here in the latter part of February, everything being in a very unsettled state and the supplies of rations inadequate to the demand.

Mr. C. F. Larrabee relieved Dr. H. R. Wilbur, March 4, 1873, as special agent. Full supplies were still very difficult to obtain, and a great deal of jealousy existed between the rival chiefs, two outlaw chiefs, Charley and Co-chi-nay, having returned to the reservation. In April one of the most troublesome chiefs, Skin-as-kism, and another Indian were killed in a quarrel.

On May 27, Lieut. Jacob Almy, Fifth Cavalry, was killed by an Indian named Des-oh, when the bands of Co-chi-nay and Clumly, to whom the murderer belonged, immediately left the reservation and fled to the mountains, the Indian Des-oh having, previous to the shooting, tried to spear Agent Larrabee, but was prevented by an Indian called Yomas. After this murder Agent Larrabee turned over to me, as representative of General Crook, all property belonging to the Indian Department, for which he was responsible, giving as his reason for leaving the agency that the Indians could only be controlled by the military authorities.

I took charge of the agency upon the 1st June, ultimo, and since that time have been gratified that the majority of the Indians are striving to obtain the confidence of all connected with them, and have cheerfully obeyed instructions, planted considerable grain, and worked in the fields, brought in all the hay and wood required by the troops, and on the 8th of this month delivered up to justice an Indian implicated in the murder of Lieutenant Almy.

A canal, for the purpose of irrigating the land, and to enable the Indians to cultivate the valley of the Gila, was commenced in March, 1873. This canal was partially completed in June last, when a portion of land was plowed and allotted to the different chiefs for their bands. Seeds and farming utensils were furnished them, and there is now a thriving crop of corn and beans, the Indians taking great interest and pride in the growth of their respective lots.

In July a number of stock-cattle were given them, in fulfillment of a promise made them by the special commissioner last year. Their cattle seem to be taken great care of, and are in good condition.

There are no schools or missions upon this reservation. The agency was formerly under the control of the Dutch Reformed Church, but no effort has been made to establish a school or mission. In my opinion the children could readily be taught, as they are naturally bright and clever; but it is impracticable to establish any school unless adequate funds are supplied, the Indians themselves being entirely destitute of any property, with the exception of the cattle given them, and a few horses owned by the Apaches.

I am, sir, very respectfully, your obedient servant,

W. H. BROWN,
Captain, Fifth United States Cavalry,
Acting Agent for the Pinal and Aravaipa Apaches and Tontos.

Hon. E. P. SMITH,
Commissioner of Indian Affairs, Washington, D. C.

60.

OFFICE CAMP APACHE INDIAN AGENCY, CAMP APACHE, ARIZ.,
August 31, 1873.

SIR: In compliance with circular letter from the Hon. Commissioner of Indian Affairs relative to annual reports, I have the honor to submit this, my first annual report.

In view of the very limited period which has intervened since my arrival here, and in consideration of the fact that this agency has been only established about one year, and up to the present date has never been furnished with funds, books, stationery, or agricultural implements, to carry on the business of the agency—under the above circumstances it cannot be expected that I shall be enabled to go much into the usual details embraced in an annual report.

There are on the reservation, according to a census taken on the 10th day of last June, 1,675 Indians, including men, women, and children, which I think is correct.

The crop of corn, this year, has been a good one, and the Indians feel very much encouraged. They have planted 283 acres.

I was unable to open an agency farm on account of not having any teams to break up the land, and there were no teams that could be hired for that purpose.

On my arrival here I found but one building belonging to the Indian Department, and that was a store-house. Through the kindness of Maj. G. M. Randall, Twenty-third Infantry, I was allowed to occupy his quarters until such time as I could get authority to build an agency building.

I made out an estimate for the necessary buildings, teams, &c., to carry on the business of the agency, and forwarded it to Dr. H. Bendell, superintendent of Indian affairs for Arizona, who informed me that he had no authority to contract for putting up of buildings at my agency, or to purchase teams, and that I would have to wait until such time as the Department at Washington ordered it done. After waiting some three months I was obliged to go to work, and with the aid of my employés I erected an agency building, one story high, 16×42 feet, which answers for a dwelling for the agent and an office besides.

I would here recommend that the agent be authorized to purchase four (4) mules, three (3) yoke of oxen, two (2) wagons, and all the necessary agricultural implements, with seeds, &c., to open an agency-farm, which is badly needed at this agency. I hope before winter sets in that I will be furnished with all of the above articles.

I would also recommend that a portable saw-mill, with a shingle-machine attached, be purchased for this agency. There is an abundance of pine timber here, and, with a good mill, I could put up all the buildings that would be necessary for the employés and Indians, and I am confident that in two (2) years the mill would pay for itself.

I would also recommend that 500 hoes, 5 dozen axes, and 1,200 blankets be purchased for the use of the Indians of this agency. The amount of hoes furnished by the Department in June last is not sufficient for the number of Indians who are willing to plant. The blankets ought to be furnished without delay, as winter will soon be upon us, and the Indians of this reserve are nearly naked.

I am pleased to report an improved condition of the tribes of this agency, in their more fully adopting agriculture as a means of subsistence. Their stock consists of cattle and horses, which are all in good condition. Some of the bands have taken good care of the cattle that Gen. O. O. Howard gave them last season. They are anxious that I should purchase sheep for them.

The Indians under my charge have been peaceful; no disturbances have occurred, and no depredations committed on the reservation, that I am aware of. The health of the Indians has been good; still, I will earnestly request that medicines be furnished this agency, as soon as possible, as there are none here to be had, and I have had to depend upon the military for medicines ever since I have been here.

There has been no missionary sent to this agency, and, up to the present, no school or schools have been established. The Indians are all anxious that a school be established this fall; but the way I am now situated, without teams to haul logs, I will have to put it off until such time as I can get teams.

I think this is the best location for an Indian reservation I ever saw. We have plenty of timber, water, and good land, and it is located away from white settlements. The winters are mild, and the grass stays green nearly all winter. I have visited the planting-grounds of my Indians as often as I possibly could, and have always been treated kindly by them. It is the general remark by all citizens who have had occasion to travel through this reservation that a remarkable change for the better has come over the Indians of this reserve within the last eight months. The head-chief of this reserve, Petone Segoski, has been of great service to me, and is learning to speak the English language very fast; he dresses in citizens' clothes, as do nearly all of his band. The Indian soldiers, forty in number, have been of great assistance to the military in fighting the Tontos.

I inclose statistics of education and farming, marked repectively A and B.

In my efforts to carry out the wishes of the Department among these Indians, I beg leave to acknowledge the kind co-operation of Maj. G. M. Randall, commanding officer of this post, who is ever ready to assist by counsel or by force.

In conclusion, allow me to express the hope that, with liberal and necessary appropriations on the part of the Government, I may, in another year, be able to make a much more flattering report of progress of this agency.

I am, sir, very respectfully, your obedient servant,

JAMES E. ROBERTS,
United States Indian Agent.

Hon. E. P. SMITH,
Commissioner of Indian Affairs, Washington, D. C.

61.

CHIRICAHUA INDIAN AGENCY, SULPHUR SPRINGS, ARIZ.,
August 31, 1873.

SIR: In compliance with instructions from the Office of Indian Affairs, per circular letter, dated June 30, 1873, I have the honor to submit the following, my first annual report of the condition of affairs within this agency.

On the 16th day of September last I was appointed by Gen. O. O. Howard, then special Indian commissioner, as a special agent to assist in making a peace with the notorious Apache chief, Cochise, and of afterward gathering the nomadic tribes of Apaches upon a reservation to be known as the Cochise or Chiricahua Indian reserve.

On the 1st day of October following, I succeeded in bringing in Cochise, with about three hundred of his people, to meet General Howard in the Dragoon Mountains, which meeting resulted, on the 12th of the same month, in the conclusion of a treaty of peace with them. I then immediately set to work to gather in the different scattered tribes, and on the 16th of the same month I issued rations to four hundred and fifty Indians. This was my first issue. On the 24th of the same month I found and brought in the Stein's Peak tribe, numbering about one hundred and fifty souls. On the 1st day of November following I found the Southern Chiricahua tribe, numbering about four hundred souls, under the Chief Natiza, and on the 3d day of the same month, concluded a treaty with them and brought them in. I learned from this last party that there were no more Indians out in large parties; they said there were still a few small parties straggling through the mountains, but that they would be brought in as fast as they could be found. On the 4th day of November I issued rations to one thousand Indians. From that time to the present date, the number of Indians drawing rations from this agency has varied from about one thousand to eleven hundred and fifty, the latter being the highest number that has been upon the reserve at any one time.

The result of the treaty with these Indians has been more satisfactory than the most sanguine friend of the present policy toward our Indians could have anticipated. For thirteen years prior to this treaty with General Howard, Cochise and his allies, the Southern Chiricahua Apaches, had waged such a bitter and unrelenting warfare against the people of these frontiers that his name had become not only a terror to the wayfarer and at the camp-fire, but to every household. It has been said, and not with any great exaggeration, that the southern overland road from the Rio Mimbres to Tucson was a grave-yard for Cochise's victims. Highways could only be traveled in safety by large and well-armed parties. Miners would leave their homes to prospect in the mountains, to be heard from no more. Farmers would be killed at the plow-handle while tilling the soil. Scarcely a family living within striking distance of his mountain fastness but mourns the loss of some of its members that have met their deaths at the hands of some of his braves. The military, although they had carried on a constant warfare against these Indians, were unable to stop their ravages. A former commissioner had been sent out by Government to treat with these Indians, but not wishing to visit them in their homes, unless accompanied by a large military escort, was unable to procure an interview with them, they declining to go near the troops, fearing treachery. This was the exact state of affairs as they existed when General Howard visited this Territory a year ago. Prior to General Howard coming, I had visited Cochise in his mountain home, and had learned from him that he wished to make peace with our Government, but I also became satisfied that he could not be brought where there were troops to make a treaty. I therefore, when sought by General Howard to assist in procuring an interview with Cochise, asked him if he were willing to visit him alone with me, and without troops. I received his frank reply in the affirmative, and I then became satisfied in my own mind, and circumstances have since proven that I was correct, that the war with Cochise and the Chiricahua Apaches was at an end. I suppose General Howard has furnished the Department with a report of his visit to and treaty with these Indians. I shall, therefore, not treat upon it here more than to state that the Department was particularly fortunate in the selection of this officer for the mission intrusted to his care. I doubt if there is any other person that could have been sent here that could have performed the mission as well; certainly none could have performed it better.

Although it is not a year since the aforementioned sad state of affairs existed, I am happy to be able to inform the Department that at present everything is exactly the reverse. Wayfarers can now be seen on our highways traveling alone and unarmed. Farmers and miners are pursuing their labors with as much unconcern as to safety as their brothers of the East, and confidence in the good faith of these Indians on the part of the settlers appears to be universal.

On the 3d day of last June I received a communication from the Office of Indian Affairs, dated the 9th of May previous, stating that Governor J. Pesqueria, of the Mexican State of Sonora, had complained to that office that Cochise's Indians had been engaged in raiding, robbing, and murdering in Sonora since the month of October previous, implying, I suppose, since they made peace with our Government. I answered this communication at length the next day. (See communication from this office dated June 4, 1873.) Since that time I have given this matter my careful consideration. I find there is a great antipathy existing against the Sonoranians in all the Apache tribes throughout the country. The Indians give as a reason for this that a few years ago they were at peace in Sonora, and the people there used to encourage them to come up here to steal, telling them they would pay big prices for the Americans' horses, as they were all large and fine. When they used to go back there off their raids the people would ply them with whisky, get them drunk, take their plunder away from them, and murder them in their houses. There are quite a large number of young people on our reserves who have lost parents in just this way, and these are the people that steal away whenever they can, organize small parties, and go on raids into Sonora. These parties are generally composed of Indians from several different reservations combined, and this reservation, bordering as it does on the Sonora line, has without doubt been made a kind of a resting-place for these parties. I have been using my best endeavors to stop this raiding, and am happy to state that I have met with some little success, and hope soon to stop it entirely, Cochise and his captains having enlisted to give me all the assistance they possibly can. On the 5th of July I took a captive boy from one of these parties that they had taken in the Mexican State of Chihuahua. I have since restored him to his parents. During this month I have also taken five horses and a mule from two different parties, each composed of Cozotur and Mimbres Apaches. They had stopped here to rest prior to proceeding on their way to their reserves, and I was informed of it by Cochise. These animals have all been restored to their proper owners. I would here state that all the robbing and murdering in Sonora is not done by Apaches from this side the line, though, by any means. There are large bands of Apaches living in Sonora who commit the greater portion of the depredations committed there.

In regard to the future prospects for farming operations by these Indians, I would state that I have conversed with Cochise and many of his head-men upon this subject repeatedly, and I am of the opinion that it will require some little time to bring them into the traces and make them submit to this exaction, which must eventually be required of them. They have never been an agricultural people, and claim that they do not know how to farm. I tell them we will learn them how, and furnish them with tools and seeds to commence with. But I must admit that thus far I have not met with much success, even in obtaining promises. However, time and perseverance work wonders, and I hope in a short time to be able to report more favorably in regard to this matter. Cochise himself admits it would be best for his people to farm, but says he is afraid his older people will not. He thinks it would be best to commence with his young people, and bring them up to farming and labor.

I would here most respectfully call your attention to the condition of these Indians in regard to clothing. A few blankets and a little manta and calico were furnished by

General Howard to the first parties that came in to make peace, and nothing has been furnished since. Those that I brought in afterward, and promised that they were to have the same treatment as the first, I have not as yet been able to give anything, and their condition is deplorable. Many of them may be seen with nothing but a piece of corn or flour sack tied around them to hide their persons. It is now nearly a year since I first brought in these people, and I think nothing will go further to show their sincerity in their peace than to know that they have waited this long to have the promises of the Government fulfilled. I would urge that my estimate for manta, blankets, needles and thread, inclosed in communication to Superintendent Bendell, dated May 31, 1873, be furnished at as early a day as possible.

I am pleased to state that, on the 8th of this month, I received instructions from your office, per communication dated July 8, 1873, to remove the headquarters of this agency to the vicinity of the San Simone Ceniga, and erect agency buildings. Immediately upon the receipt of the above instructions, I invited proposals from contractors for the erection of the buildings. Fnding their demands so exorbitant, their proposals being above the amount of my estimate, I have deemed it best to hire the labor and erect the buildings myself, knowing that I can erect them for a less cost than that of any of the proposals I have received. I would therefore request that the sum of six thousand seven hundred and fifty ($6,750) dollars be furnished me for that purpose, for laborers in this Territory cannot be hired, unless they know they will receive their pay at designated times; also, as I stated in a former communication, laborers discharged from this agency have been obliged to discount their vouchers 25 per cent. in order to get them cashed, which, I can assure you, has not helped the reputation of the agency in that respect.

The general health of these Indians has been excellent; only two deaths from natural causes have come to my knowledge since I have been here; several deaths have, however, occurred from violence.

Drinking and gambling is, apparently, a natural vice of the Indian, and these Indians are not an exception to the rule. As far as chastity is concerned, though, they are far superior to any Indians I ever knew, any deviation from that course being punished by cutting off the offender's nose.

Taking everything into consideration, I think there is every reason to feel encouraged at the future prospect of the Indians. By fair treatment I believe in a few years they can be made to rank among the best-behaved and most industrious tribes upon this frontier.

Very respectfully, your obedient servant,

THOMAS T. JEFFORDS,
United States Special Indian Agent, Chiricahua Apaches.

Hon. EDWARD P. SMITH,
Commissioner of Indian Affairs, Washington, D. C

62.

OFFICE OF THE SUPERINTENDENT OF INDIAN AFFAIRS,
Olympia, Wash., October 20, 1873.

SIR: I have the honor to submit the following as my second annual report.

A prolonged absence of two months, visiting Indian tribes east of the Cascades, and exploring and inspecting the reservation set apart for the non-treaty Indians of that region, which took a much longer time than anticipated, and from which I only returned on the 25th ult., has caused the delay in the preparation of this report.

Since making my last annual report, I have made and forwarded to your office [as] an addendum or appendix to my annual report, but not forwarded in time to be published with it, ten special reports upon the history, boundaries, area, and legal status of ten of the fourteen Indian reservations in this superintendency, and asking the proper Executive or Department action, to correct the legal status of each in accordance with law and justice.

* * * * * * *

I have since my last report, besides revisiting a portion of the twelve reservations that I had then visited, visited and inspected the two remaining reservations of this superintendency that I had not then visited, to wit, the Muckleshoot and the Colville reservations. I visited and inspected the

MUCKLESHOOT RESERVATION

on the 19th and 20th of July last, which, with further research into the history and legal status of that reservation, developed facts in addition to those stated in my special report of the 20th of January last, which I desire to urge as additional reasons for granting, at least in part, the request therein made to enlarge said reservation and make its boundaries to conform to Government surveys or the meanderings of adjoining rivers.

* * * * * * *

There is not the slightest excuse or justification for the many turns, crooks, corners, and angles in the boundary, and the very ugly shape given to this reservation, as it is situated on a beautiful, slightly rolling prairie.

* * * * * * *

It will be seen that the fellow who established this boundary came near zigzagging the western side across to the eastern side at one point, and thus dividing the reservation into two parts. * * * * * [and] cut [the Indians] off by about half a mile from access to White River on the southwest, and by about two miles from access to Green River on the northeast, from which rivers they have from time immemorial taken fish, their main reliance for food.

It will be seen by the inclosed map that the donation claims of Dominic Corcoran and James Riley (the histories of which are given in my special report of the 20th of January last) are mostly included within the lines of the reservation; one fragment of the former and two fragments of the latter are left outside the lines of the reservation. Since these two claims cover nearly the whole of the reservation, and must be paid for by the Government, and contain within their lines about the same amount of land as is contained within the lines of the reservation, the question naturally arises, why were not these two claims wholly taken and their lines made to constitute the boundaries of the reservation? * * * * *

They (the Indians) have, since the Muckleshoot reservation was agreed upon at the Fox Island conference, believed that its boundary, as established and published by Agent Simmons and other officials, as mentioned in said special report, embraced all the land in the forks of White and Green Rivers and west of the range-line between ranges 5 and 6 east, as their reservation; and this also was believed and respected by the neighboring whites as the legal Indian reservation. And it was not till I had received the telegram from your office of the 9th of May last, declining to ask an Executive order legalizing the reservation, as set apart by Agent Simmons, as requested in said special report, and made the fact known to the Indians, they knew their reservation was so small and ugly in shape.

Many of the Indians had houses and small farms outside of the legal reservation, and as soon as it became known that the reservation, as defined by Agent Simmons, was not legal, and that instead of the Indians having a legal right to about 5,000 acres they had only a legal right to about 400 acres, the whites began to jump the Indian improvements. I got six of the Indians who had valuable improvements on even-numbered sections, (the Northern Pacific Railroad grant covers the odd sections,) to come up and take the necessary oaths and homestead their improvements. But the Northern Pacific Railroad takes many of them situated on the odd-numbered sections.

The prairie on which the legal Muckleshoot reservation is situated, with the land around it, is mostly rich agricultural land, and nearly all of the reservation, with some land around it, is under cultivation by the Indians, a majority of whom, with their chief, Nelson, are an orderly, industrious people, and earnest and devoted Catholics, who have built a small, comfortable church, where Nelson assembles his people by the sound of a bell, every morning and evening, for prayers; and thus twice a day the simple, earnest prayers of these poor ignorant Indians go up to the Christian's God for blessings on themselves and our great nation and its rulers, who, in justice and equity, so far as these Indians are concerned, have a doubtful title to the benefit of these prayers.

* * * * * I therefore ask a rehearing and consideration of this case, and if the Department still thinks proper to adhere to the decision of it contained in your telegram to me of the 9th of May last, stating that the reservation "cannot now be enlarged as recommended by Agent Simmons," then, in the name of justice, I ask that sections one and twelve in township twenty north, of range 5 east, be set apart and legalized to them as a reservation. These two sections, containing their present small, ill-shaped, *legal* reservation, with nearly the whole of Muckleshoot prairie and about all of the Indians' improvements thereon, will give them an outlet to White River and a decent-shaped reservation, approaching toward justice in area and with boundaries conformable to, and easily ascertained by, the public surveys.

* * * * * * *

THE COLVILLE RESERVATION,

It will be recollected that the Colville reservation proper, including the Colville Valley, was set apart by Executive order of April 9, 1872, and with the reservation the majority of the non-treaty Indians east of the Cascades in this Territory were much pleased. But without consulting their interests or wishes, and even without their knowledge, the Government being deceived as to the true state of affairs, was induced to change the reservation by Executive order of July 6, 1872, to the west and north of the Columbia, east of the Chenagan, and bounded on the north by British Columbia as now constituted. The country embraced in this reservation was but little known to the whites.

* * * * * * *

So, on the 26th of July last, I started for Fort Colville, about 600 miles distant, via the Columbia River and Walla-Walla. At the latter place I learned that the Hon. J. P. C. Shanks was at Lewiston, in the edge of Idaho, 105 miles distant, visiting the Lapwai reservation near that place; so I took stage and went over there, and got him to kindly consent to do the non-treaty Indians of the Upper Columbia in this superintendency and myself the favor to go with me to Colville to meet these Indians in council. We arrived there on the 7th of August, and having sent out runners to collect the Indians in council on the 11th, we spent the three intervening days in traveling over and seeing as much of the new reservation as possible.

We had a satisfactory council with the Indians on the 11th and 12th of August, and on the 13th General Shanks left on his return to Idaho.

As will be seen by reference to these speeches, they insist with both logic and equity that they and their ancestors from time immemorial owned all of the country before the white man came. That the English and American governments had run an east and west line through it, dividing it between themselves without asking them anything about it. That when the white men came to settle in their country they were glad to receive them and to divide their agricultural and pasture lands with them, and to learn from them how to work and live like white men; but that the whites kept coming and, without their consent, claiming their best agricultural lands, and crowding them back into the mountains. That the Government of the United States at first set off a reservation for them with which they were much pleased, but afterward, without consulting them, and without their consent or knowledge, had changed it all to the west side of the Columbia, among the mountains and rocks, where agricultural lands were very scarce, and they could not make a living if they moved over there. Therefore they would not move over on to that reservation unless forced to do so. That the San Ports, Okanagons, and Lakes who resided on different parts of the reservation claimed the whole of it, used most of its agricultural lands, and would need the whole of them, as game continued to grow scarce; therefore, they with their women and children would starve if forced over there. In view of these facts, they asked that the Government would enlarge the reservation by extending it east of the Columbia River to the Idaho line and to include all the country in Washington Territory north of the Spokane River.

Besides the three days spent in looking at the reservation with General Shanks before mentioned, I spent from the 20th of August to the 11th of September on the reservation, every day in the saddle except three in council with the Indians residing on it. The reservation is well watered, having on it two good-sized rivers, the Kettle and San Port. One fork of the former heads in British Columbia, but the latter with its many branches and two lakes all rise and end on the reservation, while there are twelve other streams of considerable size that rise on the reservation and enter either the Columbia on the east and south and the Okanagan on the west, and then there is rock enough on the reservation to supply the world, much of it being fine marble. The timber, too, though mostly scattering and inferior in size and limited in variety, is sufficient for all necessary purposes.

The largest amount of agricultural land in any one valley on the reservation is in that of the Inespellum. Much of the land in this valley is thin, gravelly, and poor, but about five hundred acres of good agricultural land could be had in one body, which by irrigation could be made to produce wheat, oats, rye, barley, potatoes, turnips, and garden vegetables. Plenty of water can be had for irrigation, and the land is favorably situated for the construction of irrigating ditches. Probably two hundred or three hundred acres more of equally good agricultural lands susceptible of like cultivation could be had in the valley in detached bodies.

The only water-privilege for milling purposes near this agricultural land is on the Inespellum, three miles below where the good land begins. Here the stream falls about twenty feet in fifty yards. But good timber for sawing is scarce, and would have to be hauled from four to five miles.

The summer grazing advantages in and around the Inespellum Valley are excellent. The rich bunch-grass is everywhere abundant, but it is too short and scattering to be cut for hay. Therefore, the question of feed for live-stock through the snows of winter is a matter of much importance to those who would go into the stock-raising business in this valley, or indeed anywhere on the reservation, as long grass for hay is everywhere scarce, and only found in small patches along the streams, and would furnish at no place a sufficient quantity for the subsistence of a large herd through winter.

I was told that in that portion of the valley of the Okanagon around the south end of Lake Sooyoous, and for eight or ten miles south, and also in portions of the valley of the Columbia around the south and east sides of the reservation, the chinook winds prevail to such an extent through the winter as to prevent snows from interfering with the grazing of cattle and sheep, and hence that they subsist and keep fat through the winter without feed in these places. I know from undoubted authority that live-stock has been repeatedly so subsisted through winters at these points. But the grazing areas of these favored portions of valleys are too small to support large herds of cattle, and it is possible that the chinook winds may lull for a few weeks some winter at these points, and let the snow and cold so accumulate as to cause cattle and sheep to perish from hunger and cold; so that if the non-treaty Indian tribes in this Territory east of the Columbia and the reservation are forced on to it to remain, I cannot see how they can obtain a subsistence with certainty, and the greater part of them would most probably be soon starved to death. It would, therefore, be both unjust and cruel to restrict these tribes to the reservation as now constituted, and I most certainly concur with them in asking the addition mentioned.

This addition, leaving out what the Northern Pacific Railroad will take from it, would embrace about three thousand square miles, and, with the exception of the Colville Valley, is mostly a conglomeration of barren, rocky mountains. The Colville Valley is about thirty miles long and from a half to two miles wide, and though it contains much agricultural land, yet it is not all such, as much of it is too rocky, gravelly, or sandy to be fit for agricultural purposes, and then the valley is so elevated as to be liable to frosts every month in the year. But with all these disadvantages tolerably good wheat, rye, barley, oats, and potato crops can be raised with tolerable certainty, and the grazing is very good, so that with the agricultural lands of this valley, and those to be found on the Spokane and in patches along the Columbia, and on a few small streams on this addition, with the advantages for grazing, the non-treaty tribes of that region cannot only maintain themselves in comfort, but some 500 or 600 Cœur d'Alenes, over on the edge of Idaho, who had a talk with General Shanks about a reservation over there on the line of the Northern Pacific Railroad, could be willingly brought on to this reservation thus enlarged, and then maintain themselves. Also some 300 or 400 Kooteneys and Pend d'Oreilles residing mostly in Idaho would consent to come on to this enlarged reservation and maintain themselves. Thus some 800 or 1,000 more Indians besides those on this proposed addition could be brought on to it and all be made to subsist themselves. It would be a material benefit and advantage both to the whites and Indians to have the Cœur d'Alenes brought away from the vicinity of the Northern Pacific Railrord, where they claim a large reservation. All of the Indians on this proposed addition, together with those proposed to be brought on to it, with the exception of a portion of the Spokanes, belong to the Catholic Church, and are strongly under the influence of the Catholic fathers; are more or less intermarried, and would therefore readily coalesce and harmonize. All of the Lakes, the larger portion of the Okanagons, and a portion of the San Ports residing on the reservation are also Catholics.

There are four white settlers on the reservation who have made some improvements on their claims that were taken before the reservation was set apart that will have to be appraised and paid for. There are about sixty white settlers on the proposed addition who have claims or improvements that will have to be adjusted if this addition is made to the reservation. About one-half of these settlers are intermarried with or are living with Indian women.

The improvements made on the reservation and proposed addition are generally small and not of much value, but if taken for the Indians would be of great value to them as beginnings in the right direction.

In consideration of these facts and reasons, I respectfully ask that the addition shall be made to this reservation, and that an Executive order be issued defining the whole reservation, including the addition, as follows:

Begining in the middle channel of the Columbia River, two miles below the mouth of the Okanagon River; thence up the middle channel of the Columbia River to the mouth of the Big Spokane River; thence up to the south bank of the Spokane to a point where the northerly line of the lands granted to the Northern Pacific Railroad intersects the same; thence northeasterly with the line bounding said grant to a point where it intersects the boundary-line between the Territories of Washington and Idaho; thence north on said boundary-line to where the same intersects the boundary-line between the United States and British Columbia; thence west on said last-named boundary-line to a point two miles west of Sooyoos Lake; thence southerly with the course of the Okanagon River, but two miles therefrom, to the place of beginning. My reasons for placing the western boundary of the reservation two miles west of the Okanagon River are as follows: The valley of the Okanagon is the home of the Okanagon tribe of Indians. This valley from the British boundary to the Columbia River is about eighty miles in length and will average about one mile in width. It is bounded on each side by high, basaltic, rocky mountains. The land in the valley is generally rocky, gravelly alkali, and valueless except for pasturage, but there are occasional patches of rich agricultural land, affording long, rich grass for pasturage and hay. If the river is continued as the boundary, white men will settle and have cattle ranches at these occasional patches on the west side of the river, which is fordable in many places during a large part of the year. The cattle would cross from both sides and give trouble. But a greater and much more injurious source of trouble would be that whisky hells would be established at these occasional patches if left outside and adjoining the reservation, and send their streams of demoralization, misery, and death among the Indians. This valley should therefore all be for the use of the Indians and under the control of the agent.

The western boundary, being two miles from the river and among the mountains, would include all of the desirable lands in the valley, and no settler could find a footing within twenty miles of that border. I would locate the boundary along the southern bank of the Spokane, for the purpose of enabling the Indians to keep the control of their old and valuable fisheries on that river.

If the Government is really desirous of bringing up her Indian wards from barbarism to civilization, and of passing them on from pupilage to citizenship as speedily as possible, she should not hesitate to furnish all of the necessary means and appliances to that end. No equipment for civilizing operations of any kind has ever been furnished by the Government for the reservation near Fort Colville. No agency school, shop, or other buildings have yet been erected for the benefit of the Indians of this reservation. * * * *

The interpreter at Colville, George Hern, is a very capable and useful man. He speaks fluently some seven or eight different dialects, being those of all the tribes who annually frequent the great Kettle Falls fishery on the Columbia, most of whom belong to that agency. His services are therefore very valuable and indispensable to the agent, and his time is all required. I therefore ask that his pay be increased to $1,000.

I also ask that the agent's salary be increased to $2,000 per annum. The great cost of the necessaries of life at that place on account of the cost of transportation so far overland, the discount on currency in which he is paid, and the amount of service required in attending to so many Indians make the present salary inadequate.

I also ask that there be a physician appointed for this reservation, and that his salary be fixed at $2,000, with hospital, medicines, instruments, &c., furnished by the Government. * * * * * * *

On my return from the Upper Columbia I came by and stopped for a few days at the

YAKIMA AGENCY.

I found the new saw-mill in operation and every indication of the continuation of the prosperty and progress in civilization mentioned in my last annual report. (See Report Commissioner Indian Affairs for 1872, pp. 337, 338.) For particulars as to the prosperous condition of this agency under the efficient direction of Agent Wilbur I refer to his annual report, inclosed, together with the annual reports of the physician, superintendent of instruction, and farmer of that reservation. It will be seen that by the census of 1870 the Indians of the Yakima reservation numbered 3,500, now probably increased to 4,000. (See Report Indian Affairs for 1870, p. 17.) This large number of people are dependent upon one physician for medication. One of the consequences resulting from their increase in civilization is the loss of their superstitious belief in sorcery and *timanamus* in the cure of diseases, and the increase of their faith in the efficiency of our physician. This is shown by the accompanying excellent report of Dr. Kuykendall, the well qualified physician at the Yakima reservation. This report shows that his medical prescriptions to the Indians for the year averaged over nine per day, and that his professional visits to them averaged within eighteen of being one for every day in the year, besides his lectures and instructions to them on hygienic duties, &c. And yet the Government only allows this efficient physician for his valuable services to her 3,500, or perhaps 4,000, wards the paltry sum of $1,400, out of which sum he is required to furnish and pay for all of the medicines and surgical instruments needed and used, and to furnish his own wood, lights, transportation, &c., and do without any hospital accommodations for his sick, while (as hereinbefore shown) she furnishes a physician for 40 stout, able-bodied soldiers at Fort Colville, and pays him for medical attention to these 40 men a salary of $2,100, furnishes him in the most ample style all the medicines and surgical instruments he can possibly need, besides a commodious and well-furnished hospital—hospital steward, nurse, and cook—with all needed fuel, lights, and transportion both for himself and hospital.

* * * * * * *

I ask that the salary of he physician at the Yakima reservation be increased to $2,000, and that the Government furnish the necessary medicines and surgical instruments, hospitals, hospital supplies, &c., as in the Army.

It will be seen by reference to the report of the efficient superintendent of instruction at the Yakima reservation that they "labor under many embarrassments for want of means in the school department." This should not be. Failure to provide means for proper educational facilities is far more culpable, far-reaching, and disastrous in its consequence than failure to provide proper medical treatment. Failure in the latter respect occasions more suffering and death, while failure in the former perpetuates barbarism and degradation and defeats the hope of civilization.

I therefore ask an appropriation of $5,000 for school-buildings on the Yakima reservation. For many efficient reasons that will suggest themselves to the honorable Commissioner, I respectfully ask that the salary of the agent of this important reservation be increased to $2,000; and I again unite with Agent Wilbur, as in my last annual report, (see Report Commissioner Indian Affairs, 1872, p. 338,) in calling the attention of the Government to the $7,250 due his agency. The justice of this demand is not questioned, and this matter has been so pressed upon the attention of the Department by reports and letters during the last six years, that I should think it would be attended to for the same reason that induced the king to grant the widow's petition, if nothing more.

There is an appendix to Agent Wilbur's report, calling the attention of the Department to a matter of the greatest interest to the peace and welfare of the Indians over whom he is appointed to preside. I feel very sure that the honorable Secretary of the Interior did not fully consider the matter referred to, else he would not have granted permission for the erection and maintenance of Roman Catholic missions upon the Yakima and Nez Percé reservations, in violation of a clause of the second articles of each of these treaties. * * * * *

No teacher or other white man should come or be placed on an Indian reservation without the invitation or hearty consent of the agent; else inharmony and discord must follow. And it was to guard against and prevent the inharmony and discord that would be certain to follow the admission of any white man on a reservation without the consent of the agent that that wise provision contained in a clause of the second article of every treaty on this coast made by Governor Stevens was inserted, as follows: "Nor shall any white man, excepting those in the employment of the Indian Department, be permitted to reside upon the said reservation without permission of the tribe and the superintendent and agent." Therefore, no authority, not even that of the President of the United States, can legally put "*any white man*, excepting those in the employment of the Indian Department," upon either the Nez Percé or Yakima reservation without the consent of the Indian tribes belonging to those reservations, the superintendent and the agent of each, all three first had and obtained. The order of the honorable Secretary being in plain violation of this provision of these treaties is of course illegal and void. I therefore most heartily unite with Agent Wilbur in respectfully protesting against the order of which he complains, and respectfully ask its reconsideration, and I would as heartily unite with either of the Catholic agents in this superintendency in protesting against a like order placing a Protestant teacher on either of their reservations without their hearty consent first had. * * * * * *

POINT ELLIOTT TREATY—ITS RESERVATIONS AND INDIANS.

The Indians belonging to the four reservations set apart by this treaty are doing as well as could be expected from the very limited and inefficient means and machinery provided by Government for tiding them over the rough and dangerous breakers that intervene between barbarism and civilization. There were four reservations that were set apart by this treaty for the different tribes that were parties thereto. The Indians of these tribes, according to the census of 1870, (see Report of Commissioner of Indian Affairs for 1870, p. 177,) number 3,384. About one-third of this number belong to the Tulalip reservation, which, according to the treaty, ought to contain 38 sections, and is situated on the eastern shore of Puget Sound, thirty miles north of Seattle. But one agent and one set of employés were authorized by the treaty for the whole four, or rather five, reservations named in the treaty.

It will be seen by reference to Point Elliott treaty of January 22, 1855, that five different reservations are therein specified, four by the second and one by the third article, but that through a blunder or ignorance of the geography of the country the Tulalip reservation set apart by the third article of the treaty, and the largest of the five, was made to lap over and cover up one of the smaller reservations set apart by the next preceding article. In my special report upon the legal status, area, &c., of the Tulalip reservation of the 17th of February last, this matter is fully explained, and I then requested that the Government would not profit by the blunder of her officials and swindle these poor ignorant Indians out of two sections of land, (the amount of the small reservation so covered up,) and asked that the Tulalip reservation should be enlarged to the amount of two sections. That request was refused on the ground that the Northern Pacific Railroad had acquired the legal title to the odd sections, one of which was asked as part of said addition. But the Northern Pacific Railroad having since then located its western terminus at Tacoma, near sixty miles south of this reservation, and thus relinquished all legal claim to all lands in the neighborhood of said reservation, I hereby renew my request to have the Tulalip reservation enlarged by Executive order, as specified in said special report, so that these Indians may have the amount of land to which they are entitled by treaty. The agency of the reservation under this treaty is located on the Tulalip reservation, which, by the treaty, (see article 3,) was to consist of 36 sections as a "general reservation," (see article 7,) and as a "central agency," (see article 14,) "with a view of ultimately drawing thereto and settling thereon all of the Indians living west of the Cascade Mountains in said Territory." (See article 3.) By article 9 of this treaty an "agent" is mentioned and authorized, but for many years no agent has been appointed for the reservations and Indians of this treaty. The Rev. Father Chirouse, now holding the appointment over these Indians, is only a subagent, with a salary of $1,200 in currency. The same has been the case with his predecessors for a number of years. Where is the wisdom or justice of appointing a subagent over these four reservations from twenty five to sixty miles apart, the smallest of which is nearly as large as the Skokomish or Makah reservations, while each one of the latter reservations has an agent at a salary of $1,500 each?

The official duties of Subagent Chirouse are complicated and overwhelming. Indeed, with all his industry, he cannot perform one-half of them. The Tulalip reservation alone, on which the subagency is situated, is six times larger than the Skokomish and twice as large as the Makah reservation, has belonging to it twice as many Indians as the former, three times as many as the latter, and, besides, has attached to it three other reservations from 25 to 60 miles distant, each of which has from 400 to 700 Indians belonging to it.

I therefore respectfully call the attention of the honorable Commissioner to this injustice, and ask that he will make a note of it and take the proper steps to have it remedied. The proper remedy is the appointing of one agent and three subagents and allowing four sets of employés. The subagent, physician, school-teacher, farmer, blacksmith, carpenter, and saw-mill tender now at the Tulalip are of but little or no benefit to the Indians of the Port Madison and Swinomish reservations, each 25 miles distant from it in different directions, and of less benefit to the Indians of the Lummi reservation, 60 miles distant. It is great injustice that the Indians of these three last-named reservations should be deprived of the oversight, training, services, and protection of such employés as are provided for the Tulalip. The assistant farmer of this treaty has for a number of years been in charge of the Lummi reservation, and their moral and physical improvement, and superiority over the poor Indians of the Swinomish and Port Madison reservations, where there is no Government employé, are very apparent.

The better-disposed Indians of the two last-named reservations have frequently begged Subagent Chirouse to send them some good white man to supervise and care for them, and while on my visits to them they earnestly requested the same of me. This just request, to which both Subagents Chirouse and myself would gladly have acceded, could not be complied with for want of means.

The Indians of these two last reservations subsist mostly from the sale of saw-logs which they cut on their respective reservations. They are systematically swindled in the sale of these logs on account of their ignorance. Vicious white men go among them and debauch them with whisky and prostitute their women. They are a prey to ignorance, vice, filth, and disease. (See Report Commissioner of Indian Affairs, 1872, pp. 332 and 333; also addition or appendix of December 31, 1872, not published; also my special reports on each of these reservations.) These poor, ignorant, miserable, perishing wards of our great Government beg and pray their guardian to send them help, protection, and teachers. Will their prayer continue to be unheeded by their guardian?

Subagent Chirouse in his report herewith inclosed complains of the insufficiency of the pay of his employés, and asks that their salary be increased. I most heartily join with him in this request. The pay allowed to employés on Indian reservations should be such as to command the services of the best men. One thousand two hundred dollars per annum, in our depreciated currency, is the salary of the physician at Tulalip, and he is required out of this sum to furnish himself in medicine and everything else he may need. This meager sum will be no temptation to a first-class physician who can clear from $2,000 to $4,000 annually by his practice. Nor will $900 in the same currency (the pay of each mechanic and farmer on the Tulalip) be any temptation to first-class mechanics and farmers, when such men can make from $3 to $5 in coin daily by their labor. I therefore ask that the physician both here and on the other reservations on this side of the Cascades be paid $2,000 per annum, with medicines, surgical instruments, hospital, &c., supplied as requested for the Colville reservation, and that the pay of farmers and mechanics on all reservations west of the Cascades be raised to $1,200 per annum.

Subagent Chirouse, in his accompanying report, also repeats the old unavailing complaint found in almost every report made, both to the Indian Department and missionary boards, since the foundation of our Government, of the demoralizing and destructive power and influence of the whisky traffic among the Indians, and says truly that it will "destroy the whole race, if not stopped." * * * *

Skokomish reservation.—Agency and Indians thereunto belonging.

This reservation is situated at the southern extremity of the western arm or bay of Puget Sound, called Hood's Canal. The treaty by which it was set apart specified that it should be "the amount of six sections, or three thousand eight hundred and forty acres." (See art. 2d of treaty.) Under the allowance recently made for the survey of Indian reservations in this superintendency, the survey of the Skokomish reservation into forty-acre lots has been completed within the present month, much to the satisfaction of the Indians; but a large amount of it was found to be an almost wholly impassable marsh that never can be drained or used for any beneficial purpose, on account of being nearly on a level with the waters of the river and sound.

It will be seen by reference to the census of 1870 (see Report Commissioner Indian Affairs, p. 17,) that the number of Indians belonging to this treaty was 921, and it will be seen that the report of 1871 (see report Commissioner Indian Affairs for 1871, p. 278) puts their number at 1,000. If the whole number of forty-acre lots contained in this reservation were capable of being settled on as homes by the Indians, there would be but ninety-six homes for the 1,000 Indians—only about half enough. But as probably not more than half the forty-acre lots in the reservation are capable of settlement, there is not in the reservation more than a fourth of the amount of arable land needed by the Indians belonging to the reservation for homes.

It will be seen by reference to my special report on the legal status, &c., of the Skokomish reservation, under date of 21st of February last, that an addition thereto was recommended, in accordance with prior recommendations. This recommendation was refused for the alleged reason that the Northern Pacific Railroad had acquired the odd sections, some of which were included in the addition asked. It will be seen by the accompanying annual report of Agent Eells, of this reservation, that the location of the terminus of that road at Tacoma has probably operated as a withdrawal of their right to the odd sections included in the addition asked. If this is the case, he renews the application for the addition, as set forth in said special report, and I most heartily second this application, as it is right and just that it should be granted.

Agent Eells in his accompanying annual report asks special attention to the case of A. D. Fisher, whose donation-claim was included in this reservation, and has never yet been paid for. Mr. Fisher has been the victim of the grossest injustice, as will be seen from Agent Eells's statement, and my own, contained in my said special report. The claim of Mr. Fisher, with valuable improvements, was taken and appraised at $1,771. This appraisement, with others by the same appraisers, was forwarded to your office under date of February 3, 1866, and has never since been heard from. Mr. Fisher is a poor, hard-working man. His property was taken without his consent, and doubtless fairly appraised, and for over seven years, through the culpable negligence of Government officials, this poor man has been kept out of his just dues. I join with Agent Eells in asking prompt attention and action upon this case.

The Point-no-point treaty, by which this reservation was set apart, was concluded with four tribes of Indians, to wit, the Skokomish, the Too-an-hoolis, the S'Klallams, and the Chin-a-kums. The first two named tribes have always claimed the country about the mouth of the Skokomish River, and around the south end of Hood's Canal, as theirs, and have therefore mostly resided on and been content with the reservation. But the last two named tribes (of which the S'Klallams are much more numerous than either of the other three) have always refused to recognize the reservation as their home, and very few of them have ever stopped on it; they have mostly resided northwardly from the reservation, along the shores of Hood's Canal, and on the west side of Puget Sound, in the vicinity of Port Townsend, and along the southern shore of the Strait of Fuca, as far west as Klallam Bay. It will be seen by reference to the report of the Commissioner of Indian Affairs for 1859, p. 398, and the report of same for 1866, p. 195, that reservations were promised these Indians on Hood's Canal, twenty miles north of the present reservation, and at Klallam Bay, on the Strait of Fuca, and that a reservation was set off and defined for the S'Klallams, on Klallam Bay, by Agent Simmons in his celebrated pronunciamento or proclamation of December, 1859, published in the Pioneer and Democrat of Olympia, in which this reservation for the S'Klallams is authoritatively and luminously defined as follows: "About two sections of land on the Straits of Fuca, commencing at the point immediately west of Klallam Bay, and following the meanderings of the shore, eastwardly, to the eastern point of said bay; then southerly; then easterly; then, north, to the place of beginning—the last-mentioned lines to run far enough back to give the required quantity of land." The enlarged Muckleshoot reservation, as mentioned in my special report thereon of January 9, 1872, with other smaller matters, were all contained and set forth in the document above mentioned; but, unfortunately for poor Lo, none of the reservations therein set forth were ever legalized by Executive action. The Indians on the Strait of Fuca mentioned by Agent Eells have frequently, but in vain, asked that the above or some other reservation be properly set apart and legalized to them. In May last an old chief of a band of about forty, with twenty-three of his people, visited me and begged that I would give them a small reservation near Port Angelos, on the Strait of Fuca. I inquired at the land-office, and was informed that the land in the vicinity of the small tract they wanted was unsurveyed; and I wrote you, under date of the 8th of May last, asking that a small tract of land, including their village, be set apart to them. But I afterward discovered that a custom-house reservation had been set apart a number of years ago, which included the desired tract, and that said custom-house reservation had been laid off into five-acre or ten-acre lots, "ringed," puffed, and sold on speculation. The custom-house at that point was afterward washed away, and the place abandoned by the public functionaries. A single family now holds the site of Port Angelos, and the non-resident speculators are waiting for something to turn up. Some of them learning that Yoman and his band desired a reservation there, I received several communications from them, patriotically offering to sell to the United States on very liberal terms. These Indians are justly entitled to one or more reservations, and I respectfully recommend that they be set apart, or that an appropriation be made to pay the homestead fees of all Indians who will take homestead claims.

Agent Eells also reiterates the old and oft-repeated mournful complaint of the debasing and destructive effects of whisky on the Indians, and says that the scattered S'Klallam tribe, once the most numerous and warlike on the sound, is being rapidly diminished by it, and at the present rate of decrease will be about extinct at the end of the present generation. Their temporal salvation, as before stated, is in the hands of our law-makers, upon whose skirts will be their blood, if not rescued.

I refer to the accompanying report of Agent Eels for particulars concerning the status and improvement of the Indians of his charge.

Neah Bay agency and Indians.

The reservation upon which this agency and these Indians are domiciled is located at, and embraces Cape Flattery, the extreme northwestern corner or rather angle of Washington Territory, formed by the junction of the Strait of Juan de Fuca with the Pacific Ocean, and is a wild, bleak, stormy locality, and seems to be the home of the winds, snow, and rain, particularly the latter, as it has been ascertained by observation that there is a greater amount of cloudy and rainy weather and a larger amount of rain-fall at this place than at any other point within the limits of our Government, except, perhaps, Alaska. As to the situation of this reservation, and the necessities wants, and progress of the Indians belonging to it, I refer to my last annual report, (see report Commissioner Indian Affairs for 1872, p. 345,) and especially to my subreport or appendix to my last annual report, under date of December 31, 1872, not forwarded in time for publication with my last annual report; also, to the inclosed report of Agent Gibson. Since my last report a long-standing trouble, which has been the source of much difficulty to the agent and demoralization to the Indians, has been removed by the Executive order of the 2d of June last, legalizing and extending the disputed addition to that reservation so as to include the claims of those who have so long been cheating and demoralizing the Indians and giving trouble to the agent and Government employés. The principal claimant and disturber still has a large herd of cattle, which, by the terms of the treaty required to be made with him, he is permitted to keep there one year. These cattle are very breachy, and have occasioned much destruction and damage to the crops on the reservation, as will be seen by the accompanying report of Agent Gibson. When the time is out and they are removed, the reservation and Indians will have peace.

It will be seen by former reports that the Indians of this reservation are fish-eaters, and draw their subsistence almost wholly from the "great deep," and consequently have but very little disposition or taste for agricultural or pastoral "life-lines;" therefore the "fish-line" is the natural and perhaps the only "line" upon which they can be civilized. I therefore unite with Agent Gibson in recommending the purchase of a schooner, to be used, as mentioned by him, in their fishing operations.

I also join in his request to have a dike constructed for the purpose of reclaiming a large tract of rich farming land; also to have farm buildings constructed, and the boundary of the reservation, as now established, surveyed. I also join in his request to have a road constructed from Neah Bay to the Quinaielt reservation, full 75 miles over a very rough, wild, broken, unsettled country. There is no communication between these two reservations except by water. There is a good wagon-road from the mouth of the Columbia River to the Quinaielt reservation. A road from the latter reservation to Neah Bay would open land-travel along the whole Pacific coast of this Territory, and be a very great benefit to the Makah Indians, as Agent Gibson states.

I also join with Agent Gibson in recommending the increase of the salary of the physician at this reservation, and that there be allowed an assistant teacher and cook for the school. I also recommend the purchase of a portable steam saw-mill, the construction of a fishery and a hospital, as mentioned in the appendix to my last annual report. The various items of appropriation asked for in order to properly set up the machinery for civilizing the Makah Indians are as follows, to wit:

A portable steam saw-mill	$3,000 00
A fishery, complete in all its arrangements	5,000 00
Dike to reclaim farming land	1,500 00
Hospital for sick, aged, and destitute	2,000 00
Schooner for fishing	5,000 00
Road to Quinaielt	1,000 00
Physician's pay increased to	1,500 00
Medicines and surgical instruments	500 00
Assistant school teacher	600 00
Captain of schooner for one year	1,000 00
Engineer and sawyer	2,000 00
Total	23,100 00

The above would be sufficient to start the machinery, which in five years would push this agency forward to be self-supporting, and without further need of the aid or guardianship of the Government. There is not a doubt but that this can be done, if the above-named appliances and means are judiciously used and appropriated, and surely the object aimed at is well worthy the effort.

QUINIAELT RESERVATION, AGENCY, AND INDIANS.

This reservation and agency are located at the mouth of the Quinaielt River, on the shore of the Pacific Ocean, about twenty-five miles north of Gray's Harbor, in a very bleak, barren, inhospitable region. The land is mostly drift, and composed of sand, gravel, and bowlders, and only scattering small strips along the streams can be used for agricultural purposes. Occasional patches of pasture-land may also be found, but in both these respects the general aspect of the country is forbidding. The Indians belonging to this reservation are "fish-eaters;" but very few of them depend upon hunting and the products of the chase for a living. Therefore, like the Makahs, the only process for their civilization is on the "fish-line." For which reason a fishery, with all the appliances for catching, packing, canning, marketing, &c., with competent skilled men to teach and train them in running it a year, is, after a good industrial boarding-school, the most needed appliance for their civilization.

For reasons set forth in the accompanying report of Subagent Henry, of the Quinaielt reservation, and in my last annual report, (see Report of Commissioner of Indian Affairs, 1873, pp. 339, 340, 341,) I again recommend the enlargement of the reservation, as set forth on the last cited page. Two or three fisheries should be erected on the reservation when thus enlarged.

A village should be laid off at each fishery, with streets and lots, and each Indian engaged about the fishery should have a lot, with a neat house, yard, and garden, in the village, each of which should have a church and school-house, as soon as far enough advanced for primary schools, away from the principal industrial boarding-school.

I join with Subagent Henry in recommending the increase of the salary of the physician at Quinaielt, and that medicines and surgical instruments be furnished by the Government.

For reasons set forth in my last annual report, (see Report of Commissioner of Indian Affairs for 1872, pp. 332 and 333,) I recommend an appropriation for the construction and maintenance of a hospital at this reservation. As there is no harbor along the coast of this reservation, or anywhere near it, a fishing schooner would be useless to them, as their fish are mostly taken in the mouths of the rivers.

The additional appropriations needed to rig up the necessary humane and civilizing machinery for this reservation, are as follows:

For industrial boarding-school	$3,000 00
For pay of superintendent matron, two teachers, and cook	3,000 00
For provisions, clothing, books, &c., for the school children	2,000 00
Construction and finishing of hospital	2,500 00
Pay of physician	1,500 00
Medicines and surgical instruments	500 00
Construction and finishing fishery	3,000 00
Pay of fisherman one year	1,000 00
Pay of cooper and tinner	2,000 00
Portable steam saw-mill	3,000 00
Engineer and sawyer	1,000 00
Total	22,500 00

MEDICINE CREEK TREATY, RESERVATIONS, AND INDIANS.

This is the first treaty made with the Indians in Washington Territory. It was made December 25, 1854, and ratified April 10, 1855. The sum stipulated to be paid by the treaty was $32,500, in payments running for twenty years, without interest. There is a question as to whether the twenty years expires on the 26th of December, 1874, or on the 10th of April following. In either case the annuity payments under this treaty must end within the next eighteen months. It then becomes a question for the next Congress to determine whether further appropriations shall be made for the benefit of the Indians of this treaty after the expiration of the treaty obligation for such.

For reasons stated in my first annual report, (Report Commissioner Indian Affairs, 1872, pp. 336, 337,) and for the following additional reasons, I feel very sure that there are strong moral and equitable obligations upon the Government to continue to make the liberal appropriations for these Indians asked in said last year's report, p. 337. It will be seen by reference to the "records of the proceedings of the commission to hold treaties with the Indian tribes in Washington Territory," December 10, 1854, article 4, that the basis of value fixed to be paid for lands to be ceded by the Indians to be treated with, was at the rate of ten dollars for each chief, seven dollars and fifty cents for each sub-chief, and five dollars each for all other persons. That the number of Indians was estimated to be 650, which fixed the whole sum to be paid at $32,500, to be paid in annual payments or annuities running through twenty years and decreasing at the rate of 5 per cent. per annum. It will be seen by reference to the Report of Commissioner of Indian Affairs for 1859, pp. 391–394, and the report of 1861, p. 189, that there was a very grave mistake made in estimating the number of Indians included in this treaty at 650, when there were at least 1,400. This mistake is also mentioned in the report of 1858, p. 226. The great injustice occasioned to these Indians by this blunder is strongly referred to, and the attention of Congress called thereto in the Report Commissioner Indian Affairs, 1862, p. 386. It is here stated by Superintendent Hale that their number is three-fold what was supposed. So that this blunder has swindled these Indians out of about fifty thousand dollars.

It will be seen by reference to the Report of the Commissioner of Indian Affairs for 1872, p. 337, that these Indians ceded to the Government by this treaty over two million acres of land, besides the greater part of Puget Sound, for a compensation that was wholly inadequate, and it will be seen by the same report, pp. 336 and 337, that the money that has been paid on that treaty has not inured to their benefit, and that they know and complain of this. In view of these facts I ask, in the name of humanity and justice, that the appropriations and civilizing appliances I asked for this reservation in my last annual report be granted, and that in addition thereto there be an appropriation annually of $1,500 for each of the other three reservations belonging to this treaty, to wit: the Nisqually, Squaksin, and Muckleshod, for the pay of a teacher and assistant teacher for each, there being no white or Government employé on either. Also that there be an agent allowed and appointed for this treaty, with an annual appropriation for his pay.

The honorable Commissioner did a very special and much-needed favor to justice, civilization, and the Indians of this treaty by allowing $4,000, at my request, for the construction of an industrial boarding-school building on the Puyallup reservation. I have had a commodious boarding-school building erected, and it is so far completed that the teachers (the Rev. Mr. Stone and wife) have moved into it, and will open school soon. The great drawback is the want of funds to clothe and lodge the Indian school-children, furnish them with books, &c. There being only $1,500 per annum allowed for "schools, shops, &c., and providing necessary supplies for the same," after the "necessary supplies" for the blacksmith and carpenter shops is taken out, the amount left "for schools" is very limited.

I refer to the accompanying reports of the physician and farmer in charge of this reservation, especially the remarks of the former on the necessity for a hospital.

The Indians of the Puyallup reservation are greatly pleased with the survey of their reservation into 40-acre lots, which is now nearly completed. It has quieted their fears of losing it by its being absorbed by the Northern Pacific Railroad, the terminus of which was located within two miles of its border. The allotment of the surveyed lots among them will be a matter of much difficulty on account of conflicting claims, the lines passing through improvements, &c.

CHEHALIS RESERVATION AND INDIANS.

The status of this reservation, the duty of the Government toward the Indians belonging thereto, their necessities, wants, &c., were so fully set forth in my last annual report, (see Report Commissioner Indian Affairs, pp. 334, 335, and 336,) and in my special report of the 9th of January last, that but little more need be said in this report. Since my last annual report I have had the unfinished hall of a school-house (built some years ago) finished off, and a commodious boarding and lodging house erected adjoining it, with rooms for teachers, and dining, cook, wash, and sleeping rooms for pupils, a description of which is contained in the accompanying report of the farmer in charge, to which reference is made.

The items of appropriation mentioned as necessary for this reservation on the 336th page of the last annual report Commissioner Indian Affairs are still absolutely necessary, if the Government intends or desires to rig up the civilizing machinery for these untutored wards to be efficient. The survey of this reservation into 40-acre lots was recently completed, but the maps are not yet finished and returned. As soon as this is done the lands will be allotted as far as they will go. There will not be near enough to supply all of the non-treaty Indians west of the Cascades.

The school, which has been in successful operation since the 1st of January last, with from fifteen to thirty pupils, has not yet been as successful as desired, or as it would have been if properly qualified teachers had been in charge of it. * * * * I think teachers possessing these requisites pretty fully have now been obtained.

NEED FOR ADDITIONAL LEGISLATION.

The Indians of this superintendency, and of British Columbia, near the border, are more or less intermarried, visit each other, and have much intercourse. It will be seen by reference to the reports of former superintendents and agents in this Territory that this intercourse has been the subject of much trouble and demoralization, not only to the Indians in the neighborhood of northern border of this Territory, but also to the whites, more or less, especially to the Indians and whites around the shores and islands of Puget Sound. The British Columbia Indians, from Vancouver and other islands, and the mainland, come in their canoes in swarms around our logging camps and towns around the sound, get all the whisky they want, and their women engage in prostitution. A number of brothels at different points around the sound are filled with their women.

These Indians, having the same rights and privileges as British subjects within our lines, can purchase and use intoxicating liquors as freely and as openly as any other foreigners. They make a liberal use of this privilege, and supply their Indian friends and associates on this side of the line with these liquors.

The laws of the United States regulating intercourse with Indians only prohibits to "sell, exchange, give, barter, or dispose of any spirituous liquors or wine to any Indian under the charge of any Indian suprintendent or Indian agent appointed by the United States." Therefore the courts have always decided that this prohibition does not apply to Indians not "under the charge of" such superintendent or agent. This is unfortunate, and operates very injuriously along our national borders. I therefore respectfully recommend an amendment or change of this limitation, so as to prohibit the sale, giving, barter, or in any manner disposing of any wine, spirituous liquor, ale, beer, porter, cider, or any other intoxicating beverage to any Indian or Indians *who have not all of the rights and privileges of citizens of the United States.* The prohibition thus limited would not only protect the nation's wards by prohibiting the sale of these liquors to them, but would also reach and protect the Indians from British Columbia, Canada, or Mexico, when within the lines of the Government.

Our United States law, thus amended, would be almost as comprehensive and as efficient as that of British Columbia on this point, which says that "Any person selling, bartering, or giving, or attempting to sell, barter, or give intoxicating liquor *to any Indian of the continent of North America or of any of the islands adjacent thereto,* shall be liable, on conviction for such offense, to a fine not exceeding five hundred dollars." I trust that the foregoing suggestion will meet the eye and approval of Congress.

There is a matter of much importance to our Indians which I respectfully ask shall be brought to the attention of Congress. That is the enactment of a law prescribing the requisites, and fixing the *modus operandi* by which native-born Indians may acquire all of the rights and privileges of citizens of the United States. There is no law on this subject. Secretary Cox, in a letter to the Commissioner of the General Land-Office, under date of February 11, 1870, decided that under the recent amendments to the Constitution a native-born Indian could become entitled to the benefits of the homestead and pre-emption laws by disclaiming tribal relations and treaty rights, and directed the Commissioner of the General Land-Office, in accordance therewith, to prepare forms of oaths, and directions to the local officers. Many Indians in this Territory are availing themselves of this privilege by taking homesteads.

But though they become property and freeholders, and subject to taxation, and to be sued, yet he has not the right to sue in his own name or to vote, or sit on a jury, or hold office. He is, so far as citizenship is concerned, a constitutional, illegal, anomaly —a sort of an indefinable, hybrid citizen. If the right to all of the benefits and privileges of citizenship is placed in reach of the Indian, under proper restrictions, it will prove a powerful incentive to his progression upward in civilization. This is, therefore, a matter well worthy the attentionand action of Congress.

I also suggest the propriety of extending the jurisdiction of the civil and criminal laws of States and Territories over all Indians within their respective borders, except that of taxation. This would certainly be beneficial.

I have the honor to be, very respectfully, your obedient servant,

R. H. MILROY,
Superintendent Indian Affairs, Washington Territory.

Hon. E. P. SMITH,
Commissioner of Indian Affairs.

63.

TULALIP INDIAN RESERVATION,
Washington Ter., July 1, 1873.

SIR: In compliance with the regulations of the Indian Department, I have the honor to submit the following report in reference to Indians on the reservations under my charge.

Since the logging work commenced on the Tulalip reservation, quite a large number of Indians have gathered there, and are now permanently located. They are kept constantly employed, and receive sufficient remuneration for their labor to support themselves and families. Their conduct in general is very good, and their constant employment keeps them from wandering about the mills and white settlements, where they have been more or less exposed to all sorts of temptations of vice and debauchery.

Many bad Christians have totally reformed, and several infidel Indians have joined the church, and are now good and faithful members.

Our church at Tulalip is by no means large enough to give accommodation to the number of people who come there for instruction. I would therefore respectfully suggest that an appropriation be made for its enlargement. My assistant, the Rev. Father Richard, visits the Indians of Port Madison, Black and White River, Muckelshoot, Puyallup, and Nisqually four times a year, where he has quite a large number of well-disposed Indians, who seem to profit considerably by his teaching and example. They have applied for means to build a church, where they could gather for the performance of their religious duties, and it is very much to be regretted they could not obtain their request in this particular.

The average number of children attending our schools at Tulalip during the past year has been from forty-five to fifty. Their progress has been encouraging, though it is a work that requires an amount of patience and perseverance. They are required to perform a certain amount of manual labor each day in their respective departments—the boys under the direction of the Rev. Father Richard and Mr. H. De Vries, the girls under the skillful training of the Sisters of Charity, who are indefatigable in their exertions to forward their advancement in the paths of virtue and civilization.

Farming operations have commenced at the marsh; twelve acres of land have been cleared and partly put under cultivation, and from the present healthy appearance of vegetables now growing it seems to give a favorable guarantee of its future productions. I have had a good wagon road made from the agency to the marsh, and a strong substantial bridge built across the creek; it is 16 feet wide and 200 feet in length. I commenced another road from the agency to the mission, but not having means to go on with it I was obliged to stop the work. The road is very much needed and I regret not being able to complete it. There have been five comfortable houses built on the reservation for Indians who have expressed their desire to make it their permanent home. I have had a house and barn erected on the high ground convenient to the marsh, southwest from where the ditching of the marsh is now begun. I was obliged to hire white men to do this work, the farmer being mostly employed in the mill since its repair, and the carpenter being busy in repairing old buildings and erecting new ones. I find it extremely difficult to retain my employés, from the fact of their salary being so low; they say it is not sufficient to support themselves and families, and that common laborers are getting better paid for less amount of work than is expected from them. Nevertheless, as soon as an employé resigns I get another to take his place, and I have now the full number of employés, all good men and well adapted for their respective positions. I would again ask the Department to increase their salary or at least to pay them in coin or its equivalent.

The Indians who were engaged in logging during last winter did not make money enough to pay their expenses; they are now, however, doing very well, and hope to save as much money as will bring themselves and families through the winter. They have increased their stock considerably and are highly pleased to see the large clearing caused by the logging operations, where their stock may roam at large during the winter with a fair prospect of good pasturage.

From time to time I am obliged to visit the four reservations pertaining to this agency, viz, Lummi, Swinomish, Port Madison, and Muckelshoot, in order to settle many little difficulties that many times exist between the Indians and white settlers. The Lummi Indians, having now Mr. John McGlinn at their head, are doing very well under his instructions; and since Mr. William DeShaw has undertaken to look after the interests of the Port Madison Indians everything seems to go on much better than heretofore.

Of some of the numerous complaints made by a large number of Indians under my charge, I will just mention a few which seems to me to be both just and reasonable, and are of such nature as might attract your attention and also that of the Department.

The white settlers, who are increasing so rapidly in this country, and locating themselves around Indian reservations, are becoming more and more troublesome to the Indians, and I am very much of opinion that they will destroy the whole race in a short time, if some efficient means be not speedily taken to put a stop to their nefarious traffic in poisonous whisky. This is one of the chief causes of complaint against the Government, for allowing whisky shops to be established so near the reservations.

It has been a very old custom among the Indians to set fire to the woods in order to burn the underbrush and promote the growth of wild berries, which they gather, dry, and dispose of among themselves and white settlers. There are another class of Indians who live by the chase and are called Sunitees; these men destroy all the game on the reservations and elsewhere, and, disposing of them, make money by doing so. When I took charge of this agency I was requested by the Indians to allow them to cut the timber and dispose of it to the saw-mills, as they thought it would be better than have it destroyed by fire, and that they could make more money this way than any other, as their land was not adapted or in any way fit for agricultural purposes. I considered their demand and thought it very reasonable, and gave them all the encouragement I could, in order to carry on the work. They were quite satisfied to labor hard provided they got paid for it, but when I told them they should pay stumpage, as the timber they were cutting and disposing of was common property, and that all the Indians who were parties to the Point Elliott treaty were all equally entitled to their share of the proceeds or the timber, they then got quite discouraged and said they were not disposed to work and earn money and then be obliged to hand it over to support idle Indians, who did nothing but bask in the sunshine from morning till night, spending their time in gambling and drinking, when they could get the means of doing so. They then asked me why I did not impose a tax on those wild Indians who destroyed the woods by fire for the purpose of gathering wild berries, and on the hunters for destroying their game, as it also was common property, as well as the timber that was standing useless until it was cut down and converted into money; that all the Indians who desired to work were welcome to their share of the proceeds, provided they shared also in the labor. They said that they had themselves and families to support and many old and decrepit relations that depended on them, and would be starved if they had to depend on Government rations; that they did not believe the Government ever intended to tax them for trying to support themselves by hard labor, or making the most of the property the Government awarded them, and that the taxing system was got up by the agent to make money for himself and those that were in league with him.

Finally, they complain against the Department for not having their lands surveyed and secured to them, and thus save them from the trouble and annoyance they are continually receiving at the hands of the white settlers.

In conclusion, I desire to return you my most sincere thanks for the courtesy you have always shown in aiding my efforts in the management of my agencies. I have done and am still trying to do all in my power to dispense justice and maintain peace between the whites and those Indians under my charge.

Desiring your respectful attention to the accompanying report of Dr. Van Den Bergh with regard to the sanitary condition of the Indians pertaining to this agency,

I have the honor to be, sir, very respectfully yours,

E. C. CHIROUSE,
H. Sub Indian Agent.

R. H. MILROY, Esq.,
Superintendent of Indian Affairs, Olympia, Wash.

64.

NEAH BAY INDIAN AGENCY, WASHINGTON TERRITORY,
September 1, 1873.

SIR: I have the honor to submit the following as my third annual report upon the condition of affairs at this agency.

When I assumed charge of this agency, a little over two years ago, it was in a most deplorable condition, indeed. About ten years previous to that time, when the agency was established, an addition was illegally made to the treaty reservation upon which all the improvements of the agency excepting the school-house were located, and upon which nearly all the money appropriated for this tribe has been expended. The agency was really not upon the reservation. After Agent Webster, who established the agency and made most of the improvements, went out of office, several of his employés, having become informed of the condition of the reservation, took claims upon the addition which he had made and thus improved. For seven or eight years the Indian Department and these Indians had considered this addition as a part of the reservation, and had held undisputed control over it, when the persons who had located claims upon it denied the right of the Government to hold it as a reservation any longer. These persons were perhaps legally right, but certainly morally wrong in attempting to take what justly belonged to these Indians, and had been improved with money appropriated by the Government for their benefit. The Indians objected to having their lands and homes taken by white men, and made many bitter complaints to me in regard to it. A difficulty was growing out of this unpleasant state of conflicting authority, interest, and rights, which, without very prudent management, must have resulted seriously, and would probably have ended in another Modoc war. The President's executive order of January 2d last, extending the limits of the reservation, has finally (and it is to be hoped forever) settled this difficulty. After these claimants had been officially notified that their claims were included in this extension, they still refused to leave them, stating that the President had no authority to extend the reservation, and threatened to forcibly resist any attempt to remove them. After the time in which they were notified to leave had expired, in compliance with the advice of the honorable Secretary of the Interior, a request was made for a military force to remove them, and on the 24th of June last Lieut. James A. Houghey, of the Twenty-first United States Infantry, and commander of San Juan garrison, with a detachment of twenty-five men of Company H of the same regiment, arrived at Neah Bay on the steamer Favorite for that purpose. By the same steamer that brought the troops I received instruction to give Webster sixty days more in which to move, and he was accordingly not molested. After again advising McCollum and Colby to peaceably abandon the reservation, and even offering to assist them in removing their effects, which they still declined to do, Lieutenant Houghey had a sergeant and four men placed in each one of their houses, and sent McCollum under guard to the outer limits of the reservation. Colby left without any further trouble. * * * *

During August Rev. J. F. DeVore, J. B. Montgomery, and Capt. George D. Hill, the gentlemen who compose the board appointed to appraise the value of the improvements made by McCollum, Colby, and Webster, visited Neah Bay and made a personal inspection of the improvements with a view to assessing the value of the same, in order that they may be justly compensated therefor. * * * *

The Indians are highly pleased at the result, and seem much better satisfied, since they now feel that their homes are secured to them forever where they can live in peace and enjoy the fruits and blessings of their own labor. They have already purchased seven head of cattle and four horses, the first stock ever owned by the tribe; and since they are satisfied that this land now undoubtedly belongs to them they are making arrangements to purchase cattle and horses and raise stock. This of course I encourage them in doing, as I think it far better for their future interest and welfare that they should give more of their attention to pursuits of this character. * * *

The boundaries of the reservation as now extended should be surveyed and established at an early day.

The Indians have been very peaceable and well-disposed during the last year, and are steadily adopting the habits and customs of civilization. Many of them wear citizens' clothes, and some of them are learning to talk English quite well. Only in two or three instances during the past year has whisky been brought or drank upon the reservation. It is only when they visit the towns upon Puget Sound, and the different tribes that inhabit the shores of Vancouver's Island on the opposite side of the straits of Juan De Fuca from here, that they drink whisky, and then but a few of them ever become intoxicated. There are quite a number of them that cannot now be persuaded to drink whisky at any time. Captain John, one of the best chiefs in the tribe, who I am informed formerly dealt considerably in whisky, could not now be induced to taste it. The Indians who live upon Vancouver's Island visit the different villages of this tribe quite frequently and sometimes in great numbers—were formerly in the habit of bringing whisky with them, but we have been so successful in destroying it that they found it more expensive than profitable, and the past summer have not brought any.

The Makahs, as usual, have been very busily engaged during the summer catching and drying salmon and halibut for winter use, and have succeeded in laying up a good supply.

There is no road or trail leading from this reservation to any white settlement that can be traveled on horseback. The Indians recently (since they have taken the notion to buy horses and cattle) have asked me to assist them in opening a trail along the Pacific coast, from this agency to the Quinaielt reservation, which if done would open communication between this place and the Quillehute and Chehalis countries, and enable the Indians along the coast to bring stock into this coast country, which I have no doubt would be a great benefit to them. The distance from here to Quinaielt is about sixty-five miles.

Although the crops upon the reservation were put in with more care than usual last spring, they have not done well. The potato-crop (the one we most depend upon) is almost an entire failure. They are affected with the blight, and the tops are all dried and withered away; the potatoes were beginning to rot before they were half grown. Ten acres of potatoes upon the reservation farm I do not think will yield over three hundred bushels, and six acres at the agency will not yield over one hundred bushels. The Indians' potatoes are also almost an entire failure, and they will have to purchase or do without the coming winter. The Indians are very fond of potatoes, and of late years they have become one of their chief articles of food. Boiled or roasted potatoes, dried salmon or halibut, and whale-oil make a dish which is greatly relished by them. The farmer seeded about three acres in pease and about six in oats and barley. Before the pease had matured the cattle broke into the field at night and destroyed them, and very much injured the barley. The oats and barley have been harvested, and [we have] made about five tons of good hay. The farmer also seeded four acres more at the farm in timothy, which now looks very well, and next season will probably produce a good crop of hay. I also had about two acres at the agency sowed with timothy-seed. There is but little of this land that is fit for anything but grass, and much of it will not even produce that. We have harvested about twenty tons of hay, and small in amount as it may appear, it is the largest crop of hay ever produced upon the reservation. I expect to have four acres more sown in timothy and clover after the potatoes are dug. The gardens at the agency are very fine, the best I have seen in the Territory. * * * * * * * * *

In my last annual report I referred to the poor and almost worthless quality of the land upon which the reservation farm is located, it being a mere sand-bed, and recommended an appropriation of $1,500 for the construction of a dike across the Wa-ach slough, by which about five hundred acres of excellent tide-land might be reclaimed, upon which a good farm could be made with but little labor; also an appropriation of $1,500 for building a new farm-house and making other necessary improvements. I would invite your attention to that report and renew the same recommendation.

I have been asked by the chiefs of this tribe a number of times to urge the Government to furnish them a schooner, and I suppose there is nothing that these Indians have a greater desire to possess, or that would please them better or be more beneficial to them, than a good schooner of about fifty tons burden. They are natural sailors, and from infancy spend much of their life upon the water. They obtain nearly all their resources from the sea. The products of the waters about Cape Flattery, which amount to many thousand dollars annually, would be lost to the country were it not for these Indians, as there are perhaps no other people who would or could take their places and obtain a support as they do, and besides produce annually what is worth thousands of dollars to the several interests of our country. It seems to me that a race of people like this, who inhabit a portion of the country which, without them, would be desolate and almost worthless, should be fostered, protected, and cared for, and, if possible, civilized as a matter of interest, to say nothing of their claims upon our charity, or the general good that intellectual and moral advancement always produces upon society. From the 1st of January to the last of May is their sealing season, and the weather is much of the time disagreeable and stormy and the sea rough during this period; but when the weather will permit they engage in sealing, going from ten to forty miles from land in their cedar canoes on the Pacific after the fur-seal. This is an extremely dangerous business, and sometimes they are blown so far out to sea by a strong east wind that they never return. It is, however, very profitable, as they find ready sale for the skins at from two to ten dollars apiece, and sometimes kill fifteen hundred seals in a single season. Later in the season they go far out to sea in their frail canoes in pursuit of whales. Last summer they killed nine whales, some of them very large ones. This summer they have as yet killed only two. If they had a good schooner it would be of great advantage to them in sealing and whaling, as they could put their canoes, provisions, and water on board the schooner and go out to sea among the seals and whales, and, leaving the schooner, they, in their canoes, could engage in sealing or whaling all day, and return to the schooner at night to sleep and rest, and renew their supply of water and food; and in case of a storm the schooner would be a safe refuge for them. With a schooner they would be able to remain at sea for many days, or even weeks, at a time, in almost perfect safety, and would undoubtedly be far more successful in their perilous pursuits than they are. I would earnestly recommend an appropriation of $5,000 for the purpose of procuring a schooner for the use of this tribe.

There was considerable sickness in the tribe last winter, and many of the Indian children were afflicted with the measles; but through the summer the health has been generally very good. In my last annual report I urged the necessity of establishing a hospital at Neah Bay, where the old, maimed, and sick might be brought from the different villages and have care, food, and medicine, and be under the immediate supervision of the resident physician, and at least kept from dying of starvation or utter neglect. This appears to me to be an actual necessity for the proper care of these people. I cannot understand why it is that the Government does not care for all Indians alike. Many agencies, I understand, have hospitals, and it seems to be the Indians that are most favorably situated and best able to take care of themselves that are thus favored, while this tribe, located perhaps in the most unfavorable part of the United States, in an unproductive country, far remote from any settlement, with very poor, unhealthy habitations, and no mill to make lumber with which to construct better ones adapted to health and comfort, where they can never accumulate much wealth or provide for their own comfort and welfare as it should be done, are neglected, and actually many times suffer for the comforts a hospital would afford. Dr. Bryant, the resident physician, is a very competent officer, and well adapted to the service. His salary, $1,200 per annum, in currency, which is equal to about $1,000 in coin, (the prevailing currency on this coast,) is very inadequate, and does not properly compensate for the services rendered, and, besides, with this meagre salary he is required to furnish all medicines used. Will $1,000 a year properly compensate for the services of a physician and pay for all the medicines required in his practice for that time in this country, where medicines are very expensive? It certainly will not. Almost any common laborer can go into any saw-mill on Puget Sound and earn as much per annum. Dr. Bryant is making a sacrifice by remaining in the service, and should he leave, his place could not be easily filled by a competent physician. I would recommend that the salary for a physician at this agency be increased to $1,500 per annum, dating back one year, also that an appropriation of $1,500 be made for the establishment of a hospital at Neah Bay, which, with the labor that could be performed by the present employés, would, I think, be ample for that purpose, and that an additional appropriation, annually, of $300 be made to pay for the services of a person to perform the duties of cook and nurse. I would further recommend that $300 be allowed annually for the purpose of purchasing the necessary medicines for the use of the physician, and that the necessary surgical instruments, such as are furnished for the Army surgeons, be furnished for the use of the physician upon this reservation, or a sufficient appropriation be made for the purchase of the same.

With regard to the school allow me to say the children, under the supervision of Rev. C. H. Hodges, the teacher, are doing finely. * * * The boys, every day that the weather will permit, are required to perform a portion of labor in the school garden, and the girls to attend to the domestic duties of the house. On Lord's day they are thoroughly washed and dressed, and required to attend religious services. Mr. Hodges in his spare moments labors in the capacity of missionary on the reservation, looking out for the general interests of the reservation morally and spiritually, having religious services at the school-house on Lord's day, and this labor is done by him gratuitously.

The school at present numbers eighteen, and they are advancing finely. When the Indians return from their summer resorts the number of scholars will be increased. One remarkable feature of the school is the regularity of the children in their attendance. Mr. Hodges has some scholars that have not missed a day from school since he has been with them, notwithstanding the numerous "pot-latches" that are constantly going on among the Indians during the summer months. The proximity of the school-house to the Indian ranches is a great drawback to the prosperity of the school. The ideas and habits formed in school do not harmonize with the savage and barbarous habits of the Indians; not only this, but many of the old Indians are trying to persuade the children that education is a detriment to them, as it unfits them for the hardy pursuits of the Indian. The appropriation for the support of the school is small. One woman is obliged to cook and wash for the whole school, and do it at very low wages. We greatly need an assistant teacher and another cook; and I would recommend that an appropriation of $600 annually be made to pay for the services of an assistant teacher, and $300 annually to pay for the services of another cook.

In conclusion, I will say that the present employés upon the reservation are all good Christian men, and are earnestly endeavoring to instruct and elevate the Indians and better their condition; and while our efforts have not accomplished what we had desired they should, owing to the many difficulties we have had to contend with, yet we confidently hope that the aggregate good we may have disseminated among them will result in a permanent advancement and a lasting blessing to the whole tribe.

I am, sir, very respectfully, your obedient servant,

E. M. GIBSON,
United States Indian Agent.

Hon. R. H. MILROY,
Superintendent of Indian Affairs for Washington Territory.

65.

SKOKOMISH AGENCY, WASHINGTON TERRITORY,
September 23, 1873.

SIR: It becomes my duty to make my third annual report of the affairs at this agency and the Indians belonging to this reservation.

The general condition of the Indians under my charge is much the same as at the time of my last report. The year has been quiet, peaceful, and prosperous. During the month of October last I made a distribution of annuity goods to such Indians under my charge as came for them. In consequence of the great distance that most of the S'Klallams live from the agency, not half of that tribe came for their goods. Less than five hundred in all were present at the distribution. During the past few weeks I have visited most of the Indian towns of the S'Klallams. A large proportion of them live on the southern shore of the Straits of Juan de Fuca, in small villages from ten to twenty miles distant from each other. They occupy houses, some of which have floors and windows, and are as good as many whites inhabit. They subsist by fishing and working by the day or month for farmers and others. Some have declared their intention to become citizens, and have taken up claims, and are farming and accumulating property. They seem to be peaceable and industrious; but many of them often go across the straits, and get liquor in large quantities, and drink badly. Being so far from the oversight of any one, they drink without any restraint. Others live at the various saw-mills on the sound and work in them. These are doing well, except that they connive secretly to get whisky and drink badly. I have endeavored to induce them to come on to the reservation by offering to give them pieces of land of their own to cultivate. They are very slow to take in such an idea, because that, first, it removes them so far from their old homes. Then there is not a cordial good-feeling between them and the Twanas, who are in the majority on the reservation. The reservation is so small that they can have but small pieces of land, and must be thrown in close proximity with those they do not like, and who speak a different language. Then, there is not as good an opportunity to get work near the reservations as there is where they now are; and the opportunities to get and sell fish where they are are far superior to those near here. These reasons all combine to render it difficult to bring them in any considerable numbers on the reservation. They are diminishing in number, and the most discouraging feature in relation to them is that they have scarcely any children. Consequently, as a nation, when this generation passes away, they will become almost extinct.

The Twanas, who mostly live on the reservation, are improving. They are drinking less than formerly, and work more steadily. During the past year they have cut and sold 2,000,000 feet of saw-logs, which have been sold for about $10,000. They are beginning to clear up some of their land, have cut considerable hay, and are raising some potatoes. I have distributed to them three hundred fruit-trees during the last spring, which they have set out on their pieces of ground.

The school has been steadily gaining. We report this year an attendance of twenty scholars against fifteen last year. Their progress is quite satisfactory. During the past summer the teacher has worked with the boys forenoons, and had study-hours in the afternoons. They have cultivated about four acres of garden, and cut and put up for winter use over forty cords of good, dry wood.

At the agency there was produced on the farm last year 700 bushels apples, 45 tons hay, 120 bushels potatoes, 125 bushels turnips, 110 bushels beets, 30 bushels carrots, 20 bushels parsnips, 20 bushels pears, and 25 bushels plums. This summer there has been made a dike ten feet wide and about two feet high, 240 rods long, a rail fence 300 rods long, a warehouse 20 by 36 feet, a council-house 20 by 40, also other improvements on the buildings at the agency. The crops this year are good and have been well taken care of.

During the early part of the summer I made urgent request that the reservation be enlarged, but the withdrawal of all alternate sections of land by the North Pacific Railroad Company forbid such an extension. Since that time the company have located their terminus at a point south of the desired extension, so that it is presumable, at least, that the withdrawal will be rescinded. Should such be the case, I earnestly request that such extension be made.

I would call your attention to the following facts: Some ten or twelve years ago the then acting superintendent of Indian affairs for this Territory, at the urgent request of the Indians, decided upon adding to the reservation a half-section of land which was a donation-claim of A. D. Fisher. The place and improvements were appraised and the appraisement forwarded to Washington. The place was then turned over to the agent, and used for the benefit of the Indians as a part of the reservation. A portion of it was used by them as a burying-ground for their dead. At that time the land was all unsurveyed, so that no title could be given, as Mr. Fisher had none. As near as I can learn, no notice was ever taken of the appraisement, and Mr. Fisher has never received a cent for his place. During the past summer the land has been surveyed, and turns out to be on a railroad section. Mr. Fisher had, however, completed the requisite four years' residence, and is entitled to a patent ahead of the railroad company. Were he now paid what he should have been years ago, he could complete his title and give a good deed to the Department, and this would secure this tract of land to the Indians and also be an act of justice to the former owner. I recommend that this matter be investigated, and such action taken as will mete out justice to both parties, and secure to them their just rights.

In conclusion, I would say that the moral advancement of the Indians here is truly gratifying. The new council-house, which has been recently erected and is also used for a church, is filled every Sabbath with attentive listeners to the Word of Life, and the seeds of truth thus sown seem to be taking root. We are gratified also that the reservation is so soon to be sub-divided into small lots and assigned to the Indians in severalty. I believe this will be followed by marked improvement.

I have the honor to be, very respectfully, your obedient servant,

EDWIN EELLS,
United States Indian Agent, Washington Territory.

Gen. R. H. MILROY,
Superintendent Indian Affairs, Olympia, Wash.

66.

QUINAIELT INDIAN AGENCY, WASHINGTON TERRITORY,
September 1, 1873.

SIR: I have the honor submit my annual report of the condition of this agency during the past year. The condition of these Indians has improved in many respects. I have endeavored by every means in my power to awaken a desire upon their part to improve, but have succeeded only to a limited extent. Some few of them have cleared small pieces of land, and planted potatoes and other vegetables.

The land is all of a nature that requires much time and labor to bring into a state available for farming purposes. The upland is covered with a heavy growth of spruce, hemlock, and cedar, of poor quality, and the river bottom, which is narrow, and subject to overflow in winter, is covered with spruce, vine, maple, and crab-apple.

When we take into consideration the fact that nature has surrounded these people with an abundance of game, such as elk, deer, and bear, and that the river abounds in salmon of the finest quality, it is not to be wondered at that they prefer to obtain a support from the river and forest, as was done by their fathers, to going into the dense forests by which they are surrounded to clear a farm. For these reasons, I am of the opinion that they will depend principally upon fishing as a means of obtaining a living. Having in view the enlargement of this reservation, as recommended by you in your report for 1872, which is entirely too small for the support of the number of Indians included under this treaty, and to inform myself as to the character of the country, in company with Lieut. S. R. Jones, United States Army, and a party of Indians to manage the canoe, we went from the agency up the river to Quinaielt Lake, some fifty miles distant, the river being very crooked, and difficult to ascend on account of rapids.

The country along the river is generally unproductive, although there are small tracts of land in the bottoms which would produce well if cleared. The lake is a beautiful sheet of water, clear and deep, so deep that at the distance of a quarter of a mile from shore we were unable to find the bottom with 300 feet of line. It is surrounded by high mountains, upon some of which snow remains the year round. The extent of the lake is about three miles in width by five in length, lying in a northeasterly and southwesterly direction the longest way. From the west side we went out into the country to see a prairie, which our guide informed us lay about three miles distant. The country over which we passed is worthless, being nothing more than a deposit of sand and gravel. When we found the reported prairie it proved to be nothing more than an old burn, covered with gravel, unfit for farming, and affording little grass, showing signs of having been occupied by elk and deer. We were informed by our guide that it was about one day's journey to the Queets River, north from where we were, across a range of mountains in sight, which he said was the divide. From the character of the country and the elevation we had attained, I think the Queets River would be reached about fifty miles from its mouth.

Knowing what I do of the country, I respectfully ask that the reserve be enlarged as recommended by you, including the Queets River on the north, the Quinaielt Lake on the east, thence from the southern extremity of said lake to the south line of the reserve as it is. This will furnish the Indians with good hunting and fishing grounds, also enough agricultural land for their use, and would be satisfactory to them.

The number of Indians included in this treaty, as taken at the distribution of annuities one year since, is as follows: Males, 248; females, 306; total, 554. Number of deaths on the reserve, so far as I am able to learn, 9; births, 10. As not more than one-fourth of the Indians under treaty reside on the reserve, and with the above figures as a guide, it is safe to presume that the total number is not materially changed.

I would respectfully call your attention to the fact that this agency is poorly supplied with medicines, I having received no money for that purpose. The physician cannot reasonably be expected to furnish medicines for more than five hundred Indians out of his salary of $1,000 per annum and have much for his services. I think this difficulty can be remedied when it is understood. The present appropriation for employés, and a "physician who shall furnish medicine for the sick," is $4,100. Of this it requires for pay of physician, $1,000; three employés at $900 per annum each, and a herder at $250; total, $3,950—leaving a balance of $150 unexpended of the employés' fund. I would respectfully ask that $150 be added to the salary of the physician for the purchase of medicines; and if a small amount could be appropriated for the purchase of surgical instruments and hospital supplies it would greatly aid in the work of civilizing and Christianizing the Indians. The physician is a faithful and competent officer, and very successful in the treatment of complaints incident to this coast, and I am confident the additional $150 would be used for the purpose intended. I respectfully refer you to his accompanying report.

The farming operations at this agency are not large. We have about eighteen acres partly cleared as an agency farm; have slashed three acres this year, which is ready to burn, and have seeded ten acres to timothy, which in another year will yield a large amount of hay. The amount of hay cut this year is about five tons. At present we have a prospect of a good crop of potatoes and turnips for winter use. The garden at the agency has furnished plenty of vegetables for summer use. Some of the Indians have cut small amounts of hay, and have potatoes which look well at this time. If our potato crop is not injured by the "potato rot," which has made its appearance on this coast, there will be plenty for agency use.

A difficulty occurred at this agency early in the spring, which came near proving serious. The Indians became insolent, and upon my attempting to arrest two of them for disobedience of orders, and inciting others to resist my authority, they were taken away from me by superior force, and I was compelled to call upon the military for aid. The prompt and efficient service rendered by the detachment of 23 men under First Lieut. S. R. Jones enabled me to arrest the offending Indians and punish them, which I was unable to do with the force of employés I had without resorting to the use of fire-arms, which I did not feel justified in doing.

The cruel and barbarous custom of flattening the heads of their children is still practiced by some of the Indians belonging to this reservation. It was my endeavoring to, and succeeding in, taking a child out of the "press" that brought on the trouble. * * The child is kept in this press from three to five hours each day until the head assumes the required shape. It is a cruel and barbarous practice, and if it cannot be prevented by peaceable means it should be done by force.

For information concerning the school I refer you to the report of the teacher. The Indians do not support the school as they should. They are so entirely bound by superstition and ignorance that although I have endeavored, by all the means in my power, to lead them from darkness to light, I have met with poor success. A person who expects to accomplish the work of enlightening and civilizing a people who for generations have lived in ignorance and superstition will be disappointed. Still, I believe a consistent and patient course of dealing with them will meet with its reward, and that much good can be accomplished among the young, if not the old.

The agency buildings have been whitewashed and cleansed, and put in good repair for the winter. The Indians are also becoming more cleanly in their habits, and appreciate comfortable houses and good provisions. I have kept them supplied with soap in abundance, as it can always be used to good advantage by them. From experience in transportation of agency-goods, which is done with cattle over a distance of thirty miles on the ocean beach, I am satisfied that much time can be saved by the teamster employed at the agency by having a faster team. I have, therefore, purchased a good pair of mules and a wagon suitable for that purpose.

I have the honor to forward statistics of education and farming with reports of employés.

Thanking you for the courteous treatment received, officially and personally,

I am, very respectfully, your obedient servant,

G. A. HENRY,
Sub-Indian Agent.

Gen. R. H. MILROY,
Superintendent Indian Affairs, Washington Territory.

67.

OFFICE OF YAKAMA INDIAN AGENCY,
Fort Simcoe, Wash., August 26, 1873.

SIR: In accordance with instructions of the Department I have the honor to submit my annual report for the fiscal year 1873.

During the strife the Department had with the Modocs, the inhabitants east of the Cascade Mountains, many of them believed we were to have serious trouble with Indians belonging to this treaty. Reports were put in circulation that two thousand Indians, armed and well fortified, had gathered at White Bluffs, on the Columbia River, and were about to break out on the settlements. Quite a number of the white families left the country; others went into fortifications and applied to the Government for arms to protect themselves during the approaching struggle. I took five Indians from the agency and visited these places of reported danger, and found nothing that indicated hostility on the part of the Indians. I did find that a class of irresponsible whites were quite anxious to have a war, that the treaty might be broken up and the land of the reservation opened for white settlements. I am pleased to be able to report that our Indians during the war with the Modocs evinced the most perfect agreement with the Department. Such was their zeal for the right, I believe I could have raised five hundred men in a day that would have marched to the hottest part of the battle.

The difficulty said to exist on Snake River was reported to the Department on my return. (See said report.)

There has been no year since the making of the treaty with this nation of Indians when they have been so universally well disposed toward the whites. Little difficulties have arisen between the whites and Indians on the border of the reservation, but I have been prompt to go to the place of difficulty and have the parties together, and thus settle the matter. I have almost universally found the whites were first in the transgression.

FARMING.

Our farming interest has increased, over last year, among the Indians in inclosing and cultivating land at least one-fourth.

MILLS.

In my last report I asked the Department to permit me to purchase and erect a steam saw-mill, without any additional appropriation of money for such purchase and erection, which permission was given. I have the pleasure to report that said mill has been purchased, transported to the agency and erected, and is in good running order, capable of making 10,000 feet of lumber in twelve hours, or as much in one day as our water-mill would make in twelve.

The Indians are much encouraged with the expectation of making improvements in building houses, barns, and fencing their land with permanent fences. In the transportation and erection of said mill the Indians have rendered valuable service without pay. The cost of the mill in running order is a little over $4,000, and is worth, at least, $7,000. The water and steam mills can be used to good advantage, being sixteen miles apart, and accommodating different parts of the agency.

The grist-mill has been repaired the past year at an expense of about $100, and is now in good running condition.

The schools at the agency have been in operation for ten months of the year and have done well. (See report of superintendent of instruction.)

Their sanitary condition was never as good as at this time. The skill and untiring attention given to this department by Dr. Kuykendall is universally approved by the Indians and employés of the agency. There has not been money enough appropriated for the purchase of medicines. (See physician's report herewith remitted.)

The religious interests of the agency is not the least of any and all interests here represented. There is a steady coming up in character and stability of right action that merits the approval of all who observe the change.

In conclusion I wish to call the attention of the Department to that part of my report of last year to the money due this agency from the late Superintendent Waterman, $7,250. This money should have been paid in December, 1866. No good reason can be assigned why this money should be withheld from this agency. Also, I observed that there was appropriated $1,000 of school money over former years, which money has not been received. Please call the attention of the Department to this money matter, that with it we may enlarge our schools and increase the general interests of the agency.

I have the honor to be your obedient servant,

JAMES H. WILLEN,
United States Indian Agent, Washington Territory.

General R. H. MILROY,
Superintendent Indian Affairs, Washington Territory.

Appendix.

OFFICE YAKAMA INDIAN AGENCY,
Fort Simcoe, Wash., September 1, 1873.

Since the date of the foregoing report, and before mailing it, I have received a copy of a letter from the honorable Commissioner of Indian Affairs, dated June 13, 1873, addressed to Charles Ewing, esq., Washington, D. C., which letter was written in answer to the request of the Roman Catholic bishop of Nisqually for permission to build a church and residence for a Catholic priest within the jurisdiction of both the Yakama and the Nez Percé Indian agencies, and states that the honorable Secretary of the Interior had given permission to the Catholic authorities to erect such buildings.

In response to the very surprising information contained in this letter, I beg leave to submit the following considerations:

1st. The two reservations referred to have been assigned by the President, under the new Christian policy, to two Protestant denominations—that of the Nez Percés to the Presbyterian Church, and that of the Yakama Nation to the Methodist, with the expectation on the part of all Protestant Christians that, so far as the religious instruction of these tribes are concerned, those respective churches were to have entire jurisdiction without the interference of other denominations, most of all without the interference of the Catholic priesthood.

2d. In the case of reservations assigned under the new policy to the Catholic Church, as at Tulalip, under the Point Elliot treaty, where a Catholic priest is now the agent, and where the same priest has been many years the teacher, and where the whole machinery of the Catholic Church, including a school for girls, under the Sisters of Charity, has been long in operation, no denomination of the Protestant Church has ever attempted to interfere. It has been conceded on all hands that Father Chirouse had entire jurisdiction of the religious instruction of all the Indians under that treaty, and that it would be unlawful and improper under the present Indian policy of the Government. No good results could follow from instructions that would contradict the teachings of the lawfully constituted authority of the agency. Such contradiction would only confuse the minds of the heathen tribes, and weaken their confidence in Christianity altogether.

3. So far as the Yakama Nation is concerned, and I believe the same is true of the Nez Percés Indians, the steady, uniform, persistent policy of the Catholic priesthood is *now* and *always has* been, to contradict the instructions of the Protestant teachers, to defeat their influence, and drive from the mind of the Indians all confidence in their honesty, and all inspired purpose of thrift and progress. * * * *

4. To encourage, within the lawful jurisdiction of an Indian agent, an element of power and influence that is utterly hostile to all the endeavors of the constituted authority, must necessarily prove disastrous to the success of all attempts at true Christian progress not only, but it must prove disastrous to the peace of the reservation, and to the safety of the lives of the resident employés.

It becomes my conscientious duty, therefore, to remonstrate in the most distinct and positive terms against an order that I know to be fatal to every true interest of the Indians of my agency, and a violation of the precedents and the policy of the Christian administration of Indian affairs.

Respectfully submitted.

JAMES H. WILLEM,
United States Indian Agent, Wash. Ter.

68.

FORT COLVILLE, *October* 20, 1873.

SIR: In conformity with the regulations of the Indian Department I have the honor to submit my first annual report of the affairs of this agency, from the 13th of September, 1872, the date of my assuming charge, up to the present date.

I found on my arrival here that there had been no house or other buildings provided for the use of the agent and employés of the Government, but was kindly furnished with comfortable quarters at the garrison by the commanding officer, Capt. Evan Miles, Twenty-first Infantry, and to whom I am indebted for many other courtesies.

As soon as practicable I called the chiefs and head-men in council, to ascertain (as instructed from your Office) how they were pleased with the new reservation set aside for them by Executive order, and if they were willing to remove to it. The result of that council was made known to you in my special report of November 20, 1872. I will only add here that the tribes represented, viz, the Colvilles, Spokanes, Pend d'Oreilles and Lakes, were unanimous, as they still are, in their opposition to removing to the reservation north of the Columbia; their principal objections being, first, their great unwillingness to leave their own country; secondly, the reservation boundaries do not include their fisheries; thirdly, there are no root-grounds on that side of the river, and an insufficiency of farming-land whereby they could subsist themselves by agriculture. Until such time as they may be able to cultivate the soil, the different fisheries and root-grounds now frequented by them must be their main source of subsistence.

As to whether or not their objections to the reservation are well founded, you will be able to decide from your recent careful and patient examination. For myself I am free to say that I deem the reservation, as now defined, entirely insufficient for the number of Indians belonging to this agency, and would give my reasons more in detail did I not know that you are now thoroughly acquainted with it, and in your report will set forth its merits and demerits more forcibly than I can possibly do.

At the council held here on the 11th and 12th of August, by General Shanks and yourself, the Indians renewed their objections to the reservation, and asked that Colville Valley be given them for a reserve. The propriety of acceding to their wishes in that respect is now the all-important question, both to the Indians and the white settlers of the valley, which I hope will be eventually settled to their mutual satisfaction. For many reasons, which I shall soon make the subject of a special report, I would earnestly recommend that a commission be appointed to assess the value of the property of the white settlers of this valley, with a view of its being set apart as an Indian reserve.

The unsettled question of the location of this agency, the want of agency-buildings, and the insufficiency of means at my disposal, have seriously impeded the anticipated advancement of the Indians under my charge; yet, under your directions, much has been done for their advancement. A day-school for Indian children was organized January 1, 1873, and placed under the instruction of Father Tosi, at St. Frances Regis Mission, in Colville Valley. The average attendance was forty-five. The progress made much exceeded my expectation. The children generally manifested a desire to learn, and Father Tosi and his assistant were zealous and untiring in their efforts. The school was discontinued March 31 by reason of the annual visit of the Indians and their families to the root-grounds. I would state in this connection that I have recently established a boarding and industrial school, as directed by yourself, and placed the same in charge of Sisters of Charity, the Catholic Fathers having kindly proffered the necessary buildings for temporary use of the school. The school has not been sufficiently long in operation to warrant extended remarks; yet, from present indications, I am sanguine of its ultimate success.

Much difficulty has been experienced in inducing the Indians to agricultural pursuits. They are unwilling to inclose farms while the possibility of their being at any day removed from them exists. And further, I have been unable to provide with proper implements and seed all who are disposed to farm; notwithstanding, some advancement in this particular has been made; between three and four thousand bushels of wheat have been harvested, and from fifteen hundred to two thousand bushels of potatoes have been cultivated, besides sufficient hay to subsist their horses and cattle during the winter. They have also cut and corded about five hundred cords of wood, for which they have received one dollar and fifty cents per cord.

The Indians of this agency, with the exception of the San Poels, are peaceable and well-disposed, and have made considerable advancement in Christianity and civilization. There are quite a number of thrifty and intelligent farmers among them, and they show more disposition to work and make their living by the arts of civilized life than any Indians I have met with on this coast during a residence of more than twenty years. The Colvilles have this year built for themselves a large church of hewn logs, capable of accommodating nearly a thousand persons, and they take much pride in their handiwork. The San Poel Indians have a religion of their own, and are under the influence of men called dreamers. Although never in open hostility to the whites, they have never been disposed to cultivate friendly relations with them, and have uniformly refused to accept presents from the Government agents, or hold any intercourse with them. The wants of the sick and destitute have been as liberally administered to as the limited means at my disposal would allow.

I am, sir, very respectfully, your obedient servant,

JOHN A. SIMNS,
Special Indian Agent.

General R. H. MILROY,
Superintendent Indian Affairs, Olympia, Wash. Ter.

69.

PUYALLUP INDIAN RESERVATION, WASH. TER.,
October 1, 1873.

SIR: I have the honor to transmit this, my third annual report.

The Indians on this reservation during the past year have made considerable progress in the arts of civilized life. They have been farming quite extensively, with fair yields, except the potato-crop, which is almost an entire failure. The loss of this crop will go hard with them, as the potato is their main vegetable. They have an abundance of hay for their stock and the most of it very well housed.

Farming on this reservation has never been carried on as extensively as it should have been, considering the large amount of really good farming land. I have repeatedly urged upon them the advantages of large fields well fenced and properly cultivated. They have invariably answered by saying that if their reservation was surveyed so that each Indian could have his piece of land they would then feel like going to work in earnest and clear up their land and farm like white men. Now that the reservation is being surveyed and a prospect that each Indian or family will have a portion of land set apart for them, I have strong faith that they will be better satisfied and more industrious than heretofore; and I am confident that many of them will make successful farmers and good citizens. Their constant theme of conversation for the past year has been the survey of their reservation, and now that it is about being consummated they are making arrangements for building good houses, clearing and fencing large fields, and in fact begin farming in earnest.

The census taken on the 7th of September shows a population of five hundred and seventy-seven persons, being an increase of one hundred and twenty-seven in the past two years.

For want of suitable school-buildings and proper appliances the school for the past year has not been very successful, but now that a large and substantial boarding-school building is nearly finished and in a very desirable place, with plenty of good land for a school-farm, and the Rev. G. W. Sloan as teacher, I feel confident of a good showing in the future. In view of the fact that the employés' buildings on this reservation are situated on low flat land, subject to frequent overflow in the winter, and the fact that they are old, rotten, and entirely unfit to be inhabited, I would recommend an appropriation sufficiently large to put up new buildings on the site selected for that purpose adjoining the new school-house.

The health of the Indians on this reservation during the past year has been generally good. For further account of their sanitary condition I will refer you to the report of the resident physician herewith inclosed. I would also respectfully refer you to the recommendation contained in his report. In the physician's opinion as to the necessity of a hospital I fully concur.

The number of Indians (including the Nisquallies) that look to this physician for treatment is between seven and eight hundred. In view of this fact I would respectfully recommend that medicines be furnished by the Department for this reservation.

I am, sir, very respectfully, your obedient servant,

BYRON BARLOW,
Farmer in charge Puyallup Reservation.

Gen. R. H. MILROY,
Superintendent Indian Affairs, Washington Territory.

70.

CHEHALIS RESERVATION.

SIR: I submit to you my report for the year of 1873. We have this year built a boarding-house for the Indian school, 28 by 46 feet; * * * * * * barn for hay, 35 by 45 feet; built an office for the doctor, 12 by 14 feet; 22 desks for school and 40 benches for same, and a black-board; made 12 large gates and 5 smaller ones; made 25 rods of picketfence around yard and garden; also, built 250 rods of rail-fence, grubbed and broke 25 acres of new ground for Government. * * * * * * *

The Indians of this reservation are well pleased with the fruits of their labor. There is not a more moral and industrious tribe of Indians in Washington Territory. * * * * * * *

Rev. J. F. Devore established a branch of the Methodist Episcopal Church here some four months since, and the Indians are now, a majority of them, taking a deep interest in religious affairs, and are becoming, very fast, good practical men and women.

The Chehalis reservation, is naturally adapted to farming and manufacturing, having 4,500 acres of good land, abounding with splendid fir, cedar, oak, ash, and alder, with a saw-mill to convert its fir and cedar into lumber; mechanical shops to work its oak into wagons and plows, and its ash into fork-handles, its alder into ax-handles, its cedar into buckets, churns, and wash-tubs.

The reservation is surrounded with large fields of magnificent coal and iron, making it naturally a manufacturing point. Our nearest point for lumber is 25 miles, and our nearest wagon and smith shop is 25 miles. Taking the Chehalis Valley, with its rich mineral and large body of land and its splendid timber, with agricultural shops on this reservation, will in a short time become one of the most prolific valleys west of the Rocky Mountains.

There is a very large drift or jam in the Chehalis River, on the reservation; if not removed, in a short time will ruin the reservation. It is now one mile in length, and is increasing every year. Will cost $10,000 to $15,000 to remove. I close this report hoping the Government will grant our little wants. There can be a school built up on this reservation of 50 to 60 scholars if we had the necessary appropriation.

Respectfully, yours,

DAVID SIRES,
Farmer in charge Chehalis reservation.

The SUPERINTENDENT OF INDIAN AFFAIRS,
Washington Territory.

71.

UMATILLA INDIAN AGENCY, OREGON,
September 4, 1873.

SIR: I have the honor to submit this my third annual report as agent for the Walla-Walla, Cayuse, and Umatilla tribes of Indians.

These Indians, once powerful and warlike tribes, inhabiting a large scope of country in Eastern Oregon and Washington, have now dwindled down to a comparatively small remnant of their former strength. I have endeavored several times since I took charge of this agency to get a correct census of them, but have as yet found it impracticable, owing to the fact that, in accordance with their treaty-rights, there are always more or less of them absent from the reservation, in the mountains and at the fisheries, hunting, digging roots, gathering berries, and fishing. I will endeavor again this winter, when the snow in the mountains renders it impracticable for them to leave, to make an actual count. The census taken nearly three years ago by my predecessor, I believe to be as correct as it could be taken at that time, and which he reports as follows viz:

	Men.	Women.	Boys.	Girls.	Total.	
Walla-Wallas	57	87	28	29	201	Homli, chief.
Cayuses	95	140	57	42	334	Howlish Wampo, chief.
Umatillas	92	144	41	25	302	Wenap Snoot, chief.
Total	244	371	126	96	837	

This number, I think, is now too high. One great difficulty in enumerating these people exists in the fact that a portion of the Indians belonging to these tribes still remain on the Columbia River, and some of these occasionally come on the reservation and profess to have come to remain; they will stay a short time and then leave again for the Columbia.

During the past year considerable improvements have been made by the Indians; better fences have been built, and some new farms opened, though much more improvement would have been made if we had an adequate supply of lumber. As it is, the saw-mill erected by one of my predecessors is at such a distance from timber as to be almost useless. I called attention to this in my last annual report, and in that report asked that permission be given to me to remove the mill to a point farther up the river, nearer the timber. And I also asked that an appropriation of $1,000 be made for that purpose. I beg leave, respectfully, to again call your attention to the matter. Logs have now to be hauled a distance of from ten to twelve miles over a mountain-road, and as there is no team at the agency belonging to the department with which to haul logs, and I had no funds whatever to purchase any, I have furnished my own team of oxen to haul what logs have been hauled during the past year, and by this means I have been enabled to get a small amount of lumber. This I have done without making any charge to the Government. Had I not done this I would not have had any lumber at all, even enough to make a coffin to give a decent burial to any of these poor people who died during the year.

I stated above that I had no funds whatever to purchase teams. Of the appropriation of $4,000 per annum for beneficial objects not one single dollar of that fund has been turned over to me since September, 1871; and of the appropriation for incidental expenses of $40,000 per annum for the Indian service in this State, only $200 of that appropriation has been turned over to me during the same period of two years.

I would also beg leave to call your attention to that portion of my last annual report wherein I called the attention of the Department to the unfulfilled stipulations of the treaty of June 9, 1855, with these Indians, and particularly to the fourth article of said treaty, which provides as follows: "Art. 4. In addition to the consideration above specified the United States agree to erect, at suitable points on the reservation, one saw-mill and one flouring-mill, a building suitable for a hospital, two school-houses, one blacksmith shop, one carpenter and joiner shop, one dwelling for each two millers, one farmer and one superintendent of farming operations, two school-teachers, one blacksmith, one wagon and plow maker, one carpenter and joiner, to each of which the necessary out-buildings."

Of the stipulations provided in this article, all that has ever been done by the Government is the erection of the saw and flouring mills. The other buildings for the agent and employés were temporary cabins erected in 1860, made of cottonwood poles, and although these have been temporarily repaired every year, hoping that the Government would make an appropriation to fulfill the solemn stipulations of the treaty, they are now almost completely rotten, and are liable to fall down at any moment. I do not think that it is right or just to take the money belonging to the Indians, and which is appropriated to carry out the other stipulations of the treaty, to do the work which the Government agreed to do. I trust, therefore, that the appropriation which I asked for in my last annual report, viz:

For necessary buildings for agent and employés, and erecting a building for hospital	$8,000
For manual-labor school, and furnishing same	3,000
For removal of saw-mill	1,000

may be made by next Congress. This is a small amount, but it would go a great way toward carrying out the beneficent purposes of the Government.

I have not received any instructions from Washington since the abolition of the superintendency, but as soon as I was notified officially by the late superintendent, T. B. Odeneal, esq., that such was the fact, I deemed it my duty to forward a requisition for funds direct to your office, which I trust may be forwarded as early as practicable, to enable me to obtain such supplies as may be necessary before winter sets in and navigation on the Columbia River closes, which it usually does by the first week in December.

Although during the past year there has been great excitement all over the country in consequence of the difficulties with the Modocs, and the white settlers in all portions of Eastern Oregon were forming military companies for their defense, these Indians were always peaceable and quiet, and carefully avoided by word or action giving any cause of offense. There was also great excitement existing among the citizens in this vicinity, particularly in La Grande, during the summer, in consequence of the Government giving the Wal-low-wa Valley to the Indians. And as many of the Indians of the reservation go every year to hunt, fish, and dig roots in that vicinity, I deemed it necessary to go with them, taking with me the interpreter, and it was only with great effort that difficulty was avoided, as many of the settlers were disposed to prevent the Indians from going there at all.

The Indians this year have raised a large amount of grain and vegetables, although a good deal in some portions of the reservation was partially destroyed by the crickets and grasshoppers, and with what fish and game they have caught, and the roots and berries they have gathered, they will have ample, I think, to subsist them comfortably during the coming winter, with the exception of a few poor old and decrepit Indians who will require some assistance, which I shall be able to give them from the products of the agency-farm.

The health of the Indians during the past year has been generally good, although during the winter there was considerable sickness and a good many deaths, as the Indians mostly live along the streams, which during the spring of the year rise to a considerable height, and when the waters recede leave the ground wet and marshy, naturally causing a large amount of intermittent fever, which renders giving them permission to go off to the mountains during the summer a sanitary necessity.

It pleases me much to say that during the year there has been little drunkenness among these Indians; although it is perhaps impossible entirely to prevent them from obtaining intoxicating liquors, yet those engaged in the vile traffic have found out—many of them to their sorrow—that it is a perilous business. I have, since I took charge of this agency, caused the arrest of ten persons for this crime, all of whom were held to answer before the United States district court for Oregon, and eight of them were convicted and sentenced to various terms of imprisonment; one forfeited his bonds and left the country, and only one escaped through the grand jury not finding a true bill. And in addition to this number several were convicted at Walla-Walla, Wash., for selling liquor to these Indians, and two are now awaiting trial at the next term of court. I am greatly indebted to the assistance of the United States judicial officers both of this State and the first judicial district of Washington Territory, for the prompt manner in which they have constantly aided me in my efforts to punish those guilty of this offense.

I have continually urged upon these Indians the benefits that would inure to them if they would let some of their young men work in the shops and at the mills; and although some of the old men see the necessity of their so doing, they have no control over their children; and I have not yet been able to get a single one to come. I have promised to board and clothe them, and as soon as they are capable of earning anything to pay them liberally for their work. I have pointed out to them that in a few more years their treaty will expire, and there will be no more mechanics or millers to do their work for them; but they will not heed the advice.

I have several times reported to the Department the difficulties attending the proper control of the Indians of this reservation in consequence of the large number of vagabond Indians on the Columbia River; and I am glad to find that Hon. E. C. Kemble, United States inspector, who visited this agency last month, has received instructions to make some arrangements with those Indians. I understand that he has called them together to meet in council about the middle of this month.

The day-school at this agency, under the general supervision of Reverend Father G. A. Vermeersch, who has been ably assisted by Mr. Thomas Tierney and Miss M. C. Cornoyer, has been carried on during the entire year, with the exception of one week's vacation at Christmas and a few weeks during the extremely hot weather in the month of August. There has been an average attendance of 26, viz: 16 boys and 10 girls. Many of the children are able to read, write, and cipher as well as most white children of their age. The girls have made great advancement in sewing and knitting; nearly all the clothing that I have been able to give the scholars has been made up by the girls in the school, and they have knit a great many pairs of socks and stockings, both for themselves and their parents. The fact that I have had no annuity funds in my hands for the past two years, has prevented me from clothing the children as well as I could wish. Many of the children of a proper age to go to school live at a long distance from the school-house, rendering it impracticable for them to attend until we are prepared to board and lodge them; but I trust that an appropriation will soon be made for a manual-labor school; when this is done I think we will have a large increase in the number of scholars.

The divine services on Sunday are well attended, not only by the members of the church, but by many who are not, and a more orderly congregation cannot be found in the United States, or one which appears to take more interest in the matters which pertain to their eternal salvation. During the early part of last month the Right Reverend A. M. Blanchet, bishop of Nisqually, visited this agency and administered the holy sacrament of confirmation to over twenty Indians and several whites who availed themselves of the visit of the bishop to receive that holy rite at the same time.

Very respectfully, your obedient servant,

N. A. CORNOYER,
United States Indian Agent.

Hon. EDWARD P. SMITH,
Commissioner of Indian Affairs, Washington, D. C.

72.

WARM SPRINGS AGENCY, *September* 1, 1873.

SIR: In compliance with the regulations of the Indian Department service, I have the honor to submit the following as my annual report for the time intervening between the date of my last report and September 1, 1873:

I have not been able to make a new census during the year, but presume that the deaths and births are about the same, and the census of last year will therefore apply to this, making, in all, the number of Indians belonging to this reservation 626.

About thirty-nine of this number are absent without leave. They left the reservation while under charge of my predecessor. They were induced to do so by the influence of bad men; and also they are believers in a superstition known as the Smohollah. This religion, if such it may be called, is believed by nearly all the Umatillas, Spokanes, a great part of the Yakimas, and many renegades of other reservations. The religion is like that of the Mormons, and ministers and works on the evil passions. The main object is to allow a plurality of wives, immunity from punishment for law-breaking, and allowance of all the vices—especially drinking and gambling—are chief virtues in the believers of this religion. Some provision should be at once made for placing all these outlaws on a reservation where they could receive the benefit of a strict law rigidly enforced.

The Indians residing on this reservation are making a great progress in every respect. They are now nearly all professors of Christianity, and, as a natural result, are rapidly becoming civilized. They have no quarreling among themselves; are on friendly terms with their white neighbors; have been blessed with an abundant harvest; have good, comfortable houses, and are making permanent improvements on their farms; and, morally and socially, will compare with any community of whites in the United States.

Just before my arrival here, a few years ago, five of these Indians were hung for murdering white men; and they had nothing to eat or wear, and were embittered against the whites. I treated them kindly, often overlooking offenses that should have been punished; and when I did punish, did so mildly, always showing them that it was for their good; the consequence is that the large amount of iron which was used by former agents to make handcuffs to iron prisoners with has been used by me in the manufacture of plows and wagons. The guard-house likewise has fallen, and is in ruins. The Bible and the plow are the great causes of all this. Compare the cost that this agency has been to the cost of one month's extermination policy, and no other argument need be produced in favor of the humane and Christian policy of our President. I am confident that a like result may be obtained with any tribe of Indians, by a kind and patient treatment. They should be regarded and treated as children—with firmness and kindness.

During the Modoc war General Canby telegraphed to me at Salem asking for a company of scouts from this agency. I telegraphed to Mr. T. F. Smith, then in charge, to furnish them; and in six hours' time Mr. Smith had enlisted the company, and was ready to move. Their services during the war cannot be exaggerated, as they undoubtedly saved the soldiers of Captain Hasbrouck from a total massacre at Sorass Lake, May 10. They were the captors of the lava-beds, and, in fact, did all the successful fighting that was done—and never forgot their duty as Christians during the whole time. The day-school has been well attended, and the children have learned very rapidly. The Sabbath-school continues, and our new school-house is full to overflowing every Sabbath-day. The school is taught by the employés and myself. The Indians have their prayer-meetings, and also services of their own after the Sabbath-school. They open all councils with prayer, and are manifesting their religion not only by observing the forms, but by practicing in their every-day life their professions.

The mills are in good repair, but the saw-mill should be removed to the mountains, where timber could be had. As it is, we have to haul the logs the distance of eight miles, and we are thus retarded in our work.

The harvest has been abundant; and no fears need be entertained of any suffering during the winter, for all have an abundance.

My employés are all married men, and have families, and as they have everything to buy, paying high prices therefor, some provision should be made for furniture for them, as the treaty provides that they shall be furnished with houses and furniture. They are all good men, and ready and willing to work for the good of the Government and Indians, and have been selected, after long personal knowledge of them, by me, and at the request of the Indians; and as they thus have great personal influence with the Indians, and do much more than I could get other men to do, I am anxious to retain them all, and wish to have them comfortably fixed with all they are allowed by treaty.

I have to report that the salmon-fishery at the Dalles, on the Columbia, has been claimed by white men, and that the Indians are forbidden to fish thereat. The Indians reserved the right to fish at this fishery in their treaty of June, 1855. Afterward they made a treaty to visit the fishery on passes from their agent; but from some cause the treaty, as approved, makes them to give up their right. I have investigated this matter, and have the evidence of the persons who interpreted to the Indians that nothing was said as to their giving up this right; and I am therefore fully satisfied that the treaty is a great wrong, and that the fishery rightfully belongs to these people; and I trust that measures will be at once taken to restore it to them.

For report of day-school see report of teacher, herewith transmitted.

I would also call attention to the report of physician, herewith transmitted.

Very respectfully, your obedient servant,

JOHN SMITH,
United States Indian Agent.

Hon. COMMISSIONER INDIAN AFFAIRS,
Washington, D. C.

73.

OFFICE GRAND RONDO INDIAN AGENCY, OREGON,
September 10, 1873.

SIR: I have the honor to submit this my second annual report of the condition of affairs of this agency.

The prominent features of progress apparent for the past year are an increased extent of Indian farms, many new houses, barns, granaries, fencing, and improvements of substantial character; also, an increased desire among the Indians to remain on the reservation and improve their places. Formerly it was their custom to leave their reservation early in the spring, spending most of the time around the small towns of the State until fall; now but few leave the reservation, and then only to work for the farmers in the vicinity.

The allotting of their lands in severalty was an event of great importance; the benefits are clearly shown in the satisfaction of the Indians, their industry, habits, and manifest desire to improve in every way. They now require assistance from the Government to aid them in building; want windows, doors, nails, hinges, &c.; also, agricultural implements, scythes, cradles, forks, &c. The articles named and a few groceries for the old and sick during the winter months is about all they require. In connection with this subject I beg to quote from the report of ex-Superintendent Hon. T. Odeneal, page 360 report of Indian commission, 1872, in reference to the wants of these Indians:

"In order to give them a proper start in the right direction, as they now enter upon this new era, (getting deed to their lands,) and place them upon a self-sustaining basis, it is very important that they at once be supplied with the means necessary to enable them to build, move, and repair houses, barns, and fences, and get such farming implements as they now need. For this purpose I would respectfully recommend that an appropriation of $8,000 be made. To aid them now in building and finishing houses suitable for the habitation of civilized people will prove a stimulus of inestimable value, and hasten the time when they can dispense with all Government aid and become self-supporting.

"This amount should be in addition to their annuities, and for the special purposes aforesaid. At least one-half, and perhaps two-thirds, of the lots of land which will be assigned in accordance with the survey have no buildings upon them. Most of the houses, which have been built in clusters, will have to be moved, and in order to do so many of them will have to be torn down and rebuilt. Quite a large number will have to build new houses, and all of them will have to do more or less fencing. This will of course cost them much labor and some money; the labor they can perform, and are willing to do it, but the money they have not; and without it their labor is nearly useless. Believing it to be the most economical thing the Government can do for them, and knowing it will best subserve the interest of the Indians, I take the liberty of urging the importance of making the appropriation aforesaid."

The foregoing suggestions are indorsed by me, and I respectfully commend them to you for the consideration which their importance merits.

It is conceded by all who are conversant with Indian affairs who have visited this agency, that the Indians here are far in advance of any other tribes of the Pacific coast; exhibit more thrift; evince a greater aptitude in agricultural pursuits; more ambitious in their improvements; in fact, come nearer the standard of civilization. They have been stimulated with the promise that the Government would help those who helped themselves, and whenever it has been possible I have assisted those that showed the most disposition to help themselves. The indolent have received no encouragement. I feel safe in saying that it would be difficult to find any community, of the same number, a more industrious people.

There yet exists one evil among them which is difficult to overcome, their medicine men and women. They are a source of great mischief, are generally cunning, scheming, and encourage the superstition of the Indians. They practice entirely upon the credulity of their patients, making believe that their success will be according to the fee they receive; the more the fee the more speedy the cure, which often results in their getting everything the patient possesses.

The majority of the Indians employ the resident physician; his efforts, however, are often unsuccessful from not being able to attend to the administering of his remedies and seeing that his patient receives proper food. A hospital is greatly needed; the establishment of one would speedily destroy the practice and influence of the Indian doctors. No more beneficial expenditure could be made than the building and maintaining of a hospital. A special appropriation of $1,500 is required. A similar suggestion was made in my last annual report, but failed to receive attention.

The school is a success; pupils have made great progress in their studies; the majority of those who have attended regularly during the year can read and write well, and many are proficient in elementary arithmetic and higher branches.

Could not accommodate all the children last year; school building too small. A new and large school-house is now being built; expect to have a much larger attendance the present year. From the school of this agency as now conducted incalculable benefits will accrue, not only to the children, but to the State. The tuition they now receive will make them useful citizens, men and women capable of filling any position in society, thoroughly understanding their duty to their God, their country, and society. A great change is manifested by the old Indians regarding schools; where they formerly opposed; they now encourage, and all evince great desire that their children shall receive its benefits.

The success of the school here is mainly attributed to the efficiency of the teacher,

Jas. Donnally, whose zeal and attention to the scholars is worthy of special commendation. He is greatly assisted by the Rev. Father Croquet, the missionary of the reservation, who has devoted the greater part of his life to the benefit of these Indians, and whose interest for them is unabated.

Under date of August 5, I addressed a communication to you in relation to the Coast Indians, who have never been recognized by the Government. They are anxious to be instructed in the pursuits of industry, have their children attend school, &c. Col. E. C. Kemble, of the Indian Department, made this agency a visit last month; arranged to return in October; will then have an interview with the leading Coast Indians and try and make some arrangements for their benefit.

Very respectfully, your obedient servant,

T. R. SINNOTT,
United States Indian Agent.

Hon. E. P. SMITH,
Commissioner Indian Affairs, Washington, D. C.

74.

UNITED STATES INDIAN AGENCY,
Siletz, Oreg., September 13, 1873.

SIR: In compliance with the requirements of the Department I have the honor to submit this my first annual report.

I assumed charge here April 1, 1873. At that time there existed a general feeling of alarm among the people in the vicinity, caused by the Modoc outbreak, and rumors of intended hostilities on the part of these Indians were everywhere rife.

Many of them had always lived at the fisheries on Yaquina Bay, just outside the reservation, and the state of public feeling had induced my predecessor to collect them all at the agency, abandoning in their haste the provisions they had prepared for their subsistence, and relying entirely on those living here for future support. The food prepared for winter use of the Indians at the agency was soon exhausted, and I was compelled to purchase and issue food till the potatoes were sufficiently grown to afford means of subsistence. This entailed a heavy expense on the second and third quarters of 1873, and has embarrassed my operations ever since.

Notwithstanding the advanced season when we arrived here, we have sown a much larger area of ground than ever before on this reservation, aggregating nearly or quite 1,100 acres, 1,000 of which are sown to wheat and oats and the remainder planted to potatoes. About 175 acres of this is on Government account and the rest belongs to the Indians. As many of them were destitute of teams we have been compelled to use those belonging to the Government to assist them in putting in their crops. The moisture of the climate here retards the ripening of the crops; and we are now in the midst of our harvest, which promises an abundant yield. The potatoes will prove a total failure. They gave every promise of an excellent crop, but the "potato rot" has developed itself and in all probability will destroy the whole. As this crop is the sole dependence of very many families for their winter subsistence, I fear much suffering will result.

The health of the Indians has generally been good, but for further particulars on this point as well as statistics of farming operations I refer to reports of Dr. Geo. W. Whitney and superintendent of farming, Wm. Bagley.

Two schools have been in operation a part of the summer, and a part of the time were well attended, with fair prospect of improvement. The Department has now provided for a manual labor school, which will be organized as soon as the necessary preparation can be made and from which I confidently expect the best results.

Since May last we have been favored with the presence and labors of the Rev. W. C. Chattin, engaged as teacher, and who has added to his duties the labors of a missionary, at such times as not engaged in his regular occupation. The results of his labors show what might have been accomplished had the present enlightened policy sooner prevailed.

These Indians have heretofore borne the character of being the most turbulent and disorderly in the State, and were so represented by Superintendent Meacham in his report for 1871. Notwithstanding this character and the little time they have been under the influence of Christian teaching, a church of over forty members has been organized, who show by their daily lives that they comprehend and feel the power of the religion they profess. The good accomplished cannot be measured by the number admitted to church membership. There is an influence proceeding from those who have embraced Christianity that is accomplishing much for the elevation of this people.

The position of agent here is peculiarly annoying by reason of old feuds and jealousies that are constantly breaking out, taking so much of the time of the agent to settle that little is left for his other duties. The reason for this may be found in the fact that these Indians are composed of some ten or twelve different tribes always hostile in the past, each one of which has injuries to avenge or outrages to atone.

One measure I would most urgently recommend, viz, the allotment of lands in severalty. This was promised the Indians some years since and the surveys were made, but the work was suddenly stopped and the land is yet undivided. This has caused much dissatisfaction among the Indians, which I could only allay by promising to designate tracts of lands which each family might cultivate provided the allotment was not made. There is nothing stimulates man to exertion like the consciousness that he is to reap the fruits of his labors himself; and, in my opinion, the allotment of these lands would do more to stimulate this people to improvement than any other one measure that could be adopted.

I would also respectfully recommend an appropriation for a saw-mill. The money we are compelled to expend for lumber to meet only the most pressing necessities would in two or three years pay the entire cost of a mill.

In conclusion, I desire to express my gratification at the evidences of improvement already made, and my hope that this people will continue to improve till they no longer need the care of the Government.

From the evidences I see on all sides of me, from the earnest desire I continually hear to improve their condition, and from their willingness to labor to this end as well as from the progress already made, I am led to the conclusion that a very few years of judicious care will place the Siletz Indians in a position where they will be fully capable of caring for themselves.

Very respectfully, your obedient servant,

J. H. FAIRCHILD,
United States Indian Agent.

Hon. E. P. SMITH,
Commissioner Indian Affairs, Washington, D. C.

75.

OFFICE KLAMATH INDIAN AGENCY, OREG., *September* 1, 1873.

SIR: I have the honor to submit this my second annual report of the condition of this agency.

The Modoc war, which commenced about the last of November and continued until near June, has kept this section of country in a continued state of excitement, in which the Indians upon this reservation have necessarily shared. Knowing, as they did, that the hostile band of Modocs were parties to the treaty in common with themselves, they have naturally taken a deep interest in everything pertaining to the war, as well as the efforts to make peace, and have, though falsely accused otherwise, been very anxious to avoid all implication in the difficulty themselves. Had there been any great dissatisfaction among them on account of ill-treatment in the past, as has been alleged by irresponsible parties, I have no doubt that some of them would have joined Captain Jack while he seemed so successful; but not one did so, and, so far as I can obtain proof, not one approved his course of action, and nearly all of them held themselves in readiness to render the Government any assistance in their power to secure peace, even to going on the war-path against the hostile band. Some fifty or sixty of the Klamaths did render very efficient service during the early part of the war in protecting settlers, and also in co-operating with the United States forces, both as regular militia and also as scouts.

These Indians have taken an unusual interest in agricultural pursuits during the past spring and summer; and, with the assistance of employés and the aid of Government teams, have cultivated more than twice the amount of land ever planted by them before; but the frequent heavy frosts during May, June, and July have destroyed the greater portion of their crops, so that they will gather little except a few acres of rye. This is very discouraging, and demonstrates still further the absolute necessity, which I have so often presented, of supplying them with cattle, before they can ever become self-supporting. The grain on the Government farms will not yield more than a half crop from the blighting effects of frosts. (For estimate of amount raised see Statistical Report.)

Thomas Pearne, an educated Indian belonging to the Yakima reservation, has been laboring with the Klamaths religiously during the past winter and spring, and some thirty-six have united with the church, and, with a few exceptions, are trying to lead Christian lives.

I had hoped to complete the necessary buildings in season to open a boarding-school last spring, but so much labor has been needed upon the mills and other agency buildings in order to render them suitable for employés, that it has been impossible to complete them. A neat, comfortable, and commodious school-house, capable of seating some forty pupils, is now finished, and a school boarding-house up and inclosed, and is being rapidly pushed toward completion, so that I hope to open a small school during the fall or early winter at furthest; but an additional appropriation for this object will be necessary to make this enterprise an ultimate success. Being fully convinced that a radical change in the Indian character can only be wrought in childhood and early youth, I would most respectfully urge the co-operation of the Government in the prosecution of this work of taking the children from their native haunts of degradation, and clothing, feeding, and teaching them the habits and arts of civilization. Without a special appropriation for this object, little can be done to emancipate them from the thrall of ignorance and superstition which characterizes their fathers.

The saw-mill has been thoroughly repaired at considerable cost, and the flouring-mill, which was not completed for want of sufficient funds, or lack of proper care in the use of the means appropriated, is being completed from the accumulated fund for "repair of mills," &c. I think it will be in running order late in the coming autumn, and when it shall be understood that we are prepared to manufacture flour, a large amount of grain will doubtless be raised and brought here for grinding from the Link River and Lost River Valleys. The saw-mill has been kept running whenever practicable, and beside furnishing all the lumber for agency purposes, has manufactured a large amount for Indians, for which they find a ready market at Fort Klamath and in the valleys below. They are very enterprising in this matter, and keep the mill well supplied with logs. They would willingly cut many more than can be sawed or sold.

At Camp Yainax, near the eastern boundary of the reservation, are located the Wohlpapee and Yahooskin Snakes, Schonchin's band of Modocs, and Ocheo's band of Pi-Ute Snakes. These Indians, unlike the Klamaths, make but little provision for their winter's subsistence, and, consequently, have to be fed by Government. The Modocs and Wohlpapee Snakes have taken a great interest in improving their little farms and commencing new ones this season under the supervision of Commissary O. C. Applegate; but frost has blasted their hopes also. Ocheo's band have been accustomed to go to their old country, about Camp Warner, at the opening of spring, where they support themselves through the summer by fishing, hunting, &c., and, as winter approaches, return to Yainax to be fed. These Indians are very much lower in the scale of humanity than the other tribes in Oregon, and adopt more slowly the manners and customs of civilized life. With these natural obstacles their progress in the arts of civilization must necessarily be slow. I have understood, but cannot say by what authority, that this band is to be taken to the new reservation on the Malheur. This I think Ocheo will oppose. He says he wishes to consider Yainax his home. This question should be settled at once, so that they may have a permanent home. Provision should also be made for their support, as well as for the Yahooskin and Wohlpapee Snakes. It is necessary that provision be made for a full corps of employés at Yainax, except a miller and sawyer.

Three of the Yahooskin Snakes, who have lived about Summer Lake much of the time for the last year or two, were killed by the settlers in May last under the following circumstances: During great excitement caused by false reports regarding Indian outbreaks, it appears that the citizens of Summer Lake and Che-wa-kan Valleys, who had forted up for defense, determined to arrest these Indians, believing that they were acting as spies for a large band of hostile Snakes reported to be in the vicinity, and ten men went out for that purpose. They found the Indians at Summer Lake, whither they had gone for the purpose of trading with the citizens, not knowing that the settlers had all left the valley. One of the Indians was shot and killed while trying to avoid capture by running, and the other two were killed while trying to escape after their arrest. On hearing of the affair, I immediately took Chocktoot, the chief of the band, and hurried to the scene of the difficulty, and, by prompt action, succeeded in quieting matters and avoiding further trouble; but Chocktoot still expects that something will be done to punish the parties engaged in the assault. He is not disposed, however, to make trouble about it.

The military road company lay claim to every odd section of land for three miles each side of their road which runs the whole length of the reservation, and they are now advertising those lands for sale. This matter needs attention at once to avoid trouble with the Indians, as the treaty gives them all the land inside the reservation lines. If the road company have the prior right, which they claim, it will be necessary to purchase their right, as the settlement of whites within the reservation limits would cause endless trouble if not open war. The lands in question embrace some of the finest portions of the reserve.

Very respectfully, your obedient servant,

L. S. DYAR,
United States Indian Agent.

Hon. E. P. SMITH,
Commissioner of Indian Affairs.

76.

ROUND VALLEY RESERVATION,
California, September 12, 1873.

SIR: In compliance with the regulations of the Department, I have the honor to submit this, my first annual report, as agent of the Round Valley (United States) Indian reservation. Assuming charge at this agency October 1, 1872, owing to the severe illness of my worthy predecessor, Hon. Hugh Gibson, and his absence from the reservation for a number of months previous to my taking charge, together with influences referred to in his last annual report, I found things in much disorder. However, by adopting and enforcing rigid discipline for a time, and using firmness in all my transactions, order was soon restored, and prosperity was at once manifest in every department of the reservation. From a careful census taken, we had June 30, 1873, one thousand one hundred and twelve Indians who actually make this reserve their home.

	Male.	Female.	Total.
Potter Valley Indians	178	201	379
Pitt River Indians	32	46	78
Red Wood Indians	40	61	101
Uki Indians	96	114	210
Wylackie Indians	17	16	33
Concow Indians	69	90	159
Little Lake Indians	64	88	152
	496	616	1,112

In addition to these there are two hundred or more who are more or less dependent on this reservation for protection, supplies, &c. I am pleased to be able further to inform you that a considerable number, since the above census was taken, have voluntarily come to the reserve, and continue coming. I am happy to report that the Indians here are, on the whole, contented and happy, quiet, orderly, and easily governed. The maintenance of a military post here is a needless expense, and the abolishment of Camp Wright would be a financial benefit to the Government.

EDUCATIONAL.

During the past year one school has been kept in operation all the time, with eighty pupils enrolled, and an average daily attendance of fifty. This number of scholars being too great in justice to either pupils or teacher, and there being more who ought and would attend school if they had an opportunity, by authority of B. C. Whiting, then superintendent, I employed a second teacher, and since July 1st have had two schools in operation. The advancement of the Indians in learning to read and write has been much greater than even the friends of the Indians expected, and to all a matter of profound gratification.

RELIGIOUS INSTRUCTION, ETC.

We have Sabbath-school and religious services every Sabbath, in which, I am pleased to say, the employés take an earnest, active interest. Miss Colburn, who now teaches one school, and Miss Burnett, who is engaged to teach the other, after the 1st of October next, are women of established character, as experienced, earnest, Christian workers in educational matters, and religious training.

SANITARY STATE OF THE INDIANS.

The health of the Indians has been much improved in general. First, because more houses have been built, and they sheltered from the inclemency of the weather during the severe storms of winter. Second, many of them have had bed-ticking issued to them, and have been induced to sleep on bedsteads instead of the ground; they are, therefore, less afflicted with colds, coughs, consumption, rheumatism, &c.; and thirdly, I have abolished all the sweat-houses on the reservation. A hospital, however, is needed more for their health and life than anything else in the sanitary department, aside from that of physician. Without a hospital and steward the sick cannot be properly cared for; medicine is not now and never will be regularly and properly taken by the sick, and I sincerely hope that an appropriation for this purpose will soon be made.

FARMING.

All the farming land has been cultivated, and that too in excellent condition. The yield has been over an average for this season; quite a sufficiency has been raised for the subsistence of the Indians, consisting of wheat, potatoes, corn, onions, tomatoes, melons, &c. The Indians have planted about fifty acres for themselves, which contributes largely to their comfort and contentment, and we hope the quantity of land cultivated by them next year will be much greater.

Owing to the cold, dry spring, and the prevailing high winds in early summer, our corn and buckwheat will be but light, yet we expect a sufficient quantity for our own use.

IMPROVEMENTS.

We have completed the school-house commenced by my predecessor, so as to make it suitable for school purposes. There has been about one hundred and thirty acres of land grubbed and put in a state of cultivation; nearly one mile of ditching and draining, thereby reclaiming some valuable land, adding much to the appearance and healthfulness of the reserve. One carriage-house has been built, one granary 72 feet by 30 feet completed, a carpenter, lumber and blacksmith shop combined commenced and frame erected; thirteen new Indian houses made of lumber and shakes, one frame-house, and one log-house, making fifteen new houses for the natives. A great deal of fencing has been relaid, a mile of new fence made, new gates made, roads straightened, laid off, made, and repaired, &c., more than we have space here to speak of in detail. Our store-house is removed to another and more convenient part of the reserve and refitted in good style. One new house built for the clerk, 24 feet by 27 feet in length, with porch in front, one story and a half high; material in part used from a house turned over to me by George J. Prising. If we had lumber with which to build, much needed improvement could yet be made before winter sets in. A hospital, a house for the agent, one for the miller, and a turbine wheel for the grist mill, are very much needed at present.

BOUNDARIES, LAND-MATTERS, ETC.

I am pleased to inform you that the commissioners sent here to locate the boundaries of this reserve, and appraise the improvements of settlers residing north of the township-line in this valley, did their work to the entire satisfaction of every person interested in the welfare of the reservation and Indians. When the settlers are paid for their improvements, and the Government gets possession of the land embraced in the new survey, we can reasonably expect greater prosperity than we have ever yet reached. I most respectfully request the Commissioner to cause the settlers to be paid at the earliest possible convenience, so that they can leave before winter sets in, and we be not deprived of the benefits of the land and range another year.

MISCELLANEOUS.

The number of animals has been quite insufficient for the proper cultivation of the land this year cultivated, and [for] herding of stock; and with the new territory soon to be added we will need several good work-mules and riding-horses for our herdsmen. We also need wagons, harness, and farming implements. I trust Congress will make an appropriation sufficient to place the reservation in such condition that we may accomplish all the objects for which it has been established, and thus make it a blessing to the Indians and an honor to the Government.

J. L. BURCHARD,
Indian Agent.

HON. E. P. SMITH,
Commissioner of Indian Affairs, Washington, D. C.

77.

TULE RIVER INDIAN AGENCY,
California, September 10, 1873.

SIR: I have the honor, in compliance with the requirements of the Indian Department, to submit this my third annual report of the condition of the Indian service at this agency.

During the past year the Indians at this agency have been well disposed, peaceable; and a marked improvement in their moral and domestic relations it is gratifying to note. The sanitary condition of the Indians during the past year has greatly improved.

At the date of my last annual report the number of Indians living at the agency was 374; there has been no material change in the number then reported. The

Indians not properly belonging to the agency, living in this and adjoining counties, are the Wichumui, Ke-a-wah, King's River and Kern River Indians, making an aggregate of 1,000 in number.

The more destitute among them have been furnished from this agency with subsistence and clothing to some extent. It is the purpose of the agent to remove the most destitute, dependent, and helpless of them to the new agency as soon as the improvements there will permit.

The Indian school has been taught seven months during the year. The want of a school-house during the first and second quarters necessitated the discontinuance of the school. The number of pupils in attendance was 62; average attendance, 26. Many of the children made excellent progress in their studies.

Sabbath-school has been held regularly every Sabbath during the year, and meetings for religious services on Wednesday evenings. The Indians are quite regular in their attendance, and the good results are observed in their daily deportment and their observance of the Sabbath.

The crops raised at the agency the present season are, owing to the severe drought, very light. Wheat raised, 815 bushels; hay, 36 tons. The barley-crop was an entire failure for grain, a portion only being cut for hay. Vegetables of all kinds failed for want of moisture; no rain has fallen here since the 24th of February ultimo. The Water-Ditch Company, which has heretofore supplied the agency with water for irrigation purposes for the right of way over the agency lands, refused this season to supply water for that purpose, and in consequence no vegetables could be raised.

The change of the agency to Government lands will have a beneficial and permanent influence for good on the Indians in many respects. Located comparatively at a distance from those disreputable persons who take every occasion clandestinely to furnish the Indians with whisky, it is anticipated that this evil can, in a great measure, be abated. The prospects of a fixed and permanent home for the Indians will have much to do in encouraging the Indians in habits of industry and frugality. They will take pleasure and pride in planting their vineyards and orchards, in cultivating their gardens, and their moral improvement and physical and intellectual development will increase with their improvements made with the labor of their own hands.

The recent survey of the new reservation has demonstrated beyond a cavil the value of the location for an Indian reservation, with arable lands sufficient for agricultural purposes, well watered, abundance for milling and irrigation; well adapted for grazing, and stock and sheep raising, with the best pinery in the southern portion of the State, where the labor of the Indians can be made productive in preparing the timber for building and fencing to supply the demands and wants of the citizens located in the adjacent valleys and plains.

Improvements are now being commenced at the new agency, and it is expected that the buildings will be in a state of forwardness so that the Indians can be removed and the rented lands at the present agency be abandoned and possession given to the owner by the 1st of November. When this shall have been effected, the condition of the Indians at the agency, and those living in this section of the State, will be materially improved, and a more rapid advancement toward a higher civilization can reasonably be anticipated.

Very respectfully, your obedient servant,

CHARLES MALTBY,
Indian Agent.

Hon. E. P. SMITH,
Commissioner of Indian Affairs, Washington, D. C.

78.

PAI-UTE RESERVATION,
Saint Thomas, Nev., November 30, 1873.

SIR: I have the honor to submit herewith my annual report.

The Indians of this agency are divided into thirty-one different tribes or bands, and are known among white men as Pai-Utes, but, among themselves and by other Indians by as many different names as there are tribes, each tribe taking the name from the land which they occupy.

The Pai-Utes have always been an agricultural people, and their history can be traced back for more than one hundred years, which sustains this statement.

I believed it to be important to know the actual condition and number of the Indians properly belonging to this agency, and felt sensible no organized effort agreeable with the present policy of the Government for improving their condition could be put forth without concentrating all the Indians at some place to be mutually agreed upon, as at present they are scattered over the southern half of Utah, Northern Arizona, Southern Nevada, and Southeastern California.

Accordingly, I made an extended visit one year ago to most of the various tribes or bands in this agency, and I discovered most of the Indians to be in a very destitute condition, especially those in Utah, Northern Arizona, and California, and all of them desirous to have land to farm, but none of the tribes possessing enough land to meet the necessities of one-fourth their number, and living in constant fear of losing even that.

When reduced to extremity for food and clothing, these Indians have been induced to part with their best farming-lands for a trifling sum, and to-day three-fourths of their number are vagabonds. There is but little game left in all this country, and the Indians are actually forced to beg or steal, save the few who can get a little land to cultivate, or find employment among white settlers a few weeks in the year at a mere nominal amount.

In my visit among some of these tribes, I received very important aid from Prof. J. W. Powell, of the Colorado exploring and geological surveying expedition, and was enabled more fully to impress upon the Indians the importance of abandoning their present nomadic life, and consent to go on a reservation. The present policy of the Government concerning the gathering of all nomadic Indians on reservations, and the management of the same, was very fully explained, which was the first time they had ever learned that the Government was willing to aid them to a better condition of life.

Farming.—The Indians very generally expressed their approval of the wishes of the Government; many were willing to comply at once with these wishes, so far as to abandon their present mode of life, cultivate the soil, and engage in stock-raising.

Six of these bands were gathered one year ago in the valley of the Moapa, and were each given a tract of land, and not possessing either plows or harness, their land was plowed for them by white men, the seed furnished, and, with some assistance from settlers, was planted in wheat, corn, barley, melons, and squashes.

The Indians afterward cultivated the crops, carefully watering the same by irrigation, and the following was the result:

	Bushels per acre.
Fifty acres of wheat averaged	30
Seventy acres of corn averaged	20
Five acres of barley averaged	40
Five acres of melons and squashes	

The value of these crops, estimated at the ruling prices in this section, would amount to over $7,000, but this amount is not to be compared to the value derived from the influence it has had on these Indians, as well as those who have visited them from California, Arizona, Utah, and other parts of Nevada. It has been a demonstration to these Indians that farming, managed as by white men, affords them a far better and easier livelihood than in the pursuit of their usual avocations; and the effect has been to create a desire among other bands of Pai-Utes to have the same opportunity of making a living by farming.

Having traveled extensively through most of the country inhabited by the Pai-Utes, and conferring fully with Prof. J. W. Powell and Maj. G. M. Wheeler, who are thoroughly acquainted with this entire country, I was satisfied there was but one valley that possessed a sufficient amount of arable land in which they could be gathered and any general system of farming or education inaugurated among them, and that was the Moapa or Muddy Valley, Southeast Nevada. In accordance with these observations, which were communicated to the Department, an Executive order was issued March 12, 1873, establishing a reservation embracing the Moapa and a part of the Rio Virgin Valley.

The appropriations for this agency were so small for the present year, but little was done that might have been, had the amount asked for a year ago been granted. I was authorized by a letter from the Department dated June 25, "to make such preparations for raising a crop the coming year as circumstances would admit." Purchasing some farming implements and detaching some of the horses from the special commission work, several of the Indians were at once set to work preparing the ground for a fall-crop, and in a few weeks over one hundred acres of wheat was planted in the lower valley by the Indians alone, and with the aid of some of the settlers about two hundred acres of wheat was planted in the upper valley, making nearly three hundred acres that are at present planted and growing finely. One-half of this wheat is for the Indians at present on the reservation, and the other half for those who are to be brought to the reservation the coming season.

The Indians now here are irrigating and otherwise caring for all the crops until harvested. It is my intention to put in, within a few weeks, as much more wheat, barley, and corn as there can be water secured to irrigate the same. The only difficulty in the way at present seems to be a want of funds to purchase mules, harness, and plows, as well as wheat, barley, and corn, for seed.

Education.—A school has been organized and been in successful operation for three months, a temporary teacher secured, and, for want of a better place, an abandoned adobe building is used as a school-house. There are at present twenty scholars whose attendance has been remarkably good, averaging fifteen since the organization of the school. The scholars come to the school at 9 o'clock in the morning and remain until 4 o'clock in the afternoon, there being an intermission of one hour for recess, at which time all receive a piece of bacon, a cup of flour, and a little tea. The scholars make the flour into bread and cook it outside the building at a camp-fire, at the same time preparing their piece of bacon and making their tea. This furnishes a pleasant diversion from their studies, and no doubt does much to secure regular attendance at school; by remaining at home they would get neither bacon nor tea, and it would be quite uncertain what they would get, if anything; and it would be more than probable the remainder of the day would be spent in hunting rabbits or birds.

The teacher is enthusiastic in his work and feels sanguine that the same number of white scholars, without previous training, could not present a better record for order or proficiency in studies. None of these scholars could tell one letter from another when they commenced attending school, and in six weeks after entering the school five of them could read words of four letters and *understand their meaning*. The black-board is used by the teacher in illustrating the lesson, and the scholars are taught to print their lessons on the same. It is my intention to adopt the Kindergarten system of instruction, as far as practicable, believing it to be specially adapted to interest and educate Indians.

I believe it would be a matter of economy if there was a liberal expenditure of means in this department of work among the Indians, and some general plan be chosen by the Government which should, perhaps with some modification, be adopted by the different Indian teachers whose services are paid by the Government. I am most thoroughly convinced of the importance of establishing industrial or manual-labor schools on all the Indian reservations. Such schools, liberally furnished, each school supplied with good, practical Christian women of experience as teachers, selected with a view of special fitness for this work, and if economically managed after they are once started, can be carried on with comparatively little more expense than under the present system. The education of the children will be more thorough and rapid than at present, and the influence on the parents and adult Indians most beneficial. The home influence, as at present, seriously counteracts that of the school. All missionary labor can be best promoted by control, first, of the female children, and putting them in training schools; second, of the boys, and teaching them far as possible skilled labor, and training them to intelligent habits at all times and by all means, whenever possible, teaching both old and young the meaning of English words.

A majority of all the Indians west of the Rocky Mountains at one time formed one great family, called "Numas," of which the Pai-Utes were a part, and the structure of their language is the same, and their customs and religion at present are very similar. All religious as well as other instruction imparted to these Indians in their own language not only fails to impress upon their minds a clear understanding of such instruction, but in many cases does not convey any idea whatever of the subject. To illustrate: there are no words in the Numa language to express a proper conception of the Supreme Being, Saviour, hell, heaven, forgiveness, soul, &c.

Employés.—The different religious denominations who have supervision of the selection of Indian agents and religious work among Indians should share with the agent the responsibility of selecting the employés on the different reservations, and, as far as practicable, active, religious men, specially fitted for the several positions to be occupied, should be chosen; more especially should this be the case in the selection of teachers who could properly fill the place of missionaries among most of the Indians of our country, at least until they have learned to understand the English language.

Believing the office of teacher among Indians second to no other, and, save that of farmer and physician, is of greater importance than all others, and that none but the most intelligent and experienced are capable of properly instructing Indians, and only such should be employed, I would urge upon this Department the importance of granting a compensation which will enable the agent to secure such persons.

Salt.—There are valuable salt mines on the reservation which no doubt can be made a source of revenue to this agency, and at the same time give employment to a large number of Indians, whose services could be obtained in consideration of supplies, which are now given them without equivalent.

Swamps.—The arable land can be increased one-third by the drainage of three swamps in the Moapa Valley; and another and important consideration would be the great increase of the water-supply, which is greatly needed.

Roads.—The roads leading to this reservation are in such a wretched condition most of the year, the cost of transportation is made an important item of expense, which can be reduced fully one-fourth, if the roads are put in good repair. This can be done with a small expenditure of money, especially the road north leading to Pioche.

Buildings.—There are quite a number of adobe buildings now on the reservation, most of which are occupied by settlers; and as soon as the claims of these settlers are paid by the Government, many of these houses can be used for agency purposes.

Hospital.—I believe the erection of a good hospital-building will not only do much to lead other Indians to this reservation who have agreed to come, but make them satisfied to remain after getting here; and, in this connection, I beg leave to submit observations of Dr. H. P. Geib, the physician of this reservation, who, while I was absent the past season acting as special commissioner in visiting other Indians, was placed in charge of the reservation, and is entitled to great credit for the manner in which he discharged his duties as physician, and, at the same time, superintended the farming operations. I would invite special consideration of the Department to his recommendations for hospital-supplies and the employment of Indian apprentices.

MEDICAL DEPARTMENT.

"Since my arrival on this reservation a part of my time has been occupied in super intending the farming arrangements, but mainly in looking after the physical condition of the Indians, providing such measures as would be likely to benefit them for the present and future.

"During the past summer there has been a great amount of sickness among the Indians of the reservation, principally of a malarious nature and origin, due to the several swamps that exist throughout the reservation. In the months of August and September at least one-third of all the Indians living in the valley were so afflicted; but by judicious management and proper treatment but one case of death occurred during the whole season. "The Indians undoubtedly appreciate the efforts made in their behalf to alleviate their sufferings and the cure of their ailments.

"Previous to the establishment of a medical department on the reservation the mortality among the Indians of the valley was very great. Many of their superstitious ideas regarding medical treatment and the power of medicine are being eradicated as they see the results of medical skill, and the proper care of those that are sick. As a rule, the Indians show but little attention to each other while suffering from any disease. I have endeavored to impress upon their minds, by daily examples of attention, the necessity of showing proper care to all of their number who were suffering from disease. I have every reason to believe that the measures employed by this department of the agency have been the means of establishing confidence between the officers of the reservation and the Indians under their charge, so that the future labors of yourself in their behalf will be easier of accomplishment.

"During the prevalence of malarious diseases the past summer and fall, owing to the great number who were sick, it was found necessary to provide temporary shelter for the sick. In the absence of a hospital-building, this was accomplished by erecting tents in the vicinity of the Indian camps, and transferring the Indians from their 'wick-ie-ups' to these tents as soon as the condition was as ascertained. The system of prescribing and furnishing medicines at the surgeon's quarters to those Indians who were slightly ill, and then allowing them to leave, was not successful. Many of them having superstitious ideas regarding the remedies employed, if they were not benefited immediately, would throw the medicine away. To obviate this difficulty, I established a rule to furnish no medicine to Indians to take away with them. If they are not sick enough to enter the hospital, they are required to report to the surgeon's quarters at a specified time, and receive the medicine directly from the acting hospital steward. All those who were on the sick-list received daily rations of flour, tea, &c. Messes are formed from those who are convalescent, who are required to do the cooking for the sick, under the direction of the surgeon.

"As before stated, most of the sickness has been of a malarious origin. But few cases of tuberculous disease have been brought to my knowledge. Venereal diseases exist to only a limited extent among the Indians on the reservation. Cases that have presented themselves have been communicated by Indians visiting the reservation from other sections of the surrounding country. Diseases of the eye are numerous, principally acute and chronic conjunctivities, no doubt caused by particles of paint or vermilion used by the Indians to paint their faces, and coming in contact with the surface of the eye, and by its irritation causing inflammation.

"The increased number of Indians to be located on the reservation the coming season will impose a heavy burden on this department of the agency, and as a matter of justice and humanity, as well as economy, I would earnestly recommend that a sufficient amount be appropriated for the erection of a hospital-building, and the purchase of medical supplies to be furnished this department.

"The assistance of an efficient hospital steward is required, to have charge of the dispensary department of the hospital, and also to perform such duties as he may be called upon to do in taking care of the sick. I would recommend the selection of one or more intelligent young Indians who understand and speak English fluently, if such can be found, to be employed by the physician in connection with the hospital, and, assisted by the hospital steward, made acquainted with the preparation of different medicines. I am persuaded such an apprentice or student could secure aid from some religious denomination, and in course of time be placed in a school where he could complete a medical education, and with it do much to remove the superstition now prevailing among Indians concerning 'medicine men.'

"I would also recommend that a sufficient amount of funds be appropriated for the purpose of a thorough drainage of the swamps, not only as a sanitary measure, but also for the purpose of securing the large amount of land that would be thus reclaimed and rendered fit for cultivation. Were this project carried out, I firmly believe that at least five thousand acres of arable land would be added to the reservation; and these swamps are the source from which arises the main causes of the vast amount of sickness among the Indians of this valley. There is no doubt in my mind, that if a thorough system of drainage were employed to reclaim these lands, the expenses of the medical department would be materially diminished in consequence."

NUMBER OF INDIANS.

The number of Indians belonging to this agency has been very largely overestimated, an actual census of which was taken by the special commission the past season, which shows the total number of Indians properly belonging to the agency to be 2,027, all of whom have signified their purpose of coming to the reservation as soon as means are provided for keeping them there. There are also about 300 Chem-a-hue-vis, now living in the Chem-a-hue-vis Valley, in Lower California. These Indians are intermarried, and affiliate with the Pai-Utes of this agency, and formerly lived among them; therefore should be brought to this reservation.

The report of the special commissioners, consisting of Professor J. W. Powell and the writer, will speak more fully of the advantages, necessities, and present condition of this reservation, and I would most respectfully ask the Department to give such consideration to the recommendations in this report as will relieve the reservation at the earliest practicable day of all the present settlers, whose presence is a source of serious embarrassment in the management of the reservation. Most of the settlers have already expressed a willingness to surrender their improvements and leave the reservation, as soon as their claims are paid.

Very respectfully, your obedient servant,

G. W. INGALLS,
United States Indian Agent.

Hon. E. P. SMITH,
Commissioner of Indian Affairs, Washington, D. C.

79.

Table showing number of Indians within the limits of the United States, (exclusive of those in property, the number of schools, and of the scholars and teachers

Name of agency and tribes.	Population.			Wealth in individual property.	Schools.		No. of scholars.	
	Male.	Female.	Total.		Number.	Location.	Male.	Female.
INDEPENDENT AGENCIES IN NEW YORK, MICHIGAN, WISCONSIN, MINNESOTA, AND IOWA.								
New York agency.								
Senecas, Onondagas, Oneidas, Cayugas, Saint Regis, Tuscaroras on eight reservations in State of New New York.	2,531	2,610	5, 141	$341, 856	28	On the reservations ..	676	583
Green Bay agency.								
Menomonees	728	752	1, 480	100, 000	2	Wolf and Oconto Rivers, Wisconsin.	45	37
Stockbridges and Munsees	110	131	241	18, 250	1	Red Springs, Wisconsin.	30	30
Oneidas	644	635	1, 279	200,000	2	Reservation, Wisconsin.	44	22
Sac and Fox agency, Iowa.								
Sacs and Foxes of the Mississippi	161	174	335	20, 000	....	No school	....	....
Michigan agency. (*a*)								
Ottawas and Chippewas	2,847	3,192	6,039	509, 373	2	Eagle Town and Cross Village.	75	77
Chippewas of Lake Superior	564	631	1, 195	1, 200	2	L'Anse and Barroga.	27	29
Chippewas, Ottowas, and Pottowatomies.	120	133	253	....	....	No school	....	....
Pottowatomies of Huron	23	27	50	....	....	No school	....	....
Chippewas of Swan Creek and Black River.	785	845	1, 630	40, 000	4	Nebesing and three other places.	57	58
La Pointe agency. (*b*)								
Chippewas of Fond du Lac, Boise Forte, Grand Portage, Red Cliff, Red River, Lac de Flambeau, and Lac Court d'Oreilles bands.	....	....	5, 125	....	....	....	....	....
Chippewa agency.								
Pillager, Mississippi, Pembina, and Winnebagoshish bands of Chippewas.	2,087	2,558	4, 547	....	3	On reservation	46	38
Chippewa Special agency.								
Chippewas of Red Lake band	464	677	1, 141	22, 225	1	Red Lake Agency	20	10
NORTHERN SUPERINTENDENCY IN NEBRASKA.								
Santee Sioux agency.								
Santee Sioux	412	505	917	19, 460	3	On reservation	80	40
Winnebago agency.								
Winnebagos	740	782	1, 522	100, 000	3	On reservation	160	90

(*a*) From report for 1872. No report received for 1873.
(*b*) From report for 1871. No report received since that year.

Alaska Territory,) on reservations, or embraced within an agency; their wealth in individual connected therewith; churches, members of church, &c.

No. of teachers.		Denomination in charge of schools.	Amount contributed by any religious society.	Amount contributed by individual Indians.	Number of missionaries and their names and denominations.	Number of Indians brought immediately under the civilizing influence of the agency.	Number of Indians who have learned to read during the year.	Number of school-buildings.	Number of church-buildings.	Number of church-members.	Number of Indians killed by members of their own tribe.	Number of Indians killed by hostile Indians.	Number of Indians killed by white men.	Number of white men killed by Indians.
Male.	Female.													
4	24	1 Episcopal..	$250	$611	Rev. Asher Wright, William Hall, George Ford, Presbyterians. Rev. T. Cornelius, William D. Buck, W. Smith, T. Shanandoah, Thomas La Forte, Methodists. Rev. T. D. Horton, John Griffin, Baptists.	5,141	208	28	12	547	1	....	....	....
2	1	Congregatn'l, Romanist.	....	....	Catholic priest at Keshena.	1,480	15	2	1	......	....	....	....	....
1	....	Presbyterian.	....	....	J. Slingerland, Presbyterian.	241	10	1	1	......	....	....	....	....
2	....	Methodist ... Episcopalian.	400 500	} 200 {	S. W. Ford, Methodist. E. A. Goodnough, Episcopal. }	1.279	20	2	2	480	....	....	....	....
....	....	....	....	....	....	......	....	....	....	......	....	....	....	....
2	1	Catholic.....	....	....	Rev. M. Herstret, J. Wiekamp.	......	....	....	....	......	....	....	....	....
2	....	Methodist & Catholic.	....	....	Rev. C. W. Austin, W. Terhost.	......	....	....	....	......	....	....	....	....
....	....	....	....	....	....	......	....	....	....	......	....	....	....	....
....	....	....	....	....	....	......	....	....	....	......	....	....	....	....
1	3	Methodist ...	....	....	Rev. John Irons...	......	....	....	....	......	....	....	....	....
....	....	....	....	....	....	......	....	....	....	......	....	....	....	....
2	6	Episcopal....	1,260	....	Rev. J. A. Gilfillian, Episcopal.	615	85	5	1	100	8	....	....	....
....	1	Congregat'n'l.	400	....	F. Spees, Congregational.	......	....	1	....	......	....	....	....	....
4	4	Congregational & Episcopal.	11,380	310	Thirteen missionaries, Congregational & Episcopal.	917	5	6	2	512	....	....	....	....
1	2	Friends	....	....	....	1,522	30	4	....	......	....	....	....	....

Table showing number of Indians within the limits of the United

Name of agency and tribe.	Population.			Wealth in individual property.	Schools.		No. of scholars.	
	Male.	Female.	Total.		Number.	Location.	Male.	Female.
NORTHERN SUPERINTENDENCY IN NEBRASKA—Continued.								
Omaha agency.								
Omahas	486	515	1,001	$75,000	3	On reservation	65	45
Pawnee agency.								
Pawnees	1,032	1,344	2,376	75,000	3	Pawnee agency	94	46
Great Nemaha agency.								
Iowas	114	107	221	3,000	1	At agency	33	28
Sacs and Foxes of Missouri	46	49	95	2,000	....	....	....	....
Otoe ageny.								
Otoes and Missourias	218	229	447	25,000	1	At agency	50	33
CENTRAL SUPERINTENDENCY FOR KANSAS AND INDIAN TERRITORY.								
Kicapoo agency.								
Kickapoos	135	139	274	$2,975	1	On the reservation	18	28
Kaw agency.								
Kaws	279	254	533	12,700	1	At agency	29	9
Pottawatomie agency.								
Pottawatomies	234	249	483	36,668	1	On reservation	20	14
Quapaw agency.								
Quapaws	119	116	235	17,803	1	On their reservation	33	12
Confederated Kaskaskias, Peorias, Piankeshaws, Weas, and Miamies.	102	115	217	60,938	1	On Peoria reservation	20	13
Ottawas of Blanchard's Fork, &c.	75	75	150	30,500	1	On their reservation	22	21
Eastern Shawnees	37	58	95	20,000	....	....	....	....
Wyandotts	116	115	231	45,000	1	On their reservation	42	40
Senecas	104	102	206	44,000	....	....	....	....
Black Bob Shawnees	40	45	85	1,000	....	....	....	....
Neosho agency.								
Great and Little Osages	1,474	1,351	2,823	425,000	1	Mission in Kansas	17	16
Wichita agency.								
Caddoes	....	....	401					
Wichitas	....	....	300					
Wacoes	....	....	140					
Tawacamies	....	....	125	....	2	On reservation	30	20
Keechies	....	....	106					
Delawares	....	....	61					
Ionies	....	....	50					
Penetethka Comanches	....	....	345					
Kiowa agency.								
Kiowas	....	....	2,000	200,000				
Comanches	....	....	2,198	401,425	1	At agency	24	26
Apaches	....	....	774	50,015				
Delawares	....	....	30	6,200				

States, exclusive of those in Alaska Territory, &c.—Continued.

No. of teachers. Male.	No. of teachers. Female.	Denomination in charge of schools.	Amount contributed by any religious society.	Amount contributed by individual Indians.	Number of missionaries and their names and denominations.	Number of Indians brought immediately under the civilizing influence of the agency.	Number of Indians who have learned to read during the year.	Number of school-buildings.	Number of church-buildings.	Number of church-members.	Number of Indians killed by members of their own tribe.	Number of Indians killed by hostile Indians.	Number of Indians killed by white men.	Number of white men killed by Indians.
2	1	Presbyterian.	$500	....	William Hamilton, Presbyterian.	1,001	16	4	1	38	....	....	....	....
1	9	Friends	....	....	....	......	....	3	....	20	....	70	....	....
....	2	Friends ...	....	....	....	221	40	1	....	......	....	....	....	....
			....	....	....	95	....	....	....	......	....	....	....	....
....	2	Friends	200	....	....	447	10	1	....	......	....	....	....	....
....	1	Friends......	$308	....	....	274	12	1	2	133	....	....	....	....
....	1	Friends......	300	....	....	533	8	2	....	......	....	....	....	....
1	....	Friends......	....	....	....	483	3	1	....	......	....	....	....	....
....	1	Friends...	235	....	....	235	20	1				....	....	....
1	....		....	....	....	217	9	....				....	....	....
1	....		200	....	....	150	5	1	..	50	1	....	....	....
....	....		....	....	....	95		....				....	....	....
1	....		250	....	....	231	40	1				....	....	....
....	....		....	....	....	206		....				....	....	....
....	....		....	....	....	85	....	....				....	....	....
6	6	Catholic.....	....	....	....	2,823	....	....	....	300	2	....	1	1
2	2	Friends......	....	....	....	1,183	....	2	....	......	....	....	....	....
2	1	Friends......	490	....	....	1,000	15	1	....	......	....	....	....	....

Table showing number of Indians within the limits of the

Name of agency and tribe.	Population.			Wealth in individual property.	Schools.		No. of Scholars	
	Male.	Female.	Total.		Number.	Location.	Male.	Female.
CENTRAL SUPERINTENDENCY FOR KANSAS AND INDIAN TERRITORY—Cont'd.								
Upper Arkansas agency.								
Cheyennes	1,000	1,200	2, 200	52, 500	1	At agency	34	29
Arapahoes	775	875	1, 650	45, 000				
Apaches	60	60	120	1, 500				
Sac and Fox agency.								
Absentee Shawnees	326	363	€89	42, 708	1	North Fork of Canadian.	14	10
Sacs and Foxes	246	201	447	36, 350	1	Deep Fork of Canadian.	10	8
Indians in Kansas without an agency.(a)								
Chippewas of Swan Creek, &c., Munsees or Christians.	28	28	56	5, 334	1	Moravian Mission	11	5
INDEPENDENT AGENCIES, *but attached to Central Superintendency so far as respects the fulfilling of certain treaty stipulations.*								
Cherokee agency.								
Cherokees	8, 817	8, 400	17, 217	5, 000, 000	63	In nine districts	865	1, 019
Choctaw agency.								
Choctaws	7, 500	8, 500	16, 000	3, 500, 000	50	Neighborhood schools, &c.	573	556
Chickasaws	3, 000	3, 000	6, 000	2, 000, 000	13	Neighborhood schools, &c.	217	213
Creek agency.								
Creeks	6, 000	7, 000	13, 000	....	34	National schools, &c.	300	400
Seminole agency.								
Seminoles	1, 120	1, 318	2, 438	400, 500	4	At Nobletown and other places.	94	63
INDEPENDENT AGENCIES IN DAKOTA.								
Sisseton Sioux agency.								
Sisseton and Wahpeton Sioux	682	852	1, 540	50, 000	5	At agency and other places.	104	57
Devil's Lake agency.								
Sisseton, Wahpeton, and Cut-Head Sioux.	434	586	1, 020	30, 000	1	At agency; not finished.	....	....
Grand River agency.								
Lower Yanctonai Sioux	.....	.....	2, 534	....	...	No schools	....	....
Upper Yanctonai Sioux	.....	.....	1, 386	....	...	do	....	....
Uncpapa Sioux	.....	.....	1, 502	....	...	do	....	....
Blackfeet Sioux	.....	.....	847	....	...	do	....	....
Cheyenne River agency.								
Two Kettle, Minneconjon, Sans Arc Sioux, and part of Blackfeet band.	.....	.....	6, 000	....	...	No schools	....	....

(*a*) From report for 1872; no report for 1873.

United States, exclusive of those in Alaska, &c.—Continued.

No. of teachers. Male.	No. of teachers. Female.	Denomination in charge of schools.	Amount contributed by any religious society.	Amount contributed by individual Indians.	Number of missionaries and their names and denominations.	Number of Indians brought immediately under the civilizing influence of the agency.	Number of Indians who have learned to read during the year.	Number of school-buildings.	Number of church-buildings.	Number of church-members.	Number of Indians killed by members of their own tribe.	Number of Indians killed by hostile Indians.	Number of Indians killed by white men.	Number of white men killed by Indians.
1	1	Friends				1,500	35	1			3		4	4
1	1	Friends				689	12	1						
1	3					447	10	2						
	1	Moravian			Levi Ricksecker	56		1						
29	36				Baptist, Methodist, Presbyterian.									
33	19				Baptist, Methodist, Presbyterian.			50	40	2,500	15			7
12	6				Baptist, Methodist, Presbyterian.			13	20	1,000	7			3
24	19		5,200		8 Presbyterian, 6 Methodist.									
1	3				2 Presbyterian									
4	1		1,100		6 Presbyterian	1,000		2	4	313	1			
					J. B. Genet, Catholic.	800		1	1	200				
					Catholic									
					do									
					do									
					do									

Table showing number of Indians within the limits of the

Name of agency and tribes.	Population.			Wealth in individual property.	Schools.		No. of scholars.	
	Male.	Female.	Total.		Number.	Location.	Male.	Female.
INDEPENDENT AGENCIES IN DAKOTA—Continued.								
Upper Missouri agency.								
Lower Yanctonai Sioux	670	530	1,200		1	At agency	12	8
Lower Brulé Sioux	935	865	1,800		1	do	10	10
Fort Berthold agency.								
Arickarees	473	623	1,096			No schools		
Gros Ventres	232	296	528					
Mandans	196	283	479					
Yankton agency.								
Yankton Sioux (*a*)			1,947		5	At agency and other places.		
Ponca agency.								
Poncas	383	355	738	18,000	1	At agency	20	15
Whetstone agency.								
Upper Brulé Sioux (*a*)	2,350	2,650	5,000			No schools		
Flandrau special agency.								
Santee Sioux (*b*)			100					
INDEPENDENT AGENCIES IN WYOMING.								
Red Cloud agency. (*c*)								
Ogallalla Sioux			6,320			No schools		
Northern Cheyennes and Arapahoes			2,857					
Shoshone agency.								
Eastern Band of Shoshones	489	535	1,024	65,000	1	At agency	38	14
INDEPENDENT AGENCIES IN IDAHO.								
Nez Percé agency.								
Nez Percés	1,322	1,485	2,807	225,000	2	Kamia and Lapwai	16	9
Fort Hall agency.								
Bannacks and Shoshones			1,500	12,000		No school		
INDEPENDENT AGENCIES IN MONTANA.								
Blackfeet agency.								
Blackfeet	1,200	1,800	3,000	40,000	1	At agency	10	15
Bloods	750	1,000	1,750					
Piegans	1,200	1,550	2,750					
Crow agency.								
Mountain Crows	1,400	1,600	3,000	200,000	1	At agency	28	34
River Crows	500	700	1,200	50,000				
Flathead agency.								
Flatheads	216	260	476		2	St. Ignatius mission	54	23
Pend d'Oreilles	420	600	1,020					
Kootenays	135	190	325					

(*a*) From report for 1872; no report for 1873. (*b*) No report received. (*c*) From report for 1872 and 1873.

United States, exclusive of those in Alaska, &c.—Continued.

No. of teachers. Male.	No. of teachers. Female.	Denomination in charge of schools.	Amount contributed by any religious society.	Amount contributed by individual Indians.	Number of missionaries and their names and denominations.	Number of Indians brought immediately under the civilizing influence of the agency.	Number of Indians who have learned to read during the year.	Number of school-buildings.	Number of church-buildings.	Number of church-members.	Number of Indians killed by members of their own tribe.	Number of Indians killed by hostile Indians.	Number of Indians killed by white men.	Number of white men killed by Indians.
1	1	Prot. Episc'l.	....	....	4 Prot. Episcopal.	....	....	1	....	....	1	....	....	....
1	1	....do	....	....		....	....	2	....	....	2	....	....	....
....	....	....	....	....	....	....	....	....	....	....	....	14	....	....
....	....	....	....	....	....	....	....	....	....	....	....	....	....	....
1	2	Prot. Episc'l.	....	....	3 Prot. Episcopal..	738	....	....	1	28	....	5	....	1
....	....	....	....	....	....	....	....	....	....	....	....	....	....	....
....	....	....	....	....	Congregation'l and Presbyterian.	....	....	....	....	....	....	....	....	....
....	....	....	....	....	....	....	....	....	....	....	5	35	7	....
1	....	Episcopalian	....	....	....	800	11	1	....	9	....	3	....	....
2	1	Presbyterian.	....	....	1, W. H. Spalding..	800	100	2	2	700	2	....	....	....
....	....	....	....	....	....	....	....	1	....	....	5	....	....	....
1	1	Methodist	....	....	....	....	25	1	....	....	90	42	....	2
1	....	Methodist.	....	....	....	62	6	1	....	....	1	7	....	....
....	....		....	....	....	....	....	....	....	....	....	....	....	....
1	2	Catholic	2,400	....	9 Catholics	1,821	12	2	10	....	1	8	....	....

Table showing number of Indians within the limits of the

Name of agency and tribe.	Population.			Wealth in individual property.	Schools.		No. of scholars.	
	Male.	Female.	Total.		Number.	Location.	Male.	Female.
INDEPENDENT AGENCIES IN MONTANA—Continued.								
Milk River agency. (*a*)								
Santee and Yanktonai Sioux	....	....	2, 625	....	....	No schools	....	....
Teton Sioux and roaming Indians	....	....	8, 000					
Fort Belknap special agency. (*a*)								
Assinaboines	....	....	4, 790					
Gros Ventres	....	....	1, 100	....	....	No schools	....	....
River Crows	....	....	1, 240					
Fort Lemhi special agency. (*a*)								
Mixed Bannack, Shoshones, and Sheep-eaters.	....	....	677	....	....	No schools	....	....
INDEPENDENT AGENCIES IN NEVADA, COLORADO, AND UTAH.								
Walker River and Pyramid Lake agency, Nevada. (*a*)								
Pah-Utes	....	....	6 000	....	....	No schools	....	....
Southeast Pah-Ute agency, Nevada.								
Pah-Utes	....	....	3, 000	....	....	No schools	....	....
Indians in Nevada not under an agent.								
Washoes, 500; Goship Utes, 204	....	....	704					
Shoshones	....	....	2, 000	....	....	No schools	....	....
Bannacks	....	....	1, 500					
White River agency, Colorado.								
Grand River Yampa and Uintah bands of Utes.	394	406	800	....	....	No school	....	....
Los Pinos agency, Colorado.								
Tabequache Utes	983	1, 307	2, 290					
Muache Utes	213	299	512	$150, 000	1	At agency	27	13
Capote Utes	66	81	147					
Weminuche Utes	110	140	250					
Denver special agency, Colorado.								
Pe-ah's band of Utes	....	....	350	....	....	No school	....	....
Uintah Valley agency, Utah.								
Uintah Utes	450	350	800	....	....	No school	....	....
Pah Vants, 134; Goship Utes, 256; Pah-Utes, 528; in Utah not under an agent.	....	....	918	....	....	....	....	....
INDEPENDENT AGENCIES IN ARIZONA.								
Colorado River agency.								
Mohaves on reservation	502	338	840	2, 500	....	No school	....	....
Mohaves not on a reservation	....	....	3, 000	....	....	do	....	....
Yumas not on a reservation	....	....	2, 000	....	....	do	....	....
Hualapais not on a reservation	....	....	1, 500	....	....	do	....	....
Chemehuevais not on a reservation	....	....	400	....	....	do	....	....
Pah-Utes in Northern Arizona	....	....	284	....	....	do	....	....

(*a*) No report for 1873.

United States, exclusive of those in Alaska, &c.—Continued.

No. of teachers.		Denomination in charge of schools.	Amount contributed by any religious society.	Amount contributed by individual Indians.	Number of missionaries and their names and denominations.	Number of Indians brought immediately under the civilizing influence of the agency.	Number of Indians who have learned to read during the year.	Number of school-buildings.	Number of church-buildings.	Number of church-members.	Number of Indians killed by members of their own tribe.	Number of Indians killed by hostile Indians.	Number of Indians killed by white men.	Number of white men killed by Indians.
Male.	Female.													
....	....	....	....	....	....	....	....	....	....	......	....	....	....	....
....	....	....	....	....	....	....	....	....	....	......	....	....	....	....
....	....	....	....	....	....	....	....	....	....	......	....	....	....	....
....	....	....	....	....	....	....	....	....	....	......	....	....	....	....
....	....	....	....	....	....	....	....	....	....	......	1	....	1	....
....	....	....	....	....	....	....	....	....	....	......	....	....	....	....
....	....	....	....	....	....	....	....	....	....	......	....	....	....	....
....	1	Unitarian....	....	....	....	2, 663	4	1	....	......	2	....	....	....
....	....	....	....	....	....	....	....	....	....	......	....	....	....	....
....	....	....	....	....	....	....	....	....	....	......	1	....	....	....
....	....	....	....	....	....	....	....	....	....	......	....	....	....	....
....	....	....	....	....	....	40	....	....	....	......	1	....	1	....
....	....	....	....	....	....	....	....	....	....	......	....	....	....	....
....	....	....	....	....	....	....	....	....	....	......	....	....	....	....
....	....	....	....	....	....	....	....	....	....	......	....	....	....	....
....	....	....	....	....	....	....	....	....	....	......	....	....	....	....
....	....	....	....	....	....	....	....	....	....	......	....	....	....	....

Table showing number of Indians within the limits of the

Name of agency and tribe.	Population. Male.	Population. Female.	Population. Total.	Wealth in individual property.	Schools. Number.	Schools. Location.	No. of scholars. Male.	No. of scholars. Female.
INDEPENDENT AGENCIES IN ARIZONA—Continued.								
Pima and Maricopa agency.								
Pimas	2, 025	1, 991	4, 016	....	1	Pima Village	32	24
Maricopas	167	143	310	....	1	Maricopa Village	15	22
Papago agency.								
Papagoes	3, 500	2, 500	6, 000	....	1	San Xavier del Bac	20	15
Moquis Pueblo agency.								
Moquis Pueblos, in seven villages, (*a*)	.....	.....	1, 700	....	1	....	41	19
Camp Apache and San Carlos special agency.								
White Mountain or Coyatero Apaches	587	927	1, 514	....	....	No school	....	....
Pinal Apaches	375	450	825	55, 000	....	do	....	....
Aravaipa Apaches	125	150	275					
Tonto Apaches	100	100	200					
Rio Verde special agency.								
Apaches	468	442	910	....	....	No school	....	....
Apache Yumas	359	281	640					
Apache Mohaves	279	229	508					
Chiricahua special agency.								
Northern and Southern Apaches	450	650	1, 100	18, 000	....	No school	....	....
NEW MEXICO SUPERINTENDENCY.								
Navajo agency and special agency.								
Navajoes	4, 310	4, 804	9, 114	....	....	No school	....	....
Mescalero Apache agency.								
Mescalero Apaches (*a*)	781	1, 114	1, 895	....	....	No school	....	....
Pueblo agency.								
Pueblos, in 19 villages	4, 041	3, 838	7, 879	$535, 750	5	In 5 villages	73	37
Southern Apache agency, Tularosa reservation.								
Southern Apaches	200	300	500	5, 000	....	No school	....	....
Abiquin or Tierra Amarilla agency.								
Capote Utes	100	140	240	....	....	No school	....	....
Weeminuche Utes	300	330	630	....	....			
Jicarilla Apaches	200	200	400	....	....			
Cimarron agency.								
Muache Utes	.....	.....	650	....	....	No school	....	....
Jicarilla Apaches	.....	.....	560	....	....			
INDEPENDENT AGENCIES IN CALIFORNIA AND OREGON.								
Round Valley agency, California.								
Pitt River, Potter Valley, Redwood Ukies, Wylackie, Concow, and Little Lake Indians.	500	619	1, 119	28, 000	2	At reservation	66	64

(*a*) From report for 1872.

United States, exclusive of those in Alaska, &c.—Continued.

No. of teachers.		Denomination in charge of schools.	Amount contributed by any religious society.	Amount contributed by individual Indians.	Number of missionaries and their names and denominations.	Number of Indians brought immediately under the civilizing influence of the agency.	Number of Indians who have learned to read during the year.	Number of school-buildings.	Number of church-buildings.	Number of church-members.	Number of Indians killed by members of their own tribe.	Number of Indians killed by hostile Indians.	Number of Indians killed by white men.	Number of white men killed by Indians.
Male.	Female.													
1	1	Ref'd Church.	$600	....	....	280	....	1	....	....	1	1	1	1
....	1	....do....	....	....	....	130	....	1	....	....	....	....	....	....
....	2	Catholic....	....	....	1, Catholic....	....	....	1	1	1,500	....	....	....	....
1	....	....	....	....	....	....	....	....	....	....	....	....	....	....
....	....	....	....	....	....	50	....	....	....	....	14	....	....	....
....	....	....	....	....	....	....	....	....	....	....	2	....	....	2
....	....	....	....	....	....	....	....	....	....	....	3	....	....	....
....	....	....	....	....	....	....	....	....	....	....	2	....	....	....
....	....	....	....	....	....	....	....	....	....	....	....	....	....	....
....	....	....	....	....	....	....	....	....	....	....	....	....	....	....
5	1	Presbyterian.	$1,200	....	....	2,595	73	5	....	....	....	....	1	....
....	....	....	....	....	....	500	....	....	....	....	5	....	3	....
....	....	....	....	....	....	....	....	....	....	....	....	....	....	....
....	....	....	....	....	....	....	....	....	....	....	....	....	....	....
1	1	Methodist Episcopal.	....	....	....	700	45	2	....	....	....	....	1	....

Table showing number of Indians within the limits of the

Name of agency and tribe.	Population.			Wealth in individual property.	Schools.		No. of scholars.	
	Male.	Female.	Total.		Number.	Location.	Male.	Female.
INDEPENDENT AGENCIES IN CALIFORNIA AND OREGON—Continued.								
(*a*) *Hoopa Valley agency, California.*								
Hoopas	290	435	725	5,000	1	At agency	44	30
Tule River agency, California.								
Tules and Tejons	149	168	317	5,600	1	At agency	30	32
Indians in California not embraced in an agency.								
Coahuila, Manache, Mission, and other Indians.	....	....	20,000	....	....	No school	....	....
Warm Springs agency, Oregon.								
Wascoes	154	134	288	49,000	1	At agency	65	10
Warm Springs	131	158	289	33,000				
Terrinoes	16	33	49	18,000				
Grand Ronde agency, Oregon.								
Molels, Clackamas, and other bands	465	459	924	8,000	1	At agency	49	25
Siletz agency, Oregon.								
Rogue River, and thirteen other bands.	....	....	1,058	....	1	At agency	25	15
Umatilla agency, Oregon.								
Walla-Wallas, Cayuses, Umatillas	370	467	837	170,000	1	At agency	16	10
Klamath agency, Oregon.								
Klamaths	242	330	572	23,200	...	No school	....	....
Modocs	42	58	100					
Wall-pah-pe Snakes	52	76	128					
Yahooskin Snakes	52	68	120					
Piute Snakes	80	120	200					
Alsea subagency, Oregon.								
Coos	53	70	123	10,000	....	No school	....	....
Umpquas	17	27	44					
Alseas	54	54	108					
Sinselaws	23	45	68					
Malheur special agency, Oregon.								
Roving Indians in eastern and south-eastern parts of the State.	....	....	1,200	....	....	No school	....	....
Indians roaming on Columbia River, Oregon.								
Renegades and others	....	....	3,000	....	....	No school	....	....
WASHINGTON TERRITORY SUPERINTENDENCY.								
Neah Bay agency.								
Makahs	294	310	604	$100,000	1	Neah Bay	12	1
Skokomish agency.								
S'Klallams	280	320	600	....	1	At agency	15	5
Twanas	125	150	275	....				

(*a*) From report for 1872.

United States, exclusive of those in Alaska, &c.—Continued.

No. of teachers.		Denomination in charge of schools.	Amount contributed by any religious society.	Amount contributed by individual Indians.	Number of missionaries, and their names and denominations.	Number of Indians brought immediately under the civilizing influence of the agency.	Number of Indians who have learned to read during the year.	Number of school-buildings.	Number of church-buildings.	Number of church-members.	Number of Indians killed by members of their own tribe.	Number of Indians killed by hostile Indians.	Number of Indians killed by white men.	Number of white men killed by Indians.
Male.	Female.													
....	1	Methodist Episcopal.	....	....	....	....	....	....	....	....	....	....	....	....
....	1	Methodist Episcopal.	....	....	....	317	18	....	....	8	....	....	....	....
....	....	....	....	....	....	....	....	....	....	....	....	....	....	....
1	....	....	....	....	....	575	35	2	....	340	....	2	....	....
1	1	....	....	....	....	700	50	1	1	600	....	....	....	....
1	....	Methodist Episcopal.	....	....	....	....	....	....	....	....	....	....	....	....
2	1	Catholic	....	....	1, Catholic	....	26	1	....	250	....	....	....	....
....	....	....	....	....	Methodist Episcopal.	600	1	1	....	36	....	....	....	....
....	....	....	....	....	....	....	....	....	....	....	....	....	....	....
....	....	....	....	....	....	....	....	....	....	....	....	....	....	....
....	....	....	....	....	....	....	....	....	....	....	....	....	....	....
....	2	Christian	....	....	....	....	....	....	....	....	....	....	....	....
1	1	Congregat'nl.	....	....	1 Congregational	300	5	1	1	....	1	....	....	....

Table showing number of Indians within the limits of the

Name of agency and tribe.	Population.			Wealth in individual property.	Schools.		No. of scholars.	
	Male.	Female.	Total.		Number.	Location.	Male.	Female.
WASHINGTON TERRITORY SUPERINTENDENCY—Continued.								
Yakama agency. (a)								
Yakamas	1,400	1,600	3,000	....	2	Fort Simcoe	34	14
Tulalip subagency. (a)								
D'Wamish and other allied tribes	1,698	1,902	3,600	90,775	1	Tulalip reservation	23	25
Quinaielt subagency.								
Quinaielts, Queets, Hohs, Quille-Utes	248	306	554	5,000	1	At agency	8	5
Colville special agency. (a)								
Colvilles, Spokanes, Pend d'Oreilles, Lakes.	1,717	1,632	3,349	90,400	1	Saint Francis Regis mission.	30	15
Puyallup reservation. (a)								
Nisquallys, Puyallups, and others	.....	.....	1,200	....	1	On reservation	....	....
Chehalis reservation. (a)								
Chehalis and other Indians	.....	.....	600	....	....	No school	....	....
INDIANS IN NORTH CAROLINA, TENNESSEE, GEORGIA, FLORIDA, AND TEXAS.								
Not under an agent.								
Cherokees, Seminoles, Lipans, Tonkaways.	.....	.....	2,000	....	....	....	....	....

(*a*) From report for 1872.

RECAPIT

Number of Indians in the United States, exclusive of those in Alaska Territory	295,084
Wealth of Indians in individual property	$16,082,155
Number of schools upon Indian reservations	285
Number of scholars in these schools, male, 4,792; female, 4,234	9,026
Number of teachers for these schools, male, 172; female, 185	357
Number of school-houses	167
Amount contributed by religious societies for support of schools	27,173
Amount contributed by individual Indians for support of schools	1,121
Number of missionaries among the Indians	91

United States, exclusive of those in Alaska, &c.—Continued.

No. of teachers. Male.	Female.	Denomination in charge of schools.	Amount contributed by any religious society.	Amount contributed by individual Indians.	Number of missionaries and their names and denominations.	Number of Indians brought immediately under the civilizing influence of the agency.	Number of Indians who have learned to read during the year.	Number of school-buildings.	Number of church-buildings.	Number of church-members.	Number of Indians killed by members of their own tribe.	Number of Indians killed by hostile Indians.	Number of Indians killed by white men.	Number of white men killed by Indians.
1	1	Meth. Epis.			1 Methodist									
2	2	Catholic												
1	1	Meth. Epis.												
1		Catholic												

ULATION.

Number of Indians brought immediately under the civilizing influences of the agencies	38, 637
Number of Indians who have learned to read during the year	1, 019
Number of church-buildings upon the reservations	103
Number of church-members, Indians	9, 664
Number of Indians killed by Indians of their own tribe during the year	178
Number of Indians killed by hostile Indians during the year	185
Number of Indians killed by whites during the year	20
Number of white persons killed by Indians during the year	21

81.

DEPARTMENT OF THE INTERIOR,
OFFICE INDIAN AFFAIRS,
November 1, 1873.

SIR: I have the honor to submit herewith my eighth annual report upon the Indian trust-fund business.

The general plan carried out in presenting this report is the same as adopted in 1869.

Tables Nos. I, II, and III, (purchase of bonds,) should be considered collectively; also the interest-tables on non-paying stocks.

All important transactions which have occurred since the 1st of November, 1872, are explained in detail.

Special attention is invited to the subject of non-paying State bonds, which will be treated upon in closing the report.

PURCHASE OF STOCKS.

No. I.—*Schedule showing the description, amount, cost, and date of purchase.*

Kind of bonds purchased.	Date of purchase.	Amount purchased.	Per cent.	Rate of purchase.	Cost of bonds, including commission.	Commission.	
						Rate.	Amount
United States loan of 1881	Nov. 4, 1872	$1,650 00	5	109½	$1,806 75	......	....
United States 10-40s	May 15, 1873	54,200 00	5	112⅛	60,839 50	⅛	$67 75
United States loan of 1865	Sept. 24, 1873	114,000 00	6	....	127,953 68	......	....
Do	Oct. 4, 1873	20,000 00	6	....	} 33,725 52	......	....
United States loan of 1868	....do	10,000 00	6	....			
United States loan of 1865	Oct. 23, 1873	9,500 00	6	110⅛	10,461 88	⅛	11 87
Do	Oct. 27, 1873	12,000 00	6	110¼	13,230 00	⅛	15 00
Do	Oct. 28, 1873	5,000 00	6	110⅛	5,506 25	⅛	6 25
Do	Oct. 30, 1873	44,000 00	6	110	48,400 00	⅛	55 00
Total		270,350 00			301,923 58		155 87

No. II.—*Schedule showing the tribes for which the bonds exhibited in Schedule No. I were purchased.*

Kind of bonds.	Amount.	Per cent.	Fund or tribe.	Amount to each.
United States loan of 1881	$1,650 00	5	Cherokee national fund	$704 31
			Cherokee school-fund	552 52
			Cherokee orphans' fund	211 29
			Chickasaw national fund	48 75
			Chippewa and Christian Indians	14 94
			Iowas	16 44
			Kaskaskias, Peorias, &c	76 45
			Shawnees	25 30
United States 10-40s	54,200 00	5	Sacs and Foxes of the Mississippi	54,200 00
United States loan of 1865	114,000 00	6	Cherokee national fund	3,161 48
			Cherokee school-fund	7,175 11
			Cherokee orphans' fund	27,415 06
			Cherokee asylum-fund	23,874 60
			Chickasaw national fund	50 95
			Chippewa and Christian Indians	4,454 74
			Choctaw general fund	1,781 90
			Choctaw school-fund	16,928 00
			Creek orphans	414 16
			Iowas	120 19
			Kansas schools	1,781 90
			Kaskaskias, Peorias, &c	97 04
			Menomonees	8,018 52
			Osage schools	6,236 63
			Ottawas and Chippewas	8,909 47
			Pottawatomies' education	890 94
			Sacs and Foxes of the Mississippi	905 41
			Senecas and Shawnees	1,783 90
United States loan of 1865	20,000 00	6	Cherokee orphans' fund	20,000 00
United States loan of 1868	10,000 00	6	Cherokee orphans' fund	10,000 00
United States loan of 1865	9,500 00	6	Cherokee orphans' fund	9,500 00
United States loan of 1865	12,000 00	6	Cherokee orphans' fund	5,542 29
			Cherokee asylum-fund	6,457 71
United States loan of 1865	5,000 00	6	Cherokee asylum-fund	5,000 00
United States loan of 1865	44,000 00	6	Cherokee asylum-fund	32,342 96
			Shawnees	11,657 04
Total	270,350 00			270,350 00

No. III.—*Schedule showing the sources from which the funds were derived for the investments exhibited in Schedules Nos. I and II.*

Kind of bonds.	Amount of purchase.	Per cent.	Tribe or fund.	Amount drawn for investment.	Sources from whence drawn.
United States loan of 1881	$704 31	5	Cherokee national fund.	$1,542 43	Fulfilling treaty: Proceeds of lands.
	552 52	5	Cherokee school-fund.	88 95	Trust-fund stocks redeemed, due.
	211 29	5	Cherokee orphans' fund.		
	48 75	5	Chickasaw national fund.	53 38	Fulfilling treaty: Proceeds of lands.
	14 94	5	Chippewa and Christian Indians.	16 36	Fulfilling treaty: Proceeds of lands.
	16 44	5	Iowas	18 00	Fulfilling treaty: Proceeds of lands.
	76 45	5	Kaskaskias, Peorias, &c.	83 71	Fulfilling treaty: Proceeds of lands.
	25 30	5	Shawnees	27 71	Fulfilling treaty: Proceeds of lands.
United States 10-40s	54,200 00	5	Sacs and Foxes of the Mississippi.	60,872 08	Fulfilling treaty: Payment for lands.
United States loan of 1865	3,161 48	6	Cherokee national fund.	33,893 75	Fulfilling treaty: Proceeds of lands.
	2,213 03	6	Cherokee school-fund.		
	948 44	6	Cherokee orphans' fund.		
	23,874 60	6	Cherokee asylum-fund.		
	486 14	6	Cherokee school-fund.	545 65	Fulfilling treaty: Proceeds of school-lands.
	4,475 94	6	Cherokee school-fund.	5,023 79	Trust-fund stocks redeemed, due.
	26,463 12	6	Cherokee orphans' fund.	29,702 23	Proceeds of Osage diminished reserve.
	3 50	6	Cherokee orphans' fund.	3 93	Proceeds of sale of orphans' bonds.
	50 95	6	Chickasaw national fund.	57 19	Proceeds of sale of Chickasaw national bonds.
	4,454 74	6	Chippawa and Christian Indians.	5,000 00	Proceeds of Missouri bonds redeemed.
	1,781 90	6	Choctaw general fund.	2,000 00	Proceeds of Missouri bonds redeemed.
	16,928 00	6	Choctaw school-fund.	19,000 00	Proceeds of Missouri bonds redeemed.
	414 16	6	Creek orphans	8 99	Fulfilling treaty: Proceeds of lands.
				455 86	Proceeds of sale of Creek orphans' bonds.
United States loan of 1865	120 19	6	Iowas	134 90	Fulfilling treaty: Proceeds of lands.
	1,781 90	6	Kansas schools	2,000 00	Proceeds of Missouri bonds redeemed.
	97 04	6	Kaskaskias, Peorias, &c.	24 48	Fulfilling treaty: Proceeds of lands.
				84 08	Proceeds of sale of Kaskaskias, &c., bonds.
	8,018 52	6	Menomonees	9,000 00	Proceeds of Missouri bonds redeemed.
United States loan of 1865	6,236 63	6	Osage schools	7,000 00	Proceeds of Missouri bonds redeemed.
	8,909 47	6	Ottawas and Chippewas.	10,000 00	Proceeds of Missouri bonds redeemed.
	890 94	6	Pottawatomies' education.	1,000 00	Proceeds of Missouri bonds redeemed.
	905 41	6	Sacs and Foxes of the Mississippi.	32 58	Fulfilling treaty: Payment for lands.
				983 65	Fulfilling treaty: Proceeds of lands.
	1,783 90	6	Senecas and Shawnees.	2 24	Fulfilling treaty: Proceeds of lands.
				2,000 00	Proceeds of Missouri bonds redeemed.
	20,000 00	6	Cherokee orphans fund.	33,725 52	Proceeds of Osage diminished reserve.
United States loan of 1868	10,000 00	6			

No. III.—*Schedule showing the sources from which the funds were derived for the investments exhibited in Schedules Nos. I and II*—Continued.

Kind of bonds.	Amount of purchase.	Per cent.	Tribe or fund.	Amount drawn for investment.	Sources from whence drawn.
United States loan of 1865	$9,500 00	6	Cherokee orphans' fund.	$10,461 80	Proceeds of Osage diminished reserve.
	5,542 29	6	Cherokee orphans' fund.	6,110 37	Proceeds of Osage diminished reserve.
	6,457 71	6	Cherokee asylum-fund.	7,119 63	Fulfilling treaty: Proceeds of lands.
	5,000 00	6	Cherokee asylum-fund.	5,506 25	Fulfilling treaty: Proceeds of lands.
	32,342 96	6	Cherokee asylum-fund.	35,577 25	Fulfilling treaty: Proceeds of lands.
	11,657 04	6	Shawnees	12,860 27	Proceeds of sale of Ottawa of Blanchard's Fork and Roche de Boeuf trust-fund bonds.
Total	270,350 00			302,017 47	

Statement of requisitions and refundments.

Date.	Requisition and refundment.	Amount drawn.	Amount invested and refunded.
1872.			
October 21	Requisition in favor of the Secretary of the Interior	$1,830 54	$1,806 75
December 27	Amount refunded by the Secretary of the Interior	....	23 79
1873.			
April 19.............	Requisition in favor of the Secretary of the Interior	60,872 08	60,839 50
June 28	Amount refunded by the Secretary of the Interior	....	32 58
October 4	Requisition in favor of the Secretary of the Interior	178,251 45	178,251 45
October 16	Requisition in favor of the Secretary of the Interior	61,063 40	61,025 88
October 30	Balance in hands of the Secretary of the Interior	....	37 52
	Total..	302,017 47	302,017 47

Section 4 of the general appropriation act of Congress, approved February 14, 1873, (Stat. 17, p. 462,) provides that there shall be set apart from the funds belonging to the Cherokee Nation the sum of $100,000 from the proceeds of lands sold to the Osages, $80,000 thereof to be invested as a part of the orphans' fund, and $20,000 to be expended for buildings and other improvements deemed necessary for the benefit of the institution for the orphans; and the sum of $100,000 from the proceeds of the strip of land in Kansas to be set apart for an asylum for the insane, deaf and dumb, blind, and indigent persons of the Cherokee Nation, $75,000 of which to be invested as a separate fund, and its interest semi-annually applied to the support of said institution, the remaining $25,000 to be expended for its establishment.

In accordance therewith $80,000 derived from the sale of lands to the Osages, and $75,000 from the sale of the Cherokee strip in Kansas, have been invested in United States registered six per cent. stocks; and of the stocks so purchased, $71,505.41 has been added to the orphans' fund, and $67,675.27 set apart as a separate fund for the Cherokee asylum.

No. IV.—*Statement showing the sale of bonds since November 1, 1872.*

Kind of bonds.	Per cent.	Fund or tribe.	Date of sale.	Amount sold.	Premium realized on amount sold.	Amount of commission.	Net proceeds of bonds sold.
			1873.				
United States loan of 1881	5	Cherokee national fund..	Jan. 31	$600 00	$81 00	....	$681 00
United States loan of 1867.	6	Ottawas of Blanchard's Fork and Roche de Bœuf.	May 21	21, 150 00	3, 859 87	$26 44	24. 983 43
United States loan of 1881.	5	Ottawas of Blanchard's Fork and Roche de Bœuf.	May 21	574 48	83 30	71	657 07
United States loan of 1881.	5	Chickasaw national fund.	May 21	50 00	7 25	06	57 19
United States loan of 1881.	5	Cherokee orphans	May 21	3 44	50	01	3 93
United States loan of 1881.	5	Creek orphans...........	May 21	398 57	57 79	50	455 86
United States loan of 1881.	5	Kaskaskias, Peorias, &c..	May 21	73 51	10 66	09	84 08
United States loan of 1881.	5	Pottawatomies, mills.....	Oct. 28	5, 000 00	375 00	6 25	5, 368 75
United States loan of 1881.	5	Pottawatomies, education.	Oct. 28	5, 000 00	375 00	6 25	5, 368 75
Total	...	....	....	32, 850 00	4, 850 37	40 31	37, 660 06

By the general appropriation act of Congress, approved February 14, 1873, (Stat. 17, p. 462,) the Secretary of the Interior was authorized to sell all the bonds then held in trust for the Ottawas of Blanchard's Fork and Roche de Bœuf, amounting to $21,724.48, and apply the proceeds of the sale in the manner prescribed by the terms of the sixteenth article of the treaty with the Senecas and other tribes of February 23, 1867. (Stat. 15, p. 517.)

The sixteenth article of the treaty, above referred to, provides for the sale of the west part of the Shawnee reservation to the Ottawas, at one dollar per acre; and for the purpose of paying for said reservation the United States shall take the necessary amount, whenever the area of such land shall be found by actual surveys, from the funds in the hands of the Government arising from the sale of the Ottawa trust lands, as provided in the 9th article of the treaty of 1862, and the balance of said fund, after the payment of accounts provided for in article 5 of the said treaty, shall be paid to the tribe per capita.

The area of the Shawnee lands sold to the Ottawas, by actual survey, is 14,860$\frac{27}{100}$ acres, which, at one dollar per acre, would produce the sum of $14,860.27. This sum, after deducting $2,000 advanced by the United States, as provided by the 8th article of the treaty of February 23, 1867, (Stat. 15, p. 515,) has been invested, in accordance with said 8th article of said treaty, in United States registered bonds, loan of 1865, for the benefit of the Shawnees, as will appear by reference to Schedules Nos. II and III, "Purchase of stocks."

The balance of the net proceeds of the Ottawa bonds, $10,780.23, after the payment of accounts hereinbefore referred to, is to be paid to the tribe per capita.

By the same general appropriation act, (Stat. 17, p. 452,) the Secretary of the Interior was also authorized to sell eighty-six twenty-one-hundred-and-eightieth parts of the several classes of bonds held in trust by him for the Pottawatomies, to carry out the provisions of the 3d article of the treaty with the Pottawatomies of November 15, 1861, as modified by the treaty of March 29, 1866, by paying to those members of the tribe who are entitled thereto under said treaty provisions their share of the tribal funds.

In compliance therewith the following amounts were sold, viz:

Of the education fund	$5,000 00
Premium realized on sale of the same	368 75
Total proceeds	5,368 75
Amount remitted to Superintendent Hoag, October 30, 1873, to pay 86 citizens their share of the proceeds of the sale, $3,211.89, and premium, $236.88...	3,448 77
Leaving a balance of this fund to be re-invested of..........................	1,919 98
Of the mill-fund	$5,000 00
Premium realized on sale of the same	368 75
Total proceeds	5,368 75

Amount remitted to Superintendent Hoag, October 30, 1873, to pay 86 citizens their share of the proceeds of the sale, $2,621.95, and premium, $193.37	$2,815 32
Leaving a balance of this fund to be re-invested of	2,553 43

The amounts shown in Table No. IV, sale of stocks, as sold and belonging to the Chickasaw national fund, Cherokee orphans' fund, Creek orphans, and Kaskaskias, Peorias, &c., being portions of a bond in which the Ottawas of Blanchard's Fork and Roche de Bœuf had an interest, were necessarily sold, in order to realize the amount belonging to the Ottawas.

The amounts realized by the sale of that portion belonging to the Chickasaws and others have been re-invested. (See Schedules Nos. I, II, and III, "Purchase of stocks.")

No. V.—*Statement showing the redemption of bonds since November 1, 1872.*

Kind of bonds.	Fund or tribe.	Date of redemption.	Amount redeemed.
Missouri State, Pacific Railroad 6 per cent. bonds.	Cherokee school-fund	Feb. 18, 1873	$2, 000 00
	Cherokee school-fund	Mar. 8, 1873	1, 000 00
	Cherokee school-fund	July 22, 1873	2, 000 00
	Chippewa and Christian Indians	July 22, 1873	3, 000 00
	Chippewa and Christian Indians	Aug. 16, 1873	2, 000 00
	Choctaw general fund	Aug. 16, 1873	2, 000 00
	Choctaw school-fund	Aug. 16, 1873	19, 000 00
	Kansas schools	Sept. 7, 1873	2, 000 00
	Menomonees	Sept. 7, 1873	9, 000 00
	Osage schools	Sept. 7, 1873	7, 000 00
	Ottawas and Chippewas	Sept. 7, 1873	10, 000 00
	Pottawatomies, education	Sept. 7, 1873	1, 000 00
	Senecas and Shawnees	Sept. 7, 1873	2, 000 00
	Total		62, 000 00

The proceeds of the above bonds were subsequently invested in United States 6s, loan of 1865, as will appear by reference to Schedules Nos. I, II, III, "Purchase of stocks."

No. VI.—*Statement of exchange of bonds.*

Date of exchange.	Amount exchanged.	Kind of bonds exchanged.	Amount received in exchange.	Kind of bonds received in exchange.
	$90, 000 00	Arkansas 6 per cent. coupon.	$90, 000 00	Arkansas 6 per cent. coupon, interest from Jan. 1, 1874.

Recapitulation of statements effecting aggregate of bonds held in trust, &c.

Whole amount of bonds reported on hand November 1, 1872			$4, 810, 716 83⅔
Amount of bonds since purchased, (see purchase of bonds, Schedules Nos. I, II, and III)	$270, 350 00		
Add amount of bonds received from the State of Arkansas in lieu of interest	78, 000 00		
		$348, 350 00	
Deduct amount of bonds sold, (as per statement No. IV, sale of bonds)	32, 850 00		
And amount of bonds redeemed, (as per statement No. V, redemption of bonds)	62, 000 00		
		94, 850 00	
			253, 500 00
Total amount on hand November 1, 1873			5, 064, 216 83⅔

INDIAN TRUST-FUND.

A.—*List of names of Indian tribes for whom stock is held in trust by the Secretary of the Interior, showing the amount standing to the credit of each tribe, the annual interest, the date of treaty or law under which the investment was made, and the amount of abstracted bonds for which Congress has made no appropriation, and the annual interest on the same.*

Tribe.	Treaty or act.	Statutes at Large.		Amount of stock.	Annual interest.	Amount of abstracted bonds.	Annual interest.
		Vol.	Page.				
Cherokee national fund	Dec. 29, 1835	7	478	$943,550 86	$55,183 92	$68,000 00	$4,080 00
Cherokee school-fund	Feb. 27, 1819 Dec. 29, 1835	7 7	195 478	520,134 64	29,576 75	15,000 00	900 00
Cherokee orphan-fund	Dec. 29, 1835 Feb. 14, 1873	7 17	478 462	248,600 51	14,836 35	....	....
Cherokee asylum-fund	Feb. 14, 1873	17	462	67,675 27	4,060 52	....	....
Chickasaw national fund	Oct. 20, 1832 May 24, 1834	7 7	381 450	1,261,996 $73\frac{2}{3}$	75,157 84	....	....
Chickasaw incompetents	May 24, 1834	7	450	2,000 00	100 00	....	....
Chippewa and Christian	July 15, 1859	12	1105	42,792 60	2,449 79	....	....
Choctaw general fund	Jan. 17, 1837	7	605	453,781 90	27,206 91	....	....
Choctaw school-fund	Sept. 27, 1830	7	333	50,355 20	2,701 31	....	....
Creek orphans	May 24, 1832	7	366	77,015 25	4,397 90	....	....
Delaware general fund	May 6, 1854	10	1048	435,283 90	24,544 03	....	....
Delaware school-fund	Sept. 24, 1829	7	327	11,000 00	550 00	....	....
Iowas	May 17, 1854 Mar. 6, 1861	10 12	1069 1171	107,463 43	6,617 37	....	....
Kansas schools	June 3, 1825	7	244	27,267 31	1,525 48	....	....
Kaskaskias	May 30, 1854 Feb. 23, 1867	10 15	1082 519	80,047 92	4,939 40	....	....
Kaskaskias, &c., school-fund	Feb. 23, 1867	15	519	44,700 00	3,129 00	....	....
Kickapoos	June 28, 1862	13	625	131,400 00	6,570 00	....	....
Menomonees	Sept. 3, 1836	7	506	153,457 41	7,753 05	....	....
Osage schools	June 2, 1825	7	240	40,236 63	2,074 20	....	....
Ottawas and Chippewas	Mar. 28, 1836	7	491	21,209 47	1,199 57	....	....
Pottawatomies, education	Sept. 26, 1833	7	431	86,390 94	4,328 46	1,000 00	50 00
Pottawatomies, mills	Sept. 26, 1833	7	431	15,000 00	750 00	....	....
Sacs and Foxes of the Mississippi	Feb. 18, 1867	15	495	55,105 41	2,764 32	....	....
Sacs and Foxes of Missouri	Mar. 6, 1861	12	1171	21,925 00	1,217 25	....	....
Senecas	June 14, 1836 Jan. 9, 1837	5 5	47 135	40,944 37	2,047 22	....	....
Senecas and Shawnees	June 14, 1836 Jan. 9, 1837	5 5	47 135	15,439 39	867 42	....	....
Senecas, Tonawanda band	Nov. 5, 1857	11	737	86,950 00	4,347 50	....	....
Shawnees	May 10, 1854 Feb. 23, 1867	15 15	515 515	16,492 69	941 20	....	....
Stockbridges and Munsees	Sept. 3, 1839	7	580	6,000 00	300 00	....	....
Total	....	....	......	5,064,216 $83\frac{2}{3}$	292,136 76	84,000 00	5,030 00

B.—*Statement of stock-account, exhibiting in detail the securities in which the funds of each tribe are invested and now on hand, the annual interest on the same, and the amount of abstracted bonds not provided for by Congress.*

Stocks.	Per cent.	Original amount.	Amount of abstracted bonds not provided for by Congress.	Amount on hand	Annual interest
Cherokee national fund.					
State of Florida	7	$13,000 00	....	$13,000 00	$910 00
State of Georgia	6	1,500 00	....	1,500 00	90 00
State of Louisiana	6	11,000 00	....	11,000 00	660 00
State of Missouri	6	52,000 00	$50,000 00	2,000 00	120 00
State of North Carolina	6	41,000 00	13,000 00	28,000 00	1,680 00
State of South Carolina	6	118,000 00	....	118,000 00	7,080 00
State of Tennessee	6	5,000 00	5,000 00	....	....
State of Tennessee	5	125,000 90	....	125,000 00	6,250 00
State of Virginia	6	90,000 00	....	90,000 00	5,400 00
United States, issue to Union Pacific Railroad, eastern division	6	156,638 56	....	156,638 56	9,398 31

B.—*Statement of stock-account, &c.*—Continued.

Stocks.	Per cent.	Original amount.	Amount of abstracted bonds not provided for by Congress.	Amount on hand.	Annual interest.
United States registered, act of June 30, 1864	6	$118,043 06	....	$118,043 06	$7,082 58
United States registered, act of March 3, 1865	6	87,507 75	....	87,507 75	5,250 46
United States registered, act of March 3, 1865, loan of 1867	6	161,950 00	....	161,950 00	9,717 00
United States funded, loan of 1881	5	30,911 49	....	30,911 49	1,545 57
Total		1,011,550 86	$68,000 00	943,550 86	55,183 92
Cherokee school-fund.					
State of Florida	7	7,000 00	....	7,000 00	490 00
State of Louisiana	6	2,000 00	....	2,000 00	120 06
State of North Carolina	6	21,000 00	8,000 00	13,000 00	780 00
State of South Carolina	6	1,000 00	....	1,000 00	60 00
State of Tennessee	6	7,000 00	7,000 00	....	....
State of Virginia: Chesapeake and Ohio Canal Company	6	1,000 00	....	1 000 00	60 00
United States, issue to Union Pacific Railroad, eastern division	6	51,854 28	....	51,854 28	3,111 26
United States loan of 10-40s	5	31,200 00	....	31,200 00	1,560 00
United States registered, act of June 30, 1864	6	24,672 50	....	24,672 50	1,480 35
United States registered, act of March 3, 1865	6	224,204 52	....	224,204 52	13,452 27
United States registered, act of March 3, 1865, loan of 1867	6	125,270 29	....	125,270 29	7,516 22
United States funded, loan of 1881	5	38,933 05	....	38,933 05	1,946 65
Total		535,134 64	15,000 00	520,134 64	29,576 75
Cherokee orphans' fund.					
United States, issue to Union Pacific Railroad, eastern division	6	....	....	22,223 26	1,333 40
United States registered, act of June 30, 1864	6	....	....	2,002 50	120 15
United States registered, act of March 3, 1865	6	....	....	156,981 67	9,118 90
United States registered, act of March 3, 1865, loan of 1867	6	....	....	49,545 00	2,971 50
United States registered, loan of 1868	6	....	....	10,000 00	600 00
United States funded, loan of 1881	5	....	....	7,848 08	392 40
Total				248,600 51	14,836 35
Cherokee asylum-fund.					
United States registered loan of 1865	6	....	....	67,675 27	4,060 52
Chickasaw national fund.					
State of Arkansas	6	....	....	168,000 00	10,080 00
State of Maryland	6	....	....	8,350 17	501 01
State of Tennessee	6	....	....	616,000 00	36,960 00
State of Tennessee	5¼	....	....	66,666 66⅔	3,500 00
State of Virginia: Richmond and Danville Railroad	6	....	....	100,000 00	6,000 00
United States registered loan of 1862	6	....	....	61,000 00	3,660 00
United States registered, act of June 30, 1864	6	....	....	131,631 94	7,897 92
United States registered, act of March 3, 1865	6	....	....	104,150 95	6,249 06
United States funded, loan of 1881	5	....	....	6,197 01	309 85
Total				1,261,996 73⅔	75,157 84
Chickasaw incompetents.					
State of Indiana	5	....	....	2,000 00	100 00
Chippewa and Christian Indians.					
United States registered, act of March 3, 1865, loan of 1867	6	....	....	26,562 38	1,593 74
United States registered, loan of 1865	6	....	....	4,454 74	267 28
United States funded, loan of 1881	5	....	....	11,775 48	588 77
Total				42,792 60	2,449 79

B.—*Statement of stock-account, &c.*—Continued.

Stocks.	Per cent.	Original amount.	Amount of abstracted bonds not provided for by Congress.	Amount on hand.	Annual interest.
Choctaw general fund.					
State of Virginia, (registered)	6			$450,000 00	$27,000 00
United States registered, loan of 1865	6			1,781 90	106 91
United States funded, loan of 1881	5			2,000 00	100 00
Total				453,781 90	27,206 91
Choctaw school-fund.					
United States registered, act of March 3, 1865, loan of 1867	6			1,427 20	85 63
United States registered, loan of 1865	6			16,928 00	1,015 68
United States funded, loan of 1881	5			32,000 00	1,600 00
Total				50,355 20	2,701 31
Creek orphans.					
State of Tennessee	5			20,000 00	1,000 00
State of Virginia: Richmond and Danville Railroad Company	6			3,500 00	210 00
State of Virginia: Chesapeake and Ohio Canal Company	6			9,000 00	540 00
State of Virginia registered certificates	6			41,800 00	2,508 00
State of Virginia registered, loan of 1865	6			414 16	24 85
State of Virginia funded, loan of 1881	5			2,301 09	115 05
Total				77,015 25	4,397 90
Delaware general fund.					
State of Florida	7			53,000 00	3,710 00
State of Georgia	6			1,500 00	90 00
State of Missouri	6			8,000 00	480 00
State of North Carolina	6			87,000 00	5,220 00
United States issue to Union Pacific Railroad, eastern division	6			49,283 90	2,957 03
United States registered, act of March 3, 1865	6			26,200 00	1,572 00
United States funded, loan of 1881	5			210,300 00	10,515 00
Total				435,283 90	24,544 03
Delaware school-fund.					
United States funded, loan of 1881	5			11,000 00	550 00
Iowas.					
State of Florida	7			22,000 00	1,540 00
State of Kansas	7			17,600 00	1,232 00
State of Louisiana	6			9,000 00	540 00
State of North Carolina	6			21,000 00	1,260 00
State of South Carolina	6			3,000 00	180 00
United States registered, act of March 3, 1865	6			5,220 19	313 21
United States registered, act of March 3, 1865, loan of 1867	6			7,000 00	420 00
United States funded, loan of 1881	5			22,643 24	1,132 16
Total				107,463 43	6,617 37
Kansas schools.					
United States registered, loan of 1865	6			1,781 90	106 91
United States registered, act of March 3, 1865, loan of 1867	6			14,430 16	865 81
United States funded, loan of 1881	5			11,055 25	552 76
Total				27,267 31	1,525 48
Kaskaskias, Peorias, &c.					
State of Florida	7			16,300 00	1,141 00
State of Louisiana	6			15,000 00	900 00

B.—*Statement of stock-account, &c.*—Continued.

Stocks.	Per cent.	Original amount.	Amount of abstracted bonds not provided for by Congress.	Amount on hand.	Annual interest.
State of North Carolina	6			$43,000 00	$2,580 00
State of South Carolina	6			3,000 00	180 00
United States registered, loan of 1865	6			97 04	5 82
United States registered, act of March 3, 1865, loan of 1867	6			3 85	23
United States funded, loan of 1881	5			2,647 03	132 35
Total				80,047 92	4,939 40
Kaskaskias, Peorias, &c. school-fund.					
State of Florida	7			20,700 00	1,449 00
State of Kansas	7			24,000 00	1,680 00
Total				44,700 00	3,129 00
Kickapoos.					
United States funded, loan of 1881	5			131,400 00	6,570 00
Menomonees.					
State of Tennessee	5			19,000 00	950 00
United States registered, loan of 1865	6			8,018 52	481 11
United States funded, loan of 1881	5			126,438 89	6,321 94
Total				153,457 41	7,753 05
Osage schools.					
United States registered, loan of 1865	6			6,336 63	374 20
United States funded, loan of 1881	5			34,000 00	1,700 00
Total				40,236 63	2,074 20
Ottawas and Chippewas.					
State of Tennesee	5			1,000 00	50 00
State of Virginia: Chesapeake and Ohio Canal Company	6			3,000 00	180 00
State of Virginia registered, act June 30, 1864	6			2,000 00	120 00
State of Virginia registered, loan of 1865	6			8,909 47	534 57
State of Virginia funded, loan of 1881	5			6,300 00	315 00
Total				21,209 47	1,199 57
Pottawatomies, education.					
State of Indiana	5			67,000 00	3,350 00
United States registered, loan of 1865	6			890 94	53 46
United States funded, loan of 1881	5			18,500 00	925 00
Total				86,390 94	4,328 46
Pottawatomies, mills.					
United States funded, loan of 1881	5			15,000 00	750 00
Sacs and Foxes of the Mississippi.					
United States, 10-40s	5			54,200 00	2,710 00
United States registered, loan of 1865	6			905 41	54 32
Total				55,105 41	2,764 32
Sacs and Foxes of the Missouri.					
United States registered, act of March 3, 1865	6			5,100 00	306 00
United States registered, act of March 3, 1865, loan of 1867	6			7,000 00	420 00
United States funded, loan of 1881	5			9,825 00	491 25
Total				21,925 00	1,217 25

B.—*Statement of stock-account, &c.*—Continued.

Stocks.	Per cent.	Original amount.	Amount of abstracted bonds not provided for by Congress.	Amount on hand.	Annual interest.
Senecas.					
United States funded, loan of 1881	5			$40, 944 37	$2, 047 22
Senecas and Shawnees.					
State of Missouri	6			1, 000 00	60 00
United States 10-40s	5			1, 000 00	50 00
United States registered, loan of 1865	6			1, 783 90	107 03
United States registered, act of March 3, 1865, loan of 1867	6			6, 761 12	405 67
United States funded, loan of 1881	5			4, 894 37	244 72
Total				15, 439 39	867 42
Senecas, Tonawanda band.					
United States funded, loan of 1881	5			86, 950 00	4, 347 50
Shawnees.					
United States, registered, loan of 1865	6			11, 657 04	699 42
United States funded, loan of 1881	5			4, 835 65	241 78
Total				16, 492 69	941 20
Stockbridges and Munsees.					
United States funded, loan of 1881	5			6, 000 00	300 00

C.—*Statement of stocks held by the Secretary of the Interior in trust for various Indian tribes, showing the amount now on hand; also abstracted bonds for which Congress has made no appropriation.*

Stocks.	Per cent.	Amount on hand.	Amount of abstracted bonds.
State of Arkansas	6	$168, 000 00	
State of Florida	7	132, 000 00	
State of Georgia	6	3, 000 00	
State of Indiana	5	69, 000 00	$1, 000 00
State of Kansas	7	41, 600 00	
State of Louisiana	6	37, 000 00	
State of Maryland	6	8, 350 17	
State of Missouri	6	11, 000 00	50, 000 00
State of North Carolina	6	192, 000 00	21, 000 00
State of South Carolina	6	125, 000 00	
State of Tennessee	6	616, 000 00	12, 000 00
State of Tennessee	5	165, 000 00	
State of Tennessee	5¼	66, 666 66⅔	
State of Virginia	6	698, 300 00	
United States loan of 1862	6	61, 000 00	
United States 10-40s	5	86, 400 00	
United States registered, act of June 30, 1864	6	278, 350 00	
United States registered, act of March 3, 1865, loan of 1865	6	740, 900 00	
United States registered, act of March 3, 1865, loan of 1867	6	399, 950 00	
United States registered, act of March 3, 1865, loan of 1868	6	10, 000 00	
United States issue to Union Pacific railroad, eastern division	6	280, 000 00	
United States funded, loan of 1881	5	874, 700 00	
Total		5, 064, 216 83⅔	84, 000 00

D.—*Statement of funds held in trust by the Government in lieu of investment.*

Tribes.	Dates of acts, resolutions, or treaties.	Statutes at Large.			Amount in the United States Treasury.	Annual interest, at 5 per cent.
		Vol	Page.	Sec.		
Choctaws	Jan. 20, 1825	7	236	9	$390,257 92	$19,512 89
	June 22, 1855	11	614	3		
Creeks	Aug. 7, 1856	11	701	6	200,000 00	10,000 00
	June 14, 1866	14	786	3	675,168 00	33,758 40
Delawares	Sept. 24, 1829	7	327	1	37,095 25	1,854 76
	May 6, 1854	10	1049	5		
Iowas	May 7, 1854	10	1071	9	57,500 00	2,875 00
Kansas	June 14, 1846	9	842	2	200,000 00	10,000 00
Kickapoos	May 18, 1854	10	1079	2	95,945 95	4,797 29
Miamies of Indiana	June 5, 1854	10	1099	4	221,257 86	11,062 89
Miamies of Kansas	June 5, 1854	10	1094	3	50,000 00	2,500 00
Osages	June 2, 1825	7	242	6	69,120 00	3,456 00
	Sept. 29, 1865	14	687	1	300,000 00	15,000 00
Pottawatomies	June 5, 17, 1846	9	854	7	168,123 85	8,406 19
Sacs and Foxes of the Mississippi	Oct. 2, 1837	7	541	2	200,000 00	10,000 00
	Oct. 11, 1842	7	596	2	800,000 00	40,000 00
Sacs and Foxes of the Missouri	Oct. 21, 1837	7	543	2	157,400 00	7,870 00
Seminoles	Aug. 7, 1856	11	702	8	500,000 00	25,000 00
	May 21, 1866	14	757	3	70,000 00	3,500 00
Senecas of New York	June 27, 1846	9	35	2 & 3	118,050 00	5,902 50
Shawnees	May 10, 1854	10	1056	3	40,000 00	2,000 00
Winnebagoes	Nov. 1, 1837	7	546	4	886,909 17	44,345 46
	Oct. 13, 1846	9	879	4	75,387 28	3,769 36
	July 15, 1870	16	355	......	78,340 41	3,917 02
					5,390,555 69	269,527 75
Delawares	July 12, 1862	12	539	......	423,990 26	21,199 51
Iowas	July 12, 1862	12	539	......	66,735 00	3,336 75
Kaskaskias, Peorias, &c	July 12, 1862	12	539	......	44,583 27	2,229 16
					535,308 53	26,765 42

The sum of $535,308.53 belonging to the Delawares, Iowas, Kaskaskias, Peorias, &c., as above stated, was placed to the credit of these tribes upon the books of the Treasury, in accordance with an act of Congress approved July 12, 1862, being equal to the sum originally invested in bonds abstracted from the custody of the Secretary of the Interior in 1860; said act authorizing the payment of interest on the same from July 1, 1862, at 5 per centum per annum in semi-annual payments.

The whole amount of bonds abstracted was $870,000, of which $83,000 belongs to the Cherokees. Interest upon this last sum is annually estimated for by the Indian-Office, Congress not yet having made any provision for the payment of the principal, to which fact special attention is invited.

E.—*Interest collected on United States bonds, payable in coin, and premium realized on coin sold.*

Fund or tribe.	Face of bonds.	Period for which interest was collected.	Coin interest.	Premium realized.
Cherokee national fund	$122,118 06	May 1, 1872, to Nov. 1, 1872	$3,663 54	$467 10
	30,807 18	Aug. 1, 1872, to Nov. 1, 1872	385 09	47 90
	242,221 27	July 1, 1872, to Jan. 1, 1873	7,266 64	862 91
	31,511 49	Nov. 1, 1872, to Feb. 1, 1873	393 89	50 71
	122,118 06	Nov. 1, 1872, to May 1, 1873	3,663 54	622 80
	30,911 49	Feb. 1, 1873, to May 1, 1873	386 39	65 69
	242,221 27	Jan. 1, 1873, to July 1, 1873	7,266 64	1,126 33
	30,911 49	May 1, 1873, to Aug. 1, 1873	386 39	60 37
			23,412 12	3,303, 81
Cherokee school-fund	28,525 00	May 1, 1872, to Nov. 1, 1872	855 75	109 11
	38,380 53	Aug. 1, 1872, to Nov. 1, 1872	479 75	59 67
	338,447 20	July 1, 1872, to Jan. 1, 1873	10,153 42	1,205 72
	38,393 05	Nov. 1, 1872, to Feb. 1, 1873	486 66	62 66
	31,200 00	Sept. 1, 1872, to Mar 1, 1873	780 00	116 02
	28,525 00	Nov. 1, 1872, to May 1, 1873	855 75	145 48
	38,933 05	Feb. 1, 1873, to May 1, 1873	486 66	82 73
	338,447 20	Jan. 1, 1873, to July 1, 1873	10,153 42	1,573 78
	38,933 05	May 1, 1873, to Aug. 1, 1873	486 66	76 04
	31,200 00	Mar. 1, 1873, to Sept. 1, 1873	780 00	63 38
			25,518 07	3,494 59

E.—*Interest collected on United States bonds, payable in coin, &c.*—Continued.

Fund or tribe.	Face of bonds.	Period for which interest was collected.	Coin interest.	Premium realized.
Cherokee orphans' fund	$12, 225 00	May 1, 1872, to Nov. 1, 1872	$366 75	$47 76
	7, 640 23	Aug. 1, 1872, to Nov. 1, 1872	95 50	11 88
	133, 846 82	July 1, 1872, to Jan. 1, 1873	4, 015 40	476 83
	7, 851 52	Nov. 1, 1872, to Feb. 1, 1873	98 14	12 64
	12, 225 00	Nov. 1, 1872, to May 1, 1873	366 75	62 35
	7, 851 52	Feb. 1, 1873, to May 1, 1873	98 14	16 68
	133, 846 82	Jan. 1, 1873, to July 1, 1873	4, 015 40	622 39
	7, 848 08	May 1, 1873, to Aug. 1, 1873	98 10	15 33
			9, 154 18	1, 264 86
Chickasaw national fund	296, 731 94	May 1, 1872, to Nov. 1, 1872	8, 901 96	1, 135 00
	6, 198 26	Aug. 1, 1872, to Nov. 1, 1872	77 48	9 64
	6, 247 01	Nov. 1, 1872, to Feb. 1, 1873	78 09	10 05
	296, 731 94	Nov. 1, 1872, to May 1, 1873	8, 901 96	1, 513 33
	6, 247 01	Feb. 1, 1873, to May 1, 1873	78 09	13 27
	6, 197 01	May 1, 1873, to Nov. 1, 1873	77 46	12 10
			18, 115 04	2, 693 39
Chippewa and Christian Indians	11, 760 54	Aug. 1, 1872, to Nov. 1, 1872	147 01	18 28
	26, 562 38	July 1, 1872, to Jan. 1, 1873	796 87	94 63
	11, 775 48	Nov. 1, 1872, to Feb. 1, 1873	147 19	18 96
	11, 775 48	Feb. 1, 1873, to May 1, 1873	147 19	25 02
	26, 562 38	Jan. 1, 1873, to July 1, 1873	796 87	123 51
	11, 775 48	May 1, 1873, to Nov. 1, 1873	147 19	23 00
			2, 182 32	303 40
Choctaw general fund	2, 000 00	Aug. 1, 1872, to Nov. 1, 1872	25 00	3 11
	2, 000 00	Nov. 1, 1872, to Feb. 1, 1873	25 00	3 22
	2, 000 00	Feb. 1, 1873, to May 1, 1873	25 00	4 25
	2, 000 00	May 1, 1873, to Nov. 1, 1873	25 00	3 91
			100 00	14 49
Choctaw school-fund	32, 000 00	Aug. 1, 1872, to Nov. 1, 1872	400 00	49 75
	1, 427 20	July 1, 1872, to Jan. 1, 1873	42 82	5 08
	32, 000 00	Nov. 1, 1872, to Feb. 1, 1873	400 00	51 50
	32, 000 00	Feb. 1, 1873, to May 1, 1873	400 00	68 00
	1, 427 20	Jan. 1, 1873, to July 1, 1873	42 82	6 64
	32, 000 00	May 1, 1873, to Aug. 1, 1873	400 00	62 50
			1, 685 64	243 47
Creek orphans	2, 699 66	Aug. 1, 1872, to Nov. 1, 1872	33 74	4 20
	2, 699 66	Nov. 1, 1872, to Feb. 1, 1873	33 74	4 34
	2, 699 66	Feb. 1, 1873, to May 1, 1873	33 74	5 74
	2, 301 09	May 1, 1873, to Aug. 1, 1873	28 76	4 49
			129 98	18 77
Delaware general fund	210, 300 00	Aug. 1, 1872, to Nov. 1, 1872	2, 628 75	326 95
	26, 200 00	July 1, 1872, to Jan. 1, 1873	786 00	93 33
	210, 300 00	Nov. 1, 1872, to Feb. 1, 1873	2, 628 75	338 45
	210, 300 00	Feb. 1, 1873, to May 1, 1873	2, 628 75	446 89
	26, 200 00	Jan. 1, 1873, to July 1, 1873	786 00	121 83
	210, 300 00	May 1, 1873, to Nov. 1, 1873	2, 628 75	410 74
			12, 087 00	1, 738 19
Delaware school-fund	11, 000 00	Aug. 1, 1872, to Nov. 1, 1872	137 50	17 10
	11, 000 00	Nov. 1, 1872, to Feb. 1, 1873	137 50	17 70
	11, 000 00	Feb. 1, 1873, to May 1, 1873	137 50	23 37
	11, 000 00	May 1, 1873, to Nov. 1, 1873	237 50	21 48
			550 00	79 65
Iowas	22, 626 80	Aug. 1, 1872, to Nov. 1, 1872	282 84	35 18
	12, 100 00	July 1, 1872, to Jan. 1, 1873	363 00	43 11
	22, 643 24	Nov. 1, 1872, to Feb. 1, 1873	283 04	36 44
	22, 643 24	Feb. 1, 1873, to May 1, 1873	283 04	48 12
	12, 100 00	Jan. 1, 1873, to July 1, 1873	363 00	56 26
	22, 643 24	May 1, 1873, to Aug. 1, 1873	283 04	44 23
			1, 857 96	263 34

E.—*Interest collected on United States bonds, payable in coin, &c.*—Continued.

Fund or tribe.	Face of bonds.	Period for which interest was collected.	Coin interest.	Premium realized.
Kansas schools	$11, 055 25	Aug. 1, 1872, to Nov. 1, 1872	$138 19	$17 19
	14, 430 16	July 1, 1872, to Jan. 1, 1873	432 90	51 41
	11, 055 25	Nov. 1, 1872, to Feb. 1, 1873	138 19	17 79
	11, 055 25	Feb. 1, 1873, to May 1, 1873	138 19	23 49
	14, 430 16	Jan. 1, 1873, to July 1, 1873	432 90	67 10
	11, 055 25	May 1, 1873, to Aug. 1, 1873	138 19	21 59
			1, 418 56	198 57
Kickapoos	137, 400 00	Aug. 1, 1872, to Nov. 1, 1872	1, 717 50	213 61
	131, 400 00	Nov. 1, 1872, to Feb. 1, 1873	1, 642 50	211 47
	131, 400 00	Feb. 1, 1873, to May 1, 1873	1, 642 50	279 22
	131, 400 00	May 1, 1873, to Aug. 1, 1873	1, 642 50	256 64
			6, 645 00	960 94
Kaskaskias, Peorias, Weas, and Piankeshaws.	2, 644 09	Aug. 1, 1872, to Nov. 1, 1872	33 05	4 11
	3 85	July 1, 1872, to Jan. 1, 1873	12	01
	2, 720 54	Nov. 1, 1872, to Feb. 1, 1873	34 01	4 39
	2, 720 54	Feb. 1, 1873, to May 1, 1873	34 01	5 78
	3 85	Jan. 1, 1873, to July 1, 1873	12	02
	2, 647 03	May 1, 1873, to Aug. 1, 1873	33 09	5 17
			134 40	19 48
Menomonees	126, 438 89	Aug. 1, 1872, to Nov. 1, 1872	1, 580 48	196 57
	126, 438 89	Nov. 1, 1872, to Feb. 1, 1873	1, 580 48	203 49
	126, 438 89	Feb. 1, 1873, to May 1, 1873	1, 580 48	268 68
	126, 438 89	May 1, 1873, to Aug. 1, 1873	1, 580 48	246 95
			6, 321 92	915 69
Osage schools	34, 000 00	Aug. 1, 1872, to Nov. 1, 1872	425 00	52 86
	34, 000 00	Nov. 1, 1872, to Feb. 1, 1873	425 00	54 71
	34, 000 00	Feb. 1, 1873, to May 1, 1873	425 00	72 25
	34, 000 00	May 1, 1873, to Aug. 1, 1873	425 00	66 40
			1, 700 00	246 22
Ottawas and Chippewas	2, 000 00	May 1, 1872, to Nov. 1, 1872	60 00	7 65
	6, 300 00	Aug. 1, 1872, to Nov. 1, 1872	78 75	9 79
	6, 300 00	Nov. 1, 1872, to Feb. 1, 1873	78 75	10 14
	2, 000 00	Nov. 1, 1872, to May 1, 1873	60 00	10 20
	6, 300 00	Feb. 1, 1873, to May 1, 1873	78 75	13 39
	6, 300 00	May 1, 1873, to Aug. 1, 1873	78 75	12 31
			435 00	63 48
Ottawas of Blanchard's Fork and Roche de Bœuf.	574 48	Aug. 1, 1872, to Nov. 1, 1872	7 18	89
	21, 150 00	July 1, 1872, to Jan. 1, 1873	634 50	75 35
	574 48	Nov. 1, 1872, to Feb. 1, 1873	7 18	92
	574 48	Feb. 1, 1873, to May 1, 1873	7 18	1 22
			656 04	78 38
Pottawatomies, education	23, 500 00	Aug. 1, 1872, to Nov. 1, 1872	293 75	36 54
	23, 500 00	Nov. 1, 1872, to Feb. 1, 1873	293 75	37 82
	23, 500 00	Feb. 1, 1873, to May 1, 1873	293 75	49 94
	23, 500 00	May 1, 1873, to Aug. 1, 1873	293 75	45 90
			1, 175 00	170 20
Pottawatomies, mills	20, 000 00	Aug. 1, 1872, to Nov. 1, 1872	250 00	31 09
	20, 000 00	Nov. 1, 1872, to Feb. 1, 1873	250 00	32 19
	20, 000 00	Feb. 1, 1873, to May 1, 1873	250 00	42 50
	20, 000 00	May 1, 1873, to Aug. 1, 1873	250 00	39 06
			1, 000 00	144 84
Sacs and Foxes of the Mississippi	54, 200 00	Mar. 1, 1873, to Sept. 1, 1873	1, 355 00	110 09

E.—*Interest collected on United States bonds, payable in coin, &c.*—Continued.

Fund or tribe.	Face of bonds.	Period for which interest was collected.	Coin interest.	Premium realized.
Sacs and Foxes of the Missouri	$9,825 00	Aug. 1, 1872, to Nov. 1, 1872	$122 81	$15 27
	12,100 00	July 1, 1872, to Jan. 1, 1873	363 00	43 11
	9,825 00	Nov. 1, 1872, to Feb. 1, 1873	122 81	15 81
	9,825 00	Feb. 1, 1873, to May 1, 1873	122 81	20 88
	12,100 00	Jan. 1, 1873, to July 1, 1873	363 00	56 26
	9,825 00	May 1, 1873, to Aug. 1, 1873	122 81	19 19
			1,217 24	170 52
Senecas	40,944 37	Aug. 1, 1872, to Nov. 1, 1872	511 80	63 66
	40,944 37	Nov. 1, 1872, to Feb. 1, 1873	511 80	65 89
	40,944 37	Feb. 1, 1873, to May 1, 1873	511 80	87 01
	40,944 37	May 1, 1873, to Aug. 1, 1873	511 80	79 97
			2,047 20	296 53
Senecas, Tonawanda band	86,950 00	Aug. 1, 1872, to Nov. 1, 1872	1,086 88	135 18
	86,950 00	Nov. 1, 1872, to Feb. 1, 1873	1,086 87	139 93
	86,950 00	Feb. 1, 1873, to May 1, 1873	1,086 87	184 77
	86,950 00	May 1, 1873, to Aug. 1, 1873	1,086 87	169 82
			4,347 49	629 70
Senecas and Shawnes	4,894 37	Aug. 1, 1872, to Nov. 1, 1872	61 18	7 61
	6,761 12	July 1, 1872, to Jan. 1, 1873	202 83	24 09
	1,000 00	Sept. 1, 1872, to Mar. 1, 1873	25 00	3 72
	4,894 37	Nov. 1, 1872, to Feb. 1, 1873	61 18	7 88
	4,894 37	Feb. 1, 1873, to May 1, 1873	61 18	10 40
	6,761 12	Jan. 1, 1873, to July 1, 1873	202 83	31 44
	4,894 37	May 1, 1873, to Aug. 1, 1873	61 18	9 56
	1,000 00	Mar. 1, 1873, to Sept. 1, 1873	25 00	2 03
			700 38	96 73
Shawnees	4,810 35	Aug. 1, 1872, to Nov. 1, 1872	60 13	7 48
	4,835 65	Nov. 1, 1872, to Feb. 1, 1873	60 45	7 78
	4,835 65	Feb. 1, 1873, to May 1, 1873	60 45	10 28
	4,835 65	May 1, 1873, to Aug. 1, 1873	60 45	9 45
			241 48	34 99
Stockbridges and Munsees	6,000 00	Aug. 1, 1872, to Nov. 1, 1872	75 00	9 33
	6,000 00	Nov. 1, 1872, to Feb. 1, 1873	75 00	9 66
	6,000 00	Feb. 1, 1873, to May 1, 1873	75 00	12 75
	6,000 00	May 1, 1873, to Aug. 1, 1873	75 00	11 72
			300 00	43 46
Total amount of interest on gold-bearing bonds			124,487 02	
Total premium realized on sale of the same				17,597 78

F.—*Interest collected on United States bonds, payable in currency.*

Fund or tribe.	Face of bonds.	Period for which interest was collected.	Amount collected.
Cherokee national fund	$156,638 56	July 1, 1872, to July 1, 1873	$9,398 32
Cherokee school-fund	51,854 28	July 1, 1872, to July 1, 1873	3,111 26
Cherokee orphans' fund	22,223 26	July 1, 1872, to July 1, 1873	1,333 40
Delaware general fund	49,283 90	July 1, 1872, to July 1, 1873	2,957 02
	280,000 00		16,800 00

G.—*Interest collected on certain State bonds, the interest on which is regularly paid.*

Fund or tribe.	Face of bonds.	Period for which interest was collected.	Amount collected.
MISSOURI STATE, HANNIBAL AND SAINT JOE RAILROAD BONDS.			
Cherokee national fund	$2,000 00	July 1, 1872, to July 1, 1873	$120 00
Delaware general fund	8,000 00	July 1, 1872, to July 1, 1873	480 00
KANSAS SEVEN PER CENT. BONDS.			
Iowas	17,600 00	July 1, 1872, to July 1, 1873	1,232 00
Kaskaskias, Peorias, Weas, and Piankeshaws school-fund.	24,000 00	July 1, 1872, to July 1, 1873	1,680 00
LOUISIANA 6s.			
Cherokee national fund	11,000 00	May 1, 1872, to May 1, 1873	660 00
Cherokee school-fund	2,000 00	May 1, 1872, to May 1, 1873	120 00
Iowas	9,000 00	May 1, 1872, to May 1, 1873	540 00
Kaskaskias, Peorias, Weas, and Piankeshaws	5,000 00	May 1, 1872, to May 1, 1873	300 00
	10,000 00	April 1, 1872, to April 1, 1873	600 00
MISSOURI STATE, PACIFIC RAILROAD 6 PER CENT BONDS.			
Cherokee school-fund	2,000 00	July 1, 1872, to Feb. 18, 1873	75 78
	1,000 00	July 1, 1872, to Mar. 8, 1873	40 85
	2,000 00	July 1, 1872, to July 22, 1873	126 90
Chippewa and Christian Indians	3,000 00	July 1, 1872, to July 22, 1873	190 35
	2,000 00	July 1, 1872, to Aug. 16, 1873	135 13
Choctaw general fund	2,000 00	July 1, 1872, to Aug. 16, 1873	135 13
Choctaw school-fund	19,000 00	July 1, 1872, to Aug. 16, 1873	1,283 67
Kansas schools	2,000 00	July 1, 1872, to Sept. 7, 1873	142 36
Menomonees	9,000 00	July 1, 1872, to Sept. 7, 1873	640 60
Osage schools	7,000 00	July 1, 1872, to Sept. 7, 1873	498 25
Ottawas and Chippewas	10,000 00	July 1, 1872, to Sept. 7, 1873	711 78
Pottawatomies, education	1,000 00	July 1, 1872, to Sept. 7, 1873	71 18
Senecas and Shawnees	2,000 00	July 1, 1872, to Sept. 1873	142 36
	1,000 00	July 1, 1872, to July 1, 1873	60 00
MARYLAND 6 PER CENT. BONDS.			
Chickasaw national fund	8,350 17	July 1, 1872, to July 1, 1873	495 16
	159,950 17		10,481 50

Statement of appropriations made by Congress for the year ended June 30, 1873, *on non-paying stocks held by the Secretary of the Interior for various Indian tribes.*

Bonds.	Per cent.	Amount of stock.	Amount of annual interest.
Arkansas	6	$90,000 00	$5,400
Florida	7	132,000 00	9,240
Indiana	5	69,000 00	3,450
North Carolina	6	192,000 00	11,520
South Carolina	6	125,000 00	7,500
Tennessee	6	104,000 00	6,240
Tennessee	5¼	66,666 66⅔	3,500
Tennessee	5	165,000 00	8,250
Virginia	6	581,800 00	34,908
Virginia	6	13,000 00	780
Total		1,538,466 66⅔	90,788

INTEREST ON NON-PAYING STATE STOCKS.

H.—*Collections made since November* 1, 1872, *due and unpaid July* 1, 1872, *and prior thereto.*

Date of collection.	Amount collected.	Period for which collected. From—	Period for which collected. To—	On what amount of bonds.	Kind of bonds.	Deposited in the Treasury to re-imburse the United States for money appropriated.
February 13, 1873	$29, 040 00	Oct. 1, 1862	Apr. 1, 1868	$88, 000	North Carolina	$29, 040 00
February 13, 1873	18, 480 00	Oct. 1, 1868	Apr. 1, 1872	88, 000	....do	18, 480 00
February 13, 1873	9, 900 00	Apr. 1, 1863	Apr. 1, 1868	33, 000	....do	9, 900 00
February 13, 1873	6, 930 00	Oct. 1, 1868	Apr. 1, 1872	33, 000	....do	6, 930 00
February 13, 1873	13, 266 00	July 1, 1863	Jan. 1, 1872	26, 000	....do	13, 266 00
June 5, 1873	12, 453 20	July 1, 1868	July 1, 1872	69, 000	Indiana	12, 453 20
Total	90, 069 20					90, 069 20
Whole amount collected and re-imbursed the United States on account of appropriations for fiscal year ending June 30, 1872, and prior thereto						90, 069 20

J.—*Collections of interest made since November* 1, 1872, *falling due since July* 1, 1872.

Date of collection.	Amount collected.	Period for which collected. From—	Period for which collected. To—	On what amount of bonds.	Kind of bonds.	Deposited in the Treasury to re-imburse the United States for money appropriated.	Amount carried to the credit of Indian tribes.
1873.		1872.	1873.				
Jan. 7	$15, 360 00	July 1	Jan. 1	$512, 000	Tennessee, Nashville and Chattanooga Railroad sixes.		$15, 360 00
Jan. 7	3, 000 00	July 1	Jan. 1	100, 000	Virginia, Richmond and Danville Railroad sixes.		3, 000 00
Jan. 7	105 00	July 1	Jan. 1	3, 500			105 00
June 5	1, 725 00	July 1	Jan. 1	69, 000	Indiana	$1, 725 00	
			1874.				
June 28	422 20		Jan. 1	90, 000	Arkansas	122 20	300 00
		1873.	1873.				
July 7	15, 360 00	Jan. 1	July 1	512, 000	Tennessee, Nashville and Chattanooga Railroad sixes.		15, 360 00
July 14	3, 000 00	Jan. 1	July 1	100, 000	Virginia, Richmond and Danville Railroad sixes.		3, 000 00
	105 00	Jan. 1	July 1	3, 500			105 00
Oct. 18	1, 725 00	Jan. 1	July 1	69, 000	Indiana	1, 725 00	
	40, 802 20					3, 572 20	37, 230 00

The amount brought upon the books of this office, from appropriations made by Congress, for interest on non-paying stock for the fiscal year ended June 30, 1873, as previously stated, was	90, 788 00
Deduct amount deposited in the United States Treasury to re-imburse the Government, as per above table	3, 572 20
Balance re-imbursable for the fiscal year ended June 30, 1873	87, 215 80

Recapitulation of interest collected, premiums, &c., as per tables hereinbefore given.

	Table No. 1.	Table No. 2.	Table No. 3.	Table No. 4.	Table No. 5.	Total.
Coin interest on United States bonds	$124, 487 02					$124, 487 02
Interest on United States bonds, (currency)		$16, 800 00				16, 800 00
Interest on paying State stocks			$10, 481 50			10, 481 50
Total interest collected on non-paying bonds due prior to July 1, 1872				$90, 069 20		90, 069 20
Total collected on non-paying bonds due since July 1, 1872					$40, 802 20	40, 802 20
Total interest collected during time specified						282, 639 92
Add premium on coin interest on United States bonds, (see Table No. 1)						17, 597 78
Total premium and interest						300, 237 70
Deduct amount refunded to the United States						93, 641 40
Balance carried to the credit of trust-fund interest due various Indian tribes						206, 596 30

In the annual trust-fund report of November 1, 1872, attention was invited to the complicated condition of many of the trust-fund accounts, and especially to the accounts with the Chickasaw Nation, and it was then suggested "that the honorable Secretary of the Interior be requested to call upon the Treasury Department to furnish this office with full and complete statements of all financial transactions on the part of the Government with the Chickasaw Nation from the origin of their trust-funds," &c.

In compliance with a request of the Department the Secretary of the Treasury has since transmitted official statements of the original investments made for the benefit of the Chickasaw Nation, with an exhibit of the changes since occurring in their stock and interest accounts, as appears upon the records of the Treasury Department.

The information thus obtained will enable this Department to determine any arrears or balances that may be due to said nation, or by them to the Government.

In justice to the members of the various tribes for whose benefit so extensive investments have been made, and for the purpose of simplifying the accounts with them, the Government should assume the State bonds now held in trust and issue in lieu thereof United States bonds.

The investments in State bonds, the greater portion of which are still held in trust, have proved unprofitable on account of their depreciation in value, and frequent suspensions or deferments of interest due the fund. The whole amount of State bonds held in trust is $2,332,916.83$\frac{3}{8}$, of which $1,984,466.66$\frac{2}{3}$ are classed as non-paying bonds.

The arrears of interest now due, and that will accrue on said bonds prior to July 1, 1874, amount to		$1,077,522 00
Of which amount there is due the tribes the sum of	$297,890 25	
Being arrears of interest embraced in estimates for the fiscal year ending July 1, 1873, in excess of appropriations made by Congress to cover deficiencies to that date, and the sum of	89,678 00	
		387,568 25
embraced in the estimates to cover arrears of interest on said bonds accruing during the fiscal year ending June 30, 1874.		
The balance		689,963 75

will be due the Government for moneys advanced for interest in default.

Whatever reasons may have formerly induced said investments, no good reasons now exist to justify the Government in continuing them, and it is specifically stipulated in nearly all treaties providing for the investment of any portion of the proceeds of the sale of Indian trust-lands, that the investments so authorized shall be in "safe and profitable stocks."

Very respectfully, your obedient servant,

LONSVILLE TWITCHELL,
Trust-fund Clerk, Indian Office.

Hon. EDWD. P. SMITH,
Commissioner of Indian Affairs.

82.

DEPARTMENT OF THE INTERIOR,
Office Indian Affairs, November 1, 1873.

SIR: I have the honor to submit herewith a report upon the various financial transactions relating to the receipts and disbursements of moneys received on account of sales of Indian lands.

Having been unable to complete an annual report on this branch of business in 1872, the transactions which occurred during the year ending October 31, 1872, will be stated preceding the account of the transactions occurring during the last twelve months.

In order to make the whole subject understood, if possible, by the members of the various tribes interested, and for the purpose of facilitating official business which may occur hereafter in connection with the same, all transactions referred to will be stated in detail, and fully explained with complete references to all treaties and acts of Congress, upon which official action has been based.

Statement of appropriation in accordance with the 3d article of treaty with Sacs and Foxes of Mississippi, of February 8, 1867, ratified July 25, 1868, in payment for lands ceded to the United States in accordance with 1st and 2d articles of said treaty, with an exhibit of disbursements therefrom.

	Warrant No. 358, for amount appropriated by act of Congress approved April 10, 1869.	$147, 393 32	
June 17, 1869	Drawn by J. D. Cox, for payment of certificates		$55, 000 00
October 15, 1869	Remitted to Enoch Hoag, superintendent		3, 920 30
October 25, 1869	do		12, 450 00
February 17, 1870	do		10, 000 00
March 10, 1870	do		7, 550 00
May 23, 1870	Refunded by Enoch Hoag, superintendent	3, 820 68	
August 31, 1870	Interior Department transfer-account, being amount paid to Superintendent Murphy on settlement of his account.		75 00
March 1, 1870	Drawn by Hon. C. Delano, Secretary, and trustee for payment of certificates.		5, 000 00
July 17, 1870	Remitted to Enoch Hoag, superintendent		5, 000 00
October 13, 1870	do		1, 312 13
June 13, 1872	do		10, 000 00
July 24, 1872	Refunded by Hon. C. Delano, Secretary, and trustee, (portion of $5,000 drawn March 1, 1871.)	1, 965 51	
October 31, 1872	Balance on hand		62, 872 08
	Total	153, 179 51	153, 179 51
November 1, 1872	Balance on hand	62, 872 08	
April 19, 1873	Drawn by Hon. C. Delano, Secretary of the Interior, for investment, per 3d article of treaty of February 18, 1867.		60, 872 08
June 28, 1873	Amount refunded by Secretary of the Interior, uninvested balance.	32 58	
October 4, 1873	Drawn by the Secretary of the Interior for investment		32 58
October 31, 1873	Balance on hand		2, 000 00
	Total	62, 904 66	62, 904 66

Account "fulfilling treaty with Chippewa and Christian Indians, proceeds of lands." Treaty of July 16, 1859. (Statutes at Large, vol. 12, p. 1105.)

Mode of sale.—The second article of the treaty provides for an appraisement at a reasonable value, and a sale at public auction to the highest bidder in excess of said appraisement.

November 1, 1871	Amount remaining on deposit in the United States Treasury, to the credit of the Hon. C. Delano, Secretary and trustee	$12, 935 65	
	Paid for advertising		$767 50
February 12, 1872	Drawn by Hon. C. Delano, Secretary and trustee, for investment in United States bonds		12, 168 15
July 19, 1872	Refunded by Hon. C. Delano, Secretary and trustee, being balance in his hands from amount drawn for investment.	16 36	
October 21, 1872	Drawn by Hon. C. Delano, Secretary and trustee, for investment in United States bonds		16 36
	Total	12, 952 01	12, 952 01

Account "fulfilling treaty with Pottawatomies, proceeds of lands." Treaty of February 27, 1867. (Statutes 15, p. 532.)

Mode of sale.—The eleventh article of the treaty provides for the sale to certain parties of 1,014 62-100 acres of land, at $1 per acre. Number of acres sold 1,014 62-100.

December 19, 1868	Amount received in payment therefor, by warrant No. 335.	$1, 014 62	
	By the second article of the above treaty, a contract was made on the 3d of September, 1868, with the Atchison, Topeka and Santa Fé Railroad Company, for the sale to said company of certain lands described in the fifth article of the treaty of November 15, 1861, said lands to be paid for at the expiration of five years from date of contract; interest on the purchase-money to be paid annually. In accordance with said contract the Atchison, Topeka and Santa Fé Railroad Company paid five annual instalments of interest on the purchase-money, amounting to	101, 630 05	
September 3, 1873	Amount received as final payments from the Atchison, Topeka and Santa Fé Railroad Company, in payment for 338,776 82-100 acres of land, at $1 per acre	338, 766 82	

Account "fulfilling treaty with Pottawatomies," &c.—Continued.

	Disbursements.		
	From the above receipts the following payments have been made, viz:		
	To 1,604 persons who have become citizens of the United States	....	$252, 321 84
	To 570 Indians, comprising the Prairie band of Pottawatomies	....	26, 838 28
October 30, 1873	Balance on hand as follows:		
	Amount belonging to the Prairie band...... $153, 856 29		
	Amount belonging to six persons, who have become citizens, but as yet are unpaid.... 1, 195 08		
	Amount required to re-imburse the United States, for money advanced, per act of Congress, approved May 29, 1872............ 7, 200 00	....	162, 251 37
	Total	$441, 411 49	441, 411 49

The number of acres of land originally sold to the Atchinson, Topeka and Santa Fé Railroad Company was 340,180.33; but it was subsequently ascertained that a few certificates were issued for tracts that had been allotted and patented to members of the tribe, in accordance with the provisions and reservations of the treaty.

The number of acres so certified to the railroad company was 1,413.51, thus diminishing the original number of acres to 338,766.82, and the amount in payment thereof to the sum of $339,766.82.

The railroad company, having paid four annual instalments of interest on the original sum of $340,180.33, were entitled to a rebate of $84.81 on each instalment so paid, making a total of $339.24, which sum was deducted by the company on final settlement with the United States.

The whole amount received in payment for lands sold to the company was, principal, $338,766.82; and interest, $101,630.05; total, $440,396.87.

Congress having, by the act of May 29, 1872, (Stat. 17, p. 179,) appropriated the sum of $7,200 to carry out the provisions of the 4th article of the treaty of November 15, 1861, by paying to those members of the tribe who were entitled to allotments of eighty acres of land each, the cash value of the same, the said amount to be re-imbursed from the proceeds of the sales of the Pottawatomie lands, that amount should be reimbursed the United States on account of said appropriation, from the balance now on hand under head of account, "fulfilling treaty with Pottawatomies—proceeds of lands."

Account "fulfilling treaty with Osages, proceeds of lands." Second article treaty September 29, 1865. (*Stat. at Large, vol.* 14, *p.* 688,) *and section* 12 *act July* 15, 1870. (*Stat. at Large, vol.* 16, *p.* 362.)

Mode of sale.—Under the direction of the General Land-Office.

	The account stood upon the books of the Indian-Office, November 1, 1871, as follows, viz:		
	Amount brought upon the books under this head of account	$348, 701 05	
	Paid for expenses of surveys, &c	....	$16, 563 16
	Balance at that date	....	332, 137 89
		348, 701 05	348, 701 05
	Account for year ending October 31, 1872:		
November 1, 1871	Balance on hand	332, 137 89	
December 2, 1871	Warrant No. 501, from sales of land	21, 346 99	
May 11, 1872	Warrant No. 516, from sales of land	51, 854 81	
September 16, 1872	Warrant No. 541, from sales of land	71, 214 71	
March 6, 1872	Paid for expenses of surveys	....	435 64
October 31, 1872	Leaving a balance of	....	476, 118 76
		476, 554 40	476, 554 40
November 1, 1872	Balance on hand	476, 118 76	
November 26, 1872	Warrant No. 544, from sales of land	15, 630 62	
December 12, 1872	Warrant No. 554, from sales of land	10, 039 79	
January 31, 1873	Warrant No. 561, from sales of land	30, 062 88	
June 30, 1873	Warrant No. 583, from sales of land	25, 000 00	
October 31, 1873	Balance on hand	....	556, 852 06
		556, 852 06	556, 852 06

The following abstract from an official statement received from the General Land-Office will exhibit the net amount realized from sales of the Osage Indian trust-lands, sold in accordance with the provisions of the 2d article of the treaty, and of act of Congress above referred to. The amounts stated as gross receipts include interest on deferred payments authorized by act of May 9, 1872:

From January 6, 1868, to November 1, 1870.	Gross receipts	....	$107,719 40
	Expense of surveys	$88,516 76	
	Expenses incident to sale to October 1, 1870	1,133 41	
			89,650 17
			18,069 23
From November 1, 1870, to November 1, 1871.	Gross receipts	701,860 41	
	Expense of surveying diminished reserve .. $75,435 64		
	Expenses incident to sale to October 1, 1871. 1,505 80		
		76,941 44	
			624,918 97
From November 1, 1871, to November 1, 1872.	Gross receipts	812,088 56	
	Expenses incident to sale to October 1, 1872	1,720 00	
			810,368 56
From November 1, 1872, to November 1, 1873.	Gross receipts	533,078 28	
	Expenses incident to sale to October 1, 1873	2,762 60	
			530,315 68
	Total net receipts		1,983,672 44

Account "fulfilling treaty with Shawnees, proceeds of lands."

Treaty or act.—By authority of resolution of Congress, approved April 7, 1869.
Mode of sale.—Under the direction of General Land-Office.

November 1, 1871	Balance on hand, being amount refunded by Hon. J. D. Cox from funds drawn December 6, 1869, for investment in United States bonds	$77 71	....
October 21, 1872	Amount drawn by Hon. C. Delano, Secretary and trustee, for investment in United States bonds	....	$27 71
October 31, 1872	Balance on hand	....	50 00
	Total	77 71	77 71
November 1, 1872	Balance on hand	50 00	....
August 13, 1873	Carried to the Treasury of the United States by surplus warrant No. 586	....	50 00
	Total	50 00	50 00

Account "fulfilling treaty with Ottawas of Blanchard's Fork and Roche de Bœuf, proceeds of land."

November 1, 1871	Balance on hand, being portion of amount received from the Ottawa University	$56 00	....
May —, 1872	Drawn by Hon. C. Delano, Secretary and trustee, for investment in United States bonds	....	$56 00
July 24, 1872	Refunded by Hon. C. Delano, being balance from amount drawn in May, uninvested	1 67	....
October 31, 1872	Balance on hand at this date	....	1 67
	Total	57 67	57 67
November 1, 1872	Balance on hand	1 67	....
April 28, 1873	Amount paid Treasurer of the United States on account of internal-revenue tax	....	1 67
	Total	1 67	1 67

Account "fulfilling treaty with Sacs and Foxes of Missouri, proceeds of land."

Treaty.—March 6, 1861, (Stat. at Large, vol. 12, p. 1171.)
Mode of sale.—Upon sealed proposals invited by advertisement, no sale to be less than $1.25 per acre.

November 1, 1871	Balance on hand	$216 06	
April 30, 1872	Warrant No. 514, sale of land	22, 989 61	
June 19, 1872	Refunded by Hon. C. Delano, Secretary and trustee, uninvested balance	3 10	
	Paid for advertising		$1, 066 25
	Drawn by Hon. C. Delano, Secretary and trustee, for the purchase of $19,650 United States five per cent. bonds, $9,825 of which belong to the Sacs and Foxes, and $9,825 belong to the Iowas		22, 011 10
October 31, 1872	Balance on hand		131 42
	Total	23, 208 77	23, 208 77
November 1, 1872	Balance on hand	131 42	
June 5, 1873	Amount received on settlement of the account of	115 75	
October 31, 1873	Balance on hand		247 17
	Total	247 17	247 17

Account "fulfilling treaty with Iowas, proceeds of land."

December 2, 1871	Warrant No. 500, being amount received from Omaha Mining Company for royalty on coal taken from Iowa lands in Nebraska	$18 00	
October 21, 1872	Drawn by Hon. C. Delano, Secretary and trustee, for investment in United States bonds		$18 00
	Total	18 00	18 00
November 26, 1872	Warrant No. 546, from sales of lands	100 00	
December 12, 1872	Warrant No. 552, received from Omaha Coal-Mining Company for royalty on coal taken from the Iowa Indian lands	12 90	
September 13, 1873	Warrant No. 596, for royalty on coal as above	22 00	
October 4, 1873	Drawn by Hon. C. Delano, Secretary and trustee, for investment		134 90
	Total	134 90	134 90

Account "fulfilling treaty with Kaskaskias, Peorias, Weas, and Piankeshaws, proceeds of lands."

May 29, 1872	Refunded by Hon. J. D. Cox, late Secretary and trustee	$83 35	
	Amount received from Agent G. A. Colton, on settlement of his accounts	36	
October 21, 1872	Drawn by Hon. C. Delano, Secretary and trustee, for investment in United States bonds		$83 71
	Total	83 71	83 71
November 26, 1872	Warrant No. 546, from sales of lands	15 39	
March 8, 1873	Warrant No. 565, from sales of lands	9 45	
October 4, 1873	Drawn by Hon. C. Delano, Secretary and trustee, for investment		24 84
	Total	24 84	24 84

Account "fulfilling treaty with Wyandotts, proceeds of land."

November 1, 1871	Balance on hand, being amount received for right of way, &c	$1, 123 35	
	Remitted to Enoch Hoag, superintendent, for the benefit of the tribe		$1, 123 35
	Total	1, 123 35	1, 123 35

Account "fulfilling treaty with Chickasaws, proceeds of land."

Treaty.—Eleventh article of treaty of May 24 1834.
Mode of sale.—Under direction of the General Land-Office.

November 1, 1871	Balance on hand, being amount received from sale of their lands in Mississippi in 1870	$109 38	
May 3, 1872	Drawn by Hon. C. Delano, Secretary and trustee, for investment in United States bonds		$109 38
July 19, 1872	Refunded by Hon. C. Delano, Secretary and trustee, being balance from amount drawn May 3, uninvested	53 38	
October 21, 1872	Drawn by Hon. C. Delano, Secretary and trustee, for investment in United States bonds		53 38
	Total	162 76	162 76

Account "fulfilling treaty with Stockbridges, proceeds of land."

November 1, 1871	Balance on hand, being portion of amount received October 11, 1870, for sale of timber cut on their land	$228 54	
May 11, 1872	Warrant No. 516, sale of timber	178 20	
May 30, 1872	Warrant No. 526, sale of timber	1,000 00	
May 15, 1872	Remitted to W. T. Richardson, agent, to be expended for the benefit of the tribe		$406 74
October 31, 1872	Leaving a balance of		1,000 00
	Total	1,406 74	1,406 74
November 1, 1872	Balance on hand	1,000 00	
December 16, 1872	Remitted to Agent William T. Richardson, for benefit of the tribe		1,000 00
January 31, 1873	Warrant No. 560, sales of land and timber	6,998 67	
March 8, 1873	Warrant No. 566, sales of land and timber	1,806 76	
March 27, 1873	Warrant No. 570, sales of land	700 00	
April 14, 1873	Warrant No. 571, appropriated by Congress to re-imburse this fund for amount erroneously covered into the Treasury as receipts from sales of public lands	174,548 83	
September 13, 1873	Warant No. 596, from sales of land	300 00	
October 31, 1873	Balance on hand		184,354 26
	Total	185,354 26	185,354 26

Account "fulfilling treaty with Sacs and Foxes of Mississippi, proceeds of land."

	Balance on hand November 1, 1871, viz:		
	Part of proceeds of sale of lands under treaty of October 1, 1859, ratified July 9, 1860	$712 15	
	Amount received in payment for lands, under 11th and 13th articles treaty of February 18, 1867, ratified July 25, 1868	340 00	
	Amount received in payment for lands, under 11th article of treaty last named	8 00	
August 31, 1870	Interior Department transfer account, being amount paid to Superintendent Murphy on settlement of his account		$75 48
December 8, 1871	Treasurer United States, internal-revenue tax		1 02
October 31, 1872	Balance on hand		983 65
	Total	1,060 15	1,060 15
November 1, 1872	Balance on hand	983 65	
October 4, 1873	Drawn by Hon. C. Delano, Secretary and trustee, for investment		983 65
	Total	983 65	983 65

"Proceeds of Sioux réservation in Minnesota and Dakota."

Treaty or act.—Sold in accordance with an act of Congress approved March 3, 1863, (Stat. at Large, vol. 12, p. 819.)
Mode of sale.—Sold under the direction of the General Land-Office.

November 1, 1871	Balance on books of Indian-Office		$173,816 43	
	The General Land-Office reports sales as follows during the year:			
	In Minnesota, 40,463.29 acres, realizing (from October 1, 1871, to September 1, 1872)	$51,678 30		
	Improvements	250 00		
	Sold in Dakota, 954.44 acres, during August, 1872	1,676 01		
		53,604 31		

"Proceeds of Sioux reservation in Minnesota and Dakota"—Continued.

	There has been brought on the books of the Indian-Office as follows:		
December 2, 1871	Warrant No. 499	$1,202 19	
January 30, 1872	Warrant No. 510	8,189 74	
May 15, 1872	Warrant No. 518	28,724 16	
September 16, 1872	Warrant No. 540	9,984 40	
	From which there has been disbursed since November 1, 1871, under the provisions of the act of Congress approved March 3, 1863, as modified by the act of July 15, 1870, as follows:		
	For the benefit of Santee Sioux:		
November 15, 1871	Barclay White, superintendent		$1,809 66
November 22, 1871	......do		4,867 97
December, 1871	Annuities, subsistence, &c		10,979 17
March 22, 1872	Barclay White, superintendent		12,319 46
April 3, 1872	......do		1,000 00
June 13, 1872	......do		5,894 23
July 25, 1872	......do		2,965 32
October 16, 1872	......do		6,319 42
November 11, 1871	Interior Department, transfer warrant, for amount paid to late agent Balcomb on settlement of his account.		12 53
	For the benefit of Sioux of Lake Traverse:		
December 8, 1871	Treasurer United States internal-revenue tax		9 12
December 14, 1871	W. J. Worden, special commissioner, services		94 00
	Annuities, subsistence, &c		11,256 94
November 11, 1871	Interior Department, transfer warrant, for amount paid to late agent Balcomb on settlement of his account.		18 14
	For the benefit of Sioux of Devil's Lake:		
November 11, 1872	Annuities, subsistence, &c		7,273 99
May 15, 1872	W. H. Forbes, agent		737 14
November 11, 1871	Interior Department, transfer warrant, for amount paid to late Agent Balcomb, on settlement of his account.		9 31
October 31, 1872	Balance on hand		156,350 50
		221,916 92	221,916 92
November 1, 1872	Balance on hand	156,350 50	
December 12, 1872	Warrant No. 553, sales of lands	5,770 00	
January 31, 1873	Warrant No. 557, sales of lands	6,384 18	
March 8, 1873	Warrant No. 564, sales of lands	1,100 00	
June 11, 1873	Warrant No. 576, sales of lands	1,400 00	
June 12, 1873	Warrant No. 578, sales of lands	454 61	
August 15, 1873	Warrant No. 591, sales of lands	3,826 01	
September 13, 1873	Warrant No. 594, sales of lands	492 40	
September 13, 1873	Warrant No. 597, sales of lands	1,818 33	
October 7, 1873	Warrant No. 598, sales of lands	3,918 41	
	From which there has been disbursed since November 1, 1872, as follows:		
	For the benefit of the Santee Sioux:		
February 5, 1873	Barclay White, superintendent		6,468 96
February 10, 1873	......do		8,000 00
May 1, 1873	......do		2,500 00
May 6, 1873	......do		4,018 83
July 14, 1873	......do		400 00
September 18, 1873	......do		1,569 60
	Subsistence, &c		4,739 54
	For the benefit of Sioux of Lake Traverse:		
July 23, 1873	James Smith, jr., special commissioner, services, &c		260 16
July 28, 1873	Transporting commissioners		54 60
	Annuities subsistence, &c		21,059 71
	For the benefit of Sioux of Devil's Lake:		
July 23, 1873	James Smith, jr., special commissioner, services, &c		173 44
July 28, 1873	Transporting commissioners		36 40
September 5, 1873	Transportation of supplies		721 56
	Annuities, subsistence, &c		18,493 15
October 31, 1873	Balance on hand		113,018 49
		181,514 44	181,514 44

Fulfilling treaty with Cherokees—proceeds of lands.

November 1, 1871	Balance on hand	$253 02
December 2, 1871	Amount received from sales of land advertised for sale June 13, 1871.	8,966 62
May 29, 1872	Uninvested balance refunded by Secretary of Interior	100 80
July 19, 1872	..........do	24 05
July 24, 1872	..........do	1,413 79
July 24, 1872	..........do	56
September 21, 1872	..........do	3 23
January 31, 1873	Warrant No. 559, from sales of lands, (strip)	3,063 50
February 15, 1873	Warrant No. 563, from sales of lands, (strip)	3,050 85
March 12, 1873	Warrant No. 569, from sales of lands, (strip)	2,031 47
June 11, 1873	Warrant No. 575, from sales of lands, (strip)	4,460 00

Fulfilling treaty with Cherokees, &c.—Continued.

June 11, 1873	Warrant No. 575, from sales of lands	$7,080 38	
June 12, 1873	Warrant No. 577, from sales of lands, (strip)	6,449 40	
August 15, 1873	Warrant No. 590, from sales of lands, (strip)	12,847 25	
September 13, 1873	Warrant No. 596, from sales of lands, (strip)	8,242 37	
September 13, 1873	Warrant No. 596, refunded by Secretary of Interior	16 50	
October 7, 1873	Warrant No. 599, from sales of lands, (strip)	63,874 74	
October 30, 1873	Warrant No. 602, from sales of lands, (strip)	38,147 17	
	Disposition of funds:		
December 13, 1871	Amount disbursed in payment for advertising sale of June 13, 1871.		$575 75
February 12, 1872	Drawn by Hon. C. Delano, Secretary and trustee, for investment.		8,643 90
October 21, 1872	Drawn by Hon. C. Delano, Secretary and trustee, for investment.		1,542 43
February 18, 1873, April 8, 1873, June 20, 1873	Amount paid for expenses incurred in surveying the Cherokee strip of land.		13,347 97
October 4, 1873	Drawn by Hon. C. Delano, Secretary and trustee, for investment, being proceeds of sales of neutral lands.		7,096 88
	And from proceeds of sales of Cherokee strip, for investment on behalf of Cherokee Asylum, per act of Congress approved February 14, 1873, (Stat. 17, p. 462.)		26,796 87
October 16, 1873	Drawn by Hon. C. Delano, Secretary and trustee, from proceeds of sales of Cherokee strip, for investment as above.		48,203 13
October 31, 1873	Balance on hand, being proceeds of sales of the Cherokee strip, of which $25,000 is applicable for the establishment of the Cherokee Asylum, (act of February 14, 1873, Stat. 17, p. 462.)		53,818 78
		160,025 71	160,025 71

Fulfilling treaty with Cherokees—proceeds of school-lands.

November 26, 1872	Warrant No. 547, sales of school-lands in Alabama	$127 28	
June 11, 1873	Warrant No. 575, sales of school-lands in Alabama	418 37	
October 4, 1873	Drawn by Hon. C. Delano, Secretary and trustee, for investment.		$545 65
		545 65	545 65
	Fulfilling treaty with Cherokees—Proceeds of Osage diminished reserve-lands in Kansas, (transfer:)		
October —, 1873	Warrant No. —, sales of Osage lands	80,000 00	
October 4, 1873	Drawn by Hon. C. Delano, Secretary and trustee, for investment for the benefit of the Cherokee orphan fund, in accordance with the act of Congress approved February 14, 1873, (Stat. 17, p. 462.)		80,000 00
		80,000 00	80,000 00

Payment of Cherokee national warrants.

Paid in accordance with the 23d article of the treaty of July 19, 1866.			Sources from which funds were drawn for payment.		Total amount paid.
Periods during which payments were made.			Proceeds of Cherokee neutral lands.	Proceeds of sale of bonds held in trust.	
From—	To—	By whom paid.			
March 7, 1867	March 4, 1869	Hon. O. H. Browning	$3,971 64	$90,914 02	
April 1, 1869	November 1, 1869	Hon. J. D. Cox	8,955 96	16,581 25	
November 1, 1869	November 1, 1870	do	11,417 90		
November 1, 1870	November 1, 1871	Hon. C. Delano	8,598 74	3,552 00	
November 1, 1871	November 1, 1872	do		915 88	
November 1, 1872	November 1, 1873	do		664 50	
Amount paid from proceeds of Cherokee neutral lands			32,944 24		$32,944 24
Amount paid from proceeds of sale of bonds				112,627 65	112,627 65
Total amount of Cherokee funds expended in payment of Cherokee warrants prior to date of this report					145,571 89

Six hundred dollars in United States bonds, loan of 1881, belonging to the Cherokee national fund, were sold, the proceeds of which, $681, were used in the payment of Cherokee national warrants, amounting to $664.50, during the year ending November 1, 1873. The balance of said proceeds, $16.50, was refunded by the Secretary of the Interior, September 13, 1873, as will appear by reference to statement of account "Fulfilling treaty with Cherokees—Proceeds of lands."

Fulfilling treaty with Omahas—proceeds of lands.

Treaty or act of July 31, 1872.	
The lands were appraised under instructions from the Department, and advertised for sale, on sealed bids, to the highest bidder for cash. Bids were opened June 1, 1873. The whole number of acres advertised was 50,000. But few bids were received. Total number of acres awarded was 300.72, the proceeds of which amounted to the sum of $702.20. This amount was covered into the Treasury and brought upon the books of this office by appropriation warrant No. 602, dated October 1, 1873, and still stands to the credit of said appropriation...	$702 20

Account fulfilling treaty with Kansas Indians—proceeds of lands.

Treaty.—Article 4 of the treaty of October 5, 1859, (Stat. at Large, vol. 12, p. 1112.)
Mode of sale.—By awards made upon sealed proposals, invited by advertisement.

	Whole number of acres sold prior to November 1, 1871, 37,786.76, realizing	$53, 824 23	
	Receipts prior to November 1, 1871, under contract with the Union Pacific Railroad of July 4, 1869, for right of way, timber, &c	14, 000 00	
	All of which was distributed prior to date of last report		$67, 824 23
		67, 824 23	67, 824 23
	Account for the year ending October 31, 1872:		
	No sales since last annual report.		
September 10, 1872..	Received from Missouri, Kansas and Texas (formerly Union Pacific Southern Division) Railroad, for right of way, &c., under contract of July 4, 1869	7, 563 09	
September 21, 1872..	Refunded by Hon. J. D. Cox, being a balance in his hands from amount drawn for investment	5 79	
September 12, 1872..	Remitted to Enoch Hoag, superintendent, to be expended for the benefit of the tribe		7 , 563 09
October 31, 1872....	Balance on hand		5 79
		7, 568 88	7, 568 88
November 1, 1872...	Balance on hand	579	
October 7, 1873	Warrant No. 600, being proceeds of sales of a portion of the Kansas Indian diminished reserve lands in Kansas, in accordance with act of Congress, approved May 8, 1872. (Stat. 17, p. 86.)	9, 084 09	
September 19, 1873..	Amount remitted Superintendent Enoch Hoag, to pay expenses of appraisement		$4, 590 89
October 1, 1873	Amount paid J. L. Sharp, special commissioner, for services in appraising diminished reserve lands		1, 200 00
October 31, 1873	Balance on hand		3, 298 99
	Total	9, 089 88	9, 089 88

The Kansas "diminished reserve," authorized to be sold by act of May 8, 1872, as above stated, contained 80,409.06 acres, and was advertised as being subject to sale on sealed bids until June 15, 1878.

Awards were made for the number of acres bid for, amounting to	$2, 443 94
Number of acres paid for in full at the date of this report	1, 838 72
Number of acres for which accounts are in suspense	605 22
Amount received for 1,838.72, reported for patents	9, 099 09
Amount of proceeds covered into the United States Treasury, under head of "Fulfilling treaties with Kansas Indians—proceeds of lands"	9, 084 09
Balance in safe	15 00
	9, 099 09

Account proceeds of Winnebago reservation in Minnesota.

Treaty or act.—Act of February 21, 1863. (Stat. at Large, vol. 12, p. 658.
Mode of sale.—Sections 2 and 3, of said act, provides for the sale, under the directions of the General Land-Office, of the lands allotted to the Indians, as provided by the treaty of April 15, 1859. (Stat. at Large, vol. 12, p. 1101.)

	Account for the year ending October 31, 1872:		
November 1, 1871	Balance on hand	$331 16	
January 30, 1872	Warrant No. 510, sale of lands	280 00	
May 15, 1872	Warrant No. 518, sale of lands	360 00	
September 16, 1872	Warrant No. 541, sale of lands	450 00	
December 13, 1871	Paid to M. St. Cyr, guardian of three Indians		$3 21
March 23, 1872	Paid to Barclay White, superintendent, for the benefit of the tribe		607 95
July 1, 1872	Interior Department, transfer account, amount due agent, Superintendent A. D. Balcomb, on settlements of his account		145 18
October 29, 1872	Paid to M. St. Cyr, guardian of three Indians		85 57
October 31, 1872	Balance on hand		679 25
	Total	1,421 16	1,421 16

No change since November 1, 1872.

Account fulfilling treaty with Winnebagoes, proceeds of lands.

November 1, 1871	Balance on hand	$681 90	
December 20, 1871	Refunded by H. F. Denman, late superintendent	713 84	
March 23, 1872	Paid by Barclay White for the benefit of the tribe		$358 63
October 31, 1872	Balance		1,037 11
	Total	1,395 74	1,395 74
November 1, 1872	Balance on hand	1,037 11	
November 26, 1872	Warrant No. 549, from sales of lands	120 00	
January 31, 1873	Warrant No. 558, from sales of lands	240 00	
October 31, 1873	Balance on hand		1,397 11
	Total	1,397 11	1,397 11

The sale of the Winnebago trust-lands authorized by the second article of the treaty of 1859, and the act of February 2, 1863, was commenced in July, 1863, and continued in 1864, 1865, 1866, and 1867, during which period 29,152.93 acres were sold for the sum of $66,216.43.

At the date of this report a sale is in progress for the residue of said lands, amounting to 4,146,43 acres. The awards were approved October 2, 1873, and will average $3.60 per acre. Forty days having been allowed for payments to be completed, no funds have yet been received on account of this sale except the ten per cent. deposits received with bids, and since placed to the credit of the respective parties officially advised of awards in their favor.

On reviewing this report, I find it necessary to state that the various requisitions drawn in favor of the Hon. Secretary of the Interior as trustee, &c., referred to in accounting for the disposition made of the proceeds of the sales of the different classes of Indian trust-lands, were for funds subsequently invested in Government bonds, in accordance with treaty stipulations; and for further information in regard to said investments, I have the honor to refer you to the annual trust-fund report for the present year.

Very respectfully, your obedient servant.

LONSVILLE TWITCHELL,
Trust-Fund Clerk, Indian Office.

Hon. EDWARD P. SMITH,
Commissioner of Indian Affairs.

Statement showing the present liabilities of the United States to Indian tribes under treaty stipulations.

Names of tribes.	Description of annuities, &c.	Number of installments yet unappropriated, explanations, &c.	Reference to laws: Statutes at Large.	Annual amount necessary to meet stipulations indefinite as to time, now allowed, but liable to be discontinued.	Aggregate of future appropriations that will be required during a limited number of years to pay limited annuities incidentally necessary to effect the payment.	Amount of annual liabilities of a permanent character.	Amount held in trust by the United States on which five per centum is annually paid, and amounts which, invested at five per centum, produce permanent annuities.
Apaches, Kiowas, and Comanches.	Thirty installments, provided to be expended under the tenth article treaty of Oct. 21, 1867.	Twenty-four installments unappropriated, at $30,000 each.	Vol. 15, p. 584, § 10		$720,000 00		
Do	Purchase of clothing	Tenth article treaty Oct. 21, 1867	do	$26,000 00			
Do	Pay of carpenter, farmer, blacksmith, miller, and engineer.	Fourteenth article treaty Oct. 21, 1867.	Vol. 15, p. 585, § 14	5,200 00			
Do	Pay of physician and teacher	do	do	2,500 00			
Do	Three installments, for seed and agricultural implements.	Three installments of $2,500 each due.	Vol. 15, p. 583, § 8.		7,500 00		
Do	Pay of a second blacksmith, iron and steel	Eighth article treaty Oct. 21, 1867	Vol. 15, p. 584, § 8.	2,000 00			
Arickarees, Gros-Ventres, and Mandans.	Amount to be expended in such goods, &c., as the President may from time to time determine.	Seventh article treaty July 27, 1866.	Treaty not published.	75,000 00			
Assinaboines	do	do	do	30,000 00			
Blackfeet, Bloods, and Piegans.	do	Eighth article treaty Sept. 1, 1868	do	50,000 00			
Calapooias, Molallas, and Clackamas of Willamette Valley.	Five installments, fourth series, of annuity for beneficial purposes.	One installment of $5,500 due	Vol. 10, p. 1114, § 2		5,500 00		
Cheyennes and Arapahoes.	Thirty installments, provided to be expended under tenth article treaty of Oct. 28, 1867.	Twenty-four installments unappropriated, at $20,000 each.	Vol. 15, p. 596, § 10		480,000 00		
Do	Purchase of clothing, same article		do	14,500 00			
Do	Pay of physician, carpenter, farmer, blacksmith, miller, engineer, and teacher.		Vol. 15, p. 597, § 13	7,700 00			
Do	Three installments, for the purchase of seeds and of agricultural implements.	Three installments of $2,500 each due.	Vol. 15, p. 595, § 8.		7,500 00		
Do	Pay of second blacksmith, iron and steel		Vol. 15, p. 597, § 8.	2,000 00			
Chickasaws	Permanent annuity in goods		Vol. 1, p. 619			$3,000 00	
Chippewas — Bois Forte Band,	Twenty installments, for blacksmith, assistant, iron, tools, &c.	Twelve installments, at $1,500 each, unappropriated,	Vol. 14, p. 766, § 3		18,000 00		

Do	Twenty installments, for schools, instructing Indians in farming, and for the purchase of seeds, tools, &c.	Twelve installments, at $1,600 each, unappropriated.	do		19,200 00		
Do	Twenty installments of annuity, in money, goods, or other articles; in provisions, ammunition, and tobacco.	Annuity, $3,500; goods, &c., $6,500; provisions, &c., $1,000; twelve installments unappropriated.			132,000 00		
Chippewas of Lake Superior.	Twenty installments, in coin, goods, implements, &c., and for education.	One installment unappropriated	Vol. 10, p. 1111, § 3		19,000 00		
Do	Twenty installments, for six smiths and assistants, iron and steel.	do	Vol. 10, p. 1111, § 5		6,360 00		
Do	Support of smith and shop, and pay of two farmers, during the pleasure of the President.	Estimated at	Vol. 11, p. 1112	1,800 00			
Do	Twenty installments, for seventh blacksmith, &c.	Three installments unappropriated, at $1,060 each.			3,180 00		
Chippewas of the Mississippi.	Money, goods, support of schools, provisions, tobacco, as per fourth article treaty Oct. 4, 1842; eighth article treaty Sept. 13, 1854; and third article treaty May 7, 1864.	Three installments, 2d series, of $9,000.01, to be appropriated.	Vol. 7, p. 592, § 4; vol. 10, p. 1111, § 8; vol. 13, p. 694, § 3.		27,000 03		
Do	Two farmers, two carpenters, two smiths and assistants, iron and steel; same articles and treaties.	Three installments, 2d series, at $1,400, to be appropriated.	do		4,200 00		
Do	Twenty installments, in money, at $20,000 each; third article treaty Feb. 22, 1855.	One to be appropriated	Vol. 10, p. 1167. § 3.		20,000 00		
Do	Ten installments for support of schools, in promoting the progress of the people in agriculture, and assisting them in becoming self-sustaining; support of physician and purchase of medicines.	Four installments of $11,500 to be appropriated.	do		46,000 00		
Do	Forty-six installments, to be paid to the chiefs of the Mississippi Indians.	Twenty of $1,000 each to be appropriated.	Vol. 16, p. 548, § 3		20,000 00		
Chippewas of the Mississippi, and Pillager and Lake Winnebagoshish bands of Chippewas.	Pay of two carpenters, two blacksmiths, four farm-laborers, and one physician, ten years.	Two installments of $7,700 to be appropriated.	Vol. 13, p. 694, § 6		15,400 00		
Do	For services and traveling expenses of a board of visitors, not more than five persons, to attend annuity payments.		do	480 00			
Do	To be applied for the support of a saw-mill as long as the President may deem necessary.		do	1,000 00			
Do	Pay of female teachers employed on the reservation.		Vol. 13, p. 694, § 13	1,000 00			
Chippewas, Pillager and Lake Winnebagoshish bands.	Thirty installments, in money, $10,666.66; goods, $8,000; and for purposes of utility, $4,000.	Eleven installments to be appropriated, at $22,666.66 each.	Vol. 10, p. 1163, § 3		249,333 26		
Do	Twenty installments, for purposes of education; third article treaty Feb. 22, 1865.	One installment to be appropriated.	do		3,000 00		

Statement showing the present liabilities of the United States to Indian tribes, &c.—Continued.

Names of tribes.	Description of annuities, &c.	Number of installments yet unappropriated, explanations, &c.	Reference to laws: Statutes at Large.	Annual amount necessary to meet stipulations indefinite as to time, now allowed, but liable to be discontinued.	Aggregate of future appropriations that will be required during a limited number of years to pay limited annuities incidentally necessary to effect the payment.	Amount of annual liabilities of a permanent character.	Amount held in trust by the United States on which five per centum is annually paid, and amounts which, invested at five per centum, produce permanent annuities.
Chippewas of Red Lake and Pembina tribe of Chippewas.	$10,000, as annuity, to be paid per capita to the Red Lake band, and $5,000 to the Pembina band, during the pleasure of the President.	....	Vol. 13, p. 668, § 3.	$15,000 00	....	....	....
Do	Fifteen installments, of $12,000 each, for the purpose of supplying them with gilling-twine, cotton maitre, linsey, blankets, &c.	Estimated, Red Lake band $8,000, and Pembina band $4,000; five installments to be appropriated.	Vol. 13, p. 669, § 3.	....	$60,000 00	....	....
Do	Fifteen installments, to pay one blacksmith, physician, &c., miller, farmer, $3,900; iron and steel, and other articles, $1,500; carpentering, &c., $1,000.	Five installments to be appropriated, at $6,400 each.	Vol. 13, p. 690, § 4.	....	32,000 00	....	....
Do	Fifteen installments, to defray the expenses of a board of visitors, not more than three persons, to attend annuity payments.	Five installments to be appropriated, at $390 each.	......do	....	1,950 00	....	....
Choctaws	Permanent annuities	2d article treaty Nov. 16, 1805, $3,000; 13th article treaty Oct. 18, 1820, $600; 2d article treaty Jan. 20, 1825, $6,000.	Vol. 7, p. 99, § 2; vol. 11, p. 614, § 13; vol. 7, p. 213, § 13; vol. 11, p. 614, § 13.	....	....	$9,600 00	....
Do	Provisions for smiths, &c	6th article treaty Oct. 18, 1820; 9th article treaty Jan. 20, 1825.	Vol. 7, p. 212, § 6; vol. 7, p. 236, § 9.	....	....	920 00	....
Do	Interest on $390,257.92; articles 10 and 13 treaty January 22, 1855.	....	Vol. 7, p. 236, § 9; vol. 11, p. 614, § 13.	....	....	19,512 89	$390,257 92
Confederated tribes and bands in Middle Oregon.	Five installments, for beneficial purposes, at the direction of the President, treaty of June 25, 1855.	One installment of $4,000 to be appropriated.	Vol. 12, p. 964, § 2.	....	4,000 00	....	....
Do	Fifteen installments, for pay and subsistence of one farmer, blacksmith, wagon and plow maker.	One installment of $3,500 to be appropriated.	Vol. 12, p. 965, § 4.	....	3,500 00	....	....

Do	Twenty installments, for pay and subsistence of one physician, sawyer, miller, superintendent of farming, and school-teacher.	Six installments of $5,600 yet due	do		33, 600 00		
Do	Twenty installments, for salary of head chief.	Six installments, of $500 each, yet due.	do		3, 000 00		
Creeks	Permanent annuities	Treaty Aug. 7, 1790	Vol. 7, p. 36, § 4			1, 500 00	
Do	do	Treaty June 16, 1802	Vol. 7, p. 69, § 2			3, 000 00	
Do	do	Treaty January 24, 1826	Vol. 7, p. 287, § 4			20, 000 00	490, 000 00
Do	Smiths, shops, &c	do	do			1, 110 00	22, 200 00
Do	Wheelwright, permanent	Treaty Jan. 24, 1826, and Aug. 7, 1856.	Vol. 7, p. 287, § 4; vol. 11, p. 700, § 5.			600 00	12, 000 00
Do	Allowance, during the pleasure of the President, for blacksmiths, assistants, shops and tools, iron and steel, wagon-maker, education, and assistance in agricultural operations, &c.	February 14, 1833; August 7, 1856.	Vol. 7, p. 419, § 5; vol. 11, p. 700, § 5.	840 00			
		August 7, 1856	Vol. 11, p. 700, § 5	270 00 600 00 1, 000 00 2, 000 00			
Do	Interest on $200,000, held in trust, 6th article treaty August 7, 1856.	August 7, 1856	do			10, 000 00	200, 000 00
Do	Interest on $675,168, held in trust, 3d article treaty June 14, 1866, to be expended under the direction of the Secretary of the Interior.	Expended under the direction of the Secretary of the Interior.	Vol. 14, p. 786, § 3			33, 758 43	675, 168 00
Crows	For supplying male persons over fourteen years of age with a suit of good, substantial woolen clothing; females over twelve years of age, a flannel skirt or goods to make the same, a pair of woolen hose, calico and domestic; and boys and girls under the ages named such flannel and cotton goods as their necessities may require.	Treaty of May 7, 1868	Vol. 15, p. 651, § 9	23, 973 00			
Do	For the purchase of such articles from time to time as the necessities of the Indians may indicate to be proper.	do	do	10, 000 00			
Do	For pay of physician, carpenter, miller, engineer, farmer, and blacksmith.	do	Vol. 15, p. 652, § 10	6, 600 00			
Do	Twenty installments, for pay of teacher, and for books and stationery.	Sixteen installments of $3,000 each yet due.	Vol. 15, p. 651, § 7		48, 000 00		
Do	Blacksmith, iron and steel, and for seeds and agricultural implements.	Estimated	Vol. 15, p. 651, § 8	3, 250 00			
Do	For the purchase of such beneficial objects as the condition and necessities of the Indians may require.	do	Vol. 15, p. 652, § 9	20, 000 00			
Delawares	For interest on $37,095.25, at five per centum, being the value in part of thirty-six sections of land, set apart by the treaty of 1829 for education.	Senate resolution January 19, 1838.	Vol. 7, p. 327, § 1; vol. 10, p. 1049, § 5.			1, 854 76	37, 095 25
D'Wamish & other allied tribes in Washington Territory.	Twenty installments of $150,000, to be expended under the direction of the President.	Six installments to be appropriated.	Vol. 12, p. 928, § 6.		27, 000 00		
Do	Twenty installments, for agricultural school and teachers.	Six installments, at $3,000, to be appropriated.	Vol. 12, p. 929, § 14.		18, 000 00		

Statement showing the present liabilities of the United States to Indian tribes, &c.—Continued.

Names of tribes.	Description of annuities, &c.	Number of installments yet unappropriated, explanations, &c.	Reference to laws: Statutes at Large.	Annual amount necessary to meet stipulations indefinite as to time, now allowed, but liable to be discontinued.	Aggregate of future appropriations that will be required during a limited number of years to pay limited annuities incidentally necessary to effect the payment.	Amount of annual liabilities of a permanent character.	Amount held in trust by the United States on which five per centum is annually paid, and amounts which, invested at five per centum, produce permanent annuities.
D'Wamish and other allied tribes in Washington Territory.	Twenty installments, for a smith and carpenter shop and tools.	Six installments, at $500 each, yet due.	Vol.12, p.929, § 14	....	$3,000 00	....	....
Do	Twenty installments, for blacksmith, carpenter, farmer, and physician.	Six installments, at $4,600, to be appropriated.	do	....	27,600 00	....	....
Flatheads & other confederated tribes.	Twenty installments, for agricultural and industrial school, providing necessary furniture, books, stationery, &c., and for the employment of suitable instructors.	Six installments, at $2,100 each, to be appropriated.	Vol. 12, p.977, § 5	....	12,600 00	....	....
Do	Five installments, 4th series, for beneficial objects, under the direction of the President.	Five installments to be appropriated, at $3,000 each.	Vol.12, p.976, § 4	....	15,000 00	....	....
Do	Twenty installments, for two farmers, two millers, blacksmith, gunsmith, tinsmith, carpenter and joiner, and wagon and plow maker, $7,400; and keeping in repair blacksmith's, carpenter's, and wagon and plow maker's shops, $500.	Six installments of $7,900 yet to be provided.	Vol.12, p.977, § 5	....	47,400 00	....	....
Do	Twenty installments, for keeping in repair flouring and saw mill, and supplying the necessary fixtures.	Six installments of $500 to be provided.	do	....	3,000 00	....	....
Do	Twenty installments, for pay of physician, $1,400; keeping in repair hospital, and for medicine, $300.	Six installments of $1,700 to be appropriated.	do	....	10,200 00	....	....
Do	Twenty installments, for repairing buildings for various employés, &c.	Six installments of $300 each yet due.	do	....	1,800 00	....	....
Do	Twenty installments, for each of the head chiefs of the Flathead, Kootenay, and Upper Pend d'Oreille tribes, at $500.	Six installments of $1,500 each to be provided.	do	....	9,000 00	....	....

Gros Ventres	Amount to be expended in such goods, provisions, &c., as the President may from time to time determine as necessary, per 8th article treaty of July 13, 1868.	Treaty not published		$35,000 00			
Iowas	Interest on $57,500, being the balance on $157,500.		Vol. 10, p. 1071, § 9			$2,875 00	$57,500 00
Kansas	Interest on $200,000, at five per centum		Vol. 9, p. 842, § 2			10,000 00	200,000 00
Kickapoos	Interest on $95,945.95, at five per centum		Vol. 10, p. 1079, § 2			4,797 29	95,945 95
Klamaths and Modocs.	Five installments of $5,000, 2d series, to be expended under the direction of the President.	Two installments to be provided	Vol. 16, p. 708, § 2		10,000 00		
Do	Five installments of $3,000, 3d series, to be expended under the direction of the President.	Five installments due	do		15,000 00		
Do	Twenty installments, for repairing saw-mill and buildings for blacksmith, carpenter, wagon and plow maker, manual-labor school, and hospital.	Thirteen installments of $1,000 each yet due.	do		13,000 00		
Do	For tools and materials for saw and flour mills, carpenter's, blacksmith's, wagon and plow maker's shops, books and stationery for manual-labor school.	Twelve installments to be appropriated.	Vol. 16,		18,000 00		
Do	Pay of superintendent of farming, farmer, blacksmith, sawyer, carpenter, and wagon and plow maker.	Seven installments of $6,000 each yet due.	Vol. 16, p. 709, § 5		42,000 00		
Do	Pay of physician, miller, and two teachers, for twenty years.	Twelve installments to be provided, at $3,600 each.	do		43,200 00		
Makahs	Ten installments, being the 5th series, for beneficial objects, under the direction of the President.	Six to be appropriated, at $1,000 each.	Vol. 12, p. 940, § 5		6,000 00		
Do	Twenty installments, for agricultural and industrial schools and teachers, for smith and carpenter shops and tools, and for blacksmith, carpenter, farmer, and physician.	Six installments to be appropriated, at $7,600 each.	Vol. 12, p. 941, § 11		45,600 00		
Menomonees	Fifteen installments, to pay $242,686, for cession of land.	Seven installments of $16,170.06 yet due.	Vol. 10, pp. 1065 and 1067, § 5.		113,190 42		
Miamies of Kansas	Permanent provisions for smith's shops and miller; &c.	Say $940 for shop and $600 for miller.	Vol. 7, p. 191, § 5			1,540 00	30,800 00
Do	Twenty installments upon $150,000, 3d article treaty June 5, 1854.	Six installments of $7,500 each yet due.	Vol. 10, p. 1094, § 3		45,000 00		
Do	Interest on $50,000, at the rate of five per centum as per 3d article treaty June 5, 1854.		do			2,500 00	50,000 00
Miamies of Indiana	Interest on $221,257.86, at five per centum per annum.	June 5, 1854	Vol. 10, p. 1099, § 4			11,062 89	221,257 86
Miamies of Eel River.	Permanent annuities	4th article treaty 1795; 3d article treaty 1805; 3d article treaty 1809.	Vol. 7, p. 51, § 4; vol. 7, p. 91, § 3; vol. 7, p. 114, § 3.			1,100 00	22,000 00
Molels	Pay of teacher to manual-labor school, and subsistence of pupils, &c.	Treaty December 21, 1855	Vol. 12, p. 982, § 2	3,000 00			
Mixed Shoshones, Bannocks, and Sheep-Eaters.	To be expended in such goods, provisions, &c., as the President may from time to time determine as proper.	Treaty September 24, 1868		35,000 00			

Statement showing the present liabilities of the United States to Indian tribes, &c.—Continued.

Names of tribes.	Description of annuities, &c.	Number of installments yet unappropriated, explanations, &c.	Reference to laws: Statutes at Large.	Annual amount necessary to meet stipulations indefinite as to time, now allowed, but liable to be discontinued.	Aggregate of future appropriations that will be required during a limited number of years to pay limited annuities incidentally necessary to effect the payment.	Amount of annual liabilities of a permanent character.	Amount held in trust by the United States on which five per centum is annually paid, and amounts which, invested at five per centum, produce permanent annuities.
Navajoes	For such articles of clothing, or raw materials in lieu thereof, seeds, farming implements, &c.	Treaty of June 1, 1868	Vol. 15, p. 668	$45, 705 00			
Do	For the purchase of such articles as from time to time the condition and necessities of the Indians may indicate to be proper.	do	do	14, 000 00			
Do	For pay of two teachers	do	Vol. 15, p. 668, § 6	2, 000 00			
Nez Percés	Five installments, 3d series, for beneficial objects, at the discretion of the President.	One installment to be appropriated, $6,000.	Vol. 12, p. 985, § 4		$6, 000 00		
Do	Twenty installments, for two schools, &c., pay of superintendent of teaching and two teachers, superintendent of farming and two farmers, two millers, two blacksmiths, two gunsmiths, tinner, carpenter, wagon and plow maker, keeping in repair grist and saw mill, for necessary tools, pay of physician, repairing hospital and furnishing medicine, &c., repairing buildings for employés, and the shops for blacksmith, tinsmith, gunsmith, carpenter, wagon and plow maker, providing tools therefor, and pay of head chief.	Six installments to be provided, at $17,200 each.			103, 200 00		
Do	Sixteen installments, for boarding and clothing children who attend school, providing school, &c., with necessary furniture, purchase of wagons, teams, and tools, &c.	Eight installments of $3,000 each to be provided.	Vol. 14, p. 649, § 4		24, 000 00		
Do	Salary of two subordinate chiefs	Treaty June 9, 1863	Vol. 14, p. 650, § 5	1, 000 00			
Do	Fifteen installments, for repairs of houses, mills, shops, &c.	Eight installments unappropriated, at $3,500 each.	Vol. 14, p. 649, § 5		28, 000 00		
Do	Salary of two matrons for schools, two assistant teachers, farmer, carpenter, and two millers.	Treaty June 9, 1863	Vol. 14, p. 650, § 5	7, 600 00			

Nisqually, Puyallup, and other tribes and bands of Indians.	Payment of $32,500 in graduated payments, as per treaty December 26, 1854.	One installment to be appropriated	Vol. 10, p. 1133, § 4	....	1,000 00	....	....
Do	Pay of instructor, smith, physician, carpenter, &c., for twenty years.	One installment to be provided for.	Vol.10, p.1134, § 10.	....	6,700 00	....	....
Do	Support of an agricultural and industrial school, smith and carpenter shops, and providing necessary tools therefor.	......do	......do	....	1,500 00	....	....
Northern Cheyennes and Arapahoes.	Purchase of clothing, as per sixth article treaty May 10, 1868, thirty years.	Twenty-five installments to be appropriated, of $15,000 each.	Vol. 15, p. 657, § 6	15,000 00	....	....	....
Do	Ten installments, to be expended by the Secretary of the Interior for Indians roaming, and in the purchase of such articles as may be deemed necessary.	Five installments to be appropriated.	......do	18,000 00	....	....	....
Do	For the last of four installments, to furnish flour and meat.	One to be appropriated, at $66,576	......do	66,576 00	....	....	....
Do	Pay of teacher, carpenter, miller, farmer, blacksmith, engineer, and physician.	Estimated	Vol. 15, p. 658, § 7	7,700 00	....	....	....
Omahas	Fifteen installments, 3d series, in money or otherwise.	Nine installments to be appropriated, at $20,000 each.	Vol. 10, p. 1044, § 4	....	180,000 00	....	....
Do	Ten installments, to pay engineer, miller, farmer, and blacksmith, keeping in repair grist and saw mill, support of blacksmith-shop, and furnishing tools.	Estimated, engineer, $1,200; miller, $900; farmer, $900; repair of mill and support of smith-shop, $600; two installments of $4,500 yet due.	Vol. 10, p. 1045, § 8	....	9,000 00	....	....
Osages	Interest on $69,120, at 5 per centum, for educational purposes.	Resolution of the Senate to treaty January 2, 1825.	Vol. 7, p. 242, § 6	....	....	$3,456 00	$69,120 00
Do	Interest on $300,000 at 5 per centum, to be paid semi-annually, in money or such articles as the Secretary of the Interior may direct.	Treaty September 29, 1865	Vol. 14, p. 687, § 1	....	....	15,000 00	300,000 00
Ottoes and Missourias.	Fifteen installments, being the 3d series, in money or otherwise.	Nine to be appropriated	Vol. 10, p. 1039, § 4	....	81,000 00	....	....
Pawnees	Annuity goods, and such articles as may be necessary.	Treaty September 24, 1857	Vol. 11, p. 729, § 2	....	....	30,000 00	....
Do	Support of two manual-labor schools and pay of teachers.	......do	Vol. 11, p. 730, § 3	11,200 00	....	....	....
Do	For iron and steel and other necessary articles for shops, and pay of two blacksmiths, one of whom is to be tin and gun smith, and compensation of two strikers and apprentices.	Say for iron or steel, $500; two blacksmiths, $1,200; and two strikers, $480.	....	2,180 00	....	....	....
Do	Farming utensils and stock, pay of farmer, miller, and engineer, and compensation of apprentices to assist in working the mill, and keeping in repair grist and saw mill.	Estimated	Vol. 11, p. 730, § 4	4,400 00	....	....	....
Poncas	Fifteen installments, 3d series, to be paid to them or expended for their benefit.	Fifteen installments of $8,000 each yet due.	Vol. 12, p. 997, § 2	....	120,000 00	....	....

Statement showing the present liabilities of the United States to Indian tribes, &c.—Continued.

Names of tribes.	Description of annuities, &c.	Number of installments yet unappropriated, explanations, &c.	Reference to laws: Statutes at Large.	Annual amount necessary to meet stipulations indefinite as to time, now allowed, but liable to be discontinued.	Aggregate of future appropriations that will be required during a limited number of years to pay limited annuities incidentally necessary to effect the payment.	Amount of annual liabilities of a permanent character.	Amount held in trust by the United States on which five per centum is annually paid, and amounts which, invested at five per centum, produce permanent annuities.
Poncas	Amount to be expended during the pleasure of the President, for aid in agricultural and mechanical pursuits.	Treaty March 12, 1868	Vol. 12, p. 998, § 2	$7,500 00			
Pottawatomies	Permanent annuity in money	August 2, 1795	Vol. 7, p. 51, § 4			$261 47	$5,229 39
Do	do	September 30, 1809	Vol. 7, p. 114, § 3			130 74	2,614 79
Do	do	October 2, 1818	Vol. 7, p. 185, § 3			653 67	13,073 39
Do	do	September 20, 1828	Vol. 7, p. 317, § 2			522 94	10,458 79
Do	do	July 29, 1829	Vol. 7, p. 330, § 2			4,183 48	83,669 59
Do	For educational purposes, during the pleasure of the President.	September 20, 1828	Vol. 7, p. 318, § 2	5,000 00			
Do	Permanent provision for three blacksmiths and assistants, iron, steel, &c.	October 16, 1826	Vol. 7, p. 296, § 3				
		September 20, 1828	Vol. 7, p. 318, § 2			737 34	14,746 79
		July 29, 1829	Vol. 7, p. 321, § 2				
Do	Permanent provision for furnishing salt	do	Vol. 7, p. 320, § 2			114 39	2,287 80
Do	Permanent provision for payment of money in lieu of tobacco.	September 20, 1828	Vol. 7, p. 318, § 2			78 44	1,568 79
		June 5 and 17, 1846	Vol. 9, p. 855, § 10				
Do	For interest on $168,123.85, at 5 per centum	do	Vol. 9, p. 855, § 7			8,406 19	168,123 85
Pottawatomies of Huron.	Permanent annuities	November 17, 1808	Vol. 7, p. 106, § 2			400 00	8,000 00
Quapaws	For education, smith, farmer, and smith-shop, during the pleasure of the President.	$1,000 for education; $1,660 for smith, &c.	Vol. 7, p. 425, § 3	2,660 00			
Quinaielts and Quillehutes.	$25,000, 5th series, to be expended for beneficial objects.	One installment of $1,000 to be provided.	Vol. 12, p. 972, § 4		$1,000 00		
Do	Twenty installments, for an agricultural and industrial school, employment of suitable instructors, support of smith and carpenter shop, and tools, pay of blacksmith, carpenter, farmer, and physician.	Six installments to be appropriated, of $7,100 each.	Vol. 12, p. 973, § 10		42,600 00		
Rogue Rivers	Five installments, in blankets, clothing, farming utensils, &c.	One installment of $3,000 still due			3,000 00		

River Crows	Amount to be expended in such goods, provisions, &c., as the President may from time to time determine.	July 15, 1868	Vol. 16, p. 349, § 7	30,000 00			
Sacs and Foxes of Mississippi.	Permanent annuity	Treaty November 3, 1804	Vol. 7, p. 85, § 3			1,000 00	20,000 00
Do	Interest on $200,000, at five per cent	Treaty October 21, 1837	Vol. 7. p. 541, § 2			10,000 00	200,000 00
Do	Interest on $800,000, at five per cent	Treaty October 21, 1842	Vol. 7, p. 596, § 2			40,000 00	800,000 00
Sacs and Foxes of Missouri.	Interest on $157,400, at five per cent	Treaty October 21, 1837	Vol. 7. p. 543, § 2			7,870 00	157,400 00
Do	Interest on $11,615.25, at five per cent	Treaty March 6, 1861	Vol. 12, p. 1170			580 71	11,615 25
Seminoles	Interest on $500,000, eighth article treaty August 7, 1856.	$25,000 annual annuity	Vol. 11, p. 702, § 8			25,000 00	500,000 00
Do	Interest on $70,000, at five per cent. per annum.	Support of schools	Vol. 14, p. 757, § 3			3,500 00	70,000 00
Senecas	Permanent annuities	September 9 and 17, 1817	Vol. 7, p. 161, § 4; vol. 7, p. 179, § 4.			1,000 00	20,000 00
Do	Smith and smith-shops and miller	February 28, 1831	Vol. 7, p. 349, § 4	1,660 00			
Senecas of New York	Permanent annuities	February 19, 1841	Vol. 4, p. 442			6,000 00	120,000 00
Do	Interest on $75,000, at five per centum	Act June 27, 1846	Vol, 9, p. 35, § 3			3,750 00	75,000 00
Do	Interest on $43,050, transferred from the Ontario Bank to the United States Treasury.	do	do			2,152 50	43,050 00
Senecas and Shawnees.	Permanent annuity	Treaty September 17, 1818	Vol. 7, p. 119, § 4			1,000 00	20,000 00
Do	Support of smiths, and smith-shops	Treaty July 20, 1831	Vol. 7, p. 352, § 4	1,060 00			
Senecas, Shawnees, Quapaws, Peorias, Ottawas, Wyandotts, and others.	Five installments, for blacksmith and assistant, shop and tools, iron and steel for same, for Shawnees.	Last appropriated					
Do	Six installments, for blacksmith and necessary iron, steel and tools, for Peorias, Kaskaskias, &c.	One installment to be appropriated			1,123 29		
Shawnees	Permanent annuity for education	August 3, 1795; May 10, 1854	Vol. 7, p, 51, § 4			3,000 00	60,000 00
Do	Interest on $40,000, at five per cent	August 3, 1795	Vol. 10, p. 1056, § 3			2,000 00	40,000 00
Shoshones — Western band.	Twenty installments, of $5,000 each, under the direction of the President.	Ten installments to be appropriated	Vol. 13, p. 557, § 7.		50,000 00		
Shoshones — Eastern band.	Twenty installments, of $10,000 each, under the direction of the President.	do	Vol. 13, p. 177, § 5.		100,000 00		
Shoshones—Northwestern band.	Twenty installments, of $5,000 each, under the direction of the President.	do	Vol. 13, p. 663, § 3.		50,000 00		
Shoshones—Goship band.	Twenty installments, of $1,000 each, under the direction of the President.	do	Vol. 13, p. 682, § 7.		10,000 00		
Shoshones and Bannacks.	For the purchase of clothing for men, women, and children.	Estimated	Vol. 15, p. 676, § 9.	13,374 00			
Do	For the purchase of such articles as may be considered proper by the Secretary of the Interior.	do	do	30,000 00			
Do	For pay of physician, carpenter, teacher, engineer, farmer, and blacksmith.	do	Vol. 15, p. 676, § 10	6,800 00			
Do	Blacksmith, and for iron and steel for shops.	do	Vol. 15, p. 676, § 8	2,000 00			
Do	For the purchase of seeds and farming implements.	Two installments to be provided			5,000 00		

Statement showing the present liabilities of the United States to Indian tribes, &c.—Continued.

Names of tribes.	Description of annuities, &c.	Number of installments yet unappropriated, explanations, &c.	Reference to laws: Statutes at Large.	Annual amount necessary to meet stipulations indefinite as to time, now allowed, but liable to be discontinued.	Aggregate of future appropriations that will be required during a limited number of years to pay limited annuities incidentally necessary to effect the payment.	Amount of annual liabilities of a permanent character.	Amount held in trust by the United States on which five per centum is annually paid, and amounts which, invested at five per centum, produce permanent annuities.
	For Bannacks:						
Shoshones and Bannacks.	Purchase of clothing for men, women, and children.	Estimated	Vol. 15, p. 676, § 9	$6,937 00			
Do	Purchase of such articles as may be considered necessary by the Secretary for persons roaming, &c.	do	do	16,000 00			
Do	For seeds and agricultural implements, &c	Three installments to be appropriated.			$7,500 00		
Do	Pay of physician, carpenter, miller, teacher, engineer, farmer, and blacksmith.		Vol. 15, p. 676, § 10	6,800 00			
Six Nations of New York.	Permanent annuities in clothing, &c	Treaty November 11, 1794	Vol. 7, p. 46, § 6			$4,500 00	$90,000 00
Sisseton and Wahpeton of Lake Traverse and Devil's Lake.	Amount to be expended in such goods and other articles as the President may from time to time determine.	February 14, 1873, estimated		80,000, 00			
Sioux of different tribes, including Santee Sioux in Nebraska.	For second of three installments for the purchase of seeds and agricultural implements.	Two installments of $15,000 each yet due.	Vol. 15, p. 638, § 10	15,000 00			
Do	Purchase of clothing for men, women, and children.	Twenty-six installments of $159,400 yet due.			4,144,400 00		
Do	Blacksmith, and for iron and steel	Estimated	Vol. 15, p. 638, § 8	2,000 00			
Do	For such articles as may be considered necessary by the Secretary of the Interior for persons roaming.	Twenty-six installments of $236,000 yet due.			6,136,000 00		
Do	Physician, five teachers, carpenter, miller, engineer, farmer, and blacksmith.	Estimated	Vol. 15, p. 638, § 13	10,400 00			
S'Klallams	Twenty installments, being fifth series on $60,000, to be expended under the direction of the Secretary of the Interior.	Six installments due, graduated	Vol. 12, p. 934, § 5		10,400 00		

Do	Twenty installments for agricultural and industrial school, pay of teacher, blacksmith, carpenter, physician, and farmer.	Six installments of $7,100 yet due	do		42,600 00		
Do	Smith, carpenter-shop, and tools			500 00			
Tabequache band of Utahs.	Purchase of iron, steel, and tools for blacksmith-shop and pay of blacksmith and assistant.	Estimated	Vol. 13, p. 675, § 10	720 00			
Tabequache, Muache, Capote, Weminuche, Yampa, Grand River, and Uintah band of Utes.	For iron and steel and necessary tools for blacksmith-shop.	do	Vol. 15, p. 621, § 11	220 00			
Do	Two carpenters, two millers, two farmers, one blacksmith, and two teachers.	do	Vol. 15, p. 622, § 15	11,000 00			
Do	Thirty installments of $30,000, to be expended under the direction of the Secretary of the Interior, for clothing, blankets, &c.	Twenty-five installments of $30,000 still due.	Vol. 15, p. 622, § 11		750,000 00		
Do	Annual amount to be expended, under the direction of the Secretary of the Interior, in supplying said Indians with beef, mutton, wheat-flour, beans, &c.		Vol. 15, p. 622, § 12	30,000 00			
Umpquas and Calapooias, of Umpqua Valley, Oreg.	Twenty installments of annuity, for beneficial objects.	One installment to be provided	Vol. 10, p. 1126, § 3		1,000 00		
Do	Support of teachers, &c., for twenty years	One installment of $1,450 yet due	Vol. 10, p. 1127, § 3		1,450 00		
Walla-Walla, Cayuse, and Umatilla tribes.	Five installments, third series, to be expended under the direction of the President.	One installment to be provided, at $4,000.	Vol. 12, p. 946, § 2		4,000 00		
Do	Twenty installments, for pay of two millers, farmer, superintendent of farming operations, two school teachers, physician, blacksmith, wagon and plow maker, carpenter, and joiner.	Six installments of $11,200 each still due.	Vol. 12, p. 947, § 4		67,200 00		
Do	Twenty installments, for mill fixtures, tools, medicines, books, stationery, furniture, &c.	Six installments of $3,000 each yet due.	do		18,000 00		
Do	Twenty installments, of $1,500 each, for pay of head chiefs, three in number, at $500 per annum.	Six installments yet due	Vol. 12, p. 947, § 5		9,000 00		
Winnebagoes	For interest on $886,909.17, at 5 per centum per annum.	November 1, 1837, and Senate amendment July 17, 1862.	Vol. 7, p. 546, § 4			44,345 46	886,909 17
Do	Thirty installments of interest on $75,387.28, at 5 per centum per annum.	Three installments of $3,769.36 still due.	Vol. 9, p. 879, § 4		11,308 08		
Do	Interest on $78,340.41, at 5 per centum per annum, to be expended under the direction of the Secretary of the Interior.					3,917 02	78,340 41
Wal-pah-pe tribe of Snake Indians.	Ten installments, second series, under the direction of the President.	Eight installments of $1,200 each still due.	Vol. 14, p. 684, § 7		9,600 00		
Yankton tribe of Sioux.	Ten installments, of $40,000 each, being second series, to be paid to them or expended for their benefit.	Five installments of $40,000 each yet due.	Vol. 11, p. 744, § 4		200,000 00		

Statement showing the present liabilities of the United States to Indian tribes, &c.—Continued.

Names of tribes.	Description of annuities, &c.	Number of installments yet unappropriated, explanations, &c.	Reference to laws: Statutes at Large.	Annual amount necessary to meet stipulations indefinite as to time, now allowed, but liable to be discontinued.	Aggregate of future appropriations that will be required during a limited number of years to pay limited annuities incidentally necessary to effect the payment.	Amount of annual liabilities of a permanent character.	Amount held in trust by the United States on which five per centum is annually paid, and amounts which, invested at five per centum, produce permanent annuities.
Yakamas	Five installments, third series, for beneficial objects, under the direction of the President.	One installment to be provided	Vol. 12, p. 953, § 4.		$6,000 00		
Do	Twenty installments, for two schools, one of which is to be an agricultural and industrial school, keeping the same in repair, and providing books, stationery, and furniture.	Six installments to be provided, at $500 each.	do		3,000 00		
Do	Twenty installments, for superintendent of teaching, two teachers, superintendent of farming, two farmers, two millers, two blacksmiths, tinner, gunsmith, carpenter, and wagon and plow maker.	Six installments to be provided, at $14,600 each.	do		87,600 00		
Do	Twenty installments, for keeping in repair hospital, and furnishing medicines, &c., pay of physician, repair of grist and saw mill, and furnishing the necessary tools.	Six installments to be provided, at $2,000 each.	do		12,000 00		
Do	Twenty installments, for keeping in repair buildings for employés.	Six installments to be provided, at $300 each.	do		1,800 00		
Do	Salary of head chief for twenty years	Six installments to be provided, at $500 each.	do		3,000 00		
Do	Twenty installments, for keeping in repair the blacksmith's, tinsmith's, gunsmith's, carpenter's, and wagon and plow maker's shops, and furnishing tools.	do	do		3,000 00		
Total				$821,205 00	14,866,795 08	$362,291 61	$6,375,432 99

Table comprising a list of the several Indian agencies, with the names of the agents and the number of Indians at each agency, in the various States and Territories.

State or Terrritory.	Agency.	Agent.	Number of Indians.	Total.
New York	Forestville	Daniel Sherman	....	5, 141
Michigan	Lansing	George I. Betts	....	9, 167
Wisconsin	La Pointe	Isaac L. Mahan	5, 125	
	Green Bay	Thomas N. Chase	3, 000	8, 125
Iowa	Sac and Fox	A. R. Howbert	....	335
Minnesota	Chippewa	E. Douglass	4, 547	
	Red Lake	R. M. Pratt	1, 141	5, 688
Nebraska	Great Nemaha	Charles H. Roberts	316	
	Winnebago	Taylor Bradley	1, 522	
	Omaha	T. T. Gillingham	1, 001	
	Pawnee	William Burgess	2, 376	
	Ottoe	J. W. Griest	447	
	Santee	Joseph Webster	917	6, 579
Kansas	Kickapoo	B. H. Miles	274	
	Kansas or Kaw	M. Stubbs	533	
	Pottawatomie	M. H. Newlin	483	1, 290
Indian Territory	Quapaw	H. W. Jones	1, 219	
	Neosho	J. T. Gibson	2, 823	
	Sac and Fox	John H. Pickering	1, 136	
	Kiowa and Comanche	J. M. Haworth	5, 002	
	Wichita	J. Richards	1, 528	
	Upper Arkansas	J. D. Miles	3, 970	
	Cherokee	J. B. Jones	17, 217	
	Choctaw	Albert Parsons	22, 000	
	Creek	Edward R. Roberts	13, 000	
	Seminole	H. Breiner	2, 438	70, 333
New Mexico	Navajo	William F. M. Arny	9, 114	
	Mescalero Apache	Samuel Bushnell	1, 875	
	Cimarron	Thomas A. Dolan	1, 210	
	Southern Apache	B. M. Thomas	500	
	Pueblo	E. L. Lewis	7, 879	
	Abiquiu	William D. Crothers	1, 270	21, 848
Dakota	Yankton	J. G. Gasmann	1, 947	
	Sisseton	M. N. Adams	1, 540	
	Devil's Lake	William H. Forbes	1, 020	
	Cheyenne River	H. W. Bingham	6, 000	
	Whetstone	E. A. Howard	5, 000	
	Grand River	Ed. Palmer	6, 269	
	Fort Berthold	L. B. Sperry	2, 103	
	Upper Missouri, (Crow Creek)	H. F. Livingston	3, 000	
	Ponca	C. P. Birkett	738	
	Flandreau, (no report)	J. P. Williamson	250	27, 867
Colorado	White River	J. S. Littlefield	800	
	Los Pinos	C. Adams	3, 199	
	Denver	J. B. Thompson	350	4, 349
Arizona	Pima and Maricopa	J. H. Stout	4, 326	
	Colorado River	J. A. Tonner	8, 024	
	Moquis Pueblo	William S. Defrees	1, 700	
	Papago	R. A. Wilbur	6, 000	
	Camp Verde	J. Williams	2, 058	
	Camp Apache	J. E. Roberts	2, 814	
	Chiricahua	T. J. Jeffords	1, 100	26, 022
Montana	Blackfeet	R. F. May	7, 500	
	Crow and Lemhi Farm	James Wright	4, 877	
	Milk River	William W. Alderson	10, 625	
	Flathead	D. Shanahan	1, 821	
	Fort Belknap	W. H. Fanton	7, 130	31, 953
Wyoming	Shoshonee and Bannacks	James Irwin	1, 024	
	Red Cloud	J. J. Saville	9, 177	10, 201
Utah	Uintah Valley	J. J. Critchlow	....	1, 718
Idaho	Fort Hall	H. W. Reed	1, 500	
	Nez Percé	J. B. Monteith	2, 807	4, 307
Washington Territory	Neah Bay	E. M. Gibson	604	
	Yakama	J. H. Wilbur	3, 000	
	S'Kokomish	Ed. Eells	875	
	Tulalip	E. C. Chirouse	3, 600	
	Quinaielt	G. A. Henry	554	
	Colville	J. A. Simms	3, 349	

List of the several Indian agencies, &c.—Continued.

State or Territory.	Agency.	Agent.	Number of Indians.	Total.
Washington Territory ..	Puyallup	None, (farmer in charge)	1, 200	
	Chehalis	None, (farmer in charge)	600	
				13, 782
Oregon	Warm Springs	John Smith	626	
	Grand Ronde	P. B. Sinnott	924	
	Siletz	J. H. Fairchild	1, 058	
	Umatilla	N. A. Cornoyer	837	
	Klamath	L. S. Dyar	1, 120	
	Alsea	In charge of employé	343	
	Malheur	H. Linderville	1, 200	
	Not under any agent, (estimated.)		3, 000	
				9, 108
California	Hoopa Valley	E. K. Dodge	725	
	Round Valley	J. L. Burchard	1, 119	
	Tule River	J. B. Vosburgh	317	
	Mission		4, 000	
	Not under any agent, (estimated.)		15, 000	
				20, 161
Nevada	Pyramid Lake	C. A. Bateman	6, 000	
	S. E. Nevada	George W. Ingalls	3, 000	
	Not under any agent, (estimated.)		4, 204	
				13, 204
Indians in North Carolina, Tennessee, Georgia, Florida, and Texas, not under any agent, (estimated.)				2, 000

INDEX.

www.ingramcontent.com/pod-product-compliance
Lightning Source LLC
LaVergne TN
LVHW020601110826
845149LV00002B/336

9781418188153